THE INFLUENCE OF
PROPHECY IN
THE LATER
MIDDLE AGES

THE INFLUENCE OF PROPHECY IN THE LATER MIDDLE AGES

A Study in Joachimism

MARJORIE REEVES

UNIVERSITY OF NOTRE DAME PRESS

Notre Dame   London

Library of Congress Cataloging-in-Publication Data

Reeves, Marjorie.
    The influence of prophecy in the later Middle Ages :
a study in Joachimism / Marjorie Reeves.
        p.   cm.
    Originally published: Oxford : Clarendon Press, 1969.
    Includes bibliographical references and index.
    ISBN 0-268-01170-2 (alk. paper)
    1. Joachim, of Fiore, ca. 1132-1202.   2. History (Theol-
ogy)—History of doctrines—Middle Ages, 600–1500.
3. Bible—Prophecies.   4. Bible—Criticism, interpretation, etc.—History—Middle Ages, 600–1500. I. Title.
BR115.H5R4   1993
231.7′45′0902—dc20   93-24809
                                                    CIP

∞ *The paper used in this publication meets the minimum requirements of*
the American National Standard for Information Sciences—Permanence of Paper
for Printed Library Materials, ANSI Z39.48-1984.

TO
MY MOTHER

PREFACE TO THE NEW EDITION

I N THE LAST thirty years or so, interest in 'that fascinating and singular figure', Joachim of Fiore, and, more generally, in medieval apocalypticism, has developed to a remarkable degree. This has been in part due, perhaps, to our increasing perception of psychological factors in the study of historical causes. It is, above all, in the human imagination that expectations of the future work most powerfully, and the history of the images and visions in which both hopes and fears concerning a final climactic age of history have been cast can no longer be ignored or brushed aside as 'lunatic fringe'. Seminal books such as Norman Cohn's *Pursuit of the Millennium*, first published in 1957, put us on the track and modern anthropological studies have shown how, when societies or groups are under pressure of great change, the imagination feeds again on crisis images from the past. Joachim of Fiore was not a millenarian in the strict sense of the word, but the ever-expanding research of recent years is showing how powerful and pervasive an influence his theology of history has exercised, far beyond the later Middle ages, through the Renaissance and Reformation period, even down to the nineteenth and twentieth centuries. The Centro Internazionale di Studi Gioachimiti, established in the Abbot Joachim's chosen monastic location, San Giovanni in Fiore, has drawn together an international group of scholars whose periodic meetings have proved a remarkable stimulus to Joachimist studies.

I am grateful to the University of Notre Dame Press for undertaking to republish this book and wish to thank the editor and staff for their willing cooperation. In the course of revising it I have become increasingly aware of the debt I owe to the members of what one might venture to call 'the Joachite club'. First, I must recall the memory of two early collaborators, Morton Bloomfield and Beatrice Hirsch-Reich. Secondly, I must express my gratitude to more recent collaborators, Harold Lee, Warwick Gould and, presently, Martha Fleming and Jean Vereecken. A whole bevy of distinguished scholars agreed willingly to contribute to a recent volume on Renaissance prophecy. I owe a great personal debt to the scholarship as well as to the friendly criticism of Randolph Daniel, Bernard McGinn, Robert Lerner, David Burr, Roberto Rusconi, and Cesare Vasoli. Many others have sent me a rich collection of writings over the broad field of prophecy and millenarianism. The generous exchange of knowledge and ideas between scholars is at least one cause for optimism in the international scene today.

> Marjorie Reeves,
> St. Anne's College, Oxford.
> March, 1993.

PREFACE

Human beings in general can no more ignore their future than they can lose their past. Thus a theme common to all periods of history is that of attitudes towards the future. Such attitudes are determined by what one may term the contemporary rules of predictability. These in turn derive from assumptions about the determining factors of human living. From expectations of hope or of fear spring motives for decision and action. A study of prediction, therefore, has something significant to contribute to the understanding of an age. Today much decision is based on a type of prediction which is being evolved under sets of rules deriving from scientific method. Just how adequate an approach to the future this supplies remains to be seen. In this book I have attempted a study of attitudes to the future based on an entirely different set of assumptions. The medieval concept of prophecy presupposed a divine providence working out its will in history, a set of given clues as to that meaning implanted in history, and a gift of illumination to chosen men called to discern those clues and from them to prophesy to their generation. These assumptions governed the rules of predictability. Such an approach to the future was in part deterministic, but never mechanistic. Divine providence, it was believed, used human agencies and prophecy was often a call to men to involve themselves in the working out of God's purposes in history. The two determined points of the future were the appearance of Antichrist and the Last Day of Judgement. These apart, there was scope for the play of human imagination on the future forms of society and their fate. Men were called to involve themselves in a poetic dream rather than a scientifically controlled future. This style of thought became widespread in the later Middle Ages after receiving a tremendous impetus from the prophetic message of Joachim of Fiore. His doctrine of the three *status* imparted a rhythm and expectation to the course of history which appealed powerfully to the imagination. This current of thought does not slacken as one moves into the Renaissance period. Although obviously different ways of looking at the future were forming in the sixteenth century, they existed side by side with the old assumptions in the minds of rulers, churchmen, and scholars. Only reluctantly in the seventeenth century was prophecy as an attitude towards the future acknowledged to be outmoded.

I am happy at last to be able to acknowledge a long-standing debt of gratitude to Westfield College, London, where, as the holder of a research studentship, I first embarked on this subject more than thirty years ago. That I did so at all was due to the encouragement of Miss Gwyer, my Principal as an undergraduate at St. Hugh's College, Oxford. Over the years since then I have accumulated many debts to scholars. Until her death I was constantly drawing on the scholarship and insight of Dr. Beatrice Hirsch-Reich. The pioneer in modern Joachimist studies, Professor Dr. Herbert Grundmann, Präsident of the *Monumenta Germaniae Historica*, not only provided foundations for this book but generous help at various stages, particularly with regard to manuscripts. Other manuscript queries have been answered for me with unfailing willingness by Dr. Marie Thérèse d'Alverny and Dr. Jeanne Bignami-Odier. Collaboration with Professor Morton Bloomfield of Harvard marked the beginning of a continuing discourse on Joachimist problems in which I have been indebted to him both for his critical judgements and his vast knowledge of the sources. In Oxford, Miss Beryl Smalley has put me on the track of important exegetical material and Dr. Richard Hunt has watched for Joachimist references which might turn up in Bodley. Acknowledgements to other scholars who have generously supplied references will be found in footnotes. In its latest stage Professor Ernest Jacob kindly read and criticized the first part of this book, while Professor Richard Southern gave most generously of his time and thought to the improvement of the first two parts. For the sabbatical leave which enabled me to complete the book I must thank the Trustees of the Leverhulme Foundation and the Principal and Fellows of St. Anne's College, Oxford. For willing and accurate help over much tiresome typing I must thank my sister, Kathleen Reeves. At the proof-reading stage I have been saved from many foolish slips by the close scrutiny of my sister, Joan Sheppard. Finally, I owe a lasting debt of gratitude to my friend Alexandra Fairbairn, who has lived with this book for so long.

M. E. R.

Oxford
May 1968

CONTENTS

NOTE ON REFERENCES
AND BIBLIOGRAPHIES

SELECT Bibliography I is the original bibliography. All works given in this are cited throughout by the abbreviations in square brackets. The alphabetical List of Abbreviations preceding the text refers by numbers to the entries in the Bibliography.

All other works are cited in full the first time. Subsequent citations are given as 'op. cit.' if the full reference is within about the last ten references, or as 'op. cit. (ref. page and note)' if it is further back.

Quotations in the text have their own abbreviated references given at the end of the quotation, except where they are immediately preceded by a footnote which itself gives an exact reference for the quotation.

Select Bibliography II attempts to give the main publications relevant to the text from 1969 to 1992. In square brackets some brief annotations are given. Where these are followed by *cf* plus page references, these refer to the text, indicating that the cited work corrects, disagrees with or adds to the text of the book.

In quoting from early printed editions I have at times modernized punctuation and use of capital letters to make reading easier. In the spelling of personal names I have not attempted to achieve any uniformity of style, but used the most convenient forms.

ACKNOWLEDGEMENTS

I must acknowledge the use of material from articles written by myself in the following journals:

Recherches de Théologie ancienne et médiévale, xxv (1958), pp. 111–41.
Mediaeval and Renaissance Studies, v (1961), pp. 163–81.
Traditio, xvii (1961), pp. 323–70.

ABBREVIATIONS

The number before each item is that of the reference in the Bibliography.

PART ONE

THE REPUTATION OF THE
ABBOT JOACHIM

———

I

JOACHIM AND HIS CONTEMPORARIES

JOACHIM of Fiore has seldom been viewed with indifference. In his lifetime (c. 1135 to 1202)[1] he made a strong impact both upon those who sought him out and those before whom he presented himself. He was favoured by four popes, yet denounced by the Cistercian Order as a runaway. After his death the thing everyone knew about him was that he was a prophet—true or false. His sanctity guarded his personal reputation when his views on the Trinity were condemned in 1215, yet after the 'horrible scandal' of the Eternal Evangel in 1255 the Commission of Anagni set up by the Pope to examine his works condemned the whole 'fundamentum doctrine' of Joachim. St. Bonaventura dismissed him as ignorant and *simplex*, and St. Thomas Aquinas wrote off his prophecies as 'conjectures', some true, some false; yet Dante placed him in the *Paradiso*, where he made Bonaventura himself acclaim him as 'di spirito profetico dotato'. He found a place in the *Acta Sanctorum* as *beatus*, yet equally he appeared in the *Catalogus Haereticorum* of Guido of Perpignan and Bernard of Luxemburg. In the sixteenth century he was claimed in such works as Henriquez's *Fasciculus Sanctorum Ordinis Cisterciensis*, but also by Mathias Flacius Illyricus in his *Catalogus Testium Veritatis* and by other Protestants collecting medieval ammunition. In the early seventeenth century the learned still argued hotly about his reputation. The argument continues even today.

It is possible to catch something of the excitement and interest

Note: All references given in abbreviated form will be found fully set out in the Select Bibliography.

[1] The date given for Joachim's birth is based on the evidence of the interview which Adam of Persigny had with him. Adam described Joachim thus: 'videbatur autem fere sexagenarius'. This interview is usually dated 1195/6 but if, as is possible, it took place as late as 1198, the approximate date of Joachim's birth would be brought nearer the date of 1145 given in the biography written by Jacobus Graecus (cf. *infra*, p. 112). For recent discussions of this problem see Grundmann, *NF*, pp. 35–7; Russo, *Gioacchino*, p. 9; Crocco, *Gioacchino*, p. 18. For the surviving materials on the life of Joachim see Baraut, *AST* xxvi, and Grundmann, *DA* xvi. The latter supplies the most up-to-date reconstruction of all the known facts of Joachim's life.

which Joachim aroused among contemporaries from the records of a series of interviews in which he met them. Apart from these, the facts concerning his life are scanty. He appears suddenly out of the fastnesses of Calabria, makes a dramatic pronouncement, and disappears again. The first of these interviews took place at Veroli in 1184 when Pope Lucius III was in residence there. Joachim was at that time Abbot of the Cistercian monastery of Curazzo, but he had been residing at the sister house of Casamari since 1182/3, and it was Luke of Cosenza, whom he first met at Casamari, who recorded the conversation between Pope and Abbot.[1] In his memoir of Joachim, Luke stresses at the outset that he was endowed by God with *sapientia* and *intelligentia*.[2] He goes on immediately: 'tunc, coram Domino Papa et Consistorio eius, cepit revelare intelligentiam Scripturarum, et utriusque Testamenti concordiam: a quo et licentiam scribendi obtinuit, et scribere coepit' (*AS*, p. 93). Thus in Luke's mind this visit to the Pope was clearly connected with Joachim's gift of spiritual intelligence and with the particular method 'given' to him of expounding the Scriptures through the concords of Old and New Testaments. At the interview Joachim sought and obtained permission to embark on his life's task of drawing forth this spiritual intelligence through his expositions of Scripture. Luke's brief reference ties in convincingly with a fuller record of the interview at Veroli which has come to light in MS. 322 of the Biblioteca Antoniana at Padua. Here, in a thirteenth-century manuscript containing otherwise none but genuine works of Joachim, is a short tract entitled *Expositio Prophetiae Anonymae Romae repertae anno 1184* (f. 149^v). This is written in the first person and purports to be Joachim's exposition of a prophecy found in Rome among the papers of Cardinal Mathias of Angers. It is specifically stated that this exposition was made in the presence of Lucius III at Veroli and it seems likely that Joachim was invited to do so in order to test the nature of his spiritual gift. The whole tract has been dismissed as apocryphal by Mgr. Tondelli,[3] but, apart from the fact that its presence in the Antonian manuscript creates a strong presumption in favour of genuineness, it bears the authentic marks of Joachim's thought and style.[4] It is an early expression of Joachim's mind and,

[1] *AS*, p. 93.   [2] Ibid.   [3] Tondelli, *Lib. Fig.* I, p. 119.
[4] Its genuineness is maintained by Grundmann, *NF*, p. 46. The text of the prophecy which Joachim set out to interpret begins 'Excitabatur Roma contra Romanum'. Apart from some omitted lines it is identical with a prophecy published by Holder-Egger under the title *Sibilla Samia* (*NA* xv. 177). Holder-Egger thought it belonged to the

as such, is particularly illuminating. We see him when he is just beginning to move away from the conventional career of an able monk caught in the treadmill of administering a Cistercian house. His mind is venturing out into new paths of thought and meditation upon the total meaning of history and the mysterious activity of the Trinity, interpenetrating all ages. These meditations will soon drive him out of the Cistercian Order to move further up the mountain of contemplation and ultimately to found his own order of S. Giovanni in Fiore. But in 1184 he is still establishing his basic method and authority. He lays his plan before the Pope: he will elucidate the meaning of history by pondering the great concords of the two Testaments. His method is demonstrated on the spot by his exposition of the prophecy, the text of which is given in our tract. It is an enigmatic oracle foretelling woes, especially on Rome. Joachim begins, not with an explanation of the oracle at all, but with an exposition of the seven persecutions suffered by the Hebrews in the Old Dispensation, matched by the seven persecutions of the Church in the New.[1] Here at once we meet the first of Joachim's basic patterns of history, the one, indeed, with which he starts his *Liber Concordie*. Its inspiration is the Book with Seven Seals,[2] and the theme of double sevens runs like a ground bass through Joachim's many variations of pattern.[3] This is the pattern of twos, in which

same mid-thirteenth-century pseudo-Joachimist group of writings as the oracle of Sibyl Erithrea. If this were so, obviously the case for the genuine character of the whole piece would fall to the ground. But Holder-Egger, significantly, could not find in it any allusions to thirteenth-century history. It is, indeed, the kind of oracle which could be applied to many periods and there seems no reason why it should not have been a twelfth-century production belonging to the group of Sibylline oracles just then coming into vogue.

[1] MS. Ant. 322, f. 150^r: 'Fuit autem contra israel prima persecutio egyptiorum. Secunda madianitarum. Tercia aliarum nationum. Quarta assiriorum. Quinta chaldorum. Sexta medorum et persarum. Grecorum sub antiocho subsecuta est septima. . . . Prior ergo ecclesie persecutio fuit iudeorum. Secunda paganorum. Arrianorum tercia. Hec est Gothica. Wandalica. Alemanica. Lombarda. . . . Porro quarta persecutio sarracenorum loco assiriorum successit. . . . A tempore ergo Zacharie papa cuius diebus larga pace conquievit ytalia verba haec cepere compleri.' After this Joachim turns to the exposition of the oracle as the fifth persecution and onwards. These concords of persecutions correspond exactly to similar sequences in Joachim's works; see the summaries in Reeves, Hirsch-Reich, *RTAM* xxi. 216–22. Many details in the Paduan manuscript also correspond to Joachim's expositions, e.g. on Pope Zacharias cf. *Lib. Conc.*, f. 41^r, and *Lib. Fig.* II, Pl. X, where precisely the same words occur. Shortly afterwards the Paduan exposition quotes one of Joachim's favourite texts: 'Litera enim occidit, spiritus autem vivificat'; see *infra*, p. 17 n. 3.

[2] Apocalypse 5: 1.

[3] Reeves, Hirsh-Reich, *RTAM* xxi. 216–22.

the whole of history is seen as two great parallel streams rolling on towards their respective consummations in the First and Second Advents.[1] There is, as yet, no hint of any Trinitarian pattern in history: the tribulation of Antichrist closes the New Dispensation with no suggestion of an apotheosis of history in the Age of the Spirit, except in one significant detail, namely, the conversion of the Jews before the End.[2] Joachim has little of interest to say on the text of the oracle itself, and clearly the most significant point of this little exposition is that he pushes aside the prophecy and deals in trenchant terms with his own interpretation of history. We see Joachim, then, in this first interview, already known as one who interprets prophecy, whose exposition of history in terms of con-cords between the two Dispensations is approved by the Pope, and who is commissioned by His Holiness to start writing his two great works, the *Liber Concordie* and the *Expositio in Apocalypsim*.[3] From Robert of Auxerre, one of the earliest chroniclers to write about Joachim, we learn that he also visited Pope Urban III at Verona in 1186. But no reliable details of this visit are known.[4]

The second interview was the famous one of the winter of 1190/1 in which Richard Cœur de Lion met Joachim in Messina. The cultural connections between England and Sicily at this time have been stressed by Miss Jamison[5] and we may speculate as to whether

[1] On Joachim's patterns of 'twos' and 'threes', *infra*, p. 19. Also Reeves, *MARS* ii. 74–7.

[2] On Joachim's attitude towards the Jews see B. Hirsch-Reich, 'Judentum im Mittelalter', *Miscellanea Mediaevalia*, iv. 228–63. The final conversion of the Jews was a common medieval theme but one of peculiar significance to Joachim. It is significant that, according to the material preserved at Fiore, when Joachim called together three close disciples to tell them of his Eastertide vision, he spoke solely of imminent tribula-tion, not at all of *renovatio*, see *AS*, p. 106; Baraut, *AST* xxvi. 216, and *infra*, p. 23 n. 1.

[3] The fact of the commission by Lucius III is attested by Joachim's Testamentary Letter (*infra*, p. 28) and the letter of Pope Clement III, both printed at the beginning of the *Lib. Conc.* The material for the life of Joachim edited by Baraut specifically mentions the interview at Veroli (*AST* xxvi. 215–16). Curiously enough, however, this ancient *Vita* connects the permission given by Pope Lucius with the *Psalterium* rather than the other works. The story given here differs considerably from Luke of Cosenza's and arouses suspicion in some details. Luke is a prime witness and therefore I have followed his account.

[4] All recent writers accept Joachim's visit to Verona as authentic and some authoriza-tion by Urban III is implied by Joachim's Testamentary Letter and by Clement III's letter, but it should be noted that for the story that Joachim went to Verona to meet Urban the oldest authority is Robert of Auxerre, writing before 1212 (*MGHS* xxvi. 248–9).

[5] E. Jamison, (i) 'The Sicilian-Norman Kingdom in the Mind of Anglo-Norman Contemporaries', *Proceedings of the British Academy* (London, 1938), pp. 237–85;

Richard had arrived already determined to see this famous abbot. Roger Howden tells us that the King, hearing much by common fame of Joachim, Abbot of Curazzo, who was said to possess the spirit of prophecy, sent for him and willingly listened to the prophet's wise words. For Joachim was learned in the Scriptures and had written an exposition of St. John's visions.[1] Joachim was now the much-discussed abbot endowed with the spirit of prophecy, but this was firmly linked with the study of the Scriptures and especially of the Apocalypse.

So the Abbot stood in the midst of the eager group of English courtiers[2] 'tam clericis quam laicis' and expounded the vision of St. John concerning the Dragon with seven heads: 'Reges septem sunt, quinque ceciderunt, et unus est, et unus nondum venit.' The five heads that had fallen Joachim interpreted as *Herodes, Nero, Constantius, Maumet, Melsemutus.* Then, pronouncing Saladin to be the 'one that is', Joachim prophesied his downfall, and, turning to the King, said: 'Haec omnia reservavit Dominus et per te fieri permittet, Qui dabit tibi de inimiciis tuis victoriam . . .' Of the 'one not yet come', Joachim declared his belief that this was Antichrist, and that he was already fifteen years old but not yet come to power. While everyone expressed admiration at these prognostications, the King asked Joachim where Antichrist was born and where he was to reign. Joachim answered that Antichrist was already born *in urbe Romana* and that he would obtain the apostolic see, whereat the King replied: 'Si Antichristus in Roma natus est et ibi sedem apostolicam possidebit, scio quod ipse est ille Clemens qui modo papa est.' ('Haec autem dicebat quia papam illum odio habebat', remarks the chronicler.) Joachim's apparently unorthodox view of Antichrist then prompted the King to put forward the standard version of Antichrist's career: 'Putabam quod Antichristus nasceretur in Babylonia, etc.' Soon the whole assembly was absorbed in a heated discussion and refutation of Joachim's views: 'plures tamen et fere omnes viri ecclesiastici in scripturis Divinis plurimum eruditi nitebantur probare in contrarium.' It was a continuing debate: 'tamen adhuc sub judice est', wrote Howden in his first or 'Benedict' version of this interview, and, when he revised it a few years later, he took the

(ii) 'Alliance of England and Sicily in the Second Half of the Twelfth Century', *Journal of the Warburg and Courtauld Institutes,* vi (1943), pp. 20–32.

[1] Roger Howden, *Cronica,* RS, iii. 75.

[2] This account is taken from the two versions: 'Benedict of Peterborough', *Gesta Henrici II et Ricardi I,* RS, ii. 151–5; Roger Howden, *Cronica,* RS, iii. 75–9.

opportunity to insert more material on Antichrist. Thus Joachim's thoughts could spark off a continuing discussion about the central problems of history: the seven tyrannies of the Dragon, the scourge of the Saracens, the advent of Antichrist.

The authenticity of the two accounts of this encounter at Messina has been much questioned.[1] Doubts were aroused partly by the discrepancies between the two, but, since Lady Stenton has demonstrated that Roger Howden accompanied Richard on his crusade and that he was himself the author of both versions of the discussion, these may reasonably be said to have been cleared away.[2] A more fundamental criticism is that the account puts into Joachim's mouth views that were not his. Thus F. Russo has argued that the whole episode is a fabrication by Joachim's enemies, since the statement that Antichrist *iam natus est in civitate romana et in sede apostolica sublimabitur* 'è talmente contrario allo spirito di Gioacchino'.[3] Here we plunge at once into the controversy which has always bedevilled discussion of Joachim's position: were his views really heretical, or was he entangled in dangerous statements by the machinations of those who opposed him, particularly in the Cistercian Order? From the thirteenth century to the present day there have been historians who seem to be more concerned to establish either his orthodoxy or heresy than to discover what he really thought. The proper way to proceed is surely to ask quite simply whether the interpretation expounded at Messina finds corroboration in the *Expositio in Apocalypsim*, the work which Roger Howden specifically mentions, and which was indubitably Joachim's own work. There the Dragon's heads are named exactly as at Messina, except that the fifth is designated as the Emperor Henry IV. This concentrates attention on the rare name *Melsemutus* assigned to the fifth head at Messina. Russo claims that this does not occur in Joachim's genuine works,[4] but this statement is not true: twice over in the *Expositio* Joachim speaks of *Meselmutus* or the 'Mauri qui vulgo dicuntur Meselmuti', assigning these persecutors to the time of the Dragon's fifth head.[5] Clearly there is a discrepancy here in the naming of the fifth head, but we

---

[1] Notably, among recent writers, by Buonaiuti, *Gioacchino da Fiore*, pp. 156–68; Russo, *Misc. Franc.* xli. 329–31.

[2] D. Stenton, 'Roger of Hoveden and Benedict', *EHR* lxviii (1953), pp. 574–82. See also R. Southern, *Western Views of Islam in the Middle Ages* (Cambridge, Mass., 1962), p. 40 n. 8.

[3] Russo, *Misc. Franc.* xli, p. 329 (quoting Howden, loc. cit., p. 78).

[4] Russo, loc. cit., p. 331.   [5] *Expos.*, ff. 116ᵛ, 134ᵛ.

need not be disturbed by variation in the identity of the seven heads, since variation was a common habit with Joachim and his remark in the *Expositio* that he had picked up rumours of *Meselmutus* and his people from eyewitnesses of their persecutions gives this detail in the Messina story an authentic ring—indeed, this may have been the occasion when he heard of them. The final proof on this point concerning Meselmutus lies in the fact that the figure of the Dragon in the *Liber Figurarum* gives *Meselmothus* as the fifth head.[1] For those convinced of the genuineness of the *Liber Figurarum* this is a strong argument for the authenticity of the Messina interview. It is true that the coincidence has been used in the opposite sense by Russo to suggest that the Messina episode is demonstrably false because based on a later spurious work, but this argument falls to the ground once it has been demonstrated that the 'Benedict' version of the encounter must have been written within a year or two at most of the time of the interview.[2]

Turning now to Joachim's rather surprising statement that Antichrist was already born in Rome, this seems to have misled some modern historians as much as King Richard, but a careful reading of the *Expositio*—and other genuine works—makes the point quite clear. For the Church, Joachim constantly uses the term Jerusalem, and this is juxtaposed to Rome, which always means the secular realm, more specifically, the Roman *Imperium*.[3] In his patterns of concords Rome equals Babylon, a point which is strikingly made in the Babylon/Rome pair of figures in the *Liber Figurarum*.[4] Thus when Joachim says that Antichrist is born in Rome he is only translating the recognized legend into his own terms. As for the prophecy that Antichrist would usurp the seat of St. Peter, Joachim certainly expected a pseudo-pope as one of the manifestations of Antichrist, without implying in the least that the Roman Church was to become identified with a carnal church of Babylon.[5]

We may thus accept Roger Howden's double account as a record

[1] *Lib. Fig.* II, Pl. XIV.

[2] Among recent supporters of the authenticity of the English story are Jamison, loc. cit. (i), pp. 263 seq.; J. de Ghellinck, *L'Essor de la littérature latine au XIIe siècle* (Brussels, Paris, 1946), i. 200; Grundmann, *NF*, pp. 48 seq. and *DA* xvi. 499–500.

[3] For detailed references see Reeves, Hirsch-Reich, *Studies, ad indicem.*

[4] *Lib. Fig.* II, Pls. XVI, XVII.

[5] *Expos.*, ff. 166^v–168^r, expounding Apocalypse 13: 11: 'Et vidi aliam bestiam ascendentem de terra'. See especially f. 168^r: 'Ita bestia que ascendet de terra habitura sit quendam magnum prelatum, que sit similis Symonis Magi, et quasi universalis pontifex in toto orbe terrarum.'

of a genuine encounter. Nevertheless, there is a divergence between the two versions which must be noted. According to the 'Benedict' account, Howden committed himself to a prophecy of victory to King Richard over the Saracen; this was modified in the later 'Howden' version to a vague pronouncement that the time for the recovery of Jerusalem was 'not yet'. No doubt this alteration was due to the limited success of the crusade. In any case, the prophecy was made briefly in passing, and Joachim's real attention was concentrated on the exposition of the Apocalypse and the programme of Things to Come. He was concerned with exegesis rather than with literal prophecy. It is noteworthy that at this period he was still more occupied with the tribulations to be endured in the near future than with the Age of the Spirit to come afterwards, but the context of the conversation must have suggested the trials of Christians and their stern conflicts rather than the Sabbath of quietness to follow. This was certainly the focus of interest for crusaders, and, as we have seen, Richard and his companions drank in the Abbot's exposition eagerly, applied his words with alacrity to Pope Clement III, and went off at once into a debate on the where and when of Antichrist. Joachim's interpretations of history were too lofty and subtle for common understanding, but they were certainly not irrelevant to his contemporaries. This episode shows him in the midst of the European political scene, the sought-after prophet caught up in one of its major preoccupations—the menace of the Saracen and the crusade of the faithful against the infidel. We have noticed that Joachim had been collecting information on the situation of Christians in Spain and Mauretania; we know from a reference in the *Expositio*[1] that he was again in Messina in 1195, questioning a man who had escaped from Alexandria, for he reported with a thrill of horror his rumour: 'dixit se audisse a quodam magno Sarraceno misisse Patharenos Legatos suos ad illos, postulantes ab eis communionem et pacem.' Contemporary happenings form part of the material on which Joachim's mind fed. His meditations upon the inner concords of the two Testaments were not concerned with a dead history but with a continuing drama *usque ad presens.*[2] Contemporary events illumined the concords of Scripture; the study of the Testaments gave the clue to the vast events on the threshhold of which Joachim believed he stood.

---

[1] *Expos.*, f. 134ʳ.
[2] *Expos.*, f. 9ᵛ, where the phrase recurs more than once.

The next encounter shows him vividly as the prophet denouncing contemporary political wrongs by the light of Biblical prophecy. Professor Grundmann has recently published a fragmentary *Vita Joachimi Abbatis* which he has established as the work of an anonymous disciple. This contains a striking account of a whirlwind descent made by Joachim on the Emperor Henry VI when the latter came to south Italy in 1191 to claim the kingdom.[1] Joachim denounces the deeds of the *feroces barbarorum animi* but declares that in these events are fulfilled, by concord, the doom pronounced by Ezekiel upon Tyre (the kingdom of Tancred): 'For thus saith the Lord God: Behold, I will bring upon Tyrus Nebuchadrezzar king of Babylon, a king of kings from the north, with horses, and with chariots, and with horsemen, and companies, and much people' (Ezek. 26: 7). And thus it was, 'sub misterio veterum de prophetatione novorum': the Emperor Henry VI, like Nebuchadrezzar of Babylon, took the new Tyre and devastated it. There can be no doubt as to the fierceness with which Joachim proclaimed the future, for—to his retreating back—Henry's marshal remarked: 'Quanta mala latent sub cuculla illa!' Henry accepted the role of Nebuchadrezzar, however, and later honoured the Abbot, his foundation, and his family. We know from the privileges received, as well as some biographical episodes, that Joachim was later on good terms with the Imperial authority, especially the Empress Constance.[2] Yet in his interpretation of contemporary history there can be little doubt that the Roman *Imperium* was the New Babylon.[3]

In all these interviews we see Joachim impinging dramatically on the contemporary scene in his interpretations of events by means of

[1] For an account of how this material was preserved, *infra*, p. 112. The text has been edited by Baraut, *AST* xxvi. 220–5; Grundmann, *DA* xvi. 535–9. Papebroch (*AS*, p. 108) takes some of this material from the *Cronologia* of Jacobus Graecus.

[2] A famous interview with the Empress Constance is recounted by Luke of Cosenza (*AS*, p. 94): 'Sexta feria in Parasceve sedebam cum eo in claustro Sancti Spiritus de Panormo et ecce vocatus ad Palatium fuit ad Imperatricem Constantiam, quae illi confiteri volebat. Ivit et invenit eam intra ecclesiam in sella consueta sedentem; iussus (autem) sedere, in sellula pro ipso posita sedit; sed cum Imperatrix aperuit ei propositum confitendi, eam qua debuit auctoritate fraenavit, et respondit dicens Quia ego nunc locum Christi, tu vero poenitentis Magdalenae tenes, descende, sede in terra, et ita fideliter confitere: aliter enim non debeo te audire. Descendit et sedit Imperatrix in terra et humiliter confessa est peccata sua, mirantibus omnibus cum ipsa, quae retulit auctoritatem Apostolicam in Abbate fuisse.' On the privileges granted to St. Giovanni in Fiore by the Hohenstaufen see W. Holtzmann, *Papst- Kaiser- und Normannenurkunden aus Unteritalien*, ii: S. Giovanni di Fiore, *QFIAB* xxxvi (1956), pp. 5 seq. See also *AS*, p. 108.

[3] See especially *Expos.*, ff. 173ᵛ–174ʳ.

the concords of the Scriptures, but there is little to suggest the long
meditations on the concords, the mystical experiences in which his
great images were 'given', the *interna cantilena*[1] of the spiritual
psalmody with which he praised God. There is one further contemporary account of Joachim which also incorporates the record of
an interview. It occurs in the *Chronicon Anglicanum* of Ralph of
Coggeshall.[2] Joseph Stevenson, who edited this work for the Rolls
Series, thought that the inclusion and unusual length of this account
of one so far removed from English affairs was due to the common
Cistercian affiliation.[3] It is true that one part at least of Ralph's
information was derived from a Cistercian source, namely the interview which Adam, Abbot of Persigny, had with Joachim in Rome.
But this meeting evidently took place after Joachim's break with the
Cistercian Order, for Ralph described Joachim as 'ordinis Cister-
ciensis, sed Cisterciensibus minime subiectus'.[4] Is it not, then,
likely that a vital interest in this contemporary prophet inspired
Ralph's account, rather than his ambiguous connection with the
Cistercian Order, which is so quickly passed over?

Ralph's account focuses at once on Joachim's gift of divine
wisdom—'cum fere esset prius illiteratus'—and the interpretation
of the Apocalypse which flowed from it. This shows that the
Expositio, or an early version of it, was already known. The Coggeshall historian gives a clear exposition of Joachim's method of
concords between the Old and New Testaments, with his pattern
of Seven Seals and their parallel openings. He reports Joachim as
placing the contemporary moment in the persecution of the fifth seal:

dicit agi temporibus nostris a Saladino et eius successoribus qui terram
Hierosolymitanam invaserunt et matrem Syon a civitate sua Hierusalem
transmigrare compulerunt. . . . Hanc autem persecutionem quintam
quintae persecutioni Veteris Testamenti non incongrue assignare videtur,
in quo muri Hierusalem eversi sunt . . . et populus in Babylonem a
Nabuchodonosor captivus addictus fuit. Dicit etiam quod anno Domi-
nicae Incarnationis MCXCIX incipiet sexta visio et sexti sigilli apertio,
sub qua visione probat auctoritate Apocalypsis quod complebitur omnis
Antichristi persecutio et eiusdem mors et perditio. (*Chronicon Anglicanum*, RS, p. 68.)

It seems clear that this account must derive from a pre-1199 source.
The record of Adam of Persigny's interview with Joachim follows.

[1] *Psalt.*, f. 228ᵛ.
[2] Ralph of Coggeshall, *Chronicon Anglicanum*, ed. J. Stevenson, RS, pp. 67–79.
[3] Ibid., p. xi.   [4] Ibid., p. 67.

One would naturally deduce that the material in the preceding account also came from Adam, were it not that in the best manuscript the description of the meeting is a later marginal addition in the same hand. As recorded here, Adam concentrated at once in the interview on the nature of Joachim's inspiration by asking how he was able to foretell future events: 'an ex prophetia, an conjectura, seu revelatione?' Joachim replied that 'se neque prophetiam, neque conjecturam, neque revelationem de his habere'. 'Sed Deus,' *inquit,* 'Qui olim dedit prophetis spiritum prophetiae, mihi dedit spiritum intelligentiae, ut in Dei spiritu omnia mysteria sacrae Scripturae clarissime intelligam, sicut sancti prophetae intellexerunt qui eam olim in Dei spiritu ediderunt.' Adam and Joachim then went on to discuss Antichrist in terms very similar to those of the Messina interview, with Joachim emphasizing that when he declared Antichrist to be already growing up in Rome he meant in the mystical Babylon which he identified with Rome. He then made a remarkable prophecy: 'Praedixit quoque Innocentium Tertium successorem non habiturum.' Finally, when asked how many years hence the reign of Antichrist would be, Joachim replied that, unless death intervened, he might see this himself; to which answer Adam appends the observation: 'videbatur autem fere sexagenarius.'

It has been customary to date this conversation to 1195/6,[1] but the Coggeshall account does not, in fact, pin it down exactly and the reference to Innocent III obviously creates a difficulty. This might conceivably have been added later, but in the context of the sense of imminence evident in Joachim's last reply, it seems a likely enough forecast for him to make if Adam was talking to him in 1198, just after Innocent III's election. The conversation seems to be all of

---

[1] The interview has been connected with Joachim's likely presence in Rome to obtain recognition of the Order of Fiore, granted by Celestine III on 25 August 1196 (see Grundmann, *DA* xvi. 481, 504), but there is no necessary reason for tying the two events together. Two recent writers (Ghellinck, op. cit. (ref. p. 9 n. 2), i. 190; H. de Lubac, *Exégèse médiévale: Les Quatres Sens de l'Écriture* (Paris, 1961), p. 483) say that in 1195 Adam de Persigny was charged to examine the doctrines of Joachim, but the only source for this, so far as I know, is Papebroch (*AS*, pp. 138–40) who cites a manuscript in the Bibl. S. Victoris, Paris. Ralph's account of Joachim occurs between the entries for the years 1195 and 1196, but it is introduced simply by the vague words *Hac tempestate*, referring to the previous paragraph on Saracen incursions into Spain. As it stands, the account must have been written after Innocent III's election and its position in the chronology need indicate no more than that the Saracen menace of those years provided the suitable context for Joachim's prophecies. The fact that Adam wrote on the *Psalterium decem chordarum* may possibly reflect the influence of Joachim (see *PL* ccxi, col. 723).

a piece and it has an authentic ring. If, therefore, we take the complete Coggeshall account—whether derived from one source or two —as representing Joachim's state of mind in 1198, it shows us the concentrated expectation with which he was awaiting the year 1200 and what would follow it. Possibly in the last two years of his life this high excitement began to be modified. The Coggeshall account is also of great interest as evidence of the extent to which Joachim's thought was known in England before 1200, but Ralph's exposition suggests that it was only imperfectly understood. He reports the Abbot correctly as placing the death of Antichrist at the end of the sixth seal, but then makes the Resurrection of the dead follow immediately and afterwards the seventh seal, 'id est sanctorum aeterna glorificatio'. Thus the Sabbath Age of the seventh seal is clearly placed outside history. This does not represent Joachim's distinctive view of the Sabbath Age or third *status* within history. Indeed, although these Cistercians appear to understand Joachim's outlook and method better than most, the real nature of his belief in the third *status* is not grasped. It is striking that contemporaries took hold of his pattern of twos in the concords of Old and New Testaments but not of his pattern of threes. We shall see that this remains true in the first phase of Joachimist influence after his death: it took nearly fifty years for the dynamite contained in his doctrine of the three *status* to explode.

By no means all contemporary Cistercians kept an open mind on the subject of Joachim. We have one astonishingly bitter attack, inflamed no doubt by Joachim's break away from the Cistercian authority. Geoffrey of Auxerre, the friend of St. Bernard, makes his onslaught in a fragment of a sermon which has been rescued by Fr. Leclercq.[1] It is a unique attack, because as yet there is no perception of the heretical implications of Joachim's doctrines, and therefore Geoffrey, convinced none the less that the Abbot's views are dangerous, focuses attention on his supposed Jewish origin. No other allegation that Joachim was a converted Jew has survived, yet Geoffrey's accusation at once commands attention because of the evidences of Jewish thought in Joachim's writings. Dr. Hirsch-Reich made a thorough study of Joachim's relations with Judaism, but declared decisively against the idea of Jewish parentage.[2] The

---

[1] *Studia Anselmiana*, xxxi (Rome, 1953), J. Leclercq, *Analecta Monastica*, 2nd Ser., pp. 200–1.
[2] B. Hirsch-Reich, 'Joachim v. Fiore u. das Judentum' (ref. p. 6 n. 2), pp. 239–43.

point, however, cannot finally be proved one way or the other. There are many diatribes against Joachim, but this contemporary Cistercian one stands alone:

Ex iudaeis orta persona est, in iudaismo, quem necdum satis evomuisse videtur, annis pluribus educata, quae sicut per eos qui certius cognoverunt tandem nobis innotuit, licet non solus ipse sed etiam sui pares suos potissimum a vobis et suas hactenus quam studiose poterant absconderint aquas. Nec mediocrem confert ei auctoritatem ipsum barbarum nomen: dicitur enim Ioachim. Quod de nullo diebus nostris meminimus nos audisse, ut in baptismo retinuerit nomen quod in indaismo prius habuerat. Multorum etiam habitus noster ei conciliat animos, et quod cisterciensis ordinis cum voluerit monachum sese exhibet et abbatem esse. Nam et olim quidem exstitit, sed ab annis iam . . . [next page lost]. (Op. cit., p. 201.)

II

JOACHIM'S VIEW OF HISTORY

JOACHIM would never have called himself a prophet in the sense of one who foretells the future according to revelations given directly and instantly to him. His whole doctrine of spiritual intelligence expounded in the writings, as well as the accounts he gives of his own mystical experiences, corroborates the disclaimer so clearly made in the conversation with Adam of Persigny. The *spiritualis intellectus* or *intelligentia* with which he believed he had been endowed was indeed a gift from on high, but it was poured out only on those who wrestled and agonized over the hard, external realities of the Letter. The two Testaments are the indispensable framework of spiritual understanding and no one can reach it by a short cut: only to those who have disciplined themselves by long study, meditation, and prayer upon the Letter of the Scriptures will the Book be opened, the secrets revealed, and full illumination given. Under many symbols Joachim expresses his sense of the unshakable realities of the two Testaments which give shape to all his thought: they are the two cherubim guarding the Ark of the *Spiritualis Intellectus*;[1] they are the feet, like two pillars of fire, of the Angel of Apocalypse 10: 1; and whilst the rainbow about his head is the 'spiritualis intellectus qui ex utroque procedit', they are also the earth and sea upon which he plants his feet;[2] they are the two iron plates between which the Host is baked (prefigured in the cake baked for Elijah by the widow of Zarephath);[3] and they are the earth and water of Elijah's altar on Mount Carmel upon which the fire falls.[4] The *Spiritualis Intellectus* cannot be attained by abandoning the discipline of the Letter and the shapes it imposes upon thought: the preparation is an arduous labour, a pilgrimage through the desert. Like Elijah we must build the altar of the Old Testament and pour out the water of the New Testament and be expectant that the fire of the Spirit will come down:

[1] *Lib. Conc.*, f. 18ʳ. [2] *Expos.*, f. 137ᵛ–138ʳ.
[3] *Lib. Conc.*, f. 100ᵛ; cf. 1 Kgs. 17: 13–15.
[4] *Lib. Conc.*, ff. 102ᵛ–103ʳ; cf. 1 Kgs. 18: 30–8.

Construendum est nobis cum Helya altare de terra ipsa: terra collocanda inferius: ut aqua desuper locari queat: expectantibus nobis ignem de celo, que consumat terram et aquam, expectantibus spiritualem intellectum, quia terrenam illam superficiem littere que de terra est et de terra loquitur evacuando consumat: et nihilominus evangelicam doctrinam designatam hic in aqua lambendo commutet: secundum quod aqua illa crassa quam posuit in altari Neemias sacerdos, conversa est in ignem aut sicut in Cana Galilee aqua hydriarum commutata est in vinum. Et hoc quare? ut caro que interposita est consumpta usquequaque deficiat: ut omnis carnalis intelligentia a facie spiritus inanescat. Opus inquam nos in hoc opere altare testamenti prioris pro dono omnipotentis Dei ordinate componere, fundentes et statuentes desuper aquam testamenti novi: ut aliud inter aliud, ac si rota infra rotam inesse per concordiam videatur. Invisibilem autem spiritum ignem suum spiritualem, veluti de tertio celo dirigere: ut veniente quod perfectum est evacuetur quod est ex parte. (*Lib. Conc.*, f. 7ʳ.)

The study of the Letter is essential, yet it interposes a barrier. The *Spiritualis Intellectus* is sepulchred *in ventre littere* or *in corde littere*: 'Occiderunt ergo Christum et sepellierunt in monumento: occiderunt et spiritualem intellectum velantes eum sub littera . . .' (*Expos.*, f. 95ʳ). Only the risen Christ, the Lion of the tribe of Judah, can split the stone and rend the barrier. Or again, under another figure, no one can open the Book 'quousque veniret ille qui passurus erat cum littera et resurrecturus cum spirituali intellectu'.[1] To those who prepare by study and contemplation the experience of illumination and liberation is given: 'transibit itaque labor doctrine et remanebit diligendi libertas.'[2] Thus Joachim claims understanding neither by revelation without study nor by study without revelation. Although 'the Letter killeth, but the Spirit quickeneth' (as he so often quotes),[3] Letter and Spirit are inseparably bound together.

The relationship is clearly a Trinitarian one: in Joachim's phrase, the *Spiritualis Intellectus* proceeds from both the Testaments, just as the Spirit proceeds from both the Father and the Son. This relationship interpenetrates the history with which the two Testaments are concerned. In the Old Dispensation one unitary line of Fathers proclaims God the Father as far as Jacob, but from this

---

[1] *Expos.*, f. 110ᵛ.
[2] *Expos.*, f. 86ʳ.
[3] 2 Cor. 3: 6, quoted 37 times in the *Lib. Conc.* and *Expos.*

point onwards the double lines of Fathers and Judges (or Kings) show forth the procession of Son and Spirit from Father:

Ne quis extimet otiosum vel absurdum quod ita duas lineas istas ostendimus ex una procedere. Una enim fuit usque ad Jacob: et exinde ex una due, que et ipse unitate maxima connexe sunt: intelligat in illa una que precessit in patribus venerari oportere mysterium Dei Patris. In illa que propagata est per Iudam mysterium Filii: in ea vero que per Joseph et Moysen mysterium Spiritus Sancti. Super quo evidentissima similitudo potest videri de testamento novo: cum constet Luce clarius quam Mattheus qui loqui exorsus est de nativitate Christi, qua natus est de virgine secundum carnem: secutus est lineam generationum, incipiens ab Habraam et perducens illam usque ad Joseph virum Marie. Lucas autem qui locutus est de spirituali . . . illos magis patres scribere voluit qui dicebantur patres secundum legem: . . . Ut ergo in novo testamento linea quam texuit Mattheus pertinet ad carnem Filii: quam vero prosecutus est Lucas ad gratiam Spiritus Sancti. Ita et in veteri linea que propagata est per filios Iude et David pertinet secundum significatum ad Filium: que autem per iudices ad Spiritum Sanctum. (*Lib. Conc.*, f. 16ᵛ.)

Thus the two genealogies of St. Matthew and St. Luke, like the double lines of descent in the Old Testament, embody the mystery of the Son and Spirit proceeding from the Father. This Trinitarian structure of the lines of descent which form the central frame of sacred history is well expressed diagrammatically in the *Liber Concordie*.[1] Similarly, the famous three orders which characterize successively the three *status* of history emerge from the structure of history in a Trinitarian relationship: the *ordo conjugatorum* of the first *status* is initiated in Adam; the *ordo clericorum* finds its symbol in Isaiah, who appears in the days of Ozias, when the second *status* begins; the *ordo monachorum*, representing the Spirit, must have a double procession, and Joachim finds this in Elisha, under whom the *initiatio prima* or procession from the Father takes place, and St. Benedict, exactly forty-two generations later, who represents the second *initiatio*:

Igitur primus ordo initiatus est ab Adam: secundus ab Ozia rege Iuda: tertius secundum aliquid ab Helyseo propheta: secundum aliquid a beato

---

[1] Exigencies of space have forced the diagrams into a jumbled form in the printed edition, as also in some manuscripts. Though badly arranged, the conception can be clearly grasped in Bib. Ant., MS. 328, ff. 14ᵛ, 20ᵛ–21ʳ, but it is set out most clearly and beautifully in Bib. Laur., MS. Conv. Soppr. 358, ff. 10ᵛ, 11ʳ, 15ᵛ, 16ᵛ. See also Bib. Laur., MS. Plut. VIII, dextr. X, ff. 16ʳ⁻ᵛ, 24ᵛ–25ʳ, 27ʳ. For a full account of these diagrams see Reeves, Hirsch-Reich, *Studies*, pp. 31–38.

Benedicto. Quare sic? Quia Spiritus Sanctus a Patre Filioque procedit. Si enim a solo Patre procederet sicut Filius, oportunum esse videretur ut ordo clericorum et monachorum similiter inciperent: et simul ambo consumationem acciperent. Si autem a solo Filio sicut Filius a solo Patre, ita videtur pertinere tantummodo tertius status ad Spiritum Sanctum: quomodo secundus ad Filium. Quia vero unus est Pater a quo procedunt Filius et Spiritus Sanctus: unus scilicet qui a Patre simul procedit et Filio: duo qui procedunt ab uno Patre: recte primus status ascribitur Patri: secundus soli Filio: tertius communis Filio et Spiritui Sancto. (*Lib. Conc.*, f. 9ᵛ.)

Thus the third *status*, as well as the second, has its origins in the first, as both Son and Spirit proceed from the Father. This pattern, again, is set out diagrammatically in the *Liber Concordie*.[1]

Out of these early pages of the *Liber Concordie* there emerges the essential framework of all Joachim's thought about the meaning of history: the double pattern of twos and threes. There are two Testaments and these clearly give the pattern of twos, of two great eras of history governed by the Two Persons, 'una ingenita, alia genita', and culminating in the First and Second Advents respectively. Here the divine purpose is perceived in the histories of the two great peoples elected by God—*Populus Judaicus* and *Populus Gentilis*[2]—and in the concords between the two eras. But when the procession of the Spirit is added, the pattern of twos can become a pattern of threes. Joachim calls these two ways of looking at history two *diffinitiones* and assigns the pattern of threes to Alpha, the pattern of twos to Omega (ꞷ). 'Prima diffinitio designatur in A quod est elementum triangulatum. Secunda designatur in ꞷ in quo virgula de medio duarum procedit. Utrumque ergo sciri oportuit: quia utrumque plenarie pertinet ad catholicam fidem' (*Lib. Conc.*, f. 10ʳ). Joachim's working method is by concords and his double pattern gives him a double assignation of concords: according to the pattern of threes they must be assigned in three overlapping eras: from Adam to Christ, from Ozias to 'these times', from St. Benedict to the *consummatio seculi*; according to the other pattern, they must be

---

[1] *Lib. Conc.*, ff. 11ʳ⁻ᵛ, 24ᵛ (but in the printed edition the idea is completely lost). Once again, this conception needs a good deal of space to set out and is only seen clearly in certain manuscripts, e.g. Conv. Soppr. 358, ff. 10ᵛ, 11ʳ, 21ᵛ⁻22ʳ; Plut. VIII, dextr. X, ff. 16ʳ⁻ᵛ, 21ᵛ⁻22ʳ (a unique version of this diagram), 34ʳ. See also MSS. Rome, Vat., Lat. 4861, ff. 25ʳ, 38ʳ; Borghese 190, f. 37ʳ⁻ᵛ; Urb. Lat. 8, ff. 30ᵛ⁻31ʳ; Bib. Cors. 41, F. 2, f. 12ᵛ; Padua, Bib. Anton., 328, f. 26ʳ; Paris, Bib. Nat., Lat. 15254, ff. 249ᵛ⁻250ʳ; 16280, ff. 46ᵛ⁻47ᵛ.

[2] *Lib. Conc.*, f. 19ʳ; *Expos.*, f. 37ᵛ.

assigned in two eras only: from Adam to Christ and from Ozias to the *consummatio seculi*. In a passage explaining this Joachim makes it clear that this double structure derives from the mystery of the Trinity:

Propter illa que dicta sunt superius de sacro mysterio Trinitatis, duplicem esse diximus causam concordie secundum quod tres esse diximus ordines electorum, et duos populos vocatos ad fidem. Diximus etiam quod in prima assignatione concordie incipiendum ab Adam et desinendum in Christo: incipiendum est ab Ocia, et desinendum in temporibus istis: incipiendum a temporibus St. Benedicti et desinendum in consummatione seculi. In secunda assignatione incipiendum est ab Adam . . . et desinendum in Christo: incipiendum ab Ocia rege Iuda, et desinendum in consummatione seculi. (*Lib. Conc.*, f. 13ᵛ.)

It is essential for the understanding of Joachim's ideas to grasp this double method of thinking. The interplay of the Two Persons and the Third, forming the double concords of twos and threes, is very clearly seen in a passage which sums up the whole argument:

Ex duplici causa concordiarum questio mota est, et decisa, ostendente nobis veritate que ait: Ego sum Alpha et Omega: quod et propter equalitatem personarum tres ordines electi sunt a principio tribus temporibus specialiter deputati: et propter auctoritatem Patris et nativitatem Filii duo populi electi sunt ad fidem unius Dei sub duobus testamentis: Judaicus videlicet et Gentilis: et propter notitiam Spiritus Sancti, qui a Patre Filioque procedit, aliqui processerunt ex eis tam in veteri testamento quam in novo, manentes sub doctrina spiritualium virorum, in quibus et illa perfectio inventa est de qua dicit Apostolus: Ubi spiritus domini, ibi libertas. Iam igitur ostensa causa et assignata ratione de utraque concordia. Primo quidem de prima diffinitione agere incipiemus, inchoantes ab Adam et ab Ozia et pervenientes usque ad Christum: et usque ad hec tempora nostra: deinde secundum aliam diffinitionem usque ad consummationem seculi. (*Lib. Conc.*, f. 19ʳ.)

Joachim, then, founded his interpretation of history upon a belief that it reflected the nature of the Godhead, sometimes in the twofold relationship of Father and Son, sometimes in the threefold relationship of Father, Son, and Holy Spirit. He reached his interpretations of the past and his expectations for the future by a process of minute study and long pondering. Yet these historical studies are never divorced from spiritual perception. It is important to realize that Joachim's spiritual longing to approach the mystery of the Triune God was part and parcel of his Scriptural and historical studies. When he was 'given' spiritual understanding in moments of vision, this was afterwards expressed alike in theological and historical terms. Joachim's mystical experiences and his historical studies are fused together and this gives a peculiar quality to his work, at once spiritual and exalted and, on the other hand, concrete, framed by earthly events.

That spiritual understanding was given in moments of illumination we know through the autobiographical passages of Joachim's own writings. He records two such moments as crucial in his spiritual development, one at Easter and the other at Whitsuntide. Later, one of the common legends told of him relates a spiritual experience of his youth which would have preceded the other two. We have no evidence for this from Joachim's writings but since the two later ones clearly took place in the midst of his studies, it seems not unlikely that the initial impetus to contemplation of the mysteries came from some earlier experience. If this were associated in his mind with the First Person of the Trinity—and one legend which places the vision on Mount Tabor suggests this—then the Easter and Whitsuntide revelations would naturally take their place in a Trinitarian sequence.

There are three legends of the early experience. The first two have as a setting Joachim's pilgrimage as a young man to the Holy Land.[1] In one, as he lay thirsting in the desert, he was bidden in a dream to drink from a river of oil and, awakening, found he understood all the significances of the Scriptures. In the other, a vision came to him on Mount Tabor of the open Scriptures and the plan which he was to follow in expounding them. Thirdly, there arose the legend which was later the most popular, of how Joachim, walking in the garden during the early days of his monastic life at Sambucina, received at angelic hands the miraculous draught of illumination in the meaning of the Scriptures.[2] All three legends

---

[1] The best evidence that Joachim did make this pilgrimage as a young man comes from a chance remark of Joachim himself (*Quat. Evang.*, p. 93 '. . . *sicut ipsi vidimus Hierosolomis*') and Luke of Cosenza's account of an episode in Syria which Joachim himself recounted to Luke (*AS*, p. 93).

[2] None of these are given exactly in the material preserved at Fiore, but Jacobus Graecus, using this material, implies that Joachim had a mystical experience on Mt. Tabor. Papebroch adds these three legends from Gregorio de Laude's Life of Joachim (*AS*, pp. 97–9). On the history of these legends see *infra*, pp. 72, 102–3. The cult of Joachim includes a reference to Mount Tabor in the *Oremus*: 'Deus, qui gloriam tuam tribus Apostolis in monte Thabor manifestasti et in eodem loco beato Joachim veritatem Scripturarum revelasti . . .' (cited by Crocco, *Gioacchino*, p. 29 n. 24).

stress the same point: the instant gift of spiritual illumination in the meaning of the Scriptures received by one who had before been without understanding. This instantaneous understanding does not accord with Joachim's own account of spiritual strivings or the metaphors of pilgrimage towards the *Spiritualis Intelligentia* which he so often uses. Yet the persistence of these legends must carry weight and, without postulating some such early experience, it is hard to see how Joachim was led into the particular approach to the study of the Scriptures upon which he had already embarked when the Eastertide experience recorded in the *Expositio in Apocalypsim* took place.

In describing this experience Joachim emphasizes the fact that he was already 'labouring in the way' on his exposition of the Apocalypse. He had reached the verse *Fui in spiritu dominica die* when he was moved to write thus:

Et enim cum decursis precedentibus libri huius capitulis, pervenirem ad locum istum, tantam fateor difficultatem et quasi preter solitum perpessus sum angustias intellectus: ut sentiens oppositum mihi lapidem ab ostio monumenti, hebetatus subsisterem: et dans honorem Deo qui pro velle suo claudit et aperit, relicto loco ipso intacto, ad sequentia pertransirem, servans difficultatem eandem universali magistro: ut ipse qui aperuit librum et soluit septem signacula eius, cum sibi esset placitum, mihi vel aliis aperiret. Cumque me occupatum in multis hoc ipsum oblivio procul duceret: factum est verso anni circulo diem adesse paschalem mihique circa horam matutinam excitato a somno, aliquid in libro isto meditanti occurrere: pro quo confisus de dono Dei audacior factus sum ad scribendum, quinimmo in silendo et non scribendo timidior. . . . Et enim cum non nulla iam capere, et maiora adhuc sacramenta nescirem, quasi quedam pugna gerebatur in mente mea, his quidem quod patebant suadentibus ausum, ceteris autem difficultatem minantibus. Cum ergo in supra scripta nocte simile aliquid contigisset, circa medium (ut opinor) noctis silentium et horam qua leo noster de tribu Iuda resurrexisse extimatur a mortuis, subito mihi meditanti aliquid, quadam mentis oculis intelligentie claritate percepta de plenitudine libri huius et tota veteris ac novi testamenti concordia revelatio facta est . . . (*Expos.*, f. 39$^{\mathrm{r-v}}$.)

This is a vivid piece of inner autobiography. We see Joachim battling against the mental obstacle, the great stone which holds the *Spiritualis Intellectus* entombed. We see him turning to other things, and then in the midst of Easter Eve awaking and returning to the mental conflict. Then comes the great moment of liberation, when, at the hour of the Resurrection, the stone is rolled away from the mind and the light streams forth, just as the Spirit is liberated from the Letter. It is an experience explicitly connected with the power of the Risen Christ and explicitly concerned with the concords of the Old and New Testaments. The Lord of all history alone reveals the plenitude of meaning in history. Joachim, we know, was writing his two main works—the *Expositio* and the *Liber Concordie*—simultaneously.[1] Although this experience of illumination occurs in the context of the Apocalypse alone, it clearly belongs also to the *Liber Concordie* and in the Venetian edition of the *Liber Concordie*, at the end of the Testamentary Letter, the last five lines of the passage given above are quoted, beginning: 'Ego Joachim circa medium, ut opinor, noctis silentium . . .'[2]

The first two Persons of the Trinity, the concords of the two Testaments, the *Diffinitio* ⍵ which represents the pattern of twos— all these are comprehended in the Easter vision, while this whole complex of ideas finds its chief exposition in the first two main works of Joachim. Yet because the Spirit issues forth from the Letter of the two Testaments and because in the historic process the third *status* proceeds from the first two, the third Person of the Trinity is already present in Joachim's interpretations. The pattern of threes, the *Diffinitio* A is already expounded in the *Liber Concordie* and the *Expositio*, but the struggle to comprehend the nature of the Trinity is arduous, and only culminates in the moment of illumination which happened at Whitsuntide and is recorded in the Preface to the third chief work, the *Psalterium decem chorda-rum*. Between 1182 and 1184, for some time, Joachim was at the

[1] In the material at Fiore the order of Joachim's experience is puzzling. It is given as (*a*) the Whitsuntide vision at Casamari which led to the writing of the *Psalt.*; (*b*) the visit to Lucius III at Veroli; (*c*) his conversation with three disciples three days after the Easter vision described in the *Expos.* (Baraut, *AST* xxvi. 215–16). Yet Joachim himself says in the Preface to the *Psalt.* that the inception of the *Lib. Conc.* and *Expos.* preceded that of the *Psalt.* (see passage quoted *infra*, pp. 24–5); and Luke of Cosenza tells us that when he first met Joachim at Casamari in 1183 he was dictating and amending the *Lib. Conc.* and *Expos.* simultaneously, while during the year and a half there he also began the *Psalt.* (*AS*, p. 93). Moreover, all the internal evidence of the evolution of Joachim's thought points to the Eastertide experience (and the inception of the *Lib. Conc.* and *Expos.*) as preceding the Whitsuntide experience (and the writing of the *Psalt.*).

[2] The opening words, *Ego Joachim*, suggest that Joachim himself inserted this quotation preceding the *Lib. Conc.*, but, since I have been unable to find it in any of the manuscripts of this work which I have consulted, it must be concluded that the Venetian editors inserted it in the printed edition.

Cistercian house of Casamari, where Luke of Cosenza became his secretary and friend. It is from Luke that we learn that Joachim was at that time revising the first two works and starting the *Psalterium*. It is from Joachim himself that we learn of the time of mental stress through which he passed:

Eram aliquando ego ipse anxius ad verba Dei et querebam per exercitium lectionis ad veritatis notitiam pervenire. Cumque ad eam per legendi studium properare flagrarem, assumens sibi pennas velut Aquile, longius quam erat recedebat a me. Cum autem positus in fervore novissimo, cepi Dei causa diligere psalmodiam multa mihi in scriptura divina, psallenti sub silentio reserrari ceperunt, que antea legendo vestigarene quiveram. . . . Sed cum mihi qui . . . cogitatione et aviditate illius superne civitatis habitator effectus fruebar secundum interiorem hominem non modica visione pacis, accidere illud quod sibi multi . . . queruntur ut rursum ecclesie cura rei familiaris cogeret implicari negociis monasterii . . . compulsus sum iterum cum cordis gemitu . . . exclamare: Heu mihi quia incolatus meus prolongatus est: habitavi cum habitantibus cedar: multum incola fuit anima mea. . . . Accidit post annos aliquot, cum essem apud Cenobium Casemaris, . . . diem adesse solennem in quo dona Sancti Spiritus super sanctos apostolos effusa sunt . . . statui apud me die illo dicere mihi aliquot psalmos ad honorem Sancti Spiritus . . . sperans donari mihi aliquid in die ipso. . . Interea cum ingrederer oratorium et adorarem omnipotentem Deum coram sancto altari, accidit in me velut hesitatio quedam de fide Trinitatis, ac si difficile esset intellectu vel fide etiam omnes personas unum Deum, et unum Deum omnes personas. Quod cum accideret oravi valde, et conterritus vehementer compulsus sum invocare Spiritum Sanctum . . . ut ipse mihi dignaretur ostendere sacrum mysterium Trinitatis. . . . Hec dicens, cepi psallere ut ad propositum numerum pervenirem. Nec mora occurrit animo modo forma psalterii decachordi, et in ipsa tam lucidum et apertum sacre mysterium Trinitatis, ut protinus compellerer clamare Quis Deus magnus sicut Deus noster? (*Psalt.*, f. 227^{r-v}.)

Joachim immediately set to work on the first of the three books into which, as a symbol of the Trinity, he divided his *Psalterium decem chordarum*. He did not finish the work until two years later, and, indeed, on all three of the main works he probably continued making additions and revisions. In the Preface to the *Psalterium* these three works are clearly associated together in his mind as bearing a Trinitarian significance and he gives us a brief glimpse of their organic connection:

Et quamvis post opus concordie quod incepimus primo, et expositionem Apocalipsis, que (ignorante me omnimodis exitum rei) nescio qua Dei providentia ex eodem primo opere nascendo, processit Spiritui Sancto, qui et donat quod exhibemus hoc tertium opusculum, dedicare decreverim, quia tamen nihil est in rebus creatis quod sic attribuatur uni persone, ut alienum sit a regno et operatione duarum, non inconvenienter in hoc ipso mysterium Trutilat rinitatis . . . (*Psalt.*, f. 227ᵛ.)

Again in the Testamentary Letter which Joachim addressed to the Pope in 1200 the three main works stand out together. It is possible to see each work as peculiarly associated with one Person of the Trinity. Thus the *Liber Concordie*, with its focus on the concords of the Scriptures, actually makes the most intensive study of the Old Testament as prefiguring the New. The *Expositio* naturally centres in the Risen Christ of the Apocalypse and is deeply concerned with the interpretation of the New Testament era or the second *status*. The *Psalterium* is less concerned with historical concords and more with the *Spiritualis Intellectus* which belongs to the third *status*. Yet since, as Joachim says above, no one Person can be isolated from the others, each work partakes of the character of both the others, while the third in its thought does indeed seem to proceed from the first two. Thus Joachim's conception of the relationship of the Persons of the Trinity is reflected in the relationship of his works.

Around this grand Trinitarian sequence other smaller works are grouped. Some questions concerning the authenticity of certain small tracts are not yet settled, but it seems certain that the *De Vita Sancti Benedicti et de officio divino secundum eius doctrinam*[1] is genuine and probably early. This is an interpretation of the life and rule of St. Benedict in terms of historical concords from the Old and New Testaments. Here Joachim is already seeing the evolution of first Benedictinism and then Cistercianism as significant parts of the cosmic pattern of history. The emphasis is mainly on patterns of twos, but it is significant that already in this tract we find a seminal number-concept which forms a transition to the pattern of threes. The number twelve gives an obvious set of concords between the Old and New Testaments, but Joachim finds a deeper symbolism in splitting the perfect number unequally into five and seven and in seeing here a representation of the transition from exterior and literal meanings to interior and spiritual ones. The promise of a third *status* proceeds from an understanding of the five and the

[1] Ed. Baraut, *AST* xxiv.

seven.[1] This symbolism emerges fully developed in the *Vita Sancti Benedicti*, where it is specifically connected with the Trinity:

Est enim perfectissimus duodenarius numerus, propter quinarium et septenarium, quorum alter ad exercitia corporum, alter ad virtutes pertinet animorum; quia et sensus corporis quinque sunt, et septem dona sancti Spiritus . . . inde quod tribus duodecim in quinque et septem divise sunt, similiter et ecclesie totidem . . . Novissime septem tribus sedibus suis locate sunt, novissime septem ecclesie que in Asya ab apostolis fundate sunt. Oportet ergo precedere quinarium, ut septenarius oportune sequatur, ut in nomine Trinitatis deifice omne genu flectatur, celestium, terrestrium et infernorum. (*Vita S. Benedicti*, pp. 53–4.)

Elsewhere in this work the three *status* of history are directly introduced and thus we may deduce that Joachim was working out his understanding of the Trinity within history before he was able wholly to grasp its meaning theologically after the Whitsuntide experience.

There are two short tracts on the Apocalypse besides the *Expositio*. One is an alternative and fuller version of the *Liber Introductorius* to the main work. As it appears separately in early manuscripts at Pavia, Paris, and the British Museum, it seems certain that it was circulating independently in the thirteenth century.[2] This, according to the manuscript evidence, should be called the *Enchiridion in Apocalypsim*, rather than the second short tract which was edited by Huck under that title.[3] This latter is an interesting little work,

---

[1] For a fuller exposition of the five/seven symbolism see Reeves, *MARS* ii. 77–9; Reeves, Hirsch-Reich, *Studies*, pp. 13–19.

[2] MSS. Pavia, Bib. Univ., Aldini 370; Paris, Bib. Nat., Lat. 2142, ff. 103^r–135^r; Brit. Mus., Harley 3049, ff. 137^r–140^v (extract only, beginning in the middle of a sentence which corresponds to f. 12^r, line 8, of the printed edition of the *Expos.*; obviously the early pages have been lost). The expanded parts are interesting; some have been studied by Tondelli, *Lib. Fig.* I, pp. 121–2, 137–45 (with extracts) and *ASCL* xii. 3–4. If, as he argues, this represents an early version, it deserves further study. The *incipit* is as in the printed edition: 'Quam propensioribus studiis a viris catholicis'; the *explicit* differs: '. . . et consummatis ad integrum muris Jerusalem apparebit in oculis reproborum quasi sponsa circumamicta varietate et ornata monilibus suis et regnabit ex hoc nunc, magis autem ex tunc et usque in secula seculorum. Amen.' A strong reason for calling this work the *Enchiridion* is that it was quoted as such three times by the Commission of Anagni (1255) (*ALKG* i. 104–5, 122, 133).

[3] Huck, *Joachim v. Floris*, pp. 287–305, edited from MSS. Paris, Bib. Nat., Lat. 2142, ff. 96^r–103^v, and Vatican, Reg. Lat. 132, ff. 49^r–58^v. It is also found in Brit. Mus., MS. Harley 3969, ff. 216^r–224^r (lacking the beginning). In both the Paris and Vatican manuscripts this immediately precedes the *Enchiridion* dealt with in the previous footnote, and Huck actually confused the two. But this little tract is quite distinct: *Incipit*: 'Apocalipsis liber ultimus est librorum omnium'; *Explicit*: '. . . et tunc revelabitur gloria civitatis superne ad quam nos perducat dominus, etc.' See Tondelli, *ASCL* xii. 3–4.

regarded by Huck as an early one. Two other short works, the *Adversus Judaeos*[1] and *De Articulis Fidei*,[2] have appeared in modern editions, but in MS. Antoniana 322 at Padua there are still a number of short sermons, letters, and other pieces which are unedited. Finally, there is the larger but unfinished *Tractatus super Quatuor Evangelia*,[3] and beside it may be placed the *Liber Figurarum*,[4] since both probably represent the latest stages of Joachim's thinking. The *Tractatus* was at one time regarded with suspicion because it was not named in Joachim's Testamentary Letter. But Buonaiuti, in his Introduction to his edition of it, cleared away doubts and we can now see it as probably the latest and most radical of Joachim's writings. The *Liber Figurarum* has aroused great controversy. The reasons for placing it among the genuine works of Joachim have been set out fully elsewhere.[5] 'Genuineness' here can have two different meanings: it may be that the archetype was conceived and executed by Joachim himself, or it may be that the idea of the *Liber Figurarum* was Joachim's but that it was carried out by some close disciple. We know that Joachim taught by figures[6] and that he had an aptitude for expressing intricate patterns and mysterious relationships as figures. Nothing would be more natural than to attempt a gathering together of his main concepts in a set of such *figurae*. Some are related directly to one of the three main works, but the *Liber Figurarum* cannot be seen as a series of textual figures put together later into one *liber*. The cross-references and interrelations of various figures are too complex for such a simple explanation. Just as the three main works are intimately connected, so the parts of the *Liber Figurarum* are organically connected in a whole which expresses most subtly the interweaving patterns of the twos and threes. This collection of *figurae* was a popularizing device of great appeal to the visual imagination, and it may well have been through this means that Joachim's ideas were most widely disseminated.

Grundmann further distinguishes a shortened *Expositio* which, under the title *Apocalipsis Nova* appears in MSS. Dresden, A. 121 and Vatican, Lat. 4860. See Appendix A.

[1] Ed. A. Frugoni (Rome, 1957).

[2] Ed. E. Buonaiuti (Rome, 1936).

[3] Ed. E. Buonaiuti (Rome, 1930).

[4] Ed. L. Tondelli, M. Reeves, B. Hirsch-Reich (Turin, 1953).

[5] Reeves, Hirsch-Reich, *Studies*, pp. 75–98.

[6] Huck, *Joachim v. Floris*, p. 290: '... que ut fidem inquirentibus facerem, iam dudum in figuras converti.'

III

THE CONDEMNATION OF 1215

JOACHIM had been encouraged to write by three popes; he had
been permitted to leave his duties as Abbot of Curazzo, protected against the attempts of the Cistercian Order to reclaim
him as a fugitive, and given privileges for his new Order of S.
Giovanni in Fiore.[1] In particular, Celestine III had been the friend
of Joachim; and this may account for the curious little mistake
in Joachim's Tables of Concords[2] by which Celestine is listed as
the Pope initiating the fortieth generation of the Church in 1200,
whereas he died in 1198. This entry, which is probably a later
addition by Joachim or by a disciple, may represent a reluctance to
name Innocent III or a desire to include Celestine, born of the
differing attitudes of these two Popes towards Joachim. We have,
perhaps, a hint that Joachim was aware of a changing attitude on the
part of the Papacy in his so-called Testamentary Letter.[3] This was

---

[1] The three Popes were Lucius III, Urban III, Clement III; see Joachim's Testamentary Letter and the letter of Clement III prefacing the *Lib. Conc.* and *Expos.* For
Cistercian action against the fugitive see J. Canivez, *Statuta Capitulorum Generalium
Ordinis Cisterciensis* i. 154. The new Order of Fiore was approved by Celestine III in
the Bull *Cum in nostra*, 25 Aug. 1196; see Jaffé-Lowenfeld, *Regesta Pontificum Romanorum*, ii. 626, and *AS*, p. 125. Later confirmation of the privileges of the Order were
given by Innocent III (21 Jan. 1204), Honorius III (2 Dec. 1216 and 27 Dec. 1220).

[2] *Lib. Fig.* II, p. 18 and Pl. IV.

[3] The authenticity of the Testamentary Letter, dated 1200 (printed at the beginning
of the *Lib. Conc.* and the *Expos.*, also by Crocco, *Gioacchino*, pp. 67–8) together with
that of the letter of Clement III, dated 8 June 1188, to which it refers (also printed at
the beginning of the Venetian editions) was questioned by E. Anitchkof, *Joachim de
Flore et le milieu courtois* (Rome, 1931), pp. 18 seq., 249 seq., and by Buonaiuti, *Gioacchino da Fiore*, pp. 173 seq. Buonaiuti's doubts—the more serious of the two—sprang
from a view of Joachim's relations with the papacy which really attempted to make him
a crypto-Protestant. His specific arguments were (1) that these letters endow Joachim's
writings with an official character out of keeping with the nature of Joachim's works;
(2) that the letters would suppose the initiation of the *Lib. Conc.* and *Expos.* in the
pontificates of Lucius III and Urban III, which is incompatible with internal evidence,
notably the reference to a Messina visit in 1195 which indicates that at that time the
Expos. was only half-written (f. 134ʳ); (3) that the omission from these letters of all
reference to the suspect *libellus* against Peter Lombard and the unfinished, radical
Tractatus super Quatuor Evangelia reveals clearly that the purpose of forging the letters
was to establish Joachim's orthodoxy as well as his submission to the Papacy. Buonaiuti's

written, not right at the end of his life, but in 1200, that is, soon after Innocent III's accession, probably before Joachim started his last and unfinished work, the *Tractatus super Quatuor Evangelia*. There is a note of urgency and insistence in this letter. Joachim stresses his intention to submit all his writings to the Holy See for correction, but the shortness of man's days has so far defeated him. We know from Clement III's letter that Joachim had been urged as long before as 1188 to finish his work and present himself to the Pope 'quam citius se opportunitas dederit', yet still he lingered over the three main works, making additions and cross-references.[1] Now panic assails him that time will not be given to him to present his works in person, so in the most solemn words he adjures his 'coabbates et priores et ceteros fratres' to carry out this duty and represent to the Pope Joachim's unwavering devotion and obedience. The letter ends with an almost painful insistence on his submission to the Holy See:

Credens ad integrum que ipsa credit: et tam in moribus quam in doctrina suscipiens correctionem, abiiciens quos ipsa abiicit, suscipiens quos suscipit ipsa. Credens firmiter non posse portas inferi prevalere adversus eam: . . . non deficere fidem eius usque ad consummationem seculi. Hoc scriptum feci ego Joachim abbas et propria manu roboravi anno domini incarnationis 1200. Et sic me tenere confiteor sicut in eo continetur. (*Lib. Conc.*, Testamentary Letter preceding the Preface.)

general view of Joachim's relations with the papacy has been refuted and the genuine character of the two letters upheld by Grundmann, *DDJ* xiv. 225 n. 24; Foberti, *Gioacchino* I, pp. 44 seq.; Tondelli, *Lib. Fig.* I, pp. 124–5; Crocco, *Gioacchino*, pp. 66–8. Without repeating in detail the arguments against Buonaiuti's specific points, we may note (1) that there is irrefutable internal evidence for Joachim's belief that he wrote under the express command and sanction of successive popes in the *Expos.*, ff. 2ʳ, 224ᵛ; (2) that cross-references show that Joachim did not write his main two works in orderly sequence, but, working on both at once, inserted later passages in both which make it impossible to establish a hard and fast dating; (3) a number of other lesser works almost certainly written before 1200 are also omitted, besides the *libellus*, whilst there was certainly time for the *Quat. Evang.* to have been partly written after 1200. In any case no such distinction between 'orthodox' and 'unorthodox' can be drawn to correspond with inclusion and exclusion from the Testamentary Letter: the Trinitarian doctrine of the *Psalt.* is the same as that condemned in 1215, and therefore presumably of the lost *libellus*. The most conclusive external corroboration of Joachim's Testamentary Letter is the evidence of the 1215 condemnation itself, which specifically states in defence of Joachim's reputation that he submitted all his works to the Apostolic See, affirming in a letter witnessed by his own hand that he firmly adhered to the faith of the Roman Church (see passage quoted *infra*, p. 32).

[1] Although in general there is a discernible progression of thought through the three main works, there is little orderly structure within them, and a number of cross-references in the first two demonstrate that Joachim went on revising, amending, and adding.

Why did he feel so strongly the need to reiterate his obedience and to insist on the submission of all his works? May it not have been that he was aware of a new wind blowing, and had a premonition that it might develop for him into a tempest?

The storm only blew up after his death, when, at the Lateran Council of 1215, Joachim's attack on the Trinitarian doctrine of Peter Lombard in his tract *De Unitate et Essentia Trinitatis* was condemned as heretical. There is an apocryphal story that Joachim and Peter Lombard met and disputed at Sambucina.[1] This was not possible, but there can be no doubt that the Lombard's thought made a strong impact upon Joachim's mind and that he found himself deeply opposed to his Trinitarian doctrine. Joachim's writings are not, in general, polemical, but the violent attack which he must have launched against the Master of the Sentences, in the condemned and now lost treatise, finds strong echoes in some passages of his other writings, all the more striking because of their uniqueness.[2] The lost work probably used *figurae* in its exposition of false and true doctrine, for a set of such *figurae* has been recovered from the Dresden manuscript of the *Liber Figurarum*.[2]

So far as we can reconstruct it, Joachim's main attack on Peter Lombard was focused on his belief that the Lombard postulated his 'summa res non generans, nec genita, nec procedens' as something distinct from the three separate Persons of the Trinity. Joachim calls this the *perfidia (Petri)* and accuses Peter Lombard of belief in a *quaternitas*. The full evidence for Joachim's view and an exposition of his *figurae* on the subject has been given elsewhere.[2] The study of Joachim's *figurae*, in particular, has made clear his passionate belief in the *natura indivisibilis* of the Trinity, which he expounds through a striking variety of images. Why had Joachim such a deep personal antagonism to the Master of the Sentences, even aligning him with the arch-heretics Sabellius and Arius? We must recall that the formative period of Joachim's thinking coincided with the time after the Lombard's death in 1160 when an intense debate was proceeding between the protagonists and antagonists of his view. In this passionate clash of opinion anti-dialectics—great mystics like Richard of St. Victor—attacked the Lombard's teaching with full force, and at the Third Lateran Council of 1179 Pope Alexander III

---

[1] For a full examination and refutation of this legend, see Crocco, *Gioacchino*. p. 22 n. 15.

[2] See Reeves, Hirsch-Reich, *Studies*, pp. 212–23.

even proposed to condemn the *Sententiae* as heretical.[1] On the other side, Peter Lombard's faithful disciples rallied to his defence and prevented the condemnation. In this period of fluctuating views Joachim's attack would have seemed neither shocking nor unusual, but the intensity of his opposition derives from the peculiar integration of his Trinitarian doctrine with his understanding of history which, as we have seen, characterizes the Abbot's thought. To him the abstraction of a 'summa res non generans . . .', aloof from history and unable to enter into it—for so he conceived Peter Lombard's doctrine to be—was utterly repugnant. The essence of the Trinity could not be thought of apart from its interpenetration of history: its unity in the divine sphere could only be expressed in terms of the 'Three-are-One'; in the human sphere, by the unity of the three *status* in history, developing towards one goal. Threeness and Unity were of equal importance in Joachim's view, whereas the Lombard's doctrine implied that unity transcended all differentiation. No doubt Joachim failed to understand the Lombard's metaphysical concept as a notional distinction, mistaking it for a real entity, something 'fourth' which he abhorred, but his whole approach was anti-dialectical, and he believed, as we have seen, that the mystery of the Trinity could only be understood through deep spiritual experience, not by the philosophical way of the *carnalis intellectus*.[2]

Already in his life-time Joachim's views were misunderstood: in attacking a supposed quaternity it was only too easy to give an impression of falling into Tritheism. Joachim tells us that he was accused of attempting to 'scindere unitatem',[3] though he rejects this emphatically. Because so much emphasis was later placed on the Abbot's doctrine of the three *status*, it has often been assumed that Joachim was most deeply influenced by the Greek approach to the Trinity through a stress on the Three Persons.[4] The recent study of

[1] F. Pelster, 'Eine ungedruckte Einleitung zu einer zweiten Auflage des Eulogium', *Historisches Jahrbuch*, liv (1954), p. 228.

[2] Prof. Jacob comments: 'There was here a fundamental clash between metaphysician and artist.' In this paragraph I have drawn heavily on the research of Dr. B. Hirsch-Reich.

[3] *Expos.*, f. 38ʳ: 'Non enim deesse possunt qui cogitent mala in cordibus suis, arbitrantes nos unitatem scindere, quia Trinitatem in misteriis predicamus.'

[4] The chief writers to stress Greek influence on Joachim's thought were Renan, *Revue des Deux Mondes*, lxiv (1866), pp. 94–112; F. Tocco, *L'eresia nel medio evo* (Florence, 1884), pp. 387 seq.; E. Gebhart, *L'Italie mystique* (Paris, 1908), pp. 63, 78; P. Fournier, *Études sur Joachim de Flore et ses doctrines* (Paris, 1909), pp. 4 seq., 14, 16. Buonaiuti,

the *Liber Figurarum* brings out clearly the opposite point—that Joachim was equally influenced by the Latin approach through the Unity of the Three Persons. He would not, however, establish the Unity by any method which suggested an entity separate from the action of the Three Persons, and so he sought to walk a difficult knife-edge, setting forth through a variety of symbols and *figurae* his concept, not so much of a Three-in-One, as of a Three-are-One.

It is not surprising that the misunderstanding which he had met himself continued after Joachim's death and developed into the attack of 1215. Times had changed since Alexander III had thought of condemning the Lombard's views, and now Innocent III, himself a product of the Paris theological school, was determined to establish the Master of the Sentences as the authority. The strong opposition of the great Calabrian must have been well known and thus his work against Peter Lombard was selected for formal condemnation at the Fourth Lateran Council. In the decree[1] Joachim's argument against the Lombard was set out in words almost certainly taken directly from the now lost *libellus*. The Council condemned the tract and approved the central statement of Peter Lombard which Joachim had attacked. But the condemnation was carefully phrased so as to avoid branding Joachim himself as a heretic and to safeguard his reputation:

Si quis igitur sententiam sive doctrinam praefati Joachimi in hac parte defendere vel approbare praesumpserit: tanquam haereticus ab omnibus confutetur. In nullo tamen per hoc Florensi monasterio, cuius ipse Joachim extitit institutor, volumus derogari: quoniam ibi et regularis institutio est et observantia salutaris, maxime cum idem Joachim omnia scripta sua nobis assignari mandaverit, apostolicae sedes iudicio approbanda, seu etiam corrigenda: dictans epistolam cui propria manu subscripsit, in qua firmiter confitetur se illam fidem tenere, quam Romana tenet ecclesia, quae cunctorum fidelium, disponente Domino, mater est et magistra. (Mansi, xxii. 986.)

The intention to defend Joachim's name from scandal was made even plainer when, in 1220, Honorius III found it necessary to order a public declaration throughout Calabria that Joachim was not a heretic and that 'eum VIRUM CATHOLICUM reputamus'.[2]

Gioacchino da Fiore, pp. 136 seq., has brought powerful reasons to challenge this. For a recent survey of work relevant to Joachim's sources see Bloomfield, *Traditio* xiii. 271–88. See also Crocco, *Sophia* xxiii. 192–6 and *Gioacchino*, pp. 107–11.

[1] Mansi, *Sacrorum Conciliorum . . . Collectio*, xx. 981–3.

[2] *AS*, p. 104. See also Crocco, *Gioacchino*, p. 62; Foberti, *Gioacchino* II, p. 8. See

None the less, to theologians of succeeding generations this condemnation placed Joachim in a definite category of one who had
erred in his theological doctrine. It obviously influenced both St.
Bonaventura and St. Thomas Aquinas, for instance. The verdict
hung like a millstone on his reputation and earned him a place in
catalogues of heretics. It has, indeed, been a matter of controversy
right down to the present day as to whether Joachim did or did not
err in his Trinitarian doctrine, and all too seldom have the judgements been dispassionate. Fournier, writing in 1909, accused him of
Tritheism,[1] and this view has been followed by Ottaviano.[2] On the
other hand, there have not been wanting modern champions, like
Foberti,[3] to exonerate Joachim from any taint of deviation from
orthodoxy.

This affirmation of Joachim's orthodoxy was one line of defence
taken by Joachim's followers, for some claimed that Joachim had
taught exactly the same as Peter Lombard. We get a vivid glimpse
of the confusion into which the condemnation had thrown Joachim's
disciples, and of another possible attitude in the record of a vision
which was preserved at Fiore and also in a fourteenth-century
manuscript of the *Expositio in Apocalypsim*.[4] This relates how in
1215 the Archbishop of Cosenza sent his scribe to Curazzo to
transcribe the *Expositio*, how the scribe was troubled at the news of
the condemnation, and how, in two visions, one of Joachim ('quidam
senex habens in digito annulum et baculum in manu'), and the
other of Peter Lombard ('quandam umbram omni nigredine nigrio-
rem, que lacertos habens pilosos et digitos ligneos ac virgam fer-
ream in manu'), he was reassured in his faith in Joachim. This little
text may well not be immediately contemporary[5] (as Ottaviano
thought), but none the less it reveals strikingly the state of mind of
some Joachites and their defence of their master's reputation.[6]
Faith in the Abbot's orthodoxy is reasserted and, by compensation,

MS. Florence, Bibl. Laur., Ashburnham 415, f. 25[2] for an example of the embarrassment
caused by the condemnation to those who wished to cite Joachim as a prophet.

[1] Fournier, op. cit., pp. 15–16.
[2] Ottaviano, *Lib. contra Lombardum*, pp. 54–63.
[3] Foberti, *Gioacchino* I, pp. 81 seq.; *Gioacchino* II, pp. 39 seq., 63 seq.
[4] Naples, Bib. Naz., MS. Brancacciana I. F. 2, f. 288[r–v] and repeated on f. 331[v];
Rome, Bib. Casanatense, MS. 1411, f. 191[r]. The text was published and discussed by
Ottaviano, *Sophia* iii. 476–82, and republished in *Siculorum Gymnasium, rassegna
semestrale della Facoltà di Lettere e Filosofia dell'Università di Catania*, 1949, pp. 291–3.
[5] See the points made by Russo, *ASCL* xx. 68–73.
[6] This is discussed in detail in Reeves, *Sophia* xix. 355 seq.

Lombard is represented as a diabolical creature. In the vision he prophesies that the chief doctors of the Church will take the Lombard's side, but there is a characteristic Joachimist note in the expectation expressed in these words: 'Set scias quod opus illud [i.e. Joachim's work] adhuc revelabitur tali viro, per quem dolor eorum qui de ipsius operis dampnacione fuere turbati in magnum gaudium convertetur.' Here already we see signs of an attitude found later among various groups of Joachites, that they may have to endure official censure or persecution for a while, but that in the end the true orthodoxy, of which they are the guardians, will be revealed.[1]

There are hints of another line of defence. In the pseudo-Joachimist treatise *Super Hieremiam*[2] there is an enigmatic passage which was recognized at Fiore in the sixteenth century as referring to the unjust condemnation of Joachim.[3] Of course the Joachites believed that this had been 'prophecy' on the part of Joachim himself, whereas we can date the work roughly to the early 1240s. Thus it was written some time after the events of 1215, but it probably enshrines a tradition and an attitude which had developed in the interval, perhaps at Fiore itself. The passage, of which the inner meaning was still preserved at Fiore in the sixteenth century, runs as follows:[4]

Spiritualiter, quia idolum doctrine heretice est posita ante templum ecclesie, quam adorant omnes et tenent vani ceterique magistri in sanam doctrinam et fidelem: . . . ut eam extinguant et nomen doctoris, cui revelabitur sententia Danielis, evertant: futurum est enim ut Caiphas summus Pontifex veritatem insinuet, ut unus damnetur, idest moriatur doctor pro populo, ut non tota gens pereat in errore. Sic Sedechias contra Hyeremiam insurgit: damnat librum, scindit Trinitatem ab unitate scalpello sententiam scribe Doctoris. Nescio, autem, Deus scit, utrum in nobis complenda sint, vel in secuturo ordine consummanda.

The seventeenth-century writer of Joachim's life, Gregorio de Laude, continues the quotation, with his own commentary:

Designat Herodes summum pontificem post Celestinum futurum, quicunque sit ille [De Laude: his est Innocentius III], a quo, quia stella disparuit (De Laude: id est, quia auctore libri anno Domini, ut infra

---

[1] *Infra*, pp. 150–1.   [2] *Infra*, p. 56.
[3] For the whole of this paragraph see Reeves, *Sophia* xix. 358 seq.
[4] MS. Brancacciana, f. 305ʳ. Cf. *Super Hier.*, f. 23ʳ, which only differs slightly from the Fiore version.

probabitur, 1202 e vivis sublato, claritas, sensus et veritas scripturae suae disparuit), spiritualis intelligentia extinguetur in dolo: et per invidiam tradetur et perimere cogitabit. Quia autem congregaverunt pontifices ecclesiarum pharisei, scilicet abbates, priores, religiosi Cistercienses, concilium forsitan generale, invidentes Christo [De Laude: i.e. Sacerdoti Abbati Joachimi, ex eo quod novam reformationem induxerat in Cisterciensem Ordinem, tunc mira observantia celeberrimum, Florensem nuncupatam], totum ad illum doctorem veritatis referendum est quod sextus describit angelus: immo sub quo in manu alterius angeli liber demonstratur veritatis apertus. . . . Sequitur: 'Ad viros anathot qui querunt animam tuam'. A quibusdam Cisterciensium egredietur iniquitas hec: ut doctor ille 'non prophetet in nomine domini et in eorum manibus', i.e. operibus et consiliis 'moriatur', scilicet reprobetur. Sed quod inde sequitur 'Iuvenes eorum morientur gladio, filii eorum et filie in fame, et reliquie non erunt ex eis', iuvenes sunt priores, filii monaci, filie monasteria vel obedientie eorum. . . . 'Inducam enim malum super viros anathot', scilicet super prelatos maiores Cisterciensium . . . (*Apologetica*, pp. 293–4.)

Thus the tradition, embodied in the *Super Hieremiam* and preserved down to the seventeenth century at Fiore, was that the condemnation of the anti-Lombard tract had been engineered by an unjust conspiracy in which the Cistercian leaders were the chief villains, in alliance with the 'summum pontificem post Celestinum', i.e. Innocent III. The cited passage is the most explicit but it gives clues of identification which enable us to see other veiled references to the condemnation in the *Super Hieremiam*.[1] I have argued elsewhere[2] that the *Super Hieremiam* displays a double attitude towards the Cistercian Order; on the one hand, denouncing the machinations of its conspiring 'Pharisees', on the other, viewing it as the repository of true religion and the root from which will spring one of the orders of the third *status*. This attitude could only have belonged to Joachim's own circle of disciples in Calabria. It seems, then, that in this circle ranks were closed in defence of Joachim's reputation, and counter-accusations launched against the 'conspiracy' of the Pope and the Cistercian leaders. No attempt was made, apparently, to accuse the latter of deliberate falsification or of inventing Joachim's anti-Lombard tract; for these accusations we must wait until the controversy breaks out again in the seventeenth century, and, indeed, for the notion that the Cistercians actually

[1] See *infra*, pp. 149–50, for these references; also Reeves, *Sophia* xix. 360–1.
[2] Ibid., pp. 363–7.

wrote the offending tract themselves, until Foberti's defence of Joachim in the twentieth century. The thirteenth-century charge is a much vaguer one: that in some way a deadly blow had been struck at Joachim's reputation and the 'star' of spiritual intelligence temporarily extinguished. We have evidence that some monks sought to leave the Order during the pontificates of Honorius III and Gregory IX,[1] but the staunch fidelity of the congregation of Fiore in general to its master's memory can hardly be doubted. It finds expression in the unusually pointed phrase of the Antiphon to Vespers which the Order was permitted to use in commemorating its Founder: 'errore procul haeretico'.[2]

[1] Pressutti, *Regesta Honorii III*, ii. 133, Bull of 12 May 1223; 189, Bull of 2 Jan. 1224, forbidding Cistercians in Calabria to receive members of the Florensian Order without due formalities. Prohibition renewed by Gregory IX in 1234, see Potthast, *Regesta Pontif. Romanorum*, n. 9459.

[2] The whole Antiphon runs: 'Beatus Joachim, spiritu dotatus prophetico, decoratus intelligentia; errore procul haeretico, dixit futura ut praesentia' (*AS*, p. 90). We may, perhaps detect the attitude of Joachites to Innocent III in three details: (*a*) the careful repetition of Celestine III instead of Innocent III in the Tables of Concords already referred to (*supra*, p. 28); (*b*) in part of a thirteenth-century prophecy published by Tondelli (*infra*, p. 51), which begins: *Post Celestinum regnabit papa superbus* . . .; (*c*) in a passage in *De Oneribus* again associating Celestine rather than Innocent with the crucial year 1200: 'tercius [status] splendebit anno M.CC^2 quasi sub celestino papa' (f. 43^2).

IV

THE EARLY DISSEMINATION OF JOACHIMIST IDEAS

WHEN the Council of Arles condemned Joachim's doctrine in 1263 it minimized his influence, describing his works as 'qui a majoribus nostris usque ad haec tempora remanserunt intacti, ut pote latitantes apud quosdam religiosos in angulis et antris (Denifle: a nostris), doctoribus indiscussi, a quibus si ruminati fuissent, nullatenus inter sacros alios et sanctorum codices mixti remansissent'.[1] This statement has misled historians; it has commonly been assumed that until about 1240 Joachim's works and reputation remained in obscurity, cherished only in a corner by a small group of Calabrian disciples. The early 1240s were seen as the starting-point of the Joachite movement, primarily because at this time, according to the Franciscan Salimbene,[2] a Florensian abbot sought refuge in a Pisan convent of the Minorites, bringing with him the works of Joachim, which were thus introduced to the Order. Soon after, the first of the pseudo-Joachimist works, the *Super Hieremiam*, appears, and a little later evidence for Joachimist influence in the Franciscan Order begins to accumulate. This picture takes no account of Joachim's considerable reputation during his lifetime, nor of the spread of the Order of Fiore and its ramifications in the generation after his death. Joachim's fame had already gone north of the Alps before he died; the favour of Honorius III and Gregory IX in the early thirteenth century exalted the Order and spread its ties even as far as England before 1250, though its houses remained chiefly concentrated in southern Italy.[3] In Calabria itself we must probably think of three closely related groups as centres of Joachimist influence: the Florensian houses themselves,

[1] Mansi, *Sacrorum Conciliorum . . . Collectio*, xxiii, col. 1003; cf. Denifle, *ALKG*, i. 90 n. 4.
[2] Salimbene, p. 236.
[3] On the growth of the Order of Fiore and its ties and possessions, even as far as England, see F. Caraffa, *Il monastero florense di S. Maria della Gloria presso Anagni, con una introduzione sui monaci florensi e i loro monasteri* (Rome, 1940); Russo, *Gioacchino*, Part II.

those friendly Cistercian houses which continued to revere Joachim, and the newly-planted Franciscan houses, when they begin to appear in Calabria from 1221 onwards. Beyond south Italy it has been possible to collect considerable evidence to show the dissemination of interest in Joachim's views. Some of this has been set out fully in an article in *Speculum* upon which this account draws.[1] The carriers were probably disciples and visitors returning from Calabria, while one of the most effective agencies in spreading these ideas may have been *figurae*. Recent studies of the *Liber Figurarum* and its satellite figure-collections show that there must have been a number of single figure-sketches or small collections of figures in circulation.[2]

The subject of Joachim's immediate disciples and the tradition they disseminated has recently been illuminated by the discovery at Naples of an important collection of material from S. Giovanni in Fiore itself, made in the late sixteenth century and gathered together in the seventeenth by the antiquary Camillo Tutini, who left it to the Bibliotheca Brancacciana.[3] This enables us to go behind the seventeenth-century lives of Joachim by Jacobus Graecus and Gregorio de Laude (or Lauro) and the collection of material made by Papebroch in the *Acta Sanctorum*. Close study has revealed, not only the traditions of Joachim and his disciples preserved at Fiore, but fragments, at least, of the earliest biographies of Joachim.[4] Luke of Cosenza, Joachim's scribe and friend, gives us the names of his earliest disciples, Raynier of Ponza and the Cistercian abbot, John of Curazzo; the fragment of a contemporary *Vita* names three more, Peregrinus, Bonatius, and Jacobus, while Graecus's Life adds another Cistercian abbot, Alexander of Sanctus Spiritus in Palermo, and John of Aquitaine. These are all shadowy figures, except Luke and Raynier.[5] We can, however, find traces of their activities and outlook. We have already observed the line of defence they built up against the condemnation of 1215. Later we shall find evidence for a particular role assigned to the Cistercian Order in the Joachite future, and obviously the beginnings of this view go back to the first disciples. None of the major pseudo-Joachimist works appeared

---

[1] Bloomfield, Reeves, *Speculum* xxix. 772–93.

[2] Reeves, Hirsch-Reich, *MARS* iii. 170–99.

[3] *Supra*, p. 33 n. 4, for this manuscript.

[4] These have been studied and edited by Baraut, *AST* xxvi. 195–232, and Grundmann, *DA* xvi. 437–546.

[5] On Joachim's disciples see Grundmann, *ZKG* xlviii. 160–5; *DA* xvi. 440–65, especially on Raynier of Ponza.

until the second generation of Joachites, but several of these refer
to the pronouncements of Fr. Raynier.[1] Although the particular
oracles in question are clearly post-1250, there may have been
prophetic words of his in circulation. If the first generation of
disciples did not write full-scale works, there are indications at least
that they made small anthologies of Joachim's *figurae*, with some
texts, and that they ventured on modifications of some of these
figurae.[2] One small pseudo-Joachimist text, at least, emanated from
this group, the *Epistola subsequentium figurarum* attached to the first
anthology.[3] Finally, we catch an echo of the kind of message
Joachim's disciples would carry abroad with them in an interesting
reference to a Calabrian Abbot John who visited the abbey of Erbach
near Mainz in 1217. In his conversation with the Prior Gebenon
John told him that Antichrist would soon be born and referred to
the fact that a 'solitarius . . . magni nominis in partibus nostris
Cardinali cuidam id aperuit, signoque manifesto comprobavit'. This
conversation stimulated Gebenon to examine the prophecies of St.
Hildegarde on this subject, and the Preface he wrote to her writings,
entitled *Pentacron seu Speculum Futurorum Temporum sive de Quinque
Temporibus*, contains direct reference to Joachim.[4] It seems almost
beyond doubt that the Calabrian *solitarius magni nominis* is Joachim
himself, and it has been plausibly suggested that the Abbot John is
Joachim's disciple, John of Aquitaine.

Whoever were the carriers, whether returned Crusaders, Cistercian travellers, or Joachim's disciples, there can be no doubt that the
Abbot Joachim's reputation had spread to north Italy and thence
north of the Alps soon after 1200. The earliest Italian chronicle

[1] See *infra*, p. 57 n. 3.

[2] *Infra*, p. 42, for description of the earliest anthology at the end of Paris, Bib. Nat.,
MS. 11864. A fuller version of this anthology is found in MSS. Vat., Lat. 3822, and
Paris, Bib. Nat., Lat. 3595. The 'tree' which is given in Vat., Lat. 3822 (ff. 4ᵛ, 7ʳ,
originally facing each other), and in Paris, Lat. 3595 (ff. 29ᵛ–31ʳ), in a very crude,
garbled form, is a conflation of two magnificent trees in the *Lib. Fig.* II, Pls. I, II, with
additions from Pls. III, IV. For a fuller account of all these manuscripts see Reeves,
Hirsch-Reich, *MARS* iii. 177–82, 198 (*Addendum*).

[3] Printed by Tondelli, *Lib. Fig.* I, pp. 41–3. MSS.: Rome, Vat., Lat. 3822 (ff. 3ᵛ–
4ʳ); Paris, Bib. Nat., Lat. 11864 (ff. 151ᵛ–152ᵛ) and Lat. 3595 (ff. 28ᵛ–29ᵛ). Tondelli
(pp. 37–8) argues in favour of its genuineness, but see Reeves, Hirsch-Reich, *MARS* iii.
180–2, where the arguments for its spurious character are given.

[4] J. B. Pitra, *Analecta Sacra* (Paris, 1882), pp. 483–8, printed part of Gebenon's
Pentacron. B. Hauréau, *Histoire littéraire de la France*, xxx (1888), pp. 616–19, gives some
manuscripts. Besides these, it is found in MSS. Cambridge, Corpus Christi College,
404; British Museum, Arundel 337; Tours, Bibl. Munic., 520. On this encounter see
Grundmann, *ZKG* xlviii. 164–5; Bloomfield, Reeves, *Speculum* xxix. 789–90.

referring to Joachim shows that prophetic words of his concerning
the Emperor Henry VI and the fate of both *Regnum* and *Imperium*
were circulating soon after his death. Sicard, Bishop of Cremona,
writing his chronicle between 1201 and 1215, records:

1197. His temporibus quidam extitit Ioachim Appulus abbas, qui spiritum habuit prophetandi, et prophetavit de morte imperatoris Henrici et
futura desolatione Siculi regni et defectu Romani imperii. Quod mani-
festissime declaratum est. Nam regnum Sicilie multo tempore est per-
turbatum et imperium per scisma divisum (*MGHS*, xxxi. 175).

In France Robert of Auxerre, writing before 1215, gives an account
of Joachim under the year 1186 which is worth quoting in full:

Per hos dies venit ex Calabria partibus ad Urbanum papam Verone
morantem quidam abbas nomine Joachim, de quo ferebant, quia, cum
prius non plurimum didicisset, divinitus acceperit intelligentie donum,
adeo ut facunde diserteque enodaret difficultates quaslibet scripturarum.
Hic itaque dicebat, quedam Apocalypsis mysteria hactenus latuisse, sed
modo per eum clarescere in spiritu prophetiae, sicut ex opusculo quod
conscripsit legentibus liquet. Dicit enim, quia, sicut scripturae veteris
Testamenti quinque etatum seculi ab Adam usque ad Christum decur-
sarum hystoriam continent, sic liber Apocalypsis etatis sexte a Christo
inchoate cursum exponit, ipsamque etatem sextam in sex etatulas dis-
pertitam earumque singulas singulis huius libri periodis satis congrue
designatas. Dicit quoque, haec revelata fuisse in fine etatulae quintae,
atque in proximo succedere sextam, in qua tribulationes varias multi-
plicesque pressuras perhibet emersuras, sicut in apertione sigilli sexti et in
sexta libri perioda, ubi de ruina Babylonis agitur, patenter ostenditur.
Id vero in libello eius pre ceteris notabile ac suspectum habetur, quod
mundi diffinit terminum, et infra duas generationes, quae iuxta ipsum
annos faciunt 60, arbitratur implendum quicquid de Antichristo legitur
eventurum. Dicat quisque quid senserit, nos tutius iudicamus non discu-
tere quam arguere quod nescimus et rei nobis incerte presagium iudicio
relinquere posterorum. (*MGHS* xxvi. 248–9.)

We notice at once that, though the two accounts are quite independent, Robert of Auxerre stresses the same two points as Ralph of
Coggeshall: the sudden gift of divine understanding to one previously ignorant, and his elucidation of the Apocalypse. Like Ralph,
the writer is able to give a clear summary of one of Joachim's historical patterns, that of the seven over-all ages of the world in which
the sixth, beginning in Christ, is subdivided into six *etatulae*. He
reports Joachim as standing at the end of the fifth *etatula* and
expecting that, in the approaching sixth, tribulations would thicken

until the coming of Antichrist and the end of the world, which would occur in two generations, i.e. sixty years. Thus already Joachim is seen as a prophet who points towards the year which most people interpreted as 1260. Finally, we should notice that Robert of Auxerre, in a manner we shall find characteristic of many who report Joachim's views, adds his own cautious comment on these debatable matters. Thus Joachim is known for three things: his gift of spiritual intelligence, his special method of Biblical exegesis through a pattern of history, and his prophecy of approaching crisis.[1] Robert's use of the word *etatula* probably indicates that his knowledge came, not from the full *Expositio in Apocalypsim* of Joachim, but from the earlier tract which was edited by Huck.[2] The expectation of *renovatio* after Antichrist was quite clear even in this early tract, but it seems that Joachim's expectation of the third *status* had not yet caught on. In an entry under 1190 Robert of Auxerre returns to Joachim to give a report of the interview at Messina. We do not know how he acquired his information, but obviously this discussion on the burning topics of Antichrist and the fate of Jerusalem formed the type of news to circulate quickly.

A little later we find another French cleric, William of Auvergne (d. 1249), citing Joachim to illustrate in his *De Virtutibus*[3] the gift of the *donum intellectus*:

Debes etiam scire, quia istud donum, scilicet donum intellectus, tantae

---

[1] It has been claimed that Godefroy of St. Victor in lib. 2, cap. 103, of his *Microcosmus*, ed. P. Delhaye (Lille, 1951), pp. 114–15, was denouncing the heresy of Joachim when he wrote: 'Siquidem Spiritus Sanctus, huius autor scripture, previdens futuros hereticos qui dicerent Christum ad tempus regnaturum et ecclesiam desituram in tempore et fidem catholicam et cetera dona gratie que sunt in ecclesia in exterminium itura, fideles suos, quos velud luminaria in celo posuit . . . firma anchora spei eiusdem regni solidari voluit.' This work has been dated *c.* 1185 (Delhaye) or 1190–2 (Lubac, op. cit. (ref. p. 13 n. 1), pp. 483–4). To impute to Joachim the view that the reign of Christ would pass away before the end of time would only be possible if the extreme implications of the pattern of threes had already been pushed to its limit. But the whole weight of evidence suggests that Joachim's pattern of twos alone was fully grasped by the first generation of disciples. It seems incredible that as early as 1185–92, when Joachim's main works were still unfinished, these words could have been directed specifically against him.

[2] *Supra*, p. 26, on this tract. See Huck, *Joachim v. Floris*, p. 290, for the division of the sixth age into six *etatulae*. It seems probable that this early tract on the Apocalypse was also the one known to Ralph of Coggeshall (cf. *supra*, p. 12.)

[3] Gulielmus Alvernus, *Opera Omnia*, *De Virtutibus* (Venice, 1591), p. 147. Père de Lubac thinks that, like Robert of Auxerre, William was reserving judgement: 'Quel est le sens de ce "mirabitur"? Ne faudra-t-il pas prendre pour autant de réserves ces mots: "crediderunt nonnulli, etc."?' (op. cit., p. 484).

claritatis est et acuminis in quibusdam, ut valde assimiletur spiritui
Prophetiae, qualem crediderunt nonnulli fuisse in Abbate Joachim et
ipsemet de seipso dixisse dicitur, quia non erat ei datus spiritus Prophetiae, sed spiritus intelligentiae. Si quis autem inspexerit libros eius, quos
scripsit super Apocalypsim et super concordiam duorum Testamentorum,
mirabitur donum intellectus in eo.

We notice here, not only that Joachim is becoming a type of those
who receive the *donum intellectus*, but also that his own disclaimer of
the spirit of prophecy has lodged in the mind as part of his reputation. A further point is that both his main works, the *Expositio* and
the *Liber Concordie*, are cited as if well known.

Three striking examples illustrate the importance of *figurae* as
early carriers of Joachim's ideas. In Paris a volume of the works of
Isidore of Seville, written in a twelfth-century hand, has on the
back folios a little Joachimist supplement, dated to the first decade
of the thirteenth century and probably emanating from a northern
scriptorium.[1] It starts with a pair of Joachim's Tables of Concords,
taken directly from the *Liber Figurarum*[2] and set out carefully on
one big folio. This is followed by the tract *De Septem Sigillis* which,
it has been argued, is a genuine little work closely associated with the
Liber Figurarum.[3] Two small works, the *Epistola subsequentium
figurarum* and the *Universis Christi fidelibus*, fill the remaining space.
The latter is probably a genuine tract,[4] but the former, as already indicated,[5] is the work of a disciple. Its purpose was to elucidate
a tree-figure which was already a hybrid one, composed of elements
from three different figures of the *Liber Figurarum*.[6] Why the scribe
of the Paris manuscript included the *Epistola*, but not the figure
belonging to it, we cannot say. What is clear, however, is that we
have here undoubted evidence of the circulation of the first little
Joachimist textbook soon after the Abbot's death.

At approximately the same date it appears likely that the Tables
of Concords were also circulating in England. Our source here is
a fifteenth-century manuscript, which, however, clearly goes back

[1] Paris, Bib. Nat., MS. Lat. 11864, ff. 151ᵛ–152ᵛ. For description see *Lib. Fig.*
II, p. 34.
[2] *Lib. Fig.* II, Pls. IX, X.
[3] Reeves, Hirsch-Reich, *RTAM* xxi. 226–39.
[4] Ed. Bignami-Odier, *MAH* liv. 220–3, who regards it as spurious, as also does
Tondelli, *Lib. Fig.* I, p. 41. Grundmann, *NF*, p. 25, thinks it genuine and the writer
agrees with him.
[5] *Supra*, p. 39.
[6] See Reeves, Hirsch-Reich, *MARS* iii. 180–1.

to a lost exemplar.[1] The main part of the manuscript is devoted to works and letters of Peter of Blois, but towards the end the writer leaves his author to discourse on the absorbing theme of the pagan and heretic hordes believed to be even then massing in far regions against the Church. Here we get one indication of the date from which the writer is looking at the future: '. . . cumque iam a resurrectione transierunt M.CC. anni et xiii hodie credendum est quod istis ducentis et xiii annis solutus sathanas cepit operari per sarracenos et hereticos misterium iniquitatis' (loc. cit., p. 777). After expounding the Prophets on the final tribulation he passes without warning into an account of the Abbot Joachim's views. As with Ralph of Coggeshall and Robert of Auxerre, the emphasis is on the concords between the Old and New Dispensations, and the double sequences of seven persecutions. A reference to the *tabula* of Joachim and to its *sinistra* and *dextra partes* shows that the writer has before him one of Joachim's *figurae*, while a comparison of the texts establishes beyond doubt that this was one of the pairs of Tables of Concords from the *Liber Figurarum*.[2] The date of this disquisition on Joachimism is probably 1213, and it was almost certainly written in England. Since this account in many respects resembles Ralph of Coggeshall's, it is tempting to connect the two.[3] In one respect, however, the writer has moved beyond Ralph, for the latter had made Joachim place the decisive moment of history at the opening of the sixth seal in 1199, whereas our writer expects the climax of Antichrist at the seventh seal, dated 1260. In these two examples from the manuscripts of Paris and Erfurt, one probably French and the other going back to an English original, we see the continuing interest in Joachim's Biblical exegesis and his patterns of concords, an interest which could stimulate a writer to fill up the end of his book with Joachimist prophecy. The focus of interest, as with Howden and Ralph of Coggeshall, was obviously the prophetic future, and especially the approaching Antichrist. No one yet saw the seventh seal as a Sabbath Age beyond Antichrist, yet within history, completing the pattern of threes in the third *status*.

[1] Erfurt, Stadtbücherei, MS. Amplonian F. 71. For a transcript and fuller discussion of the relevant parts of this manuscript see Bloomfield, Reeves, *Speculum* xxix. 777–80.

[2] *Speculum* xxix. 778. Prof. R. Southern first drew my attention to this manuscript.

[3] It has been suggested that Ralph of Coggeshall was also the author of an English Cistercian treatise, *Distinctiones Monasticae et Morales* (*c.* 1225), which may show faint traces of Joachimist influence. But this authorship is disputed. For references see *Speculum* xxix. 776.

There is, however, one most striking exception to this general picture of first-generation Joachimism as concerned with the pattern of twos, not threes. Dr. Hirsch-Reich discovered a third example of an early writer who used the *Liber Figurarum*, but this time it was not Joachim's historical exegesis that attracted attention so much as his Trinitarian doctrine.[1] Between 1208 and 1210 the Cistercian Werner of Rochefort used the Sacred Name *IEUE* in a sermon on the Trinity.[2] He placed the Tetragrammaton in its three combinations of *IE*, *EU*, *UE*, at the angles of an equilateral triangle, with the whole Name, encircled, in the centre. Dr. Hirsch-Reich showed that this could hardly have been derived by Werner from any other source than Joachim, and has identified the figure he used as almost certainly the Psaltery in the *Liber Figurarum*.[3] Thus we find a French theologian pondering on Joachim's figurative treatment of the Unity and Trinity of the Godhead some years before the condemnation of those views in 1215.[4]

[1] Bloomfield, Reeves, *Speculum* xxix. 781–3.
[2] Migne, *PL* ccv, col. 713.   [3] *Lib. Fig.* II, Pl. XIII.
[4] A similar use of the Tetragrammaton in a *Tractatus contra Amaurianos* (see refs. *Speculum* xxix. 782 n. 45) suggests that the author was Werner. If so, his interest in Joachim may have arisen because he found similar doctrines being misused by the Amalricians. See *Speculum* xxix. 783 for discussion and references on the unsolved problem of the relationship between Joachimism and the Amalricians.

V

JOACHIMISM IN THE MID-THIRTEENTH CENTURY

As we approach the second generation after Joachim—the crucial one, according to his calculations—the double reputation of the Abbot begins to emerge more clearly. On the one hand, he is branded as one condemned for his attack on Peter Lombard. There is a revealing fragment of English evidence on the reaction of the orthodox in an anonymous Latin poem found in a Bodley manuscript of the first half of the thirteenth century.[1] The poem, which is chiefly a hexametric arrangement of phrases taken from the condemnation of 1215, was probably written in the twenties or thirties. It is interesting that one of the earliest chroniclers to record the condemnation is also English: Roger of Wendover, who, writing in the thirties, gives under the year 1179 an account of Joachim's Trinitarian views which is unusually full and shows more than formal interest.[2] He summarizes Joachim's accusation in the lost *libellus* that Peter Lombard had fallen into quaternity, and quotes one of Joachim's key sentences in formulating his own view. Then he gives the opinion expressed by the 1215 Council 'quod saepe dictus Joachim huiusmodi unitatem non veram et propriam, sed quasi collectivam et similitudinariam esse fateatur, quemadmodum multi homines dicuntur unus populus, et multi fideles una ecclesia'. But he ends on an unexpected note by stressing the fact that this question of the Lombard's views had been in the balance during several pontificates before Innocent III came down heavily against Joachim:

Stetit autem haec indeterminata altercatio a diebus Alexandri papae usque in tempora Innocentii papae per annos multos, sedentibus inter eos in cathedra Romana, Lucio, Urbano, Gregorio, Clementio et Celestino pontificibus Romanis, quibus succedens Innocentius tertius . . . libellum abbatis Joachim, quem contra Petrum et articulum ediderat praedictum, his verbis damnavit . . . (*Flores*, RS, i. 122.)

[1] Oxford, MS. Bodley 40, transcribed and discussed in *Speculum* xxix. 784–5.
[2] Roger of Wendover, *Flores Historiarum*, RS, i. 121–3. Like the author of the poem, however, he only quotes the lost *libellus* from the 1215 decree of condemnation.

Roger seems to be aware of the fact that the condemnation of Joachim rather than Peter Lombard had not been a foregone conclusion. A second notice of the condemnation, written before 1242 by a celebrated Bolognese lawyer, Johannes de Deo, also takes care to present Joachim in the best possible light.[1]

On the other hand, Joachim's reputation as a Biblical exegete was also spreading and, again, we find here some significant scraps of English information. It is well known that Adam Marsh, the Franciscan scholar, sent 'paucas particulas de variis expositionibus Abbatis Joachimi' to Robert Grossetete, Bishop of Lincoln, suggesting that he should read the *libellus* 'in cubiculo' before he returned it.[2] Adam had acquired it, he said, 'per quendam fratrem venientem de partibus transmontanis'. The description—*de variis expositionibus*—suggests one of the anthologies to which we have already drawn attention, one small enough to be called a *libellus*. Adam expressed admiration for Joachim as one who 'non immerito creditur divinitus spiritum intellectus . . . assecutus', and was eager to discuss the Abbot's message of the terrible days to come. But he reserved judgement until he could hear Grossetete's opinion. Although Salimbene mentions him as a friend of Hugh de Digne, the great Joachite, there is nothing really to suggest that Adam was himself a Joachite. The menace of Tartar attack at that time must have made all such prophecies of crisis seem immediately relevant.[3] Although undated, the letter must have been written well before the scandal of the Eternal Evangel in 1255, for Grossetete died in 1253. How illuminating his reply might be if we had it!

Roger Bacon's interest in the Abbot Joachim springs from the same kind of preoccupation. In his *Opus Majus*[4] he raises the question, much debated in his generation, as to whether the Tartar tribes were not already breaking through the gates of the Caucasus to burst forth over Christendom in support of Antichrist. In support of this rumour he cites the evidence of Franscicans, sent by the King of France, who penetrated through the gates far beyond into

---

[1] *Chronica Romana*, MGHS xxxi. 323.

[2] *Monumenta Franciscana*, ed. J. S. Brewer, RS, Letter XLIII, pp. 146–7. See further P. G. Cantini, 'Adam de Marisco, O.F.M. auctor spiritualis', *Antonianum* xxiii (1948), pp. 468–74.

[3] Salimbene, pp. 232–3, names four whom Hugh claimed as his friends, but the description '*maximi Iohachite*' only applies to Hugh himself and John of Parma. After this Salimbene names three, including Robert Grossetete and Adam Marsh.

[4] Roger Bacon, *Opus Majus*, ed. J. Bridges (London, 1900), i, pp. 268–9.

the mountains where the Tartars had been shut up. If the gates have already been broken, he argues, it is urgent that the Church should study prophecies in order to be forewarned. He concludes: 'Nolo hic ponere os meum in coelum sed scio quod si ecclesia vellet revolvere textum sacrum et prophetias sacras, atque prophetias Sibyllae, et Merlin et Aquilae, et Sestonis, Joachim et multorum aliorum, insuper historias et libros philosophorum, atque juberet considerari vias astronomiae, inveniretur sufficiens suspicio vel magis certitudo de tempore Antichristi.' Thus Joachim takes his place in the reading-list for a study-programme on Last Things.

Two further passages bring out more strongly the influence of Joachimist expectation on Bacon, although without naming Joachim himself. Addressing the Pope in his *Opus Tertium* (1267/8), he says:[1]

Sed prophetatum est a quadraginta annis, et multorum visiones habitae sunt, quod unus Papa erit his temporibus qui purgabit jus canonicum et ecclesiam Dei a cavillationibus et fraudibus juristarum et fiet justitia universaliter sine strepitu litis. Et propter istius Papae bonitatem, veritatem et iustitiam accidet, quod Graeci revertentur ad obedientiam Romanae Ecclesiae et quod pro majori parte convertentur Tartari ad fidem, et Saraceni destruentur; et fiet unum ovile et unus pastor, sicut in auribus prophetae sonuit istud verbum. Et unus qui vidit haec per revelationem dixit, et dicit quod ipse videbit haec magnifica fieri temporibus suis. Et certe infra annum unum possent fieri si Deo placuerit et summo Pontifici, et infra minus; unde temporibus vestris possunt fieri. Et Deus conservat vitam vestram ut haec per vos fiant.

Again, in the *Compendium studii philosophiae* (1272),[2] he repeats the same expectation that after the tribulations of Antichrist will come 'unus beatissimus papa qui omnes corruptiones tollet de studio et ecclesia . . . et renovetur mundus et intret plenitudo gentium et reliquiae Israel ad fidem convertantur'. Now Joachim had never actually formulated a clear concept of an Angelic Pope to be the symbol of the third *status*, though he came fairly close to it.[3] By the end of the thirteenth century, as we shall see, this figure was becoming a focal point of Joachite expectation, but, so far as we know, Bacon's was the first full statement of it. He did not acknowledge its source in Joachim; indeed, he may deliberately have omitted him

---

[1] Roger Bacon, *Opus Tertium*, ed. J. S. Brewer, RS, *Opera Inedita*, p. 86.
[2] *Compendium studii philosophiae* (ref. as in previous footnote, p. 402).
[3] *Infra*, pp. 396-7.

from the list of prophetic sources which he gave in the *Compendium*, but he acknowledged that this hope had been prophesied for forty years or so. The most convincing marks of later Joachimism are the expectation of a *renovatio* after the tribulation of Antichrist, the return of the Greek Church to Roman obedience, and the conversion of Tartars and Jews. Thus Roger Bacon really did seem to have caught some of the Joachimist hope.[1] We must observe, however, that the evidence for this comes from two late works. We have moved into the post-1260 period, when the pattern of threes was well known and the Spiritual Franciscans were disseminating their version of the expected third *status*.

To return to the earlier period, as the 1250s approached, attention focused more and more sharply on the date of impending disaster. It was no new thing to proclaim the advent of Antichrist, but the notable concentration of hopes and fears on the decade 1250–60, and especially on the year 1260, can hardly be dissociated from Joachim. This is almost ironical, for the Abbot in his writings took care to emphasize the uncertainty of all calculations of Last Things and hardly committed himself to the *year* 1260, though he did to the *number* 1260.[2] He did, however, declare that the two generations after 1200 were crucial, and, in words which communicated suspense and excitement and were therefore often quoted, he summoned the next generation to watch:

Tempus autem quando hec erunt dico manifeste quia prope est: diem autem et horam Dominus ipse novit. Quantum tamen secundum coaptationem concordie extimare queo, si pax conceditur ab his malis usque ad annum millesimum ducentesimum incarnationis dominice: exinde ne subito ista fiant suspecta mihi sunt omnimodis et tempora et momenta. (*Lib. Conc.*, f. 41ᵛ.)

Furthermore, the translation of his ideas into *figurae* may well have 'fixed' the programme of Last Things more definitely than Joachim intended. It was difficult to compose tables in which the generations were measured off in units of thirty years without implying a definite end-date, and Joachim's later pair of Tables of Concords,[3]

---

[1] 'Et unus qui vidit haec per revelationem', says Bacon, 'dixit et dicit quod ipse videbit haec magnifica fieri temporibus suis.' The *unus* was probably a Spiritual Franciscan. But in the writer's view S. C. Easton, *Roger Bacon and his Search for a Universal Science: A Reconsideration of the Life and Work in the Light of his own Stated Purposes* (Oxford, 1952), pp. 134–43, argues too easily that Bacon was a Joachite.

[2] Reeves, Hirsch-Reich, *MARS* iii. 190 n. 1.

[3] *Lib. Fig.* II, Pls. III, IV.

even with the two blank spaces for the last two generations, pointed definitely to the year 1260. We have already shown these Tables to have been in circulation for some time, heralding the solemn date in visual form.

Another sign of heightened expectation appears in a short prophetic verse which we first meet in Mathew Paris's volume of *Additamenta*, in a manuscript executed before 1256:[1]

His quoque temporibus propter terribiles rumores hujusmodi celebriter hi versus Antichristi adventum nuntiantes recitabantur:

> Cum fuerint anni transacti mille ducenti
> Et quinquaginta post partum Virginis almae,
> Tunc Antichristus nascetur daemone plenus.

The context is similar to that in which Roger Bacon cites Joachim— reports of terrible Tartar ravages, dated as 1242—but the lines are not here ascribed to Joachim and have, in fact, no particularly Joachimist note. They soon appear, however, in the pseudo-Joachimist tract *Epistola subsequentium figurarum*[2] and are persistently ascribed to Joachim in later references. The fact that in this earliest version the crisis date is 1250 indicates that the verse was written before this date.

This little verse was obviously flying around in England in the mid-thirteenth century, for it turns up in several manuscripts of this period. By this time the crisis date has been moved on to 1260. The assumption can be made that the verse would have been scribbled into a book before the date when it should have been fulfilled. A Bible from a Gilbertine house contains the prophecy added on the end flyleaf, this time clearly ascribed to Joachim:[3]

Prophetia Joachim

> Cum fuerint anni completi mille ducenti
> Et decies seni post partum virginis alme,
> Tunc Antichristus nascetur demone plenus.

It turns up again at the end of another Bible, once more under Joachim's name and applied to 1260, while a third example comes from a manuscript of Bury St. Edmunds.[4] Its circulation in other

---

[1] M. Paris, *Chronica Majora*, RS, vi. 80.

[2] Rome, Vat., MS. Lat. 3822, f. 3ᵛ, see Tondelli, *Lib. Fig.* I, pp. 42–4; Bignami-Odier, *MAH* liv. 224–6.

[3] Cambridge, St. John's College, MS. 239 (N1), end flyleaf.

[4] MSS. Brit. Mus., Harley 1280, f. 427ʳ; Royal 10 B. XII, f. 43ʳ. It is also found in MSS. Oxford, Oriel College, 76, f. 147ʳ; Lambeth, 477, f. 26ʳ; Exeter, Cathedral Library, 3514, f. 6, all with date 1260.

parts of Europe is testified by its presence in thirteenth-century manuscripts in Paris, Rome, Reggio, Padua, Strasbourg.[1] It was quoted by Alexander of Bremen before 1250 and echoed by Albert of Stade.[2] Modified to fit later dates, it continued in vogue for the next two centuries.[3]

Another short prophecy is also found in an English manuscript in the British Museum (Royal 8 C. IV, f. 66ʳ), headed *Prophecie Joachim in maiori libro de concordanciis*. It runs thus:

Anno Incarnacionis MCCL corruent nobiles et principes et multi Christiani et potentes in conspectu paganorum [et] morientur quasi pro nichillo et multi eorum captivabuntur. Item. LIIII recuperabunt Greci Constantinopolim et turpiter eicientur Latini. Item. LVII erunt duo pape, unus Lugduni et alter Rome. Lugdunensis erit iustus et equus. Alter vero iniustus et iniquus et mutuo sese excommunicabunt. Item LX anno erunt cotidie ecclesia et clerus in tanta vilitate et conculcacione in quanta non fuerunt a tempore Constantini qui dotavit ecclesiam residente Silvestro in Romana ecclesia. Item. LXV rediet [redibit] tota Grecia ad obbedienciam Romane ecclesie. Tunc audientur nova de predicatoribus antichristi.

Obviously this passage did not come from the *Liber Concordie*, but it is significant that someone had already been inserting a forged prophecy into it. Its chief point, as with the previous one, was to announce the advent of Antichrist. It contains one genuine echo of Joachim's expectation in its reference to the return of the Greek Church to the Roman, but it does not connect this with any hope of an age of spiritual blessedness. Perhaps it was this reference to the reunion of the Churches which kept it in vogue, for it is found—

---

[1] MSS. Rome, Vat., Lat. 3820, f. 37ʳ; 3822, f. 14ᵛ; Bib. Vitt. Eman., 14 S. Pant. 31. 8, f. 57ʳ; Paris, Bib. Nat., Lat. 3319, f. 38ᵛ; Padua, Bib. Ant., Scaf. V, No. 90. misc. 2a, f. 44ʳ; Reggio Emilia, Bib. Mun., Tutti D. 2, f. 131ᵛ; Strasbourg, Universitäts-u-Landes Bibl., Lat. 71, f. 158ʳ.   [2] *MGHS* xvi. 341.

[3] MSS. Brit. Mus., Kings 8. D. 11, f. 70ᵛ (1300); Cambridge Univ. Libr., Gg. IV. 25, f. 67ᵛ (1560); Paris, Bib. Nat., Lat. 14726, f. 77ʳ (1360); Rome, Vat., Reg. Lat. 580, f. 53ᵛ (1375); Chig. A. VII. 220, f. 51ᵛ (1375); Nuremberg, Städtbibl., Cent. IV. 32, f. 46ʳ; Hague, Bib. Reg., 71. E. 44, p. 188 (1360). See also appendix to P. Langtoft, *Chronicle*, RS, ii. 449; H. Corner, *Chronica Novella*, ed. J. Eccard, *Corpus Historicum Medii Aevi* . . . (Leipzig, 1723), cols. 742–3 (1360); *Super Hier.* (Venice, 1525), f. 62ʳ (1310). It is also referred to (*a*) in Henry of Harclay's *Quaestio* on the Second Advent, ed. Pelster, 'Die Quaestio Heinrichs über die zweite Ankunft Christi u. die Erwartung des baldigen Weltendes zu Anfang des XIV. Jahrhunderts', *Arch. ital. per la storia d. pietà*, i (1950), p. 74: 'Hoc est quod dicunt versus vulgate . . . unde non debet esse decies deni, ut multi dicunt, sed decies seni . . .'; (*b*) in John Quidort's *Tractatus de Antichristo* (Venice, 1516), f. 47ʳ. See also F. Saxl, *Journal of the Warburg and Courtauld Institutes*, v (1942), p. 85.

generally with the date altered to 1350—in manuscripts at the British Museum, Oxford, Cambridge, Paris, and Florence.[1]

A third early Joachimist prophecy has been studied by Mgr. Tondelli and dated by him to 1260–4.[2] He found it in manuscripts at Padua and Reggio Emilia, and it obviously belongs to the Veneto, containing many references to northern and central Italy. Its beginning, 'In die illa elevabitur Draco repletus furore', at once evokes the image of Joachim's dragon-figure. In fact, this prophecy does quote from the *Liber Figurarum*, but from the Tables of Concords rather than the text accompanying the dragon.[3] It testifies, however, to the popularity of the dragon-symbol. At the end of the prophecy our little verse on Antichrist is tagged on in a slightly different form, still with the date 1250. Later, with the date changed to 1360, we find the whole text in a Paris manuscript.[4]

There is a further accumulation of small pieces of evidence which points to a focus of interest in Joachim's prophecies in north Italy. This interest begins with Joachim's contemporary, Sicard of Cremona, and with the early notice of Joachim by Johannes de Deo of Bologna.[5] This latter was used as a source on Joachim both by a Mantuan chronicler[6] and by Albert Milioli, the notary of Reggio. Milioli knew at least the dragon-figure and text from the *Liber Figurarum*, for he reproduces them in his *Liber de Temporibus*.[7] It would be natural to think that the copy of the *Liber Figurarum* he used was that which is now in Reggio, but in form his dragon is

[1] MSS. Brit. Mus., Royal & Kings 8. C. IV, f. 66ʳ; Cotton, Vesp. E. VII, f. 70ᵛ; Oxford, Bod. Lib., Digby 218, f. 107ʳ; Digby 176, f. 38ʳ; Ashmole 393, f. 80ᵛ; Ashmole 192, p. 102; Cambridge, Corpus Christi College, 138, f. 138ʳ (fragment); Corpus Christi College, 404, f. 100ʳ; Univ. Lib., Ii. vi. 25, f. 107ᵛ; Florence, Bib. Ricc., 688, f. cxiiiᵛ. See also Paris, Bib. Nat., MS. Lat. 16397, f. 123ʳ, for another prophecy (in French) from Joachim's 'grant livre de Concordances'. Cf. *infra*, p. 92 nn. 3, for this prophecy.

[2] Tondelli, *Studi e Documenti*, iv. 3–9, text pp. 5–6.

[3] *Lib. Fig.* II, Pls. III, IV. Cf. Tondelli, *Lib. Fig.* I, p. 219 n. 3, where he says that the text is partly taken from the Dragon figure.

[4] Paris, Bib. Nat., MS. Lat. 14726, ff. 76ʳ–77ʳ. See also Florence, Bib. Laur., MS. Plut. XVIII, sin. v, at the end, where the section beginning *post celestinum* alone is given (14th-century manuscript from Santa Croce). For other manuscripts of this prophecy see Grundmann, *NF*, p. 24 n. 1.   [5] *Supra*, pp. 40, 46.

[6] *Chronica Pontificum et Imperatorum Mantuana*, *MGHS* xxiv. 218.

[7] Modena, Bib. Estense, MS. M. I. 7 (lat. II. H. 5), f. 121ʳ, reproduced by A. Cerlini in 'Fra Salimbene e le cronache attribuite ad Alberto Milioli', *Archivio Muratoriano*, i, fasc. 8 (1910), pp. 383–409. Tondelli, *Lib. Fig.* I, p. 21, draws attention to the fact that Milioli did not take this from Salimbene because the end of his dragon text differs from that in Salimbene's *Cronica*, pp. 440–1. See also O. Holder-Egger, *MGHS* xxxi. 663; xxxii, Pt. II, p. 440 n. 1.

quite different, resembling rather the figures in Vat. MSS., Lat. 4860 and 3822.[1] Milioli also cites the Joachimist oracles which were circulating under the names of Methodius, the Sibyls, Michael Scot, and Merlin.[2] The Franciscan Salimbene, a native of Parma, was living in Reggio for part of the time when Milioli was writing his *Liber*, and clearly had some connection with its compilation. It isnot possible to say exactly which drew on the other's writing,[3] but Salimbene's pronounced Joachimist sympathies may well have influenced Milioli in this direction. That the materials for Joachimist studies were available seems likely from the important early manuscripts at Reggio, Padua, and Pavia,[4] although we must note that Salimbene as well as Milioli used a text of the dragon-figure different from that in the Reggio *Liber Figurarum*. Another Franciscan from this region, Thomas of Pavia whom we quote below, also described the dragon-figure in terms which show that he had seen it. It was in Parma that there occurred in 1233 the 'year of the Alleluia' so movingly described by Salimbene.[5] Mgr. Tondelli claimed this as a Joachimist movement,[6] and, though this can hardly be proved, such an outburst of exalted and spontaneous feeling could easily be the expression of Joachimist expectations. A more certain outburst of Joachimism occurred in Parma in 1260, when Gerard Segarelli arose to found the movement of the Apostolic Brethren.[7] Later, in 1266, we find prophecies from the pseudo-Joachimist *Super Hieremiam* quoted in Piacenza,[8] while in Parma in 1282 there was

---

[1] MSS. 4860, f. 201ʳ; 3822, f. 5ʳ, reproduced *Lib. Fig.* II, Pl. XXVIb.

[2] A. Milioli, *Liber de Temporibus*, *MGHS* xxxi. 560.

[3] This problem is fully examined by Cerlini, loc. cit., pp. 385–90.

[4] *Infra*, p. 79–80.

[5] Salimbene, pp. 414 seq.

[6] Tondelli, *Lib. Fig.* I, pp. 192–6.   [7] Cf. *infra*, p. 242.

[8] *Annales Placentini*, *MGHS* xviii. 516: 'In libro enim Johachim talia inveniuntur: "Quia necesse est a sanctuario Dei cedes incipiat, a quo velud a capite ad membra languencia vulnus livoris emanat. Potens enim est Deus Franchos repelere et Alamanos contra ecclesiam revocare; et que magis de humana quam divina potentia confidit, iusto iudicio amicorum destituta subsidiis, sub incursibus hostium conculcetur. Futurum enim est prorsus ex proximo, ut orta discordia inter principes, non tantum ab imperio ecclesia corruat, sed etiam a Francorum regno diffidat. Videat itaque generalis ecclesia, si non fiet ei baculus arundineus potentia Galicanna. Cui siquidem si quis nititur, perforat manum eius. Vicinum namque est, quatinus posterus Francos Egiptios in futura congressione collidet, ut per quos regnum mater ecclesia de ursi dentibus contendit erruere, versa vice nequeat in stragem forcium respirare, donec Dominus ex alto prospiciat, ut perfecte malicie finem ponat." ' I have been unable to locate this quotation in the Venetian printed edition of the *Super Hier*. It could be another version of f. 60ᵛ (commentary on cap. 50).

a prophet, Asdente, who foretold the future from the writings of Joachim, Merlin, Methodius, the Sibyls, Isaiah, Hosea, Daniel, the Apocalypse, and Michael Scot.[1]

A sharp comment of disapproval concerning those who busy themselves with these circulating prophecies and ought to know better comes from David of Augsburg:

. . . et ideo multifariis vaticiniis iam usque ad fastidium repleti sumus de Antichristi adventu, de signis appropinquantis iudicii, de destructione Religionum, de persecutione Ecclesiae, de regni defectione et variis mundi pressuris et aliis pluribus, quibus etiam viri graves et devoti plusquam oportuit creduli extiterunt, de scriptis Joachim et aliorum vaticinantium varias interpretationes extrahentes, quae etsi vera essent et authentica, tamen Religiosi plurima invenirent, in quibus fructuosius occuparentur. (Quoted Bondatti, *Gioachinismo e Francescanesimo*, p. 52 n. 5.)

To this we may add the view of one Franciscan, Thomas of Pavia, who—although he was known and admired by Salimbene—did not succumb to these fascinating speculations. Writing before 1260, he spoke of the great debate on the subject of Last Things and quoted Joachim at length on Antichrist. His attitude of cool detachment is well expressed in his conclusion:

Joachim vero quibusdam verborum et concordantiarum connexionibus, antichristi tempus determinare praesumit, nescio suo an divino Spiritu motus, XLII generationes a Christi nativitate vel passione usque ad antichristum ponens et pro singulas generationes XXX annos computans, mille ducentos sexaginta annos ponit vel a nativitate Christi vel a passione; et tunc oportet, ait, venire antichristum et impleri omnia quae de ipso scripta sunt. Utrum autem verum vel falsum dixerit, cito apparebit. Hoc assero quod scripta eius plures stultos et mendaces ostenderunt, vel quia aliter intellexerunt ea quam intelligenda fuerint, vel quia scripta illa humano spiritu non divino sunt edita, cuius sententiae nec assertorem me facio nec contemptorem me assero. (*AFH* xvi. 26–7.)

By way of circulating prophecies and the discussions upon them we reach the famous year 1260. The great mass movements of medieval Europe will always remain mysterious, for the causes and courses of those great waves of emotion cannot be exactly tracked. No doubt there were restless forebodings and expectations abroad, for at various times in the first half of the thirteenth century independent prophets arose to cry 'Antichrist comes!'[2] The rumours

---

[1] Milioli, op. cit., p. 560.

[2] Besides the evidence of the little verse discussed *supra*, p. 49, see references given by A. Messini, *Misc. Franc.* xxxvii. 40–2.

that the gates of the Caucasus were open and the heathen masses pouring through were persistent. No doubt many factors were building up to the crisis, but it is difficult to avoid the conclusion that the fact that the Flagellant Movement took place about 1260 must be connected with Joachimism. We should note also that Salimbene specifically states that the beginning of Joachim's third *status* was acclaimed 'in illa verberatione quae facta est MCCLX'.[1] True, Joachim arrived at this number, and therefore, by implication, at this date, through a series of Biblical calculations which others might have pursued also. But, so far as we know, no one else had pointed to 1260. Certainly the date 1260 was in the air and this was the Joachimist date. It was in the air, perhaps, because of the circulation of the Tables of Concords;[2] more likely, because simple little verses like the one we have quoted were flying around. These focused attention on one moment and touched off a great outburst.

The Flagellant Movement is described by a number of contemporary or near-contemporary chroniclers.[3] It was believed to have originated in Perugia, to have spread thence through Italy, and finally beyond the Alps to Provence, Germany, and other parts. Certain points are emphasized in nearly all accounts: it arose spontaneously, and stress is laid on the fact that neither Pope, hierarchy, nor regular preachers stimulated it; it originated with the simple, but included men of all classes; besides the religious acts of penitence —processions, flagellations, devotions in church—the movement often involved social reconciliation and reformation. No one except Salimbene and Milioli specifically connected it with Joachimism, and, indeed, certain characteristics would militate against this connection. The religious devotions appear to have been focused on the Virgin and on the humanity and Passion of Christ rather than on the Third Person of the Trinity, while it was the wrath and

---

[1] Salimbene, p. 466: 'Et eodem anno debebat inchoari doctrina Joachim abbatis, qui dividit mundum in triplicem statum. . . . In tertio statu operabitur Spiritus Sanctus in religiosis. . . . Quem statum inchoatum dicunt in illa verberatione que facta est MCCLX . . .' See also Milioli, loc. cit., pp. 524–5.

[2] As suggested by Tondelli, *Lib. Fig.* I, p. 202 and Fig. 5 opposite, reproduced from *Lib. Fig.* II, Pl. IV.

[3] The most important sources are: *Annales S. Iustinae Patavini*, *MGHS* ixix. 179; *Annales Foroiulienses*, ibid., p. 196; *Annales capituli Cracoviensis*, ibid., p. 601; *Annales Ianuensis*, *MGHS* xviii. 241–2; Heinrich v. Heimburg, *Annales*, *MGHS* xvii. 714; Hermannus Altahensis, *Annales*, ibid., p. 402; *Chronicon Rythmicum Austriacum*, *MGHS* xxv. 363; *Continuatio Mellicensis*, *MGHS* ix. 509; *Continuatio Zwetlensis*, iii, ibid., p. 656; *Continuatio Sancrucensis*, ii, ibid., p. 645; Pulkova of Radevin, *Chronicon*, ed. G. Dobner, *Monumenta Historica Boemiae* (Prague, 1774), iii. 232.

judgement of God which was expected, not the Age of the Holy
Ghost. In contemporary chroniclers the Flagellant Movement of
1260 appears mysterious and puzzling, with no obvious origins. It
seems reasonable, however, to think that it derived ultimately from
Joachim's calculations, which pointed to this year, especially when
we remember that so far popular interest in Joachimism had centred
on the pattern of twos culminating in the Second Advent. But there
is no evidence that any distinctively Joachimist prophecies were
used and nothing to suggest that the flagellants went out to meet the
third *status* of the Holy Ghost. The whole episode gives evidence
rather of a widespread mood, deriving from many sources, but
inflamed by Joachimist calculations, than of any general dissemination of Joachimist ideas, or even the invocation of the Abbot as the
prophet of Last Things.[1]

In tracing the dissemination of Joachim's fame as far as the great
year 1260 we have side-stepped the activities of groups of disciples
more closely committed to his ideas. These will be studied fully in
the next part of this book, but one main aspect of their Joachimism
must be mentioned here—namely, the production of pseudo-
Joachimist writings, some of which rapidly attained a considerable
vogue and account largely for the later reputation of Joachim.

Except for the little *Epistola subsequentium figurarum*, the pseudo-
Joachimist works do not appear until the mid-thirteenth century.
Standing apart from the rest is the so-called *Liber contra Lombardum*.
This must have been written after the publication of the Decretals
of Gregory IX in 1234, but otherwise we have no clue as to its date
or author.[2] Professor Ottaviano has argued convincingly that it was
the work of a close disciple, since in argument and language it
echoes Joachim's characteristic writing on Trinitarian doctrine. It
stands apart from the other pseudo-Joachimist works in that it is
purely a piece of theological polemic, with no reference to political
prophecy, or even to the *ecclesia contemplantium* of the third *status*.
The author was a learned man, wholly absorbed in a burning

[1] F. Ermini, 'Il "Dies Irae" ', *Biblioteca dell'Archivum Romanicum'*, ii (Geneva,
1928), pp. 62 seq., establishes the author of the *Dies Irae* as the Franciscan Thomas of
Celano and connects it with Joachimist expectation concerning 1260 and the Flagellants.
He cannot, however, produce any concrete evidence of Joachimist influence within,
the poem, except the line 'Teste David cum Sibylla'. This may link the poem with the
Joachimist oracle circulating after 1250 under the name of the Sibyl Erithrea; see
infra, p. 56.

[2] Ed. Ottaviano, *Lib. contra Lombardum*, p. 81. The details in this paragraph are
drawn from Ottaviano's Introduction to his edition of this work.

theological problem and with no prophetical axe to grind. The *Liber* seems most likely to have emanated from a school of Joachimist theology in the Order of Fiore itself.

The earliest of the prophetical works put forth under Joachim's name was the *Super Hieremiam*. It initiates a new phase of Joachim-ism in that it is the first pseudo-Joachimist work to re-state the concept of the three *status*. The problems of dating this with any exactitude are bound up with the evidence for its dissemination. Salimbene recorded his first mention of it under the year 1248.[1] Alexander of Bremen cited it at length in his *Expositio in Apocaly-psim*,[2] in a different and older version from that of the printed Venetian edition. There are still some problems concerning the date and manner of its arrival in Germany,[3] but Alexander's work en-ables us to say definitely that a version of the *Super Hieremiam* was in existence at the latest by 1248 and probably by 1243. By 1250 Albert of Stade was quoting from it and citing Alexander on it.[4] As we have noticed, both quote the verse on Antichrist and this may, perhaps, have already become attached to the *Super Hieremiam*.

The next pseudo-Joachimist work to appear was the *Vaticinium Sibillae Erithreae* in 1249 or earlier.[5] This purported to be a gloss by Joachim on a sibylline oracle and is now dated to the years before Frederick II's death. Another work, entitled *De Oneribus Prophetarum*, is closely associated with it in language and attitude

[1] Salimbene, p. 237. Since Salimbene made later additions, this reference by itself does not prove that the *Super Hier.* was in circulation by 1248.

[2] Alexander Minorita, *Expositio in Apocalypsim*, ed. A. Wachtel, *MGHS* (Weimar, 1955). On this work, see J. P. Gilson, 'Friar Alexander and his Historical Interpretation of the Apocalypse', *Collectanea Franciscana*, ii, ed. C. Kingsford *et alii* (Manchester, 1922), pp. 20–30; Grundmann, *ZB* xlv. 289–334; A. Wachtel, 'Die weltgeschichtliche Apocalypse-Auslegung des Minoriten Alexander v. Bremen', *Franziskanische Studien*, xxiv (1937), pp. 201–59, 305–63.

[3] This problem is discussed briefly by Bloomfield, Reeves, *Speculum* xxix. 790–1.

[4] Albert of Stade, *Annales Stadenses*, *MGHS* xvi. 372: 'His auditis rumoribus, prophetiam abbatis Joachim quidam reduxerunt ad memoriam, qui dixit: Superabitur Francus, capietur pontifex summus, praevalebit imperans Alemannus. [*Super Hiere-miam*, cap. 46]. Sed frater Alexander in expos. apok. eandem prophetiam tangens subicit sic: Sed ecclesia orat ut quod dictum est in ultionem transeat in salutem.' His reference corresponds to p. 509 in Wachtel's edition, but Alexander cites the passage as 'quaedam prophetia', not from Joachim, thus Albert must have known the *Super Hieremiam* independently. The date here suggested for this work rests on the assump-tion that later additions were made to it, since the last part (cap. 34 onwards) contains quotations from the prophecies of Merlin and the Sibyl Erithrea which were written *c*. 1252–4. See *Super Hier.*, ff. 58ᵛ, 61ʳ, 62ʳ.

[5] *Inc.* 'Exquiritis me o illustrissima turba danaum'. I follow here the dating of Alexander (see bibl. 7. 32, pp. 76–79).

towards the Hohenstaufen; it would seem to have been written in the year 1255–56.[1] In the same group are an *Expositio super Sibillis et Merlino* and a prophecy *De tribus statibus*, both addressed to the Emperor Henry VI, and three short prophecies.[2] All these pursue the anti-Hohenstaufen line relentlessly; all use prophecies attributed to Raynier as well as Joachim.[3] About a decade later, reflecting the last phase of Hohenstaufen fortunes, came the *Super Esaiam*, a composite work probably emanating from Calabria.[4] Associated with it was a small figure-collection, containing among others the ever-popular dragon-figure.[5] Another work which was circulating by the end of the thirteenth century was the pseudo-Joachimist exposition of the *Oraculum Cyrilli*.[6] The oracle itself was supposed to have been communicated by an angel to Cyril the Carmelite and sent to Joachim. It is generally thought to have emanated from Spiritual Franciscan circles and has been dated to the decade 1280 to 1290.[7]

[1] See Appendix A, p. 520, for full reference. I have studied this in the manuscript version in the British Museum, which contains material not included in the version edited by Holder-Egger.

[2] For details of the two longer works, see Appendix A, pp. 520-1. The first of these two is confused by Russo, *Bibliografia*, p. 53, with the *Vaticinium Sibillae Erithreae*. Three short works are (*a*) a commentary on a passage of the Apocalypse, *inc.* 'Quia semper in stipendariis propriis'; (*b*) a prophecy on the kingdom of Sicily, *inc.* 'Cum ad me ruine miseriam'; (*c*) a prophetic interpretation of the plagues of Egypt attributed to Fr. Raynier, *inc.* 'Decem plagas quibus affligetur egyptus'. On these, see *infra*, Appendix B, pp. 528-9.

[3] The creation of a pseudo-Raynier as well as a pseudo-Joachim and the composition of fictitious discussions between them is an interesting feature of this group of writings. In the *De Oneribus* references to the prophecies of Raynier, all of which concern the expectation of a Third Frederick, occur as follows: B.M., f. 39^v (*NA*, 173), B.M., f. 39^v (*NA*, omitted), B.M., f. 40^r (*NA*, omitted), B.M., f. 40^v (*NA*, 182). There was clearly an interpretation of the prophecies of the Sibyls and Merlin written in the name of Raynier, for the parallel pseudo-Joachimist *Expositio super Sibillis et Merlino* refers many times to the exposition of Raynier, in most cases disagreeing or giving an alternative meaning. The oracle on the fate of the Sicilian kingdom begins by referring to a prophecy on similar lines by Raynier, while the short oracle on the ten plagues of Egypt is written in his name. Finally, the later *Super Esaiam* is addressed to him.

[4] See Appendix A, p. 521, for full details. This was dated by W. Friderich, 'Kritische Untersuchung der dem Abt Joachim v. Floris zugeschriebenen Kommentare zu Jesajas u. Jeremias', *Zeitschrift f. wissenschaftliche Theologie* (Jena, 1859), p. 495, as on the eve of the struggle between Manfred and Charles of Anjou. For discussion of the outlook of this work see Reeves, *Sophia* xix. 363 seq.; Reeves, Hirsch-Reich, *MARS* iii. 194 seq.

[5] Following the Venetian editors, this may be called the *Praemissiones*. See Reeves, Hirsch-Reich, *MARS* iii. 172, 183 seq.

[6] For details see Appendix A, p. 522, and Select Bibliography I.

[7] Bignami-Odier, *Roquetaillade*, pp. 54 seq., discusses this work, noting that F. Ehrle dated it 1280 and B. Zimmerman *c.* 1287. The oldest version occurs in Rome, Vat., MS. Borghese 205, a collection of Arnold of Villanova's writings made in 1302.

In the late fourteenth century it was popularized by a *libellus* written around it by an unknown author who called himself Telesphorus of Cosenza.

There was a second spurt of Joachimist writing in the early fourteenth century. The most important of these pseudo-Joachimist works was a set of fifteen *Vaticinia de Summis Pontificibus* which—with fifteen later ones—became the best-seller of Joachimist literature in the next two centuries.[1] Grouped with it are the *Liber de Flore, Liber Horoscopus*, and commentaries on both of these. Here the focus of attention is on the prophetic future of the Papacy rather than the fall of the *Imperium*. They share the same enigmatic style and were thought by Grundmann to emanate from the circle of Fra Angelo Clareno, the Spiritual Franciscan leader.[2]

We must also mention here a work which was persistently cited as Joachim's in the later Middle Ages. Dr. Hirsch-Reich showed that *De Semine Scripturarum* was almost certainly written by a monk of Bamberg in 1204/5.[3] It was cited by Roger Bacon before 1267,[4] but was probably first brought within the corpus of Joachimist literature by Arnold of Villanova, who ascribed it to Joachim and wrote a Commentary on it *c.* 1290. Whilst lacking the distinctive Joachimist philosophy of history, *De Semine* fitted easily into the Joachimist canon because it was essentially an attempt to find the pattern of history by assigning centuries to the letters of the Hebrew alphabet. By this method a programme for the future was announced which included the recovery of the Holy Land and the *Renovatio Ecclesie*. The end of the world was foretold for 1400, and thus this work naturally became one of particular interest for fourteenth-century readers.

[1] Russo, *Bibliografia*, pp. 41–8, gives an immense list of manuscripts and printed editions which is still not complete. See *infra*, pp. 453–62.

[2] *Infra*, p. 193.

[3] B. Hirsch-Reich, 'Alexander v. Roes Stellung zu den Prophetien', *Mitteilungen des Instituts f. Österreichische Geschichtsforschung*, lxvii (1959), p. 306.

[4] R. Bacon, *Opus Majus*, ed. J. Bridges (ref. p. 46 n. 4), p. 269; *Opus Tertium*, ed. J. Brewer (ref. p. 47 n. 1), p. 95.

VI

THE SCANDAL OF THE ETERNAL EVANGEL

Two events in the mid-thirteenth century determined the future reputation of Joachim in many quarters. One was the horrible scandal of the Eternal Evangel which blew up in Paris in 1254/5; the other was the passage of the year 1260 without cosmic cataclysm. The latter was a simple matter of the prophet proved wrong. As a later English chronicler summed it up: 'But he failed foule and erred in his counting.'[1] Salimbene himself describes a similar mood of disillusionment when the question was put to him: 'Et tu similiter Joachita fuisti?' 'Cui dixi: "Verum dicitis. Sed postquam mortuus est Fridericus . . . et annus millesimus ducentesimus sexagesimus est elapsus, dimisi totaliter istam doctrinam et dispono non credere nisi que videro." '[2] In spite of these words, he betrays a continuing interest in Joachimism and belief in the prophet was obviously tough enough to survive such little blows as a wrong date.[3] We see the Joachite resilience in the various examples of changed dates in the prophecies already cited.[4] We see it still more clearly in a revised method of calculation which appears in pseudo-Joachimist works, by which the year of the Passion rather than of the Nativity is taken for the starting-point, so that Joachim's 1260 becomes 1290.[5]

The affair of the Eternal Evangel was a much more serious matter. Here the implications of Joachim's pattern of threes burst fully upon the world for the first time, and in a most extreme form. We shall consider later the poor, ill-balanced Franciscan, Gerard of

[1] John Capgrave, *Chronicle of England*, RS, p. 138.
[2] Salimbene, pp. 302–3.
[3] Ibid., p. 456, for a vivid little scene in which Salimbene much later encounters his old boon companion, Gerard of Borgo San Donnino, now in disgrace for the Eternal Evangel: 'Dixi igitur sibi cum esset michi familiaris: "Volumus disputare de Ioachim?" Tunc dixit michi: "Non disputemus sed conferamus et eamus ad locum secretum." Duxi igitur eum post dormitorium, et sedimus sub vite et dixi sibi: "De Antichristo quero, quando nascetur et ubi?" ' And then they launch into a long stolen conversation on these matters which occupied their minds so much.
[4] *Supra*, pp. 50 n. 3, 51.
[5] e.g. *Epistola subsequentium figurarum* in Vat., MS. Lat. 3822, ed. Tondelli, *Lib. Fig.* I, p. 43.

Borgo San Donnino, who, with his fanatical belief in the immediate advent of the third *status*, cuts a rather pathetic figure in the midst of the warring academics. Here we must note the significant fact that the first public proclamation of Joachim's Age of the Holy Ghost, which clearly took place in Paris, was a singularly dramatic one that immediately pushed the doctrine to a dangerously logical conclusion and one that Joachim himself had strenuously repudiated. For the core of Gerard's message was that, with the advent of the third *status*, the Old and New Testaments were utterly abrogated and authority had wholly passed to the Eternal Evangel of the Holy Ghost contained in the works of Joachim. Thus Joachim, who had always upheld two Dispensations, even while expecting the third *status*, and had maintained that the two Testaments would last till the end of time, became the prophet of a system which might involve the overthrow of all previous institutions and authorities in a third and final Dispensation. Men who had studied the Abbot's concords of twos with interest to discover the truth about Antichrist had apparently no inkling of these dangerous possibilities in Joachimism. Now—through the proclamation of the pattern of threes—they were laid bare.

The affair in the University of Paris was,[1] of course, blown up to huge proportions by the animosity of the secular masters against the Mendicants. Papal support of the latter was drawn in and the whole dispute was caught in a set of cross-currents in ecclesiastical politics with which we are not concerned here. Gerard's compilation as circulated has been presumed lost, but it has recently been claimed that an important Dresden manuscript contains the greater part of it.[2] It was meant to consist of Joachim's three main works with a *Liber Introductorius* by Gerard, although Denifle argued that Gerard never actually labelled the three as the first, second, and third books of the Eternal Evangel. This is deduced from the report of the Commissioners appointed by the Pope, who met at Anagni to examine and judge both Gerard's work and Joachim's.[3] Denifle also

---

[1] The starting-point of all work on the Eternal Evangel is H. Denifle, *ALKG*, i. 49–142. For an early discussion of Denifle's work, with some differing opinions, see F. Tocco, *ASI*, xvii (1886), pp. 243–61. For further bibliography see Bloomfield, Reeves, *Speculum* xxix. 772 n. 2.

[2] B. Töpfer, 'Eine Handschrift des Evangelium aeternum des Gerardino von Borgo San Donnino', *Zeitschrift für Geschichtswissenschaft*, vii (1960), pp. 156–63. See *infra*, p. 189.

[3] Denifle, *ALKG*, i. 63 seq., 199. Gerard's gloss pointed the Commissioners to the dangers implicit in Joachim's symbolism, e.g. *ALKG* i. 126, quotation from *Lib. Conc.*, f. 7ʳ, and gloss on it.

deduced from the sermons and other writings of William of St. Amour, the chief protagonist of the Seculars against the Mendicants, that only Gerard's *Liber Introductorius*, together with the *Liber Concordie*, was in fact circulated in Paris in 1254. If, however, the Dresden manuscript embodies Gerard's work, it is clear that he completed his plan of putting together the three main works (in full or abridged), with his own gloss on them.

Copies of Joachim's works were brought to the Anagni Commissioners from Fiore, and from these, as well as Gerard's Introduction, they extracted the long series of passages condemned in their report.[1] Apart from statements specifically ascribed to Gerard, these are all genuine extracts from Joachim's writings, methodically and carefully examined. The outcome was the condemnation of Gerard's *Introductorius* by Pope Alexander IV on 23 October 1255.[2] It is notable that the works of Joachim himself were left unscathed, but their condemnation was inevitable once they had been placed in the context of the kind of conclusions Gerard drew from them. At the Council of Arles in 1263 the whole 'pernicious doctrine' of the three *status*, as preached by the Joachites, was condemned, together with the writings of Joachim which were its foundation.[3] This was, of course, only a provincial condemnation, but as an attack on Joachim's doctrine it was far more damaging than the limited condemnation of 1215. Joachim's Trinitarian doctrine, condemned in 1215, was the basis of his philosophy of history, but, taken alone, it constituted

---

[1] Ed. Denifle, *ALKG* i. 99–142.

[2] See E. Faral, 'Les *Responsiones* de Guillaume de St. Amour', *Archives d'Histoire Doctrinale et Littéraire du Moyen Âge*, years 25, 26 (1950–1), pp. 363, 377, for the order of events and the Papal actions. It was, of course, quite clear from the report of Anagni that the Eternal Evangel comprised the works of Joachim, and Alexander's letter states this: 'Libellum quendam qui in Evangelium Eternum seu quosdam libros abbatis Ioachim Introductorius dicebatur . . .' Yet the Papal condemnation is carefully directed against the *libellus introductorius*; thus Denifle could justifiably say: 'Die Werke Joachims blieben vorläufig unbeanstandet. Die allgemeine Kirche hat dieselben (mit Ausnahme der Schrift gegen Petrus Lombardus) nie censuriert' (p. 89).

[3] Mansi, *Sacrorum Conciliorum ... Collectio*, col. xxiii. 1001–4 (but see correction of text by Denifle, *ALKG* i. 90). Denifle also established that the Council must be dated 1263, not 1260, because of the presence of Florentius, newly created Archbishop of Arles. He had been one of the Commissioners of Anagni and it would appear that he was anxious to get a stronger condemnation of Joachimism than that of Pope Alexander, since he so rapidly proceeded to this move. Although it is specifically the doctrine of Joachim, as contained in the *Liber Concordie* and other works, which is attacked at Arles, here again we notice that it is the '*Joachitici*' who are named, not the Abbot. The official reluctance to involve Joachim himself is probably due to respect for his memory and for his Order.

only what one might call technical heresy. Joachim's philosophy of history, it was now realized, constituted an incitement to subversive thought and action that was dangerously infectious. It is always beliefs which provide a basis for action that must be watched.

The publicity given to the whole affair was great. The secular masters of Paris produced and circulated their own list of errors from the condemned book. The earliest known copy of these is in Matthew Paris's *Additamenta*,[1] but we do not know from what source he collected this document. William of St. Amour preached and wrote furiously against these pernicious Mendicants—in a manner that evoked the same sense of crisis as the Joachites he attacked.[2] In fact, he actually cited Joachim in his support, or rather pseudo-Joachim in the *Super Hieremiam*, selecting a characteristically excited phrase of suspense: 'Nos sumus in ultima aetate huius mundi. . . . Verisimile ergo quod nos sumus prope finem mundi, periculis novissimorum temporum propinquiores sumus, quae futura sint ante adventum Antichristi. . . . Item Joachim super Jeremiam: Omne tempus a 1200 ultra aestimo periculosum . . .'[3] William saw the Mendicant friars as the pseudo-prophets forming one of the Signs presaging the Last Things. In sermons and in his tract, *De periculis novissimi temporis*, he denounced them and their works, especially the pernicious doctrine contained in the 'libellum illum qui vocatur Evangelium sempiternum', of which he claimed to have seen a part.[4]

The curious position of Joachim in all this fury is most interesting. William knew that the damnable book derived from Joachim,[5]

---

[1] M. Paris, *Chronica Majora*, ed. H. R. Luard, RS, vi, *Additamenta*, pp. 335-9. See Denifle, *ALKG*, i. 70 seq.; Benz, *ZKG* li (1932), pp. 415-55, for these excerpts.

[2] William of St. Amour, *Duo Sermones*, ed. O. Gratius, *Fasciculus Rerum Expetendarum* . . . (Cologne, 1535), ii. 43 seq.; *De periculis novissimi temporis*, ed. E. Brown, Appendix to Gratius's *Fasciculus* (London, 1690), under the title *Scriptum Scholae Parisiensis, de periculis Ecclesiae compositum An. 1389*, pp. 18-41. In the same volume are two sermons of William of St. Amour, pp. 43-54. Denifle, *ALKG*, i. 68-9, 86, quotes from his writings, some unedited. See also Faral, loc. cit. (p. 61 n. 2), pp. 337-94. The *De periculis* and other tracts were also incorporated by Matthias of Janov into his *Regulae Veteris et Novi Testamenti*, iii, *Tractatus de Antichristo*, ed. V. Kybal (Innsbruck, 1911), pp. 243-332.

[3] William of St. Amour, *De Periculis*, cap. viii, ed. Brown, p. 27. Not an exact quotation, cf. *Super Hier.*, f. 1ʳ; also *Lib. Conc.*, f. 41ᵛ.

[4] Denifle, *ALKG*, i. 68, n. 2: 'De istis novis periculis jam habemus sc. librum illum qui dicitur evangelium sempiternum, et nos . . . vidimus nonnisi mediam partem illius libri, et audivi, ubicunque liber ille sit, tantum et plus contineat quam tota biblia.'

[5] He carries its origins back to Joachim's period; see *De Periculis*, ed. Brown, p. 27: 'iam transacti sunt 55 anni quod aliqui laborabant ad mutandum Evangelium Christi

and in hasty anger he seems to have accused the Roman Curia of
being so partial to the Abbot as to have been reluctant to condemn
the book,[1] yet he made no direct attack on Joachim himself and, as
we have seen, was quite prepared to cite him on his own side. The
enemies of the Friars were, of course, intent on fastening the scandal
as closely as possible on to the Franciscans, and, indeed, succeeded
in getting the infamous book ascribed to John of Parma,[2] the
General of the Order, thus causing his downfall. William's dig at the
papacy is significant, for he implied, not simply that the Pope was
anxious to protect the Mendicants, but that Joachim had many
defenders at Rome. This might explain the care with which the
condemnation of 1255 was directed at Gerard's *Liber Introductorius*
alone, and the fact that it was left to a provincial council to condemn
Joachim's doctrine outright. With the exception, perhaps, of Innocent III, the favour shown by popes to Joachim, and later to his
memory and his Order, is strikingly consistent but puzzling to
explain.

The turmoil created in Paris is also reflected in the references of
two poets to the Eternal Evangel. Jean de Meung, in the *Roman de la
Rose*,[3] writes of

> Uns livres de par le deable
> C'est l'Evangile pardurable,
> Que li Sainz Esperiz menistre,
> Si come il apareist au titre . . .
>
> (ll. 11801–4, p. 216)

in aliud Evangelium quod dicunt forte perfectius et melius et dignius quod appellant
Evangelium Sancti Spiritus sive Evangelium Eternum quo adveniente evacuabitur
Evangelium Christi.'

[1] Faral, loc. cit. (ref. p. 61 n. 2), p. 346. William responds to the following accusation: 'Dixit in sermone . . . quod "liber Joachim, qui continet multas hereses, non potest
condempnari Romae, quia sunt ibi plures defensores qui defendunt eum".' In his reply
William waters this down considerably: 'cum ego et quidam alii praedicassemus contra
errores repertos in libris qui dicuntur esse Joachim, qui fuerunt positi Parisius ad
exemplar, et diceret nobis tam clerus quam populus quare non procurabimus illos
errores per Sedem apostolicam reprobari, ideo dixi quia jam aliqui de illis erroribus
erant dampnati, ut intellexeram, reliqui vero non poterant ita cito inspici, ad dampnan-
dam, tum propter magnitudinem et multitudinem illorum librorum, tum etiam propter
multiplicem curiae occupationem et forte quia libri habebant aliquos defensores.'

[2] For John of Parma, *infra*, pp. 186–7. The contemporary Richard of Sens, however,
ascribes the authorship to the Dominicans: 'Predicatores vero quendam librum evan-
geliorum compilaverunt, in quo aliqua dicebantur contineri, que contra fidem esse
videbantur. Clerici vero nescio qua arte procuraverunt, ut copiam ipsius libri haberent,
ex quo omnia capitula fidei contraria decerpserunt . . .' (*MGHS* xxv. 328).

[3] J. de Meung, *Roman de la Rose*, Société des Anciens Textes Français, iii (Paris,
1921), p. 216, l. 118; also pp. 217–19.

Between the years 1259 and 1263 Rutebœuf refers several times to these events as a sign of the advent of Antichrist:[1]

> Ne croient pas le droit escrit
> De l'Evangile Jesu crist
> Ne ses paroles;
> En leu de vois dient frivoles
> Et mençonges vanies et voles,
> Por decevoir
> La gent et por apercevoir
> S'a piece voudront recevoir
> Celui qui vient.
>
>   (*Du Pharisien*, ll. 104–12, p. 254)

> Et fera nueve remanance
> A cels qui font nueve creance
> Novel Dieu et nueve Evangile . . .
>   (*La Complainte de Constantinople*, ll. 43–5, p. 426)
> . . . Un livres dont je me descorde.
>   (*Les Ordres de Paris*, l. 72, p. 325)

> Jacobins rompirent la corde,
> Ne fu lors bien nostre creance
> Et nostre loi en grant balance,
> Quant les prelaz de sainte Yglise
> Desmentirent toz en tel guise?
>
>   (*Des Règles*, ll. 84–8, p. 272)

Neither of these poets mentions Joachim, but the first speaks of a certain Jehan. In the contemporary *Croniques* of St. Denis the book is clearly ascribed to Jehan de Parme:[2]

Ycelui pape, qui nommés estoit Alexandre, réprouva et dampna ii faux livres . . . Li autres livres affermoit, entre les autres erreurs qui y estoit contenues, que l'Evangile Jhesu-Christ et la doctrine du Nouvel Testament ne parmena onques homme à perfection, et que elle devoit estre mise au néent et condampnée après mil CC.LX ans, et en mil CC.LX devoit commencier la doctrine de Jehan; lequel livre l'aucteur appela l'Evvangile pardurable, en actribuant à ce livre toute la perfection du

---

[1] Ed. E. Faral and J. Bastin, *Œuvres complètes de Rutebœuf* (Paris, 1959). Page references are given to the quotations. See also the reference to the *cinquième esvangelitre*, which might allude to the Eternal Evangel, in *Le Dit de Sainte Église*, p. 280, line 40.

[2] Bouquet xxi. 119–20. It should be noted that Alexander IV had also condemned William of St. Amour's attack on the Mendicants; thus, by a strange irony, the two condemned books on opposite sides are often coupled together by chroniclers and frequently described as *duo libri pestiferi*. The Eternal Evangel is also ascribed to John of Parma by Bernard Gui, *Catalogus Pontificum Romanorum*, Muratori, o.s. iii. 2.

ceulz qui sont à sauver. Item, il estoit dit en celui livre que les sacremens de la nouvelle loy devoient, en yceli an mil CC.LX estre évacués et annullez. . . . Il est affermé que l'aucteur de ce livre . . . fu un qui avoit nom Jehan de Parme, Jacobin, et fu ce livre publiquement ars.

Thus the connection with Joachim of Fiore is little noticed in the heat of the controversy with the Mendicants, although the accounts of this wicked book show clearly that the revolutionary possibilities of Joachim's pattern of threes had been fully grasped.

The Commission of Anagni and the formal condemnation at the Council of Arles, however, left little doubt as to the source from which this doctrine was derived and from this time onwards one side of Joachim's reputation was fixed: he was now, not only the author of the condemned tract against Peter Lombard, but also the begetter of the doctrine of the Eternal Evangel. In later medieval chronicles the two condemnations of Joachim figure quite frequently—sometimes one, sometimes the other, occasionally both.[1] In the case of the

---

[1] (a) 1215 condemnation: Wendover, RS, i. 121–2, copied by M. Paris; G. de Nangis, Bouquet xx. 758; *Chron. Pont. et Imp. Mant.*, *MGHS* xxiv. 218; Richard of St. Germano, *MGHS* xix. 338; Alberic Trium Fontium, *MGHS* xxiii. 879; J. de Columpna, *MGHS* xxiv. 281; Vincent of Beauvais, *Speculum Historiale*, *MGHS* xxiv. 166; J. de Deo, *MGHS* xxxi. 323; J. Longius St. Bertini, *MGHS* xxv. 821–2; *Chron. St. Martini Turonen.*, *MGHS* xxvi. 467. The Dominican, F. Pipini, who was clearly interested in Joachim's prophecies, takes particular care to exonerate Joachim by quoting the extenuating sentences of the Lateran Council's decree: 'In nullo tamen idem Innocentius propter haec Florentino Monasterio, cuius ipse Joachim institutor extitit, voluit derogari, quoniam et regularis institutio est, et observantia salutaris, maxime quum idem Joachim omnia scripta sua eidem Papae mandaverit, Apostolicae Sedis judicio approbanda, seu etiam corrigenda, dictans Epistolam, quam propria manu conscripsit, in qua firmiter confitetur, se illam fidem tenere, quam Romana tenet Ecclesia' (Muratori, o.s. ix, col. 600, cf. *supra*, p. 32).

(b) Condemnation of Eternal Evangel: Richard of Sens, *MGHS* xxv. 328; M. Paris, RS, v. 599–600, vi. 335–9; *Chroniques de St. Denis*, Bouquet xxi. 119; B. Gui, *Flores Chronicorum*, Bouquet xxi. 698; Salimbene, p. 455; A. Milioli, *Liber de Temporibus*, *MGHS* xxxi. 524.

(c) Both condemnations: Martinus Oppaviensis, *MGHS* xxii. 438, 440; *Flores Temporum*, *MGHS* xxiv. 248; Henry of Herford, *Liber de Rebus Memorabilioribus*, ed. A. Potthast (Göttingen, 1859), pp. 181–3; copied by *Liber Cronicorum Erford.*, *MGHS*, separate edition (Hanover, 1899), p. 775; *Maius Chronicon Lemovicense*, Bouquet xxi. 768; J. Capgrave, *Chronicles of England*, RS, pp. 138, 158. A fifteenth-century Dominican chronicler, Herman Corner, gives Joachim three notices: (i) under 1169 a brief notice copying Vincent of Beauvais; (ii) under 1190 an inimical notice of his own in which he refers to the *Vaticinia*, but says that 'in pluribus [Joachim] mendax et haereticus repertus est'; (iii) a unique notice of the 1215 condemnation in which he makes the condemned book the Eternal Evangel and gives the list of the errors extracted from it by the Paris Masters in 1255. There is no doubt that he meant the earlier condemnation, since, like other chroniclers, he couples it with that of Amaury of Bènes, but it seems astounding that he should have confused the two condemnations, since he had the

first, the statements are usually cool and matter-of-fact, with frequent mention of the fact that he had submitted his works and that his own sanctity was unsullied, as in the following notice in a Mantuan chronicle partly copied from Iohannes de Deo:

> Eodem tempore fuit Abbas Ioachim in Calabria qui spiritum prophetandi habuit, et plures libros super Ieremiam et Apocalypsim et de honoribus prophetarum conscripsit. Composuit etiam librum de Trinitate, quem misit Romam emendandum. Et licet male sensisset, tamen dampnatus non fuit, sed tantum liber per Innocentium III generali concilio est dampnatus. (*MGHS*, xxiv. 218.)

The second condemnation roused much more passion and called forth many adjectives of horror, such as *pestifer, detestabilis, diabolicus*. It is notable that the writers usually had a fair idea as to what the heresy was about, as in this from the *Maius Chronicon Lemovicense*:

> MCCLIV . . . deprehensus est Parisius quidam liber qui dicebatur Evangelium aeternum, cuius actor magis videtur ex melancolia sompniasse quam ex malitia scripsisse quod scripsit. . . . Dicebat enim Testamentum Novum, post annum MCCLX in proximo venturum, esse evacuandum, et quod doctrina evangelica semiplena erat, et huic Evangelio decebat aliud succedere quod futurum erat Spiritus Sancti, sicut istud specialiter fuit Filii Dei, et quod nullus tenebatur ab illo tempore ad istud Evangelium observandum; et alia multa dicebat, graviora hiis et peiora vel aeque mala, propter quae condempnatus fuit merito liber detestabilis . . . atque combustus. (Bouquet xxi. 768.)

One of the most interesting reactions was that of the irrepressible Salimbene, who stoutly maintained that Gerard had mangled Joachim's doctrine: 'Alter vero libellus continebat multas falsitates contra doctrinam abbatis Joachym quas abbas non scripserat, videlicet quod evangelium Christi et doctrina Novi Testamenti neminem ad perfectum duxerit et evacuanda erat MCCLX° anno . . .' (*MGHS* xxxii. 455).[1]

The condemnation of Joachim received the approval of the learned and the official recognition of inquisitors compiling handbooks of heresy. It is noteworthy that St. Bonaventura never openly attacked the Eternal Evangel, but in his Commentary on Peter Lombard's *Sentences* he expressed his mind clearly on Joachim's

---

document connected with the second, probably from Henry of Herford. See J. G. Eccard, *Corpus Historicum Medii Aevi* . . . (Leipzig, 1723), H. Corner, *Chronica Novella*, cols. 742, 743, 848–51.

[1] This passage was copied by A. Milioli, *Liber de temporibus*, *MGHS* xxxi. 524–5.

Trinitarian views.[1] First he stated Joachim's objections to the Lombard's doctrine and then, in a carefully reasoned reply sought to demolish them:

Respondeo. Dicendum quod Joachim non recte arguit et deficit sua ratio, quia res non accipitur uniformiter, quia cum dicitur res primo modo, ibi accipitur res pro *re naturae*; sed cum dicitur secundo modo, accipitur pro *ipsa natura* divina. Praeterea, deficit ab insufficienti quia non valet: si aliquid dicitur de aliquo et non dicitur de alio, quod propter hoc illa faciant numerum. Unde non valet: Petrus est individuum: homo non est individuum; ergo Petrus et homo sunt due. Habere enim proprietatem et nonhabere non sufficit ad distinguendum.

Ad instantiam eius dicendum, quod non recte instat; quia essentia est res una quantum ad suppositum et significatum: non enim supponit personas: sed Deus est res una quantum ad significatum, sed plures quantum ad suppositum. Et ideo ignoranter Joachim reprehendit Magistrum, et quia cum esset simplex non est reveritus Magistrum, ideo iusto Dei iudicio damnatus fuit libellus eius in Lateranensi Concilio et positio Magistri approbata.

Bonaventura's attitude towards Joachimism, as we shall see,[2] was ambivalent. No doubt he wished to clear the Order entirely from the taint of the Eternal Evangel scandal, and certain passages in his writings look like a veiled attack upon the doctrine which, perhaps, he thought it wiser not to mention openly.[3] His Commentary on the Lombard's work gave him a less compromising chance to express disapproval of Joachim's views, and one which he seized in an attack which, it has been argued, does not really do justice to Joachim's doctrine. Yet, on the other hand, there can be little doubt that Bonaventura himself fell under the influence of certain Joachimist concepts and could not remain unmoved by the spiritual expectations which infected so many of his own Order.

St. Thomas Aquinas was equally condemnatory of Joachim's Trinitarian doctrine. He set out carefully Joachim's objections to Peter Lombard's conception of the *una essentia* of the Trinity, but in demolishing Joachim's position he passed judgement on his understanding: '. . . non bene capiens verba Magistri praedicti, utpote in subtilibus fidei dogmatibus rudis, praedictam Magistri Petri

[1] Bonaventura, *Commentaria in quatuor libros sententiarum Magistri Petri Lombardi*, ed. Quaracchi, *Omnia Opera* (Ad claras Aquas, 1882), i. 121.

[2] *Infra*, pp. 179–81.

[3] See Tondelli, *Lib. Fig.* I, pp. 249–50; Bondatti, *Gioachinismo e Francescanesimo*, pp. 137–8.

doctrinam haereticam reputavit.'[1] Aquinas, however, probably saw far more danger in Joachim's doctrine of the three *status*, with all the extreme conclusions which some of his contemporaries were tempted to draw therefrom. It is notable that he attacked aspects of the Joachimist expectation on three separate occasions. Once he specifically condemned the doctrine of the Eternal Evangel, bluntly speaking of 'ipsa doctrina Joachimi':

Unde cum quidam iam Christi evangelium mutare conentur in quoddam aliud evangelium quod dicunt aeternum, manifeste dicunt instare tempora antichristi. Hoc autem evangelium de quo loquuntur est quoddam introductorium in libros Ioachim compositum, quod est ab ecclesia reprobatum. Vel etiam ipsa doctrina Ioachim per quam, ut dicunt, evangelium Christi mutatur . . . Unde cum doctrina praedicta, quam legem antichristi dicunt, sit Parisiis exposita, signum est antichristi tempus instare: sed doctrinam Ioachim vel illius introductorii, quamvis alia reprobanda contineat, esse doctrinam quam praedicabit antichristus falsum est. (Ed. cit., ii. 105.)

On a second occasion, under the title 'Utrum Lex Nova sit Duratura usque ad Finem Mundi', he argued—and at length—against the doctrine of three *status*:

Respondeo dicendum quod status mundi variari potest dupliciter. Uno modo, secundum diversitatem legis. Et sic huic statui novae legis nullus alius status succedet. Successit enim status novae legis statui veteris legis, tanquam perfectior imperfectiori. Nullus autem status praesentis vitae potest esse perfectior quam status novae legis. . . . Alio modo status hominum variari potest secundum quod homines diversimode se habent ad eandem legem vel perfectius vel minus perfecte. . . . Sic etiam status novae legis diversificatur, secundum diversa loca et tempora et personas, in quantum gratia Spiritus Sancti perfectius vel minus perfecte ab aliquibus habetur. Non est tamen expectandum quod sit aliquis status futurus in quo perfectius gratia Spiritus Sancti habeatur quam hactenus habita fuerit . . . Ad tertium dicendum quod lex vetus non solum fuit Patris sed etiam Filii. . . . Similiter etiam lex nova non solum est Christi, sed etiam Spiritus Sancti. . . . Unde non est expectanda alia lex, quae sit Spiritus Sancti. (*Summa Theologiae* [Rome, 1948], ii. 528–9.)

Finally, dealing with speculations on the millennium, he expressed scepticism about foretelling the future by the concords of the Old and New Testaments:

Ego per illas res gestas in Egypto istas persecutiones prophetice signifi-

[1] Aquinas, *Opuscula Theologica* (Rome, 1954), i. 428.

catas esse non arbitror, quamvis ab eis qui hoc putant exquisite et ingeniose illa singula his singulis comparata videantur non per propheticum spiritum sed coniectura mentis humane qui aliquando ad verum pervenit: aliquando fallit. Et similiter vero est de dictis abbatis Joachim qui per tales coniecturas de futuris aliquando vera predixit et in aliquibus deceptus fuit. (*Commentum in Lib. IV Sententiarum*, Dist. xliii, qu. 1, art. 3.)

Aquinas clearly saw in the whole Joachimist way of thought a menace to orthodoxy and declared himself unequivocally against it.

The first person to put Joachim in a catalogue of heretics on account of his Trinitarian view of history was Guido of Perpignan, a Carmelite who became Bishop of Majorca and wrote his *Summa de Haeresibus* c. 1342. The space he devoted to the errors of the Abbot Joachim and his disciple Petrus Joannis Olivi and the vehemence with which he attacked them reveal the dangerous importance he attached to these views.[1] Majorca was a place of refuge for various *fraticelli* groups and Guido would know the fascination that Joachimist ideas exercised over fanatical adherents. Thus it was no longer for speculative errors on the Trinity that he attacked Joachim but for his central doctrine of the three *status* and the deadly poison of the hope which it engendered. Guido's onslaught focused on the following points: (i) that the life of the third *status* will be more perfect than that of Christ and the Apostles; (ii) that the third *status* will be lived wholly in the Spirit, not in the flesh; (iii) that the order of the clergy will not endure to the *consummatio seculi* but will cease in the third *status*, while the order of the third *status* will be preferred above it; (iv) that to the third *status* alone belongs the *lex libertatis*, and therefore, by implication, the Gospel of Christ was not the full Gospel of liberty, nor did the Apostles preach according to the *spiritualis intellectus*; (v) that the Roman Church is the *carnalis meretrix*, the synagogue of Satan which will be destroyed in the third *status*, as the Jewish Synagogue in the second, whereas the *ecclesia spiritualis* will reign until the end of the world. In repeated attacks these and other similar statements were branded as manifest heresy, insane, blasphemous. The last point is clearly drawn from the thought of Olivi and goes far beyond any statement by Joachim. The others also parody Joachim's views, yet it is not hard to see how

[1] Guido of Perpignan, *Summa de haeresibus* (Paris, 1528), ff. xciiii^v–ciii^v. Cf. *infra*, p. 475, for a Lollard adaptation of Guido's Summary, using it in the opposite sense, i.e. to proclaim the third *status*.

Joachim's vision of the quality of life in the third *status* could be translated into these exaggerations. The Joachimist concept all too easily led to the demoting of Christ and the Apostles to second place in the spiritual economy, and Guido was surely right to make this point the chief focus of his attack. He was in no doubt about the source from which certain dangerous fanatical groups drew their fantastic claims and he set out to destroy that root.

Guido's contemporary, Nicholas Eymerich, no doubt battled against similar problems as Inquisitor-General of Aragon, but he did no more than repeat the formal condemnation of Joachim's book against Peter Lombard in 1215.[1] On the other hand, he devoted much space to the errors of Arnold of Villanova, Petrus Joannis Olivi, and groups of Joachimist Beguins and Beghards, as well as the 'pseudo-Apostoli'.[2] Earlier in the century Bernard Gui, another Dominican Inquisitor, had also described the errors of the Beguins and Beghards without tracing them further back than the writings of Olivi.[3] Guido of Perpignan alone traced the inspiration of the fanatical and revolutionary groups back to their true source and then systematically attacked Joachim's whole conception.

Joachim occasionally figures adversely in chronicles as the failed prophet. Several cautiously quote Robert of Auxerre's reserved opinion after the crucial date of 1260 was passed.[4] The clearest expression of disgust at the failed prophet belongs to a fifteenth-century English chronicler, John Capgrave, who writes:

1152. In this tyme was abbot Joachim in Calabir, that wrote many thingis upon the Apocalypse: but he erred in many thingis; first in a mater concernyng the Holy Trynyte. For the Cherch hath determined his opinion fals, in the beginning of the Decretales Ca. Dampnamus; and Mayster Pers, the Lumbard, that made the IIII bokes of Sentens, aftir bischop of Paris, mad mech thing ageyn this abbot Joachim. This same abbot mad also a othir book 'De Seminibus Literarum' where be gret craft he drove oute the zear in whech the day of dome schuld falle. But he failed foule and erred in his counting. (Ed. cit., p. 138.)

[1] N. Eymerich, *Direct. Inquis.*, p. 310.
[2] Ibid., pp. 252–5, 265–73, 281–6, 291–303.
[3] B. Gui, *Manuel* i. 108 seq.
[4] G. de Nangis, loc. cit., p. 742; Pipini, loc. cit., cols. 598–9 (refs. p. 65 n. 1); *Vita Urbani Papae III*, Muratori, o.s. iii, Pt. i, p. 476.

VII

JOACHIM'S POPULAR REPUTATION

AGAINST Joachim condemned we must set Joachim praised. He became, in the first place, almost a stereotype of one who receives the *donum intellectus*. Some chroniclers simply say of him that he received the spirit of prophecy;[1] a number copy Robert of Auxerre's more exact description that, having been unlearned, 'divinitus acceperit intelligentiae donum'.[2] One of the most perspicacious comments on Joachim's gift of spiritual illumination comes from the Franciscan Petrus Joannis Olivi. This is all the more significant because he was in important respects committed to a Joachimist outlook. He distinguishes between the fundamental principles which are 'given' by illumination and the varying applications of them which are made by human reasoning:

Et hoc modo Ioachim in libro Concordie et in expositione Apocalipsis dicit se subito accepisse totam concordiam veteris et novi testamenti quantum ad quasdam generales regulas ex quibus ipse postmodum aliqua quasi argumentando deducti, et ut sibi videtur aliquando sic quod ex hoc extimat habere certam intelligentiam conclusionis sic deducte, aliquando vero nonnisi probabilem coniecturam in qua plerumque potuit falli. Et est simile in naturali lumine intellectus nobis ab initio nostre conditionis incerto per illud enim sine aliqua argumentatione apprehendimus et scimus prima principia et deinde aliquas conclusiones necessario inferimus per illa aliquas vero solum probabiliter et in hiis plerumque fallimur. Non tamen ex hoc sequitur quod lumen illud non sit a Deo aut quod in se sit falsum. Quod signanter dico quia quidam ex hoc voluerunt concludere quod tota intelligentia Ioachim fuerit a diabolo vel coniectura spiritus humani quia in quibusdam particularibus loquitur opinabiliter et forte aliquando fallibiliter. (Quoted Manselli, *Lectura*, p. 163 n. 3.)

This limited defence of Joachim presupposes a background of discussion and censure such as St. Thomas's.

---

[1] Sicard of Cremona, *MGHS* xxxi. 175; *Chron. Pont. et Imp. Mant.*, loc. cit., p. 218; J. de Deo, loc. cit., p. 323; Milioli, loc. cit., p. 452 (refs. p. 65 n. 1); *Annales Polonorum*, *MGHS* xxix. 630, 631.

[2] *Vita Urbani*, 476 (ref. p. 70 n. 4); Pipini, loc. cit., col. 598; G. de Nangis, loc. cit., p. 742 (refs. p. 65 n. 1). Two earlier chroniclers had made the same point independently: R. of Coggeshall, loc. cit., p. 67 (ref. p. 12 n. 2); R. Niger, *MGHS* xxvii. 338.

During the later Middle Ages there developed a series of specific stories about how Joachim received the gift of spiritual intelligence. As we shall see, these probably emanated from Fiore. The earliest was inserted by Guillaume de Nangis into Robert of Auxerre's account of Joachim:[1] '. . . dicebat enim quod ei ignoranti litteras attulerat angelus Domini librum dicens: Vide, lege, et intellige: et ita divinitus fuerat instructus.' Significantly, this story is of an open book, and therefore less obviously fabulous than the later one of a magic draught, which was a popular sixteenth-century story. None of these stories, with their sudden miraculous gift of knowledge, approach an understanding of Joachim's spiritual pilgrimage towards the *intellectus* he sought. Yet all touch the truth upon which Joachim insisted—that the *spiritualis intellectus* is 'given'—and all place a true emphasis upon Joachim as the type of one gifted with divine intelligence. This was the note struck by the Antiphon to Vespers in which his Order commemorated him: 'Beatus Joachim, spiritu dotatus prophetico, decoratus intelligentia, errore procul haeretico, dixit futura praesentia' (quoted Russo, *Gioacchino da Fiore*, p. 15). This Antiphon is echoed in the famous phrase in which Dante put the final stamp on Joachim's reputation as

> il Calabrese abate Gioacchino,
> di spirito prophetico dotato.
>
> (*Paradiso*, xii. 140–1)

Secondly, Joachim became *par excellence* the prophet who foretold the coming of the two great Mendicant Orders. The earliest record of this, interestingly enough, is by a Dominican, Gerard de Fracheto, who, writing in 1256, emphasizes the visual form given to this 'prophecy': 'Joachim eciam abbas et institutor Florensis ordinis de ipso predicatorum ordine in multis libris et locis scripsit; et describens ordinem et habitum monuit fratres suos, ut post mortem suam, cum talis ordo exsurgeret, susciperent eum devote. Quod et fecerunt: recipientes fratres cum cruce et processione quando primo venerunt ad eos' (*MOPH* i. 13). Soon after it appears on the Franciscan side, in the continuation to the Minorite Chronicle of Erfurt: 'Iste idem Ioachim abbas ante inchoacionem ordinis fratrum Predicatorum super Ieremiam in exposicione tradidit de istis eisdem ordinibus. Ipsos quoque ordines nominavit et habitum distinxit et in pictura

---

[1] Bouquet xx. 742. This is copied by the *Chron. S. Martini Turonensis*, loc. cit., p. 467 (ref. p. 65 n. 1).

parietis per manum pictoris ostendit' (*MGHS* xxiv. 207). Here the pictorial element is more explicit and we get the beginnings of the legend that Joachim himself drew pictures of the coming Friars or ordered them to be depicted. This is developed in more detail in the *Flores Temporum*, written by a Swabian Minorite *c.* 1292: 'Item in pariete cubiculi sui depinxit ymaginem fratris Minoris, dicens tales cito esse venturos, funibus precinctos, sandaliis calciatos, sanctissimos et potentissimos, multa autem passuros ab universis, sed tamen usque in finem seculi duraturos' (*MGHS* xxiv. 239).

It is interesting to find a fourteenth-century monk of Malmesbury giving an independent version of Joachim's pictorial prophesyings of new spiritual men, detached from their Mendicant connections: 'Tradunt etiam de isto quod quasi prophetice effigiavit mores, actus, et numerum virorum Apostolicorum qui post venturi forent in ecclesia Dei' (*Eulogium Historiarum sive Temporis*, RS, iii. 86). For the full development of this legend into the curious and famous one that Joachim had appeared in St. Mark's, Venice, and ordered mosaics to be made depicting the two future Mendicant leaders, we have to wait until the fourteenth century. The first specific reference I have found is in an anonymous *Brevis Historia*[1] of the Dominicans, dated 1367. Here the old story of Joachim depicting the prophecy 'in quodam monasterio ordinis sui' is told, but to it is added the statement 'et etiam in ecclesia S. Marci de Venetiis opere musivo . . . fieri fecit'. It is notable that here the prophecy is claimed for St. Dominic alone, since, in the next appearance of the legend, it is claimed exclusively for St. Francis. This is in Bartholomew of Pisa's *De Conformitate Vitae Beati Francisci ad Vitam Domini Jesu* at the end of the fourteenth century: 'Sic ergo apparet, quomodo beatus Franciscus fuit per ipsum Ioachim futurus declaratus, et non solum abbas Ioachim beatum Franciscum praenuntiavit venturum verbo, sed etiam opere, quia eum depingi fecit in ecclesia sancti Marci de Venetiis super ostium sacristiae cum stigmatibus, sicut cernentibus hodierna die clarere potest, et hoc opere mosaico' (*AF* iv. 56).

Thirdly, Joachim's interview with the two kings at Messina struck the imagination and was therefore picked out for record by a number of chroniclers. The occasion was, perhaps, seen as a modern parallel to the familiar Old Testament scene in which the prophet confronted the king and spoke portentous words. The scene at Messina was certainly dramatic and the words remembered were those concerning

---

[1] Martène et Durand, *Ampl. Coll.* vi, cols. 347–8.

an issue which touched all: the fate of Jerusalem. They were heavy words, for they were reported in Howden's revised and less optimistic version. This episode is first found in Robert of Auxerre's chronicle and is picked up later by Guillaume de Nangis, the author of the *Flores Temporum*, and others.[1] The typical form of notice may be quoted from a chronicle of Metz: '1190. Philippus rex Francie et Ricardus rex Anglie mare transeunt. Qui cum consuluissent Ioachim abbatem Florensem, predixit eis, quod in hac vice Ierusalem non recuperarent, quia nondum venerat tempus eius' (*MGHS* xxiv. 519).

Finally, we find Joachim as the prophet under whose name many varying prophecies and prognostications circulate. Thus in the mid-thirteenth century Albert of Stade writes: '1188. Eodem anno abbas Joachim sic de antichristo prophetavit: Cum fuerint expleti 1260 anni, nascetur antichristus. Et hic pro sanctissimo habebatur' (*MGHS* xvi. 351). Again, under the year 1250, he says: 'His auditis rumoribus, prophetiam abbatis Joachim quidam reduxerunt ad memoriam, qui dixit: Superabitur Francus, capietur pontifex summus, praevalebit imperans Alemannis' (ibid., p. 372).[2] In 1269 the continuator of the Erfurt chronicle has another Joachimist prophecy for Germany, beginning *Regnabit Menfridus*, and purporting to have been sent into Germany by the Cardinal Bishop of Porto.[3] In the same political context, of the struggle between Manfred and the Angevins, we find the Ghibelline chronicle of Piacenza citing the *Super Hieremiam*: 'Potens enim est Deus Francos repellere et Alemanos contra ecclesiam revocare . . .', and so on.[4] In 1284 Albert Milioli recorded that a Joachite oracle associated with the Sibyl was flying about: 'Oculos eius morte claudet abscondita. . . . Vivit et non vivit.'[5] Sicard of Cremona's early record of Joachim's prophecies concerning the *Imperium* and the *Regnum* was still exciting interest, for a later marginal note reads: 'Plus dixisset

[1] Robert of Auxerre, loc. cit., p. 255 (ref. p. 6 n. 4); Guillaume de Nangis, loc. cit., p. 745; *Flores Temporum*, loc. cit., p. 239; Pipini, loc. cit., col. 599 (refs. p. 65 n. 1); Gui, *Manuel* i. 478; *Eulogium Historiarum sive Temporis*, ed. F. S. Haydon, RS, iii. 86: 'Praedixit etiam Terram Sanctam adeuntibus quod minime proficerent.' Grundmann, *HJ* xlix. 38, notes the two things always known about Joachim, as recorded in Arras, MS. 138, f. 106ᵛ; (1) his prophecy at Messina; (2) the condemnation of the book against Peter Lombard.
[2] Quoting *Super Hier.*, cap. 46, f. 60ʳ.
[3] *MGHS* xxiv. 207. *Infra*, pp. 311–12, on this prophecy.
[4] *Annales Placentini Gibellini*, *MGHS* xviii. 516.
[5] Milioli, loc. cit., p. 568 (ref. p. 65 n. 1). *Infra*, p. 308, on this prophecy.

hic auctor, si vixisset et vidisset depositionem Friderici et successus strenuos regis Karoli in regno Sicilie'.[1] Clearly the working out of Joachim's prognostications on Sicily was seen to be still operating. An anonymous history of Sicily has a more explicit prophecy:

Abbas Joachim eruditissimus dixit per spiritum prophetiae quod uxor sua [i.e. the Emperor Henry VI's wife Constance] gravida erat, quae adhuc gravedinem nullam ventris sentiens, de daemone erat praegnans . . . dixit quod filius suus nasciturus debebat mori excommunicatus, et ideo qui extra communionem ecclesiae est positus, et moritur sine ecclesiae sacramentis, recte dici potest daemonis filius, et sic fuit, prout experientia temporum manifestat. (Muratori, o.s. viii. 778–9.)

In his *De mulieribus claris* Boccaccio gave a different version of this story in which he used the well-known formula to describe Joachim: *prophetico dotatus spiritu*.[2] Even in England Bartholomew Cotton found it worth while to set down an enigmatic oracle which was circulating under the name of Joachim: 'Eisdem temporibus quidam dixerunt subscriptam esse prophetiam Joachimi: Egredietur unicornis de plaga occidentali cum vexillo leopardorum . . .'[3] Thus Joachim served as a name to cover a very miscellaneous collection of prophecies. Sometimes they would seem to have been invented for the occasion; sometimes a particular political situation suggested some enigmatic passage in a pseudo-Joachimist work which suddenly became appropriate.

---

[1] Sicard of Cremona, loc. cit., p. 175, n. 2ª (ref. p. 71 n. 1).

[2] G. Boccacio, *De mulieribus claris* . . . (Ulm, 1473), ff. cxᵛ–cxiᵛ.

[3] B. Cotton, *Historia Anglicana*, RS, pp. 239–40. I have been unable to identify this prophecy with any passage in the pseudo-Joachimist works. He also quotes another Joachimist verse *Gallorum levitas* (see *infra*, p. 83 n. 1 and p. 312, on this) and a prophecy of Merlin.

VIII

THE DIFFUSION OF JOACHIMIST WORKS
IN THE LATER MIDDLE AGES

HOW far were Joachimist works read and used in the later
Middle Ages? The evidence of chroniclers would suggest
a very limited knowledge. Apart from the tract against the
Lombard, the book most usually attached to Joachim's name was
the *Super Hieremiam*, obviously because it was associated with the
prophecies of the Mendicants. A few chroniclers cited those other
pseudo-Joachimist works, the *De Oneribus Prophetarum* and the
Super Esaiam, or vaguely ascribed to the Abbot writings on the
prophets. Some, following Robert of Auxerre's account, at least
knew of the *Expositio in Apocalypsim*. In the early fourteenth
century Francisco Pipini, Dominican chronicler of Bologna, was
acquainted with a fair range of Joachim's works.[1] But outside
the circle of the Mendicants, few writers show any knowledge of the
Liber Concordie or the *Psalterium Decem Chordarum*, let alone the
unfinished *Tractatus super Quatuor Evangelia* or the minor works.

Yet the evidence of manuscripts themselves suggests a fairly wide
circulation, even of the genuine works, while marginal notes,
especially in the spurious writings, show the continuing excitement
with which they were read. Two Vatican manuscripts—Lat. 4959
and Ross. 552—both illustrate vividly in their execution thirteenth-
century interest in the pseudo-Joachimist *Super Esaiam* and the
little figure-collection, later called the *Praemissiones*, which precedes
it.[2] The figures are beautifully executed and, though the two manuscripts differ in style, certain artistic conventions have clearly been
already established in the rendering of these enigmatic figures and
diagrams, as seen, for instance, in the shape and decoration of the
Dragon and in a little diagram of the Red Sea with fishes in it.[3]

---

[1] Pipini, loc. cit., cols. 598–600, 724, 726–8, 736, 741, 747, 752 (ref. p. 65 n. 1).
[2] On the *Praemissiones* see Reeves, Hirsch-Reich, *MARS* iii. 183–99 and *Studies*.
[3] Dragon: MSS. Rome, Vat., Lat. 4959, f. 2ᵛ; Ross. 552, f. 3ᵛ. Red Sea: Vat., Lat.
4959, f. 27ᵛ; Ross. 552, f. 26ᵛ.

Both emphasize points of interest by a marginal *Nota* or by a pointing hand or by captions which reveal a sense of the crucial issues. The following are a few examples of these:

Lat. 4959: Nota de monachis cisterciensibus.
Nota ingratitudinem clericorum.
Nota in Anno MCCLXXXX prostari prorsus mundi superbiam. conversis ad Deum infidelibus gentibus et Judeis.
Nota de aquila et eius semine.
Nota de Tartaris. Nota de antichristo.
Nota casum Romani Imperii.
Nota quod usque ad caudam seminis aquile in Regno et Imperio afflictio non cessabit.
Ross. 552: Repeats many of the above captions and others from 4959. In addition we may note:
Nota de duobus ordinibus predicatorum et minorum.
Videtur velle quod antichristus oriri debeat de ytalica regione.
Nota de ruina sycilie.

In Florence a group of three manuscripts and a single one in the Biblioteca Laurenziana tell us something of the Joachimist interests of two fourteenth-century friars, one a Franciscan and the other a Dominican. There are three manuscripts from Santa Croce which all bear the rubric (or a similar one): 'Iste liber fuit ad usum fratris thedaldi de casa quem vivens assignavit armario Florentini conventus fratrum minorum.'[1] The first contains the *Liber Concordie* and reveals a particular interest of the scribe in the intricate calculations about the generations of history, for he made several extra attempts to set them out clearly and added a new one of his own.[2] He did not execute them well, but obviously they fascinated him. It was, perhaps, Fr. Tedaldo who peppered the margins with *Nota bene*, wavy lines, and directing hands, while his interest certainly shows in three marginal notes: on f. 83^v: 'Nota de sancta religione pauperum'; on f. 94^v (against Joachim's statement about

---

[1] MSS. Florence, Bib. Laur., (i) Plut. VIII, dextr. x (*Lib. Conc.*); (ii) Plut. XXVIII, dextr. xi, ff. 189^r–235^v (*Lib. Conc.*, Bk. V only); (iii) Plut. IX, dextr. xi (*Super Hier.*, *De Ultimis tribulationibus*, *De articulis fidei*). These manuscripts are described more fully in Reeves, Hirsch-Reich, *Studies*, pp. 35–38.

[2] ff. 20^v, 21^v, 26^v, 75^v (additional diagram).

the new order typified in Joseph, Solomon, and Christ): 'Non expresse dicitur de beato francisco'; on f. 106ᵛ: *Duo Ordines.* The second manuscript contains Book V alone of the *Liber Concordie*, while Fr. Tedaldo's third book has the spurious *Super Hieremiam*, together with two of the minor works of Joachim, now judged to be genuine and not to be found in many manuscripts: *De ultimis tribulationibus* and *De articulis fidei.* This is an unusual combination, and sets one speculating about how Santa Croce acquired these works and whether we can trace here the influence of Spiritual Franciscans.

The single manuscript once belonging to St. Maria Novella is a fourteenth-century copy of the *Liber Concordie.*[1] The scribe has left us a strong impression of his delight in draughtsmanship. He did not invent diagrams, but set out the diagrams of generations so beautifully that in some cases Joachim's meaning seems to be made clear for the first time. But the most intriguing feature of this manuscript is the evidence it gives that the scribe had seen the *Liber Figurarum*, or part of it. Towards the end of the *Liber Concordie*, at a point where the text demands a figure which appears never to have been drawn, our scribe inserted on a separate double folio of its own the *Seven Etates* figure from the *Liber Figurarum*, without the text, but elaborately executed and very clear.[2] It is only indirectly related to the text of the *Liber Concordie* but demonstrates the scribe's liking for *figurae*, since so many others evaded the need to draw by omitting the figures. Even clearer evidence of this is found in the astonishing tree which he drew at a point where the original is quite problematic.[3] It is executed in an original style, though modelled on an older figure, but at the foot he introduced a bizarre feature by making the trunk spring from the upturned mouth of a cat-like devil's head. This is a figment of his imagination, but it is hard not to conclude that he got his inspiration from the

---

[1] Florence, Bib. Laur., MS. Conv. Soppr. 358. For more detailed description see Reeves, Hirsch-Reich, *Studies*, pp. 32–38, III, 125, 264–65.

[2] Across ff. 92ᵛ, 93ʳ; ff. 92ʳ, 93ᵛ are blank. Cf. *Lib. Fig.* II, Pl. XVIII. For discussion of the missing figure in the *Lib. Conc.* see Reeves, Hirsch-Reich, *Studies*. It is possible that the idea of substituting this one originated in a lost exemplar, since there appears in Vat., MS. Urb. Lat. 8., ff. 131ᵛ, 132ᵛ, 133ʳ, at this same point, the text of the *Seven Etates*, without the figure. Several details suggest a connection between the two manuscripts, hence the likelihood that both draw from a lost source.

[3] f. 13ᵛ. For the problem of the original tree intended see Reeves, *Arbores*, pp. 127–31. In Vat., MS. Lat. 4861, on the last folio, there is a beautiful and unique tree-figure which appears to be an early attempt to supply the missing textual figure.

Tree-Eagles of the *Liber Figurarum* where the trees do indeed spring from the eagles' heads.[1] Here, however, our scribe certainly did not show any understanding of Joachim's thought, for the addition makes nonsense of the tree. But it is vivid and striking evidence for the manner in which Joachim's *figurae* could excite an exuberant imagination.

It has long been recognized that in two manuscripts at the Biblioteca Antoniana, Padua, were gathered together some of the earliest and most important texts of many of Joachim's writings. Indeed these two manuscripts seem so uncorrupted by later Joachite influence that the presence of a work here constitutes a strong presumption of its genuineness. MS. 328 contains the *Liber Concordie*. Marginal notes in fourteenth-century hands show a continued interest in Joachim's thought, especially on the three *status* and the two future orders. A long note on f. 23ᵛ on the three trees sums up Joachim's exposition admirably. Most interesting of all is a note on f. 34ᵛ, part of which reads thus: 'Vide verum nunc sit tercii status exordium quando moderni doctores et specialiter sanctus thomas de aquino novo genere docendi expositionem tam copiosam, apertam et lucidam tradiderunt.' It is fascinating to find St. Thomas hailed as the harbinger of the third *status* and the exponent of the new *intellectus spiritualis*, a role he would certainly have repudiated. Two later notes give us dates at which the book was being read: one on the computation of generations was written in 1341 (f. 62ʳ), and the other, in a less hopeful vein than the note on St. Thomas, runs thus: 'Nota de istis duobus ordinibus qui non apparent adhuc in 1342 anno' (f. 86ʳ). MS. 322 contains a collection of works, including the *Psalterium decem chordarum*, the rare and unfinished *Tractatus super Quatuor Evangelia*, and a number of minor works and short tracts, some of which still need careful analysis.[2] There are letters, sermons, prophecies, some still unedited and several to be found nowhere else. The whole collection suggests that it was made by someone with access to a mass of original material, ranging from the earliest of Joachim's writings to his latest. Unfortunately we have no clue as to the provenance of these two important manuscripts.

The presence at Pavia and Reggio Emilia of important manuscripts

[1] *Lib. Fig.* II, Pls. V, VI. For the interpretation of these see Reeves, *Arbores*, pp. 132–3; Reeves, Hirsch-Reich, *Studies*, pp. 160–63.

[2] Some of these shorter works have been described by Buonaiuti, *Quat. Evang.*, p. lxviii n. 2; Huck, *Joachim v. Floris*, pp. 158–86.

of Joachim's works strengthens the probability of Joachimist studies in north Italy. Moreover, in both these cases—as at Padua—there is no taint of pseudo-Joachimist influence. The work most conspicuously absent at Padua is the *Expositio in Apocalypsim*. Now at Pavia—once in Milan—we find a very early manuscript of the *Liber Introductorius* to the *Expositio*, in the early version which we have called the *Enchiridion*.[1] At Reggio two manuscripts from the same library have been discovered in the Seminario Vescovile. One contains a number of Joachim's minor works—*De ultimis tribulationibus*, *Adversus Judaeos*, *De Articulis Fidei*—and part of the *Tractatus super Quatuor Evangelia*. The other contains only the *Liber Figurarum*. Mgr. Tondelli argued that the library which once contained these must also have had the major works of Joachim. In the sixteenth century the second of these two manuscripts was certainly at Pavia, but Tondelli believed that both might have emanated originally from Emilia, although he named as a second possibility Florence at the end of the thirteenth century, and this would tie in with the evidence of the St. Maria Novella manuscript discussed above. In any case, these manuscripts seem to belong to northern or central Italian scriptoria, rather than southern.[2]

In the Bibliothèque Nationale at Paris there are no fewer than four thirteenth- or fourteenth-century manuscripts of the *Liber Concordie*, all of which probably emanated from scriptoria in either northern or southern France.[3] The earliest, MS. Lat. 10453, betrays a special viewpoint, in a marginal note on f. 47^r: 'Nota de ordine fratrum minorum.' This interest in the *Liber Concordie* is all the more significant when we recall the very early presence in another Paris manuscript of the Tables of Concords.[4] Also now at Paris are two early manuscripts of the little tract on the Apocalypse, which circulated separately from the *Expositio* and was probably written earlier than the main work.[5] One of these manuscripts, Lat. 2142, also

---

[1] Pavia, Bib. Univ., MS. Aldini 370.

[2] The Reggio and Pavia manuscripts are described by Tondelli, *Lib. Fig.* I, pp. 3–27, 112, 121–2, 137–45. See also Tondelli, *ASCL* xii. 1–12.

[3] MSS. Paris, Bib. Nat., Lat. (i) 10453, second quarter or mid-thirteenth century, French, probably meridional; (ii) 16280, late thirteenth century, French, south; (iii) 15254, *c.* 1300, French, north or Paris; (iv) 3320, fourteenth century. I am indebted to Mlle d'Alverny for examining the first three and giving her judgement on date and place of origin.

[4] *Supra*, p. 42.

[5] MSS. Paris, Bib. Nat., Lat. 682, ff. 41^r–45^r; 2142, ff. 96^r–103^v. *Inc.* 'Apocalypsis liber ultimus est'. *Expl.* 'Et tunc revelabitur gloria civitatis superne ad quam nos

contains the *Liber Introductorius* in the Pavia version and here called
the *Enchiridion super librum apocalipsis* (ff. 103ᵛ–133ʳ). It is significant
that these two less common works should so soon have been circulating outside Italy, and we may, perhaps, connect with this fact the
very early summaries of Joachim on the Apocalypse given by Ralph
of Coggeshall and Robert of Auxerre.

The British Museum collection has not yet been fully studied. It
contains, in MS. Harley 3969 (ff. 216ʳ–224ʳ), another early copy of
the little tract on the Apocalypse which we met at Paris. When Huck
edited this text he did not know of the British Museum copy, which
is not correctly identified in any bibliography. In Harley 3049,
a manuscript from Durham Cathedral Priory, an extract from
Joachim's *Liber Introductorius*—again in the rarer Pavia version
(*Enchiridion*)—begins abruptly on f. 137ʳ, owing to the loss of a folio.
Another interesting Joachimist book in the British Museum, MS.
Add. 11439,[1] which was written in 1377, contains mainly pseudo-
Joachimist works, but also Joachim's Testamentary Letter and two
minor works now claimed as genuine—the letter *Universis Christi
fidelibus* and the tract *Contra Judaeos*. Of the spurious writings,
the *Super Hieremiam*, the tract on the *Sibyl Erithrea*, the figure-
collection of the *Praemissiones*, and the first part of the *Super Esaiam*
are included. This would seem to have been a personal selection, not
a standard anthology. We get indications of the compiler's interests
in the marginalia and the *figurae*. In the *Super Hieremiam* particularly there are many *Notas* and headings such as *De Duobus ordinibus, VII capita draconis, papa celestinus*. His figures are the most
interesting feature, for besides giving the *Praemissiones* in its most
complete form, he invented four figures of his own.[2] These are
diagrammatic variations on some of the main themes, conceived in
what one might term the genuine 'language' of the Joachimist
figurae, although at points somewhat confused in ideas. Clearly we
meet someone here who liked to think in this form and who—as

perducat dominus.' This work was edited by Huck, *Joachim v. Floris*, pp. 287–96, from
MSS. Paris, Lat. 2142 (he overlooked 682) and Vat. Reg., Lat. 132. He mistakenly
called it *Enchiridion in Apocalypsim*. Cf. *supra*, p. 26. There is also in the Bib. Nat. an
excellent thirteenth-century manuscript of the *Psalt.*, with all the figures, and the *Lib.
Introductorius*, with part of the *Expos.*, as in the printed edition: Paris, Bib. Nat., MS.
Lat. 427; it has *Psalt.*, ff. 1ʳ–45ᵛ, *Lib. Introd.*, ff. 46ʳ–93ᵛ, *Expos.* (fragment) ff. 94ʳ–103ʳ.
    [1] This has been almost completely overlooked.
    [2] See Reeves, Hirsch-Reich, *MARS* iii. 184–5, and *Studies*, pp. 288–92, for a full
discussion of the *figurae* in this manuscript.

late as the last quarter of the fourteenth century—was studying Joachimism. A later note indicates that he was probably a Minorite.

Professor Bloomfield has directed attention to the many signs that Joachimist works were widely disseminated and read in fourteenth-century England. Besides actual surviving manuscripts there is the evidence of inventories and library catalogues. Syon monastery had a copy of the *Expositio*; so had Exeter cathedral, while the Franciscan house at Oxford had both the *Expositio* and the *Liber Concordie*.[1] The library of the Augustinian Friars at York contained, besides these two, the spurious *De Oneribus Prophetarum* and a *tabula* which may have been one from the *Liber Figurarum*. We know that this group of books had formed part of a remarkable collection of prophecies once owned by John Erghome, a member of this house and a great student of these mysteries.[2]

Scattered references show a considerable vogue for Joachimist prophecies. A preacher, probably Archbishop Stratford, quoted the *De Oneribus Prophetarum* in a sermon of the 1340s[3] and Thomas Wimbledon cited the *Super Hieremiam* in a famous sermon at St. Paul's Cross in 1388.[4] The first of these provides a particular reason

---

[1] M. Bloomfield, *Piers Plowman*, Appendix I, pp. 157–60.

[2] Ibid., p. 159. See *infra*, pp. 254–6.

[3] Hereford Cathedral, MS. P. 5. XII, f. 104^{r-v}: '. . . quod contricio et infelicitas venerunt super nostrum regnum et nostram gentem pro sancto Thome probatur per prophetiam abbatis Joachim. Joachim de Flore in Calabria scripsit unum librum quem intitulavit de oneribus prophetarum . . . et in illo libro in capitulo quod intitulatur onus in Arabia dicit haec verba: Onus hoc Britannos mutuo respicit quibus quanta cedes ab Egyptiis Francis immineat obtusus eorum oculus non attendit. pro eo videlicet quod Barachie filius in Thoma rursus occiditur necesse est denuo a rege Gallico tanquam iheu altero ut ex maiori parte populus Anglicus conteratur. quantos mercenarios habeat ovile domini set quia dominus amplius sustinere non poterit huius terre deos avaros lupi rapacis filii puto morsibus relinquendos. Hec ille abbas.' [Cf. *NA* xxxiii. 148, with slight variations. The sermon continues:] '. . . dicit populum Anglicum atterendum et a rege Gallico quia filius Barachie rursus in Thoma occiditur. Et notandum ut mihi videtur quod non potuit fieri melior comparatio in mundo quam inter Thomam et filium Barachie sc. Zachariam quod sic patet . . . [goes through the whole Old Testament episode] . . . Timendum est ergo ne dominus requirat a nobis omnem sanguinem iustum.' See W. D. Macray, 'Sermons for the Festivals of St. Thomas Becket', *EHR* viii (1893), p. 89.

[4] K. F. Sunden, *A famous Middle English Sermon (Bod. Lib., MS. Hatton 57)* (Goteborg, 1925), p. 27: '. . . also abbas joachim in exposicionn of jeromye seiþ: fro þe 3eer of oure lorld a þousand and to hundryd 3er.' The preacher is enumerating proofs that the world is approaching its end; he also cites Hildegarde as a witness. Cf. *Super Hier.*, f. 1^r.

for the popularity of the *De Oneribus* in England. The sermon is for the feast of St. Thomas Becket and the passage quoted from the pseudo-Joachimist work (written, it will be remembered, in the 1250s) is an obvious 'prophecy' of the murder of Becket. The tract *De Semine Scripturarum*, which was circulating under Joachim's name, also attracted attention: it was used in *The Last Age of the Church*, a work once attributed to Wycliffe,[1] and quoted in his *Chronicon* by Galfridus le Baker of Swynebroke.[2] Professor Bloomfield has given us a list of references to Joachim in the writings of Wycliffe himself.[3] Besides all these literary evidences, at least ten manuscripts of the fourteenth and fifteenth centuries contain stray

---

[1] *The Last Age of the Church*, ed. J. H. Todd (Dublin, 1840), is a small tract on the tribulations of the Church at the end of history. Writing in 1356, the author calculates that the end will come in 1400 and that therefore only 44 years of the last age are left. The calculations are taken from *De Semine Scripturarum* and based on the letters of the Hebrew and Latin alphabets. The author cites Joachim's books under several titles: 'the seeds of the profets', 'the deedes of prophets', 'the charge of profits', 'the sayings of popes' (pp. xxiii, xxv, xxx, xxxi). The first two titles refer to the *De Semine Scripturarum*, the third is probably the *De Oneribus Prophetarum*, the fourth, the *Vaticinia de Summis Pontificibus* or the *Liber de Flore*. There is no trace, however, of a genuine Joachimist expectation. At the end, the last lines of the Joachimist poem *Gallorum levitas* are quoted (cf. *supra*, p. 75 n. 3 and *infra*, p. 312).

[2] Galfridus Le Baker de Swynebroke, *Chronicon*, ed. E. M. Thompson (Oxford, 1889), *Chroniculum*, pp. 173–4: 'Memorandum quod ille sanctissimus abbas Joachym, monachus, descripsit mundum per literas alphabeti duraturum, et posuit numerum super quamlibet literam c. annos. Et incipit a quando Roma primo fuit condita, usque ad adventum Christi . . . Et sic, per eius oppinionem et dicti alphabeti computacionem, remanet nisi litera Z, que est ultima litera, ubi ponit finem istius seculi, hoc est CC et L annos a tempore dati huius.' At the beginning of the *Chroniculum* (p. 157) he gives the ages of history, ending with the sixth *etas* from the Incarnation: 'que nunc agitur et durabit usque ad finem mundi et continet usque ad presentem annum exclusive M.CCC.XXXVI'.

[3] Bloomfield, *Piers Plowman*, 226. An unusual reference to Joachim occurs in John Gower's *Confessio Amantis*, ed. G. Macaulay (Oxford, 1901), ii, ll. 3056 seq., p. 212. Joachim is cited as foretelling the 'mercenary activities' of ecclesiastics in the last days. This is probably an echo of Joachim's denunciation of the 'merchants' of Babylon (*Expos.*, ff. 200ᵛ seq.). I owe the Gower reference to Mr. J. Bennett.

pseudo-Joachimist oracles.[1] There are also several prophetic anthologies which betray an interest in Joachimism.

One English astrologer of the fourteenth century, however, found these oracles attributed to Joachim most irritating. John of Eschenden attacked the predictions of the Abbot Joachim for the years 1357–65 as unsupported by astrological calculations. The text he knew was that early oracle attributed to Joachim in 'suo maiori volumine de concordanciis' which, as we have seen, originated before 1250.[2] Eschenden introduced it with remarks on false prophecies put about by those who used *sciencias illicitas* and relied on their own imaginations. He then gave the end part of the prophecy and pronounced verdict on this type of prophecy: 'Qualiter et quo spiritu praedictus Joachim dixit talia, nescio. Sed firmiter credo quod nec per scientiam astronomiae, nec per aliquas constellationes supercoelestes signabuntur praedicti effectus evenire praedictis temporibus prout dixit praedictus Joachim.'

Another fourteenth-century critic of Joachim was Thomas Bradwardine. In this case, however, it was the genuine but little-known tract *Dialogi de Praescientia Dei et Praedestinatione Electorum* which concerned him. It is surprising that he had found a copy to read. He disagreed strongly with what he read and, while reproducing points from Joachim's argument carefully in his *De Causa Dei*,[3] attacked it vigorously. He acknowledged that Joachim was a great doctor, but not, he maintained, one of great authority, since in his Trinitarian writing against Peter Lombard he fell into Arianism, and in this work, whilst seeking strenuously to avoid it, he was sucked into the vortex of Pelagianism. Again we see that Joachim's thought was most vulnerable from the angle of scholastic theology: Bradwardine, in fact, accused him of contradicting himself. Yet Bradwardine's attack itself seems somewhat wide of the mark.

On the other side of the picture, as Miss Smalley has pointed out, Joachim commended himself as an authority on the Apocalypse to several commentators, probably all English Minorites. John Russel

---

[1] MSS.: Brit. Mus., Harley 1280, Kings 8. D. 11, Cotton, Vespasian E. VII; Cambridge, Univ. Lib., Ii. vi. 25, St. John's College, 239, Corpus Christi College, 138; Oxford, Bodleian Lib., Digby 218, Ashmole 393; Aberystwyth, Univ. Lib., Penarth 50; Dublin, Trinity College, 347.

[2] Oxford, Bod. Lib., MS. Digby 176, f. 38^r. See also MS. Ashmole 192, pp. 101–2, for the prophecy *De concordantiis, supra*, p. 50. It is given in full in MSS. Digby 218, f. 107^r, and Ashmole 393, f. 80^v, where it follows a work of Eschenden.

[3] T. Bradwardine, *De Causa Dei . . . Libri Tres* (London, 1618), lib. i, cap. 47, p. 436.

at the turn of the thirteenth/fourteenth century was a cautious admirer who quoted Joachim frequently in his Apocalypse-Commentary.[1] He even wished to quote Joachim on some of his most dangerous ground: his Trinitarian interpretation of the Alpha and Omega. So he safeguarded himself by openly referring to the condemnation of 1215, declaring that flowers can still be plucked from thorns:

Diffuse enim tractat istam materiam et pulcherrime docet qualiter istud misterium Trinitatis et unitatis potest similiter colligi et litteris hebraicis. . . .

Notandum est autem quod ipse Ioachim aliter hoc exponit, dicens qualiter per illas duas litteras simul potest describi emanatio personarum in divinis. Nam in hoc elemento 'a' procedunt duo ab uno, in quo signari potest processus duarum personarum, sc. Filii et Spiritus Sancti ab uno originali principio, sc. Patre . . . Hec Ioachim. Docetur lib. 16 Contra Faustum in principio, quod de spinis florem debemus eligere, de herbis frugem etc. . . ., sic inter erronea que vera sunt et salubria, hiis eiectis; extra. 1, Dampnamus: Dampnamus et reprobamus libellum sive tractatum quem abbas Ioachim edidit contra magistrum Petrum Lumbardum . . . (Quotation from the decree follows: Smalley, loc. cit., p. 301.)

Russel avoided the prophecies of the third *status* but as a straightforward expositor he found Joachim most satisfactory. It is astounding that, at a time when the extreme Joachites among the Spiritual Franciscans were taking the bit between their teeth, Russel not only remained aloof from their fervid dreams but in ignoring them calmly used as quite 'safe' material from a writer whose name was now associated with explosive views which were rocking the Order.

A second English Minorite, John Ridewall, who was a regent at Oxford, quoted Joachim's *Expositio* twice in his *Lectura in Apocalypsim*, c. 1339.[2] One is a harmless reference; the other touches dangerous stuff, but without comment: 'Ioachim dicit duo tempora, unum tempus Filii, aliud tempus Spiritus sancti, quod tempus erit in fine seculi, et tunc utile erit advertere que hinc inferuntur' (Smalley, loc. cit., p. 303). A third, John Lathbury, also an Oxford regent, quoted harmless passages from the *Expositio*, without a hint that it contained more explosive matter.[3]

---

[1] Smalley, 'John Russel O.F.M.', *RTAM* xxiii (1956), pp. 300–2. The work is known in only one copy, Oxford, Merton College, MS. 172.

[2] Smalley, loc. cit., p. 303.

[3] Smalley, 'Flaccianus *De Visionibus Sibylle*', *Mélanges offerts à Étienne Gilson* (Toronto and Paris), pp. 552–4. Lathbury also quotes from the pseudo-Joachimist *De Semine Litterarum* (or *Scripturarum*).

The English Minorite of the fourteenth century who owed most to Joachim was Henry of Cossey. His *Super Apocalypsim*[1] makes a fascinating study in the assimilation of Joachim's ideas, apparently without danger. The Abbot was his major source: he cited him at least sixty times and clearly regarded him as the great oracle. In one passage in which Henry extended the master's method by assigning the seven churches of Asia to the seven *tempora* of the Church, Sardis is made to signify the period 'a tempore karoli usque ad Johachim qui scripsit apochalipsim sed istud tempus fuit usque ad annum domini MCC et duravit amplius sed nescitur quantum' (f. 75rb). Thus Joachim himself achieved a place in one of those patterns of history which Henry of Cossey took so eagerly from him. He had assimilated the Abbot's ideas thoroughly. He never quoted slavishly, indeed he hardly quoted at all, except for the odd phrase.[2] Instead, he would summarize a line of interpretation from several pages of the *Expositio*, sometimes transposing the order and moving backwards and forwards through Joachim's work at will. His main interests were in the seven *bella* of the Old Testament and the seven persecutions of the Church, the seven heads of the Dragon, the seven *etates* of the world, and the seven orders of preachers. Obviously he was most attracted to the theme of the sixth and seventh orders and Joachim's expectation 'de isto generali ordine qui in fine convertit iudeos et alios infideles per predicacionem' (f. 71^r).[3] In particular, he adopted Joachim's interpretation of the Angel of the Church of Philadelphia as 'quidam ordo qui est vel erit sexto tempore, qui habebit donum spiritualem' (f. 82va). He was also interested in Joachim's characteristic exposition of the Alpha, Omega, and Tetragrammaton.[4] The passages used by Henry were, in the main, those in which Joachim was expounding or leading up to his expectation of the climax of history in the third *status*. The astounding thing, therefore, is that Henry apparently managed, in

---

[1] I have studied this in Oxford, Bod. Lib., MS. Laud Misc. 85.

[2] This makes the identification of his references somewhat difficult. The following list gives only the most important ones, with the reference to the *Expositio* in brackets: ff. 69^v (34^{r-v}), 71^r (84^{r-v}, 87^v), 71^v (87^v, 88^r), 72^r (93 seq.), 75^r (67^{r-v}), 78^r (71^{r-v}, 75^v), 81^r (78^r), 82^v (84^v–86^v), 89^r (114 seq.), 90^r (111^r), 96^v (116^v), 103^v (127 seq.), 104^r–107^v (128^v–132^r), 108^{r-v} (133–134^r), 110^v (137^{r-v}), 114^r (148^v, 146^r), 116^v (155^{r-v}), 117^v (10^{r-v}), 118^r (155^v), 120^r–121^v (161^v–165^r), 129^v (175^r–176^r), 130^r (182^v), 130^v (183^r), 133^r (185^v), 136^r (190^v–191^r), 142^r (196^v).

[3] He adopts Joachim's interpretation of the columns of the Temple as the sixth order (f. 71^v).

[4] ff. 69^v, 71^v.

reading and using these great passages, to remove all the dramatic emotion from them. He never mentioned the third *status* and had no room in his scheme of history for a Sabbath Age. He did not even apply Joachim's prophecies concerning the new orders to the Mendicants. This avoidance of the core of Joachimism is so remarkable that one is almost forced to conclude that it was deliberate. Henry of Cossey stands in a different category from the expositors who merely wish to add Joachim to their list of references by citing some of his innocuous and more conventional thoughts. Henry wanted the whole play of *Hamlet*—without Hamlet.

If, as Miss Smalley thinks, the anonymous author of the *Postilla Vidit Jacob in somniis* was also a Mendicant,[1] we have here another friar who, to some degree, fell under the spell of Joachim's interpretation of the Apocalypse. The author makes a direct reference to Joachim on the subject of the two witnesses, the *due olive et duo candelabra* of Apocalypse 11: 3–4:

Ioachim dicit, cui Ieronimus concordare videtur hic, quod hic dicitur de duobus hiis in spiritu esse consummandum non in littera, et quod hii duo testes sunt duo ordines, qui ante finem mundi sunt venturi, qui et due olive et duo candelabra dicuntur, quia et oleo caritatis ardebunt, et splendore sapientie lucebunt. (f. 97ᵛ.)

This, of course, is one of Joachim's key interpretations, and closer investigation reveals that the passage in which the above quotation occurs is a précis and paraphrase of a more extended exposition by Joachim, occupying folios 148ᵛ–149ᵛ in the printed edition of the *Expositio*. Except for the one reference, the author does not acknowledge his source, nor does he quote verbatim, except in scattered phrases, but these, together with the sequence and individuality of interpretation, make the source quite clear. Further examination shows the author making a similar use of Joachim's *Expositio* in at least three other passages.[2] This unacknowledged use of Joachim's interpretations is interesting, particularly as he has selected characteristic ideas of Joachim. At a number of other points where he is not

---

[1] Smalley, loc. cit. (ref. p. 85 n. 1), pp. 302, 308; cf. F. Stegmüller, *Repertorium Biblicum Medii Aevi* (Madrid, 1940–55), No. 3771. I have used Oxford, Bod. Lib., MS. 444 (2385), ff. 28ʳ–177ᵛ, to which all references are made.

[2] (1) his exposition of the Dragon's head (f. 111ᵛ) follows closely *Expos.*, f. 10ʳ⁻ᵛ; (2) he gives the 'opposites' of the world's history (f. 112ʳ) almost exactly as in *Expos.*, f. 10ᵛ; (3) his sequence of peoples raised up to oppose the Church (ff. 112ᵛ–113ʳ) incorporates characteristic details and phrases from *Expos.*, ff. 162ʳ–163ᵛ.

drawing directly on Joachim he is thinking in the same categories.[1] He interprets many of the angels of the Apocalypse as orders of preachers and is attracted by Joachim's prophetic pronouncements on the two future orders. He even hints at the special role of the Mendicants.[2] He enjoys all the drama of the cosmic conflict which belongs to this mode of expounding the Apocalypse, but keeps himself completely clear of any hope in an apotheosis of history, a third *status* or a Sabbath Age within time.[3] These last two authors demonstrate that one could appreciate Joachim's vision of the patterns of history, while evading the trap set by his expectations of the future.

Minorite interest in Joachim—even when dissociated from the views of the Spirituals—is understandable. It is more striking to find that Joachim, whose name could call forth such extremes of repulsion and enthusiasm, could also be used as a straightforward biblical exegete by the great Austin friar Agostino Trionfo. Writing in the first quarter of the fourteenth century, he cited Joachim's *Expositio* extensively in his own Apocalypse Commentary;[4] indeed, Joachim was one of the authors whom he most often quoted—in all some forty times—and clearly he was regarded as worthy to be set beside standard authorities like Jerome and Bede. As Miss Smalley remarks,[5] this defender of papal *plenitudo potestatis* must surely have set the seal of orthodoxy on everything he touched. It is fascinating, therefore, to examine his handling of Joachim's work. He adopts several of Joachim's number symbols but treats them in his own way. For instance, he cites Joachim's seven *tempora* of the Church but, completing for himself the pattern of seven corresponding 'orders', gives an un-Joachimist twist to the scheme by adding: 'In sexta de antichristo et membris eius. In septima de dampnacione impiorum et remuneracione iustorum.'[6] He uses Joachim's central

---

[1] See, for example, the pattern of seven sets of liberators from persecution (f. 112^r), the third angel as the 'ultimum ordinem predicatorum' (f. 123^v), the orders of preachers (ff. 133^r seq.).

[2] Miss Smalley makes this point, loc. cit. (ref. p. 85 n. 1), pp. 308–9.

[3] At the end, dealing with Satan bound, he seems deliberately to indulge in a piece of number-symbolism which is not Joachim's: 1000 = 10 × 10 × 10, and this signifies the triplex *status* of 'conjugatorum, continentium, prelatorum' and the three stages of *ante legem, sub lege, sub gratia* (f. 162^v).

[4] I have used Oxford, Bod. Lib., MS. 138 (1908). I am indebted to Miss Smalley for drawing my attention to this; see her article cited *supra* (p. 85 n. 1), pp. 303–4.

[5] Smalley, loc. cit., p. 303.

[6] f. 3^r, cf. *Expos.*, f. 16^r. Most of Trionfo's quotations can be quickly identified, but

five/seven pattern of Tribes and Churches, but as a purely historical interpretation, without reference to the hidden Age of the Spirit.[1] Again, the seven *bella* of the Old Testament are given, with Joachim's characteristic double conflict in the sixth age to make room for the Sabbath in the seventh, but the parallel list in the New Dispensation stops short before the Sabbath Age at the end of history.[2] The seven orders equated with the seven churches of Asia are given in a form which corresponds closely to Joachim's key figure of the *Dispositio Novi Ordinis*, but—taken out of context— bears no relation to the third *status*.[3] There can be no doubt of Trionfo's interest in Joachim's number-patterns, yet, as we examine the use he made of them, the conviction grows that he was avoiding the Trinitarian interpretation of history. No single citation ever hints at the third *status*, and occasionally his quotation most pointedly cuts out such reference. Thus, when citing Joachim on the Angel of the Church of Philadelphia,[4] he breaks off precisely at the point where Joachim launched into a long, eloquent passage on the *ecclesia spiritualis* of the third *status* and the new order of spiritual men symbolized in this angel.[5] Again, on the Son of Man who descends *amictus nube*, he selects the vaguer parts of Joachim's interpretation ('quicunque erit iste predicator') rather than the delineation of the new order which Joachim found symbolized here.[6] He avoids all other passages in which Joachim prophesied the coming new orders. Trionfo, one guesses, was well aware of the dangers in Joachim's Trinitarian view of history, yet found him such an acceptable exegete in other respects that he could not resist using him, although in a highly selective way. He was fascinated by Joachim's patterns of history, but set strict limits past which he would not stray into the expectation of a third *status*. His citations from Joachim are tame but safe.

In quite another class of writings are the prophetic anthologies.

the large number of variants shows that he was using a different version from the printed edition. Some of his additions to the text are interesting.

[1] f. 5ᵛ; cf. *Expos.*, ff. 27ᵛ–28ᵛ.

[2] ff. 30ᵛ, 36ᵛ. He takes the pattern of the over-all seven *Etates* (f. 12ʳ) from *Expos.*, f. 54ʳ, but here he is selecting one of Joachim's most commonplace number-sequences.

[3] f. 15ʳ; cf. *Expos.*, ff. 17ʳ seq., and *Lib. Fig.* II, Pl. XII.

[4] f. 21ᵛ; cf. *Expos.*, f. 82ᵛ.

[5] He gives Joachim's safer identification of the Angel ascending from the Orient as Christ Himself, rather than the Minorite interpretation as St. Francis. See f. 40ʳ; cf. *Expos.*, f. 120ᵛ.

[6] f. 53ʳ; cf. *Expos.*, f. 137ʳ.

The term 'anthology' is here used to denote collections of short prophecies or extracts from longer works. A Joachimist anthology may be regarded as a kind of Joachimist textbook. Examining these, we seem to be thrust into a luxuriant forest proliferating on all sides in prophecies, oracles, enigmatic verses, and *figurae*. Often the selections made throw a vivid light on the interests and preoccupations of those who made them. The earliest of such anthologies is that at the end of the Paris MS. 11864, already described.[1] This became the basis for a more extended collection of Joachimist material which remained in circulation through the fourteenth and fifteenth centuries.

A typical Joachimist textbook is found in the late thirteenth-century Vatican manuscript Lat. 3822, which probably emanated from south Italy.[2] The first half contains thirty-three fragments of prophecies, written in various hands, in no recognizable order, and with additional material scribbled in all the odd spaces; the second half is more ordered, with fewer hands and longer extracts or whole works. It includes the early Paris anthology mentioned above,[3] to which has been added a confused attempt at a tree of history which is a conflation of two in the *Liber Figurarum*, the text of the dragon-figure from the same, and another short tract of Joachim's.[4] This little collection of short texts and *figurae* must have been just what was needed to catch the eye of those who would not tackle the long and diffuse works of Joachim. Exactly the same anthology appears in the next century in a Paris manuscript, Lat. 3595,[5] based, however, on another original. The compilers of Vat., Lat. 3822 did not stop at this: much more was scribbled in. Two folios stitched into the middle of the little anthology contain another dragon-figure and other prophecies.[6] Then follow extracts from the *Expositio* and other genuine writings alongside the spurious *De Oneribus*, oracles

---

[1] *Supra*, p. 42.

[2] Bignami-Odier, *MAH* liv. 214 seq., 219 seq. It was previously described by Holder-Egger, *NA* xxxiii. 97–105. See also Reeves, Hirsch-Reich, *MARS* iii. 177–9; *Lib. Fig.* II, Introd., pp. 25, 28–30.

[3] ff. 1ʳ–8ʳ (folios 5 and 6 were stitched in later).

[4] f. 4ʳ: *Epistola . . . Valdonum monasterii abbati . . .* This was published by J. Bignami-Odier, *MAH* liv. 226–7, who regarded it as of doubtful authenticity. Tondelli (*Lib. Fig.* I, p. 120) and Grundmann (*NF*, pp. 25–6) accept it as genuine.

[5] See Reeves, Hirsch-Reich, *MARS* iii. 180; *Lib. Fig.* II, Introd., pp. 25, 28–30. Mlle d'Alverny informs me that this manuscript is probably of Italian origin. It belonged at one time to Cardinal Mazarin.

[6] The dragon-figure is reproduced *Lib. Fig.* II, Pl. XXXVIb, and Russo, *Bibliografia*, Pl. II.

of the Sibyls, and the little verse on Antichrist.[1] *Figurae* from the *Liber Concordie* and *Psalterium* are carefully copied out, with an extract from the Sibyl Erithrea sandwiched in the middle.[2] In the second half the whole of the *Super Hieremiam* is included and, at the end, Joachim's Testamentary Letter. This compilation illustrates vividly the variety of material circulating under or in association with Joachim's name by the end of the thirteenth century. No special viewpoint or propaganda purpose can be detected: presumably this undiscriminating collection was made because people wished to read this kind of stuff.

The compiler of another anthology in the Vatican Library—Lat. 4860—was also probably from south Italy, a Franciscan, perhaps, collecting preaching notes.[3] He was certainly more discriminating in his selection of material. He chose extracts from all Joachim's three main works, and also included in whole or part the rarer tracts *De Vita Sancti Benedicti*, *De Ultimis Tribulationibus*, and *De Articulis Fidei*. His most interesting selection was a number of *figurae* from the *Liber Figurarum*, together with two from the *Liber Concordie*. The only pseudo-Joachimist work from which he copied largely was the *Super Hieremiam*.[4] Here, then, was a compiler who must have had access to a good store of Joachim's genuine works, including the *figurae*. He was clearly interested in Joachim's historical system, including Tables of Concords, Trees of History,[5] and the Dragon, but also in the liturgical and monastic aspects of Joachim's thought, as two other *figurae* of his choice show: the *Mysterium Ecclesiae* and the *Dispositio Novi Ordinis*. It is understandable that a Franciscan should choose the *Super Hieremiam* for its prophecies of the Mendicants, but in general this anthology is striking for its emphasis on the genuine writings.

An entirely different and most interesting book of excerpts is found only in Paris and London. It is entitled *Excerptiones librorum viri eruditissimi venerabilis Ioachim primi Florencium abbatis de pressuris seculi et mundi fine . . .*[6] and contains excerpts from the *Liber*

---

[1] *Supra*, p. 49.   [2] ff. 18ᵛ–20ᵛ.

[3] See Bignami-Odier, *MAH* liv. 214 seq.; Reeves, Hirsch-Reich, *MARS* iii. 174–7.

[4] The Joachimist material is found at ff. 35ʳ–58ʳ, 72ʳ–78ʳ, 85ᵛ–141ᵛ, 145ʳ–149ʳ, 160ʳ–192ʳ, 198ʳ–204ᵛ, 206ʳ–276ʳ, 281ʳ–289ʳ. On the figures see Reeves, Hirsch-Reich, loc. cit., pp. 174–7; *Lib. Fig.* II, Introd., pp. 16, 25, 27–8. From an early table of contents we learn that the manuscript also contained the *De Articulis Fidei* of Joachim.

[5] On f. 289ʳ there is an early version of the tree-figure afterwards used in the Venetian printed edition; see Reeves, *Arbores*, p. 129.

[6] Paris, Bib. Nat., MS. Lat. 16397 was studied by E. Renan, *Nouvelles Études*

Concordie, the *Liber Introductorius* of the *Expositio*, followed by the shorter letter *Universis Christi fidelibus* and, passing thence to pseudo-Joachimist works, the *De Oneribus* and the *Expositio Iezechielis Prophete* which goes with it. The latter part of the volume contains, in another hand, the full text of the Protocol of Anagni which Denifle edited. A note states that the volume was compiled for the masters of the Sorbonne. This is curious indeed, for one would not expect a genuine interest in Joachimism in this quarter and the inclusion of the Protocol emphasizes the dangerous nature of these ideas. Yet the title is respectful to Joachim and the intention of the anthology seems clear: in Renan's words, 'on a voulu reserrer sous un petit volume toute la doctrine de l'abbé Joachim'.[1] Renan was able to prove that this compilation was not identical with Gerard's but a separate collection, made 'un peu au gré du copiste' and falling probably into the category noted by the Council of Arles as 'plurima super his phantasiis commentaria facta'.[2] The masters of Paris really wanted to know about Joachim's doctrines, while a later note in French gives evidence of a continuing interest in this manuscript.[3] Further, an almost exact copy was made in the mid-fourteenth century, probably for Richard of Kylvington, Dean of St. Paul's. It is now in the British Museum.[4] Denifle did not know it nor does any later scholar appear to have noticed it.

By the fourteenth century, when the crop of pseudo-Joachimist writings was growing luxuriant, distinct groups of prophecies were

d'histoire religieuse (Paris, 1884), pp. 250–2, 270–1, and by Denifle, who used it for his edition of the Protocol of Anagni, *ALKG* i. 97. As it stands now the manuscript is a miscellany in which the Joachimist material begins on f. 61. That it was originally a separate book is indicated by fresh pagination at this point. It was described by J. Quetif and J. Echard, *Scriptores Ordinis Praedicatorum* (Paris, 1719), p. 202. Denifle also discovered a similar selection of Joachimist extracts in Milan, Bib. Ambros., MS. H. Q. 5, inf. misc., ff. 1–62ᵛ.

[1] Renan, op. cit., p. 251.
[2] Quoted ibid., p. 271.
[3] f. 123ʳ: 'Cest que leudit esprofecies de Joachim estrit ou grant livre de concordances an lan de grace mil et CC et XX et V IIII serunt batallies espleins de nerbone de quatre rois esqueles morront les tres. Et de rechief an lan apres sera leglise de Rome sanz pape. Et de rechief an lan apres seront tuit li clerc ocis et mort. Et an lan apres sera Jerusalem sanz roi et mora un roi que len apele charles. Et an lan apres sera si grant famine que le genz morront de faim per les voies. Et an lan apres cest asavour le X an regnera antichrist.' This is a curious passage. It clearly bears some relation to the *Prophecie Joachim in maiori libro de concordanciis* circulating from the mid-thirteenth century, yet represents a quite different version; cf. *supra*, p. 50, for this prophecy.
[4] London, Brit. Mus., MS. Royal 8 F. XVI, pt. i, now bound with another manuscript. At one point it belonged to 'W. Bathon', perhaps William Laud, when Bishop of Bath, 1626–8.

circulating, which we meet in varying combinations. Thus two Paris anthologies—MSS. Lat. 3319 and 3595—are linked by common elements with two Rome collections, Vat., Lat. 3820 and Vitt. Eman., 14 S. Pant. 31.[1] The contents fall entirely into the pseudo-Joachimist category, including the *De Oneribus*, the prophecy of Sibyl Erithrea, the *Oraculum Cyrilli*, a supposed exposition by Joachim of Merlin and the Sibyls addressed to Henry VI, and other short texts. Again, MS. Paris, Lat. 14726[2] has links of common elements with all four of the above manuscripts, but adds as well a north-Italian prophecy on the Dragon,[3] prophecies of the angelic popes, and of the second Charlemagne, which we shall be considering later.[4] These examples have been selected from a number in which separate groups of prophecies are combined in various ways.[5] As late as 1387 a new anthology appears to have been created in the Vatican manuscript Reg. Lat. 580, of which a copy was made in the beautiful Renaissance manuscript Vat., Chig. A. VII. 220.[6] Again, in 1448 a canon, Antonius de Petronis, made a Joachimist compilation (Vat., Lat. 3816) which is linked with a book written in Venice by Andreas, a monk of Cyprian, in 1465, which he copied from one at St. Georgio Maggiore.

In England we get a vivid glimpse of the interest in Last Things in a Cambridge manuscript, Corpus Christi College, 404, an entirely individual anthology made in the fourteenth century at Bury St. Edmunds, mainly by Henry of Kirkestede. After some earlier prophecies from the Sibyls, Methodius, and Hildegarde, he turns to a Joachimist item entitled *Prophecie Joachim abbas de papis*,[7] which

---

[1] For a fuller description of these anthologies see Appendix C. MS. Lat. 3319 belonged at one time to Charles of Orléans; see P. Champion, 'La Librairie de Charles d'Orléans', *Bibliothèque du XVᵉ siècle*, xi (1910), pp. 63–4. I am indebted to Mlle d'Alverny for this information.

[2] Mlle. d'Alverny describes this as early 15th-century; French in script; provenance: St. Victor.   [3] *Supra*, p. 51 for this prophecy.

[4] *Infra*, p. 406.

[5] Besides those mentioned, see MSS. Paris, Lat. 2599 and 3455; Rome, Vat., Lat. 3819, 3824, 5732; Reg. Lat. 132. See Appendix C, pp. 534–40 for analysis of contents. All these need further study.

[6] For contents, see Appendix C, pp. 537–8. There is another small collection of Joachimist oracles in Florence, Bib. Ricc., MS. 688, ff. cxiiʳ–cxiiiʳ and another on f. cxxiiᵛ. On f. cxiiiᵛ is the following heading: 'Incipiunt dicta Joachim praesentata Domino Clementi Papae VII A.D. 1382 per Dominum Petrum de Caffol. Thesaurarium Ecclesiae St. Petri Avenionensis qui iuravit in conscientia sua quod ista dicta fuerunt sibi praesentata sub A.D. 1349.' Another Florentine manuscript, Bib. Laur., Plut. LXXXIX, inf. 41 (13th cent.), contains a small Joachimist section (ff. 104ʳ–112ʳ).

[7] The table of Contents on f. iv does not tally exactly with the items at this point.

consists of the last five of the *Vaticinia de summis pontificibus*.[1] The author names the first of these as Clement VI and then expects only four more popes. This both dates the manuscript for us and indicates the sense of pending dissolution.[2] There follows the *De Semine Scripturarum* and a discussion *De Antichristo et Fine Mundi* which draws on various authors including Joachim. The compiler then copies out the whole account of Joachim given by Ralph of Coggeshall, ending 'Hec in libro visionum apud Sibecone et apud Coggeshale'. The latter part of the book includes the *Oraculum Cyrilli*, the short *Prophetiae Joachim in maiori libro de concordanciis* which we have met in several manuscripts,[3] and the first fifteen of the *Vaticinia*, clearly attributed to Joachim and complete with pictures.[4] The collection ends with the so-called Merlin prophecies on the kings of England and some further visions and prophecies. Near the end we read:

Subscriptos rumores scripsit frater Willelmus de Blofield in Anglia A.D. M.CCC.XLIX cuidam fratri conventus fratrum predicatorum norwicensis, quae prophetie diverse sunt in partibus romanorum sed adhuc occulte quae omnia futura predixerunt per annos multos. Et isto anno, videlicet ab incarnatione M.CCC.XLIX predicant antichristum habere sex annos etatis et puerum esse dilectissimum et doctissimum in omni scientia in tantum quod non est aliquis iam vivens qui sibi poterit coequari. (f. 102ʳ.)

This note makes further comment unnecessary.

Comparing the later collections with the earlier, we see that their character has changed. The earliest of all had consisted almost

---

[1] That is, the last five of the second sequence of fifteen (cf. *supra*, p. 58). The fact that the first fifteen occur separately in this manuscript (ff. 88ʳ seq.) under Joachim's name shows that the second set was circulating separately. This is, indeed, very early evidence of its circulation in England.

[2] The last prophecy runs: 'Et est fera ultima aspectu terribilis qui detrahet stellas, tunc fugient oves et reptilia, nihil tantummodo remanebit. O fera crudelis universa consumens, infernus te expectat. Terribilis es et quis resistet tibi?'

[3] *Supra*, p. 50.

[4] Heading: 'Incipiunt prophetie Joachim abbatis de papis.' These are written in a different hand with clear pen-and-ink drawings. The names of the popes are added in a later hand as far as Gregory XI. The latter prophecies were originally intended to portray the series of Angelic Popes (cf. *infra*, p. 194). Here they are applied somewhat inappropriately to the Avignonese popes. After Gregory there should be one more prophecy; instead there is a remarkable page, blank except for a strange black animal with webbed back feet, bear-like front feet, long thick tail, and head like a beaver. At the top is the single legend *Urban VI*. On the compiler, Henry of Kirkestede, see R. Rouse, 'Bostonus Buriensis and the Author of the *Catalogus Scriptorum Ecclesiae*', *Speculum* xli (1966), pp. 471–99.

entirely of short genuine texts and *figurae*; the compilers of the later thirteenth-century anthologies in MSS. Vat., Lat. 3822 and 4860 were still more interested in Joachim's own system of thought than in the new crop of pseudo-Joachimist writings, though they did not, of course, distinguish them; the compilations of the fourteenth and fifteenth centuries rarely draw on the genuine writings and are filled with spurious texts, sibylline oracles, and specific prophecies. The approach of Antichrist dominates their thoughts.

IX

JOACHIM'S DOUBLE REPUTATION IN THE SIXTEENTH AND SEVENTEENTH CENTURIES

IN 1516 an edition of Telesphorus's *libellus* appeared in Venice.[1] On its title-page was a picture of *Abbas Joachim magnus propheta*. He sits at his desk, books around him, pen poised, hand lifted to ear in order the better to catch the divine oracles, a devout and inspired figure. This was the popular image of Joachim in the Renaissance period: he ranked with the Sibyls and Merlin as one of the great prophets. This fame rested partly on the tremendous vogue of the pseudo-Joachimist *Vaticinia de summis pontificibus*. These went through many printed editions, in both Latin and the vernacular. As we shall see later,[2] they were subjected to many varying interpretations. One significant feature of these editions is the large number of manuscript notes in sixteenth- and seventeenth-century hands which appear in extant copies, generally making applications of the prophecies. Some of the learned, Cardinal Bellarmine for example,[3] doubted Joachim's authorship of these enigmatic pictures, but most people did not question his responsibility for prophecies which they took most seriously.

The other thing that everyone knew about Joachim was that he had appeared in Venice to give detailed instructions for depicting St. Francis and St. Dominic in the mosaics of St. Mark's, each in his own distinctive habit. The claims to this legend, made separately by the two Orders in the fourteenth century, were brought together in the fifteenth by St. Bernardino in a sermon on St. Francis,[4] while St. Antonino gave a unique version in favour of St. Dominic.[5] Then Roberto Caracciolo of Lecce picked up the legend, probably from Bartholomew of Pisa, since he also quoted the prophecy of new

[1] Cf. *supra*, pp. 57–8, and *infra*, p. 262.

[2] *Infra*, pp. 453–62.

[3] R. Bellarmine, *De Scriptoribus Ecclesiasticis* (Rome, 1613), *sub nom.*; see quotation *infra*, p. 106.

[4] Bernardino of Siena, *Omnia Opera*, iv (Venice, 1591), pt. ii, *Sermo* xvi, 88. Cf. *infra*, p. 230.

[5] Antonino, *Pars Historialis* (Nuremberg, 1484), Tit. XXIII, cap. I, 1, f. clxxxix[v].

orders beginning 'Erunt duo viri, unus hinc, unus inde', which Bartholomew had used.[1] In a fuller version the legend began to appear in Venetian chronicles,[2] and in the sixteenth century this was enlarged by F. Sansovino into two chapters of his *Venetia Città Nobilissima* . . . :[3] 'XCVII. Delle due figure notabili di S. Domenico e di S. Francesco. XCVIII. Dell'Abbate Giovanni Gioachino inventor di esse figure, e del luogo ou'egli habitava.' This embroidered version even describes the constricted place in which Joachim sojourned:

Non è dubbio alcuno, che l'inventore di esse figure non sia stato quel venerabile huomo, chiamato l'Abbate Giovanni Gioachino, il quale essendo venuto a Venetia . . . e ottenuto un luogo in detta chiesa molto angusto e rimoto, che tuttavia si mostra, per sua habitatione, e nel quale io, con molta fatica a capochino, e a ginocchi piegati sono una volta entrato, il quale è quello, che nel cantone destro della facciata della chiesa immediate sotto le colonnelle del corritore è posto; essendo, dico, venuto a Venetia, e habitando in detto luogo con molta astinenza, e con fama di santità di vita, formò quivi, e disegnò con le proprie mani le perdette figure nel modo, come quivi dipinte si veggono, senza però il nome de detti santi . . .; il disegno e esemplare delle quali dato per lui al maestro, che lavorava di mosaico, gli ordinò, che tali di effigie, di forma, di habito, e di colore ancora di habito quali egli per l'esemplare glie appresentava, depingere . . . (Cap. XCVIII, f. 58ʳ.)

The story that Joachim had been responsible for 'diverse . . . imagini, figure e altre cose, dimonstranti cose future . . . ne' muri e nel pavimento della Chiesa' created one of the tourist attractions of Venice in the sixteenth century. In 1506 a visiting Belgian, Jean Lemaire, was much intrigued by these prophetic mosaics.[4] He was told that

labbé Ioachin Calabrois, lequel avoit esprit de Prophetie . . . leur avoit prefiguré leur decadence telle que nous la voyons, par deux Lyon volans . . . lesquelz il leur ordonna tires en marbre, au pavement de leglise saint

---

[1] R. Caracciolo, *Sermones de laudibus sanctorum* (Naples, 1489), ff. 143ᵛ–179ʳ. Cf. *infra*, p. 182. Caracciolo was interested in Joachimist literature, for he also studied the *Oraculum Cyrilli*; see B. Zimmerman, *Tractatus de prioribus generalibus ord. Carmelitarum* (Lirinae, 1907), cited in Bignami-Odier, *Roquetaillade*, p. 54 n. 5.

[2] See ed. F. Ongania, *Documenti per la storia dell'augusta ducale basilica di San Marco in Venezia* . . . (Venice, 1886), pp. 6, 7, 8, 812.

[3] F. Sansovino, *Venetia Città Nobilissima et Singolare descritta già in XIIII Libri* . . . *ampliata dal M.R.D. Giovanni Stringa* (Venice, 1604), ff. 57ᵛ–58ʳ.

[4] Jean Lemaire, *La Légende des Vénitiens*, *Œuvres*, ed. J. Stecher (Louvain, 1885), ii. 361–3.

Marc. Lun diceux Lyons estoit pourtrait gros et enflé, et sembloit nager de tout le corps sur les ondes, excepté que les pattes de devant estoient en terre ferme: lautre avoit toute la corpulence estendue sur la terre et les pieds de derriere seulement en leaue: mais il estoit maisgre et deffait à merveilles. (*La Légende*, ii, p. 362.)

The legend went that, when asked for an interpretation, the Abbot Joachim had told them plainly that the first lion stood for the Venetian Republic in prosperity, as 'seigneurs de la mer', but the second signified the state of Venice if she lost her dominance at sea 'et se mettroient à usurper en terre ferme'. Lemaire saw this prophecy fulfilled in the loss of the spice trade by Venice and her attempt to gain a land empire. His curiosity was sufficiently aroused to send him searching in many books for further clues. He found a passage in the supposed oracle of the Sibyl Erithrea which he thought might fit the state of Venice,[1] but he concluded: 'ieu laisse l'investigation aux plus sages . . .'

The point that these enigmatic designs were political prophecies relating to the fate of Italy was made by a Spanish abbot, G. de Illescas:[2]

Entre muchos sanctos y doctos varones, qui vivia en este tiempo, fue uno el Abbad Joachim, de la orden de S. Benito. Disze del que tuno spiritu de prophecia, y qui hizo enlosar la Inglesia de S. Marcos de Venecia, de muchas historias, debuzadas en diversas figuras y enigmas:

---

[1] The passage runs: 'Porro, congregatio in aquis Adriaticis ex desolatione Ursi LXX pedum coartabitur, non frangetur: donec veniant duo hirci qui diminuant aurum eius' (*La Légende*, ii. 363). This does not appear in the usual text of the pseudo-Joachimist Sibyl Erithrea and must have been derived from one of the separate oracles in circulation.

[2] G. de Illescas, *Historia Pontificalis* (Burgos, 1578), p. 317. An early eighteenth-century work by J. Dubos, *Histoire de la League de Cambray* (Paris, 1709), i. 399, gives a quaint version of the political prophecies. The Venetians for long would not emerge landwards from their lagoons because they put their faith in 'celles des peintures en Mosaïque de l'Église de Saint-Marc qui sont énigmatiques et qui contiennent, dit-on, sous différentes figures allégoriques les emblèmes prophétiques d'un grand nombre d'événements arrivez long-temps depuis qu'elles ont esté faites. On croit que c'est l'Abbé Joachim qui a fourni les desseins mystérieux de celles des Mosaïques . . . dont je parle. Tout le monde sçait que cet Abbé si célèbre par tant d'autres prophéties exprimées en des figures allégoriques vivoit dans le douzième siècle en réputation d'un homme à qui l'avenir le plus éloigné estoit aussi connu que le passé.' The most famous of these, says the author, are the portraits of St. Francis and St. Dominic, but there is also one of a fox and two cocks, said to have foretold the fate of Ludovico il Moro, and, above all, one which, more than four hundred years before the event, represented the fate of the Venetian Republic: two winged lions of St. Mark's, one swimming in the sea 'peint en chair et plein de force', the other on land 'décharné et abbatu'. These prophetic designs are to the Venetians 'les oracles du pays, puisqu'il faut que chaque pays ait les siens'.

las quales dizen aversido a la letra, pronosticos y oraculo, de las calami-
dades y disastres qui en Italia han acontescido hasta oy, y de las que estan
por acontescer.

Sansovino emphasized that these mosaics were one of the marvels of
Venice which all visitors came to see and that everyone expressed
astonishment that events could have been so exactly prophesied
beforehand.[1] P. Regiselmo's Introduction to his edition of the
Vaticinia shows Joachim as a much discussed prophet in Venice at
the end of the sixteenth century, and when he wants guidance in
establishing the details of his figures Regiselmo turns naturally to
compare them with those of St. Mark, assuming that Joachim was
the designer of both sets.[2] The response of the curious sightseer
must have been merely an idle astonishment which put the Abbot
Joachim into the same category of marvel-maker as Roger Bacon in
England. But a mystical, imaginative soul might respond by reading
deep mysteries into these enigmas. Such was Guillaume Postel, one
of whose visionary experiences, as we shall see, was stimulated by
'les peintures et entaillures de St. Marc selon que les ordonna l'abbé
Ioachim'.[3]

The core of the St. Mark's legend was always Joachim's prophecy
in picture of the two Mendicant saints, and this figures in many
works of the period, not only among the Mendicants themselves,[4]
but also in writings by Benedictines, Cistercians, Augustinians, and
Jesuits.[5] In the seventeenth century the legend itself became a theme

[1] Op. cit., f. 58ᵛ.

[2] P. Regiselmo, *Vaticinia sive Prophetiae Abbatis Joachimi et Anselmi Episcopi
Marsicani* (Venice, 1589), unpag. Notes (on *Vaticinia*) IIII, XXVII, XXIX.

[3] F. Secret, 'Guillaume Postel et les courants prophétiques de la Renaissance', *Studi
francesi* I, p. 383.

[4] T. Malvenda, *Annales Praedicatores* (Naples, 1627), p. 163. L. Wadding, *Annales
Minorum*, i (Rome, 1731), pp. 14 seq.

[5] A. Wion, *Lignum Vitae* (Venice, 1595), ii. 791; G. Bucelinus, *Menelogium Benedicti-
num* (Feldkirch, 1655), p. 388; C. Henriquez, *Fasciculus Sanctorum Ord. Cist.* (Cologne,
1631), p. 736; S. Meuccio, *Super Esaiam*, Preface; F. Bivar, *Apologeticus pro F. Dextero*
(Lyon, 1624), p. 483; J. Marquéz, *Origen de Los Frayles Eremitanos de la Orden de San
Augustin* (Salamanca, 1618), p. 346. B. Viegas, *Commentarii Exegetici in Apocalypsim*
(Evora, 1601), p. 198, gives a Latin version of the statement quoted above from Illescas.
See also A. Possevino, *Apparatus Sacer* (Venice, 1606), ii. 102; Cornelius Lapierre,
Commentarii in Quatuor Prophetas Maiores (Paris, 1622), p. 46. For the purpose behind
this Jesuit defence of Joachim see *infra*, p. 282. Other references to the St. Mark's story
include G. Pepin, *Conciones de Sanctis* (Antwerp, 1657), p. 329; C. de Visch, *Bibliotheca
Scriptorum Sacri Ord. Cist.* (Douai, 1649), p. 147; A. Manrique, *Annales Cistercienses*
(Lyon, 1642), iii, *anno* 1200. An eighteenth-century mention by G. Meschinello, *La
Chiesa Ducale di S. Marco* (Venice, 1753), ii. 45-6, illustrates the growth of a critical

of art in the cloister of the Franciscan convent of Ognissanti in Florence, where Joachim is depicted pointing to the figures of St. Francis and St. Dominic.[1] There was also a similar picture in the Franciscan Observantine convent of St. Maria la Nuova at Naples,[2] where the Abbot Joachim was represented showing to his monks 'una tavola nelle quale egli haveva fatto depingere in Venetia S. Domenico e S. Francesco . . . la qual tavola si conserva in S. Marco'. Below were the words of the pseudo-Joachimist prophecy 'Erunt duo viri, unus italus, alter hyspanus . . .'.[3] To this had been added an Italian verse:

> Vede Gioachin con memoranda essempio
> Francesco al nascer suo gran tempo avante,
> Come si scorge ancor di Marco al Tempio.

How did this story about the Venetian mosaics first arise? Is it possibly a conjunction of two facts: Joachim's visit to the Pope at Verona and his known propensity for *figurae*?[4] Certainly this popular legend emphasizes one of his most characteristic activities—the designing of enigmatic *figurae*. Its vogue reveals to us the significance of *figurae* as a popularizing agency, and shows us the continuing fascination exercised by enigmatic symbols in the sixteenth and seventeenth centuries over people who still desired to believe that they represented prophecies.

It is understandable that any oracular words about the fate of Jerusalem or the infidel should be seized on in the period of the Turkish menace. Thus, next in popularity to the St. Mark's legend, was the story of Joachim's prophecy at Messina concerning the recovery of Jerusalem. In the mid-fifteenth century St. Antonino of Florence recounts the episode,[5] and its solemn warning—'nondum liberationis Hierusalem advenisse tempus'—appears in widely

---

attitude towards the legend: since Joachim, he argues, only died in 1200, this need not be a case of genuine prophecy but merely of human discernment.

[1] Bondatti, *Gioachinismo e Francescanesimo*, p. 163.

[2] This is described by G. Germano, *Vita . . . del Glorioso Padre S. Malachia* (Naples, 1670), pp. 119–20.

[3] *Infra*, p. 182.

[4] In this connection we may notice the association of the Verona visit with the other famous *figurae* of the Popes in a note which occurs in Venice, Bib. Marc., MS. Lat. Cl. III, 177, f. 13ʳ: 'A.D. M.C.LXXXV Abbas Joachim de partibus Calabrie veniens ad urbanum papa tulit secum papalistam in quo continetur status summorum pontificum ecclesie Romane revelatus sibi a Deo usque ad finem seculi.'

[5] St. Antonino, *Pars Historialis* (Nuremberg, 1484), ii, f. ccxxiʳ.

different writings of the period.[1] From a number, we may select two for mention: Hartmann Schedelius, a German, who leaves judgement on this prophecy to posterity,[2] and an Italian, Angelo Manrique, who also leaves the question open: 'pro data sibi coelitus sapientia, an pro innata audacia, iudicent alii.'[3] Manrique discusses the whole episode, with Joachim's interpretation of the Apocalypse and his pronouncement on Antichrist—as does Cardinal Baronius also[4]—but for most writers of this time the words that stuck in the mind were those on the fate of Jerusalem. By this time also other more contemporary prophecies concerning the Turk and the fall of Constantinople had been attached to Joachim's name. Leonardo of Chios, Archbishop of Mitylene, in his *Historia captae a Turca Constantinopolis descripta*,[5] applied to Constantinople one of the oracular words from the *Vaticinia de summis pontificibus*, which, of course, he attributed to Joachim. This may be the source of the later statement by Barrio, followed by Wion and others,[6] that the fall of Greece into the hands of the Turk had been predicted by Joachim. Again, Wion would seem to be the originator of another claim that Joachim foretold the glorious victory over the Turks in 1571. Here the source seems to be simply Joachim's expectation, repeatedly expressed in the *Expositio*, of the Church's triumph over the infidel. A curious little publication, *Tractatus de Ritu, Moribus, Nequitia et Multiplicatione Turcorum*, printed *c.* 1505,[7] has at the end an *addendum* with the heading 'Hic est opinio abbatis Joachimi de secta Machometi'. This quotes a long passage from the *Expositio* (f. 163ᵛ

[1] L. Alberti, *Vaticinia circa Apostolicos Viros et Ecclesia Romana* (Bologna, 1515), Preface; Rolewinck, *Fasciculus Temporum* (Cologne, 1474), f. ccxlvi; P. Aemilius, *De Rebus Gestis Francorum* (Paris, 1544), f. 118ʳ; C. Sigonius, *Historiarum de Regno Italiae Libri Viginti* (Frankfurt, 1591), pp. 346–7; J. Nauclerus, *Chronographia* (Cologne, 1579), p. 872; Polydore Vergil, *Anglicae Historiae Libri, XXVI* (Basle, 1534), p. 243.

[2] H. Schedelius, *Liber cronicarum* (Nuremberg, 1493), f. cciiiᵇ.

[3] Manrique, op. cit. (ref. p. 99 n. 5), iii, *anno* 1191. W. Cave, *Scriptorum Ecclesiasticorum Historia Literaria* (London, 1688), p. 700, mentions the prophecy on Antichrist.

[4] C. Baronius, *Annales Ecclesiastici* (Lucca, 1746), xix. 617–19. His judgement is uncompromisingly hostile: see *infra*, p. 106.

[5] Leonardo of Chios, *Historia captae a Turca Constantinopolis descripta* (Nuremberg, 1544), f. 3. The passage quoted from *Il Papalista* begins *Ve tibi Septicollis* and originally applied to Rome (see prophecy XXV).

[6] G. Barrio, *De Antiquitate et Situ Calabriae* in *Italia Illustrata* (Frankfurt, 1600), p. 1053; Wion, op. cit., p. 791, followed by Bucelinus, op. cit., p. 388, and Henriquez, *Fasciculus*, p. 736; Visch, op. cit., p. 147 (refs. p. 99 n. 5).

[7] This is an eloquent description of the terrors of the Saracen persecution under the figure of the fourth beast in the Book of Daniel. The tract had been written in the mid-fifteenth century.

in the Venetian edition), and it must be remembered that this preceded the appearance of Joachim's work in print in 1527.

The third feature of Joachim's reputation which still caught
attention was his endowment with the spirit of prophecy and the
legends of the miraculous gift of knowledge that went with it.
Joachim was selected by Agrippa of Nettesheim as an example of
one who drew prophetical knowledge from the occult meaning of
numbers,[1] by Arnold Wion as the first fruit of the ninth branch,
Prophetia, on his *Lignum Vitae*,[2] and by Gisberto Voezio[3] as a prime
example in a chapter *De Profetia*. The story of the miraculous
draught of knowledge at Sambucina was disseminated from a
curious source, the *De Rebus Turcis* of Laonikos Chalkondyles. The
author does not mention Joachim's prophecies about the infidel, but
in Book V, after writing of papal elections, he mentions Joachim's
Vaticinia de Summis Pontificibus; and then tells the Sambucina
story:[4]

Nam cum esset idiota, nec vel modicum eruditionis haberet, ianitor in
quodam Italie monasterio Nazareorum fuit, et quendam in hortum
egresso apparuit vir forma pulcherrimus. Qui assistens ad Ioachim,
manuque amphoram tenens, inquit: Ioachim, cape, bibe vinum hoc: est
enim optimum. Qui dicto audiens, bibit ad satietatem usque amphoram-
que reddidit, inquiens se satis bibisse. Cui vir respondit: O Ioachim, si
totum hausisses vinum, nulla te scientia fugisset. Deinde in colloquium et
disputationem veniens cum viris ea tempestate doctissimis, plane divinus
quantum ad scientiam attinet, apparuit. . . . Nam quaecumque praedixit
evenisse constat, licet ubique miracula eius per Italiam obvia sint.

---

[1] H. C. Agrippa, *De incertitudine et vanitate scientiarum et artium* . . . (Paris, 1531),
f. cxlvi^r; *De Occulta Philosophia Libri Tres* (no place of pubn., 1533), f. cl^r: 'De numeris
eorundemque potentia et virtute: Per illum habetur via ad omnia scibilia indaganda et
intelligenda. Per illum habetur proximus accessus ad prophetiam naturalem; atque ipse
abbas Joachim in prophetiis suis alia via per numeros formales non processit.'

[2] Wion, op. cit., ii. 791 seq. (ref. p. 99 n. 5).

[3] G. Voezio, *Disputationes theologicae* (Utrecht, 1665), ii. 1065, giving a considerable
disquisition on the argument concerning Joachim.

[4] Laonikos Chalkondyles, *De origine et rebus Turcorum libri decem* (Basle, 1556),
p. 94: 'De Pontificibus quidam Ioachim, vir vaticinandi peritus, inter doctos Italiae
connumeratus praedixit multa quomodo singuli ad Pontificatum essent perventuri et in
eo victuri. Et quemadmodum vaticinatus est, ita accidit.' The Sambucina story follows as quoted in the text. How did this Byzantine author, who died in 1463, get hold of
this story? He tells it in the midst of a digression on the Papacy and other Italian matters
which occurs in his account of the Council of Ferrara/Florence. The miscellaneous
information included sounds like bits recounted by Greek participants after their return
from the Council. This suggests that the story was picked up at the Council, but it
must have come from Fiore originally.

This passage was used by various scholars, including Daniel Mallonius in his *elucidationes* to the *Sacrae Sindonis Explicatio* of A. Palaeoto.[1] Palaeoto had merely quoted some devotional sentences from the *Psalterium decem chordarum*, but Mallonius, annotating the work, wrote at length on Joachim, citing as many authorities as possible and discussing Joachim's reputation as a prophet. Gabriele Barrio gave a different story of the gift of knowledge in his Life of Joachim, placing the episode during Joachim's pilgrimage to Jerusalem:

Cumque deserta quaedam loca esset ingressus, nimia siti confectus, mori veritus sabulo se obruit, ne insepultus feris cibus foret, ac dum scripturarum intelligentiam meditatur, sopore corripitur. Et ecce olei flumen et iuxta hominem stantem cernere, sibique dicentem: bibe de hoc flumine, eique ad satietatem bibere videbatur. Cumque evigilasset totius divinae scripturae intelligentia illi patuit. (Op. cit., p. 1052.)

Angelo Manrique also placed the experience on the pilgrimage, but makes the vision one of the open Scriptures.[2] The source of these stories is not clear but, as we shall see, they probably sprang from the cult in Calabria.[3]

Joachim's reputation, however, was still a highly controversial one. He appeared in many of the great bibliographical compilations, such as John of Trittenheim's *Liber de ecclesiasticis scriptoribus*[4] and Sixtus of Siena's *Biblioteca sancta*,[5] but also in the catalogues of heretics compiled by the Dominican Bernard of Luxemburg, the Franciscan Alphonso de Castro, and others.[6] There is often a note of

---

[1] A. Palaeoto, *Sacrae Sindonis Explicatio* (Venice, 1606), p. 2, quoting Joachim, *Psalt.*, lib. I, dist. 2, f. 234ᵛ: 'Sufficere nobis Sudarum inspicere . . . explicandum constitui'; D. Mallonius, *Elucidationes*, pp. 11–12. See also A. R. Aurelius, *Rerum Iudicatarum Libri IIII* (Paris, 1599), i, cap. 5; T. Malvenda, op. cit. (ref. p. 99 n. 4), p. 164.

[2] Op. cit. (ref. p. 99 n. 5), ii, *anno* 1165, cap. iii.

[3] The fact that most of these references precede the publication of the seventeenth-century Lives of Joachim based on the Fiore material suggests that this material must have been known and consulted before appearing in print. On the Calabrian group, *infra*, pp. 111–20.

[4] Published Basle, 1494, see *sub nom.* See also by the same author, *De Viris Illustribus* (Co. Agr., 1575), ii. 117.

[5] Sixtus of Siena, *Biblioteca Sancta* (Lyon, 1575), i. 276. See also C. Gesner, *Bibliotheca Universalis* (Zurich, 1545), *sub nom.* Gesner describes a book which I cannot identify: 'Vidi librum quendam sermone Italico impressum huius authoris, qui mirabiles quasdam visiones cum figuris depictis continet, quales in Apocalypsi divi Ioannis habemus: qui praefatur in eum librum alia quoque, praesertim explicationes in aliquot libros sacros, ab hoc Ioachimo scripta asserit, quorum non amplius memini.'

[6] Bernard of Luxemburg, *Catalogus Haereticorum* (Cologne, 1522), unpag., *sub nom.*;

ambivalence even in the judgement of those who place him among the orthodox: was he a true prophet or no? The key-note is struck by one writer who opens thus: 'Diversi diversimode de hoc abbate Joachimo scribunt et sentiunt: dum alii eum laudant, alii autem vituperant.'¹

The argument was, perhaps, sparked off by John of Trittenheim, who, although including Joachim among Catholic writers, obviously disapproved of him. He questions Joachim's prophetic gift in his very first sentence:

Joachim Abbas Florensis . . . vir in divinis scripturis studiosus et exercitatus, qui ut Propheta suo tempore habitus etiam futura praedicere conatus est. Sed mihi videtur . . . ex conjecturis scripturarum illum magis locutum quam prophetasse. Nam, ut de caeteris taceam, Fredericum Imperatorem hostem Ecclesiae futurum somniavit, quem omnes novimus usque ad mortem pacificum et Romano pontifici subjectum et fideliem perseverasse. (*Lib. de Eccl. Scrip.*, f. 59ʳ.)

The last sentence is an astounding statement if, as one naturally concludes, the reference is to the Emperor Frederick II. It is possible, however, that Trittenheim meant Frederick III, and this is the sense in which Labbé later understood him.² But the main thirteenth-century crop of prognostications ascribed to Joachim concerned Frederick II, and it was in this sense that Thomas Malvenda, championing Joachim as a true prophet, wrote in scathing terms of Trittenheim's statement:

Sed vix crediderim Trithemium talia scripsisse, quis enim tam impudenter sic mentiri esset ausus, Fredericum II (nam de hoc certum est vaticinatum Ioachimum) semper pacificum et Romano Pontifici subiectum et fidelem perseverasse? Nemo enim, nisi plane stolidus et rerum omnium oblitus, istud asseruisse potuit. Cum omnes et ipse Trithemius in Chronicis Hirsangiensibus et totus mundus apertissime sciant, Fredericum hostem

Alphonso de Castro, *Adversus omnes haereses Libri XIIII* (Paris, 1541), ff. 45ᵛ-47ʳ; G. Prateole, *De Vitis, Sectis et Dogmatibus Omnium Haereticorum* (Cologne, 1569), p. 226 (*er.* 224); Notes by F. Maro to the *De Summa Trinitate* of St. Augustine (Basle, 1515), unpag., annotation to Lib. xv, cap. xx; D. Petau, *Opus de Theologicis Dogmatibus* (Venice, 1757), Lib. iv, cap. xiii, 4, p. 215; Lib. vi, cap. xii, 4–7, pp. 40–1. Once again, we find the issue of Joachim's Trinitarian views is of sufficient moment to be discussed at some length, with citations from Aquinas.

¹ T. Petrejo, *Catalogus Haereticorum* (Cologne, 1629), p. 97.

² P. Labbé, *De Scriptoribus Ecclesiasticis* (Paris, 1660), i. 511: '. . . teste Trithemio . . . ut Propheta suo tempore habitus etiam futura praedicere conatus est. Sed aberrasse, idem auctor asserit, ac praesertim quod Fredericum III Imperatorem somniavit hostem Ecclesiae futurum, quem omnes norunt usque ad mortem pacificum et Romano Pontifici fidelem perseverasse.'

infensissimum Romanorum Pontificum et ab ipsis excommunicatum et Imperio privatum fuisse. (Op. cit., p. 164.)

Joachim's reputation was, of course, vulnerable on two counts: not only might he be doubted as a prophet, but his orthodoxy could be called in question. In his *Adversus Omnes Haereses*[1] the Minorite, Alphonso de Castro, launched a thoroughgoing attack on Joachim's whole system of the three *status* and the Trinitarian interpretation of history, expressing surprise that the Lateran Council had not made a more sweeping condemnation: '. . . mirandum est quod nullius alterius erroris concilium illum fecerit mentionem, cum tamen plures alios errores habuerit . . .' He follows Guido of Perpignan[2] in showing that the fundamental danger of Joachimism lay in the undermining of the authority of the Apostles and the Gospel which was implicit in the doctrine of the third *status*. Alphonso does not neglect Trittenheim's attack on the false prophet who 'multa scripsit in quibus meo iudicio suum leve ingenium ostendit, quoniam in omnibus ferme libris suis, ut se futurorum praescium ostenderet, consuevit miscere prognostica, quod maxime levitatis et gloriae cupiditatis indicium est: maxime cum aliter sequi posterum res habuit quam ipse praedixit.' But the heat of his attack was probably engendered by the aberrations of his fellow Minorite, Pierre Jean d'Olivi, whom he couples with Joachim because he had believed that the third *status*, initiated in St. Francis, would supersede in all respects the second *status*.[3] Here we see that the old bitterness against the Spirituals could still be active. Yet against one Franciscan view we must set another, that of the great Luke Wadding, who accepted Joachim as a true prophet: 'Plura etiam in Commentariis in Apocalypsim praedixit de Ordinibus Mendicantibus quorum veritatem rei probavit eventus.'[4]

The main argument, however, did not spring from a consideration of Joachim's doctrines but from the question of whether he was a true or a false prophet. Obviously the editors of Joachimist works acclaimed him as a true prophet: 'Hoc unum dicam,' one of them says, 'hominem hunc occasionem mortalibus omnibus praebuisse cur attentiores et circumspectiores circa futura tempora fierent. Cum norint cuncti, quicquid in suis obscuris dictis Abbas involvit, eventus suos ad unguem sortitum fuisse.'[5] Some writers, such as

---

[1] *Supra*, p. 103 n. 6 for ref.   [2] *Supra*, p. 69.
[3] On Olivi, *infra*, pp. 194–201.   [4] Wadding, *Annales* i. 16.
[5] P. Regiselmo, *Vaticinia*, Preface.

Cardinal Bellarmine, were doubtful: 'Circumferuntur quaedam vaticinia sub eius nomine, de futuris Pontificibus Romanis, quae quam fidem mereantur, aliorum sit iudicium: illud mirum est quod cum ea vaticinia ad solos quindecim Pontifices pertineant: tamen curiositas hominum ad nostra usque tempora extendere illa conatur.'[1] The Dominican Sixtus of Siena, although he included Joachim in his *Biblioteca Sancta*, was disparaging:

. . . suo tempore verissimus propheta creditus, scripsit . . . in totum Esaiam prophetam stylo rudi et obscuro commentariorum librum unum: in quibus multa de septem temporibus ecclesiae et de oneribus sexti temporis quasi futurorum praescius disseruit, multas immiscens prophetias ac vaticinia de futuris temporibus: quae an impleta, vel adhuc implenda sint, alii viderint. (Op. cit., p. 276.)

It was Cardinal Baronius, who, in his *Annales Ecclesiastici*, launched a really fierce attack against this pseudo-prophet, devoting an amount of space—and heat—to this topic which indicates how alive the controversy was. He chooses the story of the Messina encounter in 1190 as the occasion to give his judgement on Joachim 'qui propheta Dei circumferebatur esse': 'plane tam suis ipsis vanis responsis [to Richard I], quam inanibus prophetiis, inventus est non Dei propheta, sed pseudopropheta esse' (op. cit., p. 617). In three respects during that famous interview, says Baronius, Joachim gave false prophecies, whence he concludes: 'ex eo plane longe diverso ab ipsa praedictione convicit, toto coelo Joachim pseudoprophetam fuisse.'[2] When these *Annales Ecclesiastici* were later edited by Pagius, he could not resist entering the dispute, coming out as strongly for Joachim as Baronius had been against. The Abbot, he says, has been called *Sanctus*, *Doctor*, and *Propheta* by some and *Illusor*, *Hypocrita*, *Pseudo-Propheta* by others. Yet truly events prove him to have had the gift of prophecy and Pagius piles up the list of witnesses in his favour.[3]

Several seventeenth-century writers without a special axe to grind reflect the continuing debate on the Abbot Joachim. One of these, Leonardo Nicodemo, writing his *Addizioni* to the *Biblioteca Napoletana* of N. Toppi, seems to go out of his way to discuss this controversial figure.[4] He describes the editions of various Joachimist works in considerable detail and then piles up the opinions for and

---

[1] Op. cit. (ref. p. 96 n. 3), *sub. nom.*   [2] Op. cit. (ref. p. 101 n. 4), p. 618.
[3] Op. cit. pp. 617–19 (notes).
[4] N. Toppi, *Biblioteca Napoletana* (Naples, 1678), pp. 112–13, and L. Nicodemo, *Addizioni copiosi alla bib. Nap.* (Naples, 1683), pp. 91–100.

against Joachim. He quotes the strictures of Malvenda on Trittenheim's view of Joachim, and lists a wide range of Joachim's admirers,
including Dante. 'Ma vaglia il vero, che sarebbe piu facile, per dir
così, l'annoverare le stelle del Cielo e l'arene del Mare, che coloro,
che hanno parlato con lode dell'Abbate Gioiacchino.'[1] Of course,
like all learned and saintly men, he had his enemies, and so Nicodemo adds the condemnations and the opinions of those who have
placed him in the catalogues of heretics. He defends the Abbot by
remarking that the Lateran Council only condemned one error
and that Joachim submitted all his writings to the Holy See: 'Che
avesse egli sottomesso universalmente tutti i suoi scritti all S.
Chiesa Romana, è una cose piu chiara del Sole, il perchè non si dee
in alcuna maniera chiamarsi Eretico . . .'[2] Drawing to a conclusion,
he remarks: 'Sono infinite le cose, che dir si potrebbono intorno
a questo Scrittore', but he cannot conclude without remarking on
the extraordinary opinion of Baronius who has written 'con tanta
acerbità' against 'un huomo molto celebre per altro appresso coloro,
i quasi studiosi son di sapere quello, che forse a niuno di sapere è
dato dal Cielo . . .'.[2]

Not only was Joachim a subject of controversy in himself, his
reputation also became entangled in other controversies. Thus his
'prophecies' became a major weapon in the Protestant attack on the
history of the Roman Church. As we shall see later, Reformers early
fastened on the *Vaticinia de summis pontificibus*, producing several
editions with anti-papal annotations. The Messina interview, with
Joachim's famous pronouncement that Antichrist 'Romae iam diu
fuisse natum', struck the Protestant imagination immediately and
was used by anti-papal writers, both German and English.[3] The
story as told by John Bale is worth quoting in full:[4]

---

[1] Nicodemo, op. cit., p. 96.   [2] Ibid., p. 99.
[3] See J. Foxe, *Rerum in Ecclesia Gestarum Commentarii* (Basle, 1563), p. 57; M.
Flacius Illyricus, *Catalogus Testium Veritatis* (Lyon, 1597), p. 681; R. Abbott, *Antichristi
Demonstratio . . .* (London, 1603), p. 62.
[4] J. Bale, *The First two parts of the Actes or unchast examples of the English votaryes
gathered out of their own legendes and Chronicles* (London, 1551), f. cviiiᵛ; also *Scriptorum
Illustrium maioris Britanniae . . . Catalogus* (Basle, 1558), p. 233. J. Jewel, *A Defence of
the Apologee of the Churche of Englande* (London, 1567), p. 434, translates Joachim's
famous remark thus: 'Antichriste is longe sithence borne in Rome, and yet shal be
higher avaunced in the Apostolique See.' For other Protestant references to this episode
see P. Duplessis-Mornay, *Le Mystère d'iniquité, c'est-à-dire l'histoire de la Papauté*
(Saumur, 1611), pp. 325–6; H. Bullinger, *A Hundred Sermons on the Apocalypse* (London, 1561), Preface; J. Wolf, *Lect. mem.*, p. 497; N. Bernard, *Certain Discourses* (London,
1659), p. 122.

Antichrist detected by Ioachim abbas

Whils kynge Richarde was yet in the lande of Palestyne, he sent to the Ile of Calabria for abbas Ioachim, of whose famouse learnynge and wonderfull prophecyes he had hearde muche. Among other demandes, he axed hym of Antichrist, what tyme and in what place he shulde chefely apere. Antichrist (sayth he) is already borne in the cytie of Rome and wyll set hym selfe yet hyghar in the seat Apostolyche. I thought (sayd ye king) that he shuld have bene borne in Antyoche or in Babylon . . . Not so (sayth Joachim) . . . For where as the lorde is called but holye, he is called the most holy father. Thus Antichrist shall be opened . . . Whan thys was ones knowne in Englande and in other quarters of the kynges dominyon, the prelates begonne to starkle. Yea Walter Coustaunce . . . with other . . . prelates . . . cast their heades togyther, impugnynge thys new doctryne with all power possyble. And though they brought fourth many stronge argumentes in aperaunce (saith Roger Hoveden) yet could they never to thys daye brynge their matter to a full conclusion but left it always in doubt.

On the other hand, the scandal of the Eternal Evangel was used as evidence of the corruption of the Roman Church. John Foxe fastened the guilt for this 'most detestable and blasphemous book' squarely on the friars.[1] Stillingfleet knew that it was associated with John of Parma and had unearthed the articles of the Paris Masters, from which he gave a selection in his own version.[2] The first reads: 'That the doctrine of the Abbot Joachim (a great Fanatick) excelled the doctrine of Christ and consequently the Old and New Testaments.' P. Duplessis-Mornay used this episode in his *Le Mystère d'iniquité*, drawing on both Matthew Paris and the writings of William of St. Amour.[3] Finally, it is worth quoting from a sermon of John Donne at St. Paul's on Whitsunday, 1628:[4]

About foure hundred yeares since, came out that famous infamous Booke

[1] J. Foxe, *The First Volume of the Ecclesiastical History contayning the Actes and Monumentes* (London, 1570), p. 403: '. . . there was a most detestable and blasphemous booke set forth by the friers . . . whiche they called Evangelium aeternum or Evangelium Spiritus sancti . . . In whiche booke many abhominable errours of the friers were conteyned, so that the gospell of Jesus Christ was utterly defaced: which this booke sayd was not to be compared with this everlasting gospell, no more than the shell is to be compared with the carnell: then darkness to light . . .' I owe this reference to Dr. C. A. Patrides.

[2] E. Stillingfleet, *Discourse on the Idolatry of the Church of Rome* (London, 1672), pp. 238–46.

[3] Duplessis-Mornay, op. cit., pp. 398–400.

[4] *The Sermons of John Donne*, ed. E. Simpson and G. Potter (Berkeley and Los Angeles, 1956), viii. 264–5. For a further reference see E. Leigh, *Foelix Consortium* (London, 1663), p. 115. I owe these references to Dr. C. A. Patrides.

in the Roman Church, which they called *Evangelium Spiritus Sancti, The Gospel of the Holy Ghost*; in which was pretended, That as God the Father had had his time in the government of the Church, in the Law, And God the Son his time, in the Gospel, so the Holy Ghost was to have his time; and his time was to begin within fifty yeares after the publishing of that Gospel, and to last to the end of the world; and therefore it was called *Evangelium aeternum*, The everlasting Gospel. By this Gospel, the Gospel of Christ was absolutely abrogated, and the power of governing the Church, according to the Gospel of Christ, utterly evacuated; for, it was therein taught, that onely the literall sense of the Gospel had been committed to them who had thus long governed in the name of the Church, but the spirituall and mysticall sense was reserved to the Holy Ghost, and that now the Holy Ghost would set that on foot. And so (which was the principall intent in that plot) they would have brought all Doctrine and all Discipline, all Government into the Cloyster. . . . He that first opposed this Book was *Waldo*, he that gave the name to that great Body . . . who attempted the Reformation of the Church . . . who were . . . especially persecuted for this, that they put themselves in the gap, and made themselves a Bank, against this torrent, this inundation, this impetuousness, this multiplicy of Fryars and Monks that surrounded the world in those times. And when this Book could not be dissembled . . . yet all that was done by them who had the government of the Church in their hands was but this, That this Book, this Gospel of the Holy Ghost should be suppressed and smothered, but without any noyse or discredit; and the Booke which was writ against it should be solemnly, publiquely, infamously burnt. And so they kindled a Warre in Heaven, greater than that in the *Revelation*. . . . For here they brought God the Son into the field against God the Holy Ghost, and made the Holy Ghost devest, dethrone, disseise, and dispossesse the Sonne of his Government.

Again, in the sixteenth and seventeenth centuries Joachim's prophecies become a weapon used by Augustinian Hermits in their perpetual quarrel with Augustinian Canons.[1] This focused attention on Joachim himself, since a common method of learned argument at this time was to pile up a formidable weight of evidence in support of the reputation of one's chief witness, to which the opposing side would reply by attempting to marshal an equally strong body of evidence against him. Thus when, in 1618, J. Marquéz, replying to M. Rodriguez on behalf of the Hermits, claimed that his Order fulfilled Joachim's prophecy, he strengthened his case by citing a noble list of witnesses to the prophetic gifts of the Abbot.[2] In 1624

---

[1] *Infra*, pp. 251–73, for the influence of Joachimism in the Order of Augustinian Hermits.   [2] Marquéz, op. cit. (ref. p. 99 n. 5), pp. 346–7.

a reply for the Canons came from G. Pennottus Novariensis, who, in a chapter entitled 'The fifth argument solved and the Abbot Joachim discounted',[1] picked out Joachim from the authors cited by the Hermits for an attack of special bitterness. He declared that he had looked up the prophetic passage, but who could say that it applied to the Augustinian Hermits, since it might not even yet have been fulfilled? In any case, can this Goliath stand against twenty, for is not he himself worthy of condemnation? So he looses his best shot, for what was the use of claiming as prophet a man who had so often been condemned? As Marquéz had wound up with a list of those who had praised the Abbot, so Pennottus rounds off his point with the opinions of those who have called him pseudo-prophet or heretic.

Marquéz had rested his argument with regard to the early origin of the hermits not on Joachim but on the so-called chronicle of Flavius Lucius Dexter; Pennottus had replied by an attack on its authenticity. So the reputation of the Abbot Joachim, which had first become entangled in the quarrel of the Canons and Hermits, now gets caught up in a controversy over a chronicle. Francis Bivar was not an Augustinian but a Cistercian engaged in writing an *Apologeticus pro Flavio Dextro*. Having defended the chronicle, however, Bivar is side-tracked on to the other argument.[2] Here one is at once struck by the fact that his chief interest is the reputation of Joachim which has been bandied between Canon and Hermit. Bivar wishes that Pennottus, whose vehement attack on Joachim had run into two chapters, knew how blessed the venerable Abbot was accounted in Calabria and how often his memory had been defended by the Holy See. It is clear, he says, that Pennottus has read little of the works of Joachim which he quotes, for both his references to the *Expositio* are wrong, and this is most reprehensible, seeing that he could so easily have consulted the book in several libraries of Rome.[3] Whether Pennottus likes it or not, Joachim is manifestly the prophet of the Hermits of St. Augustine. This leads to a consideration of Joachim's prophetic gifts and Bivar sets

[1] G. Pennottus Novariensis, *Generalis Totius Sacri Ord. Clericorum Canonicorum Historia Tripartita* (Rome, 1624), pp. 166–8.

[2] Bivar, op. cit., pp. 481–9 (ref. p. 99 n. 5).

[3] Ibid., p. 482: 'Certe in re tanti momenti, unde honor viri unius sancti pendebat, nemo erit qui Pennottum absolvat a culpa notabilis incuriae non legendi Joachimum, cum facillimum illi esset adire sive in biblioteca Vaticana sive S. Petri in Monte aureo, egregie a R.P. Lu. Wadingo instructa, sive Aniciana collegii Gregoriani, sive illustr. D. Io. Baptistae Coccini sacrae Rotae decani, in quibus et in aliis Urbis bibliotecis opera illius reperire licere.'

against Pennottus's handful of critics a host of those who have praised Joachim. Even for this period, with its love of cumulative evidence, this list of witnesses is of noble proportions, and Bivar generally quotes fully to show that he, at least, consults his documents.[1] He then sets out to remove the sting from the charge of heresy. He shows where writers have condemned because they did not read and assimilate fully, dealing especially with two charges, the usual Trinitarian one of 1215 and the accusation from Guido of Perpignan that Joachim held the Apostles to have preached according to the letter of the Word only. The first he answers with the argument, which he draws from Fiore itself, that the book on the Trinity condemned in 1216 had been tampered with by enemies, probably Cistercians.[2] On the second charge Bivar gives a correct exposition of Joachim's doctrine of the three *status*, in the course of which he betrays a considerable interest in the whole Joachimist conception of history.[3] One of the most interesting features of the argument is Bivar's use of something approaching a scientific historical method in the defence of a man whose reputation as a prophet he accepts.

It is strange that in an apologia for a supposed early chronicle a Cistercian monk should devote seven out of forty pages to a defence of Joachim, who had only become fortuitously associated with this work. We can detect here, I think, an echo of the cult of Joachim which can be traced in south Italy, particularly among Florensians and Cistercians in the late sixteenth and seventeenth centuries.[4] Until quite recently our knowledge of this was based on printed material alone, notably the rare volume of Gregorio de Laude, *Magni Divinique Prophetae B. Jo. Joachimi Abb. Sacri Cist. Ord. Monasterii Floris et Florensis Ord. Institutoris Hergasiarum Alethia Apologetica, sive Mirabilium Veritas Defensa*, published at Naples in 1660, and the material collected by Papebroch in the *Acta Sanctorum*. The discovery of the Tutini manuscript has enabled us to go behind these to their sources. It contains, first, a *Liber Visitationis* of the Cistercian houses made in 1597 by Cornelius

---

[1] Bivar, op. cit., pp. 483–5, declaring in conclusion that he has more than twenty witnesses against Pennottus's four or five.

[2] Ibid., p. 486: '. . . et verba libri de unitate Trinitatis in alienum a mente Auctoris sensum distorta fuere . . .' He says he has taken this allegation from Graecus's Life, c. 22; for this see *infra*, p. 112.

[3] Bivar, op. cit., pp. 488–9.

[4] On this whole subject see Reeves, *Sophia* xix. 355–8, 370–1.

Pelusius, Prior of S. Giovanni in Fiore and Vicar and Visitor of the Cistercian Order in the Kingdom of Naples. A second section is headed *De Abbatia Florensi et eius filiabus Liber IIII, 1598* (f. 64ʳ). Into this Pelusius evidently incorporated material at Fiore which is now lost, for one of the headings reads: 'De regressu Beati Joachimi Abbatis a Hyerusalem et terra sancta ubi visitavit loca insignia, et de miraculis ipsius paulo diffusius enarrandis, et que quidem cuncta sequentia in quodam vetustissimo Chyrographo in bibliotheca florensis monasterii conscripta fideliter sed difficulter exemplavimus' (f. 68ʳ). Then follows the fragment of the early *Vita*, which Professor Grundmann has now edited, and Luke of Cosenza's memoir. On f. 297ᵛ 'quedam epistola Beati Joachimi' is transcribed, and on f. 299ᵛ this section ends thus: 'Hec sunt que potuimus ex illo prefato chirografo in florense bibliotheca reperto, non minus fideliter quam difficulter exemplare et de verbo ad verbum dictando exarare . . .'

Thus we learn of an anonymous book of miracles and other material which existed at Fiore in the sixteenth century and part of which Pelusius incorporated into his manuscript. It was further transcribed by a certain Fr. Jacobus Graecus Syllaneus who put together a selection of material from it in his *Chronologia Joachimi Abbatis et Ordinis Florensis*, published in 1612. He left at Fiore his transcript and, apparently, his own selection of miracles in an un-published manuscript. So far as I know, the *Chronologia* of Graecus has not survived in the 1612 edition, but various parts of this and of the manuscripts at Fiore were used by the seventeenth-century scholars concerned to foster the cult of the Abbot Joachim. Gregorio de Laude used the material of both Pelusius and Graecus. Another Cistercian, Angelo Manrique, refers specifically to Grae-cus's manuscript of *Miracula*: 'Jacobus Graecus in speciali quodam tractatu de Joachimi miraculis quem ex archivio Florensis monasterii bona fide excerptum, atque ab urbe transmissum apud me habeo.'[1] Ferdinando Ughelli had clearly seen and used the Pelusius manu-script, remarking: 'Pelusii vero MS liber extat apud amicum nostrum eruditum Camillum Tutinum.'[2] Copies of both the *Chronologia* and the Graecus book of miracles came into the hands of Papebroch, and it is on his incorporation of this material into the *Acta Sancto-rum* that we have to rely for our knowledge of Graecus's work.[3]

[1] Manrique, op. cit. (ref. p. 99 n. 5), iii, *anno* 1211.
[2] F. Ughelli, *Italia Sacra*, ed. Coleti (Venice, 1721), ix. 185.
[3] *AS*, pp. 91 (on Graecus), 94 seq. (for extracts from Graecus's *Chronologia*). On the

Papebroch was unable to find at Fiore the original anonymous book of miracles which he conjectured to have been compiled in 1346, when a deputation went from the Order of Fiore to Rome to bear witness to the miracles of their founder.[1] He apparently did not know of the Tutini manuscript. This has now added considerably to the material collected by De Laude, Manrique, Ughelli, and Papebroch, and we can recover something of the viewpoint of those Calabrian admirers who were busy defending the Abbot Joachim at this time.

One thing stands out clearly in the Tutini manuscript—that the monks of Fiore were extremely sensitive about Joachim's reputation and that they still cherished the tradition that Joachim had been wrongfully condemned in 1215. On f. 288[r-v] there occurs the vision of the disciple at Curazzo in 1215 to which we have already referred,[2] and this is copied out again (f. 331[v]) with the heading 'Lector, nota visionem scriptam in codice quodam antiquo in Bibl. Mon. Flor.'. This was obviously regarded as dangerous material, for the first record of the vision is ringed round with a line while the word *delenda* in another hand appears in the margin. Following the extracts from the old manuscript (ending on f. 299[v]) there is a specific defence of Joachim in sections dealing with the various charges against him (ff. 300[r]–306[v]). The headings run as follows:

De errore eorum qui dicunt beatum virum Joachimum tenuisse quaterni-tatem.
De errore eorum qui dicunt beatum virum Joachim fuisse in subtilibus fidei dogmatibus rudem.
De errore eorum qui dicunt beatum virum Joachim presumpsisse et non prenunciasse cum attentaverit determinare tempus futuri iudicii uni-versalis.
De errore eorum qui dicunt beatum virum Joachim Astrologie concordia futura prenunciasse.

The first is obviously regarded as the most serious charge, re-ceiving a longer and more elaborate rebuttal than the others. There is naturally no attempt to defend the view condemned at the

Book of Miracles, Papebroch says: 'Horum narrationem ex MS. quodam Florensis monasterii libello, usuque et vetustate pene evanido transcripsit Fr. Jacobus Graecus, et paulo post annum MDCXII in archivium reposuit: unde acceptum ecgraphum nobis, ut plura alia anno MDCLXI humanissime donavit Reverendissimus Ferdinandus Ughellus ...: quod accurate examinatum, invenimus evidentia eius quem diximus cultus religiosi indicia continere' (*AS*, p. 90).
[1] Ibid., p. 91.   [2] *Supra*, p. 33.

Lateran Council: this is specifically renounced. The first line of defence is to declare that Joachim cannot on this account be called a heretic. His Testamentary Letter is quoted in full to prove his submission to the Holy See, followed by the sentences in the Lateran Council decree in which, on account of this letter, Joachim's name is cleared from obloquy. Then Honorius III's letter in defence of his memory is quoted and the opinion of St. Antonino that, although Joachim's view had been condemned, 'non tamen ipse hereticus iudicatur quia omnia scripta sua supponit iudicio ecclesie corrigenda'.[1] Next the adverse opinions of St. Thomas Aquinas[2] and Duns Scotus are carefully cited at some length. There is no attempt to refute them but instead the reader is directed to turn to Joachim's own work, the *Psalterium decem chordarum*. A number of passages from this follow, occupying some three pages and designed to demonstrate Joachim's fundamental catholicity in his exposition of the Trinity.[3] Reference is also made to the passage in the *Expositio* in which, in his exegesis of the text *Ego sum Alpha et Omega*, Joachim expounds the doctrine of the Trinity 'non minus diffuse quam catholice.'[4]

After these demonstrations of Joachim's orthodoxy the writer comes to the nub of his argument:[5]

Verum enim vero adsit veritati fides et Deum et dict . . . textor quum legenti mihi opera Be(a)ti Joachim et meditanti verba illius nihil occurrere visum est quod fidei esset obnossium. Reprobatum autem contra Magistrum Sentent. ipsius editum libellum. Nos ibidem reprobantes mirari oportet simulatque vereri, an libellus ille fuerit proprius et per manus Be(a)ti Viri Joachim: ne forte ei contigerit, quod et origeni: cum constet typographiam a Joanne guthimberg alemano repertam anno Domini circiter M.4.40 itaque de facili tempore Beati Joachim precedente typographiam per huiusmodi chyrographa, exemplaria, et apochriphas scripturas poterat quispiam innocenter de aliquo maledicto sugillari. (ff. 304ᵛ–305ʳ.)

Thus it is plain that the sixteenth-century defenders of Joachim at Fiore clung to the old thirteenth-century myth that Joachim had been the victim of a plot, and this is confirmed in the next sentence, where the writer clinches the point by quoting one of the key pas-

[1] Cf. St. Antonino, op. cit. (ref. p. 96 n. 5), f. ccxxiʳ (not an exact quotation).
[2] *Supra*, pp. 67–9.
[3] ff. 303ʳ–304ᵛ. Cf. *Psalt.*, ff. 228ᵛ–229ʳ, 229ᵛ, 229ᵛ, 230ᵛ, 230ᵛ 233ʳ 233ᵛ.
[4] *Expos.*, ff. 33ᵛ–38ᵛ.
[5] Notice the quaint reference to the invention of printing.

sages from the *Super Hieremiam*, which makes this charge under the veil of its enigmatic 'prophecy'.[1] Once again, this passage is ringed round and marked *delenda* in another hand.

The second count against Joachim is obviously an echo from Aquinas. The defence against it does little except eulogize Joachim and express astonishment at such a charge. The third is countered by quotations from the *Expositio* and *Liber Concordie*[2] in which Joachim avers that God alone knows when the final hour will be. Against the fourth, appeal is made to those who have regarded him as a prophet, with specific mention of Cyril the Carmelite, Dante, and William of Auvergne (Gulielmus Parisiensis).

Obviously the really sore spot for these monks of Fiore was the 1215 condemnation, which could not be explained away. On this they still preserved the thirteenth-century point of view of the *Super Hieremiam*. It was from Fiore itself that the seventeenth-century Cistercian defenders of Joachim almost certainly acquired their ammunition. We have already noticed the passionate defence of Francis Bivar in 1627.[3] He accepts the story that Joachim in the *Super Hieremiam* had 'prophesied' his unjust condemnation, quoting exactly the passage used in the Fiore manuscript. This he probably derived from Jacobus Graecus's work. His own reading of Joachim's writings has convinced him of their orthodoxy, so the plot is the only possible solution: 'Caeterum quantum ex lectura operum Ioachimi coniicio, quorundam sui ordinis monachorum astu, quos zelus imprudens urebat, apud Innocentium et Concilium accusatus est et verba libri de unitate Trinitatis in alienum a mente Authoris sensum distorta fuere' (op. cit., p. 486). The probable reason for this devotion to Joachim appears in a further quotation from the pseudo-Joachimist prophecy in which a great future for the Cistercian Order is foretold.[4] The point is emphasized in a marginal

[1] f. 305ʳ: 'Spiritualiter inquit quia idolum doctrina heretica est, posita ante templum ecclesie, quam adorant omnes et tenent vani ceterique magistri insanam doctrinam et fidelem: ut eam extinguant, et nomen doctoris, cui revelabitur sententia Danielis, evertant. Futurum est enim ut Caiaphas summus Pontifex veritatem insinuet, ut unus damnetur, idest moriatur, doctor pro populo, ut non tota gens pereat in errore. Sic Sedechias contra Hyeremiam insurgit, damnat librum, scindit Trinitatem ab unitate, scalpello sententiam scribe Doctoris. Nescio autem, Deus scit, utrum in nobis complenda sint, vel in securo ordine consumanda.'

[2] f. 306ʳ. Cf. *Expos.*, f. 72ᵛ; *Lib. Conc.*, f. 11ᵛ.

[3] *Supra*, pp. 110-1.

[4] Op. cit., p. 487: 'Sed nihilominus inferius ad cap. 35 perpetuitatem eiusdem Ordinis in nonnullis filiis eius praedicit' (quoting from the *Super Hieremiam*, f. 59ʳ: 'quod Jonadab . . . usque saeculi processura').

note: 'Ordo S. Bernardi semper duraturus'; Bivar's championship of Joachim surely springs from a belief that the Abbot was the prophet of Cistercian greatness.

That the reputation of Joachim was very much a live issue in the Cistercian Order at this time comes out clearly in the *Annales Cistercienses* of Angelo Manrique.[1] Manrique was Abbot of Casamari, the Cistercian house in which Joachim had received the vision of the psaltery with ten strings and worked on his three chief books. It is understandable, therefore, that he should be in the thick of the controversy. He devotes a large amount of space to Joachim, and from the outset, while assuming a careful attitude of impartiality, stresses the extreme opinions of those who write about Joachim:

> . . . de quo, ut nihil medium ab Authoribus, sic omnia extrema dicta: quibusdam Sanctum, Doctorem, Prophetamque; quibusdam illusorem et hypocritam; utrisque magnum, orbique insignem usque in hodiernam diem concertaturis. . . . Certe in Joachimo Prophetiae donum comprobavit eventus; sanctitatem miracula; doctrinam scripta; auctoritatem Florensis congregatio, cui ab ipso principium; et ni Petro Lombardo succensuisset Sententiarum Magistro, in quo gravi errori permissus est; haud dubie hodie conferretur Ecclesiae Patribus. Caeterum, ut laudatores bonorum operum, sic perperam scriptorum delatores Cistercienses expertus, quod suo loco trademus; nobis neque amore, neque odio dicendus erit. (*Annales* ii, *anno* 1165.)

His account of Joachim's life is notably full, drawn in large measure from Graecus. Throughout he is continually participating in this still living debate as to whether Joachim is a true or a false prophet. The quarrel with the Cistercians is traced out, leading up to a climax in the 1215 condemnation. Here, although he declares his impartiality, he brings Bivar's argument and the concealed prophecies of the *Super Hieremiam* into play. He is really obsessed by the extraordinary diversity of opinion on Joachim in the Church, and all the last part of his account is focused on juxtaposing the *laudatores* and the *reprobatores*:

> Mirum est quantum diviserit Ecclesiam, si ita fari licet, Joachimus Abbas, qui Catholicos multos laudatores, veneratoresque, reprobatores alios, et detractores etiam usque in hanc diem experiatur. Sed et haereticos adeo partitos habet, ut quibusdam irrisui contemptuique, aliis in ea veneratione fuerit, ut (quod catholicae et piae aures abhorrent) vel ipso Christo

---

[1] Manrique, op. cit. (ref. p. 99 n. 5), i, *anno* 1100; ii, *annis* 1165, 1168; iii, *annis* 1183, 1186, 1188, 1189, 1190, 1191, 1197, 1200, 1211.

maior, et in quibusdam eidem praeferendus, petulanti, et insania bla-
sphemia praedicaretur. Rarum utrunque, et fere sive exemplo, sive quod
Catholici ita dividantur; sive quod hominem ab eorum multis laudatum,
extollant Haeretici; qui more suo reptilia tantum terrae, seu venenosa, et
quae omnes pii exhorrent, colere solent. Satis, superque excusati sunt
Authores, qui detrahunt Joachimo, si haereticorum de eo laudes obten-
dant, nedum blasphemias, quae sanctissimum quemque possint suspectum
reddere. (*Annales* ii, *anno* 1211.)

Here we see that heretical support for Joachim weights the scales
heavily against him. In spite of adverse opinions, however, and his
own paraded impartiality, Manrique, on balance, comes down on the
side of a favourable verdict, for, he says, the saintliness of the
monks of Fiore is impressive and bad trees cannot bear good fruit.

The most complete defence is that of Gregorio de Laude, Abbot
of the Cistercian house of Sagittario.[1] The controversy breaks
straight into the Preface to his Life of Joachim, where he acknowledges the need to defend Joachim against detractors. His main
defence, however, forms the climax of the Life in a whole series of
chapters devoted to this theme.[2] He states the core of the problem
clearly: '. . . duas siquidem opiniones inter se oppositas scripsisse
reperio, quarum una fidelissima et catholica; altera vero haeretica et
damnata.' The latter, he says, was to be found in the condemned
book against Peter Lombard, but the former can be found in most of
Joachim's works, especially in the *Expositio* and the *Psalterium*. It
would, he contends, be presumptuous to suggest that the Lateran
Council had erred, therefore the book was heretical. If Joachim did
write it, it is possible for saintly men to fall into error, and Joachim's
Preface to the *Psalterium* shows how ineffable a mystery he held the
doctrine of the Trinity to be, far beyond his understanding until
he received a revelation of its meaning. The tract against Peter
Lombard might have been written before this. There follows a
long debate on possible explanations of this enigma, ending with De
Laude's firm opinion that it is the ascription of the Peter Lombard
tract to Joachim that is wrong. He quotes at length from the *Liber
Concordie* and the *Expositio* to show that Joachim's views 'omnino
catholica sint', and, since he started these at Curazzo, neither before
nor after his revelation could he have erred on the Trinity. This is
proved by his *consuetudines* for the liturgy of Fiore in which the

[1] *Apologetica* (see Select Bibliography for full title).
[2] Ibid., capp. lxiii–lxvii, pp. 267 seq.

distinctive features show his grasp of the meaning of the Trinity. The climax of the argument is the claim that Joachim was the victim of a plot by enemies, particularly Cistercians, who produced this book to blacken his name. Here De Laude makes full use of the hidden 'prophecies' in the *Super Hieremiam*, quoting at length and interpolating his own gloss to drive the interpretation home.[1]

Throughout De Laude speaks of 'noster Joachim' and his devotion clearly springs from Cistercian pride, that curious pride in their prophet which was as characteristic of one Cistercian point of view as bitter dislike was of the opposite one. But there is also an element of Calabrian, or south-Italian, patriotism in De Laude's attachment. Another interesting example of this local devotion to Joachim is seen in Matteo Guerra who, after making a reputation at the Council of Trent, was translated in 1576 to the see of St. Marco in Calabria. He appears to have written *Notuli super Psalterium B. Joachimi*, which De Laude knew from a manuscript in the house of the Capuchins at Cosenza. In the passage from this work which De Laude—and after him Papebroch—quotes, Guerra acclaims Joachim: 'compatriota meus, Caelici natus (locus distat a civitate Cosentina quatuor milliaribus), Monachus Cisterciensis, Institutor Ordinis Florensis, in vita, in morte et post mortem miraculis claruit.'[2]

Interest in Joachim may have been stimulated by the researches of local antiquaries. A local priest, Gabriele Barrio, produced a Life of Joachim as part of his *De Antiquitate et Situ Calabriae*.[3] This is a conventional piece of work, but the detail in it must have been drawn from the Fiore manuscripts. Ferdinando Ughelli, the Cistercian abbot of St. Vincent and St. Anastasius, reveals in his *Italia Sacra* a close attachment to Joachim's memory. He has used the Tutini manuscript and studied the records of Fiore. From these he has extracted the chief imperial and papal privileges to Fiore. He writes with approval of Joachim's recent defenders: 'Franciscus Bivarius . . . egregie eundem vindicat a multorum calumniis. Novissime amicus noster Gregorius Laurus . . . Joachimi scripta acriter vindicat.'[4] He also finds space for a long poem in praise of Joachim.[5] We have already referred to a Neapolitan bibliographer,

[1] See quotation *supra*, pp. 34–5 and Reeves, *Sophia* xix, p. 359.
[2] *Apologetica*, p. 135; *AS*, p. 91.
[3] *Supra*, p. 101 n. 6 for ref. This same Life was also printed as a preface to Regiselmo's edition of the *Vaticinia* (ref. p. 99 n. 2).
[4] Ughelli, op. cit. (ref. p. 112 n. 2), p. 202.   [5] Ibid., pp. 200–1.

Leonardo Nicodemo,[1] who gives a notably full and careful account
of Joachim's works—genuine and spurious, of course—with references to manuscripts. Finally, in his *Calabria Illustrata* Giovanni
Fiore celebrates Joachim's fame, particularly as the prophet of many
Orders: the Dominicans, Franciscans, Carmelites, Augustinian Hermits, Theatines, Priests of the Oratory.[2]

A curious by-product of Calabrian interest in historical tradition
was the manufacture of forgeries on a considerable scale by Ferdinando Stocchi of Cosenza. The history of the Abbot Joachim
becomes entangled in this fraud in a strange way. Graecus had
mentioned, among other disciples of Joachim, a Joannes Bonatius
and a Joannes de Aquitaine. De Laude, writing about half a century
after Graecus, quoted from a work purporting to have been written
in his old age by Bonatius, entitled *Opusculum de prophetis sui
temporis*.[3] From De Laude, Papebroch drew his references to this
same work in the *Acta Sanctorum*,[4] and thus the tradition of an
(apparently) lost work by Bonatius has come down to us. Now there
is in the British Museum a copy of a rare work entitled *Historia de'
Suevi nel conquisto de' regni di Napoli e di Sicilia per l'imperadore
Enrico Sesto, con la vita del beato Giovanni Calà, capitan generale che
fu di detto imperadore.* This was written by Don Carlo Calà and
published in Naples in 1660. One of the author's purposes was to
laud his reputed ancestor, Joannes Calà or Kalà, who, after a military
career under the Hohenstaufen, was supposed to have become a
hermit in Calabria and a companion of Joachim. Thus, in Part Two
of this *Historia*, Carlo Calà printed five short works relating to the
Blessed John Calà and purporting to have been written by his
companions. The last of these is the so-called *opusculum* of Bonatius,
in which three prophets, Joannes de Aquitaine, Joannes Calà, and
Joachim, prophesy before the Emperor Henry VI. The author adds
biographical notes, giving details not to be found elsewhere. This
would be an important discovery were it not that the work of Don
Carlo Calà has been shown to rest on a colossal fraud for which he
paid large sums of money. Ferdinando Stocchi of Cosenza, seeing
an opportunity to play on Don Carlo's desire for an illustrious
ancestry, invented a distinguished career for two brothers named
Calà, who were descended from Hohenstaufen and royal British

[1] *Supra*, pp. 106-7.
[2] G. Fiore, *Calabria Illustrata* (Naples, 1743), pp. 53-61.
[3] De Laude, *Apologetica*, p. 106.   [4] *AS*, pp. 91, 107.

stock and came to south Italy with Henry VI; he then forged the manuscript sources to establish this tale.[1] Since De Laude and Papebroch both used the work published by Carlo Calà and this was apparently unknown to Graecus earlier in the century, it seems almost certain that Bonatius's work is part of the forgery and that he never wrote such a work at all.

The problem of Stocchi's forgery has a further ramification. There is in the Vatican library a curious manuscript (Rossiano 480), entitled *Prophetiae et Epistolae Joachim Abbatis Florensis, pertinentes ad res Kalabras*, and consisting of eight prophecies and eight epistles. Part of its curiosity lies in its style of handwriting and ornamentation: it is obviously late, but gives the impression of being consciously archaic, of copying or imitating an older document. This manuscript is closely linked with the work of Carlo Calà. On the one hand, Calà possessed a copy of it, for he gives the title in full exactly as in the manuscript,[2] transcribes epistles 2, 3, and 5, and expounds some of the prophecies.[3] On the other hand, one of the epistles refers to the Blessed Joannes Kalà,[4] which at once makes it suspect. Suspicion is further aroused by the fact that Graecus apparently made no reference to either prophecies or epistles, and, indeed, no other writer appears to know anything of them except Gregorio de Laude and, following him, Papebroch. De Laude transcribes epistles 1, 2, 3, 5, 6, and 8,[5] always with the marginal reference *Ex libro Epistolarum Joachimi Abbatis Florensis*, and from him Papebroch takes numbers 1, 2, 3, and 8.[6] Of seventeenth-century writers only Carlo Calà and De Laude appear to know at first hand both the *opusculum* of Bonatius and the Prophecies and Epistles. Thus there is a strong presumption that both are Stocchi's forgeries, which De Laude obtained through Calà. There is a further fragment in the Vatican, MS. Ferraioli 728, ff. 371^r–372^v, which should be connected with Stocchi's activities, for it transcribes part of the so-called *Opusculum de prophetis sui temporis* of Bonatius. One can

---

[1] See D. Zangari, *Anonimi, pseudonimi, eteronimi scrittori calabresi o di opere attinenti alla storia letteraria delle Calabrie* (Naples, 1930), pp. 112–14; *Catalogo di manoscritti della biblioteca di Camillo Minieri Riccio*, Parte IV (Turin and Florence, 1866), pp. 11–12. For a further discussion of this problem see Reeves, *Sophia*, xix, pp. 369–71.

[2] C. Calà, *Historia de' Suevi nel conquisto de' regni di Napoli e di Sicilia per l'imperadore Enrico Sesto, con la vita del beato Giovanni Calà, capitan generale che fu di detto imperadore* (Naples, 1660), p. 97.

[3] Ibid., pp. 63–4, 96–7, 178–9.   [4] *Epistola* V, f. 5^r.

[5] De Laude, *Apologetica*, pp. 90–1, 95–6.   [6] *AS*, pp. 107, 126, 135.

almost say that Joachim's name seems to attract forgeries. The interesting point about these late ones is that the Abbot appears as a striking and dramatic figure around whom legends can be woven which feed both family pride and Calabrian patriotism.

The whole battle over Joachim is reflected in the way Daniel Papebroch handles the subject in the *Acta Sanctorum*. The very fact that Joachim is included here presupposes a judgement in his favour, but Papebroch is much aware of the need to justify this judgement. He begins by remarking that both the monastery of Fiore and the memory of its founder had fallen into ill repute, so much so that, in the opinion of some, Joachim's name should be deleted not merely from the ranks of the saints but from the very company of Catholics. To attacks both on the Order and the Founder, however, the Apostolic See has given the lie in re-establishing their fame. For Papebroch himself Joachim's claim to sanctity rests on three attributes: his great virtues, his spirit of prophecy, 'quo toti mundo vivus celebrabatur', his miracles.[1]

The authorities he uses and the manner in which he discusses them reveal the extent of his researches and his critical approach, yet also the limitations of his outlook. He has examined a copy in the possession of Ferdinando Ughelli of the transcript which Graecus made from the old collection of miracles at Fiore. From this he takes Luke of Cosenza's memoir, *Virtutum Beati Joachimi Synopsis*. Then he incorporates large portions of Graecus's own *Vita*. Thirdly, he uses the work of De Laude, including quotations from the supposed *opusculum* of Bonatius and the suspicious *Liber Epistolarum Joachimi*. These last two sources give a deceptive appearance of ancient documentation to his work. It is perhaps surprising to find that he accepts both the *Super Hieremiam* and the *Vaticinia* as genuine works, but here his critical sense was undoubtedly obscured by his passionate belief that Joachim really prophesied events in detail. On the other hand, he reveals a much more modern approach in his discussion of the San Marco story, which he dismisses as impossible on grounds of dating, remarking how easily such stories attach themselves to a great name.[2] Altogether, the impression left by Papebroch's account is of one trying to maintain the high

---

[1] *AS*, pp. 89–90.

[2] Ibid., p. 141. It is interesting to find the forged *libellus* of Bonatius used again by the Bollandists in connection with a prophecy of the World Emperor; see *AS*, May II, pp. 821–2.

standards of Bollandist scholarship whilst treating a subject in which
his emotions were engaged. The real reason for this engagement
does not emerge until his final pages.

The two issues on which Joachim most needs to be defended are
seen by Papebroch to be, first, his orthodoxy (as a necessary attribute of his sanctity), and, secondly, his true prophetic gift. These
two questions are tackled in the concluding chapters,[1] in which he
discusses and sums up all the evidence on Joachim. The first he
approaches by way of the dating of Joachim's works. Matthew Paris
had asserted that Joachim wrote the *Libellus* against Peter Lombard
in diebus Alexandri Papae, but, if so, it was a very early work.
'Quando autem et utrum revera editus ab illo fuerit', pronounces
Papebroch firmly, '. . . unum dico et uti spero dilucide probabo,
Ioachimum . . . omnia prorsus retractasse in Psalterio, non jam
libello, sed justo trium ut (ipse appellat) voluminum seu librorum
opere.'[2] This leads on to a massive defence in a chapter headed:
'Quam solide catholiceque de mysterio Trinitatis Joachimus in
Psalterio scripserit.'[3] He piles up the quotations from the *Psalterium* to demonstrate that Joachim, in attacking various heresies,
teaches an entirely orthodox doctrine of the Three Persons, and
finally declares that, whether the contradiction is resolved in terms
of the *Libellus*' being a very early work, or a forgery under Joachim's
name, the Abbot's doctrine as finally evolved in the *Psalterium* is
irreproachable:

Ex dictis satis liquido constat quam pura et orthodoxa fuerit Joachimi
Abbatis doctrina circa mysterium sanctissimae et individuae Trinitatis
saltem ultimis quindecim aut sedecim vitae annis, intra quos elaboratum
Psalterium fuit, quaecumque demum fuerit sententia iunioris. Ex hoc
posito multiplex subnascitur quaestio circa Libellum citra controversiam
haereticissimum meritoque damnatum in Lateranensi; ipsiusne revera,
an alterius Auctoris, Joachimi nomine et auctoritate abusi, ille fuerit . . .
(*AS*, p. 134.)

The theory of forgery leads straight on to the question of prophecy,
for one of the most telling points made by those who claimed that
Joachim was the victim of a plot was that he had foretold this
persecution in the *Super Hieremiam*. Papebroch believes that this
was true prophecy and quotes the key passage prophesying against
the Cistercians under the figure of the men of Anathoth.[4] He tries,

[1] *AS*, pp. 125–43.   [2] Ibid., p. 129.
[3] Ibid., pp. 131–4.   [4] Ibid., p. 137.

however, to approach the issue of Joachim's gift of prophecy in a critical spirit, rejecting examples for which he judges the authority to be insufficient. Unfortunately, he rests his true examples on 'impeccable evidence' which we know to be false—the collection of *Epistolae* and the *Super Hieremiam*. These provide him with such clear proofs that he cannot understand how St. Thomas Aquinas could have thought Joachim foretold events 'non prophetico spiritu, sed conjectura mentis humanae'.

Salva enim sancti Doctoris reverentia, persuademus nobis, libros Joachimi levi dumtaxat oculo et mente praeoccupata lectos ei fuisse, aut ne lectos quidem, sed incerto relatu perlata ad ipsum in quibus praedicendis deceptus fuerit; vel in genere tantum secutum esse sui seculi sensum, quo multa sub Joachimi nomine circumferebantur, fictitia prorsus atque inania, quorum nugacitas efficiebat, ut suspensi haererent sapientissimi quique, quo loco haberent Joachimum, vel quid de spiritu illius statuerent. (*AS*, p. 137.)

In Papebroch's view the trouble has chiefly arisen because of the *figmenta* 'quae sub nomine eiusdem circumferebantur, tamquam vaticinia celeberrimi Prophetae'.[1] His chief example of this type of story is Roger Howden's account of the Messina meeting, evidence which had been used by Baronius to show that Joachim was a pseudo-prophet. Of Baronius's account of Joachim, Papebroch speaks with considerable irony,[2] and Trittenheim's strictures come in for similar treatment. Perhaps Trittenheim was ignorant of the age in which Joachim lived; perhaps he got hold of the wrong Frederick, i.e. Frederick III, instead of Frederick II.[3] Papebroch

[1] *AS*, p. 137.
[2] Ibid., p. 138 (after quoting from Howden and Baronius): 'Quibus Beato Ioachimo usque adeo injuriis, nec satis cum scriberentur pensitatis, aliter non respondemus quam optando ut ad Annales ecclesiasticos prosequendos ulterius vita et otium Baronio suffecissent: vix enim dubitamus quin pro sua ingenuitate emolliisset sententiae praecipitate rigorem: ut enim, tum ex ipso Concilii Decreto, tum ex Pontificum consequentium Bullis cognovisset, unicum dumtaxat qui sub nomine Ioachimi ferebatur libellum fuisse damnatum, idque citra praetitulati Auctoris notam; ita fortassis etiam ad ipsam Apocalypseos expositionem legendam aliquando applicuisset animum, agnovissetque, quam falsis praejudiciis plerique eius accusatores nitantur.'
[3] Ibid., p. 139: 'Nam quae praedixit in Frederico huius nominis II impleta esse nemo negaverit . . . adeo ut merito admiremur, quomodo Ioanni Trithemio . . . exciderit haec de Ioachimo censura. . . . Fortassis aetatem Ioachimi ignorans Trithemius huc impegit, et neque Henricum Aucupem ab aliis quoque in numerandis Imperatoribus praeteriri solitum, neque Henricum Thuringiae et Hassiae Lantgravium subrogatum Frederico viventi et usque ad mortem se pro Imperatore gerenti, numeravit; itaque factum fuerit ut Henricum Luxemburgium sextum huius nominis faciens, eum esse crediderit, qui Ioachimus librum scripserit hoc principio "Pie petis aliquid": atque adeo

has no doubt whatsoever that Joachim truly prophesied concerning the Hohenstaufen, especially Frederick II, and also that the prophecies of the two Mendicant Orders are entirely credible, excluding the Venetian story. Perhaps, he hazards, the origin of this story lies in the fact that some admirers of Joachim took the theme of the figures from his works and said that in St. Mark's the prophecies of Joachim were depicted. 'Quidquid sit, non est opus istius modi tam incertis argumentis propheticum Beati Joachimi spiritum confirmari, cum alia longe certissima habeamus.' Then he turns to the *Expositio* and the *Super Hieremiam* to quote key passages on the new orders of spiritual men.[1]

This last argument occupies the concluding chapter, entitled 'Oracula Florensi monasterio a Beato Fundatore relicta, circa religiosos Ordines noviter nascituros'. It is here that we finally reach the clue to Papebroch's strong championship of Joachim, for from Joachim's prophecies 'varii religiosorum Ordines varie ad se trahunt et ad nostram Iesu Societatem etiam nonnulli'.[2] Although the belief is thus cautiously attributed to *nonnulli*, it is clear that Papebroch himself believes that Joachim, in announcing the dramatic crisis of history, had foreseen his own order as called to destiny in this time. The third of the three great tribulations of the Church has now come, in the shape of the Lutheran and other heresies, and after it the Seventh Angel is expected, 'id est, spiritus Dei septiformis, resuscitabit intelligentiam spiritualem'. Papebroch modestly expresses hesitation as to the agencies of which Joachim speaks: 'sive de Ordine praedicto quem designat Jesus, sive de spirituali intelligentia, id est, operosa efficacique doctrina Scripturarum', but there seems little doubt that he really believes the Society of Jesus to be the Seventh Angel. He has indeed been gripped by Joachim's

putaverit ea, quae legebas de Henrici successore operibus Ioachimi insparsa vaticinia, ad Fredericum Austriacum, eius nominis Tertium spectare. . . . Ut ut est, non debet contra Ioachimum recipi tam evidenti errori innixum Trithemii de illo iudicium . . .'

[1] *AS*, p. 141. On the San Marco story he writes: 'Profecto cum consideramus plerorumque Ioachimi operum idem quod horum emblematum esse argumentum, cogimur suspicari, ob argumenti similitudinem visum esse non nemini, eundem librorum et marmorum fuisse compositorem; idque a nonnullis absque ulteriori indicio receptum, eiusmodi quorumdam opinioni fundamentum dedisse apud vulgus hominum. Fortassis etiam admirator aliquis librorum Ioachimi ex ipsis desumpsit picturarum eiusmodi argumenta ea, quorum praedictio iam cernebatur ipso eventu completa; et sic dictae sint "Prophetiae Ioachimi" esse depictae.' The key passages quoted from Joachimist works are *Expositio*, ff. 83^v, 175^v–176^r; *Super Hier.*, ff. 1^r, 12^v–13^r; *Super Esaiam*, f. 11^v.

[2] *AS*, p. 142.

great vision of a 'mixed order', combining the life of Martha and Mary, sending missions to the heathen, resuscitating the spiritual intelligence through the true study of the Scriptures: 'hoc est ipsum Ordinem quem designat Jesus.'[1]

This brings Papebroch, finally, to the greatest stumbling-block. If he is to claim Joachim as a true prophet of new orders, he must justify the doctrine of the three *status*. But this was precisely the doctrine attacked as heretical by Guido of Perpignan and others. Papebroch counters by his usual method of quoting from the genuine works and then asserting that Guido travestied Joachim's views. His strictures on those who distort meanings are strong:

Ita nempe male tractantur Auctores, de quibus formato semel unde-cumque praejudicio, judicant alii, secundum quae vel perfunctorie legunt vel quae alii in ipsis pro affectu suo somniant se legisse.

Quod si contingat eos, qui talia sic excerpta et in sensum minus bonum Catholicumque detorta usurpant, homines esse in fide suspectos aut haereticae pravitatis palam convictos; tum enimvero hoc quoque neces-saria consecutione sequitur, ut fidei puritatem zelantibus suspecti quoque fiant ipsi auctores, quorum illi se testimoniis armant, siquidem alias ignoti sint. (*AS*, p. 143.)

Above all, heretics such as the Fraticelli have harmed Joachim's reputation by distorting his doctrine into blasphemy. It was this kind of pestiferous error which led St. Thomas to obtain a copy of one of Joachim's works and mark in it all the errors. Here Papebroch has to play down St. Thomas's dislike of Joachim as best he can: '. . . nemo mirari potest', he writes, 'quod sanctus Doctor, minus cognitam habens Joachimi sanctitatem et suspectum eiusdem spiri-tum, ob plurima figmenta . . . mirari, inquam, nemo poterit quod dictum opus ita lectum non valde probaverit Doctor Angelicus . . .'[2] It is on a somewhat doubtful note that Papebroch concludes his account of Joachim, and, indeed, the ambivalence of his attitude between attraction to Joachim's vision of new orders and repulsion from the fantasies of those who carry the doctrine of the three *status* too far expresses exactly the dilemma of a sober Joachite.

---

[1] *AS*, pp. 142–3. *Infra*, pp. 277–8, for this conception of Jesuit mission.
[2] *AS*, p. 143.

X

ORTHODOX OR HETERODOX?

THE scent of controversy still lingers around modern discussions of Joachim. In the late eighteenth century G. Tiraboschi devoted some ten pages in his great *Storia della Letteratura Italiana*[1] to the Abbot, focusing attention once more on the disagreement among authorities as to whether he was a true or false prophet. He cites, among contemporaries, Sicard of Cremona for, and Roger Howden against; then Dante and St. Thomas are set in similar juxtaposition. At this point he remarks: 'Or se gli antichi scrittori che vissero insieme, o non molto dopo Gioachimo, non poterono accordarsi nel formarne il carattere, qual maraviglia che discordui tra loro i moderni? . . . In ciò ancora io non seguirò i moderni scrittori, che non bastano a persuadermi, ma sol gli antichi, che sembrano assai più degni di fede' (op. cit., p. 178). With these words we finally step from the era when a case was argued by the uncritical piling up of many witnesses, good and bad, to the beginnings of modern historical method. Even the contemporary sources Tiraboschi sifts with a critical eye, dismissing prophecies which have obviously been put into Joachim's mouth or adapted, but noting that all these show Joachim to have been universally regarded as a true prophet. Of the 'moderns' he trusts Papebroch because he consulted Joachim's own works, but even Tiraboschi himself is only at the beginning of the process of determining which really are Joachim's works. He dismisses the *Vaticinia*, which any wise man can see to be an imposture,[2] but accepts the *Super Hieremiam* and thus establishes Joachim as a true prophet both of the Mendicant Orders and of the tribulation brought upon the Church by Frederick II. His concern is still with the issue of prophecy: '. . . che quando i codici su' quali si è fatta l'edizione dell'opere dell'abate Gioachimo siano originali, o almeno antichi, per modo che non v'abbia luogo a temere d'interpolazione, o d'impostura, le predizioni in esse inserite si debbon avere in conto di vere e sopranaturali profezie' (op. cit., p. 182). It is fascinating

[1] G. Tiraboschi, *Storia della Letteratura Italiana* (Milan, 1823), iv. 170–86.
[2] Ibid., p. 184.

to observe this early modern scholar seeking to establish genuine criteria of critical scholarship in a subject so long bedevilled with controversy, yet still posing the question of Joachim's reputation in the medieval terms of whether or no he was a true prophet.

With the application of modern historical criticism to the canon of Joachim's works in the second half of the nineteenth century and the gradual establishment of a reasonably clear line between genuine and spurious writings, the question of true or false prophet disposes of itself. Thus the Joachimist battleground has finally moved away from the subject which had for so long engaged the emotions of those who fought over Joachim's reputation. But the question of heresy remains, and recently we have seen that this can yet touch off a lively debate.

The charge of heresy is today still levelled against Joachim on the two counts of his doctrine of the Trinity and his doctrine of the third *status* which flows from it. On the first A. Crocco says that the work condemned in 1215 'costituisce ancor oggi per molti come l'irremovibile pietra di scandalo della dottrina di Gioacchino'.[1] Early in this century P. Fournier judged Joachim to have fallen into the error of Tritheism,[2] and on varying grounds a similar verdict of heresy has been given by the German scholar Huck and by Ottaviano in Italy.[3] Against these the modern defence has followed several lines. F. Foberti, taking his stand, like Papebroch, on the discrepancy between what he claims as the orthodoxy of the *Psalterium* and the condemned views in the *libellus* against Peter Lombard, has resurrected the hypothesis that the latter was a fabrication of the Cistercians to blacken Joachim's name.[4] This can hardly stand. There is not a shred of evidence, and the 'proof' which earlier writers found in the supposed prophecies of the *Super Hieremiam* is now seen to be neither prophecy nor proof. Moreover, the point so long made by defenders of Joachim that because the doctrine of the *Psalterium* is orthodox it is difficult to account for Joachim's writing of the *libellus* has been undermined by the work of Dr. Hirsch-Reich, who has shown that, in so far as we can reconstruct the viewpoint of the *libellus*, it is all of a piece with the

---

[1] Crocco, *Gioacchino*, p. 54.

[2] P. Fournier, *Études sur Joachim de Flore et ses doctrines* (Paris, Picard, 1909), pp. 15–16.

[3] Huck, *Joachim v. Floris*, p. 236. Ottaviano, *Lib. contra Lombardum*, pp. 58–61. Grundmann, however, in effect rebuts the charge of heresy (*Studien*, p. 112).

[4] Foberti, *Gioacchino* I, pp. 82 seq.

exposition in the *Psalterium*.[1] This leads on to a new line of defence which, briefly put, runs thus: the point at issue between Joachim and Peter Lombard was one upon which the Church long hesitated; in the Third Lateran Council there was even a suggestion of condemning the Lombard's view; Joachim developed this anti-Lombard view strongly, both in the *libellus* and in the *Psalterium*, but after the elevation of Innocent III—once a student at Paris—to the papacy, the pendulum swung heavily the other way, and so, by a narrow margin, it as Joachim's view which finally received condemnation. Thus the 'heresy' arises from an emphasis which Joachim makes in the heat of combat and which is misunderstood at a point where the line between orthodoxy and heresy is extremely fine.[2] This defence leads on to Buonaiuti's extreme view that the Fourth Lateran Council came down on the wrong side and supported the less orthodox doctrine.[3] This is not a judgement likely to find favour among other Italian historians. Far more typical is F. Russo, who accepts that Joachim wrote the *libellus* and that it was heretical, but argues that his error 'è puramente materiale, non essendoci nè ribellione all'insegnamento della Chiesa nè pertinacia nell'errore'.[4] Thus, in spite of the condemnation, Joachim remains for his Italian defenders 'uomo cattolico'. Perhaps the most searching examination of the problem has been made by Crocco. In an article in 1957 he gave a detailed exposition of Joachim's Trinitarian theology in which he characterized the concept of Unity as 'non come sostanza unipersonale, ma tripersonale', and the distinction of Persons thus: 'L'indivisibilità, o insecessibilità, non implica indistinzione delle Persone, che sussistono indivise e distinte nelle rispettive proprietà.'[5] In his later book he sums up his judgement thus:

Per valutare con esattezza ed obiettività la posizione uni-trinitaria di Gioacchino, occorre distinguere fra la sua professione di fede e le sue formulazioni teologico-concettuali. La sua professione di fede è pienamente conforme all'ortodossia, ma la spiegazione teologico-concettuale, che egli tenta di dare dei termini del dogma, non è del tutto adeguata alla sua fede.

[1] Reeves, Hirsch-Reich, *Studies*, pp. 215–18.

[2] Ibid., pp. 218–19.

[3] Buonaiuti, *Religio*, xii (1936), pp. 71–4; *Scritti minori*, pp. xlvi seq. See also *Gioacchino da Fiore*, pp. 215 seq.

[4] Russo, *Gioacchino*, p. 31.

[5] A. Crocco, 'La teologia trinitaria di Gioacchino da Fiore', *Sophia* xxv (1957), pp. 226, 231. See bibliography, no. 5.15, for a new view on Innocent's part.

Ma da questo a classificare Gioacchino come un eretico 'triteista' c'è evidentemente un abisso. (*Gioacchino*, p. 129.)

The issue of whether Joachim was heretical in his concept of the third *status* is debated on a different plane. Here is no question of technical intellectual formulation and the degree of precision required to walk the knife-edge between charges of quaternity and tritheism. What is under scrutiny is rather the nature of a hope concerning the future of history, and the question is whether the optimism engendered thereby swept Joachim into proclaiming what the Italians call 'una terza economia'. Of course the one doctrine springs from the other, but in the concept of the third *status* emotions springing from a mystically apprehended faith became crystallized into a faith which was a basis for action. As we have seen, although the implicit danger was only slowly realized, once the point had been grasped that the Joachimist hope provided a dangerously revolutionary basis for action, the doctrine of the third *status* was attacked far more energetically than Joachim's formulation on the Trinity. Today, of course, the distinction between what Joachim taught and what certain crazy Joachites proclaimed is well taken; thus we no longer consider seriously the accusation that Joachim expected a third Testament to supersede the first two. Nevertheless, the debate on whether Joachim's doctrine at this point does in fact constitute heresy still continues.

The main issue is whether Joachim expected his third *status* to supersede the second in such a way as to undermine the once-for-all character of the revelation of Christ and to substitute a more spiritual authority for that of the Church as He founded it. All modern scholars discussing this question emphasize the difficulty of deciding precisely what Joachim expected, since in the moments of eloquent, sometimes lyrical, writing he could throw off extreme phrases which are contradicted in other passages. Disagreement is therefore natural. On the one hand stand the Germans, Dempf, Grundmann, Benz, and, to a certain extent, Huck, together with the Italian Buonaiuti, maintaining that Joachim envisaged an *Ecclesia Spiritualis* without clergy or sacraments, although possibly not without an 'Angelic Pope'.[1] On the other side, Joachim's eager band of Italian champions rush to the defence.

---

[1] Grundmann, *Studien*, pp. 112 seq.; A. Dempf, *Sacrum Imperium* (Munich and Berlin, 1929), pp. 280 seq.; E. Benz, *Ricerche religiose*, viii (1932), p. 238; Buonaiuti, *Gioacchino da Fiore*, pp. 239 seq.; Huck, *Joachim v. Floris*, p. 236.

'Ammettere una terza economia', writes Russo, '—quella della Spirito Santo—è evidentemente contro il senso della Chiesa che non conosce altro che l'economia del Vecchio e del Nuovo Testamento. Ma il pensiero di Gioacchino non può essere interpretato nel senso che una terza economia . . . debba sostituirsi a quella del Figlio o del Nuovo Testamento' (*Misc. Franc.* xli. 334). But here the defence divides sharply over the *Liber Figurarum*, for whereas Tondelli, asserting its genuine character, uses it to show that Joachim never envisaged a third age without clergy or sacraments,[1] Russo and Foberti, finding unorthodox elements in it, use their assumption of Joachim's orthodoxy to argue for the spurious character of the *Liber Figurarum*![2]

Tondelli's defence of Joachim's orthodox intention is a weighty one and it has lately been reinforced by Crocco, who also accepts the genuineness of the *Liber Figurarum*.[3] Both use this to good effect, and Tondelli also draws on another recently edited tract of Joachim's, the *De Articulis Fidei*, to show Joachim's orthodoxy on the sacraments. Two important points may be picked out from his general defence: first, that Joachim's allocation of each *status* to a specific Person of the Trinity '*proprietate mysterii*' does not mean that the other Persons are absent from that *status*;[4] second, that Joachim's whole attitude towards the Papacy embodies a sense of continuity even in the midst of transformation: 'Sono elementi fondamentali, che dànno un significato spirituale di continuità alla trasfigurazione profonda che Gioachino attendeva nella Chiesa per il terzo stato del mondo.'[5] Yet a question-mark clearly remains in the minds of some, Professor Bloomfield, for instance,[6] and Cardinal de Lubac. The latter weighs all the differing views with great care, but, while unwilling to commit himself too far, he seems to feel that Joachim's expected *renovatio* does constitute a revolution in which the Papacy and the whole hierarchy disappear. Reluctantly he concludes: 'Joachim a

---

[1] Tondelli, *Lib. Fig.* I, pp. 156 seq.   [2] Russo, *Misc. Franc.* xli. 334 seq.
[3] Crocco, *Gioacchino*, p. 47.
[4] Tondelli, *Lib. Fig.* I, p. 159: 'Ma una caratteristica non va scambiata con una esclusione degli altri elementi.' Cf. Crocco, *Gioacchino*, 80–1: 'Gioacchino nell'attribuire a ciascuna delle Persone una fase peculiare nel suo disegno di teologia della storia, indica con assoluta precisione teologica il fondamento di tale attribuzione, cioè la "proprietas" personale, e protesta inoltre esplicitamente di non voler in alcun modo scindere l'unità divina. In ciascuno dei tre "stati" la Trinità opera *unitariamente*: e l'attribuzione dei singoli "stati" alle singole Persone non è altro che *un'applicazione, sul piano storico e cronologico, delle "appropriazioni"* divine.'
[5] Tondelli, *Lib. Fig.* I, pp. 164–5.   [6] Bloomfield, *Traditio* xiii, p. 267.

compromis dans ses explications—sans le vouloir, il le semble bien
—la pleine suffisance de Jésus Christ.'[1]

To reach a conclusion on this age-long debate requires close
examination of the subtle nuances in Joachim's often complex and
sometimes apparently contradictory expositions. Out of a mass of
arguments on both sides, three points emerge as fundamental for
forming a judgement. First, it seems clear that Joachim throughout
used the double pattern of concordances in twos as well as in threes;
from this it follows that he did not waver from belief in two historical
dispensations, in two Testaments, in two 'churches' (the Synagogue
and the Church of Christ). However he intended to relate his pattern of threes to that of twos, however he conceived of the *Spiritualis
Intelligentia* springing from the two Testaments and the *Ecclesia
Spiritualis* from the two Churches, the reality of the two dispensations remained, and therefore one cannot say that his third *status*
was to supersede or abrogate the regime of Christ. History for
Joachim still falls into two great divisions, closed respectively by the
First Advent of Christ and the Second: thus the Lordship of Christ
endures to and dominates the end of history.

But secondly, Joachim does speak under various figures of a
transition from the second to the third *status*, and more particularly
he uses the figure of the transition from the 'church' or the 'life'
designated in Peter to that designated in John in such a way as to
lead to the conclusion that something in the second *status* really
does pass away, leaving the life in John alone to endure to the end.
This is the most damaging point in relation to his orthodoxy, all the
more so because St. Peter in some passages clearly stands for the
Papacy. We shall examine Joachim's attitude towards the papacy in
greater detail at a later point,[2] but here we must note that Joachim's
terminology can only be understood in the context of the particular
juxtaposition he is making at the moment. Thus his statements on
the transitoriness of the life symbolized in Peter are always set in
juxtaposition to the life represented by John. Here—whether the

---

[1] H. de Lubac, *Exégèse mediévale, les quatres sens de l'Écriture*, 2 (1) (Paris, 1961),
p. 558. Altogether Lubac devotes over a hundred pages to Joachim (pp. 437–558) and in
his summing up he clearly expresses his sense of Joachim's greatness and attractiveness:
'Cet homme fut grand. . . . De ces rêves grandioses, tout n'était pourtant pas chimère.
Dans l'esprit tumultueux du prophète une haute vérité se cherchait, sans réussir à se
trouver. C'est pourquoi la figure de Joachim exerce un attrait fascinant. . . . On trouve
chez Joachim "dans le même fâcheux mélange, les plus graves erreurs et les plus per-
spicaces inspirations". Refuserons-nous absolument de l'entendre?' (pp. 555–7).

[2] *Infra*, pp. 395–7.

word *ecclesia* or *vita* is used—Joachim is surely thinking in terms of two ways of life, not two institutions. The coupling of Peter and John determines the meaning. In contrast to these passages, we must set certain others in which *successor Petri* or *Ecclesia Petri* stands alone, like a monument, transformed but immovable, through the great transition: here Joachim is expressing his unshakeable fidelity to the great institution which is to him the one Church, true through all time.[1] It is the *significatum Petri* as embodying the spiritual life of the second *status* that alone passes away, not the institution which Christ founded upon the rock of St. Peter. The 'pattern of twos' remains unimpaired at this point.

Thirdly, there is the question of whether Joachim really looked forward to the achievement of human perfection in the third *status*, that is, within history. In spite of his great lyrical outbursts on the glories of the Age of the Spirit, he does not fail to remember its finitude: as the Seventh Day it is held distinct from the Eighth Day of Eternity; like the other *status*, it too will end in a tribulation; there are indications, albeit not very clear ones, that a decline in virtue must be expected at the end even of the third *status*.[2] Joachim's optimistic expectation in history did not lead him into the error of belief in the perfectibility of Man within this mortal life.

By a rather narrow margin we reach the conclusion that in intention and in the broad outline of his conception Joachim was faithful to the orthodoxy of the Latin Church as he understood it. Mgr. Tondelli has stressed the fact that Joachim was an exegete rather than a theologian;[3] thus his exegesis in detail could carry him into statements which were theologically compromising without sufficient awareness of the danger. Perhaps one might go further and say that in some respects he was a poet rather than a theologian—a poet of the meaning of history. His intention was entirely faithful to the Church, but when his imagination took eagle's wings it swept him far, and sometimes beyond the bounds.

[1] See *Lib. Conc.*, ff. 95ᵛ, 122ᵛ, 132ᵛ; *Quat. Evang.*, p. 86. Cf. Crocco, *Gioacchino*, pp. 94–6.

[2] See *Lib. Conc.*, ff. 52ʳ, 56ʳ⁻ᵛ; *Expos.*, ff. 212ʳ–214ʳ; also 9ʳ–11ʳ, 24ᵛ, 207ʳ; *Vita S. Benedicti*, pp. 63 seq., 67, 69; *Lib. Fig.* II, p. 75. On the Eighth Day, as distinguished from the Seventh, see *Lib. Conc.*, ff. 37ʳ, 132ᵛ; *Expos.*, ff. 110ᵛ–113ᵛ; *Vita S. Benedicti*, pp. 50–1, 71; *Quat. Evang.*, pp. 6, 29, 57, 308; *Lib. Fig.* II, p. 75.

[3] Tondelli, *Lib. Fig.* I, pp. 149 (n. 2), 151.

PART TWO

NEW SPIRITUAL MEN

———

I

THE AGE OF THE CONTEMPLATIVES

A PROPHET foretells the future: he can also create it. For the historian the history of prophecy contains the delicate problem of the interplay between word and action. Are prophecies fulfilled because of their far-seeing diagnosis or because of the response they evoke in action? The historical significance of Joachim lies in the dynamic quality of certain key ideas which he proclaimed. They worked underground in the following centuries, from time to time springing to new life in a group or an individual. Their vital quality arose from the fact that they worked in the imagination, moving to hope and so to action; thus their impact was emotional rather than intellectual. As the leaven acted, Joachim's conceptions become debased, but in so far as his ideas stirred the expectations of men, we can legitimately call these movements Joachimist. In this sense many expressions of religious hopes and fears for the future can be called Joachimist in inspiration right down to the sixteenth century. This can be shown by tracing the history of certain themes in the tradition of Last Things. Here one of Joachim's key ideas was the expectation of new orders of spiritual men sent 'ad vesperum huius seculi', that is, in 'fine huius sexte etatis'.[1] From the thirteenth to the sixteenth century, and even beyond, there were those who fastened on this conception of future spiritual orders and found in it the understanding of their own mission in the world. In this chapter we shall study some manifestations of this idea, but first we must analyse the conception in Joachim's own writings.

The Abbot's famous three *status* of mankind were characterized by three orders of men. He states this at the outset of the *Liber Concordie*: 'Secundum quod tres status seculi mutationes temporum operumque testantur, licet totum hoc presens seculum unum esse dicatur: ita tres esse ordines electorum, licet unus sit Dei populus . . . Et eorum quidem ordinum primus coniugatorum est: secundus clericorum: tertius monachorum' (*Lib. Conc.*, f. 8ᵛ). These reflect the three persons of the Trinity:

[1] *Lib. Conc.*, f. 76ᵛ.

Habet ergo coniugatorum ordo imaginem Patris: quia sicut Pater ideo
Pater est quia habet Filium, ita ordo coniugatorum non nisi ad procrean-
dos filios institutus est a Deo. . . . Habet et clericorum ordo imaginem
Filii qui Verbum Patris, quia ad hoc constitutus est ipse, ut loquatur et
doceat populum viam Domini, et ostendat ei continue legitima Dei sui.
Habet et monachorum ordo imaginem Spiritus Sancti qui est amor Dei,
quia non posset ordo ipse despicere mundum et ea que sunt mundi nisi
provocatus amore Dei et tractus ab eodem spiritu qui expulit Dominum in
desertum: unde spiritualis dictus est, quia non secundum carnem ambu-
lat sed secundum spiritum. (*Lib. Conc.*, f. 9ᵛ.)

Their characteristics follow: 'Et scimus quod primus ordo qui
institutus est primo, vocatus est ad laborem legalium preceptorum:
secundus qui institutus est secundo, vocatus est ad laborem passionis: tertius qui procedit ex utroque, electus est ad libertatem
contemplationis, scriptura attestante que ait: Ubi Spiritus Domini,
ibi libertas' (*Lib. Conc.*, f. 20ʳ). Each arises, develops, and fructifies
within a given period of history, the second and third orders overlapping with the previous one in their initial stage: 'Coniugatorum
ordo initiatus ab Adam, fructificare cepit ab Habraam. Clericorum
ordo initiatus est ab Ozia. . . . Fructificavit autem a Christo qui
verus est rex et sacerdos. Monachorum ordo . . . incepit a beato
Benedicto, viro utique claro miraculis, opere et sanctitate, cuius
fructificatio in temporibus finis' (*Lib. Conc.*, f. 8ᵛ).

This pattern of threes, laid down so clearly in the early chapters of
the *Liber Concordie*, is, as we have seen, one of the two fundamental
patterns upon which Joachim built up his system of thought.¹ The
three orders recur many times in the *Liber Concordie*, where the
Abbot's mind is playing almost equally on the 'twos' and 'threes'.²
In the *Expositio in Apocalypsim*, where attention is concentrated
mainly on the double pattern of Seven Seals and their Openings, the
three orders are mentioned infrequently.³ In the *Psalterium Decem
Chordarum* Joachim returns, with his contemplation of the Trinity,
to the pattern of threes, devoting a whole section to the three orders
and giving us a fine interpretation of their characteristic works: since
the Father creates, the Son teaches, and the Holy Spirit exults, the
primary works of the orders belonging to them are *operatio, doctrina*,
and *jubilatio*.⁴ It is interesting that the *Liber Figurarum*, built up on

¹ *Supra*, pp. 18–20.
² e.g. *Lib. Conc.*, ff. 8ᵛ, 9ᵛ, 10ʳ, 20ʳ, 33ʳ, 56ᵛ, 70ᵛ, 83ʳ, 96ᵛ, 112ʳ.
³ e.g. *Expos.*, ff. 18ᵛ, 37ᵛ, 141ʳ, 147ʳ⁻ᵛ.
⁴ *Psalt.*, ff. 224ᵛ–247ᵛ. See also ff. 249ʳ⁻ᵛ, 250ʳ–256ʳ, 266ᵛ, 277ᵛ–278ʳ.

a subtle combination of the 'twos' and 'threes', embodies the three orders only once—in the three sides of the Psaltery itself,[1] so poetically interpreted for us in the treatise. The *Super Quatuor Evangelia* has the three *status* much in mind and gives us some further symbols of the three orders: they are the fir tree, the pine tree, and the box, which together are the glory of Lebanon;[2] they are the sparrow, pigeon, and turtle-dove offered at the Purification in the Temple;[3] they express, in the first *status*, the maturity of the old, in the second, the patience of young men, in the third, the sincerity of boys.[4] In his *De Vita S. Benedicti et De Officio Divino secundum eius doctrinam* Joachim again speaks of the three 'works': '. . . operando, legendo, psallendo, quorum primum proprie laycorum est, secundum clericorum, tertium monachorum'.[5]

The order which characterizes the third *status* is a constant theme in the Abbot's writing. It is elusive, for all that, since Joachim did not attempt a specific description of the third order. Its general character, however, appears in its many designations. Besides the frequent *ordo monachorum*, Joachim speaks of the *ordo* or *ecclesia contemplantium* or *quiescentium*,[6] always in contrast to the life of activity and labour, and sometimes of the *ecclesia spiritualis* or *populus ille spiritualis*.[7] It is typified in Joseph in the Old Testament and S. John the Evangelist in the New, and because these represent the Holy Spirit, it is a sevenfold order.[8] It is found also in Sarah and Mary, contrasted with Hagar and Elizabeth.[9] It is the Virgin Church 'que nescit virum, que requiescit in silentio heremi'.[10] According to the Trinitarian structure of history the third order must have a double origin, proceeding from the two previous orders. Using his

---

[1] *Lib. Fig.*, Pl. XIII.

[2] *Quat. Evang.*, p. 76. See Isa. 60: 13: 'The glory of Lebanon shall come unto thee, the fir tree, the pine tree, and the box tree together to beautify the place of my sanctuary.' Joachim interprets the box as the laity, the fir as the clergy, and the pine as the order of monks.

[3] *Quat. Evang.*, p. 84; cf. Luke 2: 24. The sparrow signifies married men, the pigeon clergy, the turtle-dove monks.

[4] *Quat. Evang.*, p. 92. See also pp. 20–5, 84–5, 91–2, 155. For a passage with the reverse symbolism of the laity as children, the clergy as young men, and monks as old men see *Psalt.*, f. 246ʳ.

[5] *Vita S. Benedicti*, 77.

[6] *Lib. Conc.*, ff. 67ʳ, 83ʳ 83ᵛ, 85ᵛ, 96ᵛ, *Expos.*, ff. 53ᵛ, 141ᵛ, 156ʳ.

[7] *Lib. Conc.*, ff. 58ᵛ, 61ʳ, 70ᵛ, 85ᵛ, 96ʳ; *Expos.*, ff. 49ʳ, 82ᵛ.

[8] *Expos.*, ff. 22ʳ, 48ʳ, 93ᵛ, 204ᵛ.

[9] *Lib. Conc.*, f. 61ʳ; *Expos.*, f. 83ʳ.

[10] *Expos.*, f. 83ʳ.

calculations by generations, Joachim finds its first seed in Elijah, Elisha, and the sons of the prophets, and its second in St. Benedict, who assumes a crucial role in the germination and growth of the third order: 'incepit a beato Benedicto, viro utique claro miraculis, opere et sanctitate, cuius fructificatio in temporibus finis.' Indeed, in the initiation of the third *status* and the third order, Joachim almost endows St. Benedict with the messianic significance which later the Spirituals recognized in St. Francis. The Rule of St. Benedict was not to Joachim a third Testament, but it was an instrument of the Holy Ghost, and his tract on the *Vita et Regula S. Benedicti* was essentially an exposition of its significance in the third *status*.[1]

When he tries to delineate the third order more closely Joachim is driven to poetic metaphor: its likeness must be sought in 'illa suavissima et speciosissima columba',[2] in the birds that fly upwards to the heavens,[3] in the clarity of the sun,[4] in all the metaphors of his famous and oft-quoted passage on the sequence of threes.[5] Its marks are liberty and spiritual understanding.[6] This does not mean that it is free from the authority of the two Testaments, but that to it is entrusted the glorious treasure of spiritual intelligence which proceeds from both.[7] So the spiritual men will still feed joyfully in the pastures of the Scriptures,[8] until in the silence of contemplation, the illumination of spiritual understanding, and the jubilation of psalmody[9] the third order will find its life. Although obviously Joachim upheld a strict adherence to the monastic rule, only once does he emphasize poverty as a special characteristic of the third order.[10]

There is one important question to which Joachim never gives a clear answer. What part is to be played in the third *status* by the orders pertaining to the two previous ages? The answer might contain the seeds of a dangerous revolution against the established hierarchy. Some of the Abbot's pronouncements appear uncompromisingly revolutionary:

[1] *Lib. Conc.*, ff. 8ᵛ, 10ʳ, 20ʳ, 23ʳ, 48ʳ, 57ᵛ, 67ʳ, 82ʳ–84ᵛ; *Expos.*, f. 82ᵛ. See E. Benz, 'La messianità di San Benedetto', *Ricerche religiose*, vii (1931), pp. 336–53.

[2] *Expos.*, f. 95ᵛ. See also *Lib. Conc.*, f. 83ᵛ: 'suavitas vite contemplative'.

[3] Ibid., f. 68ᵛ.   [4] Ibid., ff. 66ᵛ, 68ʳ.

[5] Ibid., f. 112ʳ⁻ᵛ.   [6] Ibid., f. 95ᵛ.

[7] Ibid., ff. 9ʳ, 10ʳ, 103ᵛ; *Expos.*, ff. 86ᵛ, 99ʳ, 128ᵛ.

[8] *Lib. Conc.*, f. 133ʳ: 'Gaudium ergo onagrorum sunt pascua gregum donec effundatur super nos spiritus de excelso. Quia tamdiu viri spirituales qui designantur in onagris gaudent in pascuis scripturarum, quamdiu abundantiam illam spiritus non habent.' Cf. Isa. 32: 14, 15.

[9] *Expos.*, ff. 84ʳ–86ᵛ.   [10] *Lib. Conc.*, f. 67ʳ.

Sicut ordo conjugatorum initiatus ab Adam, fructificavit ab Abraam . . . consumatus est in Christo. . . . Et ordo clericorum initiatus ab Ozia, fructificavit a Christo et consumabitur ut putamus circa finem generationis 42ᵉ ab incarnatione Domini. Consumabitur dico secundum id quod pertinet ad verbum Domini dicentis Petro, Sequere Me, circa finem generationis 42ᵉ ab incarnatione dominica. Ita ordo monasticus accipiens ut iam dixi initium secundum regulam monasticam quam Latini utuntur a beato Benedicto tempus fructificandi generatione 20ᵃ ab eodem sancto viro. Cuius consumatio in consumatione seculi est. (*Lib Conc.*, f. 57ʳ.)

This dangerous idea of the order of clergy passing away before that of contemplatives springs from the symbolism of Peter and John: Peter who enters the Sepulchre first, Peter whose death is foretold by the Lord, typifies the *ordo clericorum*, whilst John who arrives first but enters last into the Sepulchre, John who is told to tarry till the Lord's coming, is the *ordo monachorum*, enduring until the end of time.[1] He repeatedly emphasizes this in the *Expositio in Apocalypsim*, in such words as these: 'Primus ergo duorum (ordinum) patietur cum Petro. . . . Secundus relinquetur cum Joanne ad predicandum Evangelium Regni. . . . De hac serotina predicatione quam facturus est ordo ille quem designat Joannes, consumato iam pene illo ordine quem significat Petrus . . .' (f. 142ʳ⁻ᵛ). Here a later scribe, picking at once on the exciting idea, has directed attention to it by the marginal note (twice repeated in the printed edition): 'Clerus consumabitur.'

Yet Joachim's conception is so much more subtle than that of a revolutionary fanatic. When the 'populus tertii status qui erit spiritalis et sapiens, pacificus, amabilis, contemplativus' comes to domination, the Roman pontiffs, typified in Joseph and Solomon, will still rule from shore to shore.[2] The *ecclesia contemplantium* will have its prelates.[3] The *ordo contemplantium* itself is not, as one might suppose, narrowed to the hermits who practise what is, for Joachim, the supreme way of life: it is a many-divisioned order;[4] it includes the sun, moon, and stars, i.e. anchorites, cenobites, and monks living in separate cells;[5] it contains many mansions designed for different types;[6] it is sevenfold, according to the seven gifts of the Holy Spirit.[7] Joachim's is no esoteric sect: even the *ecclesia*

[1] *Expos.*, ff. 141ᵛ–143ʳ; also ff. 47ʳ, 77ʳ, 83ʳ, 93ᵛ, 204ᵛ; *Lib. Conc.*, f. 18ʳ. Cf. John 20: 4–8; 21: 18–21.

[2] *Lib. Conc.*, ff. 95ʳ–96ᵛ; *Expos.*, ff. 48ʳ, 93ᵛ.   [3] *Lib. Conc.*, ff. 57ᵛ seq.

[4] Ibid., f. 57ᵛ.   [5] Ibid., ff. 66ᵛ–67ʳ.

[6] Ibid., f. 71ᵛ.   [7] *Expos.*, ff. 22ʳ, 48ʳ.

laycorum has its place in the divine scheme,[1] and his concern is to bring all men into the new religious life. There is no precise statement about the structure of society in the third *status*, but form and authority there will be, and religious life will be many-sided. This is most strikingly embodied in one of the figures of the *Liber Figurarum*—the 'Dispositio Novi Ordinis pertinens ad tercium statum ad instar superne Ierusalem'.[2] The geometrically-designed 'ground-plan' of the new society is built up on that mystical equation $5+7 = 12$ which, as we have seen, embodies the transition to the third *status*.[3] The four Animals of the Gospels, *Leo*, *Vitulus*, *Homo*, *Aquila*, symbolizing the four traditional orders of Apostles, Martyrs, Doctors, Virgins, together with the *Sedes Dei* (*Columba*) in the midst,[4] form the five main 'oratories' of the design, to each of which one of the five senses is allotted. But to these are added—at carefully specified distances—the oratories of prophets and patriarchs respectively, thus transforming the five into a seven to which the seven gifts of the Spirit can be assigned, balancing the senses. This sevenfold figure gives Joachim the sevenfold form of his *novus ordo*, five divisions of which belong to the monastic life, the sixth to the clergy, and the seventh to married men. It is true that only the five lie truly within the City, while the other two are situated in the 'suburbs', yet it is striking that the clergy and laity are needed to complete the mystical seven belonging to the third *status*, and the symbolism of this figure seems to prove conclusively that all the previous orders of history were to be subsumed into the final one. Indeed, Joachim's sketch, in the two lowest oratories, of a spiritualized order of clergy and one of married men suggests a sympathy with contemporary experiments in these directions which one might not expect from a contemplative.

Thus a most interesting aspect of the Abbot's thought is his concern for the general body of Christian people. Here is no esoteric mystic who locks up the spiritual future within a select group while the masses perish. Sometimes he even visualizes the conversion of *all* peoples, including the Jews, to a new spiritual intelligence.[5] A transition period is therefore necessary during which there will be a great preaching as well as the greatest conflict with Antichrist.

---

[1] *Lib. Conc.*, f. 100ʳ.   [2] *Lib. Fig.*, Pl. XII.   [3] *Supra*, pp. 25–6.
[4] Cf. the many references to the four *Animalia* and the *Sedes Dei* in the works, of which the following are most relevant to the figure: *Lib. Conc.*, ff. 25ᵛ–26ʳ; *Expos.*, ff. 50ʳ, 107ʳ, 111ʳ, 189ᵛ; *Psalt.*, ff. 247ᵛ seq.   [5] *Lib. Conc.*, f. 85ᵛ.

The agents thus to bring the Church through the desert and across Jordan into the Promised Land are the *viri spirituales*.[1] This is a designation constantly used by Joachim, sometimes to denote the contemplatives of the third *status* in general, but more often to describe the agents of God active in bringing the world through the great transition stage. Here the emphasis is on their function as preachers. They are the *predicatores veritatis*[2] sent to lay bare hidden mysteries through spiritual intelligence,[3] and to sound the Word of God throughout the world with the solemn voice of the Seventh Trumpet.[4] Once Joachim speaks of a great individual preacher,[5] once of three great preachers,[6] and several times of twelve, typified in the twelve patriarchs and apostles,[7] but more often he seems to have in mind preaching orders.

Here we meet a problem which was present with Joachim all his life. He was a mystic to whom the supreme life was to be found only in the silence of contemplation, yet he was always aware of the needs of the people at the mountain-foot: the hermit must agonize over the sins of men;[8] there must be a mediating body between those at the top and those at the bottom, and for 'animal men', who could not bear the blazing sunlight of the full hermit life, there must be the gentler moonlight of an active order by which to teach them.[9] This great problem of the relation between the life of contemplation and that of evangelical preaching can be traced in Joachim's life and runs throughout his writings. How could the contemplative rise towards God without heeding the perils of men? Yet, if the solitude were exchanged for the crowd, how could the vision fail to be obscured in the dusty whirl of happenings? He expresses the inherent contradiction between the two duties thus: 'Quia et proprium est monachorum continere se per silentium in quiete contemplationis, ut audiat quid loquatur in se Dominus Deus. Et proprium clericorum loqui in medio populi verba Dei' (*Lib. Conc.*, f. 93ʳ). Yet the *ordo monachorum* bears responsibility for all: it must be like the columns of the Temple, high and lifted up towards heavenly things, yet bearing the roof of the whole Temple, beneath which it gathers

---

[1] *Lib. Conc.*., ff. 16ᵛ, 19ʳ, 21ᵛ, 67ʳ–68ᵛ, 76ʳ–78ᵛ, 83ᵛ, 85ᵛ, 88ᵛ–90ʳ, 103ᵛ, 115ᵛ, 133ᵛ; *Expos.*, ff. 49ʳ, 64ʳ⁻ᵛ, 75ʳ, 84ʳ, 128ᵛ, 137ʳ, 184ᵛ–187ʳ, 196ʳ, 209ʳ, 217ᵛ, 222ʳ.

[2] *Lib. Conc.*, ff. 76ʳ, 78ᵛ, 80ᵛ, 88ᵛ, 117ʳ; *Expos.*, ff. 137ʳ, 147ᵛ.

[3] Ibid., f. 222ʳ.   [4] Ibid., f. 152ʳ.

[5] Ibid., f. 137ʳ.   [6] Ibid., f. 147ᵛ.

[7] *Lib. Conc.*, ff. 21ᵛ–22ʳ, 57ᵛ, 102ʳ, 113ᵛ; *Expos.*, f. 103ʳ.

[8] Ibid., f. 185ᵛ.   [9] *Lib. Conc.*, f. 68ʳ.

laity and clergy.[1] Upon the spiritual men, therefore, is laid the heavy responsibility of mediation. They must be able to intercede for souls, like Abraham for Sodom;[2] like Moses, remaining on the mountain of contemplation, they must know how to deliver to Aaron the word for the people;[3] like Elijah they must call down rain upon thirsty souls.[4] The spiritual men will be called to descend from the contemplative to the active life,[5] to maintain a life of ascending and descending,[6] to labour before they attain the rest pertaining to them.[7]

Joachim's famous prophecies of two new orders must be seen as his solution to this problem of mediation. They are conceived as great evangelistic agents whose task lies in the sixth age and who, although already embodying the new life, must be distinguished from the general order of contemplatives pertaining to the third *status* or seventh age. Later these prophecies became so inextricably associated with the two great Mendicant Orders that they were popularly supposed to refer to two parallel orders. From Joachim's writings, however, it is clear that his original conception was of two bodies of men fulfilling different functions: one to lead a hermit life, praying for the world and gathering vision for its need upon the mountain-top; the other an active preaching order to carry the vision downwards, following an intermediary way of life, contemplative in comparison with the world's, active as against the hermit's.

He finds these two orders in many Scriptural symbols. Two angels were sent to lead Lot and his family from the destruction of Sodom; two prophets in the days of Zacharias (i.e. John Baptist and Christ, 'licet dissimiliter magni') saved the faithful remnant from the Hebrew synagogue; in the last days the elect remnant must be led forth by two prophets from the synagogue of Satan.[8] Again, the angels sent to Sodom are equated with Moses and Elijah, and both typify 'duo . . . genera spiritualium virorum qui mittuntur a Domino predicare in mundum, unum quod sicut Moyses populo spirituali preest simpliciter in deserto, aliud quod quasi Helias vitam solitariam seorsum a conventibus ducit'.[9] Elsewhere it is Elijah and Elisha who represent the two types of order: 'quia post viros illos spirituales qui sequentes vitam Helie noctis consortia nescierunt, dati sunt alii viri sancti imitatores Helisei, qui incedentes inter

---

[1] *Expos.*, f. 85ᵛ.
[2] *Lib. Conc.*, f. 76ʳ.
[3] Ibid., f. 93ʳ.
[4] Ibid., f. 103ᵛ.
[5] *Expos.*, f. 137ʳ.
[6] *Lib. Conc.*, f. 68ʳ.
[7] Ibid., f. 83ᵛ.
[8] Ibid., f. 24ᵛ.
[9] Ibid., f. 76ᵛ.

utramque vitam et iustis prebuerunt sanctitatis regulam et pecca-
toribus ostenderunt bone actionis exempla.'[1] In the *Expositio* the
two orders designated in Moses and Elijah are distinguished as an
order of clergy and one of monks,[2] while in the *Liber Concordie*, at
one point, they are described as orders of clergy and laity, clearly
distinct from that of monks.[3] He finds them also in the two olive
trees of the prophet Zechariah[4] and in the raven and dove sent forth
by Noah.[5] In the thirteenth century this last became a famous symbol of the Friars Preacher and Minor; it is interesting, therefore, to
note that in this case Joachim does not work out the differences
between the two orders in terms of the two birds: 'omitto differentias
ordinum in quibus aut corvina rapacitas aut simplicitas columbina
notatur.'[6]

It is in the *Expositio*, as he meditates on the various angels of the
Apocalypse, that Joachim's prophecies of the new orders become
most explicit. His commentary on Ch. 14 contains the passages most
often quoted later, and at this point the margins of the 1527 edition
are thick with notes, such as: *Duo ordines. Ordo monachorum. Ordo
heremitarum.* Here Joachim sees his two orders most clearly typified—in the One like unto the Son of Man seated upon a white
cloud and in the angel who descends from the Temple in heaven[7]—
and here we must quote the most important passages in full:

Arbitramur tamen in eo qui visus est sedere supra nubem candidam et
esse similis filio hominis significari quendam ordinem iustorum cui datum
sit perfecte imitari vitam filii hominis et . . . habere nihilominus linguam
eruditam ad evangelizandum evangelium regni et colligendum in aream
Domini ultimam messionem. . . . Qui bene etiam supra nubem candidam
sedere describitur quia nubes quidem corporea res est, nec tamen gravis
et ponderosa, sicut terra, sed levis, et conversatio illius non erit ponderosa
et obscura, sed lucida et spiritualis. . . . Ita felices homines illius status
quia de rebus mundanis nihil cupient, velut in aere positi, super nubem
candidam requiescent. . . . Nunc videndum est de eo qui exivit de templo

---

[1] *Lib. Conc.*, f. 68ʳ. [2] *Expos.*, ff. 146ʳ–149ᵛ.

[3] *Lib. Conc.*, f. 80ʳ: 'Duo vero filii qui orti sunt ex eis [i.e. Leah and Jacob] duos novis-
simos ordines designare puto quorum unus erit laicorum, alius clericorum qui et ambo
regulariter vivent, non quidem secundum formam monache perfectionis, sed secundum
institutionem fidei Christiane, imo secundum regulam illam generalem actuum apostolorum . . .' This recalls the two lowest orders in the *Lib. Fig.*, Pl. XII; cf. *supra*, p. 140.

[4] *Lib. Conc.*, f. 124ʳ; *Expos.*, f. 148ᵛ. Cf. Zech. 4: 3.

[5] *Expos.*, f. 81ᵛ. [6] Ibid., f. 81ᵛ.

[7] Cf. Apocalypse 14: 14, 17. It is notable that as Joachim approaches this exposition
of the state of that Church 'que futura est in novissimo tempore', he expresses great
diffidence about his ability to interpret it; cf. *Expos.*, f. 175ʳ.

quod est in celo habens et ipse falcem acutam. . . . De templo quod est in celo: . . . quia vita illa que designatur in nube humilior est ea que designatur in celo, utique quia et aer medius est inter terram et celum. . . . Quamvis ille qui ascendet super nubem candidam contemplative vite insistat respectu eorum qui terrenis implicantur negociis, altioris tamen vite videtur esse ille qui egreditur de templo quod est in celo: quia alia est libertas magisterii et doctrine spiritualis designate in nube, alia libertas amoris contemplationis divine. Quocirca, ut in eo qui erat similis filii hominis aliquis ordo futurus perfectorum virorum servantium vitam Christi et apostolorum intelligendus est, ita in angelo qui egressus est de templo quod est in celo, aliquis ordo heremitarum emulantium vitam angelorum. . . . Et rursum iis qui filii hominis similis esse perhibetur continue manifestus apparet, hic autem de celo in quo manebit occultus, velut repente egressus est, quia hi qui militant Deo in humiliori perfectione ad utilitatem intuentium in conspectu electorum hominum dati sunt, quatenus ab eis accipiant salutis monita et pie conversationis et perfectionis exemplum; qui autem ut perfectius vivant remotiora petunt, si quando suggerente Spiritu egrediuntur ad homines veluti de archanis celorum advenisse putantur, adeo ut multorum corda hominum timore concutiant admirantium, seu vite perfectionem seu penitentie novitatem. . . . Surget enim ordo qui videtur novus et non est. Induti nigris vestibus et accincti desuper zona, hi crescent et fama eorum devulgabitur. Et predicabunt fidem quam et defendent usque ad mundi consumptionem in spiritu Helye. Qui erit ordo heremitarum emulantium vitam angelorum. Quorum vita erit quasi ignis ardens in amore et zelo Dei ad comburendum tribulos et spinas, hoc est, ad consumendum et extinguendum perniciosam vitam pravorum. . . . Puto enim quod in tempore illo vitam monachorum erit quasi imber ad irrigandum superficiem terre in omni perfectione et iustitia fraterne charitatis. Vita autem heremitarum erit quasi ignis ardens . . . Erit ergo ille ordo tanquam mitior et suavior ad colligendas segetes electorum Dei, velut in spiritu Moysi. Iste vero ferocior et ardentior ad colligendam vindemiam reproborum, ac si in spiritu Helye. (*Expositio*, ff. 175ᵛ–176ʳ.)

II

CLAIMANTS OF JOACHIM'S PROPHECY

THE Friars Preacher and Friars Minor appeared so aptly to fulfil Joachim's expectations of new spiritual orders that contemporaries at once acclaimed the miraculous foreknowledge of the Abbot. Why was Joachim able to gauge so well these developments in the next generation? Was this a case of diagnosis or response? Some historians have been tempted to try and trace a direct influence of Joachim upon St. Francis at least, but so far all attempts to prove that the latter was inspired by or even knew of the Abbot have failed. The answer must be diagnosis, and the clue probably lies in the relation between Joachim's thought and contemporary religious experiment. He was greatly concerned, as we have seen, both with the new quality of life belonging to the Age of the Spirit and with the orders of men to mediate the new spiritual intelligence to the world. The period in which he lived was characterized by a search for new forms of religious life, which included a desire to follow the vocation of the evangelical preacher. Thus the twelfth and early thirteenth centuries are full of religious experiments— orthodox and heretical: some reflect Joachim's sense of tension between the call to contemplation and the vocation of preaching; some embody his idea of religious orders of clergy and laity; all express dissatisfaction with existing forms of religious life.[1]

The Cistercian Order had, in part, met this need, but not wholly, since it went no further than a reformed Benedictinism. Joachim's own life and thought form part of this movement, for he sought to embody the new quality of religious life in his Order of Fiore, while proclaiming the need for preaching orders in his writings. But, so far as we can judge it, Joachim's order, like the Cistercian from which it sprang, was conservative: it took the shape of a reformed monasticism, the cenobitism to which Joachim only gave second place in his expectations. It is curious that the Abbot, so bold in

---

[1] H. Grundmann, *Religiöse Bewegungen im Mittelalter* (Hildesheim, 1961).

prophecy, was so timid in experiment. He appears never to have seen himself as an innovator nor his order as one of the new ones to revolutionize the future. Like Moses he only viewed the Promised Land afar off. As we shall see,[1] in certain enigmatic passages Joachim seems to foreshadow a great future for the Cistercian Order at an unspecified time, but immediately neither the Order of Fiore nor its greater parent met the need of the time. Joachim's prophecies still looked into the future, awaiting the new spiritual men. When the Orders of St. Dominic and St. Francis emerged in the early thirteenth century, they crystallized all these aspirations of the twelfth; in particular they expressed in definitive form the life of evangelical preaching. Thus they also gathered up Joachim's prophecies, embodying perfectly the mediating orders of Joachim's expectation. Moreover, the Franciscans possessed a mystical quality which made them apt for Joachim's description of spiritual men midway between the contemplative and the active life.

As we have seen, some of Joachim's ideas were circulating in the first half of the thirteenth century and, in spite of the 1215 condemnation, his reputation as a holy man with the gift of prophecy was established. It is significant that in the Bull canonizing St. Dominic Gregory IX coupled the Order of Fiore with the two Mendicant Orders and the Cistercian as the four pillars of the Church.[2] By the mid-thirteenth century Joachim's prophecies of two new orders of spiritual men were being appropriated by both Dominicans and Franciscans. In 1255 their two Generals, Humbert de Romanis and John of Parma, issued a joint encyclical.[3] This contains a striking expression of the idea of two orders sent to save the world 'novissime diebus istis in fine seculorum'. They are symbolized in a number of parallel twos: 'duo magna luminaria, duae tubae vere Moyses, duo Cherubim, duo ubera sponsae, duo filii olivae splendoris, duo testes Christi, illae duae stellae lucidae quae secundum Sybillinum vaticinium habent species quatuor animalium in diebus novissimis nomine Agni vociferantes in directione humilitatis et voluntarie paupertatis.' There is no direct reference to Joachim here, but the language suggests the influence of his characteristic imagery. All but the last are Biblical symbols,[4] of which Joachim uses all but the

[1] *Infra*, p. 155.
[2] *AS*, May, p. 125.
[3] Wadding *Annales*, iii. 380.
[4] Cf. Gen. 1: 16; Exod. 19: 16, 25: 18; S. of S. 4: 5; Zech. 4: 3; Apocalypse 11: 3–4.

second,[1] and it is noteworthy that the most unusual—the two olive trees from Zechariah—occurs both in the *Liber Concordie* and the *Expositio*. The last (*duae stellae lucidae*) is a direct quotation from the pseudo-Joachimist oracle of the *Sybil Erithrea*.[2] There are also echoes from Alexander of Bremen's commentary on the Apocalypse,[3] in which he quotes from the *Super Hieremiam*, where the theme of the two new orders is played many times, with variations, and where we see beyond doubt that the Mendicants were commonly held to fulfil Joachim's prophecy. Humbert de Romanis writes in the same vein in his *Legenda*:[4] 'Nos autem sumus in quos fines seculorum devenerunt. Missus est igitur hora cene, i.e. novissimis diebus, ordo novus. Novus, inquam, pariter et antiquus' (*MOPH* xvi. 369). In 1256 Gerard de Fracheto accepts the prophecy for the Dominicans in his official *Vitae Fratrum*,[5] recording the well-known story of how the monks of Fiore had come forth to hail the first-approaching Friars Preacher as those whom their master had foretold. On the Minorite side the chronicle of Erfurt gives us the first version of the famous story that the Abbot Joachim had drawn pictures of the future Franciscans and Dominicans.[6] The crop of spurious works which followed the *Super Hieremiam* provided corroboration,[7] and scribes began to identify the prophecies in their marginal captions.[8]

The idea thus disseminated was that Joachim had prophesied the appearance of two *parallel* orders which were symbolized in all the twos of Scripture: for example, the raven and dove, the two angels sent to Sodom, Moses and Aaron, Caleb and Joshua, two spies in Canaan, Esau and Jacob, Elijah and Elisha, Peter and John, the two on the Emmaus road, Martha and Mary, Paul and Barnabas, and the

[1] See, for example, *Lib. Conc.*, ff. 63ʳ⁻ᵛ, 18ʳ, 124ʳ, *Expos.*, f. 148ᵛ.

[2] *NA* xv. 165.

[3] Wachtel, *Expositio*, p. 437.

[4] *Legenda Humberti de Romanis*, *MOPH* xvi (1935), p. 369. One is tempted to find a direct echo of Joachim's prophecy in the description of the *ordo* as *novus et antiquus*; cf. passage quoted from Joachim's *Expositio*, *supra*, p. 144.

[5] *MOPH* i (1897), 13, quoted *supra*, p. 72.

[6] *MGHS* xxiv. 207, quoted *supra*, p. 72. See also *Flores Temporum*, *MGHS* xxiv. 239, quoted *supra*, p. 73.

[7] Cf. *Super Hier.*, ff. 12ᵛ seq.; *Super Esaiam*, ff. 7ʳ, 11ᵛ; *Sibyl Erithrea*, *NA* xv. 165; *De Oneribus*, Brit. Mus., MS. Royal & Kings, 8. F. xvi, ff. 39ᵛ, 42ᵛ, 43ʳ.

[8] e.g. MSS. Rome, Vat., Ross. 552, f. 6ᵛ; Lat. 3819, f. 134ʳ; Lat. 4860, ff. 24ᵛ, 272ᵛ; Bib. Corsini, 41. F. 2, f. 72ʳ; Florence, Bib. Laur., Plut. IX, dextr. xi, ff. 14ʳ, 17ᵛ, 31ᵛ, 34ʳ, 46ᵛ; Plut. VIII, dextr. x, f. 94ᵛ; Paris, Bib. Nat., Lat. 10453, f. 47ʳ; Lat. 2599, f. ccxlvᵛ.

two witnesses in the Apocalypse.[1] Joachim's original conception of an active and a contemplative order was lost and that of two active preaching orders substituted. The Mendicants were not, in general, concerned to understand Joachim's view of history or claim the role of his spiritual men; their desire was to appropriate a jewel of fame for the crown of their founders. Yet some caught the excitement of those cast for a decisive role in history. Even less temperamentally sympathetic Dominicans were somewhat infected. In the Franciscan Order, of course, there emerges about the middle of the century the group of Spirituals who plunge intensely into Joachim's expectations.

Apart from the Mendicants, there is one other quarter to which one might look for whole-hearted disciples of Joachim—Calabria. The evidence is slight, but there are signs of a circle of disciples in the Order of Fiore itself and in some Cistercian houses closely associated with it. In the first place we have the story of the scribe sent by the Archbishop of Cosenza to Curazzo (a Cistercian house) to transcribe the *Expositio*, who was terrified by the bogy of Peter Lombard and reassured by the apparition of Joachim himself.[2] In the second place, we can presuppose the gathering together of reminiscences and legends concerning their master into a collection which has come down to us through the sixteenth-century Tutini

---

[1] Raven and Dove: Gen. 8: 7, 8; cf. *Super Hier.*, ff. 2ʳ, 12ᵛ–13ʳ, 18ᵛ, 23ᵛ, 45ʳ; MS. *De Oneribus*, f. 39ᵛ; MS. Flor. Ricc., f. 28ʳ; Salimbene, p. 20.

(2) Two Angels at Sodom: Gen. 19: 1; cf. *Super Hier.*, f. 12ᵛ; *Super Esaiam*, 30ʳ; Salimbene, p. 20.

(3) Esau and Jacob: Gen. 27; cf. *Super Hier.*, f. 24ʳ⁻ᵛ; Salimbene, p. 20.

(4) Moses and Aaron: Exod. 4: 29 seq.; cf. *Super Hier.*, ff. 12ᵛ, 27ᵛ, 38ʳ, 40ʳ; *Super Esaiam*, f. 5ʳ; MS. *De Oneribus*, f. 43ʳ; Salimbene, p. 20.

(5) Two explorers in Canaan: Josh. 2; cf. *Super Hier.*, ff. 12ᵛ, 40ʳ; *Super Esaiam*, f. 5ʳ; Salimbene, p. 20.

(6) Caleb and Joshua: Num. 14: 6, 30, 38; cf. *Super Hier.*, f. 12ᵛ; *Super Esaiam*, 5ʳ; Salimbene, p. 20.

(7) Elijah and Elisha: 2 Kgs. 2: 1 seq.; cf. *Super Hier.*, ff. 12ᵛ, 13ᵛ; Salimbene, p. 20.

(8) Two men in Dan: 12: 5; cf. *Super Hier.*, ff. 18ᵛ, 35ʳ; *Super Esaiam*, f. 30ʳ; MS. Flor. Ricc., f. 28ʳ.

(9) Martha and Mary: John 11; cf. *Super Hier.*, f. 24ʳ⁻ᵛ.

(10) Peter and John: John 20: 2 seq. and Acts 3: 1; cf. *Super Hier.*, ff. 1ᵛ, 2ʳ, 12ᵛ, 13ʳ; MS. *De Oneribus*, f. 39ᵛ; Salimbene, p. 20.

(11) Two on the Emmaus road: Luke 24: 13; cf. *Super Hier.*, f. 12ᵛ; Salimbene, p. 20.

(12) Paul and Barnabas: Acts 13: 2; cf. *Super Hier.*, ff. 12ᵛ, 40ʳ; *Super Esaiam*, f. 5ʳ; Salimbene, p. 21.

(13) Two witnesses: Apocalypse 11: 3; cf. *Super Hier.* ,ff. 18ᵛ, 40ʳ, 58ʳ; *Super Esaiam*, ff. 28ᵛ, 38ᵛ, 48ʳ; MS. *De Oneribus*, f. 39ᵛ, 43ʳ; Salimbene, p. 21.

[2] *Supra*, p. 33; also Reeves, *Sophia* xix. 355–6.

manuscript.[1] This included the memories of Joachim's two close disciples, Raynier of Ponza and Luke of Cosenza, and emphasized his spirituality and his gift of prophecy. There must also have been a gathering together of Joachim's sermons and occasional pieces, for the material found together in MS. Antoniana 322 at Padua could only derive from a collection made by intimate friends and disciples.[2] In the third place, the *Liber contra Lombardum* gives us clear proof that Joachim's Trinitarian doctrine was kept alive at least as late as 1234, probably among his immediate disciples.[3] Finally, we can detect the building up of the legend that Joachim had been 'unjustly' condemned by the machinations of enemies. As we have seen, the evidence of this process emerges in the *Super Hieremiam* about the mid century.

Leaving aside for a moment the problem of its authorship, we may glance at its enigmatic allusions under various Scriptural figures to the persecution of Joachim. In the utterance of Caiaphas, the High Priest, as well as the action of Zedekiah the King, who slashes Jeremiah's book with a knife and burns it, the writer sees the condemnation of the Abbot.[4] As Christ lay three days in the tomb, so must spiritual intelligence be entombed in the letter, watched by doctors and masters.[5] Again, Herod prefigures the future supreme pontiff after Celestine III, under whom 'the star' will disappear and spiritual intelligence be extinguished in grief, whilst the priests of the Church and the Pharisees, i.e. the leaders of the Cistercian Order, gather together in general council.[6] All this refers to 'illum doctorem veritatis' against whom the men of Anathoth, i.e. certain Cistercians, have conspired, saying 'Prophesy not in the name of the Lord that thou die not by our hand', i.e. suffer condemnation through our works and counsels. For this the Cistercian Order will suffer the doom which Jeremiah pronounced against the men of Anathoth.[7] In these and other passages, the identifications, veiled or open, are unmistakable: Innocent III is Caiaphas, Zedekiah, and Herod; the

---

[1] Naples, Bib. Naz., MS. Brancacciana 1. F. 2. Cf. *supra*, pp. 38, 111–12.

[2] There is still work to be done on this manuscript before its contents have been fully analysed. There are, for example, unpublished sermons and tracts on ff. 72ʳ–80ᵛ, 136ᵛ–140ᵛ, 149ʳ–156ʳ. See Appendix A, pp. 516–17.

[3] *Supra*, p. 55.

[4] *Super Hier.*, ff. 23ʳ, 59ʳ, cf. Jer. 36: 11–23; John 11: 50–2. Note that the king in Jeremiah is actually Jehoiakim. One of the key passages is quoted *supra*, pp. 34–5.

[5] *Super Hier.*, f. 23ʳ.

[6] Ibid.; cf. Matt. 2.

[7] *Super Hier.*, f. 23ᵛ, cf. Jer. 11: 21–3.

Cistercians are the Pharisees and the men of Anathoth; Joachim is Jeremiah and also 'the star'. One passage in particular is important as a key to the milieu in which this book was produced.[1] The vanity of secular learning, pertaining to the Letter, is contrasted with that of the future spiritual men.[2] They will be forced to flee from Herod and remain hidden in Egypt, until they can take refuge in Galilee, which is identified with the Cistercian religion. There they will live in poverty of spirit 'quousque tempus veniat perfectionis eorum'. They cannot, however, escape the opposition of pope and prelates. The writer drops an enigmatic hint: 'Summus pontifex prioris ordinis caput diminuet doctrinam magistrorum subtrahendo, et alteri ordini addet prioris officium.' He foresees, under the figure of the trial of Christ by Herod and Pilate, the persecutions of spiritual men under the *pseudo papa futurus Herodes*, followed by their figurative death, burial, resurrection, and ascension into the contemplative life. In succeeding pages other hints of persecution and of God's judgement are thrown out: 'Dissipabo consilium Iude, scilicet decretalium generalis ecclesie consultores';[3] 'quia forte in uno illorum [i.e. predicatorum veritatis] ordine multi silebuntur'.[4] As the first Zedekiah sent two priests to Jeremiah who were rebuffed, so the second will send 'quosdam magistros tam in clero quam in religioso collegio monachorum. Sed quia summus pontifex superbie nititur, ab exauditione repellitur.'[5]

Throughout the *Super Hieremiam* there runs the theme of the unjust persecution of Joachim and his disciples, the spiritual men. These so-called prophecies, which record the experiences of the generation following Joachim's death and condemnation, reveal a group of faithful followers who cling to Joachim's teaching on true spiritual understanding as opposed to vain learning, who expect persecution, who feel themselves in eclipse, like their great star, and have retreated into secret places from their enemies, but who

[1] *Super Hier.*, ff. 43ᵛ–44ᵛ.

[2] This is part of the commentary on Jer. 19, where doom is pronounced on the valley of Hinnom, identified with Bologna.

[3] *Super Hier.*, f. 44ʳ.

[4] Ibid. See also: ' "Rex Sedechias" summus pontifex futurus, "sedens super solium David ipse et servi eius", sc. prelati et cardinales, "et populus", i.e. clerus. "Porte" dignitates sunt et potestates ecclesiastice, quas hortatur Dominus per scripturas et evangelistas novos, ut "iudicium faciant iustum", quia perverse iudicant' (f. 48ᵛ; cf. Jer. 22: 2–3).

[5] *Super Hier.*, f. 47ʳ; cf. Jer. 21: 1. For other veiled references to the same theme see *Super Hier.*, f. 1ʳ (men of Anathoth); 3ᵛ, 52ᵛ (Herod); 53ʳ, 58ʳ (Zedekiah).

confidently hope for 'the time of their perfection'. This is certainly the
mood of a Joachimist group, but what group is it? We are faced with
the problem of the authorship, not only of the *Super Hieremiam*, but
also of the *De Oneribus* and *Super Esaiam*, which, although written
later, show many similar traits,[1] the figure-collection associated with
the latter,[2] and possibly other spurious works of Joachim, all of
which seem to emanate from south Italy in the mid-thirteenth century. Are these imitators of Joachim to be sought in his own order,
or among the Franciscans as has been commonly supposed? The
enigmatic character of the allusions makes it impossible to be certain, but I suggest that the persecuted spiritual men of the last
references are not Franciscans but Joachim's disciples in his own
order and in the Cistercian houses associated with him. A Franciscan
would be unlikely to harp so much on the 1215 condemnation of
Joachim, and would hardly feel it to be so closely intertwined with
his own tribulations as the writer here, for whom the silencing of
Joachim is intimately bound up with the troubles of the spiritual
men. The clearest hint which supports this view—though there are
others as well[3]—is the identification of the place of retreat in Galilee
with the Cistercian religion.[4] This is an unlikely statement for a
Franciscan. Surely the writer is here hinting at a fact, the possibility of which we have neglected too much in our study of Joachimism; namely, the presence in Calabrian monasteries of Joachim's
immediate disciples, driven in upon themselves after the condemnation of 1215 (when their Order was 'diminished'), but studying,
copying, and imitating the writings and figures of their master,
whilst waiting for the vindication of his prophecies. A point of
significance here is that the *Super Hieremiam* embodies the first
clear enunciation of the concept of three *status* since Joachim's
death. It seems to initiate a new phase of Joachimism in which the
emphasis shifts from the pattern of twos to that of threes. If we see

[1] The *De Oneribus* contains two veiled hints of an attitude towards the 'unjust'
condemnation of Joachim similar to that of the *Super Hier.* i, f. 43^r: '. . . tercius (status)
splendebit anno MCC quasi sub celestino papa' (i.e. avoiding the association of the third
status with Innocent III); ii, f. 45^r, a reference to the *stella veritatis* which disappears
under Herod *ob arroganciam prelatorum*. The *Super Esaiam* contains two references to
Zedekiah and Herod (f. 33^v–34^r, f. 14^r in the geographical section) which carry the same
implications as the *Super Hier.*
[2] For this see Reeves, Hirsch-Reich, *MARS* iii. 183–97.
[3] For a discussion of this whole question see Reeves, *Sophia* xix. 362–7; Reeves,
Hirsch-Reich, *MARS* iii. 194–7.
[4] *Supra*, p. 150.

the *Liber contra Lombardum* as stimulated by the desire to defend the master's Trinitarian theology, the revival of interest in the historical concept of the three *status* would follow naturally, finding expression in the *Super Hieremiam*.

The feature which has usually been regarded as a clear pointer to Franciscan authorship of the *Super Hieremiam* and *Super Esaiam* is the prominence of the theme of two new orders, the prophecy so completely appropriated by the two Mendicant Orders.[1] But when one reads these works without the presupposition that all the prophecies of new spiritual men refer to the Mendicants, the identification does not seem so plain. The direct applications to Franciscans and Dominicans are often in marginal captions which were probably added later. Without these, many of the passages on new spiritual men seem to derive directly from Joachim's own works and therefore to carry no specific reference to the two Mendicant Orders. A few, however, do seem to allude quite clearly to the Friars Preacher and Minor.[2] Unless these were touched up later—the addition of a few words would suffice—we must assume that the authors accepted the current identification of the two orders with the Mendicants. We remember that the monks of Fiore, taught by their master to expect these two new orders, went forth to hail the Friars Preacher at their first appearing as the fulfilment of this prophecy.[3] They could accept this identification of Joachim's two orders of the transitional period and still look for the fulfilment of Joachim's greater concept of the general spiritual order belonging to the third *status* itself. Both the *Super Hieremiam* and the *Super Esaiam* appear to be written from a viewpoint which is not directly concerned to push the application of Joachim's prophecies to the two Mendicant Orders or to the Franciscans in particular, but is occupied rather with the concept of spiritual men in general. The fact that the two Orders are given equal status in itself suggests outside authorship, since when Joachim's prophecies were appropriated by writers of either Order they were apt to exclude the other or give it lower place.

Once the preoccupation with the Mendicants has been cleared away, attention focuses on the curious and paradoxical role accorded to the Cistercians in these works; on the one hand, condemnatory, in so far as the Order has opposed Joachim, but, on the other

---

[1] *Supra*, p. 148 n. 1, for a list of some principal references.
[2] Cf. *Super Hier.*, ff. 12ᵛ seq.; *Super Esaiam*, ff. 7ʳ, 11ᵛ.   [3] *Supra*, p. 147.

hand, hinting prophetically at its great future in the third *status*. Thus at the outset of the *Super Hieremiam*, in the Dedication to Henry VI, the author describes the precursors of the third *status* in a sequence of threes, instead of the more common twos. The first three to whom Christ appeared at the Sepulchre were Mary, St. Peter, and St. John: 'Maria Cisterciensium religionem, Simon predicantes de evangelio, Joannes laudantes Deum de resurgente Christo significat; tandem Maria ingressa est sepulchrum, quia etsi in ordine illo revelata est et apparuit stella magna, tamen ultima noscet quid debeat percipere veritatis' (*Super Hier., Prefatio*). The modification of the usual two orders to three is significant; significant, too, is the symbolism of the fact that Christ appears first to Mary but that she enters the tomb last. The *magna stella*, as in other passages, is surely Joachim himself. Here the Cistercians are portrayed as reluctant to recognize their salvation, but there are other indications that the writer believes the life of the third *status* to be hidden within the Cistercian Order. A clear claim is made for it in the following words: 'In tertio [statu] vero retorquendum est totum ad Cistercienses et alios futuros religiosos, qui post antichristi ruinam multiplicandi sunt.'[1] Then there is the passage already quoted from f. 43ᵛ in which the spiritual men take refuge in the Galilee of the Cistercian religion. Later, Jonadab, the son of Rechab, is interpreted as St. Bernard, and the Cistercians are the Rechabites to whom the promise of the Lord to Jonadab is applied: ' "Non deesse de semine Jonadab, sed stare semper in conspectu Domini" videtur quod Cisterciensis religio sit usque in finem seculi processura.'[2] Finally, the Cistercian Order is the City of the Sun which shines as the sun in relation to the other four Churches: 'Civitas autem solis, que est in terra Egypti, una vocabitur Cisterciensis religio, que et in Claravalle claruit, et respectu aliarum quattuor ecclesiarum, clericorum, canonicorum nigrorum et aliorum ordinum more solis refulsit' (*Super Hier.*, f. 60ᵛ).[3]

The *Super Esaiam* carries echoes of the same viewpoint, both in harsh criticism of the Cistercian Order[4] and in expectation of its

---

[1] *Super Hier.*, f. 14ʳ.

[2] Ibid., f. 59ʳ, cf. Jer. 35: 14. *Supra*, pp. 115–16, for the comment of a seventeenth-century Cistercian, Francis Bivar, on this passage.

[3] Cf. Isa. 19: 18.

[4] It is identified with the order of Pharisees, *Super Esaiam*, f. 1ʳ⁻ᵛ. In what is probably the earliest manuscript of this work (Vat., Lat. 4959, f. 4ᵛ) this point is picked out in a bold red marginal note: 'Nota de monachis ordinis cisterciensis.'

New Spiritual Men

special place in the future. In a passage which draws directly on
Joachim's own symbolism the Cluniac and Cistercian Orders are
equated with Manasseh and Ephraim respectively, carrying the
hidden meaning which would be clear to Joachim's followers that in
the true spiritual succession the greater and more enduring inheritance goes to Ephraim.[1] Again, a note on the famous words 'Egredietur virga de radice Iesse et flos de radice eius ascendet' (Isa. 11 : 1)
runs thus: 'Nota Esaiam oraculum texere de flore et de virga,
Paulum de Christo et ecclesia, Gabrielem de Filio Dei et Matre
Virgine, Bernardum de Cisterciensi ecclesia et ordine.'[2] On the
words 'Ascendet Dominus nubem levem' (Isa. 19: 1) the comment
is: 'Nubes levis: religio. Bernardus est mons moris.' This gains
added meaning from another passage where the clouds are the new
spiritual men.[3] The Valley of Vision (Isa. 22) is the Cistercian
Church,[4] whilst the Fifth Angel of the Apocalypse is St. Bernard.[5]
Finally, we must notice, in the geographical section of the *Super
Esaiam*, a significant note on Cosenza.[6] This likens it to Jezreel in
Carmel, an identification which would at once carry the suggestion
of Elijah, prototype in the Old Testament of the new spiritual men.[7]
Thither, as to another Bethlehem, the angel will guide the true sons
into the life of solitude, while another Herod rages in the kingdom.
There seems no reason for this sudden allusion to Bethlehem and
Herod, unless at the back there lies the idea of the *magna stella* and
its disappearance under Herod's 'condemnation'. The whole passage
suggests that the region of Cosenza holds a special significance:[8]
whether Jezreel or Bethlehem, it is the place of retreat for the new
spiritual men—the Galilee of the *Super Hieremiam*.

Closely connected with the *Super Esaiam* is the most popular of
all the figure-collections made by Joachim's followers, that which we
call the *Praemissiones*. It has been argued elsewhere[9] that this was in

[1] *Super Esaiam*, f. 8ʳ. For this symbolism in Joachim's works see *Lib. Conc.*, ff. 27ʳ–29ᵛ; *Expos.*, ff. 32ᵛ, 49ᵛ; *Lib. Fig.*, Pl. XXIII.

[2] *Super Esaiam*, f. 8ʳ.   [3] Ibid., ff. 16ᵛ, 33ᵛ.

[4] Ibid., f. 37ᵛ.

[5] Ibid., f. 54ᵛ. Another passage on three *testes* or *ordines*, taken in conjunction with that in the *Super Hier.*, also probably alludes to the Cistercians, ibid., f. 58ᵛ, cf. Apoca-lypse 14: 6–9.

[6] *Super Esaiam*, f. 14ʳ.

[7] Cf. 1 Kgs. 18: 46. For the significance of Elijah in Joachim's writings see *Lib. Conc.*, ff. 20ʳ, 48ʳ, 63ʳ, 67ʳ seq., 76ᵛ, 97ʳ seq.

[8] In two early manuscripts, Vat., Lat. 4959, f. 16ʳ, and Vat., Ross. 552, f. 15ʳ, Cosenza is represented by a distinctive diagram.

[9] Reeves, Hirsch-Reich, *MARS* iii. 194–7.

fact put together to elucidate the enigmatic references in the *Super Esaiam*. If the *figurae* do indeed emanate from the same circle as the two main spurious works, then certain characteristics in the *Praemissiones* can be used to identify and describe that circle. It can be shown conclusively,[1] I think, that the *Praemissiones* are based on genuine *figurae* of Joachim, often early and simple ones; that these have been worked upon by Joachites not wholly comprehending the master's mind; that no interest whatsoever is taken in the claims of the Mendicants to be Joachim's new orders; finally, and most significantly, that in one figure, the Two Trees of Orders, the future is clearly given to the Cistercians. This, the boldest claim made for the Cistercians, is actually based on Joachim's own expectation. He did not openly assign a leading part in the drama of Last Things to his own Order, yet in his writings he hints several times that out of the Cistercian stock would spring some part of the order of contemplatives.[2] He ventured most in a figure in the *Liber Figurarum*.[3] Here two Trees of Orders have offshoots on one side of the main trunk, each representing an 'order' which is juxtaposed to one on the main stem. In the first tree the sap flows up the trunk through *Ysaac, Jacob, Joseph,* and *Effraym,* while the corresponding offshoots are *Ysmahel, Esau, Ruben,* and *Manasses.* In the second the sap of the true religion rises through the *Populus Gentilis,* not the offshoot of the *Populus Judaicus;* the *Populus Latinus,* not the *Populus Grecorum;* the *Ordo Monachorum,* not the *Ordo Clericorum;* finally, the *Ordo Cisterciensium,* not the *Ordo Cluniacensium.* Immediately above the Cistercians the stem of the tree breaks into all the luxuriant foliage and fruit of the third *status.* This figure must surely have been regarded as clear prophecy by Joachim's disciples. Their imitation in the *Praemissiones* is a much clumsier, less logical, figure, but its intention is quite plain.[4] Once more the design is of two Trees of Orders, but here the artist carries the claim further, for instead of contenting himself with the topmost place on the trunk, he crowns the two trees, the one of the Old Dispensation in the *Tribus Effraym in Joseph* and the other of the New Dispensation in the *Ecclesia Claravallensis in Bernardo.* Other tribes and orders have places as branches, but as Ephraim symbolized the true inheritance

---

[1] Reeves, Hirsch-Reich, *MARS* iii. 185 seq., for all the following points.

[2] e.g. *Lib. Conc.*, ff. 11^r, 23^r, 57^v–60^r.

[3] *Lib. Fig.*, Pl. XXIII.

[4] MSS. Vat., Ross. 552, f. 1^v; Brit. Mus., Add. 11439, f. 100^r; Vienna, 1400 (Theol. 71), f. 21^v.

of the past, so St. Bernard's followers crown the future. Beside this expression of Cistercian expectations we may set a parallel adaptation of Joachim's two trees in the Dresden copy of the *Liber Figurarum*,[1] where—if the ascription of the manuscript to Spiritual Franciscan circles is correct—the extra unnamed place at the top of the tree bears silent witness to Franciscan hopes. Joachim's trees could arouse strong aspirations.

We have been examining these mid-thirteenth-century Joachimist writings solely from the viewpoint of their religious fears and hopes. There are, of course, strong political themes in them as well, the treatment of which helps to confirm the south Italian provenance. The picture that emerges on the religious side is of a Joachimist circle which follows very closely the master's thought and symbolism, and which is characterized by this curious double attitude to the Cistercian Order, as at once the source of their persecution and the root from which will spring the *Ecclesia Spiritualis*. Where would this attitude be more likely to be found than in the Calabrian houses of Fiore, together with closely associated Cistercian houses?[2]

[1] *Lib. Fig.*, Pl. XXV.

[2] The suggestion made here that the *Super Hieremiam*, *De Oneribus*, and *Super Esaiam* emanated from a Florensian/Cistercian circle rather than a Franciscan has been challenged by Dr. Töpfer (*Das kommende Reich*, pp. 108–15). Until further light can be thrown on the origins of Joachimism in the Franciscan Order, this question cannot be settled, but, on balance, I still think a Florensian/Cistercian authorship more likely.

(i) Dr. Töpfer himself has demonstrated the likelihood that the *Super Hieremiam* was written between 1238 and 1243. This date seems to me too early for a conscious interpretation of the Spiritual Franciscan tribulations in a Joachimist sense (cf. *infra*, pp. 184–6). It is true that the persecution of the nascent Spiritual group under Elias's generalship had already taken place, but there is no evidence that the resistance of the purist party to modifications of the Rule had yet been placed in the eschatological setting of Joachim's third *status*. Hugh de Digne, the leading Franciscan Joachite of the later 1240s, never enlarged on the theme of the three *status*, and his defence of absolute poverty did not draw on a Joachimist view of history. Yet the *Super Hieremiam* is explicitly based on the doctrine of the three *status* and antedates by ten years at least the first certain application of this doctrine to the Franciscan sense of mission by Gerard of Borgo San Donnino. The *Super Hieremiam*, in fact, gives the first clear enunciation of Joachim's pattern of threes since the Abbot's death, and thus forms the starting-point of the second phase of Joachimism. The most likely source for this new development must be sought among Joachim's close disciples. We have evidence of a continuing school of Joachimist theological thought in the *Liber contra Lombardum*, *c.* 1234, which Ottaviano ascribes to a direct disciple (cf. *supra*, p. 55), and this study of Joachim's Trinitarian theology might naturally have led the attention on to the historical doctrine of the three *status*.

(ii) In the absence of any evidence that the Spiritual Franciscans were as yet linking their defence of the Rule with life in the third *status*, it seems much more likely that the persecutions 'prophesied' in the *Super Hieremiam* are those of Joachim and his followers. One of the persecution passages which clearly points to the condemnation of

If, therefore, we use these works to throw light on what was happening in Joachim's immediate circle, we can trace how they were

1215 ('damnat librum: scindit Trinitatem ab unitate . . .') concludes: 'Nescio autem, Deus scit, utrum in nobis complenda sint vel in sequuturo ordine consummanda' (f. 23ʳ). Here the context surely demands that the *nobis* should mean Florensians.

(iii) The many passages on the two new orders do seem to be pointing obviously to the Preachers and Minorites, but two points must be borne in mind: (*a*) the two orders, explicitly differentiated, already appear frequently in Joachim's works, and almost all the Biblical symbols applied to them by the author of the *Super Hieremiam* are taken from the genuine works; (*b*) the references to *praedicatores* and *ordo praedicatorum* could also be derived directly from Joachim, and all that would be needed to turn a general prophecy of the two new orders into a specific reference to Dominicans and Franciscans would be the addition of *minor* to the description of the second order. Small adaptations of the text, with the addition of marginal captions, could quickly appropriate to the Mendicants prophecies not originally intended for them. There were certainly various recensions of the *Super Hieremiam*, and until the oldest text can be established we cannot be sure to what extent and for what purpose adaptations were made. Even if certain passages were intended from the beginning to indicate the Dominicans and Franciscans, this does not by itself prove Franciscan authorship, since the Florensians themselves, as we know from Gerard de Fracheto's story, were ready to salute the fulfilment of their master's prophecies in others.

(iv) The general religious viewpoint of the *Super Hieremiam* does not seem characteristic of Franciscan Spiritualism. There is very little mention of poverty and the overriding religious quality of absolute poverty does not appear at all. In its use of concepts like *ecclesia contemplantium*, *spiritualis intelligentia*, *viri spirituales*, the work stands close to the thought of Joachim, whereas the Spiritual Franciscans, when they do adopt a Joachimist view, transform the quality of the third *status* into their own terms (cf. *infra*, pp. 208–10). It is difficult to believe that a Franciscan author would not have extolled the high doctrine of poverty. On the contrary, we find a long passage in praise of the monastic life which would seem to be written by a monk, not a friar (f. 30ᵛ).

(v) The general political viewpoint of anti-Hohenstaufen, anti-German propaganda could equally well indicate Florensian or Franciscan authorship. In spite of the patronage which Joachim received from the Hohenstaufen, we know from his encounter with the Emperor Henry VI (cf. *supra*, p. 11), as well as from his writings, that prophetically he saw the German nation in the role of one of God's scourges. The *Super Hieremiam* and others in this group of pseudo-Joachimist works are ostensibly addressed to Henry VI. This is a touch of verisimilitude far more likely to have been thought up by a Florensian who knew the story of Joachim's meeting with Henry VI than by a Franciscan. Furthermore, a Florensian abbot is not so likely to have fled from Frederick II with all the works attributed to Joachim (Salimbene, p. 236), unless the Order of Fiore were known for its anti-Hohenstaufen attitude.

(vi) Finally—and most important—it seems extremely difficult to attribute to Franciscan authorship a work which allots such a peculiar and distinctive role to the Cistercian Order, implying in a veiled manner that the future religion of the third *status* is in some way bound up with it. The ambiguity with which this Order is treated has already been indicated. By far the most reasonable explanation is that this was a Florensian viewpoint.

I have concentrated here on the authorship of the *Super Hieremiam*, since, in my view, that of the *De Oneribus*, of a group of shorter writings belonging probably to the same period, and of the *Super Esaiam* hangs on the attribution of what is clearly the earliest of these works. I believe they are all from the same milieu. There is supporting evidence

[*continued on p. 158*]

thrown into confusion by the 1215 condemnation; how they adjusted themselves by developing the persecution defence; how they retired within themselves to safeguard the almost-extinguished spiritual intelligence; how they studied and defended Joachim's Trinitarian doctrine against the Lombard and were led on to reaffirm his doctrine of the three *status*; how they bolstered morale by the production of the pseudo-prophecies; how, through the period of waiting, they did not lose the firm expectation that the order or Church of the third *status* would spring from their midst. The advent of the Mendicants confirmed belief in Joachim's prophecies without disturbing confidence in their own role, for Joachim's programme allowed room for both. But though they manufactured prophecies and *figurae*, this was a curiously quiescent group, waiting to be revealed as the true spiritual men. From this soil of Calabria there appeared no crop of passionate fanatics, moved by prophecy to action. The Order of Fiore pursued an even, undistinguished course, and it is only by hints that we can deduce its continued devotion to the master whose revolutionary thought it had lost. There seems to have been no prophetic zeal to blow up the fires. Yet, like old embers which suddenly glow for a moment, there was a remarkable recrudescence of enthusiasm for the Abbot Joachim in Calabria three centuries later. Aswe have seen, three of his champions at that time were Cistercians, of whom two go out of their way to assist at his rehabilitation. It is true that Manrique, Abbot of Casamari, maintains an ambivalent attitude, yet when he declares with warmth that Joachim was a true prophet whom his Order wrongfully opposed, his feelings have almost certainly been kindled by the still-held belief that the Abbot had foretold a great future for the Cistercian religion.

In a more general sense it is possible that Joachim's conception of the origin, development, and future of the contemplative life may have stimulated the thinking of the older monastic orders and quickened devotion to their peculiar role. There are traces in fourteenth-

for the view taken here in all of them. A significant point is that Frater Raynier appears prominently in this group of works, with reference to prophetic expositions attributed to him, only one of which appears to have survived (cf. *supra*, p. 57). These were clearly spurious writings fathered on to the original Raynier. The name of Raynier as a disciple of Joachim would be well known in the Florensian circle, but it is hardly likely that anyone outside would use it at this late date. We may, I submit, see the production of these works and the figure-collection accompanying the *Super Esaiam* as the last phase of a positive Joachimism which appears to die out in the Order of Fiore after this time.

century England, for instance, of a viewpoint on monasticism similar to Joachim's, which seems to spring from Bury St. Edmunds but becomes quite widely disseminated. Dr. Pantin has drawn attention[1] to a treatise on monastic origins which is found in the early fourteenth century at Bury and is later copied or imitated at Glastonbury, Durham, St. Albans, and other houses. The similarity to Joachim's conception is striking: the history of cenobitism starts in the Old Testament with Samuel, Elijah, Elisha, and the Sons of the Prophets; in the New Dispensation, St. Benedict is the fountainhead. The tract even expresses a Trinitarian interpretation of the orders of history which is exactly Joachimist: the *ordo conjugatorum* has the image of the Father, the *ordo clericorum*, the image of the Son, the *ordo cenobitarum*, that of the Holy Ghost, while within the latter the hermit life is the flower and end of the monastic life. As an authority for the three orders the tract names 'Januensis in libro quaestionum de antichristo'. So far we have no real clue as to the identity of Januensis.[2] It has been suggested that this is a corruption of Joachim,[3] and certainly one of the manuscripts in which this treatise on monastic origins appears gives Joachim in a list of monastic writers.[4] With this work we may perhaps link the prophetic anthology from Bury St. Edmunds which we have already described,[5] since in a considerable amount of pseudo-Joachimist material it includes prophecies on the two new orders. Again, Dr. Pantin has brought to light a sermon for a Chapter General of the Black Monks in which the historical perspective is much the same as that of the treatise.[6] The messianic role of St. Benedict in Joachim's scheme of history would obviously attract Benedictines, and no doubt this appeal to the historic and prophetic role of monks was useful in the fourteenth-century contest with Mendicants and other claimants,

[1] W. Pantin, 'Some Medieval English Treatises on the Origins of Monasticism' in *Mediaeval Studies presented to Rose Graham* (Oxford, 1950), pp. 189–215. See also Bloomfield, *Piers Plowman*, pp. 81–9, 201–3.

[2] This problem is discussed by Bloomfield, op. cit., p. 75 and *Anglia*, lxxvi (1958), p. 251 n. 2. *Januensis* may be Bartholomew *Ianonesis* of Majorca whose *De adventu Antichristi* was condemned in Barcelona in the 1360s (see Eymerich, *Direct. Inquis.* ii. 200, 226; Menéndez y Pelayo, *Heterodoxes* i. 495). There was also a Gabriel *de Janua* who seems to have been a Fraticelli (see Tocco, *Archivio storico napoletano*, xii [1887], p. 40).

[3] Hirsch-Reich, *RTAM* xxvi (1959), p. 136.

[4] Oxford, Queen's College, MS. 304, f. 62; see Pantin, loc. cit., p. 197.

[5] *Supra*, pp. 93–4.

[6] W. Pantin, 'A Sermon for a General Chapter', in *Downside Review*, li (1933), pp. 291–308.

but no group among the old orders really seized the future in the way which the Joachimist prophecies demanded. It was in the new Orders of Mendicants—Preachers, Minorities, Austin Hermits, and (later) Jesuits, as well as in heretical groups—that Joachim's prophecies of new spiritual men found a genuine response.

III

DOMINICANS

S t. Thomas Aquinas was in Paris at the time of the scandal of the Eternal Evangel. Later, as we have seen, he threw the whole weight of his learning against Joachimism. His biographer, Guglielmo da Tocco, tells a story which reveals the thoroughness with which he proscribed these views:[1]

Et quia ex dictis Abbatis Joachim praedicti haeretici fomentum sumunt praefati erroris pestiferi, praedictus Doctor in quodam monasterio petivit librum praefati Abbatis, et oblatum totum perlegit, et ubi aliquid erroneum reperit vel suspectum, cum linea subducta damnavit, quod totum legi et credi prohibuit, quod ipse sua manu docta cassavit. (*AS*, 7 Mar., p. 667.)

It is, indeed, hard to envisage a favourable reception for Joachim's ideas among Dominicans—though we notice that a book of his was available in a Dominican house. Yet the Order did not escape his influence.

The general sense of impending crisis in history, and of the peculiar role of St. Dominic called forth for this moment, was widely felt. Vincent of Beauvais, using the traditional sevenfold division of history in his *Pars Historialis*, quotes the popular Joachimist words from the *Super Hieremiam* which express so well the tension of the time: 'Ab anno domini MCC et ultra suspecta sunt mihi tempora et momenta . . . '[2] In his conception of the ages of history he uses one idea which is close to Joachim's thought, namely, the concurrent

---

[1] The preceding statement shows the Dominican view of the most obnoxious tenets held by Joachites: 'Quorum dementia ad fundandas in ruina sine fundamento haereticas pravitates, tertium novum fingit statum et sine testatore Christo novi spiritus Testamentum, sub quo status Ecclesiae debet hoc novo tempore immutari. Quorum errores praedictus Doctor in suis scriptis in diversis locis elisit: ostendens post Christi Evangelium et filii Dei ultimum Testamentum . . . nullum alium statum Ecclesiae debere succedere, sed istum . . . usque ad finem seculi permanere. Et quia ex dictis Abbatis Joachim praedicti haeretici fomentum sumunt praefati errores pestiferi . . .' (*AS*, 7 Mar., p. 667).

[2] *Speculum Historiale* (Venice, 1591), f. 488ᵛ. This often-quoted sentence is really a conflation of a genuine sentence from *Lib. Conc.*, f. 41ᵛ, and a spurious one from *Super Hier.*, *Prefatio*.

running of the sixth age and the seventh of quietude from the Ascension to his own day. But Vincent's actual account of Joachim[1] is the conventional one from Robert of Auxerre and he shows no inclination to appropriate to the Dominicans any part of Joachim's prophecy, although, as we have seen,[2] Gerard de Fracheto was quick to do so.

We must emphasize the point that in Gerard de Fracheto's story it was a group of Dominicans, not Franciscans, whom the monks of Fiore went forth to hail as the fulfilment of their founder's prophecy. This may have been a matter of chance, but the episode possibly set up a current of expectancy in the Order which encouraged some members to see their role in the cosmic setting provided by Joachimism. Thus a vision, edited from three manuscripts and studied by Fr. Oliger, places St. Dominic and St. Francis in the midst of a mysterious apparition of indescribable beauty, based on the vision of the living creatures and the wheels seen by Ezekiel.[3] All the patriarchs, prophets, apostles, doctors, etc., are there, and to the two saints is given the continuation of their work. These two transport the mystical apparition (*similitudo*) throughout the world; they fight and conquer the Dragon and the Beast which threaten it; they bring in the triumph of the *similitudo* in which it expands its wings to the ends of the earth. The vision is ascribed to John, a hermit of Asturias, but Fr. Oliger has shown that the author was probably a Dominican writing in the decade 1290–1300. Although Joachim is not mentioned, the vision is in a Joachimist vein and centres on an image dear to Joachim and prominent in his *Liber Figurarum*.[4] Moreover, this vision was quickly picked up by a Dominican who certainly knew the Joachimist prophecy. Dietrich of Apolda, writing in 1297, endows his great Order with the full Joachimist expectation. God in times past has sent many messengers inviting mankind to the Great Supper, but in the eleventh hour, 'novissime istis diebus, missus est . . . Ordo novus, novus, inquam, pariter et antiquus, novus institutione, antiquus auctoritate'.[5] This is the order of Preachers,

---

[1] *Speculum Historiale*, Bk. XXX, cap. xl.

[2] *Supra*, p. 147.

[3] L. Oliger, 'Ein pseudoprophetischer Text aus Spanien über die heiligen Franziskus u. Dominikus', in *Kirchengeschichtliche Studien P. Michael Bihl, O.F.M.* . . . (Kohner, 1941), pp. 13–28. Cf. Ezek. 1.

[4] *Lib. Fig.*, Pl. XV. References to the four *animalia* and the *rotae* of Ezekiel are innumerable in Joachim's work.

[5] Dietrich (Theodoricus) of Apolda, *Acta Ampliora, AS*, 1 Aug., p. 562. Dietrich is here quoting from the *Legenda* of Humbert de Romanis, cf. *supra*, p. 147. On the

and this is the order foretold by Joachim and hailed by his disciples.[1]
In support of his claim to this eschatological role Dietrich gives the
vision of John the Hermit.[2] Here he necessarily extends the role to
the Franciscans. In his exposition of the vision he uses an Old
Testament figure for these two latest orders which might have been
drawn from Joachim's own writings: 'Hi sunt duo filii novissimi
Jacob patriarchae senescentis, qui extremitate geniturae, singula-
ritate amoris, nominumque significationibus duos Ordines prae-
figurant.' Again, from the closing crisis of the Old Dispensation he
draws a parallel with the expected crisis of the New which also
echoes Joachim: 'sicut enim, imminente eversione Babylonica, regem
sanctum Josiam, zelatorem legalis iustitiae, synagoga Moysi pro-
genuit, ita, imminente Antichristi tyrannide, generabit Ecclesia Agni
Sponsa statum duorum Ordinum perfectionis altissimae, qui fideles
contra draconem virulentum confortabunt' (*AS*, 4 Aug., p. 627).
There seems little doubt that, whether consciously or unconsciously,
Dietrich placed the destiny of his own Order within a Joachimist
framework. Again, about 1333, another Dominican, Fr. Galvagneus
de la Flamma, recounted the same vision of John the Hermit, and
added immediately afterwards: 'Abbas Joachim in suis libris depinxit habitum predicatorum . . .' and the rest of the usual story.[3]

A little later we find in circulation a new version of Joachim's
prophecy which shows that a pseudo-Joachimist text had been
specially created in support of the single Order of the Dominicans.
It is first found in an anonymous *Brevis Historia* of the Order, preserved at St. Sabina in a manuscript of 1367:[4]

Venerabilis etiam abbas Joachim, Florensis ordinis institutor, fratribus
suis habitum, quem dictus magister Raynaldus a B. Virgine acceperat,
prophetice demonstrans, in quodam monasterio ordinis sui depingi fecit
in Calabria, dicens: 'Cito surrecturus est in ecclesia Dei ordo novus
docentium, cui praeerit unus major et cum eo et sub eo erunt duodecim
praefatum ordinem regentes: quia sicut patriarcha Jacob cum duodecim
filiis ingressus est Aegyptum, sic ipse cum illis duodecim in illo ordine
post ipsum majoribus ingredietur, et illuminabit mundum. Parcat illi

Dominican appropriation of Joachimist prophecies see also H. Haupt, *ZKG* vii (1885),
pp. 401 seq.
[1] *AS*, 1 Aug., p. 574.
[2] Ibid., pp. 625–7.
[3] Galvagneus de la Flamma, *Cronica*, ed. B. M. Reichert, *MOPH* ii, Fasc. i,
pp. 7–10.
[4] Edited Martène et Durand, *Ampl. Coll.* vi (Paris, 1729), *Brevis Historia Ord.
Fr. Praed. Auctore Anonymo*, col. 335.

Dominus, qui causam et occasionem dederit, ut per provinciarum divisionem hic propheticus et apostolicus numerus tolleretur.

One is struck at once by the Joachimist overtones in this prophecy,
which obviously could only emanate from a Dominican circle. The
extension of the concords between the twelve Patriarchs and twelve
Apostles (here implied) to the expectation of a third twelve derives
directly from Joachim's thought, and it is only the Trinitarian conception of history which really makes this possible. The last sentence
indicates that the writer is aware of the tremendous claim he is
making, yet none the less he sets out a parallel which would appear
more characteristic of Spiritual Franciscan thinking.

In his work entitled *De Quatuor in quibus Deus Praedicatorum
ordinem insignavit*[1] Stephen of Salaniaco gives as part of his first
'sign' his own version of this same story. He quotes the supposed
words of Joachim exactly, showing that this prophecy must have
been in circulation. He adds the story told by Gerard de Fracheto,
ending '"Cum venerint, cum omni honore illos excipite." Quod et
faciunt, et fecerunt, nam quando primo fratres venerunt ad eos,
exiverunt eis obviam cum crucibus et cum canticis spiritalibus et in
omnibus locis suis sicut fratres proprios exhibent et pertractant'
(*MOPH* xxii. 10). We get another hint of interest in this prophecy
from Jacob Susato, who interpreted the *duodecim illos maiores
Ordinis nostri* as the twelve provinces established in 1228.[2]

If some Dominican group invented the Joachimist prophecy of
the Preachers, it is also possible that the story of the pictures in St.
Mark's originated in the same quarter. For it is in a St. Sabina
manuscript that we meet the first reference to it in a *Brevissima
Chronica* which repeats the prophecy of the *Brevis Historia*, quoted
above, inserting in it these words: 'et etiam in ecclesia S. Marci de
Venetiis opere musivo, sive fieri fecit . . .'[3] It has been thought that
the earliest mention of the Venetian legend was by the Franciscan
Bartholomew of Pisa, but this Dominican reference is clearly earlier.
The Joachimist legend among the Dominicans had always stressed
the visual miracle of depicting them in the distinctive habit, itself
miraculously given by the Virgin in a vision to Fr. Reginald, and this
preoccupation with the form of the habit may have generated the
story of Joachim's prophetic representation of the Dominican Order

---

[1] *MOPH* xxii (Rome, 1949), pp. 9–10.
[2] Quoted by T. Malvenda, *Annales Praedicatorum* (Naples, 1627), p. 163.
[3] Martène et Durand, *Ampl. Coll.* vi, cols. 347–8.

at St. Mark's. It is significant that this earliest version speaks of the one order only.

In the next century the Dominican Archbishop of Florence, St. Antonino,[1] uses several of the Joachimist images to praise the two Mendicant Orders: 'Hi utique sunt due olive pinguedine dilectionis et devotionis: et duo candelabra lucentia ante dominum orbem doctrina illustrantia. Hi duo cherubin sapientia plena obumbrantia propiciatorum: necnon et duo seraphin caritate ardentia clamantia Sanctus . . .' (*Pars Historialis*, f. clxxxix[r]). He then quotes Joachim's exposition of Zechariah 11, adding to it a unique version of the St. Mark's story:

Exponit Abbas Joachim duas virgas esse duos ordines mendicantium qui tamen fuit ante eorum institutionem. Virgas rectas sanctitate, exiles et graciles austeritate, percutientes doctrine auctoritate. Decor est ordo predicatorum per habitum decorum quasi prelatorum. Funiculus dicitur ordo minorum quia funiculo manifesto cinguntur . . . Sed apertius prenunciatus fuit et declaratus particularius in pictura quadam que reperta est in ecclesia Sancti Marci Venetie, ubi antequam Dominicus nasceretur in mundo ymagines duorum depicte cernebantur a cunctis quarum una erat ad modum religiosi in habitu ordinis predicatorum cum lilio in manu: altera similitudinem habebat apostoli Pauli prout pingi consuevit. . . . Sub figura [i.e. St. Paul] vero ad pedes sic: Per istum itur ad Christum. Super figuram alteram scriptum erat Agios Dominicus. Sub ipso vero: facilius itur per istum. Nec mireris de scriptura huiusmodi, quia doctrina Pauli sicut et ceterorum apostolorum erat doctrina inducens ad fidem et observantiam preceptorum, doctrina Dominici ad observantiam consiliorum et ideo facilius per ipsum itur ad Christum. (f. clxxxix[v].)

St. Antonino is prepared to allow that the Joachimist prophecies concern two orders of Mendicants, but when it comes to the *figurae* of St. Mark's, he excludes St. Francis and makes a most astonishing claim for St. Dominic which I have not met elsewhere.[2]

How far did the interest of Dominicans in Joachimism go beyond claims for their founder and their order? Did they pay attention to Joachimist works? Salimbene tells a vivid little story of two Friars Preacher who passed through Hyères in 1248 and found themselves

---

[1] St. Antonino, *Pars Historialis* (Nuremberg, 1484), iii, ff. clxxxix[r–v], cxciii[v].

[2] This story is picked up by the Protestant writer Stillingfleet, who says in his *Discourse on the Idolatry of the Church of Rome* (see p. 108 n. 2 for full reference): 'I shall not insist on any more of Dominicus; nor on the blasphemous Images set up in St. Mark's Church, Venice, one of which was of St. Paul with this inscription *By him we go to Christ*: the other of Dominicus with this *but by him we go easier to Christ*' (p. 137).

momentarily in the Joachite circle of Hugh de Digne.[1] After supper the test question is put to one of them, Peter of Apulia, lector of the Neapolitan house: 'Fr. Petre, quid vobis videtur de doctrina abbatis Joachim?' To which he replies: 'Tantum curo de Ioachym quantum de quinta rota plaustri!' This sends the questioner hurrying to Fr. Hugh, saying: 'Hic est quidam Fr. Praedicator qui nichil credit de doctrina ista.' From the discussion between the sceptical Dominican and the ardent Hugh which follows it is clear that the former had read some of the Joachimist writings. He chooses as the focal point of the discussion prophecies from the *Super Hieremiam* concerning Frederick II, and in a long argument Hugh seeks to prove the truth of the Joachimist and other prophecies. The Preacher puts up a good resistance, but appears to have been saved from capitulation by a call to hurry to his boat, now ready for departure. One suspects that he went away still sceptical, but the episode shows that the Dominicans could not ignore Joachimist doctrine at this time.

Miss Smalley has drawn attention to a Dominican whom she believes 'dabbled in Joachimism', the anonymous author of a *Postilla* on Proverbs who was possibly John of Varzey, a regent in Paris *c.* 1270.[2] In his interpretation of Proverbs 30: 29–33 'John' converted the four orders represented by the Lion, Cock, Ram, and King into four ages of history, of which the third was the present and the last would extend to the end of time. In this entirely individual interpretation the author used a method which came close to that of Joachim, i.e. finding in Biblical symbols prophecies covering the whole span of history which enabled him to divide it up into specific ages. But if he had been gripped by the method—and we have no proof that he derived it consciously from Joachim—this author had certainly reacted against the view of history which Joachim and his disciples drew from it. His fourth age contained no trace of the Age of the Spirit, but was simply the Age of Antichrist directly prior to the Last Things. In his emphasis on the need for discretion in interpreting the ages of history he may actually have intended to dissociate himself from the wilder Joachimist views. As Miss Smalley says: 'It sounds as if "John" were trying to turn the Joachimist method against its exponents. He would find in Scripture an accurate

[1] Salimbene, pp. 239 seq.
[2] B. Smalley, (i) 'Some Thirteenth-century Commentaries on the Sapiential Books (concluded)', in *Dominican Studies*, iii (1950), pp. 260–5; (ii) *The Study of the Bible in the Middle Ages* (2nd edn., Oxford, 1952), pp. 290–1.

forecast of current events instead of wild predictions of the future.'[1] This may have been a typical Dominican attitude: to read the works of Joachim critically, but to draw back with caution from involvement in their extreme hopes.

Not all, however, could remain aloof from these speculations. John Quidort, or John of Paris, was a Dominican and a scholastic who yet could not keep away from speculations on Last Things and the advent of Antichrist. From his treatise *De Antichristo* it appears that he read Joachimist literature for this purpose. From the *Super Hieremiam* he quoted at length that most popular passage beginning 'Ab anno domini 1200 [here altered to 1260] suspecta sunt mihi tempora et momenta'.[2] The emphasis of his quotation is on the new order which will triumph over the threatened ruin of the Church, like Samuel over the disasters of Eli. He actually cited prophecies of the elect in the third *status* and—most astonishing— that dangerous sentence from the *Super Hieremiam*: 'Puto etiam quod sicut olim Deus patres elegit seniores prophetas: 2° apostolos iuniores: ita nunc etiam pueros ad litteram eligat . . .' He also quoted the little verse on Antichrist, with the date 1300.[3] This, he says, is popularly supposed to come from Joachim's works, but he cannot find it there. In his scheme of the ages of the Church designated by orders he found a place for the *ordo pauperum praedicatorum*, which suggests that he saw his own order in a special role. Quidort's work was popular and is later to be found in the same volume as a collection of Joachimist material from which Silvestro Meuccio drew one of his Venetian editions. Although moderate, Quidort's speculations on the imminence of Antichrist roused discussion in the University of Paris.[4] The popularity of such speculations makes Aquinas's strictures upon them all the more comprehensible.

An enigmatic figure, difficult to place in relation to Joachimism, is the Dominican Robert d'Uzès.[5] His visions enjoyed a certain

---

[1] *The Study of the Bible in the Middle Ages*, p. 291.

[2] Joannes Parisiensis, *Tractatus de Antichristo* (Venice, 1516), ff. 46ᵛ–47ʳ. This long quotation is interesting, because it is clearly drawn from a text which differs considerably from the sixteenth-century Venetian printed one. It is made up of selections from the prologue and from Ch. I, with substantial omissions. Quidort had obviously read the work. It is difficult to say whether he was responsible for revising the date 1200 to 1260. On John Quidort see M. Grabmann, 'Studien zu Johann Quidort v. Paris, O.P.', *Sitzungsber. der Bayer. Akad. der Wiss.*, 1922, pp. 1–60.

[3] Op. cit., f. 46ᵛ. [4] Cf. *infra*, p. 315.

[5] The best study is J. Bignami-Odier, 'Les visions de Robert d'Uzès, O.P. (†1296)', in *AFP* xxv (1955), pp. 258–310.

vogue right down to the sixteenth century. They belong to the same genre as the *Oraculum Cyrilli* and other pseudo-Joachimist writings, and although he did not mention Joachim, his fears and hopes ran along Joachimist lines. He expected tribulation and judgement to fall on the Church—having a vision of Rome covered thickly in dust[1]—yet his faith in the renewal of the true Church, the rock of St. Peter, was unwavering. He expected Antichrist, yet also the *renovatio*.[2] His affinity to the Joachites is most clearly seen in the visions representing the drama of Celestine V and Boniface VIII.[3] Here in striking images he expressed the exultation at the advent of the Hermit Pope and the horror at his deposition shared by many Spiritual Franciscans, and enlarged these portents into cosmic symbols of the great hope and the great dread. That he expected renewal through the agency of an Angelic Pope appears in two visions at least, but it is extraordinary to find that in one of these the great saviour of the future appears in the garb of a *Minorite*.[4] Nowhere did Robert specifically assign a great future to his own Order as such, yet he clearly envisaged, within the eschatological framework, crucial roles for the 'two white birds' of the Mendicant Orders[5] and for the Hermit Pope who exemplifies evangelical poverty. His belief that revival would come only through certain authorized agencies appeared in a reiterated denunciation of one contemporary, would-be agency, the 'Secta que vulgo Saccatorum dicitur'.[6] It should be emphasized that, although a radical critic of the contemporary ecclesiastical hierarchy, Robert d'Uzès reiterated his devotion and obedience to the Roman Church. In an agony, when tempted by the Devil, he repeated the whole Creed, concluding: 'Ego, Domine, fidem istam catholicam, quam docet et predicat sancta mater ecclesia catholica Romana, credo, confiteor. . . . Abnego et reprobo omnes scismaticos et divisos ab unitate sancte matris ecclesie Romane catholice' (*AFP* xxv. 306). Like that of other visionaries, his view was foreshortened by an eschatological immediacy, making

---

[1] *AFP* xxv (1955), pp. 274–5: *De futuro statu ecclesie et quibusdam pontificibus. Visio III.*
[2] Ibid., pp. 273, 274, 278, 282, 287.
[3] Ibid., pp. 281–2, 285–7.
[4] Ibid., p. 279, also pp. 281–2. [5] Ibid., p. 275.
[6] Ibid., p. 282; *Visio* XXI, 283; *Visio* XXII, 284. The Friars of the Sack, officially *Fratres de poenitentia Iesu Christi*, were founded *c.* 1251 and suppressed as an Order in 1274. See R. W. Emery, 'The Friars of the Sack', *Speculum* xviii (1943), pp. 323–34. It is interesting to find that, besides this attack, they also came under Salimbene's fire, op. cit., pp. 254–5, and are doomed in the pseudo-Joachimist prophecy beginning 'Erunt duo viri, unus hinc, alius inde' (cf. *infra*, p. 182).

judgement imminent and denunciation correspondingly sharper, but, *sub specie eternitatis*, he knew that the ultimate verities and obediences were immovable.

At the beginning of the fourteenth century the Bolognese Dominican Francesco Pipini reveals himself as a reader of Joachimist prophecy. In a chapter headed *De Abbate Joachimo et scriptis eius*[1] he followed Robert of Auxerre in the first part but then added his own notes. He quoted at some length from the *Super Hieremiam* on the two new orders,[2] mentioned the *Super Esaiam* and the *Liber Concordie*, and then gave a short summary of the recently circulating *De Semine Scripturarum*, which he ascribed to Joachim. It would seem that he liked collecting the latest writings of this type, for later he gives us one of the earliest references to the *Vaticinia* (first series), which he called 'Libellus qui intitulatur Incipit initium malorum'. For each pope from Nicholas III to Clement V he described the relevant picture in easily identifiable terms. Of its authorship he says cautiously: 'Fertur a nonnullis Abbatem Joachimum Libelli huius spiritu prophetico fuisse auctorem.'[3] It is possible that Pipini's interest in Joachimist writings should be connected with an otherwise isolated episode of heresy later in the century at Bologna. There was a controversy in the university concerning the Trinitarian doctrine and other views of a Dominican, Franceschino da Imola. Writing against his views, Ugolino of Orvieto declared that 'dicit . . . aut scribit cum abbate Joachim'.[4] A process against him was instituted by Gregory XI in 1372 and sentence given in 1374. We do not know how he was first stimulated to strike out on this dangerous line, but the episode is unique, first, because it concerns a Friar Preacher, and secondly, because he dared to uphold once more the Trinitarian doctrine of Joachim condemned in 1215. It might be that the stimulus came from books in the Dominican house at Bologna. But this was an academic, theological dispute: there is nothing to show that Franceschino was interested in Joachim's view of history or the prophecies associated with his name.

Two Dominican writers show a particular interest in the condemnations of Joachim's doctrine which may indicate awareness of

[1] Muratori, O.S. ix, cols. 598–600.
[2] The familiar passage beginning 'Nam ab anno MCC et ultra suspecta sunt . . .'; see *supra*, p. 161 n. 2, for the source of the first sentence.
[3] Op. cit., cols. 724, 726–8, 736, 741, 747, 752.
[4] Cf. C. Piana, 'Nuovo contributo allo studio delle correnti dottrinali nell'Università di Bologna nel sec. XIV', *Antonianum* xxiii (1948), p. 243.

its danger within their order. Both Henry of Herford[1] and, after him, Herman Corner,[2] give in full the list of errors extracted by the Paris masters from the Eternal Evangel. Corner also makes a further attack of his own on Joachim:

Abbas . . . Joachim sparsit haeresim suam in corda hominum simplicium. Hic fertur spiritum habuisse propheticum et composuisse librum de sex aetatibus, ubi tempus praesens posuit in sexta aetate. Prophetavit de Summis Pontificibus futuris, depingens eos in diversis figuris et imaginibus iuxta conditionem vitae cujuslibet, quam acturus esset. Sed quia in pluribus mendax et haereticus repertus est, ideo non videtur habuisse spiritum veritatis sed potius falsitatis. (*Chronica novella*, col. 794.)

To more sober Joachites the aberrations of fanatics must have been particularly painful. In the mid-thirteenth century Gerard of Borgo San Donnino was obviously a thorn in the flesh to the Spiritual party in the Franciscan Order. In the same period in Germany there was a heretical Dominican, Fr. Arnold, who applied Joachimism to politics. In 1248 Albert of Stade mentions his 'abominable sect' which had arisen in Swabia.[3] Once again the central theme of this Joachite appears to have been the necessity of judgement on the Church, to be followed by *renovatio*. But this time the agent of renewal was the Emperor, who would forcibly reform the Church in the sixth age and bring in the seventh of *renovatio*.[4] This, as we shall see later,[5] probably ties in with a cult of the Hohenstaufen which drew some inspiration from Joachimism. How far Fr. Arnold saw his own order, or the group in it which followed him, as special agents in the programme is not clear.

We do not know how far the Preachers were infected by the type of fanatical belief in their own role in history which inspired the Spiritual Franciscans. It is significant, however, that in 1321 a letter on this subject had to be circulated to the Order after the meeting of the Chapter General in Florence.[6] We learn that in the Roman province accusations had been brought against 'Fratres aliquos . . . qui spirituales ab aliquibus vocabantur'. Accordingly, an inquiry

[1] Henry of Herford, *Liber de Rebus Memorabilioribus*, ed. A. Potthast (Göttingen, 1859), pp. 181–3.
[2] Ed. J. Eccard, *Corpus Historicum Medii Aevi* . . . (Leipzig, 1723); H. Corner, *Chronica Novella*, cols. 849–51.   [3] *MGHS* xvi. 371.
[4] Fr. Arnold's views were put forward in a tract, *De correctione Ecclesiae* (ed. E. Winkelmann, Berlin, 1865), written *c.* 1248–50.
[5] *Infra*, pp. 310–11.
[6] Printed by Quétif-Échard, *Scriptores Ord. Praed.* (Paris, 1719), i. 534. See also Ehrle, *ALKG* iii (Berlin, 1887), pp. 611–13.

had been held into their faith and habits which exonerated them from all taint of heresy. It was, however, deemed necessary to broadcast this acquittal in order to avoid scandal and publicly to forbid any peculiarities—'ne aliquis Frater singularitatem haberet in modo vivendi, quae de se induceret in scandalum vel errorem' or any use of the name *spirituales*. Obviously one sees in the background to this pronouncement a desire to keep clear of Franciscan scandals, but may one not also deduce that there had been trouble within their own ranks which the authorities wished to hush up?

St. Vincent Ferrer affords an example of a Dominican who became a prophet almost in spite of himself.[1] Trained in the Dominican intellectual tradition, he found himself impelled to proclaim a message of Last Things by the horror of the Great Schism and by a vision of Christ, with Sts. Francis and Dominic, who committed to him the mission of preaching penitence throughout the world before the imminent crisis. From 1399 to 1419 he travelled and preached unceasingly. His belief in the approach of Antichrist was profound, yet it seems—though the evidence is not quite clear—that he also believed in a *renovatio mundi* between the death of Antichrist and the end of the world. In the seventh age after the death of Antichrist the clergy would return to true poverty and all nations would revert to Christ.[2] Likening the twelve *status* of the Church to the twelve Signs of the Zodiac, he describes the eleventh thus:[3]

Aquarius . . . et figurat undecimum statum mundi huius futurum post mortem Antichristi, quia tunc sol iustitiae erit in aquario: nam tunc omnes generationes infidelium baptizabuntur. O qualis pressura erit ad baptismum, non sufficient clerici! . . . Tunc complebitur prophetia Ezechielis: Tollam quippe vos de gentibus et congregabo vos de universis terris et adducam vos in terram vestram, scilicet ecclesiam militantem . . .

Since the twelfth would see the Last Judgement, it is clear that this preceding state represented the Joachimist seventh age before the *consummatio mundi*. Furthermore, in Vincent's eschatological scheme

[1] See H. Fages, *Notes et documents de l'histoire de Saint Vincent Ferrier* (Louvain and Paris, 1905); M. Gorce, *St. Vincent Ferrier (1350–1419)* (Paris, 1935); J. M. de Garganta and V. Farcada, *Biografia y Escritos de San Vicente Ferrer* (Madrid, 1956).
[2] In the *Mirabile opusculum de fine mundi* (no place of pub., 1483, unpag.), the two Antichrists, '*mixtus*' and '*purus*', appear. After the first there will be a *renovatio*, with a true pope and a return to apostolic poverty, before the final Antichrist. In the *Sermo de Sancto Dominico* (*Sermones de Sanctis*, Antwerp, 1573), p. 299, the seventh age of the Church is clearly placed *post mortem antichristi* and described as *perfecta*, 'quia tunc omnes ad finem Christi revertuntur'.
[3] *Sermones Hyemales* (Antwerp, 1572), pp. 60–1.

the Mendicant Orders held a key role. Like earlier messengers of God—Noah, Moses, etc.—St. Dominic and St. Francis and their Orders had been sent *ante adventum Antichristi*.[1] Their task was to accomplish the preaching of the Gospel to the whole world which must precede the advent of Antichrist. St. Vincent likened one of these preachers to the Angel with the Eternal Evangel in the Apocalypse, and soon this symbol became firmly attached to St. Vincent himself.[2] There are, he says, in all three great preachings: the first was by the Apostles; the second by St. Dominic and St. Francis and their followers; the third will be: 'in universo mundo post mortem Antichristi per fideles aliquos qui in unaquaque gente erunt mirabiliter conservati a Deo ad conversionem aliorum et tunc veniet ultima consummatio mundi' (Fages, op. cit., p. 220). In a striking image of the Cross as a tree, described in terms reminiscent of Joachim himself, St. Vincent writes thus of three great future Preachers:

Nam tria que apparuerunt in recto stipite ipsius crucis celestis significant tres futuros Predicatores circa finem mundi significatos per tres Angelos, de quibus scribitur Apocalypse c. 14. Itaque per radicem stipitis intelligitur primus, per medium pomum secundus, per supremum vero pomum tertius, qui in summo statu prosperitatis et fidelitatis Christiane veniet, scilicet post mortem Antichristi. (Fages, op. cit., p. 202.)

Here the Joachimist apotheosis of history seems fully entertained. It is not clear if St. Vincent assigned a special role to his own order, although he did accord it special praise and his whole emphasis on the activity of the preacher tended to exalt its function.[3] Joachim was nowhere quoted or referred to, yet the emphases given by Vincent were often Joachimist in tone. Thus at the end of his *De Vita Spirituali*[4] there occurs a series of three which surely betrays the influence of Joachim:

Tria sunt a nobis singulariter et quasi assidue meditanda. Primum est Christus crucifixus . . . Secundum status apostolorum et fratrum preteritorum nostri ordinis. . . . Tertium status virorum evangelicorum futurus. Et hoc debes die noctuque meditari, sc. statum pauperrimorum

[1] Fages, op. cit., p. 215.
[2] Ibid., pp. 210, 221; *Gorce*, op. cit., p. 92. The bull of canonization makes this comparison.
[3] See, for instance, the *Sermo de Sancto Dominico* (ref. p. 171 n. 2), p. 299: 'Sed dixit Heliseus, Habeatur vas novum. Ecce ordo praedicatorum dicitur vas, quia continet plures fratres, dicitur novum et vetus plus quam omnes.'
[4] Published *c.* 1500, no place of pub., date, or pag.

simplicissimorum et mansuetorum humilium abiectorum charitate ardentissima sibi coniunctorum nihil cogitantium aut loquentium, nec saporantium, nisi solum Iesum Christum et hunc crucifixum . . . supernam Dei et beatorum gloriam contemplantium et ad eam medullitus suspirantium. . . . Et per conversationes imaginari debes eo ipsos: ut cantantes canticum angelicum cum iubilo citharizantium et citharis cordis sui, hec imaginatio ducet te plus quam credi potest in quoddam impatiens desiderium adventus illorum temporum. Ducet te in quoddam admirabile lumen . . .

In the mid-fifteenth century, besides St. Antonino, we find a Venetian Dominican, Fr. Rusticianus, studying Joachimist prophecy and making his own compilation. This is preserved in a copy made in 1469.[1] Its core was the work of a fourteenth-century Joachite, Telesphorus of Cosenza, which Rusticianus, according to his Dedicatory Epistle, had received from another Venetian, Dominico Mauroceno. To this he added prophecies from St. Bridget, Vincent Ferrer, and a certain Fr. Antonius de Yspania. Rusticianus also worked over the text of Telesphorus, adding pictures and additional comment. The most interesting of these additions are pictures of the expected Emperor Frederick III, with his advancing army and eagles, and of the Angelic Pope being crowned by an angel.[2] As we shall see,[3] in the next stage of its history this compilation was appropriated by Augustinians, but there can be little doubt that Rusticianus was genuinely interested in the Joachimist programme and was known for this taste among the Venetians. Writing a little later, Giovanni Annio of Viterbo, O.P., directed his Gloss on the Apocalypse towards a Joachimist age of felicity, expecting a Pope and a Prince who together would bring in the final state of beatitude.[4] Neither of these two Dominicans made special prophetic claims for their own Order, but they reveal a continuing concern with Joachimist expectations.

Thomas Malvenda was a seventeenth-century Dominican who took St. Vincent Ferrer's eschatological view seriously. As a historian he dealt at some length with Joachim and his reputation. As we have seen,[5] he defended that reputation with warmth and recognized

[1] Venice, Bibl. Marc., MS. Lat. Cl. III, 177. See J. Valentinelli, *Bibliotheca manuscripta ad S. Marci Venetiarum* (Venice, 1868), ii. 215. For a fuller account of this manuscript see *infra*, pp. 343–5.
[2] ff. 28ʳ, 29ʳ.   [3] *Infra*, p. 262.
[4] Giovanni Annio of Viterbo, *Glossa super Apocalypsim de statu ecclesie ab anno domini MCCCCLXXXI usque ad finem mundi* . . . (Louvain, undated, unpag.).
[5] *Supra*, p. 104.

him above all as the prophet of the Mendicants. The reason for this championship may be sought in his view of the cosmic role which orders of spiritual men were to play in the Last Things. He adopted from St. Vincent the concept of the three preachings and discussed the length of the period of *renovatio* between Antichrist and Judgement,[1] resting his belief in this renewal on the text much used by Joachim: 'Elias cum venerit omnia restaurabit.' This is not to say that Malvenda shows interest in the concept of the third *status*, but there is, as in the case of St. Vincent, an optimistic note in his view of the end of history which suggests Joachimist influence. This is strengthened by his vision of the Gospel preaching throughout the world, a vision tinged with an excitement unknown to St. Vincent. For Malvenda sees the opening up of the world by new exploration as part of the eschatological pattern. Before Antichrist comes, the Gospel must be preached throughout the whole world: now at last this condition is being fulfilled by the *viri apostolici*:

Denique toto complectimur pectore admirabilem illam ac solida veritate subnixam viri Apostolici S. Vincentii Ferrarii assertionem, sacrum Christi Evangelium per Fratres Praedicatores ac Minores, adde etiam Augustinianos, Iesuitas et alios aliorum Ordinum . . . praedicari, ac tandem plenarie, atque generaliter praedicandum in totius orbis humano genere culti regionibus, nimirum in cunctis terris ac insulis tam Veteris quam Novi orbis, tam apertis, quam aperiendis, tam cognitis quam co-gnoscendis. . . . Atque ut interim vetustiora omittamus, quis non videat S. Patrem Vincentium certissimum extitisse vatem, cum aperte cernamus in omnibus regionibus, insulis ac Provinciis quas tum Lusitani, tum Castillii aperuerunt, atque Imperio subdiderunt, que sane tam in Africa quam in Asia et amplissimo Novo Orbe, vastissimoque Oceano sunt innumere atque plane latissimae per Dominicanos, Francescanos, Augustinianos, Iesuitas et alios Evangelii ministros a Romano Pontifice missos Evangelium praedicatum . . . Christianam Religionem plantatam, indiesque longius latiusque per novas terras et insulas quae aperiuntur, continenter diffundi atque propagari? (*De Antichristo*, p. 171.)

We shall meet this theme again: the sense that the opening up of unimagined geographical vistas enhances the cosmic role of the new spiritual men and reveals more fully the meaning of history. It is a strange and significant marriage between the Renaissance view of the expanding universe and medieval expectation of God's will in history.

[1] T. Malvenda, *De Antichristo Libri Undecim* (Rome, 1604), pp. 115, 171, 177–9, 531 seq.

IV

EARLY FRANCISCANS

IT is, however, chiefly within the Franciscan Order that we perceive that strong emotional response to Joachimist prophecies which places them within a context of urgent meaning and finds in them incitement to radical action. Several recent writers analysing the controversy between the Conventual and Spiritual parties in the Franciscan Order have laid stress on the Joachimist thread running through this. Yet they seem to leave it as a thread apart, a separate and additional element which threw the Spirituals off their true path, bedevilled the controversy on Absolute Poverty and distorted perspectives on both sides. Few seem to have understood the deep connection between the passion of the Spirituals for evangelical poverty and the Joachimist expectation in history. This connection was often quite unconscious: it is to be detected in such characteristics as the belief that St. Francis's Testament had the imprimatur of the Holy Spirit, the heightened significance given to contemporary events, the exaggerated claims made first for St. Francis and later for Petrus Joannis Olivi. The background to all these is the belief that a new age on a new plane of history is dawning. From the Joachimist view of history, therefore, three characteristics of radical Franciscan thought derive: a sense that the extreme crisis of history is about to break upon the world; a belief in the supreme mission of the Order to match this moment; an attitude towards the papacy and the ecclesiastical hierarchy in which obedience strives with the conviction that the Order holds the key to the future, which cannot be wrested from it. A Joachimist view of history produced a mood somewhat akin to that of an early Marxist, a mood of certainty and urgency. The Spiritual Franciscan knew he was right because he had the clue to history; he could expect the imminent crisis confidently, since history was on his side.

History had come to a focus in St. Francis. He stood, so they believed, at a moment in time that laid on him a unique mission. In the *Vita Trium Sociorum* Cardinal Colonna's words embody this sense that the world was waiting for St. Francis: '... per quem credo quod Dominus velit in toto mundo fideles sanctae ecclesiae refor-mare.'[1] Even the official *Legenda Maiora* gave the same heightened significance to St. Francis as the 'Spiritual' legends it was to replace. He is declared to have come in the spirit and power of Elijah and to be in very truth the Sixth Angel of the Apocalypse 'ascending from the sun and having the sign of the living God'.[2] Both these identifi-cations carried Joachimist overtones. It was probably the 'great Joachite' John of Parma who first hailed St. Francis as the Sixth Angel,[3] but the first certain reference is in the excerpts made by the Commissioners of Anagni from the lost *Liber Introductorius* of Gerard of Borgo San Donnino.[4] The fact, however, that this Joa-chimist identification was acknowledged by Bonaventura[5] and incor-porated into the official legend made it safe for the orthodox; hence it appears in innumerable writings during the next two centuries.[6]

Most of those using this ascription would not have realized that this superlative claim concerning the unique mission of Francis belonged to the Joachimist scheme of history. Nevertheless, the reason why St. Francis was identified as the Sixth Angel was pre-cisely that he embodied the quality of life in a new and expected age. When the Spirituals spoke of evangelical perfection or evangelical poverty, they meant much more than mere righteous living, and in the phrase *status evangelicae perfectionis* we catch the echo of Joachim's third *status*. It is not surprising to find the scribe of a copy of the Abbot's *Liber Concordie* making the identification in a mar-ginal note: 'tertius status sub evangelica perfectione incipit'—and in another making an explicit equation between the liberty of the

---

[1] Quoted *ALKG* iii. 554 n. 1.

[2] Bonaventura, *Legenda Maiora*, *Opera Omnia* (ed. Quaracchi), viii, Prologue, cf. Apocalypse 7: 2.

[3] This is asserted by Ubertino da Casale, *Arbor*, f. ccvi[v].

[4] *ALKG* i. 101.

[5] Petrus Joannis Olivi solemnly avers that he heard Bonaventura declare this in a ser-mon: '...et hoc ipsum per claram et fide dignam revelationem est habitum, prout a fratre Bonaventura...fuit Parisius in fratrum nostrorum capitulo, me audiente, solempniter predicatum' (quoted from Olivi's *Super Apocalypsim* by Manselli, *Lectura*, p. 211 n. 1. It seems most likely that Olivi was the 'solemn doctor' who recounted the episode to Ubertino da Casale; see op. cit., f. ccvi[v]: 'Et ego audivi a solenni doctore istius ordinis quod frater Bonaventura tunc generalis minister et doctor solennis pre-sente prefato doctore qui mihi dixit quod in capitulo parisiensi solenniter predicavit quod ipse erat certus et certificatus quod beatus Franciscus erat angelus sexti signaculi et quod ad litteram de ipso et eius statu et ordine evangelista Ioannes intellexit.'

[6] See, for instance, Vat., MS. Lat. 4860, f. 24[r]. For a full list of references to this identification of St. Francis see S. Bihel, 'S. Franciscus Fuitne Angelus Sexti Sigilli (Apoc. 7: 2)?', *Antonianum* ii (1927), pp. 59–90.

Spirit, which is the mark of Joachim's third *status*, and the life of Francis: 'Nota quod libertas Spiritus est vita apostolica que in beato Francisco renovata est.'¹ This sense of the unique quality of St. Francis crystallizes in the idea that, in a special sense, his life conforms to and parallels that of Christ. Again, the extravagance of the language used in making this claim can only be understood in a Joachimist context, for it was only Joachim's Trinitarian pattern of threes which made it possible to extend the well-known concords of twos between the Testaments into the future, by making claims for St. Francis that were otherwise well-nigh blasphemous. St. Francis stood on the threshold of the third *status* as Christ on that of the second, and the parallels which Joachim had found between the first and the second *status* must now be sought between the second and the third. From one such parallel Joachim himself had explicitly drawn back: for him there could be only two Testaments and the spiritual interpretation proceeding from both could never be embodied in a third. But to some Franciscans the temptation to give the Rule and Testament of St. Francis the immutability and authority of the Third Testament was irresistible. St. Francis himself was in part responsible when he based his command to preserve the Rule on the assertion that 'ego ista verba in regula non posui sed Christus',² and it was indeed, in all but name, a third Testament which the Spirituals came to defend with such passion.

It must be emphasized that one did not need to be a committed Joachite to share in this general attitude towards the role of St. Francis and his Order in history. The moderate position is well represented by Alexander of Bremen's *Expositio in Apocalypsim*. At the outset he echoes Joachim's own spiritual experience in his account of how he came to understand the meaning of the Apocalypse,³ and his work includes many quotations from the first of the

---

¹ These notes became incorporated into the Venetian edition of the *Lib. Conc.*, ff. 11ᵛ, 21ʳ.

² Quoted *ALKG* iii. 602. See also the words of the Testament: 'Sed, sicut dedit mihi Dominus simpliciter et pure dicere et scribere regulam et ista verba, ita simpliciter et pure intelligatis et cum sancta operatione observetis usque in finem' (*Opuscula S. Francisci Assisiensis* (Ad Claras Aquas, 1949), p. 82).

³ Wachtel, *Expositio*, pp. 6–7. On Alexander and his *Expositio* see also A. Wachtel, 'Die weltgeschichtliche Apokalypse. Auslegung des Minoriten Alexander von Bremen', in *Franziskanische Studien*, xxiv (1937), pp. 201–59, 305–63; H. Grundmann, 'Über den Apokalypsen-Kommentar des Minoriten Alexander', in *Zentralblatt für Bibliothekswesen*, xlv (1928), pp. 713–23; J. Gilson, 'Friar Alexander and his Historical Interpretation of the Apocalypse', in *Collectanea Francescana*, ii (1922), pp. 20–36.

spurious Joachimist works, the *Super Hieremiam*, as well as one from the *Liber Concordie*.[1] Several of his interpretations contain echoes of the Abbot's: the pre-eminence given to the *felicissima tempora Silvestri*; the identification of one of the Angels of the Apocalypse as St. Benedict; the identification of Cosdroe, King of Persia, the Emperor Henry IV, and Saladin as manifestations of the Dragon.[2] His work reflects strongly the Joachimist mood of crisis and expectation: with Joachim he 'suspects all times and moments after 1200'. To meet the needs of these times God has raised up the two great lights Dominic and Francis, that through their new Orders the light of revelation might stream forth 'per septem orbis climata'.[3] Alexander quotes the *Super Hieremiam* at length on this theme and claims for the two Orders that they will reign with Christ for a thousand years.[4] A noteworthy point is that he cites from the *Super Hieremiam* a sequence of threes with dangerous implications: 'puto quod sicut olim [Deus] elegit patres seniores, secundo apostolos iuniores, ita et nunc pueros eligat.'[5] Using such figures as the raven and the dove, he writes of both Orders as jointly fulfilling God's mission, but there are hints that the Franciscans hold the treasure of the future. Thus he interprets the vision of the New Jerusalem coming down out of heaven in terms of the two new Orders: the two saints are its foundation stones, but to Francis is allotted the jasper stone which, being green, signifies Christ, and in the life of the City it is the quality of voluntary poverty which is emphasized.[6] Again, writing on Chapter 22 of the Apocalypse, he hails Francis as the 'novus evangelista quasi unus de paradysi fluminibus in toto terrarum orbe fluenta evangelii pia irrigatione diffudit.'[7] Alexander's Commentary never appears to have fallen under any suspicion of unorthodoxy: when treated moderately, the Joachimist role of the two new Orders could be assimilated without difficulty.

---

[1] See pp. 351 (quoting *Lib. Conc.*, f. 41ʳ), 429 (quoting the spurious verse on Antichrist), 436–7 (*Super Hier.*, ff. 10ʳ, 12ᵛ, 13ʳ), 493 (*Super Hier.*, ff. 1ʳ–2ʳ, 13ʳ, 24ᵛ, 26ʳ, 61ᵛ), 509 (*Super Hier.*, f. 60ᵛ). To justify his citations from Joachim, Alexander says: 'cuius paene omnes libri recepti sunt ab apostolicis, sicut fuit Lucius papa et Urbanus papa' (p. 493). On the importance of Alexander's *Expositio* for dating the *Super Hier.* see Grundmann, op. cit. (last note), pp. 718–20; Bondatti, *Gioachinismo e Francescanesimo*, p. 16; Bloomfield, Reeves, *Speculum* xxix. 790–1.

[2] Wachtel, *Expositio*, pp. 412 seq., 162, 260, 409, 427–30.

[3] Ibid., p. 436.   [4] Ibid., pp. 437–8.

[5] Ibid., p. 493; cf. *Super Hier.*, f. 1ᵛ.

[6] Ibid. pp. 469–81.   [7] Ibid., p. 498.

In considering St. Bonaventura's attitude towards St. Francis and his place in history, it is necessary to look more closely at the argument that the peculiar eschatological place accorded to St. Francis implies a Joachimist view of history. For in his *Commentaries on the Sentences* Bonaventura had vigorously repudiated the condemned Trinitarian doctrine of Joachim,[1] and in his latest work, the *Collationes in Hexaemeron*, he seems to be deliberating writing against this dangerous view of history without mentioning it. As if to invite comparison, he uses, like Joachim, the symbols of the Days of Creation for the ages of history, and, indeed, in his *Breviloquium* we find a summary of the seven ages practically in Joachim's words.[2] But in the *Hexaemeron* he sets another pattern of four *tempora* against Joachim's three *status*.[3] These he designates as *tempus ante legem* or *naturae, tempus legis, tempus prophetiae,* and *tempus gratiae*. The latter encompasses the whole period from the First to the Second Advent, thus emphasizing one of Bonaventura's basic principles: the centrality of Christ in history. He is, in fact, taking his stand on the two Dispensations (to which his *tempora* are allotted as three-to-one) and he emphasizes pointedly the duality of the Testaments: 'Post novum testamentum non erit aliud, nec aliquod sacramentum novae legis subtrahi potest, quia illud testamentum aeternum est.'[4] No doubt he was particularly anxious to dissociate himself from any Trinitarian conception of history, for he stresses the point that all three Persons operate equally in all the ages.

Yet he cannot free himself from the fascination of this view. He uses a number of sequences of threes,[5] including actually one of three orders corresponding to the three Persons which echoes Joachim's words closely: 'Ordo laicalis sive activorum respondet Patri, quia est producens clericalem et monachalem et non producitur; ordo clericalis respondet Filio, qui ordo producitur ab ordine laicali et producit monachalem; ordo monachalis respondet Spiritui Sancto, sc. quia ille ordo producitur et non producit' (*Collationes*, ed. Delorme, p. 255). But the most significant use of threes is the actual periodization of each of his four *tempora* into three sub-*tempora*, each representing the particular operation of one of the Persons.[6]

---

[1] Bonaventura, *Omnia Opera*, ed. Quaracchi, i, *Commentaria in quatuor libros sententiarum Mag. P. Lombardi*, p. 121.

[2] *Breviloquium*, ed. Quaracchi, v. 203–4.

[3] *Collationes in Hexaemeron*, ed. F. Delorme (Florence, 1934), pp. 160–3.

[4] Ibid., p. 180.   [5] Ibid., pp. 242–55.

[6] Ibid., pp. 162–3.

Thus Bonaventura does after all commit himself to the concept of particular manifestations of the Trinity in history and his culminating sequence brings him close to Joachim's Age of the Holy Ghost, for the fourth *tempus revelatae gratiae* is subdivided into *tempus redemptionis hominum*, *tempus diffusionis charismatum*, *tempus reserationis Scripturarum*, and the latter, pertaining to the Spirit, is especially linked with the Apocalypse. Bonaventura, it would seem, while reacting intellectually against the clear dangers of Joachim's system, was gripped emotionally by a belief in a culminating period of spiritual illumination when the Scriptures would be fully opened. In a number of passages he makes plain his expectation of an ultimate flowering of the Church within history and he follows Joachim exactly in the expression of this hope by placing the seventh age between the destruction of Antichrist and the Last Judgement and by distinguishing it from the eighth age: 'Sic erit etiam tempus pacis in fine. Quando enim Antichristus post maximam Ecclesiae ruinam occidetur a Michaele post illam summam Antichristi tribulationem, veniet tempus ante diem judicii tantae pacis et tranquillitatis quale non fuit ab initio mundi, et invenientur homines tantae sanctitatis sicut fuit tempore Apostolorum' (*Collationes*, ed. Delorme, p. 185).

Bonaventura may not have perceived that in taking his stand on two Dispensations and two Testaments he was actually in accord with Joachim, any more than he may have realized that Joachim, too, affirmed the operation of all three Persons in all stages of history. Whatever he thought about Joachim's view of history, he does in fact envisage at the end of history a crisis and a stage beyond, which form a new *status*.[1] In this he was a Joachite. It was in this context that he set St. Francis, though perhaps he did not clearly perceive that to elevate a human being into the eschatological position of the Sixth Angel of the Apocalypse, or Elijah in his second coming, implied the initiation of a new *status* in history. Yet some of his statements come near to this concept:

Et necesse fuit, ut in hoc tempore veniret unus ordo, sc. habitus propheticus, similis ordini Iesu Christi, cuius caput esset Angelus ascendens ab ortu solis habens signum Dei vivi et conformis Christo. (*Collationes*, ed. Quaracchi, p. 405.)

---

[1] See *Collationes in Hexaemeron*, ed. Quaracchi, v. 408–9; ed. Delorme, pp. 192–3. On the influence of Joachim on Bonaventura's thinking see further Tondelli, *Lib. Fig.* I, pp. 249–50; Lambert, *Franciscan Poverty*, pp. 115–16; Manselli, *Lectura*, pp. 125–30; Bondatti, *Gioachinismo e Francescanesimo*, pp. 137–9.

Tertius ordo [i.e. third of the *Ordo contemplantium*, ninth in the hierarchy, the *Ordo Seraphicus*] contemplantium est eorum qui sursum-aguntur in Deum: de quo videtur fuisse sanctus Franciscus qui in fine apparuit. . . . Isti autem de tertio hoc ordine sunt prope Ierusalem nec habent nisi evolare; nec florebit iste ordo nisi prius Christus patiatur in suis. (Ed. Delorme, p. 256.)

[After quoting again the text on the Sixth Angel:] Et sicut sex diebus factus est mundus et sexta aetate venit Christus, ita post sex tempora Ecclesiae in fine generabitur Ecclesia contemplativa. (Ed. Delorme, p. 265.)

Unde oportet quod in Ecclesia appareat aliquis status qui huic angelo [i.e. Sixth Angel] respondeat habens ultimatum et perfectum Dei cultum et hanc triplicem lucem elevantem tripliciter. (Ed. Delorme, p. 269.)

St. Bonaventura was a Joachite *malgré lui*. Although on the actual issue of Absolute Poverty he served as a moderating influence, he added fuel to, rather than dampened down, the fires of prophetic expectation which kept the controversy at white heat.

Before turning to the origins of the real Joachimist party within the Order, it will be convenient to mention three examples of four-teenth-century Franciscans who used the categories of Joachimism without being drawn into controversy. The first is Bartholomew of Pisa. Little is known of him save that he is thought to have been Bartholomew de Rinonico of Pisa, first mentioned in 1352 as living in the convent at Pisa and last met with in the Chapter General of Assisi in 1399.[1] He apparently began his *Liber de conformitate vitae beati Francisci ad vitam domini Jesu* in 1385. The elaborate parallel-ism which he sets out to establish between Christ and St. Francis is symbolized in the figure of a tree which at once recalls Joachim's trees in the *Liber Figurarum*. He chooses twelve of the fruits or 'conformities' of the tree, of which the first is headed: 'Jesus prophetis cognitus: Franciscus declaratur.' Here he expounds at length how Francis 'ad instar Christi fuit declaratus aenigmatibus et prophetarum eloquiis'.[2] Joachim is one of the chief prophets cited, with many well-known passages from the *Super Hieremiam* and quotations from Joachim's supposed expositions of the *Oraculum Cyrilli* and the Sibyl Erithrea.[3] The most interesting citations, however, are from Joachim's own

---

[1] Bartholomew of Pisa, *AF* iv, Preface. See also Ehrle, *ALKG* iii. 412.
[2] *AF* iv. 33.
[3] Ibid., 33, 40, 43–4, 45–52, 53–6, 71, 435, 437, 563–4.

Liber Concordie. One is an easily identifiable passage in Book V on the new order to appear in the sixth age symbolized in Man created on the sixth day.[1] The other is a long quotation, specifically ascribed to the *Liber Concordie*, but obviously an interpolation, beginning thus:[2] 'Erunt duo viri, unus hinc, alius inde, qui duo ordines inter-pretantur, unus Italus, scilicet de Thuscia et alter Hispanus, primus columbinus, secundus corvinus, et post istos duos ordines veniet alter ordo saccis vestitus . . .' The points of the prophecy seem to lie in the *brevissimum tempus* ascribed to the third order, in the bitter opposition of the clergy and the *ordo corvinus* to the *ordo columbinus*, and in the liquidation of the second order as *contumax et rebellis* in contrast to the promise that the first order will endure until the *novissima tempora*. The *ordo columbinus* will preach throughout the world, converting many nations and prevailing against the Moham-medans. It would be interesting to know how this prophecy ori-ginated. If it was really inserted in the *Liber Concordie*, a likely place would be Book V, cap 118 (f. 133ᵛ), where Joachim is interpreting Daniel 12: 5: 'Et ecce quasi duo viri stabant, unus hinc, alius inde . . .' We recall that it was to the Franciscan convent at Pisa that, according to Salimbene, the Florensian Abbot fled from the wrath of Frederick II, carrying with him the works of Joachim.[3] Here the first Franciscan group of Joachites may have gathered,[4] and it may well be that the interpolated passage was composed by one of these. A clue may lie in the third order, *saccis vestitus*, which probably re-fers to the Saccati, or Friars of the Sack. As we have already noted, these incurred the wrath of Salimbene and are doomed in the vision of Robert d'Uzès.[5]

Bartholomew well understood Joachim's system of seven seals or ages in the Old Testament, matched by seven in the New, and he constructed his own Joachimist scheme of history, which enabled him to establish St. Francis as the angel of the sixth seal in the New

---

[1] *Lib. Conc.*, f. 69ᵛ; *AF* iv. 54.

[2] *AF* iv. 53–4. This text is also found in Florence, Bibl. Riccard., MS. 414, f. 28ʳ⁻ᵛ, and Bibl. Laur., MS. Ashburnham, 415, f. 54ʳ⁻ᵛ. It is quoted by R. Caracciolo of Lecce, *Sermones de Sanctis* (Venice, 1490), p. 141, probably from Bartholomew, and by Wadding, *Annales* v. 15. All ascribe it to the *Lib. Conc.*, but it is obviously a spurious text, perhaps inserted at *Lib. Conc.*, f. 133ᵛ, where Daniel's words on the 'duo viri, unus hinc, alius inde' (Dan. 12: 5) are commented on.

[3] Salimbene, p. 236; A. Callebaut, 'Le Joachimite Benoit, abbé de Camajore et Fra Salimbene', *AFH* xx (1927), pp. 219–22.

[4] As suggested by Benz, *Ecclesia Spiritualis*, p. 175.

[5] *Supra*, p. 168.

Testament.[1] He does not wish, he says, to detract from other saints such as Bernard or Dominic, but Francis arises from the east—'ab ortu solis'—whereas these others are only from the west: 'fuit etiam ipse solus magis conformis Christo quam ipsi . . . his ex causis solum Franciscum dico antonomastice a Deo destinatum tali tempore et specialiter talibus finibus et fine.'[2] Thus the constant twin themes of his work are the unique significance of Francis and the preservation of the Minorite Order for the special work of God until the Judgement Day, 'aliis ordinibus deficientibus'.[3] The unqualified approval with which his book, together with the tree he had painted, was received by the Chapter General of 1390[4] shows once again that a Joachimist interpretation of the historic role of St. Francis and his Order could be given without raising a suspicion of heresy. Only when belief was pushed to the point of defiance of authority did trouble arise.

A second fourteenth-century Franciscan who 'thought in the categories of Joachim',[5] yet remained entirely on the side of orthodoxy, was Pietro Aureoli. Ernst Benz has shown how in his Apocalypse-Commentary he is immersed in a way of thought closely akin to Joachimism. The *intelligentia spiritualis* is for him an understanding which emerges from the study of history; he adopts the framework of the seven ages of the Church; he sees the various angels of the Apocalypse as historical agents and assigns a high role to the two great Mendicant saints. Yet he separates himself from Joachim and his disciples in one crucial respect: he does not believe in the third *status* or expect the seventh age within history. Repudiating

---

[1] *AF* iv. 75–8. The scheme is as follows:

1st Seal or Age		Adam–Noah	Chief Man: Adam
2nd	,,	Noah–Abraham	Chief Man: Noah
3rd	,,	Abraham–Moses	Chief Man: Abraham
4th	,,	Exodus	Chief Man: Moses
5th	,,	David–Elijah	Chief Man: David
6th	,,	Elijah–Babylonish Captivity	Chief Man: Elijah
7th	,,	Babylonish Captivity–Christ	Chief Man: Simon Onias
1st Seal from		John Baptist	
2nd	,,	Advent of the Holy Spirit	Chief Man: Paul
3rd	,,	Nero to Constantine	Chief Man: St. Laurence
4th	,,	Constantine to S. Benedict	Chief Man: S. Anthony
5th	,,	Barbarian invasions	Chief Man: St. Benedict
6th	,,	Frederick II (1206)	Chief Man: S. Francis

[2] Ibid., p. 82.   [3] Ibid., p. 435.   [4] Ibid., p. xxiv.

[5] Benz, *Ecclesia Spiritualis*, 433. For this paragraph I have drawn chiefly on Benz's studies in the foregoing work, pp. 432–72, and in *ZKG* lii (1933), pp. 90–121.

this expectation of fulfilment within time, he ranges himself against the Spirituals. We have already examined the similar case of the English Minorite, Henry of Cossey.[1] He is interested in much the same thoughts as Aureoli, only, in this case, he is not afraid to cite Joachim extensively. He plays confidently with fire, without burning his fingers.[2] The significant point which emerges from such examples is that these Mendicants could be captured by a mode of historical exposition without succumbing to the infection of the radical hope which it was apt to engender.

Returning to the mid-thirteenth century, we find an unsolved problem concerning the origins of the Joachimist party within the Franciscan order. No evidence connects the early Franciscan houses in Calabria with the Florensians, and, although it has been suggested that the first focus of Joachimist studies was in the Franciscan convent at Naples, the earliest indication of contact comes in Salimbene's story of the Florensian Abbot who brought Joachim's works to the convent at Pisa. Our first direct evidence of a Franciscan group of Joachites belongs to the 1240s, when Salimbene gives us a vivid account of the group which gathered round Hugh de Digne at Hyères in Provence.[3] We see the enthusiastic circle—which included 'iudices et notarii atque phisici et alii litterati'—congregated in Hugh's room while he expounds the doctrine of the Abbot Joachim; we listen while they seek to convert a passing traveller who calls in between boats. The curious thing about these conversations is that they turn entirely on Joachim's prophecies of the days of crisis and Antichrist, and not at all on the ushering in of the third *status*. Although Salimbene elsewhere claims the prophecies of new orders as a matter of course, the group around Hugh de Digne does not seem to have concerned itself openly with the Abbot's pattern of threes or the special role which his third *status* might give them. In his writings Hugh upholds the ideal of absolute poverty with all the passionate zeal of the later Spirituals, but, again, he makes no

---

[1] *Supra*, pp. 86–7. The unknown author of the Apocalypse-Commentary in Florence, Bibl. Laur., Ashburnham 415, also makes extensive use of Joachim, going further towards the Spirituals' position than Henry of Cossey.

[2] If the author of *Vidit Jacob in somniis* was also a Franciscan, he belongs to the same category of those who made considerable use of Joachim's expositions without drawing revolutionary conclusions (cf. *supra*, pp. 87–8).

[3] Salimbene, 238 seq. On the early Franciscans in Calabria see F. Russo, *Misc. Franc.* xxxviii. 431–56; xl. 49–71; and *Storia dell'arcidiocesi di Cosenza* (Naples, 1956), pp. 102–6. In the latter work Russo asserts that in the thirteenth century neither Florensians nor Franciscans in Calabria had any connections with the Spiritual party.

open claim that the strict Franciscan party holds the key to the third *status*.[1] So far as the evidence goes, this group in Provence seems still to belong to what we have called the first phase of Joachimism, in which emphasis is placed on the pattern of twos and the crisis of history rather than on the pattern of threes and the *renovatio mundi*.[2] Since Hugh de Digne almost certainly died in 1255 or 1256 and not later, as has been supposed,[3] he finds a natural place in the first generation of Joachimists. Thus we may conclude that, while by the 1240s Joachimist discussions were going on among Franciscans, it was not until the 1260s that the full implications of the threefold doctrine of history were realized.

This view is supported by evidence from Thomas of Pavia in the 1250s.[4] His *Distinctiones* show that the focus of attention was Antichrist and that Joachim was not yet known for the doctrine of the three *status*, but still as the prophet of Antichrist. Thomas quotes a substantial passage from the *Expositio* on the two manifestations of Antichrist, the beast from the sea and the beast from the land, which Joachim here parallels with Nero and Simon Magus.[5] Thomas reserves judgement, but cannot refrain from recounting the vision of a 'certain religious' who dreamt that the Lateran Palace at Rome collapsed about him and a great voice cried 'Ecce Nero resuscitatus est et ipse est Antichristus!' In the passage from Thomas, already quoted in the first part, we see that Joachim's calculations on the forty-two generations were also the subject of discussion, that the year 1260 was expected to bring the climax, but that already there was talk of moving it on by calculating from the Passion instead of the Nativity. Thomas continually protests his neutrality, as if in argument, but we notice that he has read the pseudo-Joachimist commentary on the Sibyl Erithrea and studied the Dragon from the *Liber Figurarum*. Perhaps the argument was with Salimbene, who says of Thomas: 'multum fuit amicus meus quia multis annis . . . habitavi cum eo.'[6] Thomas remains a sceptic, but one who hopes for a denouement: 'Sed utrum haec spiritu suo vel Spiritu divino

[1] See his *De Finibus Paupertatis*, ed. C. Florovsky, *AFH* v (1912), pp. 277–90; *Expositio super regulam Fratrum Minorum* and *Dialogus inter zelatorem paupertatis et inimicum eius*, ed. in *Firmamentum trium ordinum B. Patris Francisci* (Paris, 1512), ff. 34ᵛ–54ʳ, 105ʳ–108ᵛ.
[2] Cf. Bloomfield, Reeves, *Speculum* xxix. 786–7, 792–3.
[3] See J. Albanes, *La Vie de sainte Douceline* (Marseille, 1879), pp. l–lii; *AFH* v (1912), p. 277.   [4] *Supra*, p. 53.
[5] *AFH* xvi (1923), pp. 25–6, cf. *Expos.*, f. 168ʳ.
[6] Salimbene, p. 430.

[Joachim] dixerit, penitus ignoro, sed cito futurum est ut sciatur an verum vel falsum dixerit' (*AFH* xvi. 28). There must have been a number of Franciscans between 1240 and 1260 who would have echoed these words.

Possibly the decisive influence in the full appropriation of Joachim's third *status* by the Franciscan Zealots was that of John of Parma. In the intense joy with which these greeted his election to the Generalship in 1247 there is a note of heightened significance: 'Well and truly you have come, but you have come late' are the prophetic words with which Brother Giles greets him.[1] Yet, once again, it is difficult to discover the precise content of his Joachimism. Perhaps we get closest to his mind in words attributed to him by Fra Angelo Clareno, the historian of the Spirituals:

Dicebat enim, cum status evangelice perfectionis a fratribus promissus sit altissimus, altissimam fidem, caritatem et operacionem requirit ab eis Deus. . . . Dicebat eciam ipse . . . quod fratres debebant in summa reverencia habere testamentum, tunc propter mandatum et benedictionem sancti, tunc quia Christi spiritus loquebatur in eo, qui post illam mirabilem sacrorum impressionem stigmatum plenius et perfectius habitavit in eo. . . . Et sicut in caritatis mandato et sacramento tota lex et prophete et evangelium pendet, ita in testamento beati Francisci omnis perfectio et intencio regularis et fidelis et spiritualis intelligencia clauditur . . . Et quia est necesse vitam evangelicam per Franciscum Christo iubente innovatam finaliter reformari, ideo Spiritus Sancti per Franciscum in fine post regulam edidit testamentum. (*ALKG* ii. 271–6.)

Here, although there is no explicit reference to Joachim, familiar notes are struck: the *status* of evangelical perfection which it is the Order's mission to guard is so high as to suggest a new spiritual plane; the Testament of St. Francis embodies the *spiritualis intelligencia* and stands on a level with the Scriptures; beyond crisis, reformation is inevitable. From the reminiscences of another Spiritual, Ubertino da Casale,[2] we learn that John of Parma did indeed

---

[1] Angelo Clareno, *Historia septem tribulationum*, *ALKG* ii. 263.

[2] *Arbor*, f. ccvi^v: 'Hic autem plenissime asserebat: sicut et ego auribus meis indignis ab eius sancto ore audivi: quod sextum signaculum in Francisco et eius statu accipiat ortum et quod in confusione vite et regule sue per transgressores filios et eius faventes malos prelatos debebat iniquitas ecclesie consumari. Illius inquit que non Hierusalem et sponsa Iesu nominatur, sed Babylon et meretrix et impudica: cuius iudicium clarificationem Christi vite plenissimam reddet et pro cuius damnatione in sexta visione Apocalypsim tam solenne a sanctis cantatur alleluia. . . . Nam et ego tunc iuvenis . . . expressum verbum audivi ab eius ore sanctissimo, intuens in eius angelicam faciem.'

see St. Francis and his order in the setting of the sixth seal of history, and the certain triumph of those that kept the Rule as the triumph of the saints over the Fall of Babylon. If we may trust Angelo, John of Parma defended his confidence in the ultimate *reformacio* by explicit reference to the prophecies of Joachim,[1] and the fact that a considerable part of his examination by Bonaventura turned on the doctrine of the Abbot, whom John and his companions stoutly defended from the charge of heresy, suggests that everyone knew this to be the foundation of their optimism, although the discussion is actually devoted to Joachim's doctrine of the Trinity rather than to his view of history.[2]

In this examination John's two fellow Joachites were Leonard and Gerard of Borgo San Donnino. It was the latter who first explicitly appropriated the Joachimist future for the Franciscan Order.[3] In announcing the Third Testament, the Eternal Evangel, Gerard was the first to proclaim the advent of the third *status* and to attempt the completion of the Abbot's pattern of threes in a sense which Joachim would have repudiated absolutely. Gerard's book dropped like a stone into the pool of Paris University in 1255, creating a series of ever-widening ripples. Here we are not concerned so much with its repercussions as with its content. According to the Protocol of the Commission of Anagni, Gerard had intended to publish the three main works of Joachim, the *Liber Concordie*, the *Expositio in Apocalypsim*, and the *Psalterium decem chordarum*, as the Eternal Evangel, together with a *Liber Introductorius* and a gloss of his own. Today we only know Gerard's *Introductorius* from the excerpts made by the commissioners and from the list of errors compiled by the Paris masters.[4] The latter probably exaggerated his heresies, while the former are not very full. Thus the work that would probably tell us most about the ideas of a mid-thirteenth-century Joachite in part eludes us. Perhaps Gerard's expectations can best be glimpsed in the emphases laid by the commissioners when making their selection from Joachim's writings.[5] These suggest that there were three main points in Gerard's gospel: the proclamation of the imminent third *status* of the Holy Spirit, which will be 'sine enigmate et sine figuris'; the declaration that about the year 1200 'exivit spiritus vite

[1] *ALKG* ii. 283.
[2] Ibid., pp. 276–7; also pp. 183–4. See also Wadding, *Annales* iv. 4–6.
[3] *Supra*, pp. 60–2.
[4] Apart from the Dresden manuscript mentioned *supra*, p. 60.
[5] *ALKG* i. 99–142.

de duobus testamentis ut fieret evangelium eternum'; the belief that
the Eternal Evangel was especially committed to a barefoot order
which would proceed equally from the clerical and lay orders.[1] The
commissioners further noted that Gerard himself identified St.
Francis as the angel of the sixth seal of the Apocalypse.[2] The Paris
masters added that in the third *status* Gerard expected the active
life of the clerical order to cease to be fruitful, giving place to the
contemplative life of the monastic order and especially to the *ordo
parvulorum.*[3] At this point the commissioners clearly saw the focus
of danger; after a long quotation from Joachim on the new order,
they burst out against the 'incredible exaltation' of this order:

Hactenus verba Joachim, quibus nititur mirabiliter et incredibiliter
exaltare nescio qualem ordinem venturum, ut dicit, in fine secundi status,
de quo iam non supersunt nisi quinque anni, sicut patet per predicta,
exaltare dico non solum super omnes alios ordines, sed et super totam
ecclesiam et super totum mundum. . . . Ex prenotatis videtur quod iste
novas et falsas opiniones confingat, et hoc maxime vane glorie causa, id
est, ut exaltet huiusmodi ordinem incredibiliter et intempestive super
alios ordines, immo super totam ecclesiam. (*ALKG* i. 112, 115.)

They then examined evidence in Joachim's writings for the depression or even supersession of the clerical order.

Gerard was apparently the first Joachite to exploit fully Joachim's
Trinitarian conception of history. Previously attention had been
directed towards the Abbot's twofold pattern of Seals and Openings.
The prophecies of two new orders had been appropriated without
their full implications. Now the fanatical Franciscan focused attention on the much more revolutionary idea of the three *status*, and
thereafter this was accepted as the key to Joachim's system of
thought. Gerard picked out, not the prophecies of the two new
orders which would effect the transition from the sixth age to the
seventh, but the concept of the final order which would embody the
life of the third *status* and might be claimed to supersede all others.
In so doing he was probably making a claim for the Franciscans
which had not been explicitly voiced before. The measure of his
confidence in the Joachimist view of history is seen in the fact that

[1] *ALKG* i. 101: 'Quod evangelium eternum traditum et commissum sit illi ordini
specialiter qui integratur et procedit equaliter ex ordine laicorum et ordine clericorum,
probatur xiii capitulo circa medium, quem ordinem appellat nudipedum xxvi capitulo in
fine.' See p. 126 for the Commission's comment on the *incredibilem exaltationem* of the
new order.   [2] Ibid., p. 101.
[3] M. Paris, *Chronica Maiora*, vi, *Additamenta*, RS, p. 338.

he entered rejoicing into his eighteen years' imprisonment, and nothing could shake his faith in the coming *status caritatis* which would be *sine enigmate figurarum*.

The writings of Joachim were never again publicly proclaimed as the Eternal Evangel, but one Dresden manuscript, so Professor Töpfer has claimed, still embodies the main part of Gerard's compilation and gloss, though not his Introduction.[1] The clues lie first in partly-erased *Explicits* and *Incipits*, such as that on f. 36ʳ, at the end of the *Liber Concordie*: 'Explicit primus liber evangelii spiritus sancti', corrected to 'Explicit quintus liber;[2] secondly, in a number of glosses incorporated in the text which, from the Protocol of Anagni, we know to have been Gerard's. Dr. Töpfer believes that Gerard's *Liber Introductorius* has been removed—probably by the same anxious hand as effected the erasures—and that with it the beginning of the *Liber Concordie* has gone. Fear of heresy has caused these mutilations, yet the original copyist must have shared Gerard's views. It seems much more likely that he was a thirteenth-century Franciscan Joachite than a later one, and some characteristics of the manuscript bear out this dating. It is tantalizing that experts cannot agree as to whether it was written in west Germany, France, or Italy, for the copyist—whoever he was—could lay his hands, not only on Gerard's dangerous work, but also on unique Trinitarian *figurae* of Joachim's, and other parts of the *Liber Figurarum* in a genuine form.[3] At the same time, he did not hesitate to add pseudo-Joachimist touches to the *figurae*, and he incorporated one spurious work into his collection, the *Super Hieremiam*. He would seem to have been a committed Joachite of the second generation, with access to genuine and spurious sources and more boldness than discretion in using them. Among the *figurae* there is one most suggestive addition to the Two Trees of Orders described above: Joachim had allowed the main stem of the second spiritual tree to burst into full foliage and fruit directly out of the Cistercian Order; the Dresden figure interposes a further stage of growth before the

---

[1] B. Töpfer, 'Eine Handschrift des Evangelium aeternum des Gerardino von Borgo San Donnino', *Zeitschrift f. Geschichtswissenschaft*, viii (1960), pp. 156–63.

[2] See also Dresden, MS. A. 121, f. 83ᵛ: illegible erasure; f. 100ᵛ (in a less obvious place and so escaping erasure): 'Explicit prologus in secundum Librum Librum evangelii eterni spiritus sancti. Incipit Liber secundus evangelii eterni abreviatus'; f. 131ʳ: 'Explicit apocalipsis nova, i.e. Liber [evangelii *erased*] spiritualis qui non tamen est integer, sed abreviatus.'

[3] See Reeves, Hirsch-Reich, *Studies*, pp. 102–05.

tree is crowned, a stage represented by a blank space for a nameless order.[1] The implication is surely clear that the copyist, not quite so blatant in his statement as Gerard, expected the Franciscans to fill this space.

We have little evidence that Gerard had any following. His book was, however, copied in Rome and brought to the Franciscan house at Imola in the 1270s, where Salimbene was asked—as a student of Joachim's works—to pronounce on it. His derisory comments (*verba frivola et risu digna*) reveal how completely Gerard's movement had failed.[2] When the real Spiritual group emerged, it represented a much more subtle blend of rigorist Franciscan observance and Joachimist eschatology. The Trinitarian conception of history was put in the background—only implicit in the claims made for St. Francis and the Rule—and the pattern of history which gave shape to their expectations was that of the seven Seals and Openings. No more was heard of a third Testament and little directly of a third *status*, but attention was focused on the opening of the sixth and seventh seals, which in Joachimist thought carried overtones of the emerging third *status*. Thus the Joachimism of the Spirituals could remain implicit and unrealized in large measure, concealed within a pattern of history which appeared orthodox in form.

[1] MS. Dresden, f. 89ᵛ, cf. *Lib. Fig.*, Pl. XXV.

[2] Salimbene, pp. 457–8, still praises Gerard, however, and Clareno's little sketch of him is sympathetic: 'Erat fr. G. memorie tenacis et diserte lingue et acuti intellectus et flumen auctoritatum sanctorum egrediebatur de ore eius et non poterant eum convincere racionibus nec auctoritatibus sanctorum' (*ALKG* ii. 284). On the question of the survival of Gerard's work, Renan, *Nouvelles Études* (ref. p. 91 n. 6), p. 260, points to evidence that the College of Navarre had in its library a book ascribed to Joachim, entitled *Evangelium Aeternum*, distinct from an *Introductorium in Evangelium Aeternum*.

V

SPIRITUAL FRANCISCANS AND FRATICELLI

OUR chief source for the Spiritual movement is Fra Angelo Clareno's great and moving account, the *Historia Septem Tribulationum*.[1] Clareno did not join the Order until 1270 and probably did not write the *Historia* until *c.* 1320. It contains mistakes and is certainly a partisan work, but it gives us, above all, the historical perspective in which the Spirituals viewed their sufferings. Its very structure, with its drama of seven acts rising to a climax in the seventh tribulation, embodies the Joachimist pattern of history, for the Church in the opening of the Sixth Seal must suffer the seven persecutions which will symbolize the world's history in microcosm. It can hardly be an accident that Angelo makes the number of the persecuted brethren in 1246 exactly seventy-two. This had been a significant number for Joachim, who discovered seventy-two *seniores* appointed by Moses in the wilderness and seventy-two disciples sent out by Christ. He used this concord in representing the transition of the Church from bondage to freedom, and the same symbolism must surely be in the Spiritual leader's mind.[2] In Angelo's narrative the brethren follow their foreordained pattern of tribulation through the wilderness, and they expect to cross Jordan into the promised *reformacio*. Theirs is not the optimism of an evolutionary view of history, but a cataclysmic: 'De gradu in gradum usque ad septimum religio corruet. . . . sed semper erit ad peiora prolapsus, donec miraculo grandi et stupendo reparatio per illum qui hedificavit, et reformacio per illum qui creavit et fundavit fiet' (*ALKG* ii. 278). Thus the mood of the Zealots was a mixture of foreboding and hope: they expected both the worst and the best, but their confidence was unbounded, for the key to the future was in their hands.

[1] Ed. F. Tocco, *Le due prime tribolazioni dell'ordine dei minori* (*Rendiconti della Reale Accademia dei Lincei*, xvii) (Rome, 1908), pp. 97–131, 221–36; remainder ed. F. Ehrle, *ALKG* ii. 125–55, 256–327.

[2] *ALKG* ii. 261; see also Wadding, *Annales* iii. 100. For Joachim's use of these numbers see *Lib. Conc.*, f. 12ʳ; *Vita S. Benedicti*, pp. 56, 58; *Septem Sigillis*, p. 240. The Biblical references are to Num. 11: 16, 26; Luke 10: 1. The number is really seventy. For Joachim's reasoning in making this 70+2 see *Lib. Conc.*, f. 12ʳ.

This belief in the future was the driving force of the Spiritual group; it lay behind their bitter opposition to the growth of the Order in terms of buildings, legacies, and libraries, their passionate devotion to their patched and skimpy habits, their audacious defence before the Provincial Chapter in 1274.[1] From 1278 to 1289 Fra Angelo, together with Peter of Macerata (Fra Liberato) and others, suffered brutal imprisonment at the hands of the brethren, only to be ended by Raymund Gaufridi, the new General. He dispatched them on a mission to Armenia, where they laboured successfully until jealous attacks of their enemies drove them back to Italy about 1294. As Angelo reached in his history the advent of Pope Celestine V in 1294, the sense of crisis deepened. Intense joy on the part of the Zealots greeted the Hermit Pope, perhaps the joy of those who believed him to be the Angelic Pope.[2] Conviction as to their own high mission had now reached the point of seeking separation rather than relinquishing their role. So Peter of Macerata and Angelo Clareno obtained from Celestine absolution from the vows of obedience made to the Minorite Superiors, and permission to follow the strict Rule and Testament of St. Francis as a group within Celestine's own Order of poor hermits. But the renunciation of Celestine followed immediately, and under Boniface VIII the little new Order was abandoned to the fury of the enemies from whom they had thought to escape.[3]

With the swift downfall of hope Celestine became to Angelo the herald of the great tribulation of the Church which would endure for twenty-eight years.[4] Now indeed the world was plunging into the crisis of all time: it was the Opening of the Sixth Seal, heralded by visions to the expectant brethren, in one of which the Sealed Book of the Apocalypse itself appeared.[5] For the little group gathered around

[1] On all this period in their history see *ALKG* ii. 293–308.
[2] Ibid., p. 309.   [3] Ibid., pp. 309 seq.
[4] Ibid., p. 126.
[5] Ibid., pp. 126–7: 'Preterea ille, qui vidit et audivit aliqua particularia, que non communicanda suscepit nec communicavit alieni, quando terminum illum XXVIII annorum didicit, circa finem VIImi anni papae Bonifacii, rem valde notabilem et specificam et temporum ordinis distinctivam. In sexta die et diei hora sexta in medio positus multorum servorum Dei vidit nam subito in medio cuiusdam ospicii monasterii magni nominis domine, ubi XL et amplius erant viri religiosi, pulpidum tobalea co-opertum positum est. Et ecce dyaconus leviticis indumentis paratus apparuit et liber VII signacula habens clausus in pulpito ponitur. Et accessit dyaconus apperire librum et apperuit sextum signaculum libri que erant in sexta parte libri lecturus. Et cum inspexisset ea, que in apercione VI continebantur, totus mente et corpore immutatus legere, que lecturus venerat, non valebat, sed resolutus in lacrimas silencio et inenarrabili gemitu,

Liberato and Angelo the fury of persecution which drove them into Greece in 1295 was rising into the scale of the final sixth and seventh tribulations. Perhaps they remembered Gerard of Borgo San Donnino's prophecy of a pseudo-pope who at the end of the sixth age would embody the abomination of desolation,[1] and applied this to Boniface VIII, who had pulled down the holy Hermit Pope and pursued them into Greece with anathemas. Perhaps something of their intense mood of expectation has been preserved for us in a curious group of writings, of which the best known is the *Vaticinia de Summis Pontificibus* (first series).[2] Professor Grundmann's study of these has shown that they derive from a Byzantine source but were written in Italy, perhaps by one of Angelo's circle, about the time of Benedict XI's death in 1304.[3] The Zealots had returned after Boniface's death to seek papal favour once more and were gathered at Perugia awaiting the future. This first series of *Vaticinia* consists of fifteen prophecies, each representing a pope by means of a picture, a key phrase, and an enigmatic description. The series begins with Nicholas III, and the 'unholy' portraits are identifiable as far as Boniface VIII, with the dramatic exception of Celestine V, who is represented as a monk with the key caption *Elatio, Obedientia, Paupertas, Castitas, Temperantia, Ypocrisorum Destructor*.[4] After

que continebantur in libro, videnti reservavit, quod universaliter que (ad) VIam ordinis tribulacionem pertinebant . . .'

Another vision of a tree recalls the tree-figures of Joachim: Fr. Jacobus has a vision of a tree representing their Order, with John of Parma on the topmost branch. Christ from His throne gives St. Francis a chalice 'spiritu vite plenus' which he takes to his Order. John of Parma and a few more drink the whole. John 'totus factus est luminosus sicut sol' and the few also are similarly illumined. Some pour it away and become devils; some drink part. 'Pre omnibus autem, qui in arbore erant, luce splendebat fr. Johannes, qui totus ad vere lucis abissum infinitam contemplandam conversus intellexit tempestatis insurrecture contra arborem turbinem, et recedens de suprema rami illius altitudine, in quo stabat, ramis omnibus omissis in solidiori loco stipitis arboris se abscondit.' Bonaventura succeeds him in the tree, drinks part of the chalice, and pours out part. Then there is a great storm in the tree and those brethren who poured out the cup of life fall from it, while those who drank are translated. The tree is uprooted: 'arbor radicibus evulsa in terra corruit et confracta comminuta a turbine tempestatis in omnem ventum dispersa evanuit. Turbine autem illo ac tempestate cessante de aurea radice pullulavit aurea plantacio, aurea tota, que et flores et folia et aureos fructus produxit; de cuius arboris dillatacione, profunditate, altitudine, odore, pulchritudine tacere melius quam exprimere' (*ALKG* ii. 280–1).

The same vision, in almost identical words in Italian, is found in *I Fioretti*, ed. G. Fiore (Florence, 1943), pp. 123–5.

[1] *ALKG* i. 123.   [2] *Supra*, p. 58.
[3] Grundmann, (i) *AK* xix. 107; (ii) *HJ* xlix. 41.

[4] No. 5 where this series of 15 is given alone; No. 20 where the double series of 30 is given.

Boniface VIII there follows Benedict XI, and then begins an imaginary series of which the last six in the original order are clearly the 'holy' portraits of Angelic Popes.[1] The *Vaticinia* must, then, have been written before the election of Clement V, probably in the summer of 1304, and at that moment the *reformacio* seemed very near. Professor Grundmann has established the fact that, shortly after this series of prophecies, three other works in the same vein, the *Liber de Flore*, the *Horoscopus* of an unknown author named Dandalus, and commentaries on each of these, were written in 1304–5 or, in the case of the last, perhaps a little later.[2] In the *Liber de Flore* there is a series of portraits of four Angelic Popes which has an interesting later history; and the series of *Vaticinia*, with a later fifteen added to it, had, as we have seen, a tremendous vogue in the fifteenth and sixteenth centuries. For the moment, however, our concern is with the evidence these writings afford of the expectations of Spiritual Franciscans in the year 1304/5. Their hope was now focused on the Holy See itself. The new age must be ushered in by a mystical revolution in the very seat of authority, and in this year that revolution seemed to be at hand. How little in touch this group of visionaries were with political actualities is sharply underlined by the events of Clement V's pontificate.

Meantime, seeds of Joachimism, probably sown by Hugh de Digne, had germinated in Provence in a plant of which the chief fruit was the strange and enigmatic Petrus Joannis Olivi. It is probably impossible now to appraise him justly, for most of his contemporaries were unable to view him except through the spectacles of a heightened emotional significance. Both friends and foes placed him within the context of Last Things. To the latter he was a manifestation of Antichrist, to the former one of the prophets of the final age. The place ascribed to him by Spirituals, both in Provence and Italy, well illustrates the influence of Joachim's system upon their thoughts. Joachim had hinted several times at the fulfilment of the sequence of threes in terms of great leaders to match those of the first and second *status*. The Spirituals had already allotted the tremendous role of Christ in the third *status* to St.

---

[1] Numbers 10–15 in the original series; 25–30 in the double series. But in some versions the order is changed slightly. The captions are: *Bona gratia Simonia cessabit, Bona oratio, Bona intentio caritas, Pro honorata concordia erit, Bona occasio, Reverentia devotio.*

[2] Grundmann, op. cit. (ii), p. 41. Cf. *infra*, pp. 402–3.

Francis; now we find Olivi ranked with the Apostles and matched with St. Paul:[1]

Item dicunt ipsum esse ita magnum doctorem quod ab apostolis et evangelistis citra non fuerit aliquis maior eo. . . . Item, aliqui ex eis dicunt quod non fuit aliquis doctor in ecclesia Dei, excepto S. Paulo et dicto fratre Petro Johannis, cuius dicta non fuerint in aliquo per ecclesiam refutata; sed tota doctrina S. Pauli et fratris Petri Johannis est tenenda totaliter per ecclesiam, nec est una littera dimittenda.

Angelo Clareno, who probably never met him personally, believed him to have been foretold by the prophets, and particularly by the Abbot Joachim, who had applied the prophecy of St. Cyril to him.[2] In a letter Angelo listed him among the 'saints' of the Spirituals— 'hinc Deus celestes homines Iohannem de Parma, Corradum de Offida, Petrum de Murrone, Petrum Johannem [*sic*] clarificare miraculis voluit'[3]—and elsewhere we are told that he was the holy but uncanonized father of his sect.[4]

It is difficult now to understand the nature of the leadership exercised by Olivi, for much of his writing is in a key of moderation and sound scholarship that seems out of keeping with the high notes of fanaticism. Dr. Manselli has shown that his attitude to Joachim was not that of the slavish follower, but the admirer who regarded him as a great but not infallible authority, to be cited with due critical discrimination.[5] Nevertheless, the Joachimist overtones

---

[1] B. Gui, *Manuel* i. 138. My examination of Olivi's Joachimism was written before the appearance of Dr. Gordon Leff's *Heresy in the Later Middle Ages* (Manchester, 1967), with its important account of Olivi (pp. 100–39). [2] *ALKG* ii. 289.
[3] *ALKG* i. 558. [4] Gui, *Manuel* i. 138.
[5] Manselli, *Lectura*, pp. 163–4. Manselli quotes from Olivi's *Super Ysaiam*, MS. Padua, 1540, ff. 15–16: 'Et hoc modo Ioachim in libro Concordie et in expositione Apocalipsis dicit se subito accepisse totam concordiam veteris et novi testamenti quantum ad quasdam generales regulas ex quibus ipse postmodum aliqua quasi argumentando deducti [*sic*] et ut sibi videtur aliquando sic quod ex hoc extimat habere certam intelligentiam conclusionis sic deducte, aliquando vero nonnisi probabilem coniecturam in qua plerumque potuit falli. Et est simile in naturali lumine intellectus nobis ab initio nostre conditionis incerto per illud enim sine aliqua argumentatione apprehendimus et scimus prima principia et deinde aliquas conclusiones necessario inferimus per illa aliquas vero solum probabiliter et in hiis plerumque fallimur. Non tamen ex hoc sequitur quod lumen illud non sit a Deo aut quod in se sit falsum. Quod signanter dico quia quidam ex hoc voluerunt concludere quod tota intelligentia Ioachim fuerit a diabolo vel coniectura spiritus humani quia in quibusdam particularibus loquitur opinabiliter et forte aliquando fallibiliter' (p. 163 n. 3). Cf. a comment which Olivi made in the *Postilla* that Joachim made some statements not authoritatively but 'opinative sicut ex naturali lumine intellectus' (Rome, Bibl. Angelica, MS. 382, f. 66ᵛ). All references are to this manuscript.

are there and these must have sounded more insistently in his preaching, for it is with the passion and confidence of Joachimists that his followers defended his teaching. The clue lies in his *Postilla super Apocalypsim*, written late in life, though Dr. Manselli has found many of the ideas in this work already present in earlier ones. In the *Postilla*, where he expounds his view of history, Olivi was dealing with matters which concerned him deeply: the crucial times approaching, the cosmic forces of good and evil, the supreme mission of those who defended evangelical perfection. It was Joachim's pattern of double sevens on which he fastened most strongly; he believed the Church to be standing in the sixth age of the second seven, the age which was to be 'notabiliter preeminens quinque primis', the end of the old and the 'initium novi seculi'.[1] Dr. Manselli has argued that because Olivi, like Bonaventura, consciously disavowed Joachim's Trinitarian doctrine as condemned by the Church, his conception of history was also cut loose from Joachim's Trinitarian reading of it.[2] I do not think this judgement is correct. The *Postilla* shows that Olivi not only took his structure of history straight from Joachim's pattern of twos, but that, although he emphasized it less, Joachim's pattern of threes was also an essential part of his whole design. He specifically related the seven *status* of the Church to the second and third of the three 'general' *status* of the world, elevating the sixth and seventh *status* of the Church into the *tertius status generalis*, and this conception he explicitly attributes to the Abbot Joachim (f. 52^r). Again, he takes directly from Joachim the belief that, just as the synagogue had been propagated by twelve patriarchs and the Church of the Gentiles by twelve apostles, 'sic finaliter ecclesia . . . est per xii viros evangelicos propaganda', to which he adds: 'unde et Franciscus habuit xii filios et socios per quos et in quibus fuit fundatus et initiatus ordo evangelicus' (f. 56^v).

The question of Olivi's Joachimism seems to me to be clinched by a passage in which he expounds the *clavis David* given to the Church of Philadelphia. He uses this to develop a full statement of the three *status* in direct relation to the three Persons of the Trinity. Significantly, he does not name Joachim as his source here, but, in fact, part of the passage is a direct quotation from the *Expositio*, part is a paraphrase, and the images and language of the rest reflect Joachim's style of thought. In the following extract the direct borrowings from *Expositio*, ff. 84^v–85^v, are italicized:

[1] *Postilla*, f. 1^v.   [2] Manselli, *Lectura*, pp. 165 seq., 186–7.

Significatur etiam per hoc proprium donum et singularis proprietas tertii status mundi VI° statu ecclesie inchoandi et spiritui sancto per quandam antonomasiam appropriati. Sicut enim *in primo statu seculi ante Christum studium fuit patribus enarrare magna opera Domini incohata ab origine mundi, in secundo vero statu a Christo usque ad tertium statum cura fuit filiis quaerere sapientiam mysticarum rerum et mysteria occulta in generationibus seculorum. Sic in tertio nil restat nisi ut psallamus et iubilemus Deo laudantes eius opera magna et eius multiformem sapientiam* et bonitatem in suis operibus et scripturarum sermonibus clare manifestatam. Sicut enim in primo tempore exhibuit se Deus pater ut *terribilem* et metuendum, unde tunc claruit eius *timor,* sic in secundo exhibuit se Deus filius ut magistrum et revelatorem et ut verbum expressimum sapientiae sui patris. Ergo in tertio tempore spiritus sanctus exhibebit se ut flammam et fornacem divini amoris et ut cellarium ebrietatis spiritualis et ut apothecam divinorum aromatum et spiritualium unctionem et unguentarum et ut *tripudium* spiritualium *iubilacionum* et iocunditatum, per quam non solum simplici intelligentia, sed etiam gustativa et palpativa experientia videbitur omnis veritas sapientie verbi Dei incarnati et potentia Dei patris. Christus enim promisit quod cum venerit ille spiritus veritatis, docebit vos omnem veritatem et ille me clarificabit. (*Postilla,* f. 31ᵛ.)

To this Olivi adds a sequence of three *opera* and orders: *labor corporalium operum* appropriate to the laity, *eruditio scripturarum* appropriate to the clergy, and *suavitas contemplationis* appropriate to monks. These *opera* are paralleled in the *Expositio* by *labor, lectio, iubilatio* (f. 85ᵛ), while the orders are obviously Joachim's famous sequence.[1]

[1] The *Postilla* is still unpublished. I have examined only parts of it in detail in Rome, Bibl. Angelica, MS. 382. In these parts the references to Joachim are numerous, outnumbering any others. Olivi draws most of his interpretation of Old Testament and Church history from the *Liber Concordie* (see especially ff. 1ᵛ–13ᵛ). In his expositions of the Apocalypse Olivi uses characteristic ideas of Joachim, e.g. his five/seven division of Tribes and Churches (f. 13ʳ⁻ᵛ), his Trinitarian interpretation of the Alpha and Omega (f. 17ᵛ), his symbolism of the trumpet (ff. 60ᵛ, 62ʳ). The exposition of Apocalypse 17–20 demonstrates clearly Olivi's reliance on Joachim. The Abbot is cited specifically fourteen times, and when one compares the *Postilla* closely with Joachim's *Expositio* on these chapters, it is evident that Olivi is drawing on large portions of the latter, though not necessarily quoting verbatim or using ideas in the same order. A rough collation can be made thus:

Postilla	Expositio
f. 105ᵛ	ff. 156ᵛ, 196ʳ, echo of 203ʳ
f. 106ᵛ	f. 198ᵛ
f. 107ʳ	ff. 198ᵛ–199ᵛ
f. 107ᵛ	f. 200ʳ⁻ᵛ
f. 108ᵛ	ff. 201ʳ (summarizes this page on the evils of the carnal church), 202ʳ

[Footnote continued overleaf.

There is no doubt that Olivi expected a flowering of history between the triumph of Antichrist and the *consummatio seculi*, and that St. Francis held in his mind a unique position as the initiator of this final epoch. In one line of thought he combined a Christocentric view of history with a threefold pattern which exalted the epoch of St. Francis into a special category: this was the concept of three Advents of Christ: first in the flesh, second in the spirit of evangelical reform when there would appear 'quoddam novum seculum seu nova ecclesia', third in final judgement.[1] The conformity of St. Francis with Christ was specifically placed within this eschatological framework of history:

Sicut etiam in sexta aetate, reiecto carnali Judaismo et vetustate prioris seculi, venit novus homo Christus cum nova lege et vita et cruce, sic in sexto statu, reiecta carnali Ecclesia et vetustate prioris seculi, renovabitur Christi lex et vita et crux. Propter quod in eius primo initio Franciscus apparuit, Christi plagis characterizatus et Christo totus concrucifixus et configuratus. (*Postilla*, f. 13ʳ.)

In this context of history St. Francis assumed the cosmic role of Christ Himself to wage war on Antichrist.[2] He was the Elijah of the sixth age sent to initiate that *status evangelicus* which is and ought to be in all things *immobilis et indissolubilis*.[3] As Olivi had earlier declared: '. . . teneo et scio regulam S. Francisci statumque minorum esse vere evangelicum et apostolicum et finem omnium aliorum, in quo et per quem sollempniora suorum operum consummaturus est

Postilla	Expositio
f. 109ʳ	f. 202ᵛ (continues to follow Joachim's sequence in 203ʳ seq.)
f. 109ᵛ	f. 204ᵛ
f. 110ʳ	related to 206ʳ, adaptation from 203ʳ
f. 111ʳ	f. 209ʳ⁻ᵛ
f. 122ʳ	ff. 209ᵛ–212ʳ
f. 113ᵛ	long summary of passage from the pseudo-Joachimist work *De semine scripturarum*

In the parts studied I have found six direct references to the *tertius generalis status* (ff. 12ʳ, 32ᵛ, 52ᵛ, 55ʳ, 109ʳ, 113ʳ). Manselli, *Lectura*, p. 190, warns against using the extracts given by Baluze, since they over-emphasize points and take them out of context, but in the comparisons I have been able to make this is not the case: the quotations correspond closely and genuinely reflect the thinking of the work. For Manselli's view of Olivi and the three *status* see *Lectura*, pp. 187–8. Olivi's disciples among the Provençal Beguins later asserted specifically that they derived the doctrine of the three *status* from Olivi's *Postilla*; see *infra*, pp. 204–5.

[1] *Postilla*, ff. 7ᵛ–8ʳ.
[2] Ibid., f. 52ʳ; Manselli, *Lectura*, p. 266.
[3] Manselli, *Lectura*, p. 214; *ALKG* iii. 528.

Christus tanquam in opere et requie sexte et septime diei' (*ALKG* iii. 619 n. 3). It was to St. Francis and his order that the final eschatological task of converting the whole world was assigned.[1] The supreme duty imposed by Olivi's reading of history was to preserve the Rule inviolate:

Si quis autem profundius inspiceret, quomodo per vitam Christi et renovationem eius circa finem ecclesie consistat illustratio et exaltatio universalis ecclesie et ineffabilis appertio scripturarum et destructio antichristi et omnium testamentorum et introductio Judeorum et consummatio omnium, . . . videret clarius, quomodo istius status et regule laxatio et obfuscatio in tantum est pestilens, quod ex ea sequatur denigratio totius fidei, introductio antichristi et omnium temptationum finalium et dissipatio omnis perfecti boni, et tunc indubitabiliter certissimum esset, quod a nullo vivente dispensationem recipere potest. (*ALKG* iii. 530.)

Thus we see the consummation of the whole of history bound up with the Rule of St. Francis.

On the problem of authority Olivi, like Joachim, drew back from logical extremes. As the synagogue had once been rejected when the *ecclesia plenitudinis gentium* was elected, so in the sixth age the carnal church or adulterous Babylon must be rejected, since 'opus est spiritualem ecclesiam exaltari'.[2] Olivi certainly looked for a mystic Antichrist, a false pope, as well as an open one, a mighty king, and the new age was to be ushered in by cataclysmic events.[3] Did he, then, repudiate the existing hierarchy? Nowhere is this stated, and in his own life he opposed separation and submitted to authority.[4] Yet the elect of the sixth age were to be as superior to those of former ages as men to animals, and they would form the

---

[1] Baluze, *Miscellanea*, p. 266. Olivi borrows from Joachim's great passage on the two orders, quoted *supra*, pp. 143–4 (*Postilla*, f. 96ʳ). A marginal note to this passage of the *Postilla* reads: 'Nota secundum ioachim de sancto francisco.'

[2] *Postilla*, f. 109ʳ (after referring to Queen Vashti rejected in favour of Esther). See also f. 32ᵛ for a strong statement on the transfer of glory from the adulterous church of the fifth *status* to the elect of the sixth.

[3] Baluze, *Miscellanea*, pp. 261–9.

[4] Manselli, *Lectura*, pp. 174–5, 219–29, argues that Olivi never conceived of the carnal church as a concrete reality which could be identified in time and space, and that therefore it is a complete error, already made by contemporaries, to accuse Olivi of identifying the carnal church with the Roman Church and the *Antichristus mysticus* with the Pope. From the section I have studied (*supra*, p. 197 n. 1) it seems clear that Olivi adopted exactly Joachim's position. The *mercatores* and *negotiatores* of New Babylon are interpreted as various types of carnal ecclesiastics, and here Olivi quotes Joachim extensively (ff. 107ʳ–108ᵛ). New Babylon and the carnal church seem to be clearly synonymous, but nowhere—any more than in Joachim's *Expositio*—is there any hint of identifying it with the Roman Church.

Holy Jerusalem of the seventh age and third *status*. Like Joachim's, his view of this blessed state was mystical rather than institutional: it was characterized equally by the spiritual intelligence of the contemplative and the evangelical poverty of the friar. As we have already seen, Olivi could write on the Age of the Spirit in the language of Joachim: equally he could borrow from Joachim the image of the hollow *cithara* as the symbol of evangelical poverty: 'Secundum Joachim vacuitas cithare significat voluntariam paupertatem; sicut enim vas musicum non bene resonat nisi sit concavum, sic nec laus bene coram Deo resonat nisi amore humili et a terrenis evacuata procedat' (*Postilla*, f. 93ᵛ, quoting *Expositio*, f. 172ʳ). Like Joachim, too, he distinguished the great seventh age of history from the eternal bliss of the Eighth Day: at the close of the former mankind would once more degenerate, Gog and Magog would burst forth, and Christ would appear in judgement.[1]

It was not until he was over forty—in 1282—that Olivi was accused of putting forth strange and erroneous doctrines.[2] Before this his views on poverty had, on the whole, met with approval and there seems no obvious reason for a storm to have broken just then. The examination which took place concerned his theological and philosophical theories as well as his teaching on poverty: on the former, the errors raised do not seem to have been grave; on the latter, as Olivi himself said, Bonaventura and Pecham would have been condemned with him. It is difficult to believe that the real ground for attack lay here; probably it is to be found in the fact that Olivi was gathering a band of disciples around him in Provence and that already his doctrine of poverty, moderate though it was in itself, was being set in a framework of Joachimist prophecy. In 1285, in fact, he was accused of being the head of a superstitious sect in Provence. The storm once raised could not be stilled. Olivi was sent in 1287 as lector to Santa Croce, Florence, there to exercise his magnetic influence over the group of Tuscan Zealots including Ubertino da Casale. On his return to a lectorship at Montpellier he was forced to defend his views on poverty again at the Chapter General of Paris in 1292, and behind this probably lay the excessive statements of his followers. He died in 1298, having lived out his last years much respected in the convent of Narbonne, and, according to tradition, declaring on his death-bed that, as a loyal son of the Church, he

---

[1] Manselli, *Lectura*, pp. 235-6.
[2] Douie, *Fraticelli*, pp. 84 seq.; Lambert, *Franciscan Poverty*, pp. 155 seq.

committed all his written works to her judgement.[1] In this he followed Joachim, who was unaware of the dangerous matter his works contained. Perhaps Olivi, too, remained unaware that in adopting Joachim's expectation of a new epoch he was handling an idea far more explosive than any of the speculations he had dealt with in the Schools. Whether he knew it or not, it was his Joachimist expectation that was Olivi's chief legacy to his followers and the source of all their stubborn confidence.

The persecution of his followers, which began in his lifetime, broke in a storm after his writings had been condemned at the Chapter General of Lyons in 1299 and their possession forbidden under pain of excommunication. It is bound up with the history of the great inquiry into the split between Conventuals and Spirituals in the Franciscan Order which was initiated by Clement V in 1309. The accusations against Olivi's followers focus on their veneration for Olivi himself, their refusal to surrender his books, and their devotion to the symbols of absolute poverty. These points suggest that their real crime was a form of Joachimism, i.e. the investing of these issues with a cosmic importance. We get a hint of this in the assertion of the four who were burned at Marseilles in 1318, that to force them to give up their habit was akin to the action of the Jews in casting Christ out of the synagogue.[2] The evidence of a Joachimist faith comes out most clearly in the case of Bernard Délicieux, whose connection with the Provençal Spirituals begins *c.* 1310 and who came to the fore as their leader when they were summoned before John XXII in 1316.[3]

This popular hero of Carcassonne and Albi had been leading opposition to the Inquisition since 1296 and was feared by both lay and ecclesiastical authorities for his power to incite a crowd by his

[1] The text of Olivi's dying testimony of faith is suspect, but Manselli points to the conclusion of his *Postilla* as indubitable evidence of his attitude of submission. Here Olivi quotes from both Joachim and Richard of St. Victor: 'Ut autem verbis Joachim utar, referamus et nos gratias ei qui nos decursis tantis pelagis perduxit ad portum orantes ut si in aliquibus locis aliter locuti sumus quam ipse voluit prestet indulgentiam delinquenti. Quod si est qui pie corrigat, dum adhuc vivo, paratus sum suscipere correctionem. Si autem velox vocatio Domini subtraxerit ex hac luce, Romana ecclesia cui datum est universale magisterium, si qua indigna esse perspexerit dignetur, obsecro emendare . . .' (Manselli, *Lectura*, p. 220 n. 2). Cf. *Expositio*, ff. 223ᵛ–224ʳ.

[2] Douie, *Fraticelli*, p. 20.

[3] On Bernard Délicieux see B. Hauréau, *Bernard Délicieux et l'Inquisition Albigeoise* (Paris, 1877); M. de Dmitrewski, 'Fr. Bernard Délicieux, O.F.M., sa lutte contre l'Inquisition de Carcassonne et d'Albi, son procès, 1297–1319', *AFH* xvii (1924), pp. 183–218, 313–37, 457–88; xviii (1925), pp. 3–22; Douie, *Fraticelli*, pp. 18–20.

preaching. For a moment in 1303–4 it looked as if he might win the King of France to his side against ecclesiastical tyrannies, but Philip le Bel's relations with the new Pope, Benedict XI, were more important to him. In 1304 Benedict ordered the arrest of Bernard and it is at this moment, when he resisted arrest and carried the town of Carcassonne with him in defiance, that we first discover the faith in a Joachimist future which was the ground of his intrepid confidence. He preached to the people of Carcassonne on 'the sibyls and other prophecies, on an order of ravens and one of doves'.[1] All the people kissed his hands as he left and hailed him as an angel sent from God. A 'Papalarius' attributed to Joachim came into his hands a little later: it had pictures of popes past and future[2] and was clearly the *Vaticinia* recently produced.[3] Whether he obtained it directly from them or through his friend Arnold of Villanova, we cannot tell, but it speedily became his strength and shield. He told Arnold he had irrefutable proof that Benedict XI would shortly die[4]—and behold, he did! This raised an accusation of having compassed the Pope's death and in 1305 he was summoned before Clement V at Lyon. He did not return to the south until 1310, but came back as the convinced Joachite, absorbed in the study of Joachimist prophecies and speculating on the coming of Antichrist.[5] It is at this point that we begin to hear of his veneration for Olivi and his belief in the cause of the Spirituals. In 1316 he spoke for them with great intrepidity before John XXII. In the trial which followed, his faith in the *Vaticinia*—'in quodam libro in quo erant multi characteres et multae rotae et diversae scripturae in suis circumferentiis'—and his willingness to suffer for Olivi were both mentioned among the articles of accusation.[6] Bernard was unfrocked and imprisoned for life. When he disappeared from view he was still, like Gerard of Borgo San Donnino, a Joachite. On the journey from Avignon to his prison at Toulouse he spoke openly of the *Vaticinia* of Joachim.[7] When asked how he could read the future, he replied: 'Isaiah and Joachim, how did they know the future?' Affliction, however, brought to the forefront of his mind the necessity of martyrdom, in place of confidence in the future:

Dixit, quod sibi erant tot et tanta revelata et se invenisse per doctrinam

---

[1] *AFH* xvii. 332. [2] Ibid., p. 332 and n. 3.
[3] *Supra*, p. 193. [4] *AFH*, vol. cit., p. 333.
[5] Ibid., pp. 463–4. He was even reported to have said that if he were pope he would annul the decretal condemning Joachim's Trinitarian views.
[6] Ibid., pp. 472, 473. [7] Ibid., p. 332 n. 3.

dicti Ioachim et per dicta prophetarum, quod non credebat quod a ducentis annis citra essent alicui viventi tot revelata, et quod inter caetera erat sibi revelata persecutio quam patitur ipse idem frater Bernardus et persecutio illorum qui fuerunt combusti in Massilia, et quod de ordine Minorum affectionis suae et evangelicae paupertatis debeant esse septuaginta duo martyres Dei et in brevi. (*AFH* xvii. 466 n. 1.)

From 1317 onwards the followers of Olivi are to be found in the heretical sect called Beguins. Bernard Gui, the Inquisitor, describes them thus: '. . . qui fratres Pauperes se appellant et dicunt se tenere et profiteri tertiam regulam sancti Francisci, modernis temporibus exsurrexit in provincia Provincie et in provincia Narbonensi et in quibusdam locis provincie Tholosane. . . .' (Gui, *Manuel* i. 108). His analysis of their beliefs, written before 1325, reveals in the clearest possible way the extreme consequences of arrogating to themselves the role of new spiritual men within the framework of a Joachimist future.[1] The most perfect state in the Church is that of evangelical poverty; after Christ and His Mother, St. Francis is the highest observer of the evangelical rule and its renovator in the sixth age of the Church; the Rule of St. Francis *is* the Evangel of Christ. As no one can change the Gospel, so no one can change the Rule: neither Pope nor Council can prevail against it. Against the might of the visible Church the small sect stands and judges it by this standard of the future: they distinguish two churches—a carnal, 'quam dicunt esse ecclesiam Romanam quantum ad multitudinem reproborum', and a spiritual, 'quantum ad viros quos vocant spirituales et evangelicos qui vitam Christi et apostolorum servant',[2] and this spiritual church they claim to be theirs. At the end of the sixth age, 'in quo statu dicunt nos esse',[2] the carnal church will be rejected by Christ, whom it has crucified again in the persecuted *pauperes*, as once the synagogue was rejected. In the persecution of Antichrist all religious orders will perish except a third part of the Order of St. Francis from which will be drawn the handful, perhaps a dozen, of chosen men, *spirituales, pauperes evangelici*, who will found the 'ecclesia spiritualis que erit humilis et benigna in septimo et ultimo statu Ecclesie'.[2] Then the Holy Spirit will be poured out on these men as once at Pentecost.[3] After the death of Antichrist they will convert the whole world, which will become

---

[1] Gui, *Manuel* i. 108–74 (Latin and French).   [2] Ibid., p. 144.

[3] Ibid., p. 146: '. . . aliqui ex eis dogmatizant quod Spiritus Sanctus effundetur in majori habundantia vel saltem in equali super illos viros electos spirituales et evangelicos per quos fundabitur ecclesia spiritualis et benigna in septimo et ultimo statu, quam

bonus et benignus . . . et omnia erunt communia quoad usum et non erit
aliquis qui offendat alium vel sollicitet ad peccatum, quia maximus amor
erit inter eos et erit tunc unum ovile et unus pastor; et talis hominum
status et conditio durabit secundum aliquos ex ipsis per centum annos;
deinde deficiente amore, paulatim subingredietur malitia et in tantum
excrescet paulative quod Christus propter excessum malitie quasi cogetur
venire ad generale judicium omnium. (Gui, *Manuel*, i. 150–2.)

Some believe that during this golden age, before the final defection,
St. Francis will return to the earth in the body and will inspire all
men with his spirit. This is an eloquent Franciscan version of the
Joachimist Age of the Holy Ghost and one observes how exactly they
have caught his point that this is the seventh age—within history and
therefore subject to inevitable decay—not the timeless eighth age.

Bernard Gui's account is corroborated and amplified by depositions taken in the Inquisition at Toulouse *c.* 1322.[1] These bring
out clearly two further points: that the source of their inspiration
was the *Postilla* of Olivi, which they read in the vernacular, and that
from this they derived in the clearest and most complete terms
Joachim's doctrine of the three *status* linked with the three Persons of
the Trinity:

[Raymundus de antu sano believes the doctrine of Olivi to be true Catholic
doctrine, especially the *Postilla super apocalipsim*] quam habuit et tenuit
transpositam in vulgari et frequenter legit in ea etiam aliis personis
audientibus . . . in qua audivit legi . . . de tribus temporibus seu statibus
generalibus mundi et de septem statibus ecclesie. . . . Item in dicta
postilla legit vel audivit legi quod in secundo statu generali mundi qui
concurrit cum sexto statu speciali ecclesie in fine illius status fiet judicium
de babilone, i.e. de ecclesia carnali, quia ipsa persequitur et persequetur
veritatem Christi in pauperibus suis. (Limborch, *Hist. Inquis.*, pp. 311–12.)

[Raymundus de buxo confesses that he read the *Postilla*] et subdit in
dicta postilla quod sicut in fine primi status ecclesie fuit factum iudicium
de synagoga que Christum crucifixerat propter quod fuit destructa . . . sic
in fine secundi status ecclesie qui durat ad Antichristum fiet iudicium de
ecclesia carnali que persequitur vitam Christi in viris spiritualibus qui
volunt tenere paupertatem Christi secundum regulam sancti Francisci et
destructa ecclesia carnali post mortem Antichristi, erigetur ecclesia tercii

fuerit effusus super apostolos discipulos Jesu Christi in die penthecostes in ecclesia
primitiva'; 148: 'et dicunt quod descendet super eos tanquam flamma ignis in fornace
et hoc exponunt quod non solum anima replebitur Spiritu Sancto, sed etiam Spiritum
Sanctum in suo corpore sentient habitare.'

¹ Limborch, *Hist. Inquis.*, pp. 298 seq.

status in viris spiritualibus et . . . dixit in postilla de ecclesia Romana carnali quam Babilonem meretricem magnam vocat dejiciendam et destruendam . . . (Limborch, *Hist. Inquis.*, p. 298.)

No doubt some distortion and exaggeration took place—as in the statement that in the *Postilla* the Roman Church was identified with the Babylonish Whore—but in other statements one recognizes the *Postilla*, and it is difficult to understand from what other source the Beguins took the doctrine of the three *status*, since Joachim is not specifically mentioned in connection with it.[1]

Repeatedly the identification of the Roman Church with the carnal church and therefore with the Babylonish Woman is made in these depositions, and Pope John XXII is branded as the *Antichristus misticus*.[2] When the dual tribulation of the two Antichrists has been suffered, this church will be destroyed. This will happen within fourteen years when, as at the end of the first *status* the synagogue was destroyed, so at the end of the second, the Roman Church will be rejected and destroyed. The clearest impression left by these depositions is of their authors' fanatical belief in their own role as those who will usher in the Church of the third *status* and already embody its life. The conformity of St. Francis to Christ is now extended to his true followers, so that the four martyred Spirituals of Marseilles represent Christ crucified once more: '. . . habuerunt similitudinem quatuor parcium vel capitum crucis Christi et in eis fuit vita Christi et per consequens ipse Christus spiritualiter iterum crucifixus . . .' (Limborch, *Hist. Inquis.*, p. 299). But the gates of hell

---

[1] See, for instance, Limborch, *Hist. Inquis.*, p. 308: 'Item dixit se credidisse quod tria tempora erant ecclesie, sc. ab Adam usque ad Christum, quod tempus appropriatur Patri, quia fuit tempus potencie. Secundum tempus incepit a Christo et durabit usque ad Antichristum vel usque ad persecucionem vite evangelice, quod tempus est appropriatum Filio. Et tercium tempus erit usque ad finem mundi, quod erit tempus benignitatis, et est appropriatum Spiritui Sancti. Item dixit . . . quod sicut synagoga Judeorum fuit reprobata et rejecta adveniente ecclesia primitiva quia crucifixit Christum, ita adveniente nova ecclesia in tercio statu reprobabitur et rejicietur ecclesia ista nostra, quia persequetur . . . vitam . . . Christi in viris evangelicis et succedet tertia ecclesia.' Here we clearly have a statement of the Joachimist three *status*, but couched in the language of the Spirituals and derived from Olivi, since a little later in the same deposition we read: 'Item dixit se audivisse quod frater P. J. dixerat quod antichristus debebat esse de altiori religione fratrum minorum, quia lucifer fuit de supremo ordine angelorum et quod in quodam libro qui est de adventu antichristi est ymago depicta monialis . . .' A further deposition (p. 312) specifically states that they read in the *Postilla* of Olivi 'de tribus temporibus seu statibus generalibus mundi et de septem statibus ecclesie'. See also L. Fumi, *Eretici e ribelli nell'Umbria* (Todi, undated), pp. 159–60.
[2] Here, of course, they go beyond Olivi, although they specifically state that they read in the *Postilla* that the Roman Church is 'illam babilonem meretricem magnam' (p. 312).

cannot prevail against the true Spirituals, though persecuted, and therefore no ecclesiastical authority, not even the papacy, can destroy their order or transfer them to another. In this their Order is unique: all others will disappear but theirs will endure to the end of the world: '. . . fuit promissum sancto Francisco quod ordo eius duraret usque ad finem mundi, sicut legitur in vita eius. . . . Credit tamen quod dominus papa possit omnes alios ordines et omnes religiones tollere et destruere seu cassare. Item credidit et credit quod dom. papa non possit transferre fratrem minorem ad aliam religionem . . .' (Limborch, *Hist. Inquis.*, p. 299). The secret of this unique position lies in the affirmation 'quod veritas vite Christi magis fuit revelata Sancto Francisco et ordini eius quam cuicunque alteri sancto vel cuicunque alteri ordini',[1] and therefore 'Regula Sancti Francisci est perfectior . . . et alcior status et magis imitatur vitam Christi quam aliquis alter status . . . sive sit status prelatorum sive religiosorum . . .'.[2] The founders of the Church of the third *status* will be drawn from a very small remnant, for even the order of St. Francis has apostatized:

[After the death of Antichrist] ecclesia alia erigetur et fundaretur que esset pauper, humilis et benigna. Item credidit quod omnes religiones seu ordines destruentur ante finem mundi, excepto ordine S. Francisci, cuius ordinis dixit esse tres partes unam videlicet in communitate ordinis et secundam in illis qui vocantur fratriselli et isti duo partes finaliter destruentur, et terciam in fratribus qui vocantur spirituales et in beguinis de tercio ordine eis adherentibus, et ista tercia pars, sicut S. Francisco promissum fuit, usque ad finem mundi perduraret et in ea veritas regule remaneret. (Limborch, *Hist. Inquis.*, p. 303.)

Item . . . quod rejecta ecclesia carnali Romana eligerentur pauci viri spirituales in quibus fundaretur ecclesia tercii status . . . (Limborch, *Hist. Inquis.*, p. 306.)

Item dixit . . . quod Deus ante adventum antichristi debebat eligere XII personas que resisterent ipsi antichristo, super quas postea fundabitur ecclesia Dei tercii status. (Limborch, *Hist. Inquis.*, p. 308.)

. . . et rejecta ecclesia carnali, tunc ecclesia spiritualis succedet, que pro majori parte fundabitur per fratres minores pauperes qui petunt observanciam puritatis regule. (Limborch, *Hist. Inquis.*, p. 316.)

The confidence of this saving remnant is astonishing, as they prepare for ordeal by fire:

[1] Limborch, *Hist. Inquis.*, p. 301.   [2] Ibid., p. 305.

Opinantur etiam quod tempore persecutionis beguinorum debebat eis
dari Spiritus Sanctus taliter sicut flamma est in fornace et quod illi qui
sic acciperent Spiritum Sanctum erunt perfectiores virtute et gracia
apostolis quia forcior pugna eis instabit quam apostolis institerit, et tam
gravis debet esse eorum persecucio quod unus asinus poterit portare illos
in quibus veritas permanebit . . . (Limborch, *Hist. Inquis.*, p. 309.)

Like a recurring theme they reiterate the source of their confidence
in St. Francis as interpreted by Olivi:

Item quod tota doctrina fratris Petri Johannis Olivi est vera et catholica
et habuit eam per illuminacionem Spiritus Sancti per quem cognovit
veritatem evangelicam et regule St. Francisci quem vocant sanctum
patrem et magnum doctorem et quod est ille angelus . . . [Sixth Angel] . . .
Item quod Deus specialiter elegerat ipsum ad revelandum tempus finale
ecclesie et ad premuniendum ecclesiam contra persecuciones antichristi
et tribulaciones que in novissimo tempore ecclesie sunt future. (Limborch, *Hist. Inquis.*, p. 316.)

The evidence from these depositions shows conclusively that in this
group of Provençal Beguins expectation was once more openly
focused on the third *status* of Joachim, as recast by the Spirituals.[1]

That Olivi's speculations attracted finer minds as well as the
simple is best exemplified in his greatest disciple, Ubertino da
Casale. Ubertino's career shows him as a Joachimist preacher in
central Italy, yet also as an able dialectician when called to argue
with the learned in defence of the Spiritual party. His great work,
the *Arbor Vitae Crucifixae*, shows the profundity of his mystical
thought. He looked for a symbol of the inner growth of all history
and found it in the image of the Tree of History, so dear to Joachim.
Its roots were in the early ages from Creation to the Incarnation, its
branches were the works of Christ, its fruits the deeds of the elect.
Ubertino had not, however, assimilated Joachim's most original
conception of the tree which grows through the generations of history and reaches its climax at the end of time. He could not, in fact,
accommodate his tree image very well to his desire to write on the
pattern of history, but his Book V,[2] in which the key to his faith and
expectation lies, is, in a sense, the crown of his tree. Here the
appropriation of Joachim's scheme of history, as adapted by Olivi,

[1] It may be noted that some identified the *Papa Angelicus* as Angelo Clareno or
Philip of Majorca; see Douie, *Fraticelli*, p. 251.
[2] Ubertino da Casale, *Arbor*, ff. cc–ccxl.

appears most clearly. For a framework he took the seven *status* of the Church, thus substituting the word that Joachim reserved for the three stages of the world for the Abbot's *tempora*. But Ubertino recognized also the three general *status* and identified the sixth and seventh *status* of the Church with Joachim's third *status* of the world. The five preceding ages belonged successively to apostles, martyrs, doctors, anchorites, monks, and clergy possessing temporalities; the sixth, initiated in the time of the seraphic man Francis, 'est renovationis evangelicae vite et expugnationis secte antichristiane sub pauperibus voluntariis nihil possidentibus in hac vita'; the seventh would see 'quedam quieta et mira participatio future glorie ac si celestis ierusalem videatur ascendisse in terram'.[1]

Joachim's distinction between the activity of the sixth and the contemplation of the seventh age was still kept: 'in sexto (statu) reformatores vite evangelice, in septimo pregustatores eterne glorie.'[2] There was, however, a subtle change of ideal: in place of the *spiritualis intellectus* of Joachim the new quality of life for Ubertino and the Spirituals was the *renovatio evangelice vite* or the *renovatio forme Christi*, whose foundation was true poverty, the perfection and queen of all virtues.[3] Although couched in terms of *renovatio*, the vision looked forward, rather than backward, since the *plena clarificatio* would be new in the sixth age.[4] The word *clarificatio* suggests a link with Joachim's thought, but it is interesting that Ubertino used words of heat as well as light to express the new life: 'restituetur . . . sub vitali et vivifico calore et lumine vite Christi.'[5]

Ubertino adopted from Olivi the concept of the three Advents of Christ. In St. Francis the Second Advent of Christ had actually occurred. In words which echo those of Olivi, Ubertino declared that as in the second *etas* there came the new man Christ Jesus, so in the sixth *status* appeared the new man Francis *cum evangelico statu*.[6] Thus the sixth age (or *status*) was of all ages momentous, 'ut videatur quoddam novum seculum seu nova ecclesia tunc formari'.[7] Uniquely in Francis the life of Christ was re-embodied: 'quia vite

[1] *Arbor*, f. cc^r.   [2] Ibid., f. cc^v.   [3] Ibid., f. ccviii^r.
[4] Ibid., f. ccii^r.   [5] Ibid., f. ccii^v.
[6] Ibid., f. ccv^r: 'Sicut in secunda etate reiecto carnali iudaismo et vetustate prioris seculi venit novus homo Christus cum nova vita, lege et cruce, sic in sexto statu apparuit novus homo Franciscus cum evangelico statu quinque plagis a Christo Jesu crucifixus et configuratus in carne: cuius vita et regula sicut et Christi persona tunc fuit non dubium crucifixa et sepulta.'
[7] Ibid., f. cciii^r.

Christi renovator singulariter apparebit.'[1] Ubertino recalled hearing from an eyewitness of the occasion when St. Bonaventura first gave his approval to the belief that St. Francis was the Sixth Angel of the Apocalypse,[2] and he added his own testimony on John of Parma's similar belief.[3] St. Francis had foretold persecution and Ubertino expected the conflict with Babylon, for must not St. Francis be figuratively killed and buried before he could rise in glory?[4] The concentration of attack on the Spirituals who guarded the Rule and Testament with their lives was nothing less than the final and tremendous conflict with Antichrist, and in so far as the ecclesiastical hierarchy identified itself with this attack it ceased to be the New Jerusalem and became part of Babylon *meretrix et impudica*.[1]

Ubertino's pages mirror exactly the mood of a 'saving remnant'. They are the little flock of Christ, content to be 'quendam populum novum et humilem in hac novissima hora, qui esset dissimilis in humilitate et paupertate ab omnibus aliis'.[5] Their duty to the future requires that they should keep the holy Rule and Testament— 'illa summa perfectio quam beatus Franciscus asserit se a Christo accepisse'[6]—and wait. One band, says Ubertino, has retired into Asia to wait for the fall of Antichrist: '. . . cum non posset in medio Babylonis in observantia evangelii vivere, ad partes Asye declinare consuluit: donec reformatores evangelici status pius Jesus ecclesie dignaretur concedere: eis prophetice predicens eos illic salvandos a facie tempestatis' (*Arbor*, f. ccvii^r). The consummation for which the Spirituals wait is expressed by Ubertino in phrases which show how closely their ideal was assimilated to Joachim's third *status*, for he speaks of the contemplative and evangelical *status* designated in St. John and of the future perfection of the contemplative Church which is the sum of all things.[7]

The Spirituals adapted to themselves the role of Joachim's new spiritual men. Their philosophy of history was more Christocentric than Joachim's. The manifestation of the Third Person of the Trinity was identified with a renewal of the life of the Second Person in St. Francis, who sought the re-enactment of the Passion in his own body. St. Francis stood at the transition from the second to the third *status*, as Christ stood between the first and the second. Only the

---

[1] *Arbor*, f. ccvi^v.
[3] *Arbor*, f. ccvi^v, quoted *supra*, p. 186 n. 2.
[5] Ibid., f. ccix^r.
[6] Ibid., f. ccxi^v.

[2] *Supra*, p. 176 n. 5.
[4] Ibid., f. ccv^r.

[7] Ibid., ff. cciii^v, cciv^v.

pattern of threes made it possible to claim for St. Francis such a
unique role and to permit the adaptation to him of words written of
Christ. Thus Angelo Clareno without any sense of unfittingness
paraphrased sentences from the Epistles to exalt St. Francis as the
embodiment of the new dispensation: 'God has in times past spoken
to us in Fathers, Apostles, Prophets, Martyrs, Doctors, and Saints,
but in these newest days He has spoken to us in His seraphic son
Francis whom He has constituted heir of all things following
. . . who, being in this world in the form of Christ crucified, humbled
himself. . . wherefore God has exalted him and given him a name
. . .'[1] Thus the 'new age' was the age of a re-enacted Word as much
as of an illuminating Spirit, and the essence of the third *status* was
now expressed as evangelical perfection, but the source of their
ardent and inflexible purpose was the Joachimist expectation of the
new and last age. The *viri spirituales* had become evangelical men
and the *spiritualis intellectus* evangelical poverty, yet the two ideals
were not far apart. Joachim had been deeply aware of the claims of
the world and the need for a mediating order of evangelical men; the
Franciscans, on their side, were drawn towards the contemplative
life.[2] The early Franciscan emphasis on spiritual understanding of
the Scriptures as the only true form of learning is easily linked with
Joachim's conception of spiritual understanding.[3]

The flight towards the hermit life developed most markedly
among the Italian Spirituals. At first the crisis seemed very near:
in 1305 Fra Angelo Clareno's group looked for the Angelic Pope
almost immediately, but Clement V came. Like other Joachites, the
Clarenists then probably revised their interpretation of events in

---

[1] *ALKG* i. 558 (cf. Heb. 1: 1–2; Phil. 2: 6–9).

[2] St. Francis himself wrote under the title *De Religiosa Habitatione in eremitoriis*
a pattern of life for a hermit group; see *Opuscula*, ed. Wadding (Antwerp, 1623), p. 290.
Wadding comments on this: 'Frequenter igitur oriebatur in primaevis illis Minoribus
solitudinis desiderium, non ob aliud, nisi propter turbam tribulationum et popularium
scandalorum a quibus liberari volebant. Hominum fugerunt commercium, ut Dei
haberent consortium; homines noluerunt amicos, ut Angelos haberent familiares. . . .
Franciscus ergo eremiticam culturis vitam socios dedit, signavit et Matres, voluit eos
habere a quibus materna sollicitudine foverentur, alerentur, custodirentur . . .' (ibid.,
p. 291). In the early days there was conflict between the two ideals of solitude and
preaching; Celano records a debate 'utrum inter homines conversari deberent, an ad
loca solitaria se conferrent' (quoted *ALKG* iii. 556 n. 4). See also Bonaventura, *Legenda
maiora*, ed. Quaracchi, viii. 533–4.

[3] Celano stresses St. Francis's gift of penetrating hidden mysteries of Scripture (see
ALKG iii. 577 n. 3) and St. Bonaventura links this gift of understanding with the
spirit of prophecy (see Bonaventura, op. cit., p. 535).

order to retain their faith. Finally they were allowed to withdraw
into the separatism of those who wait for events to vindicate their
faithfulness. In the March of Ancona Fra Angelo formed his disciples once more into the Order of poor hermits.[1] The problem of
relations with authority faced them acutely. This was, indeed, the
crucial problem of all the Spirituals, and, though Olivi and Ubertino
both maintained their obedience to authority, the logic of their
reading of history was steadily driving the extremists towards the
conviction that they alone, in their separation, represented the true
Church. Fra Angelo must have been sorely tried. On the one hand,
he vehemently repudiated in his *Epistola Excusatoria* the charge of
being schismatic, and declared his unwavering loyalty to the Roman
See.[2] On the other hand, his disciples looked for the manifestation
of Antichrist in a pseudo-pope and the final overthrow of the 'carnal'
church. Until Angelo's death in 1337 the restraining influence of his
sanctity and moderation held the group in a midway position. Angelo
himself found asylum for most of the period at Subiaco. There the
history of the true followers of St. Francis took its Joachimist shape
in the *Historia Septem Tribulationum.* As he wrote, Angelo again felt
himself to be standing at a crucial moment: the twenty-eight years
of the sixth tribulation from the renunciation of Pope Celestine had
been endured and the threshold of the seventh and last had been
reached, so he prayed: 'A sex tribulacionibus liberati oremus ut in
septima liberet nos a malo. Amen.'[3] His confidence remained firm,
however, that the Dragon would be beaten down, the last darkness
be dispelled, and the faithful dwell in the full sunlight of love.[4]

The Clarenists were imposing upon themselves a well-nigh impossible tension in seeking to sustain at the same time their sense of
mission and their duty of obedience. This stands out clearly in Fra
Angelo's letters. On the one hand, he sets the Rule which they guard
above all other obediences: in it Christ speaks and the gates of hell
shall not prevail against it.[5] On the other hand, he enjoins obedience
to prelates who hold the place of Christ and His Apostles.[6] If the
Supreme Pontiff declares heretical that which doctors and saints of
the Church have taught to be the highest peak of catholic perfection,
no one may judge him except himself. We, says Angelo to his

---

[1] Douie, *Fraticelli*, pp. 64 seq.; Wadding, *Annales* viii. 300.

[2] *ALKG* i. 522–3. See also V. Doucet, 'Angelus Clarinus ad Alvarum Pelagium.
Apologia pro Vita Sua', *AFH* xxxix (1946), pp. 131–2.

[3] *ALKG* ii. 135.   [4] Ibid., 155.

[5] *ALKG* i. 563–4.   [6] Ibid., p. 555.

disciples, occupying the place of humility, ought not to speak or write anything against him, but await the judgement of Christ.[1] So Fra Angelo cannot resolve the tension for his brethren, but only exhort them to patience, in moving words: 'Vos igitur ab humilitatis iustitia et rectitudine neque verbo neque scripto debetis declinare, sed agere in silentio et tranquillitate pacis, que agitis, et confirmare sermone et opere, que dixistis' (*ALKG* i. 568).

It was hardly possible for the rank and file to preserve this position, and it seems certain that from the Clarenists, after Fra Angelo's death, as well as from other remnants of the Spirituals, there sprang many of the groups of Fraticelli who in the middle and later fourteenth century stood in declared separation from the Roman Church and attacked the Papacy fiercely. Our information on these groups is mainly drawn, on the one hand, from depositions made during proceedings against heretics and, on the other, from a series of letters or short tracts which they addressed to fellow Christians. The Processes against Rieti, Todi, Amelia, for instance,[2] show how the Clarenists were caught up in the swirling cross-currents of heretical opinion which rose to flood level during and after the appearance of Louis of Bavaria. Dualism, pantheism, Ghibellinism of an extreme type, all mingled together, and with them the fanatical defence of absolute poverty which distinguished the descendants of the Spirituals. The confession of Fr. Francesco di Vanne at Rieti gives us something of their viewpoint:

. . . quod audivit a fraticellis de paupere vita . . . quod dictus dom. papa Johannes non est papa, . . . quod dictus dom. papa Johannes amputavit capud vite Christi quia cassavit fraticellos et quia fecit decretalem quod Christus habuit in propria et comuni, quod ipse est hereticus; et dixit quod audivit ab eisdem quod habetur una profezia quod Ecclesia Romana est facta meretrix et ad hoc ut possit melius fornicari, transivit ultra montes . . . audivit ab eis quod nos qui vocamus fratres minores ab Ecclesia non sumus fratres minores, sed ipsi fraticelli sunt vere fratres minores. . . . Et dixit quod dictus fr. Angelus [Clareno] scripsit, sicut

[1] *ALKG* i. 567.
[2] L. Fumi, 'Eretici e ribelli nell'Umbria dal 1320–1330', *Bollettino della Regia Deputazione di Storia Patria per l'Umbria*, v (Perugia, 1899), pp. 412 seq.; idem, *Eretici e ribelli nell'Umbria* (Todi, undated). See also N. Papini, *Notizie sicure della morte, sepultura, canonizzazione e traslazione di S. Francesco d'Assisi* (2nd edn., Foligno, 1824), pp. 273–6, especially p. 275, where a Fraticelli, Francesco Nicolai, claims that the Church 'debet renovari et in hac renovatione debet esse summus Pontifex Jacobus de Columna fraticellus propter calvitiam quam habet in capite, quod dicit fore signum Papae futuri.'

generalis, ipsis fraticellis . . . in qua lictera continebatur quod confortarent se, quia cito habebunt bonum statum et quod dom. Phylippus, frater Regine, erit effectus Papa . . . (*Bollettino*, pp. 412–14.)

The Fraticelli tracts show clearly whither the logic of the Joachimist hope led. If the whole hierarchy of the Church opposed the perfection of the future *status* entrusted to the few, then it could not be the true Church but the expected Antichrist. Thus the mentality of the exclusive sect developed, for 'senpre gli molti hanno gli pochi fedeli de Christo perseguitati'.[1] The fatal agent of the Church's seduction was John XXII. If anyone persistently contradicted the truth of the poverty of Christ, be he pope or bishop, he was a manifest heretic whom to obey was contrary to God, the soul, and the Rule.[2] Pope John and his successors, therefore, had departed from the true Church and become schismatics. Some went so far as to assert that John XXII was the mystic Antichrist, and to all it was clear that the pope had no power to touch the Rule and Testament of St. Francis. It has been argued, says the letter of the Fraticelli to all the faithful, that the pope always has the power to create new law and this is agreed, but he has no licence to go against the express word of Christ and the Apostles[3]—and the implication is clear that the Rule of St. Francis is in this category. Thus, whilst clinging pathetically to their assertion that they believed in one catholic, apostolic Church, these Fraticelli groups set up the Rule and Testament as the criterion of orthodoxy and source of authority.

The Fraticelli saw themselves as the saving remnant gathered in the frail bark of the true Church, the Noah's Ark of the last age. The navigators who had charted their voyage were St. Francis, Petrus Joannis Olivi, and the Abbot Joachim.[4] One of their writings draws directly on the *Liber Concordie*[5] to establish their role in the new Ark of the new Deluge:

Dovete adunque sapere che secondo l'abate Giovachino nel libro delle

---

[1] L. Oliger, 'Documenta inedita ad historiam Fraticellorum spectantia', *AFH* iv (1911), p. 697.

[2] Oliger, 'Documenta inedita . . .', *AFH* iii (1910), *Epistola Fraticellorum ad universos Christi fideles*, p. 265; ibid. iv. 699. A letter to the Perugians (1379–82) says: 'Certamente tale chiesa non è santa e chattolica, ma heretica e scismatica. . . . Allora non è chiesa di Xo, ma sinagogha del diavolo' (ibid. iv. 707).

[3] Ed. Vanzolini, *Scelta di curiosità . . .* (Bologna, 1865), *Lettera de' Fraticelli a tutti i cristiani*, p. 22; Oliger, *AFH* iii. 265; ibid. vi (1913), p. 280.

[4] Tocco, *SF*, p. 515.

[5] *Lib. Conc.*, ff. 74 seq. The theme of taking refuge in Noah's ark recurs in the Fraticelli polemic; see Tocco, *SF*, pp. 504, 506.

Concordia della scrittura, il quale libro fece ad instantia d'uno Papa et
di molti prelati, ove nel quinto libro sopra dell'istoria di Noè dice che
lli cinqueciento anni di Noè innanzi che fabrichasse l'archa, significano
li cinque stati della Chiesa da Christo per infino a llui, et poi nel primo
anno del secentesimo egli comandò che fabrichasse l'archa, cioè nel
principio del sesto istato Christo dovea mandare un uomo nel mondo, il
quale dovea fabricare un'altra archa a modo di quella di Noè, nella quale si
dovea riserbare un'altra volta lo seme delli heletti dal diluvio delli infedeli,
li quali debbono ancora venire a distruggiere la chiesa di Christo, et
anche dal diluvio di molti falsi Christiani et falsi profeti cioè falsi papi o
vescovi et religiosi, li quali si cominciarono a llevare et sono levati in
questo sesto stato. E questo huomo fu il venerabile patriarcha messer
sancto Franciescho . . . (*SF*, pp. 502–3.)

St. Francis, the Sixth Angel of the Apocalypse, had descended from
the celestial contemplative life, 'vestito di novella cioè della dottrina
evangelica' in order to build 'l'archa della regola evangelicha'. After
a hundred years, 'subitamente cominciò ad venire il diluvio delli
heretici e scismatici e delli molti falsi religiosi e Christiani et questo
si cominciò più principalmente nel tempo d'uno falso papa [John
XXII].' After the Deluge, however, would come revival, when the
gospel of the true Church would be preached by twelve evangelical
men, the last twelve in a long sequence of twelves—patriarchs,
prophets, the twelve *schiatte d'Israel*, apostles, monasteries, twelve
Benedictine abbots, twelve companions of St. Francis, and finally
twelve 'poveri evangelici che debono rinovare la chiesa'—in which
again we recognize the Joachimist touch. Here we see clearly how
the sense of being the few elect holding the treasure of the future
stemmed directly from Joachim's genuine thought.

   A pessimistic note, however, is struck by the second set of *Vaticinia de Summis Pontificibus*. This second fifteen, similar in character
to the first fifteen, is attributed by Professor Grundmann to a group
of Florentine Fraticelli,[1] and, although his dating is too late, since
this series was already known to Jean de Roquetaillade in 1356,[2]
the attribution seems likely. It begins, as before, with Nicholas III,
and the tradition of the Spirituals concerning Celestine V and Boniface VIII is well preserved in the representation of a saintly pope at
prayer with a wolf tugging from behind, the caption 'Vox vulpina
perdet principatum', and a text beginning: 'Benedictus qui venit in
nomine Domini celestium omnium contemplator, qui simplex eductus

---

[1] Grundmann, *Die Papstprophetien*, pp. 117–24.
[2] On Roquetaillade see *infra*, pp. 225–8.

de terra tenebrosa ascendit et descendit . . .',[1] followed by a fierce pontiff with a sad, resigned monk behind and the caption: 'Fraudulenter intrasti, potenter regnasti, gemens morieris.'[2] John XXII is given the caption: 'Contra columbam haec ymago turpissima clericorum pugnabit', while his text begins: 'De infimo genere ascendet cruenta bestia prima et novissima que filium minimum et innoxium crudeliter devorabit.'[3] If the series was produced just before 1356, all the popes down to Innocent VI (1352) are portraits, leaving the last three only as representations of the future. The last is clearly intended for Antichrist: it is the only pope actually drawn as a beast and it has the caption: 'Terribilis es, quis resistet tibi?' while the text begins: 'Haec est ultima fera aspectu terribilis.'[4] If this series represents the pitch of hatred for the papacy now attained by some of the Fraticelli, it is curious that it could be quoted with interest by the orthodox Giovanni delle Celle.[5] The anxious puzzlement with which the final symbol was being discussed is well caught in his conclusion on these *Vaticinia*: '. . . questa bestia è Antichristo, e di vero che alcuno m'ha detto, che dee essere un altro papa; per la qual cosa delle due cose è l'una: o che il libro, che vidi, è corrotto, o alcuno v'ha aggiunto di suo proprio senso; e però sto a vedere' (*SF*, p. 426).

Although, on the whole, authorities struck hard at these groups, there were certain political and social situations which favoured them. Thus in Florence in the 1370s and 1380s the anti-papal feeling which culminated in the War of the Otto Santi and the reaction against the Great Schism, together with a general social unrest seen both in the expectation of Antichrist and in the explosion of the Ciompi revolt, all combined to provide a fertile soil for Fraticelli beliefs. Both the danger and the attraction of their hopes were felt by Giovanni delle Celle, the famous Vallombrosan hermit, who

---

[1] No. 5 in the original order. [2] No. 6 in the original order.
[3] No. 9 in the original order. [4] No. 15 in the original order.
[5] Tocco, *SF*, p. 426: Letter to Guido del Palagio: 'Io voglio aver materia di poterti scrivere più volte di quello che desideri sapere, cioè della fine del mondo; avvegnachè Jesu Christo non la volesse rivelare a' suoi apostoli, perchè non era allora di necessità, nondimeno e' pare che poi l'abbia voluto rivelare, acciocchè la gente si apparecchi, veggendo che vi siamo così presso; e primo che il rivelasse all'abate Gioacchino, abate in Calavria e uomo di grande scienza e che ebbe spirito di profezia e predisse l'avvenimento di Santo Francesco e di Santo Domenico, e disse che ne' tempi loro il mondo fiorirebbe. Questo fu nel 1138 e fece un libro, il quale si chiama il Papale, dove egli infino all'avvenimento di Antichristo dipinse tutti i papi e scrisse loro sopra ciò che doveano fare . . .' (and he proceeds to describe some of the figures down to the last).

wrote letters both against them and to them.[1] Prophetic expectations were in the air, and it seems clear that the Florentine Senate, if it did not favour the Fraticelli, for a time turned a blind eye to their increase.[2] An anonymous Florentine diary of the period records the prophecy of a Minorite in 1368. This is, in fact, part of the *Vade Mecum* of Jean de Roquetaillade, to whom we shall be turning shortly.[3] The expected programme is one of terrible tribulations and violent upheavals, of a Church forcibly reduced to evangelical poverty, of a great Pope, the *Riparatore del mondo*, and a French Emperor who will reform the world. The significant thing is that this work of a French Joachite was circulating in Florence at this time.

After Florence had made peace with the Church, however, and the Ciompi had collapsed, orthodoxy very soon reasserted itself in full force. There is a final flicker of these Fraticelli in Florence in the trial of Michael da Calci, a Minorite who had become a Fraticelli preacher.[4] In his trial he urged confidence and steadfastness on his companions on the grounds of 'la dottrina del santo abbate [i.e. Joachim] e di Pietro Iohanne' and he expects the 'papa santo da venire'.[5]

Prophetic verses in the vernacular seem to form a fringe-land between heretic and orthodox in fourteenth-century Italy. Florence was a focal point for these prophecies and many of them belong to a Joachite–Franciscan milieu.[6] Thus the vision in 1361 of a Fr. Giovanni of Florence, probably a Fraticelli, exhibits the typical Joachimist expectation of deep tribulation, followed by *renovatio*, combined with an imperialist sentiment which contains echoes of Dante.[7] The ship of the Church is sinking and St. Francis appears with Joachim:

[1] For these letters see (i) A. Wesselofsky, *Il paradiso degli Alberti, Scelta di curiosità* . . . (Bologna, 1867), pp. 335–67; (ii) Tocco, *SF*, pp. 431–94; (iii) P. Cividali, *Memorie della Reale Accademia dei Lincei*, xii (1907), pp. 354–477. See *infra*, p. 254, for Giovanni delle Celle's viewpoint.

[2] Tocco, *SF*, pp. 412 seq., deals with Florentine attitudes towards the Fraticelli.

[3] *Diario d'Anonimo Fiorentino dall'anno 1358 al 1389*, ed. A. Gherardi in *Documenti di storia italiana*, vi (Florence, 1876), pp. 389–90. See *infra*, pp. 225–8, for J. de Roquetaillade. For the source of the prophecy see Bignami-Odier, *Roquetaillade*, pp. 164, 165, 170, 171, 172.

[4] Ed. Zambrini, *Storia di Fra Michele minorita, Scelta di curiosità* . . . (Bologna, 1864). [5] Ibid., pp. 22–3.

[6] Messini, *Misc. Franc.* xxxvii. 39–54; xxxix. 109–30.

[7] Ibid. xxxix. 113. The poem was published by E. Narducci, *Manoscritti ora posseduti da D. B. Boncompagni* (Rome, 1862 and 1892).

> . . . e con pianti pregavano
> gridando Iddio dirizza la navicula:
> Vedi ch'ella pericola.
> Vedi ch'ella formicola . . .
> Vedi che in terra non truova ricovero!
> Francisco vidi e' l' Calavro isciovero,
> che dier nuovo ricovero
> alla chiesa, e gridar: O sangue povero,
> i nuovi farisei in te s'inzuppano . . .

Finally, after great tribulations and wars, the Dragon and the Beast are bound for a thousand years:

> e io che sempre coll'occhio secondolo
> vidi l'alta reina con sua tria
> che face uno ovile e una patria.
> Vidi poi nuovo cielo queto e lucido
> e terra nuova sanza nuovo mucido
> e' l' luogo ch'era sucido
> colle sante virtù tutto mondandolo.
>   (Narducci, op. cit., pp. 193, 199)

A popular poem which belongs to the same milieu and may be by the same author begins 'O pelligrina Italia'.[1] It has the same Ghibelline–Joachite viewpoint and also contains a direct reference to Joachim—'E Gioachin che pone la bestia per secento sesansei.' Significantly, this poem ends with a quotation from Dante—'Vero frutto veranne dopo il fiore' (*Par.* xxvii. 148)—which has been claimed to contain a reference to Joachim's vision of the future.[2] Two well-known names to whom such prophetic poems were ascribed are Fr. Tommasuccio of Foligno and his disciple, Fr. Stoppa. Towards the mid-fourteenth century a poem beginning 'Appri le labbra mie' was circulating under the name of Fr. Stoppa.[3] It refers back to the struggle of Louis of Bavaria with John XXII

---

[1] Ed. F. Trucchi, *Poesie italiane inedite di 200 autori* (Prato, 1846), ii. 82–95; R. Renier, *Liriche edite ed inedite degli Uberti* . . . (Florence, 1883), pp. 191–210. On this poem, see Messini, *Misc. Franc.* xxxix. 119–20.

[2] Cf. Tondelli, *Lib. Fig.* I, pp. 236–8.

[3] Published by G. Carducci, *Rime di Cino da Pistoia ed altri del secolo XIV* (Florence, 1862), pp. 264–7. Cf. Messini, *Misc. Franc.* xxxix. 120–2. Messini says that the author is not Fra Stoppa but 'un converso dei frati di Santo Agostino', and gives a reference to Sercambi's chronicle. But this refers to another prophecy in verse which has also been attributed to Fra Stoppa; see *Le croniche di Giovanni Sercambi Lucchese*, ed. S. Bongi, in *Fonti per la storia d'Italia* (Rome, 1892), iii. 274–5, 415. This is dated 1315–28.

and attacks Clement VI, but finally expects the Church to be renewed:

> Poi fie la Chiesa ornata di pastori
> Umili e santi come fui gli autori.
>
> (*Misc. Franc.* xxxix. 122)

A prophecy beginning 'Vuol la mia fantasia', attributed to both Tommasuccio and Stoppa, was circulating *c.* 1370, while manuscripts in Florence, Bologna, and elsewhere contain other similar prophetic verses under these two names which belong to the time of the Great Schism. They usually end on an optimistic note, expecting a World Emperor and/or Angelic Pope, and are sometimes attributed to Joachim himself.[1] Thus:

> Li sancti preti de novello stato
> Predicheranno,
> Tutti l'infideli converteranno,
> Vestiti tolti d'un aspero panno
> Et sempre senza proprio viveranno
> In povertade.
>
>   .   .   .   .   .
>
> Remarrà sopra terra poca gente
> Et omne spiritual sarà gaudente;
> Pregam Dio che conduca ogni gente
> Ad quello stato.
>
> (*Misc. Franc.* xxxix. 125–6)

And again:

> E sarà un Papa vero e naturale
> Santissimo, giusto e governarà piano,
>
>   .   .   .   .   .
>
> Da poi avranno un giusto per Signore
> Che fia al mondo degno Imperadore.
>
>   .   .   .   .   .
>
> E fia seguito da ogni cristiano
> E ogni sua fattura sarà buona,
> E torrà la signoria al gran soldano
>
>   .   .   .   .   .

---

[1] 'Vuol la mia fantasia' was published by F. Trucchi, op. cit. ii. 132; C. Frati, *I codici danteschi . . .*, p. 149. Cf. Messini, *Misc. Franc.* xxxvii. 48; xxxix. 122. On other poems, see Messini, *Misc. Franc.* xxxix. 124 seq.; C. Frati, *I codici danteschi della Biblioteca Universitaria di Bologna* (Florence, 1923), Appendix iv, pp. 154–74; Mazzatinti, *Misc. Franc.* ii (1887), pp. 1–7; E. Filippini, 'Una profezia medioevale in versi, di origine probabilmente Umbra', *Bollettino della R. Deputazione di Storia Patria per l'Umbria*, ix (1903), p. 19 n. 2. For a collection of these poems see the fifteenth-century Florence, Bibl. Nat. Cen., MS. II, X, 57, ff. 64 seq.

E della terra santa fia Signore.

. . . . .

E fia tranquillità, pace e unione,
Come al tempo del buon Ottaviano;

. . . . .

De' cristiani universal Signore,
E manterrà l'imperio romano,
Ai cristiani darà pace ordinata
E nulla guerra sarà ricordata.
(*Misc. Franc.* xxxix. 127–8)

Geographically, the Fraticelli who sprang from Angelo Clareno's group appear to have been widely scattered through Italy; Angelo left communities in the March of Ancona, in Naples, and in Rome itself; Umbria, especially Todi, Rieti, and Amelia, produced many accused of Fraticelli beliefs, while depositions of the later fourteenth century show their continued presence in these parts as well as in the regions of Perugia and Narni and in Tuscany.[1] The spread of Spiritual and Joachimist tenets to the Two Sicilies and to Spanish territories is an obscure story.[2] It probably began with Arnold of Villanova's interest in Joachimism, which led him to espouse the cause of the Spirituals *c.* 1303, and the friendship between Philip of Majorca and Angelo Clareno who first met *c.* 1316. The former probably influenced Frederick I of Sicily, under whom the island became a refuge for fugitive Spirituals.[3] The latter was inspired by Angelo to try and found a new order wholly based on the Rule and Testament of St. Francis. This he never fully achieved but his influence certainly helped to make Majorca and Naples receptive of Spiritual influence. Moreover, in Naples the Angevins, Robert the Wise and his Queen, also favoured them. Thus, before the middle of the fourteenth century, there must have been a considerable gathering of refugees in these parts, drawn from various Spiritual groups. In Naples there were Clarenists, and also *fratres fratris Philippi de Maioricis*, as well as survivors from the Provençal group and other Franciscan malcontents. We get a glimpse of their organization and beliefs from a process of 1362 instituted by Cardinal Albornoz against their patron Louis of Durazzo.[4] Thomas of Boiano, once

---

[1] Douie, *Fraticelli*, pp. 210 seq.; Lambert, *Franciscan Poverty*, pp. 202 seq.

[2] Douie, *Fraticelli*, pp. 211–13; Lambert, *Franciscan Poverty*, pp. 180–3.

[3] See H. Finke, *Acta Aragonensia* (Berlin, 1908), pp. 611 seq., for correspondence concerning Frederick's protection of the Spirituals in Sicily.

[4] F. Tocco, 'Un processo contro Luigi di Durazzo', *Archivio storico per le province napoletane*, xii (1887), pp. 31–40.

Franciscan Bishop of Aquino, now the head of a sect called the Brethren of the Poor Life or the Followers of Br. Philip of Majorca, was the striking personality at this time and his group held firmly to the schismatic position that since the time of John XXII the Roman Church had altogether ceased to be the true Church.

A little light on the ferment of opinion in Majorca and Roussillon is cast by the process against Adhémar de Mosset, a knight of Roussillon and counsellor to Philip of Majorca. Accused in December 1332, Adhémar appeared before the Cardinal Fournier as Inquisitor at Avignon in 1333.[1] From the interrogation it appears quite clearly that the authorities were looking for Joachimist beliefs in the 'Beguins of the Third Order' with whom he was associated. Amongst other questions he was asked if he had heard or believed the following views:

que así como después de la muerte de Cristo cesaron los ritos legales del Antiguo Testamento y empezó la obligación de los preceptos y Sacramentos evangélicos, así en el tercer estado, llamado del Espíritu Santo, habían de cesar los Sacramentos y preceptos evangélicos, y debía sucederles la ley del Espíritu Santo y sus Sacramentos y mandatos por haber terminado los preceptos y Sacramentos evangélicos.

que la ley y el tercer estado llamado del Espíritu Santo comenzó en tiempo de San Francisco . . .

que los pocos varones espirituales que se habían de separar de la Iglesia Romana, . . . recibirían el Espíritu Santo con mayor abundancia y fervor que los Apóstoles . . .

que durante el tercer estado, cuando el Espíritu Santo se comunicase tan copiosamente a los hombres, éstos no habían de pecar ni tener tal propósito . . .

que dicho tercer estado, llamado del Espíritu Santo, sería establecido en los profesores de la regla de San Francisco y Hermanos de la Penitencia o de la Tercera Regla del mismo santo . . .; la cual regla y estado tenía que durar hasta la fin del mundo sólo en aquellos de dicha regla que esto creyeren y defendieren, pereciendo con Babilonia, esto es, con la Iglesia carnal . . .; que las demás Ordenes, como la de Predicadores, por haber impugnado a los Hermanos de la Penitencia . . .; los Agustinos y Carmelitas que defendieron lo mismo . . .; los monjes Negros y Blancos y los Canónigos Regulares . . .; los reyes, príncipes, barones y demás nobles . . . que consintieron en la persecución expresada, todos tenían que ser exterminados en la destrucción de la Iglesia carnal para no resucitar jamás . . . (Pou y Marti, *Visionarios*, pp. 175–7.)

[1] Pou y Marti, *Visionarios*, pp. 165 seq.

He was also interrogated on attitudes towards the teaching of Pierre Jean d'Olivi.[1] The whole set of questions, indeed, presumes a close affinity between Adhémar's associates and the Provençal Spirituals. Although Adhémar denied these beliefs, the deposition of King James of Majorca against him goes far towards proving his connection with the group led by Philip of Majorca.[2]

In Aragon and Catalonia the chief carriers of Joachimist ideas may well have been the works of Arnold of Villanova. In his *Expositio super Apocalypsim* Arnold expounded the three *status* with their three orders, as well as the Seven Days of Creation, and Pou y Marti has studied the influence of this and others of Arnold's works in Spain.[3] The canons of the Council of Tarragona in 1317 reveal the continuing presence of his disciples in the province, while similar traces of a 'Beguin' group are found again in Tarragona in 1345.[4] For Catalonia Pou y Marti has brought to light an anonymous work, *De Statibus Ecclesiae secundum Apocalypsim*, written *c.* 1318 and known to us only from the forty-two articles extracted from it by Inquisitors.[5] These show us a thoroughgoing Catalan Joachite. The first article begins:

In prima pagina dicit: Oportet primo scire quod sunt tres status generales mundi. Primus fuit et duravit a principio mundi usque ad Christum. Secundus ab adventu Christi usque ad antichristum. Tertius a morte antichristi usque ad finem mundi. Et sciendum quod primus generalis status appropriatur Deo Patri, secundus Filio Dei, tercius Spiritui Sancto. . . . Et sicut in primo tempore Deus ostendit se tamquam terribilem et magni timoris . . . sic in isto secundo tempore Dei Filius ostendit se plenum pietate et magistrum, doctoremque seu manifestatorem veritatis . . . Sed in tertio statu ostendet se Spiritus Sanctus et dabit se sicut flammam et fornacem divini amoris et sicut cellarium vini spiritalis et sicut apotheca unguentorum spiritualium, et tunc non solum simplici intelligentia videbitur tota veritas sapientie Dei Filii incarnati et potentie Dei Patris, imo poterit homo experimentaliter palpare et gustare, unde Christus promisit: Cum venerit Spiritus veritatis docebit vos omnem veritatem. Et primus status, qui fuit operum corporalium, magis pertinet ad laicos; secundus vero, quia est status scripturarum, magis pertinet ad clericos; tertius vero, in quo est pura contemplatio, magis pertinet ad religiosos. (Pou y Marti, *Visionarios*, pp. 483–4.)

[1] Ibid., p. 181.
[2] Ibid., pp. 184–9. See also Vidal, 'Procès d'inquisition contre Adhémar de Mosset, noble Roussillonais, inculpé de Béguinisme', *Analecta Gallicana*, i. 555–89, 689–99, 711–22.   [3] Pou y Marti, *Visionarios*, pp. 36 seq.
[4] Ibid., pp. 100, 198–200.   [5] Ibid., pp. 255–8, 483–512.

This passage, based on a passage from Olivi,[1] shows a kinship with the Abbot's thought both in the images used and in its grasp of the full implications of the spiritual liberty promised in the third *status*. The rest of the articles show the writer following closely the beliefs of the Provençal Joachites and drawing constantly on views attributed to Olivi, who is held to be 'illum angelum fortem descendentem de celo, Apoc. X.'[2] The eighth article proclaims the unique divine mission of St. Francis and the Spirituals,[3] while the thirty-fifth article again characterizes the expected third *status*: '. . . dicit tercium statum generalem appropriari Spiritui Sancto, quia tunc erit plena experientia et degustatio spiritualis intelligentie et perfectio vite contemplatiue' (Pou y Marti, *Visionarios*, p. 508).

The influence of Joachimist prophecy in Spain was not confined to the heretical Beguin or Fraticelli groups. In the mid-fourteenth century we meet the Franciscan Infante Pedro of Aragon, whose visions have been preserved for us.[4] His imagination fed on a whole range of Joachimist prophecies—of Joachim himself, of Arnold of Villanova, Jean de Roquetaillade, 'Merlin', and others. He plunged into an interpretation of the well-known *Prophetia Tripolitana*, with many political applications to the Iberian peninsula.[5] Although there is no evidence that he used the Joachimist frame of three *status*, he certainly derived from the Abbot an expectation of the Age of Triumph when peace and material goods would abound, Jew and Infidel be converted, and Jerusalem would be glorified. These views drew on him an official examination, in the report of which opinions were divided as to whether his visions were of God or no.

Another powerful Franciscan mystic of the Joachimist school was Francesco Eximenis, Patriarch of Jerusalem.[6] His work *De triplici statu mundi* was written in 1398 but has never been published. A second work, *Vida de Jesuchrist* (*c.* 1404), also deals with the pattern of history and its future. Apart from Joachim himself, the chief influence upon Eximenis is that of Ubertino da Casale; he also uses the writings of Arnold of Villanova and Jean de Roquetaillade. The doctrine of the three *status* is set out uncompromisingly in his works: the second ends with the death of Antichrist and the *reformatio ecclesiae*, the third endures till the end of the world. In the

[1] Quoted *supra*, p. 197.
[2] *Visionarios*, p. 501.   [3] Ibid., p. 495.   [4] Ibid., pp. 369–96.
[5] Ibid., pp. 370–2. A later student of prophecies in the Court of Aragon was the knight Diego Ruiz, who influenced the Infanta Isabel in the early fifteenth century.
[6] Pou y Marti, *Visionarios*, pp. 397–415.

second, which is the *status* of secular clergy, Eximenis paints the
state of the Church in the usual dark colours, leading up to the
appearance of the new spiritual men who will usher in the *renovacio
ecclesiae*. The final triumph is seen in the terms of Roquetaillade:
an Angelic Pope and Good Emperor who will establish the reign of
Christ in Jerusalem, while the world will be converted by the spiritual
men of the Franciscan and Dominican Orders. Eximenis refuses
to assign dates or allot the role of universal monarch: he is a true
Joachimist rather than a collector of prophecies for a particular purpose.

The clearest evidence of a Spanish Joachite who was searching
the writings of Joachim at this time and adapting them to contemporary needs is the unknown writer of a *Summula seu Breviloquium
super concordia Novi et Veteris Testamenti*, who can be identified
with some confidence as a Catalonian Franciscan writing *c.* 1351–
54[1] His work is a full-scale presentation of the Joachimist structure
of history: the three *status*, the seven ages of the world, the double
Seven Seals and Openings. There are large excerpts from the *Liber
Concordie*, but the book is in no sense a summary of this. It is written
in the living faith that the third *status* is at hand: 'Tunc status
mundi tercius intrabit a secundo. Et regnabit sublimius Christus in
toto mundo . . . Nunc septima apercio sigilli gloriosa fiet et revelacio
per orbem radiosa. Nam grandis jubilacio erit et lux serena. Et
grandis proclamacio cunctorum laude plena. Tunc plenitudo gen-
cium solempniter intrabit ad Christum qui Rex omnium reliquias
salvabit' (MS. Egerton, f. 2ᵛ). This passage from the prologue is not
a quotation from Joachim but it is written completely within the
Joachimist expectation.

This hope has been entirely assimilated to the Spiritual Franciscan sense of mission. The writer boldly extends Joachim's pattern of
threes:

Et sicut Jacob fuit genitus ab Ysaach carnaliter in primo statu. Et Iesus
Christus a Johanne babtista sacramentaliter in secundo statu. Ita et in
tercio statu sanctus Franciscus fuit genitus a beato Bernardo simpli-
tudinaliter quo ad formam habitus. Et sicut Abraam tenuit tipum Patris,

---

[1] I have studied this in MSS. Madrid, Bib. Nat., 6972 (formerly S. 247) and Brit.
Mus., Egerton, 1150. See below, bibliography, no. 6.281, for the edition published in 1989.
The British Museum manuscript is a copy made for Pedro Fortez, a merchant of Barcelona,
in 1455 and later presented by him to the church at Barcelona. Dr. Lee informs me of
another copy made at Barcelona in 1488, now Vat. MS. Lat. 11581, ff. 1–65. It is indicative
of the continuing interest in the Joachimist scheme that this work was thought worthy of
copying at a time when its concluding table of generations was already out of date.

Ysaach tipum Filii et Jacob tipum Spiritus Sancti. Sic beatus Benedictus tenuit tipum Patris et Bernardus tipum Filii et sanctus Franciscus tipum Spiritus Sancti. . . . Et sicut Jacob in numero duodecim patriarcharum Dan emisso de medio. Et Christus in numero duodecim apostolorum Juda scariotis emisso de medio. Sicut sanctus Franciscus fructificavit in numero duodecim sociorum, uno emisso de medio ut in vita eius legitur . . . (Ibid., f. 16ʳ.)

Again, he quotes from Olivi on St. Francis as the initiator of the sixth age of the Church:[1]

Sic etiam in sexta etate mundi reiecto carnali Iudaismo et vetustate prioris seculi convaluit novus ordo cum novo duce scilicet Christo Jhesu cum nova lege et vita et cruce. Sic in sexto statu ecclesie reiecta carnalium Christianorum ecclesia et vetustate prioris seculi convalescet novus ordo cum duce novo quo renovabitur Christi lex et vita et crux propter quod in eius principio sanctus Franciscus apparuit plagis Christi passionis veraciter insignitus et Christo totius confixus et configuratus. (Ibid., f. 34ʳ⁻ᵛ.)

In the Tables of Concords which the author constructs for himself the two Mendicant Orders appear in key positions. We shall turn later to this Catalan's conception of Last Things, but here we see him as a full disciple of Joachim working out the role of the Franciscans in the programme of history.

Certain significant features emerge from this brief survey of the Spanish material. First, we must note the evidence of a considerable dissemination of Joachimist works, particularly those of Arnold of Villanova, Pierre Jean d'Olivi, Ubertino da Casale, and Jean de Roquetaillade.[2] Second, the main centre of Joachimist inspiration lay among the Franciscans, not only, as one would expect, in the heretical groups of Beguins and Fraticelli deriving from the Spiritual Franciscans, but also in orthodox Franciscan circles. Third, the Joachimist ferment in Aragon and Catalonia produced several examples of genuine Joachites, that is, those who expounded the future of history within the framework of the three *status*.

What Wadding calls the 'pestifera secta Fraticellorum' was still growing like a hydra in many parts of Italy in the fifteenth century.[3]

---

[1] Cf. *supra*, p. 198.

[2] A typical list of 'prophets' occurs in one process: 'et los noms dels profetas que allegava eren Swnt Isidre, l'abat Joatxin, Merli, Casandra, Sibilla, l'ermitá de la Lamposa, fra Johan de Rochatallada, un sant hom monje de Roma, lo qual dehia que havía fet un llibre de visions et revelacions, et lo dit frare Anselm . . .' (Pou y Marti, *Visionarios*, 439). For Catalan translations of Roquetaillade's *Liber Secretorum Eventuum* and *Vade mecum in tribulatione* see Bignami-Odier, *Roquetaillade*, pp. 241, 248.

[3] Wadding, *Annales* x. 101.

He gives us an account of a book which they issued. This shows that the Fraticelli still expected the *Papa Angelicus* and with him the World Emperor. They were entrenched in the kingdom of Naples, and the account written by the Observantines who preached against them tells of a Neapolitan noble who claimed to be the 'Emperor of the Christians' and a secular priest who claimed to be Pope. The missionaries found in Majoreti an inscription which read: 'A.D. MCCCCXIX tempore fratris Gabrielis, Episcopi Philadelphiae, Pastoris universalis, Fratrumque Minorum Ministeri generalis. Christus, Maria, Franciscus: Papa vester hoc se vocabat pastorem Philadelphiae Ecclesiae, quam vocabatis universalem et ultimam Ecclesiam Christianorum.'[1] This is a curious and interesting statement, which recalls Joachim's interpretation of the *Ecclesia Philadelphiae*.[2]

We must now retrace our steps to the mid-fourteenth century to consider a Minorite who, although a passionate Joachite, remained apart from all the groups of Beguins and Fraticelli: Jean de Roquetaillade or Rupescissa.[3] He was born near Aurillac, but the first date which can be given is 1322, when he entered the Minorite Order. Before this, he tells us, he had studied philosophy at the University of Toulouse. What he seems to have carried away from Toulouse was no liking for secular learning but a deep admiration for the works of Petrus Joannis Olivi and sympathy with those of his followers whom the Inquisition was persecuting for their adherence to the doctrine of absolute poverty. In the same year in which he joined the Franciscans, Jean de Roquetaillade had his first vision concerning Antichrist, and from this time it would seem that his mind was peculiarly receptive of any prophecies, visions, or oracles that came his way. He must have roused the suspicions of the authorities in his Order—no doubt particularly sensitive to such symptoms at this time—for in 1344 without warning he was clapped into prison at the convent of Figeac. From this time on he suffered a long series of imprisonments, vividly recorded in his writings, first in Franciscan convents and then in the papal prison at Avignon. He was persecuted ferociously by Fr. Guillaume Farinier, Provincial and then General of the Minorites, and although the intervention

---

[1] Ibid., p. 105.   [2] *Expos.*, ff. 84ᵛ seq.

[3] This account draws heavily on J. Bignami-Odier's definitive study. For the full title of this work see Select Bibliography. See also E. Jacob, 'John of Roquetaillade', *Bulletin of John Rylands Library*, xxxix (1956–7), pp. 75–96.

of the Curia took him out of the clutches of his Order, it did not release him from prison until some date after 1356. At the last, however, we find him in 1365 receiving papal charity as a sick person at the Franciscan convent in Avignon. Unlike the Beguins and Fraticelli, he never wavered in obedience to the papacy and to the Church. This cost him much heart-searching and labour in argument, for, on the other side, he embraced the extreme doctrine of absolute poverty with great eagerness and it was difficult to reconcile these two positions. He managed to convince himself that the popes had never denied the doctrine of the absolute poverty of Christ and the tenets which followed from this—not even John XXII—and that the guilt for the martyrdom of Olivi's followers belonged to the Dominican Inquisitors. Martyrs, however, they clearly were, the elect of God who defended the true secret of the future.[1]

Jean de Roquetaillade wrote much—it is puzzling to think how, since all his surviving works were written in prison. Mme Bignami-Odier has cut a clear path for us through the confused jungle of these works, of which the most important are a Commentary on the *Oraculum Cyrilli* (which he believed to be the work of Joachim), the *Liber Secretorum Eventuum*, the *Liber Ostensor*, and *Vade Mecum in Tribulatione*. All his work is inspired by a deep sense of the responsibility which rests upon the 'elect', and of his own role as the interpreter of the cosmic future. In words which contain an echo of Joachim's he disclaims the title of prophet, but affirms that to him, unworthy though he was, had been given by Christ the understanding of prophecies, so that he could uncover those secret things hidden therein.[2] The qualities needed by the elect, if they are to receive the secrets, are described in the opening to his Cyril Commentary, where he says that this book can be revealed only to those who observe the evangelical rule, who retreat to the solitary life of hermitage (or prison), and who study the Scriptures with devotion and sweetness.[3] Here we can trace a genuine flowing together of religious inspiration from both Joachim and Francis. Discoursing in the *Liber Ostensor*[4] on the various grades of perfection to be attained by the elect, Roquetaillade touches mystical heights and writes with an ardour that suggests the influence of Olivi, with Joachim in the background. In many passages he shows that the elect are the

---

[1] *Liber Ostensor*, Bignami-Odier, *Roquetaillade*, p. 45.
[2] *Vade Mecum*, ibid., p. 159.　　　　　[3] *Cyril*, ibid., p. 64; also p. 159.
[4] *Liber Ostensor*, ibid., p. 147.

saving remnant of the Franciscans. They must study the secrets and watch for the signs; they must flee the society of the reprobate,[1] yet—and here Roquetaillade dissociates himself from the Beguins— they must never separate themselves from the unity of the Roman Church, but, as the *pauperes gregis*, those who guard the faith of the most high poverty, they must suffer in silence, sowing no discord. God will preserve His elect.[2]

Roquetaillade, apparently, hardly knew Joachim's genuine works, but he regarded the Abbot as a great prophet to whom God had revealed the key to the future,[3] and, besides the *Oraculum Cyrilli*, he studied other pseudo-Joachimist works. His 'Joachimism', however, probably came to him chiefly through Olivi. It consisted in a clear and unshakeable belief that after great tribulations and several Anti- christs the world would reach the Age of Blessedness, the apotheosis of history. Once, at least, he uses Joachim's concept of the third *status* for this,[4] but more often he speaks in terms of the millennium, which (unlike Joachim) he interprets as literally a thousand years of peace until Gog and Magog herald the *consummatio seculi*. We shall be looking later at his political programme of Last Things.[5] The part allotted to his own order is reiterated. The religious orders in general will be destroyed because they have opposed the rule of holy poverty and are the cause of the great tribulation.[6] Even the Order of St. Francis will be split into parts, of which only a very small remnant, the true sons of St. Francis, will be saved, by taking refuge in caves. This handful will be the true seed with which, when the false Minorites have been destroyed, the world will be sown. The seed will spring up everywhere and multiply.[7] Again and again Roquetaillade insists that the pure seed of the Minorites will be preserved to replenish the whole world and that the Franciscan religion alone will endure till the end of the world. From its ranks in the Church of the *renovatio* will be chosen the reforming pope, the great *Reparator*, and many cardinals.[8] They will inherit the papal

[1] *Cyril*, ibid., pp. 67, 70, 95.

[2] *Lib. Ostensor*, ibid., p. 146.

[3] See *Liber Secretorum Eventuum*, ibid., p. 125, referring to a passage in which he says, concerning Satan bound for a thousand years, that St. Augustine did not interpret this well and that Joachim, who prophesied that after Antichrist the world would endure for the period of a further *status*, was closer to the true interpretation.

[4] *Vade Mecum*, ibid., p. 170.   [5] *Infra*, pp. 321–4.

[6] *Cyril*, ibid., p. 95; *Vade Mecum*, ibid., p. 165.

[7] *Cyril*, ibid., pp. 83, 89.

[8] *Cyril*, ibid., p. 96; *Lib. Ostensor*, ibid., p. 146.

power itself and provide the two prophets in sackcloth of the Apocalypse.[1] The pope himself will go on foot as a Mendicant. But this glorious future hangs on a future Saviour of the Friars Minor who will entirely reform their Order. Otherwise they would be cast away like the rest; but, thanks to the prayers of St. Francis, after the tribulation the Order will renew itself and spread throughout the world, like the stars of the heavens for multitude.[2] This was the dream of the poor Jean de Roquetaillade in his prison; one must hope that he was still expecting it when he died, for, according to his dating, the Millennium was to begin in 1400.

[1] *Lib. Ostensor*, ibid., p. 146.   [2] *Vade Mecum*, ibid., p. 166.

VI

OBSERVANTINE FRANCISCANS

IT would be a mistake to assume that the Joachimist sense of high
mission, set against an eschatological background, was entirely
channelled off into the Beguin and Fraticelli groups. In the mid-
fourteenth century, when opposition to the Fraticelli was most
fierce, we meet the congregation of the Gesuati, founded in 1360 by
a Sienese, Giovanni Colombini. This group desired to keep the pure
Rule of St. Francis, while remaining in strict obedience to the
Church. Giovanni delle Celle showed his sympathy with their ideal
of evangelical poverty in a letter of encouragement, yet they had
a hard struggle to gain approval from Urban V because of their
likeness to the Fraticelli.[1]

Still more significant is the fact that a certain Franciscan, Giovanni
delle Valle, who entered the Order in 1325, was a disciple of Angelo
da Clareno. Under his influence Giovanni founded a hermitage in
the Umbrian mountains where he and a group of companions could
live under strict observance of the original Rule. From this eventually
sprang the Observantine branch of the Order. It would be natural to
expect that these new Zealots would draw on the inspiration of the
earlier Spirituals and in fact recent research has confirmed the links
between Spirituals and Observantines.[2] An analysis of *Querimoniae*[3]
presented by a group of Observantines to the Council of Constance
has shown how closely the points, and sometimes the very words,
are linked with one of Ubertino da Casale's tracts beginning *Sanctitas vestra*. The significance of this dependence on the great Spiritual
Franciscan leader lies in the fact that the complaint is a defence of
the high vocation of evangelical poverty and of the Church's need

---

[1] Wadding, *Annales* vii. 168; viii. 45, 298–9; Tocco, *SF*, pp. 423–4.

[2] Lambert, *Franciscan Poverty*, p. 246: '. . . in some respects . . . [the Observantines
were] . . . nothing but continuators of the Spirituals of the thirteenth and fourteenth
centuries, and . . . nourished on their writings which they sought diligently and read in
secret.' See also F. Ehrle, 'Das Verhältniss der Spiritualen zu den Anhängern der
Observanz', *ALKG* iv. 181–90.

[3] L. Oliger, 'De relatione inter Observantium querimonias, Constantienses (1415) et
Ubertini Cesalensis quoddam scriptum', *AFH* ix. (1916), pp. 3–41.

for a return to the pure Rule of St. Francis. Thus we have clear
evidence that some Observantines saw their mission to the world
in terms similar to the conception of the Spirituals. The question for
us here is how far, through this inheritance from the Spirituals,
the Observantines drew on Joachimist hopes.

St. Bernardino of Siena exemplifies the connection between the
peculiar veneration of St. Francis, the high sense of mission, and
the Joachimist pattern of history. In a sermon on St. Francis under
the text 'Et vidi alterum Angelum ascendentem, etc.' he brought the
Abbot Joachim as the first witness to the claim that this Sixth Angel
of the Apocalypse was St. Francis.[1] In so doing he made it clear that
the foundation of this claim lay in the concords of the Scriptures as
established by Joachim:

Primum (testimonium) est Abbatis Ioachim qui exponendo Apocalypsim
dicit intelligendo de Sancto Francisco: hic est ille Angelus, quem Christus
per concordiam respicit. Et nota quod ille Abbas Ioachim fuit mirabiliter
illuminatus: quia mirabiliter concordat sacras scripturas: ecce concordiam quam Sanctus Franciscus habet cum Christo, quia habuit stigmata
plagarum Christi, in concordantia passionis et Evangelicae imitationis,
pacis et paupertatis. (*Sermo XVI*, p. 88.)

Moreover, he used the Joachimist scheme of Church history, as
adapted by the Spirituals, and when he declared that from St.
Francis onwards is the sixth *status* of the Church, this carried all the
Joachimist overtones. Possibly Bartholomew of Pisa was his source
in this sermon, for he gave an early version of the San Marco story.[2]
He elaborated the parallels between St. Francis and Christ in high
terms and great detail, concluding:

Unde dicebat ipse Christus: . . . ponam te quasi signaculum: nam filius
Dei est signaculum et Sanctus Franciscus fuit quasi signaculum, et non
signaculum, sed per imitationem, quasi Christus et fuit Christus per
transformationem. Unde in rima quasi transformato per humilitatem fuit
quasi Christus effectus, quoniam ego elegi te, quasi velut dicere, ego elegi
te Angelum sexti sigilli. (*Sermo XVI*, p. 89.)

He also paralleled the twelve companions of St. Francis with the
twelve Apostles, even identifying the Judas amongst them. From
this sermon, at least, it would seem that, indirectly through the

---

[1] Bernardino, *Omnia Opera*, iv, ii (Venice, 1591), *Sermones Extraordinarii, Sermo
XVI: De Sancto Francisco*, pp. 88–91.
[2] *Supra*, p. 96.

Spirituals, St. Bernardino's sense of mission was nourished on Joachim's expectation.

It has been conclusively proved that in his sermons Bernardino drew heavily on the *Arbor Vitae Crucifixae* of Ubertino da Casale.[1] In the *Itinerarium*, in which Bernardino noted the sources of his sermons, the citations from Ubertino are numerous. Of the greatest interest are those drawn from Book V of the *Arbor Vitae Crucifixae*, in which Ubertino expounded the Joachimist view of history.[2] This material was used by Bernardino for a series of Advent sermons at Genoa probably in 1418. Here he adopted the complete pattern of the seven ages of the Church with the characteristic symbolisms worked out by Ubertino. But we have to ask how far Bernardino followed Ubertino in the expectations pertaining to the sixth age of the Church. It is likely that the Genoese sermons belonged to an early stage and it is surely significant that in the final version of his sermons the *Arbor Vitae* is never openly cited. Did Bernardino deliberately draw back from the Joachimist implications of Ubertino's expectation in history? If so, was this because of the fantastic lengths to which it was pushed by the fanatics? We have a hint of this in another sermon, *De Inspirationibus*, in which Bernardino turns in revulsion from fanatics who feed on prophecies. He cites a hermit who in his own day had led a crazy crowd naked into the sea, expecting it to open before them.[3] Then he hits out at the Joachimist type of prophecy with which, he says (quoting David of Augsburg), we are stuffed to repletion:

Plerique etiam seducuntur, putantes per Spiritum Sanctum fieri quod ipsi prius finxerunt, vel quod spiritus erroris suggessit eis. Proinde vaticiniis iam usque ad nauseam repleti sumus: ut puta de Antichristi adventu, de signis iudicii propinquantis, de Ecclesiae persecutione et reformatione et similibus, quibus etiam viri graves atque devoti plusquam oportuit creduli exstiterunt, de scripturis Ioachim et aliorum vaticinantium interpretationes varias extrahentes; quae etsi vera et aucthentica forent; attamen servi Dei plurima alia reperirent, in quibus possent fructuosius occupari . . . (*Sermo III*, p. 267.)

[1] E. d'Isegem, 'L'influence d'Ubertin de Casale sur les écrits de S. Bernardin de Sienne', *Collectanea Francescana*, v (1935), pp. 5–44. It would seem that he also drew on Olivi's *Postilla* and through this on Joachim's *Expositio*; see *Quadragesimale de Christiana Religione Sermones*, *Omnia Opera*, ed. Coll. S. Bonaventura, ii (Ad Claras Aquas, Florence, 1950), pp. 465 (n. 4), 472.
[2] *Supra*, pp. 207–9.
[3] Bernardino, *Omnia Opera*, vi (Ad Claras Aquas, Florence, 1954), *Sermo II: De Inspirationibus*, p. 256.

Like St. Bonaventura, Bernardino shows towards Joachimism an ambivalent attitude which, in its mixture of attraction and repulsion, can be studied in his *Expositio in Apocalypsim*. This is a very eclectic work, without much system of thought, but clearly Bernardino wished to interpret the Apocalypse in terms of the whole history of the Church, future as well as past. This led him straight towards Joachim, and so we find a number of interpretations which seem to echo the Abbot's: the parallels of twelve Patriarchs and Tribes with twelve Apostles and Churches, the seven ages of the Old Testament matched with the seven of the New, the seven heads of the Dragon, almost identical with Joachim's, the interpretation of the four *animalia* and the contrast of the hard outer 'letter' with the inner meaning which lies 'in cortice'.[1] Joachim is never once cited, but it is difficult not to believe that Bernardino knows his works well, and this impression is suddenly confirmed when, without any warning, one comes upon two passages quoted directly from the little-known tract of Joachim, *De Septem Sigillis*.[2] These quotations are inserted straight into the text without even an indication that they are quotations, let alone any reference to their source. Significantly, these passages record Joachim's pattern of twos: the detailed parallels between the first and second Seals in the Old Testament and their Openings in the New. Bernardino obviously wants to use this framework of parallel ages and parallel symbols in the two Dispensations as the clue to the understanding of the Apocalypse, though it is noticeable that he does not use the rest of Joachim's sequences for the Seals and Openings. Bernardino follows Joachim in another point, for he sees in many of the Angels of the Apocalypse symbols of the orders of spiritual men sent to preach the Gospel. The theme of the *praedicatores universi* or the succession of the *ordines praedicantium* is a recurring one. After Antichrist there will be a final order— *ultimus ordo praedicantium*—to proclaim the end of the world.[3] Against a cosmic background the high role of St. Francis receives full emphasis. The Eagle flying through the heavens, the Sealed Book itself, the Angel with the sign of the Living God, the returning

---

[1] *Commentaria in Apocalypsim*, *Omnia Opera* (ed. J. de la Haye, Paris, 1636), v. 39, 46, 47, 59, 105, 145. See particularly the Dragon's Heads: *Herod, Nero, Constantius arrius, Cosras rex Persarum, rex Babylonis novae, sc. Henricus rex Germanorum* . . ., *quidem* [sic] *rex innominatus, Antichristus* (p. 110).

[2] Ibid., pp. 39, 77; cf. Reeves, Hirsch-Reich, *RTAM* xxi. 239, 41.

[3] *Commentaria in Apocalypsim*, pp. 47, 77, 79, 82, 84, 90–2, 98, 119–20, 127, 130, 134–5.

Elijah—all may be interpreted, according to one sense, as St. Francis.[1] Even the New Jerusalem at the end of the Apocalypse may be expounded in terms of the two Mendicant Orders, with St. Francis and St. Dominic as the foundation stones.[2] Yet at this point Bernardino draws back. There was too dangerous an attraction in this vision: the Orders were by no means immaculate, and he dared not take this interpretation too literally. Thus Bernardino would not ascribe the final role confidently either to his own Order or to the two Mendicant Orders together. Moreover, he turns away resolutely from the Joachimist vision of the Age of the Spirit. Between the defeat of Antichrist and the Last Judgement there seems to be a space for preaching and conversion, but the seventh Age of Tranquillity is beyond Judgement.[3] At some points Bernardino seems to be deliberately avoiding Joachim's interpretations, notably in the case of the Angel with the Eternal Evangel, which, he says, is simply the Gospel, called eternal 'vel quia non succedit aliud, vel quia permittet aeterna ad discrimen legis quae promittebat terrena'.[4] Whether caution or repulsion kept the great Franciscan preacher as far as possible from the dreams and claims of such as the Fraticelli, the Joachimist way of thought certainly drew him, and the mission of the *praedicatores* assumes for him its full dramatic significance in the last ages of history.[5]

Another fifteenth-century Franciscan who still responded to the Joachimist expectation was the Blessed Amadeus of Portugal (Joannes Menesius de Silva).[6] Born in 1431, after various religious vicissitudes he became a Minorite in 1452 and, coming to Italy, founded his own strict congregation of Amadeites, centring on St. Pietro at Montorio in Rome, which was given to him by Sixtus IV. Later, in the time of Leo X, the congregation became part of the Observantine Order. Amadeus was a visionary who became widely known for his *Apocalipsis nova*, which had been dictated to him, so said the legend, by the Angel Gabriel, who revealed the hidden and inner meanings.

---

[1] *Commentaria in Apocalypsim*, pp. 47, 51, 67, 96–7. [2] Ibid., p. 166.
[3] Ibid., pp. 75, 98, 159–60. [4] Ibid., p. 120.
[5] In this assessment of Joachim's influence on Bernardino I have given much more weight to it than did A. Ferrers Howell, *S. Bernardino of Siena* (London, 1913), pp. 234, 307–8, who, of course, did not know that Bernardino had directly utilized one of Joachim's writings. On Bernardino's preaching see also Wadding, *Annales* x. 33.
[6] On Amadeus see N. Antonio Hispalensis, *Bibliotheca Hispania Vetus* (Madrid, 1788), ii. 317–18; Wadding, *Scriptores*, pp. 30–1; Wadding, *Annales* xiv. 313–23. In MS. Oxford, Bod. Lib., Laud Misc. 588, ff. 4ᵛ–7ᵛ, there is a Latin text of what appears to be Amadeus' vision.

His writings were disseminated in manuscript in a number of religious houses, and certainly influenced another Franciscan, Pietro Columna (or Galatinus), a Jesuit, Cornelius Lapierre (or a Lapide), and the strange Guillaume Postel. The latter probably discovered his book when in Rome in 1547. He tells us that 'le livre dudict Amodaeus espagnol se trouve en la famille ou postérité de la plus grand [*sic*] part des cardinaux et de beaucoup de Romains qui iusques au temps du Pape Farnese ont vescu, et moyennant ladicte profétie d'Amodaeus se sont promis le Papat Angélike, mais en vain pour estre vestus de la robe de Symon Samaritain.'[1] The core of Amadeus's message concerned this Angelic Pope, whom he expounded in prophecy and—like a true Joachite—in picture. Thus his desire to reform the Franciscan Order must be placed in the Joachimist setting of the *renovatio* under the *Papa Angelicus*. The Blessed Amadeus was much venerated and his *Apocalipsis nova* aroused lively interest[2] and some controversy. This was still heated in the time of Luke Wadding. He discussed the doctrine attributed to Amadeus at considerable length,[3] and while refuting graver charges brought against the mystic, expressed the view that Amadeus's book of revelations on the Angelic Pope had been tampered with by many.[4]

In the first half of the sixteenth century, Pietro Columna, or

---

[1] F. Secret, 'Guillaume Postel et les courants prophétiques de la Renaissance', *Studi francesi* I, p. 378.

[2] Thus N. Antonio Hispalensis, op. cit., pp. 317–18, says: 'De revelationibus et prophetiis pulcherrimum libellum composuit', but adds: 'De quo opere iam per manus omnium curiosorum passim eunte, iudicium abstinere satius est, quam ut viri praestantissimi, totiusque ordinis sui Generalis olim Praefecti et aliorum prius laudatorum, censurae quicquam adiungamus . . .'.

[3] Wadding, *Annales* xiv. 313–23.

[4] After considerable discussion Wadding concludes: 'Haec prolixius, quam soleam, de Amadei doctrina explicanda, ne propter spurium foetum et apocryphum opus vir vere bonus gravem pateretur nominis jacturam . . .' (*Annales* xiv. 323).

[5] A somewhat shadowy contemporary of Amadeus was the German Franciscan, Johann Hilten, later well known as a prophet among Protestants. He wrote commentaries on the book of Daniel and the Apocalypse in which he proclaimed that *c.* 1516 there would be a *reformatio* of the Church, when the Roman pontiff would be overthrown by a reformer, and that *c.* 1600 the Turks would rule in Germany before the end of the world in 1651. In the *reformatio* we may see a lingering trace of Joachimism. The Reformers saw this announcement of a great reformer as a direct prophecy of Luther; see Myrconius's letter to Luther in 1529 (*ZKG* iii (1879), pp. 305–6), and Melanchthon's reiterated references to Hilten (*Corpus Reformatorum* (Halle, 1834 onwards), i. 1108; iv. 780; vii, cols. 653, 999, 1006, 1112; xiv. 841; xxiv, cols. 64, 225; xxv, cols. 14, 80; xxvii. 627). On Hilten see *Realencyklopädie für protestantische Theologie u. Kirche* (Leipzig, 1900), viii. 78–80; M. Flacius Illyricus, *Catalogus Testium Veritatis* (Lyon, 1597), ii. 898.

Petrus Galatinus of Puglia, was an enthusiastic disciple of Joachim and Amadeus.[1] He was a provincial minister of the Observantines, a theologian, and a humanist interested in linguistics. He spent much of his life in Rome, where he plunged into Greek and Hebrew studies and perhaps belonged to the circle of Egidio of Viterbo, who appears later in this book.[2] It is clear that Amadeus exercised a strong influence over his thinking and his imagination also fed on the symbolic interpretations of Joachim and the Joachites. As a commentator on the Apocalypse he compared Joachim favourably with Albertus Magnus, who was confused in his exposition, while Joachim 'praeceteris eleganter et spiritualiter Apocalypsim elucidat'.[3] He also gathered together the prophecies of Cyril, Petrus Joannis Olivi, Robert d'Uzès, Jean de Roquetaillade, an alleged oracle of St. Cataldus—in fact, a great deal of the regular Joachimist material. His chief published work was the *De arcanis catholicae veritatis*, but a number of others survive in Vatican manuscripts. In his *De septem Ecclesiae temporibus*, the three works, *De Ecclesia Instituta*, *Destituta*, and *Restituta*, and his Commentary on the Apocalypse, all written in *c.* 1523, Galatinus put forward his view of history, and in two of his latest tracts, *Vaticinii Romani explicatio* and *De Angelico Pastore*, he gathered together his expectations of the future.

Reading the manuscript works of Galatinus,[4] one realizes with astonishment that here is a fully-fledged sixteenth-century Joachite. It is not that he directly quotes Joachim so constantly—though he does cite the Abbot frequently in some works—but that he has assimilated so much from Joachim, whether he acknowledges the source or not. He states the doctrine of the three *status* in its full Trinitarian form;[5] he interprets the Alpha and Omega as the Trinity and the Unity of the Godhead;[6] he adopts the five/seven number-symbolism of Tribes and Churches as representing that

---

[1] On P. Galatinus see P. Kleinhans, 'De Vita et operibus Petri Galatini, O.F.M., scientiarum biblicarum cultoris (*c.* 1460–1540)', *Antonianum* i. 145–79, 327–56.

[2] *Infra*, pp. 268–71.   [3] Vat., MS. Lat. 5567, f. iii[v].

[4] The most important of these are MSS. Vat., Lat. 5567, *In Apocalypsim . . . Commentaria*; 5568, *De Ecclesia destituta* (pars 1a); 5569, *De Ecclesia destituta* (pars 2a); 5575, *De Ecclesia instituta*; 5578, *De Angelico Pastore* and *Libellus de Republica Christiana pro vera eiusdem reipublicae reformatione, progressu et felici ad recuperanda Christianorum loca expeditione*; 5579, *De septem ecclesiae tum temporibus tum statibus opus*; 5580, *De sacra Scriptura recte interpretanda opus*; 5581, *Vaticinii Romani explicatio*.

[5] Vat., MS. Lat. 5567, ff. xxiii[v]–xxiiii[v].

[6] Ibid., f. xxxvi[r]; see also on the Tetragrammaton, f. cii[r–v].

which is prior and posterior;[1] he sees in the *Tuba* the *litere superficies* and in the *flatus* the *spiritualis intellectus*;[2] he makes Peter symbolize the *ecclesiasticus ordo* and John the *monasticus [ordo] seu contemplantium status*.[3] In spite of his humanist training and interests, his approach to history is the same as Joachim's: every detail in the Old Dispensation prefigures the New, and the most important task is to seek an understanding of this symbolism through the *spiritualis intellectus*. Not that Galatinus follows Joachim slavishly: there are interesting variations,[4] and occasionally an application of the Joachimist method in a way which had not occurred to the Abbot himself.[5] The surprising thing is that the Joachimism of these writings was not detected and attacked. In the Commentary on the *Apocalypse* the unequivocal statement of the doctrine of the three *status* is emphasized by a marginal caption, and though, in this work, Joachim is not often directly cited, in others there is no hesitation in sprinkling the margins with references to him. Perhaps doubts about orthodoxy prevented the appearance in print of most of Galatinus's works, but clearly these views were no longer regarded as dangerous and, indeed, others in Galatinus's circle were eager to share his optimistic expectations about the future.

Galatinus adopted the full Joachimist framework of reference: the seven ages of the world, the two parallel seven *tempora* of the Synagogue and the Church, the three *status*. But he adapted Joachim's programme of the last stages, since—he said—Joachim, living in the fifth *tempus* of the Church, could not see the future so clearly.[6] He believed, therefore, that the sixth *tempus* was now beginning and that this would be the great Golden Age of the Church. It would end in the sharp tribulation of the last Antichrist, after which the seventh, the Sabbath Age of quietude, would last until the *consummatio seculi*. But this last age would be brief and in Galatinus's expectation it appears somewhat colourless. It is in the sixth age that the third *status* of the Spirit will begin, and here are concentrated all Galatinus's most vivid hopes for the apotheosis of history. The exaltation

---

[1] MS. 5567, ff. xxxiii^r–xxxiiii^v; on five senses and seven virtues, f. clxxxxiii^v.

[2] Ibid., ff. lii^v–liii^r. Part of this passage is more or less directly quoted from *Expos.*, f. 40^v.

[3] Ibid., ff. lxxxv^r–lxxxvi^r.

[4] Ibid., ff. clxxiiii^r–v, clxxxxii^v; also MS. 5579, f. 11^r–v for disagreement with Joachim.

[5] MSS. 5567, f. xxxiiii^r, and 5578, ff. 32^v–35^v, for applications of symbolism which had not occurred to Joachim.

[6] MS. 5567, f. iiii^r.

of Joachim's seventh age has been transferred to the sixth, 'cuius initium iam tenemus'.[1]

The programme of this *foelicissimum tempus*[2] follows the usual lines, with the conversion of the Jews, conquest and conversion of the infidels, and the gathering of all the world into one flock under one shepherd by the Angelic Pope, who will be aided by the great World Emperor. The function of the preachers receives due emphasis, but the outstanding characteristic is one which brings Galatinus close to Joachim, yet also expresses his humanist enthusiasm: spiritual illumination, that is, the laying bare of all mysteries. The *viri spirituales* of the sixth *tempus*, disciples of the Angelic Pope, will be contemplatives who are elevated to the third heaven, although they will also be preachers who descend to the people.[3] Again and again Galatinus uses metaphors and symbols to describe the *spiritualis intellectus* which echo those of Joachim,[4] and his understanding of illumination belongs to the mystical, symbolical school, concentrating attention on the elucidation of prophecies and enigmatic figures. Yet unexpectedly he will plunge into textual criticism of the new type and draw upon the scholarship of humanists like Erasmus.[5] In this he is perhaps typical of the strange flowing together of currents in the early sixteenth century.

Galatinus no longer assigned to his own Order a leading role in bringing in the *reformatio mundi*. St. Francis and St. Dominic were, he believed, the chief agencies of God in the fifth *tempus*, and Galatinus accepted the validity of Joachim's supposed prophecies concerning them. But he rejected the identification of St. Francis with the angel having the sign of the Living God, since this angel belonged to the sixth age and was therefore one of the symbols of the Angelic Pope.[6] It is remarkable that he did not attempt to assign either the Angelic Pope himself or the twelve *sancti viri* who were to assist him to any specific order, although he thought they would certainly be regulars. The Joachimism of Galatinus was thus free from the desire to claim a place in the last age. His claim was for the sixth

---

[1] MS. 5567, f. iiii^r.   [2] Ibid.

[3] Ibid., f. ci^v, where, like Joachim, he uses the figure of the Temple columns to symbolize the dual role of the *viri spirituales*.

[4] e.g. MS. 5567, ff. iiii^r ('cuncta eius mysteria ad liquidum reseratum'), xcvi^v ('quasi ex noctis caligine splendescere et ad lucis meridiane claritatem venire'), cxxix^v ('sub cortice'), clxxxx^r ('apertum est littere sepulchrum et spiritualis intelligentia simul cum Christo resurgens, patefacta est').

[5] e.g. MS. 5567, ff. lxiiii^v, cxxxxiii^v.

[6] MSS. 5567, ff. clx^{r–v}, clxxix^r, ccxl^v–ccxli^v; 5579, f. 7^r.

tempus itself: 'sextum ecclesie tempus . . . reliqua eiusdem ecclesie tempora perfectionem excellit.' In contemplation it would be more perfect and 'limpid' than the fourth *tempus*; in zeal of preaching more perfect than the fifth *tempus* of Francis and Dominic; even in peace and quiet it would exceed the length of the seventh age.[1] Here Galatinus approached the danger-point of Joachimism: the claim that the third *status* will surpass all others. Again we marvel that no one apparently took him up on this, although the expectation is clearly and urgently reiterated in his writings: 'iam iam in januis esse creditur'.[2]

Galatinus's works were not only dedicated to well-known leaders but also read by many, especially in Rome. It was in the Franciscan house of Ara Coeli that the unbalanced Postel studied them and came to believe that he was himself the Angelic Pope.[3] The Jesuit Cornelius Lapierre quoted them a number of times.[4] Later Luke Wadding was obviously interested in Galatinus's writings and hoped to publish some. But here at least was someone who was aware of playing with fire and put in a warning: 'Non omnibus omnia placebunt. Multa habet de Thalmudicis commentis, aliqua de arte Cabalistica, plurima de Pastore Angelico, ab Amadeo Hispano, cui fortassis plus aequo tribuit, excerpta, et aliquanto liberius in deformatos Ecclesiasticorum mores invehitur' (*Scriptores*, p. 192).

Luke Wadding himself forms the proper conclusion to this study of Franciscan attitudes towards Joachimism. As the great annalist of the Order he could not avoid the cardinal theme of the split between Spirituals and Conventuals, and he betrays his sympathy with the Spirituals in the amount of space he devotes to their struggles, in his defence of great leaders such as John of Parma and Petrus Joannis Olivi, and in his use of the two great classics of the Spirituals, Angelo Clareno's *Historia Septem Tribulationum* and Ubertino da Casale's *Arbor Vitae Crucifixae*.[5] At a safe distance in time he can view the impassioned controversy with a calmer eye, in due perspective, and perceive the sanctity and singlemindedness of the *Zelanti*.[6] There is, however, no ambivalence in his distinction

---

[1] MS. 5567, ff. xxii^r–v, xxiii^r, clxxxvii^r. [2] Ibid., f. iiii^r.
[3] *Infra*, p. 479. [4] *Infra*, p. 281 n. 5.
[5] Wadding, *Annales* iv. 4–12; v. 52, 108, 211, 217, 324, 378–93, 417–18; vii. 168. He justifies the length of his discussion of P. J. d'Olivi thus: 'His prolixius, sed necessario productis pro asserenda hominis innocentia' (v. 393).
[6] His balanced attitude, endeavouring to justify both Spirituals and Conventuals, appears clearly in an early discussion of the *Zelanti*, iii. 100 (*anno* 1244).

between orthodox and heretic: the true *Zelanti* (e.g. the Clarenists) remain within the true Church, they never abandon their obedience, they occupy a similar position to that of the Observantines; the Fraticelli and Beguins, in contrast, are a heretical sect and Wadding will not admit that they derive from the *Zelanti* at all.[1]

The basis of Wadding's sympathy with the Spirituals is the belief he shares with them that the Rule of St. Francis was a divine revelation.[2] As we have seen, the elevation of the Rule was carried to such heights as to be only possible if set against a Joachimist expectation in history. Wadding, of course, did not perceive this close connection, but he cannot avoid the Abbot Joachim as the prophet of the Order, and his treatment of Joachim gives us a particularly interesting example of the early seventeenth-century historian handling controversial material. In the first place, Joachim appears quite conventionally as the prophet of St. Francis.[3] Here Wadding is obviously drawing on Bartholomew of Pisa and St. Antonino of Florence.[4] The crucial discussion of Joachim, however, arises when Wadding has to deal with the examination of John of Parma and his associates by Bonaventura in 1256. In Wadding's account the Spirituals answer 'fideliter et sincere' until the 'caput accusationum omnium' is reached and they are asked 'quid sentirent de Joachimo Abbate eiusve doctrina?'[5] Here they stubbornly persist in defending Joachim; and, although taxed with the Trinitarian heresy of Joachim condemned in 1215, Gerard of Borgo San Donnino, in particular, contrives to give the impression of immovable adherence to the Abbot's doctrine.

This raises in Wadding's mind the whole thorny question of whether they were justly condemned and, therefore, whether confidence in Joachim was misplaced. It is true that the Lateran Council condemned this *libellus* of Joachim and one cannot impugn the clear verdict of a General Council, but later Honorius III in his bull to

[1] *Annales* v. 390; vi. 279–82, 316–19. He defends the Clarenists vigorously, see vi. 281–2. In dealing with the Observantines he is well aware of how easily they could be confused with the Fraticelli. On Wadding and the Spirituals see F. Casolini, *Luca Wadding, O.F.M.* (Milan, 1936), pp. 170–8.

[2] *Annales* ii. 69, where, after discussing the divine inspiration of the Rule, he quotes this praise of it: '. . . librum esse vitae, spem salutis, arrham gloriae, medullam Evangelii, viam crucis, statum perfectionis, clavem paradisi, pactum foederis eterni . . .'.

[3] Ibid. i. 14–16.

[4] He cites the spurious prophecy beginning *Erunt duo viri* which Bartholomew ascribes to the *Lib. Conc.* (cf. *supra*, p. 182) and also the San Marco story.

[5] *Annales* iv. 4 seq.

rehabilitate the reputation of Joachim defended him as 'virum catholicum'.[1] Many since have also defended Joachim, including recently Francis Bivar, 'amicus intimus, vir probus et doctus'.[2] Here Wadding seizes hold of the defence put forward by the monks of Fiore and adapted by Bivar, that Joachim had been unjustly accused and had foretold this himself. Of Joachim's orthodox intentions his Testamentary Letter is proof, and therefore there may be substance in the theory of falsification. Here the instincts of the historian appear and Wadding hopes that 'puriores codices' may be found from which the spurious additions may be detected.[3] So far, in this suggested line of defence of the Spiritual adherence to Joachim, Wadding has avoided all mention of the real difficulty—the notorious Eternal Evangel—concentrating instead on the Trinitarian heresy. He brings it in almost casually at the end of his discussion, but not until he has buttressed the sanctity of John of Parma by a long list of witnesses. Then he remarks that, by reason of the weighty testimony of so many, he cannot believe that the 'Joannes Parmensis, monachus Italicus' whom Nicholas Eymerich accuses of writing the Eternal Evangel can possibly be the Franciscan John of Parma.[4] He then cites some of the heresies from this notorious book, as given by Eymerich, arguing that these could not conceivably be the views of the Spiritual leader. What is notable here is that he neither mentions the attribution to Gerard of Borgo San Donnino, nor does he pick out any errors which relate the Eternal Evangel in any way to Joachim: it is simply an insane book that somehow got mixed up with the Spirituals because of an ascription to a John of Parma. Thus, very skilfully, Wadding diverts the whole attack from the deeply compromising adaptation of Joachim's theory of history in the Eternal Evangel back to the 'technical' heresy on the Trinity, on which he has a good line of defence. The marginal captions to this whole section reinforce the argument: 'Joachim Abbas nequaquam damnatus a Concilio Lateranensi.' 'Ita declarat Honorius III.' 'Bivarius in Apologia contra Pennottum.' 'Id amplius probatur.' 'Protestatio Joachimi.' 'Bonorum auctorum de Parmense elogia.' 'Defenditur Parmensis a gravi calumnia.'

In some instinctive way Wadding felt that the Abbot Joachim was

---

[1] *Annales* iv. 6, where Wadding quotes the Bull, for which see *supra*, p. 32.
[2] Ibid. iv. 6–7. For Bivar, *supra*, pp. 110–11.
[3] Ibid. iv. 7.
[4] Ibid. iv. 8–12.

necessary to the true spirituality of the Franciscans.[1] This is surely true. The sense of unique mission which burned in the Order could only be kindled from a particular historical hope, and it is the incandescent quality of the great Franciscans that is most remembered. The extravagances and aberrations of those who carried this sense of mission too far form a tragic chapter in the history of spiritual enthusiasm, but zeal is always dangerous. If the *Zelanti* had not raised the temperature of the Order to white heat, the Order would have been infinitely the poorer. If the Abbot Joachim had not delineated two new orders of spiritual men, one of the most moving chapters in the history of religious enthusiasm would never have been written.

[1] The sympathy which he always accords to the Clarenists, as for example in *Annales* viii. 300–1, betrays his feeling.

VII

POPULAR MOVEMENTS

J OACHIMISM was a doctrine for religious orders. Yet we have already seen that in Provence it could percolate among popular groups who used vernacular writings. There were other popular movements, more loosely connected with Joachimism, but sharing the same expectation of a new Dispensation in history. It is difficult to trace the direct origin of their inspiration because they drew little from literary sources, but since Joachimism was the most powerful and widespread form of belief in the coming Age of the Spirit during the thirteenth and fourteenth centuries, this was probably the ultimate source from which they derived. The distinctive characteristic that linked them with Joachimism rather than with a general Pantheism was the concept of the structure of history culminating in a definite historical era of the Spirit. Thus Joachim's idea of new spiritual men had a wider meaning and appeal than the Abbot could contain within his orders of monks and hermits.

In the same period in which the Spiritual party was forming in the Franciscan Order, Gerard Segarelli was founding the sect of Apostolic Brethren. He appeared in Parma in 1260, the significant year for Joachimists. Low-born and illiterate, he was refused admission by the Minorites, yet his doctrine attracted considerable numbers in northern Italy. Salimbene, who was in the Franciscan convent at Parma when Segarelli appeared, had bitter, abusive words for him: *illiteratus, ydiota, stultus.*[1] He averred that it was from the representations of the Apostles in the Franciscan Church at Parma that Segarelli took his ideas, and accused him of seducing certain Franciscans and outbidding the Minorites for the support of the Parmese. In the new movement, according to Salimbene, twelve were set apart as Apostles and a further seventy, while great propaganda was made with a boy-preacher. Here Salimbene clearly implies that Segarelli was invoking the prophecies of Joachim of the 'twelve', the 'seventy', and the 'boys' to come.[2] Indeed, Salimbene's account of

---

[1] Salimbene, p. 256. The whole account of this sect occupies pp. 255–93.
[2] Ibid., pp. 267, 290; cf. *Lib. Conc.*, ff. 57^v–58^r, 12^r, 112^r.

the *Apostolici* is interspersed with discussion of what was obviously a sore point: the claim of the new sect to be the new spiritual order of Joachim. Salimbene admits that Joachim had certainly prophesied the election of 'boys' in succession to patriarchs and apostles, but these applied to the Orders of Friars Minor and Preacher 'in quibus intrant pueri litterati, nobiles moribus et honesti', not to these 'stulti et ydiote, rudes et bestiales, qui se dicunt apostolos esse et non sunt'.[1] Salimbene is able to prove to his satisfaction from Joachim's figure of the *Novus Ordo*[2] that these pseudo-apostles are not included in the prophecies, but by discussing them in this context, and by linking them deliberately with the year 'in which the Joachites say the *status Spiritus Sancti* begins',[3] he indicates their kinship with the Joachites. Thus, although at first sight this appears to be a typical movement of return to apostolic poverty and preaching, the 'perfection of evangelical poverty' which they embrace belongs to the future and final state of the Church, rather than to the first. It is the Joachimist view of history, once more, that is the ground of their confidence.

This becomes clearer in the teaching of Fra Dolcino, who succeeded to the leadership after Segarelli's death by burning in 1300 and may well have been the real author of much of their teaching. In his manifesto of 1300 Dolcino proclaimed that in these last days God had specially sent this group (*congregatio*), under its divinely-commissioned leader, to preach the salvation of souls.[4] He claimed the inspiration of the Holy Spirit in interpreting the Scriptures and revealing the future, and put forward a view of history which, though departing somewhat from the Joachimist, is clearly related to it.[5] He believed that there were four *status*: the first belonged to the patriarchs, prophets, and other just men of the Old Testament, who lived in the good state of matrimony until, before the coming of Christ, the spiritual state of man declined from virtue. The second state, initiated by Christ and His Apostles, provided the perfect remedy for the maladies of the preceding one and carried life on to a new spiritual plane; chastity was set above marriage and poverty above riches. This age endured until the epoch of the Blessed St. Silvester and the Emperor Constantine, but declined from this time.

[1] Salimbene, p. 267.   [2] Ibid., p. 293; cf. *Lib. Fig.* II, Pl. XII.
[3] Salimbene, p. 293.
[4] B. Gui, *De Secta Illorum qui se dicunt esse de ordine Apostolorum*, Muratori, N.S. ix, Pt. v, p. 20. On Dolcino see E. Anagnine, *Dolcino e il movimento ereticale all'inizio del Trecento* (Florence 1964).   [5] Gui, op. cit., pp. 20-1.

The third *status*, beginning with St. Silvester, saw the mass conversion of the Gentile peoples. It was better at this period for the popes to take possession of rich lands and to rule over these peoples than to renounce all riches and power, but as love once again grew cold, so the more perfect way of life became, first that initiated by St. Benedict, and finally that of St. Francis and St. Dominic. Now that prelates, clergy, and religious had all grown cold in the love of God and neighbour, it was better, instead of embracing any other way of life, to return to that true apostolic life which God had reserved for these last times. This was the way of life pertaining to the fourth and last *status*; it differed from that of St. Francis and St. Dominic in being more radical in its poverty, 'et propter hoc vita nostra major est et ultima omnibus medicina'.[1] It alone would endure until the end of the world and bear its fruits up to the Judgement Day.

Following Joachim's liking for alternative divisions, Dolcino also subdivided the history of the Church into four *mutationes*. In the first she remained pure and chaste under persecution until Constantine. In the second she remained good, though rich, while clergy and religious followed the examples of Sts. Silvester, Benedict, Dominic, and Francis. The third, which was the contemporary period, saw the Church in decline, 'malitiosa, dives et honorata'.[2] It would endure for less than three years, when all the clergy and religious would be cruelly killed. In the fourth period, the Church would become truly herself: 'bona et pauper, et persecutiones passa in proprio modo vivendi apostolico reformata'. This period was initiated by Gerard of Parma 'quem dicit a Deo esse delectissimum, et perseverabit perfecta et durabit et fructificabit usque ad finem mundi'.[3]

The Apostolic Brethren carried repudiation of ecclesiastical authority to the extreme. All the authority once conferred by Christ on the Roman Church had now departed because of the evil of prelates. The Roman Church was no longer the Church of God but 'illa Babilon meretrix magna'.[4] All spiritual power had now passed to the sect or order of the *Apostoli*, upon whom had descended the power conferred on St. Peter. Since these alone constituted

---

[1] Gui, op. cit., p. 21.

[2] Ibid. Dolcino's schemes of history were an integral part of his propaganda, for we find clear echoes of them in the interrogation of Apostoli at Bologna 1299–1303. (Muratori N.S. ix, Pt. v, *Acta Sancti Officii Bononie*, pp. 53, 57–61).

[3] Gui, op. cit., p. 21.

[4] Ibid., p. 24.

the Church of God and possessed the perfection of the first apostles, they owed obedience to no man and could not be called by any authority to abandon this rule of liberty or this most perfect life, for to do so would be to descend from the more perfect to the less perfect.[1] Expectation of the transfer of authority was focused on the years immediately following 1300. It would be accomplished by the violence of revolution. Pope Boniface VIII, the cardinals, prelates, clergy, and all religious would be exterminated by the sword of God, wielded by a new Emperor and his kings. This Emperor would be Frederick, King of Sicily,[2] in support of whose claim Dolcino cited many passages from the Old and New Testaments. After the holocaust, a new and holy pope would be chosen by God and under his obedience would be placed the Apostolic order, with all those clergy and religious who were saved by divine grace from the sword and chose to join themselves to it. Then there would again be an outpouring of the Holy Spirit, as on the Apostles of the primitive Church, and the Church would be renewed, bearing its fruits until the end of the world.[3]

At the end of the manifesto of 1300 Dolcino gave a scheme of history according to the Seven Angels and Seven Churches in the Apocalypse:[4] the Angel of Ephesus was S. Benedict, his church the monastic order; the Angel of Pergamon was Pope Silvester, his church the clerical order; the Angel of Sardis was St. Francis with his Friars Minor; the Angel of Laodicea, S. Dominic with the Friars Preacher; the Angel of Smyrna was Fra Gerard of Parma, the Angel of Thyatira was Fra Dolcino, the Angel of Philadelphia would be the holy pope to come, while the last three 'churches' would constitute 'ista congregatio apostolica in istis diebus novissimis missa'.[4]

No doubt events demanded a revision of this programme, originally proclaimed for the years 1300–3. Thus in December 1303, following the death of Boniface VIII in October, Dolcino issued a second manifesto.[5] Here he gave a scheme of four popes, of whom the first and the last were good, the second and third bad. The first

[1] Gui, op. cit., p. 24.
[2] Ibid., pp. 21–2.
[3] Ibid., pp. 21–2: 'et dicit quod tunc omnes Christiani erunt positi in pace et tunc erit unus papa sanctus a Deo missus mirabiliter et electus, et non a cardinalibus . . . et sub illo papa erunt illi qui sunt de statu suo apostolico et etiam aliis de clericis et religiosis qui unientur eis . . . et tunc accipient Spiritus Sancti gratiam sicut acceperunt apostoli in ecclesia primitiva, et deinde fructificabunt in aliis usque ad finem mundi.'
[4] Ibid., p. 22.
[5] Ibid., pp. 22–3.

was Celestine V, the second Boniface VIII, the third his recent successor, who was not named by Dolcino. Against him in the next year, 1304, Frederick of Sicily would advance to destroy him and the perfidious Roman court utterly. So the advent of the holy pope was only postponed by one and he would appear shortly under the same conditions and with the same results as those outlined in the first manifesto. According to the revised schedule the three years would run as follows: 1303, in which ruin would fall on Boniface VIII and the 'king of the south' (Charles II, Angevin King of Sicily); 1304, which would see the ruin of the cardinals and Boniface's successor; 1305, when the general holocaust of clergy and religious would take place. At the time of writing Dolcino was absolutely convinced, by revelation, of this future order of events; for the present he remained hidden, to appear publicly at the given moment. In neither of his letters did Dolcino assign to himself the role of Angelic Pope, but this claim was made in the anonymous *Historia Fratris Dolcini Haeresiarchae*,[1] and repeated by Bernard Gui, who stated that, according to a revelation, Frederick, King of Sicily, would win the Empire in 1305 and that, after the death of the whole ecclesiastical hierarchy, the Church would be reduced to Apostolic poverty, and Dolcino, if he were still alive, would become *ille Papa sanctus*.[2] Upon him and his sect would be poured out the fullness of the Holy Spirit. They would preach the immediate advent of Antichrist, and when he appeared Dolcino and his followers would be removed to Paradise, while Elijah and Enoch descended to combat. When Antichrist was disposed of, they would descend again to convert all nations, while Frederick ruled over the last world-empire.[3] Thus an Age of the Spirit, after the crisis of Antichrist, was expected, one in which all the spiritual gifts of Joachim's third *status* would belong to the Apostolic Brethren alone, and their Church alone flourish until the end of time.[4]

[1] Muratori o.s. ix. 436. In interrogation Apostoli claimed both that Segarelli ought to have been pope and that Dolcino was 'sanctum et illuminatum immediate de Deo et futurum papam' (Muratori N.S. ix, Pt. v, pp. 58, 69).
[2] Gui, op. cit., p. 26.　　　　[3] Muratori, o.s. ix. 436.
[4] Gui, op. cit., p. 23: '. . . et tunc ipse Dulcinus et sui de congregatione apostolica erunt liberati ubique et omnes spirituales qui sunt in omnibus ordinibus aliis tunc unientur predicte congregationi apostolice et recipient gratiam Spiritus Sancti et sic renovabitur ecclesia; et tunc, destructis maliciosis predictis, ipsi regnabunt et fructificabunt usque ad finem mundi.' It is worth noting that the continuator of G. de Nangis's chronicle clearly thought of the Dolcinists as Joachites, describing their doctrine in terms of the three ages (Bouquet, xx. 594–5).

In 1304 Dolcino had gathered his partisans together into the mountains between Vercelli and Novara to await the fulfilment of events. They were undaunted by the passing of 1305; and when, in 1306, Clement V preached a crusade against them, Dolcino and his flock resisted to the death. The burning of Dolcino, together with the failure of prophetic fulfilment, should have put an end to the sect, but the astounding vitality of this conviction concerning the new spiritual role of the future is well demonstrated by the survival of the Apostolic Brethren and their dissemination in various regions. According to Clareno they wormed their way among the Franciscans.[1] In 1311 two fervent *Apostoli* were convicted in Bologna,[2] while in 1315 they appeared in Spain.[3] Traces of the sect appear in the depositions of the Inquisition at Toulouse,[4] and in 1318 John XXII warned the Bishop of Cracow against the *Apostoli*.[5] References can be found up to the early fifteenth century.

The manifestos of Dolcino show clearly that this sect did not belong to the category of simple evangelical movements preaching a return to Apostolic poverty. The Dolcinists based themselves on an interpretation of history and derived their high courage from the perspective which this gave them: their order was to be the culminating point of history rather than its return to a primitive purity. The use of the periodization of history, the particular symbolic meaning given to the figure of the Seven Churches, and especially to the Church of Philadelphia, the hope of the *papa sanctus*, all these point to Joachimism as the likely source from which Dolcino drew his philosophy of history.[6] He is unusual among Joachites, however, in that he makes his own scheme of periodization, providing an original variant on the Joachimist model. His scheme of fours instead of threes shows that he has no awareness of the relationship in Joachimism between Trinitarian doctrine and the meaning of history. Yet it is an Age of the Spirit to which the Apostolic Brethren

[1] *ALKG* ii. 131: 'Nam et quidam de secta illa apostolorum nomine Bentevenga ordinem minorum intravit et spiritus libertatis dyabolice spurcissimam labem in beati Francisci provincia seminavit.'
[2] B. Girolamo, 'Inquisitori ed eretici lombardi (1292–1318)', *Misc. di storia italiana*, 3rd ser. xix (1922), pp. 492–500.
[3] Gui wrote a warning letter against them to the clergy of Spain and the Archbishop of Compostella's reply speaks of several captured in that part (Gui, op. cit., p. 33).
[4] Limborch, *Hist. Inquis.*, p. 66. In this deposition Segarelli and Dolcino are claimed as founders of the *Apostoli* and the carnal church is fiercely attacked.
[5] *DTC* i. 1632.
[6] Cf. F. Tocco, 'Gli Apostolici e Fra Dolcino', *ASI* xix (1897), pp. 272–3.

look forward. This adaptation shows that the power of Joachimism lay in its use of history as the source of inspiration, even when the Trinitarian basis of this was lost.[1]

In contrast to Dolcino stand two female heresiarchs, whose heresy consisted in pushing the Trinitarian pattern of history to the point of claiming to be the incarnation of the Holy Ghost. Prous Boneta[2] lived in Montpellier and belonged to the milieu of the Provençal Beguins, though she appears to have worked independently. Her confession of 1325 shows a strange, ill-assorted mixture of Catharism and Joachimism, but its chief emphasis is on the new era of history just beginning. To usher this in, the Holy Ghost must be incarnate, undergo passion and death, and rise again. This second Crucifixion was being accomplished in the condemnation of Olivi's works and the persecution of Prous herself. For she had been chosen to be the abode of the Trinity and the giver of the Holy Ghost to the world. Whoever believed the writings of Olivi and the words of Prous would be baptized with the Holy Spirit. As Eve had been the downfall of human nature, so Prous would be the instrument of all men's salvation. While St. Francis was the angel with the sign of the Living God and Olivi the angel with the face of the sun, she herself was the angel with the keys of the abyss. Whatever her dualistic leanings, the confession of Prous Boneta ends by affirming strongly the dawning Age of the Spirit: '. . . asserens quod tempus novum dicti Spiritus Sancti et novus status ecclesiae habuit initium in dicto fratre Petro Joannis et consequitur in ipsa quae loquitur . . . et sic nunc est status ecclesiae novus in quo credere oportet in opere Sancti Spiritus . . .' (loc. cit., p. 25).

The second woman, Guglielma, appeared in Milan *c.* 1271, quickly established a remarkable religious influence there, gathered a group of disciples, and died in the odour of sanctity in 1282.[3] She

---

[1] The *Apostoli* probably regarded themselves as representing the next stage of perfection after the Minorites, as witness their nickname *Minimi* (Muratori N.S. ix, Pt. v, 57; *Acta S. Officii Bononiae* in *Atti e memorie della R. Dep. di storia patria per le provincie di Romagna*, 3rd ser. xiv (1896), p. 259). They expected, however, that the best of the Friars, Preachers, and Minors would be incorporated into the new order of spiritual men (Muratori, vol. cit., pp. 59–60).

[2] This paragraph is based on the work of W. May, 'The Confession of Prous Boneta Heretic and Heresiarch', *Essays in Medieval Life and Thought Presented in honour of Austin Patterson Evans* (New York, 1955), pp. 3–30.

[3] On the Guglielmites see *Annales Colmarienses Maiores, MGHS* xvii. 226; B. Corio, *L'historia di Milano* (Venice, 1554), f. 159ʳ; O. Raynaldus, *Annales Ecclesiastici* (Lucca, 1750), v, *anno* 1324 n. 9, p. 262; A. Ogniben, *I Guglielmiti del secolo XIII*

was buried in the Cistercian monastery of Chiaravalle and a cult developed around her tomb. In 1300, however, an investigation convinced the Inquisitors of a dangerous heresy:[1] Guglielma's bones were burnt, and the heads of her sect, a woman, Manfreda, and a man, Andreas Saramita, together with another woman, were also burnt. The circle of the initiated appears to have been very small— about thirty were inculpated—but an interesting aspect of the whole episode is the fact that they belonged mostly to the rich and cultivated classes. Manfreda was probably the cousin of Matteo Visconti and several members of the powerful Garbagnate family were implicated.

It is not easy to determine how much of the doctrine sprang from Guglielma herself and how much was worked out by Saramita. The *Process* is ambiguous, but in the end Saramita declared that he had the foundation and origin of his errors from Guglielma herself, and made the significant statement that she had dated the inauguration of her sect from 1262, close to the great Joachimist date.[2] The main tenets of Manfreda and Saramita were quite unambiguous: they declared that, as the Word had been incarnate in a Man, so the Holy Spirit had become incarnate in a woman, Guglielma. She, too, would rise from the dead, ascend into heaven in the sight of her disciples, and send upon them the Holy Spirit as tongues of flame. Once more the extreme implication is worked out: all authority has now departed from the existing ecclesiastical hierarchy and Boniface VIII is no true pope.[3] Once more the new spiritual roles are allotted, this time to women, for Manfreda will be the new pope and her cardinals will be women. She will baptize Jews, Saracens, and all other infidels, entering into peaceable possession of the Holy See.[4] The four Gospels will be superseded by new ones written by four sages chosen by the Holy Spirit. Obviously in the writing of the new Scriptures Saramita was to play a large part:

sicut discipuli Christi scripserunt Evangelia, epistolas et prophetias, ita et ipse Andreas, mutando titulos, scripsisset Evangelia et epistolas et prophetias sub hac forma, vid.: In illo tempore dixit Spiritus Sanctus

(Perugia, 1867); C. Molinier, *Revue historique*, lxxxv (1904), pp. 388–97; *DTC* vi. 1982–8; references in next footnote.

[1] See F. Tocco, (*a*) *Il processo dei Guglielmiti* (Rome, 1899); (*b*) 'Guglielma Boema e i Guglielmiti', *Atti della R. Accad. dei Lincei*, ser. v, Cl. di Scienze Morali, Storiche e Filologiche, viii (Rome, 1903), pp. 3–32.

[2] Tocco, (*b*) in last note, p. 12.

[3] Ibid., pp. 11, 14, 18, 19.   [4] Ibid., pp. 13, 20.

discipulis suis, etc., et: Epistola Sibilie ad Novarienses, et: Prophetia Carmei prophete ad tales civitates et gentes, etc. (Quoted *DTC* vi. 1986.)

In spite of the attempts of John XXII later to implicate the Visconti family,[1] there seems to have been little that was political in the programme of this sect. Its doctrine was startlingly simple and bold. When Tocco first examined the Process in detail he reached the clear conclusion that the sources of this heresy were to be sought in Joachimism, not—as some previous historians had suggested—in early Christian heresies. It is the historical character of the belief that gives us the clue. This was not a general pantheistic faith, but a set of tenets based on a specific pattern of history, a Trinitarian pattern. The originality of the Guglielmites lay in the daring logic that, if the revolution was to be absolute, there must be a new incarnation of the Godhead, and this must be in the opposite sex. Tocco calls the dream of Guglielma the most beautiful and seductive of all contemporary hallucinations.[2] It reveals the most unassailable and the most absurd lengths to which the logic of a Trinitarian interpretation of history could be pushed.

[1] See Raynaldus, vol. cited p. 248 n. 3 above, pp. 262 seq., giving John XXII's Bull accusing Galeazzo and Matteo Visconti of favouring the sect.

[2] Tocco, (*b*) in p. 249 n. 1, p. 26.

VIII

AUGUSTINIAN FRIARS

WE have seen that the Spiritual Franciscans found the essence of the third *status* in evangelical poverty rather than in spiritual illumination, yet preserved something of the *ecclesia contemplantium* in their instinctive retreat to the hermit life in solitary places. Here they found affinities with the Order of Augustinian Hermits. Thus, in 1360, the Bishops of Perugia, Città di Castello, and Fermo gave the Rule of St. Augustine to certain Fraticelli[1] and there may well have been other similar groups. On the other side, some Augustinians were attracted to the ideals of the Spirituals, for the letters of Angelo Clareno name four disciples belonging to this Order: the Blessed Simon of Cassia, Fr. Gentile of Foligno, Fr. Accamandolus of Foligno, and Fr. Philip of Castro Mili. Of these, Simon of Cassia is best known.[2] After Angelo's death he wrote a letter of mourning, saying that in Angelo he had found the foundations of his faith and his guide to peace.[3] He appears to have had a collection of Angelo's letters made,[4] and tradition, confirmed by Bartholomew of Pisa,[5] makes Angelo his interlocutor in the decisive experience of his youth which led him to the Augustinian Order. It seems clear that Simon was attracted to the extreme ideals of the Spirituals, but it is difficult to determine if he shared their Joachimist expectations, although he was described as 'endowed with the spirit of prophecy'.[6] He was a great preacher, and one sermon, at least, suggests an affinity with the Joachites. Preaching in Florence in 1348, he maintained that Christ and His disciples

---

[1] N. Papini, *Notizie sicure della morte, sepoltura, canonizzazione e traslazione di S. Francesco d'Assisi* (Foligno, 1824), p. 274; *AFH* vi (1913), p. 269.

[2] See N. Mattioli, *Il beato Simone Fidati da Cascia ... e i suoi scritti editi ed inediti* in *Antologia agostiniana*, ii (Rome, 1898).

[3] Mattioli, op. cit., p. 336; *ALKG* i (1885), pp. 535–6, especially 536; 'Nam in ipso post Deum iactaveram totius mee fiducie fundamentum et suis directionibus navigabam, sperans per ipsum portum quietis attingere.'

[4] *ALKG* i. 535. The collection was probably made by his disciple, Johannes de Salerno, to whom he addressed the letter on Angelo's death.

[5] Bartholomew of Pisa, *AF* iv. 513.

[6] L. Torelli, *Secoli agostiniani* (Bologna, 1659–86), v. 472.

had embraced perfect poverty and that they had thus pointed to the
way of perfection, saying openly that those who held the contrary
were heretics. When attacked by the brethren of St. Maria Novella,
he quoted the prophecies of the Abbot Joachim.[1] This account
suggests the preaching of a Joachimist who sees in evangelical
poverty the quality of life in the third *status*, a deduction which is
strengthened by the statement in one of his works that Sts. Dominic
and Francis had been sent by God as divine agents of the final
renewal.[2]

Little is known of Gentile of Foligno, apart from the letters of
Clareno to him. In one of these[3] Angelo speaks of the company of
contemplatives, anchorites, and virgins who in the fifth age of the
Church rose to heaven as in Elijah's chariot of fire; after these came
Francis and Dominic to prepare a perfect people, and of Francis he
says: 'To the perfect service of this poverty Christ chose and called
Francis in this latest hour.' Now Angelo looks for the advent of an
Elijah who will 'restore all things in bareness of poverty and love of
truth'. In the margin against this is written: 'Credo sequitur ordo
futurus'—we do not know by whom. Angelo is certainly here teaching Gentile the significance of the new spiritual men within the
Joachimist scheme of history.[4] Of Gentile himself we can only say
that he probably belonged to the Augustinian hermitage given by
the Bishop of Foligno and that he was probably the author of
a fourteenth-century translation into Italian of the *Scale of Paradise*
by St. John Climacus. The prologue to this suggests an affinity with
Angelo in his Greek studies and devotion to the contemplative life.
Finally, we must notice a fifteenth-century Florentine manuscript
which ascribes to Gentile of Foligno a Commentary on a prophecy of
Arnold of Villanova, entitled *Ve mundo in centum annis*.[5] The author

---

[1] Tocco, *SF*, p. 412.

[2] Mattioli, op. cit., p. 221: '. . . quasi all'ultimo mandò Dio due lucerne nel mondo,
cioè san Domenico e san Francesco, e fu nel loro tempo una grande renovazione nella
chiesa di spirito e di santità, e fecero loro ordini di scienza della madre ecclesia, i quali
andarono perfettamente un buon tempo' (from 'L'ordine della vita christiana', written
c. 1333).

[3] *ALKG* i. 559–60.

[4] There is, too, an *Apologia pro Vita Sua* which Angelo addressed to Alvaro y Pelayo and
also to brothers Gentile and Guido. The first is almost certainly Gentile of Foligno. In this
letter Angelo stresses, on the one hand, the absoluteness of the Rule and the highest
perfection attained in following it, and, on the other hand, his obedience to the Catholic
Church (*AFH* xxxix (1946), pp. 63–200).

[5] 'Infrascriptam prophetiam que incipit Ve mundo in centum annis ego frater Gentiles
de Fulgineo extraxi de quodam tractatu magistri Arnaldi de Villanova sancti viri, qui

must have been in Paris in 1300, but, although there are other possible Gentiles, he could have been our Augustinian. If the Florentine ascription is correct, we have clear evidence of the Joachimist leanings of this Augustinian. Of the other two Augustinians to whom Angelo wrote we know nothing except that they were connected with Simon of Cassia, and that Angelo tells them to hold fast the 'secrets' and to strive towards perfection.[1]

Both Simon of Cassia and Gentile of Foligno had some connection with Giovanni delle Celle; indeed, the famous Vallombrosan hermit had a number of friends among the Augustinian Friars. These included Fr. Gulielmus de Anglia, Fr. Johannes de Salerno, a disciple of Simon of Cassia, and Fr. Luigi Marsilio. Around Marsilio in the Florentine convent of Santo Spirito there gathered a group which met for daily disputations and included many leading literary, religious, and political figures. Their conversations

tractatus intitulatur de cimbalis ecclesie, in quo tractatu clare et lucide ostendit . . . quod adventus Antichristi et ipsius persecutio erit in mundo infra annos Domini 1576 . . . cui ego quamvis presumptuosus videar, exponam pro consolatione rudium cum quibusdam declarationibus mihi aliquantulum perspicuis, tam ex factis rerum iam completarum, quamque ex aliis prophetiis quasi autenticis, que alias ante plura tempora ad meam notitiam, Domino concedente, pervenerunt. Et istam prophetiam scripsit dictus fr. Gentiles Parisius in anno Domino MCCC cum predicto tractatu' (quoted in S. Giovanni Climaco, *La scala del paradiso*, ed. A. Ceruti, *Collectiones di opere inedite o rare* (Bologna, 1874), f. xxxviii).

This work, which has been identified in other manuscripts under the authorship of Fr. Gentile without the additional *De Fulgineo*, is vaguely ascribed by H. Finke, *Aus den Tagen*, p. 218, to the monk of Paris, while K. Burdach, *Vom Mittelalter* ii, Pt. i (1), p. 28 n. 2, speaks of 'jener rätselhafte Gentilis . . . falls er wirklich Mönch gewesen ist und in Paris gelebt hat'. This ascription is accepted by Grundmann, *HJ* xlix. 39, and Bignami-Odier, *Roquetaillade*, p. 312, but no clear grounds for the description 'a monk of Paris' have been given. The author must have been in Paris in 1300, but the Commentary was clearly written later, probably before 1345 (Finke, *Aus den Tagen*, p. 220). It could have been the Augustinian Gentile of Foligno, although there were other possible Gentiles (Burdach, op. cit., p. 28 n. 2). If the ascription in the Florentine manuscript were correct, it would give clear evidence of the Joachimist leanings of this Augustinian friar. The prophecy itself, *Ve mundo in centum annis*, is a Joachimist production (though not by Arnold of Villanova) and Gentile's Commentary on it envisages a Joachimist future: after a Babylonish captivity in France and other tribulations, the first of a series of Angelic Popes will be elected to bring the Church back to the 'statum primum paupertatis et sanctitatis'. The third in the series, in alliance with the Emperor, will re-enter Jerusalem and receive the submission of the Saracens (Finke, op. cit., p. 220 n. 1). Cf. *infra*, p. 418, for a link here with the *Liber de Flore*. The Florentine copy of the work was transcribed in 1494 by a layman, Luke of S. Gemignano, who collected the prophecies of Joachim, Merlin, the Sibyls, and several friars. See *infra*, p. 434, for the significant comment he added to his collection.

[1] *ALKG* i. 553.

represented a blend of humanist interests and prophetic studies.[1] From the letters of Marsilio and Giovanni delle Celle we catch their expectation of a Joachimist *renovatio mundi*. Giovanni warns friends against the false doctrines of the Fraticelli,[2] yet he himself regards Joachim as the key prophet, singled out by Christ to receive the revelation of the time when 'il mondo fiorirebbe'.[3] In a letter to Guido del Palagio he expounds with approval the *Vaticinia de summis pontificibus* (second series), which he accepts unquestioningly as Joachim's.[4] He also quotes with approval the Spirituals Ubertino da Casale, Angelo Clareno, and Jacopone da Todi.[5] An Eastertime vision of 1394 which is ascribed to him points to the advent *c.* 1400 of a *Renovator Ecclesie*. The voice of the vision proclaims: 'Erit in tote orbe Renovatio. . . . Et erit unus pastor et unum ovile.'[6] While denouncing the Avignonese papacy, the Santo Spirito group focused attention on the *renovatio mundi*. Marsilio quoted three prophetic sonnets of Petrarch to express this expectation.[7] Other members devoted themselves to the cult of the mystic prophetess St. Bridget of Sweden,[8] and hailed St. Catherine of Siena as the Fifth Angel of the Apocalypse.[9] The spiritual revolution which was to accomplish the *renovatio mundi* seemed very near.

It is curious to find, far removed from this Florentine group, another Austin friar, John Erghome of England, pursuing during

[1] A. Wesselofsky, *Il paradiso degli Alberti* (Bologna, 1868), i. 93, describes these discussions as characteristic of 'quella molteplice civiltà che stava per decidersi, tra le aspirazioni del passato e quelle dell'avvenire'.

[2] Ibid., pp. 93, 336–55; Tocco, *ASI*, ser. V, xxxv (1905), pp. 343–8; Tocco, *SF*, pp. 411–26; B. Sorio, *Lettere del beato Don Giovanni delle Celle* (Rome, 1845), p. 56.

[3] See passage quoted *supra*, p. 215 n. 5. Notice the Joachimist overtones of the verb 'fiorirebbe'.

[4] Ibid. For the *Vaticinia* see *supra*, p. 214.

[5] Tocco, *SF*, p. 423; Cividali, loc. cit., pp. 101–7, 469. A letter of encouragement to the Gesuati shows his sympathy for the extreme ideal of evangelical poverty.

[6] Florence, Bibl. Laur., MS. Ashburnham 896 (827), f. 19ʳ.

[7] Tocco, *ASI*, art. cit., p. 349; letter of Luigi Marsilio to Guido del Palagio. The three sonnets of Petrarch referred to are: 'L'avara Babilonia, Fiamma dal cielo, Fontana di dolore.

[8] See the following lines from a poem by Antonio degli Alberti:

> Mercè, giusto Signor, grazia divina
> Danne dal ciel per riformare il mondo,
> Un Cesare secondo,
> Il qual ciascun che t'ama ognora aspetta
> Si che l'Italia tua non sia dispetta.

(Wesselofsky, op. cit., p. 218)

On his connection with St. Bridget, ibid., pp. 91, 142, 195–6.

[9] Cividali, loc. cit., p. 89.

the same period his own studies in prophecy. The Augustinian bibliographers stress his search for such writings:[1] 'Quaesitis itaque authoribus qui in similibus aperiendis sensibus excelluerunt, nempe Methodio, Joachimo Abbate, Cyrillo Carmelita, Johanne Bridlingtono, Roberto Userio, Johanne Rupescissa, Johanne Barsignacio, Sibillis, aliisque eos diligenter pervolvit, emedullavitque ac suis studiis adauxit.' From these he was said to have put together *Compilationes Vaticiniorum*, which he dedicated to the Earl of Hereford.[2] The catalogue of his private library, which was afterwards incorporated into that of the Augustinian house at York, gives clear proof of his unusual tastes,[3] including music, mathematics, astrology, black magic, and prophecy. Furthermore, one item in the catalogue dovetails with the description of his writings given above:[4]

Prophecie et supersticiosa

361.   Ambrosii merlini prophecie
　　　　Joachim de seminibus literarum
　　　　Joachim de oneribus prophetarum
　　　　Joachim de duobus ordinibus
　　　　Joachim de successione papali [i.e. Vaticinia de summis pontificibus]
　　　　versus cuiusdam canonici de actubus anglie [i.e. John of Bridlington]
　　　　multe prophecie de anglia breves
　　　　prophecia Roberti de usecio
　　　　oraculum cirilli cum exposicione ioachim
　　　　excerpiones prophetie fr. Johannis de rupescissa

---

[1] J. Ossinger, *Bibliotheca Augustiniana* (Ingolstadt, 1768), p. 316. See also J. Pamphilius, *Chron. Ord. Fratrum Eremitarum S. Augustini* (Rome, 1581), f. 92ᵛ; P. Elssius, *Encomiasticon Augustinianum* (Brussels, 1654), f. 92ᵛ.

[2] Pamphilius, op. cit., f. 92ᵛ; M. R. James, 'Catalogue of the Library of the Augustinian Friars at York', *Fasciculus J. W. Clark dicatus* (Cambridge, 1909), p. 9.

[3] James, art. cit., pp. 9–14.

[4] Ibid., pp. 53–4. With the addition of Methodius, Ossinger's list of authors quoted above exactly corresponds to those named in the catalogue, including the unusual Johannes Barsignacius. Ossinger's description was adapted from J. Bale, *Scriptorum Illustrium Maioris Brytanniae* (Basle, 1557), p. 623. Bale must have had for reference a copy of the now lost *Compilationes Vaticiniorum*. For the authors named see as follows: Methodius: Sackur, *Sibyllinische Texte*; Cyril the Carmelite: Burdach, *Vom Mittelalter* ii, Pt. iv, pp. 223–327; John of Bridlington: T. Wright, *Political Songs and Poems*, RS, i, pp. xxviii–liv, 123–215; Robert of Uzès: Bignami-Odier, *AFP* xxv. 258–310; Johannes de Rupescissa: Bignami-Odier, *Roquetaillade*; the Sibyls: Sackur, op. cit.; Holder-Egger, *NA* xv. 143–78; xxx. 323–86. Johannes Barsignacius or de Basyngeio is John of Bassigny, who predicted the Black Death; see L. Thorndike, *History of Magic and Experimental Science* (Columbia, 1934), iii. 312.

prophetia iohannis de basyngeio
prophetia cibelle cum multis aliis
compendium literale petri aureole super apoc.
prophetia canonici. *frebribus* [i.e. John of Bridlington]

It will be observed at once that there are a number of pseudo-Joachimist and Joachite writings in this list, and another copy of the *Vaticinia de summis pontificibus* is included later. That Erghome also knew the most important of the Abbot's genuine works is almost established by another item in the catalogue, probably from his collection, which lists both the *Expositio* and the *Liber Concordie*.[1] The items described as 'versus cuiusdam canonici de actubus anglie' and 'prophetia canonici' are the curious prophecies often ascribed to John of Bridlington, a well-known Austin Canon. In 1362 Erghome wrote the commentary on these which exists in one manuscript.[2] The whole was dedicated to Humphrey de Bohun, Earl of Hereford, and thus corresponds to the *Compilationes* mentioned above. The work was in part a political satire on the times, but its purpose was also, it seems, to give apocalyptic meaning to Edward III's struggle with France, and it reveals something of the Joachimist optimism in its expectation of an Age of Glory which is forecast to begin shortly under the Black Prince.[3] Erghome had certainly caught some Joachimist infection from his reading.

We recall that another fourteenth-century Augustinian friar read Joachim's *Expositio* with appreciation, but the use which Agostino Trionfo made of Joachim's idea stands in sharp contrast to that of Erghome, the dabbler in prophecy.[4] If he was fascinated by Joachim's patterns of history he withdrew himself resolutely from the temptation of forecasting the future, or of assigning great spiritual roles in a coming Age of the Holy Ghost. Was there any half-way house in which a sober appropriation of Joachim's concept of the *ordo heremitarum* could be made by an Augustinian? There was, in fact, one fourteenth-century Augustinian friar who found this position.

---

[1] James, art. cit., p. 36.

[2] James, ibid., pp. 9–15, and A. Gwynn, *The English Austin Friars in the Time of Wyclif* (Oxford, 1940), pp. 130–7, both thought that Erghome had written the prophetic verses himself, as well as the commentary, but this has been disproved by P. Meyvaert, *Speculum*, xli (1966), pp. 656–64.

[3] The so-called Prophecies of John of Bridlington were published by T. Wright, *Political Songs and Poems*, RS, i. 123–215; see especially 204.

[4] *Supra*, pp. 88–9. His *Tractatus contra divinatores et sompniatores*, ed. R. Scholz, *Unbekannte kirchenpolitische Streitschriften* (Rome, 1911/14), i. 190–7; ii. 481–90, seems to have been a direct attack on Spiritual Franciscan fantasies.

Henricus de Urimaria wrote his *De origine et progressu Ordinis Fr. Eremitarum S. Augustini* in 1334.[1] There were four persons of this name, of whom three belonged to the Augustinian monastery at Erfurt; our author has been identified as Henry of Friemar, the oldest and most important of these friars. He was teaching in Paris in 1301–12, then returned to Germany, and died in 1340.[2] Although his numerous works are preserved in about 300 manuscripts, only seven are known of the *De Origine*. It was said to have been printed in Venice in 1514,[3] but no trace of this edition has been found and the modern editors of the work argue against its existence.[4] We shall refer later to one straw of evidence pointing the other way.[5] In this work the author makes high claims for his Order. Although, he says, the communal religious life is a state in which perfection is being acquired, the anchorite life is a state of perfection achieved. Therefore it is not for every man but only for the perfect man who is moved by a special impulse from the Holy Spirit to embrace this 'artissimam et sanctissimam vitam'.[6] With this lead it is not surprising to find Henry shortly afterwards claiming for his Order the prophetic role of Joachim's *ordo contemplantium*. It is, perhaps, a significant detail that he introduces the passage from Joachim with the symbol of a tree:

Et quia virtute radicis rami in longum et altum naturaliter producuntur, ideo virtute sanctitatis talium patrum, qui fuerunt sanctitatis eximii et nostri ordinis primarii fundatores, verisimiliter presumendum est quod super eorum filios et posteros per divinam clementiam benedictio copiosa descendat, quod utique videtur abbati Joachim in spiritu revelatum, qui loquens in Expositione super Apocalypsim sic dicit: Surget ordo qui videtur novus et non est, induti nigris vestibus et amicti [*Expositio*: accincti] desuper zona (hoc est cingulo); hi crescent et fama eorum divulgabitur et predicabunt fidem, quam etiam defendent, usque ad finem mundi in spiritu Helye, qui erit [*Expositio*: ordo] heremitarum emulantium vitam angelorum, quorum electio velut [*Expositio*: vita erit quasi] ignis ardens in amore et zelo Dei ad comburendum tribulos et spinas, hoc est ad extinguendum et consumendum pernitiosam vitam pravorum, ne mali amplius abutantur patientia Dei. (*Analecta Augustiniana*, p. 323.)

---

[1] Edn. in *Analecta Augustiniana*, iv (1911–12), pp. 279–83, 298–307, 321–8, and by R. Arbesmann, *Augustiniana*, vi (1956), pp. 37–145.

[2] *Analecta Augustiniana*, p. 279. See also Ossinger, op. cit., pp. 952–5; Pamphilius, op. cit., ff. 40ᵛ–41ᵛ. He figures in J. Capgrave, *De Illustribus Henricis*, RS, p. 181.

[3] Ossinger, op. cit., p. 953.

[4] *Analecta Augustiniana*, p. 279; *Augustiniana*, p. 81 n. 171.   [5] *Infra*, p. 265.

[6] *Analecta Augustiniana*, p. 322; *Augustiniana*, p. 107.

His quotation, it will be observed, is from the celebrated prophecy of Joachim in the *Expositio* which we have cited in full above.[1] He follows it by a reference to Joachim's exposition of the four angels in Chapter 7 of the Apocalypse (*Expos.* f. 120ʳ⁻ᵛ): 'Ob hoc autem dicit eos emulari vitam angelorum, quia personas illius ordinis asserit debere intelligi per illos quatuor angelos in Apocalypsi descriptos capito septimo. Et subdit: Gaudeant ergo heremite, quorum pater est Paulus primus heremita' (ibid., p. 323). According to Joachim the four angels are *quatuor genera predicatorum* who appear at the time of crisis which is the opening of the sixth seal. They are followed immediately by the angel of the sixth seal, the angel having the sign of the Living God, and it is interesting to note that Henry of Friemar makes no attempt to appropriate this symbol. He must, almost certainly, have been aware of its widespread application to St. Francis.[2] So, too, we notice how cleverly he has chosen his main prophecy. In Joachim's scheme it referred to the contemplative or hermit order, the higher of the two orders to come in the sixth age. By going thus to the genuine prophecy instead of to the prophecies of two parallel orders in the spurious writings, he has avoided those already appropriated by the Dominicans and Franciscans and claimed a higher place for his own Order. In the following paragraph he argues that the Order of Friars Hermit is much older in institution than that of the Friars Preacher or Friars Minor,[3] but he does not use Joachim—as later members of his Order did—to support this claim of antiquity. Whether or no Henry of Friemar's interest in the role of Joachim's new spiritual men was stimulated by a sense of rivalry with the other Mendicants, he restored the idea of the *viri spirituales* to Joachim's original conception, in which the keynote was contemplation rather than evangelical poverty.

There is, unfortunately, no evidence to show what Henry's contemporaries in the Order thought about his high claims for it. But rather more than a century later a curious episode at Erfurt itself reveals clearly that Augustinian hermits were still reading and thinking about Joachim's works. What has come to light is the record of a debate on Joachimism. Following a university disputation in 1465, Johann Bauer de Dorsten, a member of the Augustinian house, wrote a *quaestio* against Joachimist heresy.[4] There is no doubt about

[1] *Supra*, pp. 143–4.   [2] *Supra*, p. 176.
[3] *Analecta Augustiniana*, p. 323; *Augustiniana*, pp. 109–10. Cf. *infra*, p. 260.
[4] L. Meier, 'Die Rolle der Theologie im Erfurter Quodlibet', *RTAM* xvii (1950),

his own orthodoxy, but it is significant that the doctrine Dorsten attacked was the genuine Trinitarian view of history as developed by the Abbot himself, and that he was able to quote extensively from Joachim's own writings. His account of the conception of the three *status* and the role of the new spiritual men is an unusually clear one.[1] The occasion for his attack was probably the penetration into Erfurt of the Joachimist sect led by the Wirsbergers,[2] but the careful exposition of Joachim's writings and the familiarity with his central doctrine suggest strongly that these had been the subject of prolonged study and debate. It is possible that Henry of Friemar's use of Joachim's prophecy had attracted members of the Erfurt house in this direction.

Pastor[3] points out that the fifteenth century was the age of great Augustinian preachers in Italy, who proclaimed the imminence of Antichrist in an Apocalyptic style.[4] There is, however, no real evidence that these preachers used Joachimist categories. But towards the end of the fifteenth century there was a revival of interest in Joachim among Augustinian Friars in Italy when they perceived that he provided a powerful weapon in their controversy with the Augustinian Canons. The perpetual rivalry between the two Orders assumed many forms.[5] The dispute we must now trace briefly was yet another form of the literary warfare common between the two Orders.

In 1477, when the city of Milan was planning to adorn her cathedral with statues of the four great Church Fathers, there arose the question as to whether St. Augustine should be represented in the habit of Hermit or Canon Regular.[6] Both parties insisted strongly on their claims, and a congregation of learned men, called in to arbitrate, gave the point in favour of the Hermits. The Canons

pp. 296–7: 'Inc. Quaestio utrum tertius mundi status quem Joachim Abbas imaginatur et haereticorum conventiculum minatur catholice venturus astruatur priusquam A.D. 1471 compleatur.' Dorsten's *Quaestio* has recently been edited and studied by R. Kestenberg-Gladstein, 'The "Third Reich" ', *Journal of the Warburg and Courtauld Institutes*, xviii (1955), pp. 258–82.

[1] Ibid., pp. 267–74.

[2] Ibid., p. 259; cf. *infra*, p. 477.   [3] Pastor, *History of the Pope* v. 176.

[4] See, for instance, the appearances of apocalyptic preachers in the *Annales Placentini*, Muratori o.s. xx. 878, 890, 905.

[5] Gwynn, op. cit., pp. 137–8, thought that Erghome, the Austin friar, had tried to damage the reputation of the saintly canon, John of Bridlington, by foisting disreputable prophetic verses on him, but cf. *supra*, p. 256 n. 2.

[6] Torelli, op. cit. vii. 253; G. Tiraboschi, *Storia della letteratura italiana* (Modena, 1790), vi. 294.

retorted instantly that this could only be the judgement of unlearned
men, and one of them, Domenico of Ticino, set out to marshal
a crowd of worthier witnesses to their claims as the original Augustinians. He published his pamphlet about 1478,[1] and at once the
quarrel was removed to a wider sphere, for a local dispute had become a burning argument on origins and the new appeal to print put
a keen edge on it. He was followed in 1479 and 1481 by another
canon, Eusebio Corrado of Milan,[2] but already in 1479 an answer
had appeared from the pen of Paolo Ulmeo of Bergamo.[3] Earlier in
the fifteenth century a similar dispute had broken out in Pavia over
the custody of the relics of St. Augustine in St. Pietro in Celo
Aureo.[4] This attracted attention throughout Italy and it is not surprising to find a general warfare of pamphlets issuing from these
disputes. The first writers based their arguments mainly on what
they regarded as historical witnesses on origins. Paolo Ulmeo, who
first took up the retort for the Hermits, used an argument reminiscent of Joachim—that the stream of contemplative life had come
directly down to the Augustinian Hermits from the days of Elijah,
Elisha, and the sons of the prophets;[5] but Joachim himself, who
was cited towards the end of the pamphlet, appeared not as a prophet
but as a witness to origins, for, says the writer, in the *Expositio* he
placed the Hermits fourth in his list of Orders, but the Canons only
fifth, as instituted by St. Rufus in the twelfth century.[6]

The dispute went on heatedly both in pamphlet and sermon, for
in 1484 Sixtus IV was obliged to intervene with a lecture on Christian
charity and a command to speak and write no more of controversial
things.[7] Probably just before this the General of the Augustinian
Hermits, Ambrogio Massari da Cori, addressed a defence of his Order
to Sixtus IV himself.[8] This was a spirited pamphlet written expressly

---

[1] I have not seen this pamphlet but it is referred to by Torelli, op. cit. vii. 320, and
P. Ulmeo of Bergamo, *Libellus de apologia religionis fratrum heremitarum ordinis S.
Augustini contra falso impugnantes* (Rome, 1479, unpag.), f. 1ʳ.

[2] *Responsio adversus fratrem quendam . . . ordinis heremitarum* (Milan, 1479); *De dignitate canonicorum regularium . . .* (Rome, 1481).   [3] *Supra*, n. 1.

[4] *Codex diplomaticus Ord. Erem. S. Aug. Papiae*, ii (Pavia, 1906), p. 261 n. i; Torelli,
op. cit. vii. 253.

[5] Op. cit., f. 7ʳ, cf. *Lib. Conc.*, ff. 8ᵛ–11ᵛ.

[6] Ibid., f. 28ᵛ, cf. *Expos.*, f. 19ᵛ.

[7] *Bullarium Ord. Erem. S. Aug.* (Rome, 1628), pp. 321–4.

[8] A. *Choriolani Gen. Aug. in defensorium ord. eiusdem sc. Fratrum herem. S. Aug.
responsivum ad maledicta canonicorum assertorum regularium congregationis Frisonariae*
(Rome, 1484), f. 20ᵛ. On the date of this work and the fact that it was written before and
not after the command to silence see Tiraboschi, op. cit. vi. 295.

against the canons Domenico and Eusebio, and in his account of the rise of the Canons Regular the Abbot Joachim's statement becomes his chief argument. Joachim was still, however, treated solely as a historical witness, although we know that Ambrogio was concerned with the hermit ideal and about 1476 had published a treatise *De vita contemplativa et celsitudine*. No notice appears to have been taken of the papal command to silence, for Eusebio wrote a further reply to the Hermits,[1] while in his chronicle the Augustinian Hermit J. P. Foresti of Bergamo gave the respective dates of origin of Hermits and Canons as 398 and 1107, 'abbate Joachim teste'.[2] The original points of dispute were now becoming buried under the weight of argument.[3] The quarrel had become one of general interest and one result was to quicken the interest of some Augustinian Hermits in the Abbot Joachim.

They could not read far without realizing the appropriateness of his prophecy concerning the Hermit Order, especially the passage delineating this future order which had already been claimed for them by Henry of Friemar. It is curious that no reference to Henry's claim occurs in any of the controversial writings just cited, nor, so far as I can discover, in any other fifteenth-century Augustinian works. On the other hand, strangely enough, Joachim's prophecy is applied to the Augustinian Friars by St. Antonino of Florence, in his *Pars historialis*.[4] The fact that a Dominican devotes several pages of careful discussion to the controversy that had arisen over the Augustinian Friars' claim to antedate all other Orders shows how heated and widespread the argument had become. St. Antonino introduces Joachim's prophecy with the words 'Quidam religiosus dicti ordinis sic scribit', and he is clearly quoting from

---

[1] *Eusebius Corradus med. can. reg. congr. lat. ad sanctiss. dom. nostr. Sixtum IV Pont. Max. pro auferendo de ecclesia errore scribentium S. Aug. ecclesie doctorem fuisse heremitam* (Padua, 1484).

[2] *Omnimoda historia novissime congesta Cronicarum Supplementum appellata* (Venice, 1486), ff. 174ᵛ–175ʳ, 220ᵛ.

[3] For further accounts of disputes in Milan, Pavia, etc., see Torelli, op. cit. vii. 253–4, 320, 338–40, 444–5, 518–21, 577–8, 605–10.

[4] *Pars historialis* (Nuremberg, 1484), iii, ff. ccliiiiᵛ–cclvʳ. He treats the issue of the origin of the Augustinian hermits in a cool, judicious way, points in the argument being dealt with in a manner which illustrates the growth of a scientific historical approach. He gives Henry's argument carefully, but concludes that the evidence does not support it, and that, in fact, the Augustinian hermits, as finally constituted, are younger than the two chief Mendicant orders. As we have seen (*supra*, p. 165), for S. Antonino, Joachim is *par excellence* the prophet of St. Dominic, and he does not yield this title to any other order.

Henry of Friemar. Now the manuscripts of this particular work of Henry's are very few,[1] and it seems far more likely, therefore, that St. Antonino had met the claimed prophecy quoted as a weapon in the controversy than that he had picked it out for himself from Henry's writings. Thus the prophecy was probably current in the fifteenth century.

The full force of the Joachimist prophecy was not, however, realized until it was seized on by a small group of Augustinians in the neighbourhood of Venice in the early sixteenth century. The centre of this group, Silvestro Meuccio of Santo Cristoforo della Pace, was engaged between the years 1516 and 1527 in editing and publishing all the works of Joachim upon which he could lay hands. In all probability it was the controversy with the canons that first caused him to look for ammunition in this direction and it may well have been from St. Antonino, who was his favourite historical authority,[2] that he first learnt of the application of Joachim's prophecy to his Order. Venice was rich in Joachimist material and the manuscript which apparently first caught his eye was Frater Rusticianus's compilation of the mid-fifteenth century.[3] His first publication, based on this compilation, was entitled *Expositio magni prophete Joachim in librum beati Cirilli de magnis tribulationibus et statu sancto matris ecclesie* . . . From this point Silvestro proceeded with great industry to publish all the works of Joachim he could find, taking the false along with the true quite uncritically. From the Venetian printing presses there went forth in steady succession his editions of the *Super Hieremiam* (1516 and 1526), the *Super Esaiam* (1517), the *Liber Concordie* (1519), the *Expositio in Apocalypsim* (1527), and the *Psalterium decem chordarum* (1527).[4]

Silvestro Meuccio was known to the Venetians as a great preacher, to his Order as a learned theologian, and to his age as the editor of

---

[1] *Supra*, p. 257.

[2] See marginal notes in Silvestro's editions of *Lib. Conc.* and *Expos.* This is the only historical work to which he refers.

[3] For Frater Rusticianus, *supra*, p. 173.

[4] That these editions were planned from the beginning appears from the notice in the 1516 edn. of Telesphorus's work, f. 1ᵛ: 'Opuscula autem post presens de proximo ab eodem Lazaro imprimenda atque iam correctori tradita sunt haec subiecta, videlicet:

Abbas Joachim super Apochalypsim
Eiusdem concordantiae novi et veteris testamenti
Idem super Hieremiam
Eiusdem opusculum super prophetas (i.e. the *Super Esaiam*)
Et caetera omnia alia sua opera que ego reperiam.'

Joachim's works.[1] Of his Augustinian circle of friends we meet three in his prefaces to these works. Anselmo Votturnio (Bochturnus) of Vicenza possibly helped Silvestro in his labours, for in 1516 the first edition of the Telesphorus prophecies was dedicated to him, and when it was reprinted a few months later his letter of reply, written from Padua, had been added to it.[2] Filippo of Mantua wrote *lucubrationes* on the Apocalypse.[3] The third was a hermit mystic, Bernardino Parentino of Padua. Silvestro writes of him as the much-venerated, devout, illumined, and ecstatic slave of God, and Anselmo, replying, says:[4] 'Est enim unicum priscorum patrum vestigium hac nostra tempestate. Qui nos die noctuque monet, instruit et infestat ad spiritualia consequenda' (*Libellus*, 2nd edn., f. iii). They cling to him, like the earlier Joachites to their prophets, as the only interpreter of God's mysteries. Silvestro writes to him: 'Idcirco te pater mi Bernardine vir Dei extatice (quem spiritum prophetie habere proculdubio novi) obsecro ut solitas previas, crebras, charitatisque fervore conspersas preces ad Dominum fundas, quem non ambigo tibi ea revelaturum que vera sunt proficuaque fidelibus suis' (*Libellus*, 1st edn., f. 4ᵛ). So highly do they prize his utterances that on one occasion Silvestro inserts his words into the Joachimist prophecies he is editing: 'De hoc autem sancto patriarcha mihi interroganti multas egregias virtutes retulit quidam venerabilis eremita Parentinus spiritum prophetie habens qui adhuc vivit meque charitatis vinculo non parum diligit' (*Libellus*, f. 22ʳ).[5] The little

[1] On Silvestro Meuccio see Pamphilius, op. cit. (ref. p. 255 n. 1), f. 108ᵛ; Elssius, op. cit. (ref. p. 255 n. 1), f. 108ᵛ; Torelli, op. cit. (ref. p. 251 n. 6), viii. 23–5, 197; Ossinger, op. cit. (ref. p. 255 n. 1), pp. 587–8; Burdach, *Vom Mittelalter* ii, Pt. iv, p. 232 n. 1.

[2] Silvestro's Dedicatory Letter (ff. 2–4 in first edn., ff. ii–iiii in second edn.) is dated Nones of March; Anselmo's reply (f. iiii in second edn.) is dated 10 Kalends April.

[3] Apparently Silvestro published these *lucubrationes*, for they are mentioned in the Preface to the *Expositio* as if bound up with it. Ossinger gives two editions, Padua (1516) and Venice (1527) (op. cit., p. 542). Torelli gives only the Venetian edition (op. cit. viii. 145). But they have not apparently survived.

[4] Dedicatory Letter to the 1516 edn. of Telesphorus.

[5] Cf. *infra*, p. 377, for the passage in which Silvestro cites 'quidam venerabilis eremita Parentinus'. The text of the 1516 edn. represents four different layers:

(1) the original *Oraculum angelicum* attributed to Cyril the Carmelite, but really a mid-thirteenth-century work with a pseudo-Joachimist commentary on the oracle (ed. P. Piur in Burdach, *Vom Mittelalter* ii, Pt. iv, pp. 220–327);

(2) The *Libellus . . . de causis, statu, cognitione ac fine instantis scismatis et tribulationum futurarum . . .* of Telesphorus of Cosenza, written *c.* 1386 and extant in numerous manuscripts, of which Paris, Bibl. Nat., Lat. 3184 (written 1396) is the oldest. This incorporates part or all of chs. i, iii, vi, vii, viii, ix, x, xi of the Cyril oracle and gloss;

group of searchers is closely bound together: 'We two are one and you a third most intimate with us', writes Anselmo to Silvestro.[1]

A fourth inquirer into Joachimist mysteries was Paolo Angelo, a 'Byzantine stranger'. Once, on a bridge in Venice, Silvestro encountered a friend who showed him a newly-published book entitled *In Sathanae ruinam tyrannidis*. With the book under his arm Silvestro went home and did not cease reading until he had finished it. Apparently, in three days he was dedicating his edition of the *Super Hieremiam* to its author, and hailing this stranger as a man after his own heart whom he desired greatly to meet.[2] This wish was soon fulfilled, for Silvestro became spiritual adviser to this Byzantine and evidently drew him into the Joachimist circle.[3] In 1530 Paolo Angelo published *Profetie certissime . . . dell'Antichristo*, which was practically an Italian translation of Silvestro's first Joachimist edition. Into the tangled pattern of this work Rusticianus and Silvestro had introduced a thread of unmistakable Venetian patriotism; Paolo Angelo, therefore, lays his translation as a suitable offering before the Doge, Andrea Gritti, urging upon his attention all the voices that have been crying out on these things in recent years.[3]

In its approach to Joachimist prophecies this Augustinian group was clearly much influenced by the dispute with the Canons. Silvestro drew attention to the question of origins in his Preface to the *Expositio*:

Ipse enim ordo a parente nostro beato Augustino fundatus extitit: a quo regulam vivendique formam accepit: nec in dubium verti potest. Quod et idem Joachim hic in parte prohemiali testatur dicens: Ordo Eremitarum

(3) Fr. Rusticianus's version of Telesphorus's work composed in 1456 and preserved in the Venetian manuscript (p. 173) written in 1469, with the main additions of a Dedicatory Letter, prophecies of S. Bridget and Fr. Antonius de Yspania, pictures, and additional text; and

(4) Silvestro Meuccio's additions in the two 1516 Venetian edns.: the Dedicatory Letter and reply and extra pictures and text, of which the most important are on the German Antipope and Emperor (suppressing the earlier identification with Frederick III), a great sea-battle of Venice in alliance with France and England against the German Emperor, a great land-battle *in agro Brixiano* between the French King and the German Emperor, the summons by an angel of the Angelic Pope, clad in the habit of the Augustinian Hermits, a holy patriarch of the Venetians, and a description of the King of England and the Venetian captain of a united fleet of English, French, and Venetians, which would win a final victory against the infidel.

[1] 2nd edn., f. iiii. See Torelli, op. cit. viii. 23–5.
[2] *Super Hier.*, Dedicatory Letter.
[3] P. Angelo, *Profetie certissime, stupende et admirabili dell'Antichristo et innumerabili mali al mondo* (Venice, 1530), Dedicatory Letter.

fundatus fuit a beato Augustino in Aphrica, Ordo vero Canonicorum regularium in partibus occiduis a beato Rufo, quamvis et ipsi teneant regulam ipsius Augustini. (*Expos.*, Dedicatory Letter.)

It is clear, however, that these Augustinian Hermits did more than cite Joachim's witness on their origins: they also claimed his high promises as belonging to their future. Whether or not Silvestro first encountered these through St. Antonino, he quoted in his Preface to the *Expositio* directly from Henry of Friemar's work.[1] An edition of this was said by Ossinger to have been printed in Venice in 1514,[2] but its existence has, as we have seen, been questioned by its modern editors.[3] Surely, however, the coincidence of Silvestro's knowledge of a rare work—only two manuscripts are known in France and two in Rome[4]—with the date and place of the supposed edition makes its existence more likely? It may well have been published as part of the Augustinian Hermits' campaign against the Canons, and Silvestro may have been stimulated by it to pursue his Joachimist studies.

In his Preface to the *Expositio* Silvestro stated the high claim of the Hermits to be Joachim's new spiritual men quite clearly:

Adde quod hanc (nostram Eremitarum familiam) idemmet Abbas Joachim: et piis celebret honoribus laudeque augeat prae caeteris: ita ut in extrema mundi aetate, ordinem ipsum Eremitarum viribus divinae gratiae fultum, in zelo ac dei amore veluti inardescentem ignem, Christi fidem eiusque ecclesiae collapsa reformaturum, ac universa restauraturum fore asserat. (*Expos.*, Preface.)

Then he immediately quoted Joachim's great prophecy 'Surget ordo qui videtur novus et non est', and who would not thrill at the prospect of such a future?—'They shall increase and their fame shall be spread abroad; they shall preach the faith and defend it until the consummation of the world in the spirit and power of Elias. They shall be an order of hermits living like angels, whose life shall be as a burning fire to consume all tares.'[5] Silvestro frankly admitted that many of his contemporaries wished to appropriate Joachim's prophecies of new orders for their own Orders; he was therefore obliged to make plain what this author states concerning

---

[1] *Expos.*, Prefatory Letter, where he refers both to St. Antonino and Henry of Friemar.

[2] Ossinger, op. cit., p. 953. [3] *Supra*, p. 257.

[4] Two other pre-1550 MSS. exist in Munich and Vienna.

[5] Cf. passage quoted *supra*, p. 144.

'our order of hermits'. It will be remembered that Joachim distinguished two different orders of hermits and monks, whereas the spurious writings describe two parallel orders in terms which were very easily applicable to the two great Mendicant Orders.¹ Silvestro's method was to appropriate in the genuine works, by means of such marginal notes as *Ordo Eremitarum S. Aug.*, all the references to the hermit order,² whilst assigning to the Friars Preacher and Minor the passages in the spurious works which clearly belong to them.³ He could not, indeed, evade the claims of these two Orders, for, with many of his contemporaries, he believed that Joachim had caused the figures of St. Francis and St. Dominic to be depicted in their habits in the old sacristy of St. Mark's, Venice, 'qui usque in presentem diem manent'.⁴ But even so, wherever possible, he turned the attention back to the original distinction between the two orders of monks and hermits. Thus, although the raven and dove of Noah's ark were commonly held to signify the Dominicans and Franciscans, he says, commenting on this prophecy in the *Super Hieremiam*:⁵ 'By the raven and dove are designated two orders, namely of hermits and of monks, as the author himself shows in ch. 14 of his *Expositio in Apocalypsim*'—and this is the chapter in which occurs the prophecy so specifically claimed by Silvestro for his own Order.

An even bolder claim had already been made in Silvestro's edition of the *Expositio . . . in librum Cyrilli*. Silvestro's insertions in this generally take the form of pictures with an explanatory text. One of these shows the future Angelic Pope kneeling in prayer whilst ambassadors approach to summon him forth. The text runs thus: 'Hic angelus ostendit manu legatis seu ambassatoribus sancte unionis ecclesie religiosum nigra cucula indutum ut sunt Eremitani sancti Augustini' (*Libellus*, f. 21ʳ).

No doubt some of the Augustinian Canons protested against this presumptuous claim, for in one copy of the book the words *nigra* and *Eremitani* have been deleted and a manuscript note substitutes the name of the Canons.⁶

---

¹ *Supra*, pp. 147–8.

² For examples of such marginal notes see *Expos.*, ff. 19ᵛ, 77ᵛ, 89ʳ⁻ᵛ, 147ʳ, 162ʳ, 175ᵛ, 176ʳ.

³ e.g. *Super Hier.*, Preface, ff. 2ʳ, 13ʳ, 13ᵛ, 14ʳ, 18ᵛ, 20ᵛ, 23ᵛ, 24ᵛ, 25ᵛ, 28ʳ, 38ʳ 44ᵛ, 58ᵛ.

⁴ *Super Esaiam*, Dedicatory Letter.

⁵ f. 13ʳ. A number of marginal notes merely say *predicatores futuri* or a similar vague phrase, suggesting his desire to leave open the field for other claimants besides the two Mendicant Orders; see *Super Hier.*, ff. 3ᵛ, 5ʳ, 10ᵛ, 11ʳ, 12ʳ⁻ᵛ, 13ᵛ, 15ᵛ, 60ʳ.

⁶ Second Venetian edn., 1516, copy in the British Museum.

Silvestro's prefaces reveal a man who views the future with deep foreboding. Any sane man, he writes, will battle with all his powers against overwhelming waves, but in unknown calamities he sinks.[1] How great, then, the value of a prophet who marks out for us a way through the tempests. So the circle of Silvestro looks out upon the world with the eyes of Joachim—'noster divinus magnus modernusque propheta'[1]—expecting at once the greatest and bitterest tribulation of all time and the angelic state of reform and peace to follow. They weep for the 'innumerable abominations and unutterable blasphemies of these bad days',[2] and expect unparalleled woe: 'in our time we have seen things which until lately were incredible and it is to be feared that worse lie in the future.'[3] This they look for in the shape of a threefold scourge upon the carnal church: the German Emperor, the mystic Antichrist or the Heretic, and the open Antichrist, the Saracen.[2] From the depths of this sharp fear they look towards the vision of the Abbot Joachim; with him they expect the Church to be raised from her ruined state into that contemplative and celibate life which was to be the third *status*, enduring until the consummation of the ages.[4] This double emotion of dread and hope is expressed in Silvestro's marginal *Nota* or other notes, underscoring on the one hand tribulation and on the other blessedness to come.[5]

There was a genuine sense of vocation in this little Joachimist group. Its members wrote to warn men of impending tribulation and to prepare them for their part in the *renovatio mundi*. How far did they influence the Augustinian Order beyond their own circle? I have only found one clear instance of an interest in their Joachimist studies, but this is a significant one, for it is that of Egidio of Viterbo, the famous General of the Order.

---

[1] *Super Hier.*, Dedicatory Letter.

[2] *Super Hier.* (1526 edn.), Dedicatory Letter.

[3] *Expositio . . . in librum beati Cirilli*, Dedicatory Letter.

[4] Silvestro expresses the essence of the Joachimist hope in his Dedicatory Letter to the *Super Hier.* (1526) when, referring to Joachim's *Psalterium decem chordarum*, he says '. . . in quo contemplantium ac coelibem vitam ducentium describitur forma, quae quidem vita post nove Babylonis casum et ecclesiae reformationem in tertio videlicet mundi statu maxime vigebit.' See also the title-page to the *Expositio* in the 1527 edn.: 'Opus illud celebre . . . de statu universali reipublice Christiane: deque ecclesia carnali in proximo reformanda atque in primevam sui etatem redigenda: triplici prius tamen percutienda flagello . . .'

[5] e.g. *Expos.*, ff. 131ʳ, 134ʳ⁻ᵛ, 147ᵛ, 163ʳ, 164ᵛ, 165ʳ, 167ᵛ, 168ʳ, 170ʳ, 186ᵛ, 194ᵛ, 207ʳ, 210ᵛ; *Lib. Conc.*, ff. 21ᵛ, 25ʳ, 103ᵛ.

Silvestro Meuccio dedicated his edition of Joachim's *Expositio* to the General, describing in his Prefatory Letter how once in Venice he had had the privilege of an audience with him and how the great Cardinal had asked Silvestro to bring him certain works of the Abbot Joachim published by him. 'Which, when I had brought and he had read, pleased him not a little, so that he urged me to publish other works of the same author and especially the *Expositio in Apocalypsim.*'[1] Silvestro saw Egidio as a worthy General to lead the Order into its great Joachimist future—it is significant that his Dedicatory Letter is concerned rather with the prophecies of the new order than with more general prognostications—and he offered him the *Expositio* 'above all, because I do not doubt that in days to come our Order will be reformed under your leadership'.

Was Egidio really influenced by a Joachimist view of history? The older assessment of him as 'the polished priest of Renaissance circles'[2] has recently been challenged by a deeper study of his sermons and writings. His oratorical powers have perhaps obscured his real passion, but his zeal for reform emerges clearly. His great address at the opening of the Lateran Council of 1512 was full of a sense of the urgency of the tempestuous times.[3] He proclaimed its true mission to still the tempest of the times, to pacify Christian princes, to convert the Mohammedans, and to bring the whole Church into tranquillity. The keynote of the speech was the expected tribulation and emendation of the Church—a conjunction typical of Joachimism.

Between the years 1513 and 1517 Egidio wrote his great work on the philosophy of history, *De Historia Viginti Saeculorum.*[4] In this he sought to embody the faith of those Christian humanists with whom he had most affinity[5]—that classical and Christian culture did not

---

[1] *Expos.*, Dedicatory Letter.

[2] See F. Martin, *The Problem of Giles of Viterbo* (Louvain, 1960), p. 5.

[3] J. Hardouin, *Acta conciliorum* (Paris, 1714), ix, cols. 1576–81. See also Martène et Durand, *Ampl. Coll.* iii, *Aegidii Viterbiensis Epistolae selectae*, col. 1247.

[4] This is unpublished. The archetype is MS. Lat. IX B14 in the Bibl. Naz., Naples. See bibl., no. 8.815. It has recently been studied by E. Massa, 'Egidio da Viterbo e la metodologia del sapere nel Cinquecento', *Pensée humaniste et tradition chrétienne aux XVᵉ et XVIᵉ siècles*, ed H. Bédarida (Paris, 1950), pp. 185–239. See especially p. 199: 'E per tale presupposto la teologia richiesta da Egidio sarà essenzialmente una teologia storica. La storia è elemento essenziale della sapienza: ha un valore ed un significato metafisico.'

[5] He belongs to the Platonist following of Marsilio Ficino, whom he calls 'a messenger of divine providence who had been sent to show that mystical theology everywhere

stand in opposition but rather formed part of one harmony in the Divine purpose. Yet, although in other branches of learning he showed the new scientific spirit,[1] his approach to history was fundamentally medieval. He was not concerned with 'facts' but with the divine thoughts or ideas embodied in historical actions,[2] and he believed it possible to read these through the symbolism of history, especially through number-symbolism and concordances. His method was to take ten Psalms as symbolizing ten periods of history before Christ which must be paralleled by ten periods of history after Christ, for the ages of the Old and New Testaments corresponded perfectly. It is obvious that this method is closely akin to that of Joachim, though Egidio's pattern is far wider in range, and he is anxious to establish concords, not only between the Old and New Dispensations, but also between secular and sacred history, especially classical and Biblical. He believed that as humanity moved inevitably towards a first culminating-point in the coming of Christianity, so now it was tending towards a second great spiritual unfolding.[3] All the signs of the times, including the movement of overseas expansion, showed that humanity was approaching a future unity in an age of peace. His programme for the future Egidio dedicated to Pope Leo X, whom he confidently expected to bring all things into

concurred with our holy institutions and was their forerunner' (quoted H. Jedin, *Papal Legate at the Council of Trent, Cardinal Seripando*, tr. F. C. Eckhoff (London, 1947), pp. 56–60). See also L. Pélissier, *De 'Historia Viginti Saeculorum' Aegidii Viterbiensis* (Montpellier, 1896).
a good new translation from the Hebrew (see Pélissier, op. cit., p. 5).

[2] Massa, loc. cit., p. 206: '. . . la filosofia della storia deve cogliere non i fatti, ma le idee che movimentano i fatti. Se non sono le idee a movimentare la storia, impossibile è una filosofia della storia. . . . I "numeri" sono i rapporti in cui si definisce il pensiero divino. Pensiero divino non astratto, ma concreto, amoroso e libero. . . . Il pensiero è il principio del movimento e delle azioni. . . . Il concetto egidiano dell'Essere è tale da giustificare una Metafisica della Storia, cioè una conoscenza della storia, non nella entità fisica dei fatti che la compongono (considerazione statica) ma nella idealità che i fatti costituisce, ordina e finalizza (considerazione dinamica).' His method of concords is akin to Joachim's, but he seeks concords between secular and sacred history, especially biblical and classical, as well as between Old and New Dispensations; see, for instance, the parallels he works out between the twelve patriarchs and twelve Etruscan kings, between Moses and Jason, between the Babylonish Captivity and the Trojan War (Pélissier, op. cit., pp. 4–5). On his desire to discover 'a secret harmony between the pagan, Jewish and Christian mysteries' see E. Wind, 'The Revival of Origen', *Studies in Art and Literature for Bella da Costa Greene*, ed. D. Miner (Princeton, 1954), pp. 416–18. Massa, loc. cit., p. 208, expresses Egidio's sense of the unity of history thus: 'Non solo una "storia sacra" o una "storia laica" . . . ma una "storia assoluta" della umanità "sub specie aeternitatis".'

[3] See Massa, loc. cit., p. 209: 'Cristianesimo, prima, e Umanesimo, poi, sono la pienezza storica della spiritualità e delle "harmoniae". La perfezione spirituale del secondo assorbe a perfeziona ulteriormente la perfezione del primo.'

harmony, especially classical and Christian culture. The Pope's name, lineage, and all the events of his life were interpreted prophetically, for Egidio believed that Leo 'ab initio orbis electus est ut Christi mandata atque opera perficeret, Christianorum fidem in aeternum confirmaret, pacemque Ecclesiae reduceret'.[1]

The *Historia* shows Egidio deep in Scriptural studies as well as classical. By 1513 he was also immersed in Hebrew literature, especially the Jewish mysticism of the Cabbala.[2] This did not represent a departure from, but rather a deepening of, his search for the key to the meaning of history. In 1517 he wrote a *Libellus de litteris Hebraicis*,[3] dedicated to Cardinal Giulio de Medici, and in 1530 undertook at the request of the same man, now Pope Clement VII, the deeper searchings of the meanings of the sacred Letters and Numbers which are embodied in his *Scechina*.[4] It was no longer the outer frame of history with its concords of centuries which concerned him, but the inner seminal clues of Hebrew alphabet and number. He looked for an outpouring of the Holy Spirit in 'foelicissimo illo sabbato',[5] yet it was a future with a definite political framework that Egidio expected.

Egidio's twin stars of destiny were the Medici—under whom classical learning had flourished and the Muses been restored—and the great Imperial Charles, called to bring in 'the Kalenda' or 'the Sabbath'. The *Scechina* is dedicated to Charles V, and interwoven with its mysterious outpourings is the theme of Imperial power as the divinely appointed agency, with a reiterated apostrophe to Charles to assume his role.[6] The scene is dark—Italy torn by invading armies, the moon of the Church obscured by clouds of heresy—yet how thrilling the more distant prospect! To lift the eyes to the horizons is to see an expanding universe that calls for faith in the future, especially on the part of the Emperor: '. . . tot regna; tot imperia: tot terras: tot maria illi subdit: ut novum iam Alexandrinum nostris inminentem cervicibus videamus.'[7] This vast new world is a theme of such exhilaration that Egidio returns to it again and again. Now is the *decimum saeculum*: it began in the Medicean

---

[1] Pélissier, op. cit., p. 37.   [2] Martin, op. cit., p. 9.

[3] Egidio da Viterbo, *Scechina e Libellus de Litteris Hebraicis*, ed. F. Secret (Rome, 1959).

[4] Ed. Secret, with the *Scechina*; see previous note.

[5] *Scechina*, p. 68.

[6] Ibid., pp. 69, 77, 80, 81, 99, 106, 133, 140, 145, 160–1, 219, 220, 222, 224, 225, 228, 231, 233.   [7] *Lib. de Litteris Hebraicis*, p. 30.

Leo X, and now, to open the door of the 'celebrated Kalends', the fifth Charles is summoned.

It is significant that a cardinal of the Church, the head of a great order, a practical and respected reformer, could write thus, and still more so when we remember that Egidio was at the centre of a group at once classical and mystical in its interests, pursuing Renaissance letters and also concerned with the spiritual life. The old mistaken antithesis between pagan and Christian in the Renaissance need no longer detain us, but it is worth emphasizing the fact that classical and mystical studies could also go together. One of the clues to the fascination of cabbalistic studies for Renaissance scholars lies in their use for the interpretation of history—history conceived, that is, not so much as a scientific study but as the clue to the future.[1] In Egidio of Viterbo, as also in another member of his circle, Petrus Galatinus, we find the expectation of the apotheosis of history running like a strong current, and though this obviously had classical and Jewish as well as medieval sources, one of its fountain-heads was the Joachimist faith in the Age of the Spirit, the *renovatio mundi*. Thus we cannot regard it as a casual occurrence that Egidio should have asked Silvestro Meuccio for the works of Joachim and expressed eagerness to have them published. The drive behind his tireless work as a reformer was a belief in the *renovatio mundi*, and Joachimist thought may well have been one of the elements nourishing this. We do not know if Egidio fastened on the prophecy of the new spiritual men in the *Expositio*, so carefully pointed out to him by Silvestro in his Dedicatory Letter. Egidio's career was drawing to a close when he received it; perhaps he felt that the prophecy belonged to others to come.

Apart from Egidio's interest, the Joachimist hopes of Silvestro and his circle do not appear to have influenced the Order to any extent, but in the controversy with the Canons the Abbot's prophecy continued to be an important weapon of the Hermits. Thus in 1572, when he published his history of the Friars Hermit, Hieronymo Roman cited Joachim as a historic witness and translated into Spanish the prophecy from the *Expositio*.[2] This called forth a reply in 1598 from M. Rodriguez on behalf of the Canons.[3] In return,

---

[1] Cf. G. Signorelli, *Il Cardinale Egidio da Viterbo* (Florence, 1929), pp. 112–16.

[2] H. Roman, *Primera parte de la historia de la orden de los frayles hermitaños de San Augustin* . . . (Alcala, 1572), Preface, ff. 227ᵛ–228ᵛ.

[3] M. Rodríguez, *Quaestiones regulares et canonicae* . . . (Salamanca, 1598), p. 19.

J. Marquéz repeated in 1618 the claim of the Friars to be the fulfilment of Joachim's prophecy.[1] We have already noted how this 'slanging match' between Hermits and Canons developed into a heated argument about Joachim's reputation. To Marquéz's noble list of witnesses to Joachim's prophetic gifts the Canon G. Pennottus Novariensis replied with a longer list of those who had called him pseudo-prophet or heretic.[2] Finally, the Cistercian Francis Bivar intervened with the noble defence of Joachim which we have examined.[3] As far as the Augustinians were concerned, I have not found a further reply from either side.

The Augustinian Hermits had not to fight for their ideal like the Spiritual Franciscans. Apart from small groups of mystics and preachers, they do not seem to have felt themselves charged with the high mission of showing forth the spiritual life of the future. They claimed Joachim's prophecies for their honour, but did not, apparently, share to any large extent his vision of the spiritual Church to be. Yet one remembers that in the sixteenth century the Augustinian Hermits were moved by an extraordinary zeal to go forth to preach the Gospel in newly-discovered lands, and that, in the very years when the Spanish historians of the Order were quoting these prophecies, missionary work from Spain was expanding. Did some of these missionaries feel themselves to be Joachim's evangelical men, sent to lead the world into the new spiritual understanding? At any rate, a last echo of Joachimism among Austin Friars which comes from the year 1643 can perhaps be linked with this missionary zeal. Athanase of St. Agnès, writing in praise of the Hermits, paraphrases the prophecies of Joachim thus:[4]

... qui parle hautement de cette religion, lors qu'il la compare au Lionceau de Juda, qui ravit tout et par son rugissement donne la vie a son faon. ... L'habit noir et la ceinture de cuir est la marque des Pères de cette religion, laquelle s'estendra par tout et respandra par l'Univers les plus brillans rayons de la Predicator et les plus claires lumières de la parole de Dieu; c'est cette religion laquelle subsistera usque a la consommation du siècle et desployera tous ses efforts pour deffendre la

[1] J. Marquéz, *Origen de los Frayles Ermitaños de la orden de San Augustin* ... (Salamanca, 1618), pp. 346–7.

[2] G. Pennottus, *Generalis totius Sacri Ordinis Clericorum Canonicorum historia tripartita* (Rome, 1624), pp. 166–8, also 235–7, 485.

[3] *Supra*, pp. 110–11.

[4] Athanase of St. Agnès, *Le Chandelier d'or du Temple de Salomon* (Lyon, 1643), pp. 151–2. He partly quotes, partly paraphrases in the margin, part of Joachim's prophecy, *Expos.*, ff. 175ᵛ–176ʳ (quoted *supra*, pp. 143–4), and also a passage from f. 77ᵛ.

Foy de Jesus contre la puissance de l'Anté-Christ. Ailleurs il dit . . . c'est cette Religion laquelle n'a point éclipse parmy toutes les iniures du temps; c'est cette religion laquelle est assurée de sa grandeur et de sa durée: c'est cette religion laquelle jouyra du temps de la justice et de l'abondance de la paix: c'est cette Religion qui brisera la statue que fut montrée a Nabuchonazare: Bref, c'est cette Religion qui régnera sur toutes les Nations et les Royaumes, qui s'opposent a l'Empire Chrestien.

IX

JESUITS; CONCLUSION

THE sixteenth century did, however, give birth to a new Order which bore to a remarkable degree the characteristics of Joachim's prophesied 'monastic 'or mediating order, and within the Society of Jesus there were those who saw their vocation as that of Joachim's spiritual men. The Friars Minor and Preacher had claimed to fulfill the parallel prophecies of the spurious writings of Joachim; the Austin Friars had seen themselves designated in the *ordo heremitarum* of the genuine works; there yet remained unclaimed in the *Expositio* the interesting concept of an *ordo monachorum* that should be the link between the contemplative life and the world, charged especially with the work of evangelizing the world and gathering in the harvest of souls, whilst living a life half active and half contemplative, seated, as it were, upon a cloud between heaven and earth. In this picture of an order of men to whom would be given perfectly to imitate the life of the Son of Man and who would be designated in the name of Jesus, certain of the Jesuits saw their own vocation most vividly portrayed.[1]

The early Jesuits had a sense of the drama and urgency of their times which perhaps made some of them peculiarly receptive of ideas which issued from so dramatic a sense of history as Joachim's. They saw the world as the battlefield of two mighty 'opposites', under whose banners of good and evil the whole of humankind was encamped. Ignatius, the Soldier of God, was locked in deadly contest with the arch-devil, Martin Luther, whilst the members of Ignatius's society followed hard behind in battle against the heretics. This theme is developed by F. Montanus in his *Apologia pro Societate Jesu*, where he shows, in a chapter on 'opposites', how good and bad are always raised against each other, reborn ever in the same relationship, Jacob against Esau, Loyola against Luther.[2] The same idea was applied to the Jesuits by Florimund de Raemond:[3]

---

[1] Cf. passage quoted from the *Expos.*, *supra*, pp. 143-4, also *Expos.*, f. 83ᵛ.

[2] F. Montanus, *Apologia pro Societate Jesu* (Ingolstadt, 1596), p. 259.

[3] F. de Raemond, *L'Histoire de la Naissance, Progrez et Decadence de l'Heresie de ce siècle* . . . (Paris, 1620), Dedicatory Letter to Pope Paul V; also pp. 520-5.

God always counterbalances evil by good; thus against the calamities of heresy in the Old World must be set the marvels of a 'new Christianity' whose messengers were converting millions of people in far lands and marching in noble squadrons under the generalship of Ignatius Loyola to rout the heretic.

The final stage of this battle is now approaching and the Jesuits' own part in the drama of Last Things begins to emerge. One of the first prophecies to be applied to the Jesuits was that of St. Vincent Ferrer. Under the year 1538 N. Orlandino, the historian of the Order, notes:[1] 'Hoc porro tempore multi ex externis cum Patrum vitas et instituta perpenderunt, vehementer addubitarunt an ii forsitan essent Evangelici illi viri, de quibus tanto ante B. Vincentius Ferrerius divino instinctu praedixerat. Multa quippe videbantur ex eo praedictionis oraculo cum eorum vitis moribusque congruere.' The popular version of St. Vincent's preaching contained a prophecy of new evangelical men who, succeeding to the place forfeited by the Franciscans and Dominicans for their sins, would live in true evangelical simplicity, proclaiming the Gospel throughout the world before the Second Advent.[2] According to Orlandino, some found this prophecy quite obviously fulfilled in the Society of Jesus, for who were more simple in their zeal for poverty, or more world-wide in their missionary calling? But, he adds, the Fathers themselves, when questioned, modestly denied all claim to this role, 'cum tamen, si verum quaerimus, in eos multa quadrarent'.[3]

The theme that the Last Things must be heralded by the preaching of the Gospel in the entire world had suddenly taken on a new significance, for in the vast new exploration of the globe and the universal preaching which followed it men saw the striking fulfilment of prophecy. The next step was to claim a special eschatological role for one's own Order. Thus the official Life of St. Ignatius by P. Ribadeneira[4] expatiated on the marvels of the new discoveries, and then continued: 'Hoc igitur tempore tam opportuno, tam necessario, admirabili ac plane divino consilio, Deus nostrum elegit Ignatium, ut crucis trophaeum in disjunctissimas terras atque

[1] N. Orlandino, *Historia Societatis Jesu* (Antwerp, 1620), p. 39.

[2] See *De vita spirituali*, published *c.* 1500, undated, unpag., in which he speaks at the end of 'status virorum evangelicorum futurus'; *De tempore Antichristi et fine mundi* (ed. Fages, op. cit., p. 171 n. 1), pp. 219–20.

[3] Orlandino, op. cit., p. 39. A claim to St. Vincent's prophecy was also made by members of St. Vincent de Paul's Order and denied by their founder; see H. Brémond, *Histoire littéraire du sentiment religieux en France* (Paris, 1921), iii. 242–3.

[4] *AS*, 31 July, vii. 694–6.

provincias inferret, et gentes infinitas, agrestes ac barbaros, depulsis
ignorantiae atque infidelitatis tenebris, Evangelii clarissima luce,
per filios suos collustraret . . .' (*AS*, 31 July, p. 696). Again, J. F.
Lumnius, in his *De extremo iudicio Dei et Indorum vocatione*,[1] expounded the glorious future of the Indies, which would be called to
righteousness by the Jesuits; under the fine symbol from Isaiah—
'Who are these that fly as a cloud and as the doves to their windows?'[2]—he described the flight of these chosen angels to the
Indies. Drawing on the letters of Fr. Gaspar, a Belgian Jesuit from
Ormutius, he showed that prophecy was already being fulfilled,[3] and
throughout his work he conveyed a sense of standing on the verge of
portentous events.

Just as St. Francis had been identified as the Sixth Angel of the
Apocalypse, and St. Vincent as the Angel of the Eternal Evangel, so
Jesuit thought turned also to the Apocalypse for symbols adequate
to the life of St. Ignatius. In 1595 J. Osorius, preaching on his death,
hailed him as the Fifth Angel of the Apocalypse, at the sound of
whose trumpet there fell a great star from heaven.[4] The star is
Luther and the army of locusts which fights for him is the whole
pernicious sect of Protestant heretics. This identification was officially adopted at the Council of Tatra in 1602, where Loyola was
again referred to as the Fifth Angel of the Apocalypse.[5] In 1622
a Jesuit play, published in Latin and German, pictured the whole
action in dramatic form:[6] the first scene shows the Angel poised
with his trumpet, the Star falling, the Abyss opening to breathe
forth locusts, and the rest of the play represents the life of St.
Ignatius. Again in 1651 we find the saint hailed by the same title in
the German vernacular of a sermon.[7] Another identification, with
the 'Angelum fortem descendentem de caelo', was made by P. Deza
in a sermon of 1611.[8]

[1] J. F. Lumnius, *De extremo iudicio Dei et Indorum vocatione* (Antwerp, 1567), cap.
vi: 'De commendatione Ord. Soc. Jesu et quare qui ad Indos missi sunt angeli vocentur'.

[2] Isa. 60: 8.

[3] Loc. cit.; see also Gasparus, *Epistolae Indicarum* (Louvain, 1566).

[4] J. Osorius, *Tomus Quartus Concionum de Sanctis* (Venice, 1595), p. 153; cf. Apocalypse 9: 1–3.

[5] Cited J. Nieremberg, *Honor del Gran Patriarcha San Ignacio de Loyola* (Madrid,
1645), pp. 1–4.   [6] *Sanctitas Ignatii Loyolae* (Ingolstadt, 1622).

[7] *Catholische Lobpredig von dem Glorwürdigen Patriarchen u. Heiligen Vatters Ignatii
Loyolae* . . . (Langingen, 1651), p. 40.

[8] P. Deza, *Trois tres-excellents predications prononcées au jour et feste de la beatification du glorieux patriarche . . . Ignace fondateur de la Compagnie de Jesus* (Poitiers, 1611),
pp. 110–11; cf. Apocalypse 10: 1.

Thus the background of thought against which the vocation of the Order and its founder was frequently viewed contained elements akin to Joachimism. It is not surprising, therefore, to find some writers turning to Joachim himself. When Lumnius, in the work cited above, wished to convey the sense of standing on the threshold of greater days, it was Joachim whom he quoted:

Non igitur miretur quisquam si et nos postremis hisce temporibus quod ad quarundam attinet scripturarum intelligentiam, apertiorem veritatis notitiam ascribamus, quando iam et propinquius ad finem accedimus et per quotidianam veri experientiam quae hactenus ex parte latuerunt, lucidius revelari videmus. 'Aliter videtur civitas', sicut Abbas Joachim (*Apoc.* par. 4. dist. 7), 'cum adhuc per diaetam longius distat; aliter cum venitur ad ianuam, aliter cum pergitur intus. Nos igitur qui ad ianuam sumus, multa quidem loqui possumus quae aliquando ex toto vel ex parte latebant; sed non sicut hii qui erunt intus et oculo ad oculum videbunt.' Quod de nostris dictum quis neget temporibus? (Op. cit., cap. xiiii.)

Here he enters into the deepest expectation of the Abbot that the fullness of the *spiritualis intellectus* would be attained in the third *status*, sharing with him the excitement of the approach to that goal. It is significant that the passage he quotes immediately precedes, in Joachim's *Expositio*, the prophecy of the *ordo monachorum*,[1] but he does not attempt to claim it explicitly for the Jesuit Order.

This claim was openly made by Osorius in the sermon of 1595 from which I have already quoted. He appropriated from the *Expositio* nearly all the principal passages referring to the new order of monks. The striking aptness of the prophecies is best shown by giving Osorius's quotations from Joachim in full:

. . . in li. 20 expositione super Apocalypsim, f. 83 sic ait: Erit quidam ordo designatus in Jesu qui clarebit sexto tempore Ecclesiae, id est, in fine mundi, qui erit prae caeteris spiritualis, praeclarus et Deo amabilis. Et in f. 98 ait: Deus diliget istum ultimum ordinem quemadmodum Jacob Patriarcha Beniamin filium suum, eo quod in senectute genuerit eum. Et in f. 175 exponens illa verba Johannis Et vidi . . . filio hominis, ait: Arbitramur tamen in eo quod visus est sedere super nubem candidam significari quendam ordinem iustorum cui datum sit perfecte imitari vitam filii hominis et habere linguam eruditam ad evangelizandum et colligendum in aream Domini ultimam messionem. Qui dicuntur sedere super nubem propter contemplationem, et hic erit ordo perfectorum virorum servantium vitam Christi et Apostolorum. Et idem Abbas

---

[1] Cf. *Expos.*, f. 175^{r-v}.

Joachim super Hieremiam 1 cap. sic ait: Revelandi sunt in Ecclesia doctores praedicatoresque fideles, qui terrena ac carnalia corda omniplaga percutiant ac erectis et tumidis magisteriis silentium studiis suis imponant. (Op. cit., p. 166.)

We notice how Osorius, in quoting from the spurious *Super Hieremiam*, avoids the obvious 'prophecies' of the Franciscans and Dominicans, selecting a more general passage promising doctors and preachers.[1]

It is clear that, to a remarkable degree, Joachim's concept of the half-way order found its embodiment in the Society of Jesus. This claim to be the fulfilment of Joachim's prophecy must have attracted much discussion, for Blasius Viegas, writing about 1601, spoke of many who argued concerning it.[2] Two bishops supported the claim: Rutilius Benzonius, Bishop of Recanati, recognized in the Jesuit Order the fulfilment of the prophecies of both Joachim and St. Vincent;[3] Antonius Zara, Bishop of Petina, quoted from the *Expositio, Liber Concordie*, and *Super Hieremiam* to prove the point.[4] Again, T. Stapleton, praising the Society, quoted, as certainly applying to it, Joachim's words in the *Liber Concordie*: 'Insurget una nova religio sanctissima, quae erit libera et spiritualis, in qua Romani Pontifices . . . se continebunt. Quam religionem et ordinem Deus super omnes alios diliget quia perfectio illius vincet omnes alias aliorum ordinum.'[5] Even in the vernacular one finds in the German sermon cited above all the more trenchant phrases from Joachim's prophecies translated and arranged as a convincing description of the Jesuit Order.[6] In Spanish, J. Nieremberg in *Honor del Gran Patriarcha San Ignacio de Loyola* gathered symbols and prophecies from every quarter.[7] St. Ignatius was a new Dominic, fighting the

---

[1] Cf. *Super Hier.*, f. 1ᵛ. These words occur in the midst of a section full of prophetic references to the two Mendicant Orders, often emphasized by marginal notes, e.g. *Ordo Praedicatorum et Minorum.*

[2] B. Viegas, *Commentarii Exegetici in Apocalypsim* (Evora, 1601), p. 198.

[3] Cited Nieremberg, op. cit., p. 2.

[4] A. Zara, *Anatomia ingeniorum et scientiarum* (Venice, 1915), p. 185. He quotes *Expos.*, f. 83ᵛ (two passages to the second of which he gives the wrong reference f. 98); *Lib. Conc.*, f. 95ʳ (again with a faulty reference); *Super Hier.*, f. 1ᵛ.

[5] T. Stapleton, *Promptuarium morale super Evangelia Dominicalia* (Paris, 1617), p. 105, quoting the same passage as that cited by Zara. The quotation does not correspond exactly to any passage in the edn. of the *Lib. Conc.* Most of the phrases come from cap. 65 (f. 95), but the last sentence is based on the end of cap. 64, though going further in its claim. Stapleton's application of the prophecy is noted by De Lauro, *Apologetica*, pp. 202–6.

[6] Op. cit. (p. 276 n. 7), pp. 32, 40.   [7] Op. cit., pp. 1–5.

forces of heresy; he was more than one Angel of the Apocalypse; he fulfilled all the prophecies of Joachim and St. Vincent. Once again, he translated the prophecies of the *Expositio* into the vernacular.[1] That this application was well known is suggested by the fact that Bail, writing on Joachim's reputation in his history of General Councils, commented that some had applied his prophecies to the Jesuit Order, although modesty forbade a general assent to these claims within the Order.[2]

Here Bail was probably indicating a common Jesuit attitude. An example of a certain 'modesty' is to be found in the Commentary on the Apocalypse of Viegas. This contains one quite disproportionate passage[3] in which he digresses upon Joachim as the prophet of his Order at such length as to underline the importance which this question had now assumed. The section, headed 'Joachim Abbas de Philadelphiae Angelo vaticinium', begins with a very favourable account of the Abbot and of those who have written in his praise. Viegas notices the condemnation of 1215, the defence of Joachim by various pontiffs, and the astounding and unmerited condemnation meted out by Alphonso de Castro.[4] All this and more he mentions in order to vindicate this most celebrated man from calumny. Then he turns to the prophecies of the *Expositio* and especially to that associated with the Angel of the Church of Philadelphia.[5] He notes, in passing, the prophecies of St. Dominic and St. Francis which have been amply fulfilled, and, declaring that these under present consideration are quite distinct from those pertaining to the Mendicants, goes on to show how the Jesuits might apply Joachim's words in every particular to themselves. But upon this prophecy he will pass no judgement; nor upon that of St. Vincent Ferrer, though he will quote its most pertinent points. 'All these are wonderful and marvellous words, so mighty that no one could venture to assume for himself even the least part of them. Yet great is the sanctity of those who apply them to the Jesuit Fathers and strong is their conviction when they see the Society preaching everywhere the evangelical doctrine, obedient in everything to the Pope, practising perfect poverty'—and so on, accumulating the proofs; 'when, finally, they

[1] He quotes *Expos.*, f. 175ᵛ.
[2] L. Bail, *Summa Conciliorum omnium* . . . (Paris, 1675), i. 438.
[3] Op. cit., pp. 196–200.
[4] *Supra*, p. 105.
[5] Cf. *Expos.*, f. 83ᵛ. The whole passage occurs at the beginning of Viegas's exposition of Apocalypse 3: 7–13, on the letter to the Church of Philadelphia.

see in how small a space of time our smallest of societies has converted the world, establishing itself in almost all the heathen parts,
then not without justice do they believe these to be the men whom
Vincent and Joachim most wonderfully summoned forth. Such are
the persuasions of many notable men.' 'Yet', concludes Viegas, 'we
believe all these things to have been spoken of some other order,
we who hold ourselves to be the least and most useless of servants.'
So, dismissing prophecies, he exhorts the brethren to concentrate
wholly on the fulfilment of their office.

The assumed modesty of this passage certainly deceived some. In
the sermon cited above,[1] Deza expressed his astonishment that
Fathers Ribeira[2] and Viegas, having so carefully expounded the
Apocalypse, did not see how much its prophecies stood in their
favour. The various Angels of the Apocalypse must be interpreted
as God's messengers in history, and these culminate in this latest
manifestation of Divine agency. Paraphrasing the words of the
Epistle to the Hebrews, Deza declares:[3] 'Novissime autem diebus
istis loquutus est nobis (Deus) in filio suo Ignatio quem constituit
haeredem universorum.' Here Deza, no doubt unwittingly, is echo-
ing the words of the Spiritual Franciscan, Angelo da Clareno.[4] When
the Spiritual Franciscans made their extravagant claims for St.
Francis, boldly adapting New Testament words concerning Christ
to this new purpose, they did so on the basis of an implied Joachimism. For, as we have argued, the only possible ground for such
a claim was the threefold pattern of history. When the Jesuit was led
into a similar mode of thought, he was probably quite unaware of its
implications, although he must have caught something of its spirit.
His bold adaptation of New Testament words went altogether too
far for the theologians, and Deza found himself under the censure of the Sacred Faculty of Theology of Paris for scandalously,
erroneously, and blasphemously altering the words of St. Paul.[5]

There were obviously two schools of thought among the Jesuits
on the validity of such prophetic interpretation. These can best be
studied from the group of Jesuit commentators on the Apocalypse
who appeared in the late sixteenth and early seventeenth centuries.
Those of the 'scientific' school of thought emphasized the historic

[1] *Supra*, p. 276 n. 8.
[2] Cf. F. Ribeira, *Commentarius in Apocalypsim* (Salamanca, 1591).
[3] Op. cit., p. 112; cf. Heb. 1: 1–2.   [4] *Supra*, p. 210.
[5] *Censure de la Sacrée Faculté de Théologie de Paris sur trois sermons prétendus, faicts en
l'honneur de P. Ignace* . . . (no place of pub., 1611), pp. 5, 9–10.

setting of prophecy and its literal interpretation. They held that the Apocalypse did not describe in detail any events except those of the First Age of the Church. Some interpreted it entirely as past history, but others, whilst believing that most of it related to the first century, could not resist the desire to jump thence in their interpretation to the Last Age of the Church. Thus Ribeira believed that five seals of the Apocalypse described the history of the Church to Trajan and that the sixth and seventh concerned the end of the world; he was therefore able to work out his interpretations in a past and a future safely remote from his present.[1] Ribeira's great Commentary, published in 1591, did much to set the study of the Apocalypse on sane, historical lines,[2] but Viegas, whose interest in the prophecy of Joachim we have just examined, reproached him for being too slavishly bound to the letter.[3] As we have seen, Viegas himself felt the intoxicating power of prophecy, so much feared by others, and nearly succumbed to the temptation of applying it to his own age.

The existence of another school of thought is clearly realized by Cornelius Lapierre in his Commentaries on the Apocalypse and the four Major Prophets.[4] He takes Joachim as its prototype, calling him the founder of the method of historic parallels and associating with him Ubertino da Casale and certain more recent thinkers.[5] Cornelius knows most of the Joachimist writings and his analysis of their method is clear: their fundamental principle is that nothing occurs in the Old Testament which is not paralleled in the New and to be fulfilled in the future.[6] Both the Old and the New Testaments must be treated as symbols of the future. While careful not to identify himself with this school of interpretation, Cornelius shows a marked preference for those commentators on the Apocalypse who believe that it foretells the whole history of the Church right down to the Last Judgement. He does not actually cite Joachim on the interpretation of the great chapters in the Apocalypse dealing with the final crisis of history—perhaps because the Abbot on this subject was too suspect—but he does select from him a number of passages, chiefly

---

[1] See E. Allo, *St. Jean. L'Apocalypse* (Paris, 1921), pp. ccxxviii–ccxxx, on the different schools of interpretation.

[2] Ibid., p. ccxxxv.   [3] Ibid., p. ccxxxvi.

[4] Cornelius Lapierre (Cornelis Cornelissen van den Steen), *Commentarius in Apocalypsim* (Lyon, 1627); *Commentaria in Quatuor Prophetas Maiores* (Antwerp, 1622).

[5] *Com. in Apoc.*, p. 6; *Com. in Quat. Proph.*, p. 51. He mentions particularly Serafino da Fermo (see *infra*, pp. 469–70) and P. Galatinus (see *supra*, pp. 235–8).

[6] *Com. in Quat. Proph.*, p. 51.

on orders in the Church and their spiritual functions. He is undoubtedly interested in Joachim's concept of new orders of spiritual
men in the Last Days, citing his 'prophecies' of the Franciscans,
Dominicans, and Augustinian Hermits,[1] as well as the passage on the
new future order symbolized in the Angel of the Church of Philadelphia which was claimed by his own Order. Here he quotes from
Viegas three reasons for which men believe the Jesuits to be designated in this prophecy.[2] Later he quotes Joachim again on the two
witnesses who represent two species of orders to fight Antichrist,
and with Joachim he significantly links St. Teresa, who had also
prophesied a double order—'sc. S. Dominici et Societatis nostrae'—
to combat the army of Antichrist.[3] It is true that Cornelius cautiously
pronounces Joachim's prophecy of the Jesuits obscure and uncertain, a mystical, not literal interpretation.[2] Moreover, he twice
expresses his doubts about the whole Joachimist method.[4] Yet the
Joachimist vision of new spiritual men in the Last Days certainly
moved him, and their role is connected with a question to which he
reverts more than once: whether there will be a final time of peace
for the Church either before or after Antichrist. In a passage discussing the symbol of Satan bound for a thousand years[5] Cornelius
shows himself much attracted to the hope of a great future age of
peace and felicity in the Church. Joachim, Ubertino, Serafino, and
others place this after Antichrist; from this view he dissociates himself, but even while accepting the orthodox view that the thousand
years began with the First Advent of Christ, he lingers over the
hope that it will culminate in a future great age of splendour under
the Angelic Pope to come. In this the new spiritual men will play
a decisive role. Thus, whilst avoiding some of the doubtful implications of Joachim's philosophy of history, this Jesuit is yet moved by
the Joachimist symbols of *renovatio*, in which the destiny of his own
Order is involved.

The attraction of the Joachimist method of interpretation to
Jesuit thinkers is again implied by the strong attack made on it by the
Spanish Jesuit Alcazar in his *Vestigatio arcani sensus in Apocalypsi*.[6]

---

[1] *Com. in Apoc.*, pp. 10, 238; *Com. in Quat. Proph.*, pp. 50–1.
[2] *Com. in Apoc.*, p. 58.   [3] Ibid., p. 186.
[4] Ibid., p. 6; *Com. in Quat. Proph.*, p. 51.
[5] *Com. in Apoc.*, p. 289.
[6] Alcazar, *Vestigatio arcani sensus in Apocalypsi* (no place of pub., 1614). Once more
Ubertino da Casale and Serafino da Fermo are grouped with Joachim, this time as
representatives of a dangerous method.

He writes convinced of the profound obscurity in which the true meaning of the Apocalypse is veiled, buried far deeper than any circumstantial interpretation of events. He digresses at some length on the famous pseudo-Joachimist *Vaticinia de Summis Pontificibus*:[1] there is, he holds, a vast difference between the sort of enigma which by some judicious juggling can always be squared to any event and the true prophetic mysteries to which the answer, when it appears in due course, corresponds entirely. Such is the measure of the difference between the foolish puzzles which Joachim contrived on the popes and the profound prophecies of the Apocalypse. 'He who will may hold the Abbot Joachim to be a prophet of God, but not I.'[2] And again, 'Far from holding that prudent expositors of the Apocalypse ought to follow in the footsteps of the Abbot Joachim, it seems rather to me that those who take him as their guide through the Apocalypse and adhere to his interpretations are enslaved to vain errors and illusions.'[2]

If the good sense of the Order on the whole rejected the more fantastic interpretations of Joachimism, the worthier elements in the Abbot's thought on new spiritual men did, I think, exercise a real influence on some Jesuits. They caught the sense of standing on the threshold of great events which filled the heart with hope. One, at least, of the Jesuit commentators on the Apocalypse, Benito Pereyra, drew considerably on Joachim's thought. Pereyra, like other commentators, recognizes the special method of Joachim.[3] He uses Joachim's division of the history of the Church into seven ages, and like so many Joachites places himself somewhere at the end of the fifth age.[4] He adopts from Joachim the idea of the different agencies appropriate to each age: Apostles, Martyrs, Doctors, Anchorites and Monks, Virgins, Pastors and Prelates, and, for the seventh age, spiritual men, for whom he adds his own description: 'septimus est religiosorum virorum, exemplo vitae et sanctitate conversationis, et frequenti, ardentique praedicatione divini verbi populum fidelem reformantium atque renovantium. . . . [Such were the] Religiosi et sancti Ordines Fratrum Mendicantium et in hoc saeculo nostra Societas, ut novissima, sic etiam minima' (op. cit., pp. 769, 766). This is the only explicit reference which Pereyra makes to the

---

[1] Alcazar, *Vestigatio arcani sensus in Apocalypsi*, p. 45; cf. *supra*, pp. 58, 193, 214.
[2] Ibid., p. 76.
[3] Benito Pereyra, *Disputationes super libro Apocalipsis* (pub. Lyon, 1606; edn. used here, *Opera Theologica*, i [Cologne, 1620]), pp. 763, 769, 830.   [4] Ibid., p. 875.

role of the Jesuits, but it is clear that he sees his Society as the embodiment of the true spiritual life of the seventh age. Developing the idea of seven adversities and seven prosperities in the Church, he expounds the seventh prosperity as manifested in his own age in the discovery of new worlds and especially in the innumerable peoples converted to Christianity.[1] He believes passionately that before the end of time the 'spiritual men' must plant the Church in every race on earth.[2] Without committing himself to a belief in an earthly millennium after Antichrist, he sees in the silence at the Opening of the Seventh Seal the period of peace and quietness between the death of Antichrist and the Second Advent which will be given to the Church for the conversion of all peoples and the edification of the saints.[3]

Pereyra's chief interest in Joachim's thought, however, centres in the problem of the relation between the life of contemplation and that of active evangelism. He selects certain long quotations from Joachim's writings, and these, almost without exception, are taken, not from his interpretations of history, but from his reflections on the tensions between the two aspects of the spiritual life. One of the most interesting of these is a characteristic passage from the *Expositio*[4] in which Joachim speaks of the true pastors of the people as the columns of the Temple which, in the midst of tempestuous commotions, aspire upwards continually towards higher things. Then, changing his image to that of the double gift of his spirit which Elisha sought from Elijah,[5] Joachim reflects that it is a rare and difficult thing to have this double gift, to be able, at the same time, to provide for the brethren in the active life and also to enjoy the sweetness of contemplation. Again, shortly after, Pereyra quotes from the same passage on the vocation of those who have the spiritual cure of souls,[6] and, later again, a revealing passage on the tragedy of those religious who remain lukewarm and are never emancipated from the life of fear into the liberty of love.[7] For the true life of contemplation Pereyra adopts Joachim's interpretation of the girdle of gold in the first chapter of the Apocalypse:[8]

---

[1] Pereyra, op. cit., p. 767. [2] Ibid., p. 904–5.
[3] Ibid., p. 912; cf. Apocalypse 8: 1.
[4] Pereyra, op. cit., p. 815; cf. *Expos.*, f. 89ʳ⁻ᵛ. [5] Cf. 2 Kgs. 2: 9.
[6] Op. cit., p. 816. [7] Ibid., p. 821; cf. *Expos.*, f. 97ᵛ.
[8] Op. cit., p. 784; cf. *Expos.*, ff. 42ʳ–43ʳ. Pereyra's quotations vary somewhat from the printed edition. For other passages quoted from the *Expos.* see pp. 785, 786, 788, 803, 807, 808–9, 816, 822, 823, 832, 837–8, 848–9, 857, 875.

In Ioannis [Baptistae] ergo zona et esca veteris testamenti iustitia designata est: per Christi vero zonam sive escam novi testamenti iustitiam que de celo descendit significata est: quamvis in eisdem rebus duas vitas ecclesiae assignare possimus activam scilicet et contemplativam. . . . Infirmorum ergo et imperfectorum est habere zonam circa lumbos pelliceam: . . . perfectorum autem, maxime vero monachorum, est habere zonas aureas ad mamillas: quia illis aliquid est, si corpus impollutum servent: istis est, pene nihil autem hoc nisi habeant et munditiam cordis. . . . In zonis quoque maxima est distantia: quod enim inter zonas pelliceas atque aureas inter est, hoc differt inter corporis castitatem et mentis: illic enim exterior homo, hic interior . . . qui zonis aureis circa pectora constringuntur, id est qui fulgore sapientiae qua pascuntur, ad coelestia contemplanda et amanda trahuntur, et quasi potestate regia, immundas a se ipsis cogitationes abiiciunt. Praeterea, cinctum esse zona pellicea, significat castum esse ex necessitate, vel timore poenae; cinctum vero esse zona aurea denotat amore iustitiae atque aeternae gloriae virtutem spiritualis munditiae toto studio, totisque viribus complecti et tenere.

Thus it is upon some of Joachim's most characteristic passages concerning the life of the *viri spirituales* that Benito Pereyra draws.

Perhaps the most surprising example of a Jesuit who felt the attraction of Joachim's prophecy was Daniel Papebroch. We have already seen how his account of the Abbot in the *Acta Sanctorum* betrays his position of *parti pris*.[1] In the chapter dealing with Joachim's expectations of new spiritual men he is cautious in making claims for his own Order, but manifestly moved by the vision Joachim offers. Rejecting such 'figments' as the St. Mark's story,[2] he goes straight to the *Expositio*: 'Quidquid sit, non est opus istiusmodi tam incertis argumentis propheticum B. Joachimi spiritum confirmari, cum alia longe certissima habeamus. Quapropter libenter praeterimus quaecumque ex eiusdem operibus varii Religiosorum Ordines varie ad se trahunt et ad nostram Iesu Societatem etiam nonnulli . . .' (*AS*, p. 142). He then quotes from the two key passages in the *Expositio* in which Joachim prophesies the mediating order designated in Jesus, and also from the *Super Hieremiam*,[3] again avoiding the passages appropriated by the Mendicants. His interpretation of these passages shows how fully he has entered into Joachim's conception:

Haec aliaque eiusmodi sunt, ut praeter eos, qui tum in Ecclesia vigebant

[1] *Supra*, pp. 121–5.   [2] *AS*, p. 141.
[3] *Expos.*, ff. 83ᵛ, 175ᵛ–176ʳ; *Super Hier.*, ff. 1ᵛ, 15ʳ.

florebantque Ordines Monachorum, uni fere contemplationi ex instituto deditorum, alios nascituros praeviderit Joachim, qui in gradu Clericali operosam Marthae actionem conjungerent cum quiete Mariae: et ex utroque mixti genere, non tantum suae sed proximorum etiam saluti perfectionique promovendae vacarent: de quorum ad barbaros et infideles missionibus fructuosis, egregiisque contra vitia, haereses, ipsumque Antichristum certaminibus cum multa dicat, operosum foret omnia congerere: multo autem operosius et longe invidiosissimum foret, singula velle applicare singulis, post Joachimum natis, ad exclusionem aliorum, qui eadem de se pari vel majori jure aestimarent intelligi potuisse. (*AS*, p. 142.)

He then quotes from the *Expositio* another passage on the 'Ordinem quem designat Jesus' (f. 85ᵛ), and after this continues:

Ad Ordinis istius sic praedicti tempora existimamus pertinere sacrorum studiorum resuscitationem, quorum multo tempore tractatio sterilis atque intra meras Dialecticorum argutias, et Metaphysicorum abstractiones, implicatissimorumque terminorum farraginem multiplicem, velut in sepulchro concludenda esset; ac demum, post triplicem Ecclesiae tribulationem, a Ioachimo praevisam, in vitam quodammodo revocanda per eos, qui Divinarum rerum et Scripturarum cognitionem ita sectarentur ipsi, et aliis traderent; ut extra Scholasticae exercitationis umbram, in solem pulveremque educti, eadem uti scirent atque docerent, ad redarguendos Catholicae fidei adversarios, haereticos confutandos reducendosque, convertendos idolatras rudes ac barbaros instruendos . . . [He quotes the *Super Hieremiam* on the threefold tribulation] . . . tertia denique, ab haereticis imminens sub Luthero aliisque haeresiarchis, et in magna Ocidentalis Imperii parte . . . maxime in regionibus Borealibus, repraesentatur in Christi morte. Postquam, velit nolit mundus, septimus Angelus, i.e. spiritus Dei septiformis, resuscitabit intelligentiam spiritualem, qua caeci videant et intelligant mysteria Trinitatis totiusque fides Christianae.

Illa autem tam praeclara atque illustria, sive de Ordine praedicto 'quem designat Jesus', sive de spirituali intelligentia, i.e. operosa efficacique doctrina Scripturarum qua esset Ecclesiae restituenda . . .; an hoc quo vivimus seculo impleri coeperint, aliis relinquimus judicandum; . . . (*AS*, p. 142.)

I have quoted at length because this passage illustrates so vividly both the appropriation of Joachim's characteristic vision, in which after the tribulation the *Spiritualis Intelligentia* is to be resurrected from the tomb, and, at the same time, the characteristic Jesuit attitude in which a desire not to claim too high a place for one's own Order mingles with an emotional response which identifies Joachim's vision with its sense of mission.

A somewhat pathetic *addendum* must end this study of Joachimist ideas in the Jesuit Order. Guillaume Postel first met some of the future Jesuits in Paris before 1535 and quickly began to see their emerging purpose as part of an eschatological pattern.[1] We shall be considering later the whole of his great programme for the *renovatio mundi* through a World Emperor and Angelic Pope; here we must concern ourselves only with the eager way in which he seized on the new Order of Jesus as the principal agency of reform. He followed them to Rome and in 1543 was received into the Order as a novice by Ignatius himself. His ardour and the grandeur of his expectations for the future touched everyone and he was welcomed with high hopes. He planned to give himself to the conversion of infidels, and at first all spoke well of him, but by 1545 doubts about his extravagant fantasies were being expressed. His opinions and writings were scrutinized and he was subjected to discipline. He submitted but could not keep his fantasies under control. Reluctantly—for they admired his enthusiasm—the Jesuits were forced to expel him.[2] This was a tremendous blow, for Postel had trusted that here he had found the great instrument of the *renovatio mundi* which he never doubted was to come. He wrote of the Order in glowing terms: 'décorée du nom même de celui qui doit être reconnu pour le Roi de l'univers et déjà célèbre par le bonheur qu'elle a de remplir toutes les Indes de la lumière de l'Évangile et de préparer ainsi les voies de la Légation universelle qui se manifestera sous un autre nom' (cited Bernard-Maître, *Le Passage*, p. 238), and continued to hope for re-admission as late as 1562, when he wrote a letter of supplication to Lainez. His desire to be thought well of by the Jesuits appears even after this, in his *Retractationes* of 1564:

[1] On Guillaume Postel see Bernard-Maître, (i) *Le Passage*; (ii) *RSR* xxxviii; Secret, *Studi francesi* I; Bouwsma, *Concordia Mundi*.

[2] The judgement of the Jesuits on Postel is worth quoting in full from J. de Polanco, *Vita Ignatii Loiolae et Rerum Societatis Jesu Historia, Monumenta Historica Societatis Jesu*, i (Madrid, 1894), pp. 148–9: '. . . quidam Guilielmus Postellus, natione gallus, et eruditione (praesertim Mathematicis et linguarum multarum) satis clarus, est ad probationem admissus. Sed cum spiritu, ut ipsi videbatur, prophetiae, ut autem Ignatius et alii de Societate judicabant, erroris multa sentiret, diceret ac scriberet, quae nec vera, nec ad aedificationem et unionem cum Societate fovendam, facere viderentur, frustra remediis multis tentatis, dimissus est. Vir alioqui pius et moribus bonis praedictus, si humilius et ad sobrietatem sapere et suum judicium in obsequium fidei ac obedientiae captivare didicisset.' For the whole story see Bernard-Maître, *Le Passage*.

... ie me allay a Rome avec les dicts Iesuites, la ou ie maintins tousiours ladicte profecie, combien que par plus d'un an, continuellement quasi, par l'obedience de M. Ignigo de L. . . . ie priasse Dieu qui m'ostast de la fantaisie ceste profecie . . . de sorte que la ou ie la vouloys chasser elle croissoit maulgre moy. . . . Car a la verite j'eusse aultrement desire a tousiours vivre avec eulx [i.e. the Jesuits] . . . a cause qu'aultrement leur maniere de proceder [?] . . . est la plus parfaiete apres les Apostres qui onc feust au monde, comme ie le pense et iuge, et qui avec nous reformeroit le monde. (Cited Bernard-Maître, *Le Passage*, p. 241.)

As we shall see, Postel's expectation for the future was certainly a Joachimist one. It was a pathetic tragedy that, having tried so hard to obey them, Postel should have been shut out of his Promised Land by the sobriety of the *viri evangelici* from whom he expected everything. It was inevitable: the Order perforce interpreted its role in other terms and Postel went off into wilder fantasies and absurder claims for himself. That the Jesuits were right to expel these seductive ideas quickly from their midst appears from the fact that, in spite of his speedy departure, the infection of Postel's views spread at least a little.

In 1555, when a plan was going forward for the establishment of the College of Auvergne, it was found that Jérôme le Bas, chosen to organize the new college, had been tempted to entertain some of Postel's glowing dreams of the future, and with him another Jesuit, Jean Arnauld. In 1553 Postel had dedicated to the Bishop of Clermont a work in which he saluted the Bishop as the first in France to patronize this Society of Jesus, and declared its glorious future, destined by God to bring all peoples of the world under the supreme Pontiff, supported by the universal monarchy of the French Crown.[1] The two Jesuits had been carried away by this vision. As soon, however, as this was realized by the authorities, the two were summoned to Rome and instructed in the true assessment of such chimerical expectations. Not until he had renounced all the fantasies of Postel and submitted himself unreservedly to his superiors was Jerome le Bas allowed to return to start the college.

There was another danger in the Jesuit association with such a character as Postel: that it would be seized as a weapon against them by anti-Jesuit propaganda. This some opponents were not slow to do. An attack on the Jesuits by Master Pasquier in 1564 taxed them with

---

[1] H. Forquerary, *Histoire de la Compagnie de Jésus en France*, i (Paris, 1910), pp. 182–3.

the impieties of Postel,[1] while a later work against the Jesuits devotes a whole chapter to the *Impietez de Guillaume Postel Iesuite*.[2]

In spite of its dangers, prophetic expectations of an age of gold within history continued to attract some Jesuits. Two outstanding examples of the seventeenth and eighteenth centuries are the Portuguese Antonio Vieyra (1608–97)[3] and the famous Manual de Lacunza y Diaz (1731–1801).[4] Both held millenarian views of some kind. Vieyra's *Historia do Futuro* was partially printed at Lisbon in 1718; this does not contain any obvious Joachimist material. His chief work, *Clavis prophetarum de Regno Christi in Terris consummato*, exists only in manuscript, as also another work *Quinto Imperio do Mundo*. These titles themselves show clearly the direction of Vieyra's thought. In support of his expectations he argued that the millenarian belief had never disappeared from the Church and cited Ubertino da Casale as one of a number of witnesses to this fact. Lacunza's great work, *La Venida del Mesias en gloria y majestad*, was finished in 1790. He was probably no more of a Joachite in the strict sense of the word than Vieyra, although it seems likely that he borrowed certain ideas from Joachim. Petrus Joannis Olivi and Johannes de Rupescissa have also been suggested as precursors, but no direct influences can be traced. In general, however, Lacunza seems to belong to the Joachimist school of thought. In his emphasis on a terrestrial millennium in the future, placed between the Second Advent and the end of the world, he reveals to us that the currents of expectation we have been tracing continued to flow in the Jesuit Order for some time.

It would have been unlikely indeed to find within so rational a society as the Order of Jesus a group of Joachites comparable to the Spiritual Franciscans. It was one thing to accept the Abbot Joachim as the prophet of one's Order; it was quite another to

---

[1] I have only seen Pasquier's pamphlet in an English translation: *The Jesuite displayed . . . openly discoursed in an oration against them made in the Parliament house at Paris, by one Master Pasquier . . . translated out of French by E. A.* (London, 1594, unpag.). After describing Postel's appearance in Paris, he concludes: 'Now truly if youre societye hatcheth such monsters: if it engendereth us so damnable effects, God forbid that ever we should follow such a societie of Jesus.'

[2] *Le catechisme des Iesuites: ou Examen de leur doctrines* (Villefranche, 1602), Ch. x: *Impietez de Guillaume Postel Iesuite*, pp. 42ʳ–45ᵛ.

[3] A. F. Vaucher, *Une célébrité oubliée: Le P. Manual de Lacunza y Diaz . . .* (Collonges-sous-Salève, 1941), p. 68, gives some notes on Vieyra and his writings and further references.

[4] On Lacunza see Vaucher, *ibid.*, and *Lacunziana* (Collonges-sous-Salève, 1949).

accept his view of history and to see oneself as belonging to the order of the future, the order of those who knew the secret of life in the third *status* and were the divine agents to usher the Church into it. Few Jesuits probably went further than claiming, or allowing others to claim, the prophecies of Joachim and Vincent for the glory of their founder and Order. Yet their own dramatic interpretation of their role in history made some more prone to succumb to the temptations of a Joachimist interpretation. When new worlds were being conquered, it was easy to believe that one stood on the threshold of a new stage in history. If the good sense of the Order on the whole rejected the more fantastic claims of Joachimism, some members did, I think, turn to the Abbot's conception of new orders for the understanding of their own vocation, and those who read more deeply in Joachim's works drew therefrom inspiration for their own calling as *viri spirituales*.

The possibilities of new spiritual men had not even been wholly exhausted by the Jesuits, for we find in the second half of the sixteenth century Theodore Graminaeus still expecting Joachim's *novus ordo*.[1] He writes of the *reformatio* in the Roman Church to be expected after the ruin of Babylon, and the rebuilding of the *sancta civitas*: 'per ordinem videlicet Eremitarum, in extrema mundi aetate. . . . Surget enim ordo, ut Abbas Ioachim ante quadringentos fere annos prophetico spiritu clarus praedixit . . . qui videtur novus et non est . . .' Graminaeus gives the whole of Joachim's key passage on the hermit order and one from the *Super Hieremiam* on the *novus ordo praedicantium*. But he names no candidates for this still-awaited role.

[1] T. Graminaeus, *Mysticus Aquilo, sive Declaratio Vaticinii Ieremie Prophetae* . . . (Cologne, 1576), pp. 25–6.

CONCLUSION

IT may be thought that many of those who pursued this ideal of the *viri spirituales* were really seeking to return to the primitive purity of the Apostles. This motif of the backward aspiration had, of course, an important place in the history of medieval religious movements. But the distinctive characteristic of all the groups we have studied is that their faith sprang from a 'myth of the future'— not the past. Their reading of past history enabled them to complete the pattern of things to come in the Last Age and to find their own cosmic role within this pattern. Their models might be drawn from the past, but their belief was that the life of the future would far exceed that of the past. It was not so much a recapturing of the life of the first Apostles that they expected as the creating of the life of new apostles. It was this claim, which so easily passed into arrogance, which most shocked and offended the orthodox. Again and again in Inquisitorial proceedings the claim to greater perfection than Christ and the Apostles was a major accusation against them. Thus the most unpalatable part of the Joachimist view was the claim that the future could transcend the past. From this position it was almost impossible for the Joachite to retreat very far, for it was in the nature of the 'myth' that the achievement of the future must transcend that of the past. Perhaps it was an instinctive avoidance of the extreme consequences of this logic that led Spiritual Franciscans to try to combine faith in the future with a special devotion to the Person of Christ, and to find the focus of this combination in the life of St. Francis. The leap forward into the future was made possible by Joachim's doctrine of the Third Age, with its more abundant outpouring of the Spirit. Yet among the Spiritual Franciscans particularly there was a great emphasis on conformity to the life of Christ. The faith of these groups seems more directly Christocentric than that of Joachim. But still the role of Francis is not simply that of imitating the earthly life of Christ as closely as possible: it is to be conformed to Christ in order that at the opening of the Third Age Francis might stand as Christ had stood at the crossing from the First into the Second. The fusion of their own emphasis upon Christ with Joachim's on the Spirit is best seen in their concept of the three Advents of Christ, with Francis embodying the Second, and the orthodox Second Advent becoming the Third at the end of history.

Whether the new age was conceived in terms of a Second Advent or an Age of the Spirit, the dynamic quality of the conception lay in the belief, received from Joachim, in a new spiritual understanding which would be poured out upon men. These disciples were brought up into the high mountain and shown both the Promised Land and the crossing of Jordan which must first be accomplished. Then they saw their own calling: on the one hand, to embody the true spiritual life of the future, and, on the other, to lead the pilgrimage towards the Age of the Spirit. Thus one aspect of this great spiritual adventure was the evangelization of the world, but in essence it led towards the silence of perfect contemplation which was to be the fulfilment of history.

This study of Joachim's conception of the *viri spirituales* and its influence in the following centuries must end with one of the eloquent passages in which he summoned men to this spiritual adventure:

Clear the eyes of the mind from all dusts of earth; leave the tumults of crowds and the clamour of words; follow the angel in spirit into the desert; ascend with the same angel into the great and high mountain; there you will behold high truths hidden from the beginning of time and from all generations. . . . For we, called in these latest times to follow the spirit rather than the letter, ought to obey, going from illumination to illumination, from the first heaven to the second, and from the second to the third, from the place of darkness into the light of the moon, that at last we may come out of the moonlight into the glory of the full Sun. (*Lib. Conc.*, ff. 5ᵛ–6ʳ.)

PART THREE

ANTICHRIST AND
LAST WORLD EMPEROR

———

I

THE END OF HISTORY

FROM its birth Christian thought held within it both a pessimistic and an optimistic expectation concerning history: its
end could be conceived either as a mounting crescendo of evil
or as the Millennium, a Messianic Age of Gold. The first view, based
on such passages as Matthew 24, was the more cautious, orthodox
position: the world was doomed to age and deterioration, iniquity
would increase and love would grow cold, the final tribulations would
come suddenly upon it, and immediately after, the Son of Man
would appear to judge the human race and make an end to history.
The hope in a future Age of Gold finds its origin in the concept of
the Jewish Messianic Age, when a Holy People was expected to
reign in Palestine in an era of peace, justice, and plenty, in which the
earth would flower in unheard-of abundance. The agent of this
triumph is at first expected to be an earthly king chosen by God, but
later the apocalyptic element takes over and the Messiah becomes
a superhuman figure of divine intervention.[1] Yet the Messianic Age
is conceived as within history, not beyond it. It is the very apotheosis
of history, embodying a lineal rather than a cyclical conception of
time. It is not a recurring phenomenon, a return to an Age of
Innocence, but a climax towards which the whole of history was
moving. The optimistic strand in the Christian expectation of history derives from this Jewish hope of a Messianic Age.

In the Christian thought of the early centuries three concepts were
developed which might be used to support the idea of a future age of
bliss. The first was that of the Millennium, based on the mysterious
words of Apocalypse 20: 1–3, in which Satan is bound for a thousand
years. The second was the concept of a Sabbath Age, symbolized in
the Seventh Day of Creation when God rested from His labours.[2]
Third, at least one early thinker, Montanus, believed that a
further illumination by the Holy Ghost was to be expected.[3] The

---

[1] N. Cohn, *The Pursuit of the Millennium* (London, 1957), pp. 1–6, sketches the ideas
of Jewish apocalyptic.

[2] Gen. 2: 2–3.   [3] Cohn, op. cit., pp. 8–9.

Millennium, as described in the Apocalypse, has the following characteristics: it will be ushered in by direct divine intervention in history; it will be a definite limited period of time, that is, within history and distinct from eternity; during it Satan will be bound, but not finally; it will be enjoyed by a privileged and elect group, not by a whole generation of the human race; it will end in a further and final struggle with evil, further divine intervention, and the winding-up of history. Only after this will the Holy Jerusalem descend: the new heaven and earth will be beyond history, not its fruition. An ambiguity soon developed in the interpretation of this programme. It could be seen as an earthly Age of Gold at the end of time. Thus among early Christians Papias (*c.* A.D. 60–130) expected an abundance of earthly fruits, while Justin Martyr believed that the Millennium would see a rebuilt, adorned, and enlarged Jerusalem in which the saints would dwell for a thousand years.[1] On the other hand, Millenarianism was attacked as a dangerous hope by Origen, who in the third century argued for a purely spiritual Millennium and attacked crude materialistic dreams;[2] while in the early fifth century St. Augustine was teaching that the Millennium had begun at the birth of Christ and had already been fully realized in the Church.[3]

Again, there is an ambiguity inherent in the concept of the Sabbath Age: as the Seventh Day of Creation, distinct from the Eighth Day of Eternity, it was expected to fall within time and history; yet if it were to be ushered in by direct divine intervention, still more if it were placed after the Last Judgement, it would seem to fall beyond history. This difficulty emerges clearly in Lactantius's exposition of the conception:

Et sicut Deus sex illos dies in tantis rebus fabricandis laboravit: ita et religio et veritas in his sex millibus annorum laboret necesse est, malitia praevalente ac dominante. Et rursus, quoniam perfectis operibus requievit die septimo, eumque benedixit, necesse est, ut in fine sexti millesimi anni malitia omnis aboleatur e terra, et regnet per annos mille iustitia; sitque tranquillitas, et requies a laboribus, quos mundus iamdiu perfert. (*PL* vi, cols. 782–3.)

Here the Millennium and the Sabbath seem to be united. Lactantius expects first a growing crisis of evil: 'ita iustitia rarescet, ita impietas

<hr />

[1] Cohn, op. cit., p. 10.   [2] Ibid., p. 13.
[3] St. Augustine, *De Civ. Dei*, xx, capp. vi–xvii (ed. J. Welldon, London, 1924, ii. 458–84).

et avaritia et cupiditas et libido crebrescent.'[1] The Roman Empire must decline into senectitude and Lactantius elaborates the theme of rising wars, plagues, and abominations, of an evil king, 'perditor generis humani', and of a false prophet. Finally, the righteous are besieged in a mountain by Antichrist. Then they call to God and He sends a liberator—'regem magnum de coelo'—to their aid. Shortly after this Christ Himself appears in judgement with an army of angels. He does final battle with Antichrist and destroys him, but immediately the Resurrection of the Dead and the Last Judgement follow, and the Sabbath Age is explicitly stated to take place afterwards:

Verum ille, cum deleverit iniustitiam, iudiciumque maximum fecerit, ac iustos qui a principio fuerunt ad vitam restauraverit, mille annis inter homines versabitur, eosque iustissimo imperio reget. . . . Tum qui erunt in corporibus vivi non morientur: sed per eosdem mille annos infinitam multitudinem generabunt, et erit soboles eorum sancta et Deo cara. . . . Sub idem tempus etiam princeps daemonum . . . catenis vincietur; et erit in custodia mille annis coelestis imperii, quo iustitia in orbe regnabit. . . . Post cuius adventum congregabuntur iusti ex omni terra; peractoque iudicio, civitas sancta constituetur in medio terre in qua ipse conditor Deus cum iustis dominantibus commoretur. (*PL* vi, cols. 808–9.)

Yet, although the Sabbath Age takes place after the Last Judgement and General Resurrection, it is clearly an Age of Gold of the earth, in which the stars will be brighter, the land will flower and fruit more abundantly, and so on. Although achieved through a supernatural agency, it is an age of Creation and it has a definite time-span. Again, the emphasis on a final flowering of the earth is well illustrated by the expectations of Commodianus in the fifth century.[2]

Yet again, St. Augustine, while ensuring that the pattern of the Seven Ages became the basic ground-plan of medieval historiography, was himself uncertain about the nature of the Sabbath Age. He recognized explicitly that the Seventh 'Day' of Creation was distinct from the Eighth 'Day': '. . . haec tamen septima erit sabbatum nostrum, cuius finis non erit vespera, sed dominicus dies velut octavus aeternus.'[3] Yet he placed the Sabbath after the Second Coming and Last Judgement and emphasized the contrast between

---

[1] Lactantius, *Divinarum Institutionum Liber Septimus*, PL vi, cols. 786–808, for the following summary of Lactantius' programme.
[2] Cohn, op. cit., pp. 12–13.
[3] St. Augustine, op. cit., xxii, cap. xxx (ed. cit. ii. 646).

the imperfect tranquillity of human existence and the supernatural state of blessedness then to be attained:

Sed hic sive illa communis sive nostra propria talis est pax, ut solacium miseriae sit potius quam beatitudinis gaudium. Ipsa quoque nostra iustitia . . . tanta est in hac vita, ut potius remissione peccatorum constet quam perfectione virtutum. . . . In illa vero pace finali . . . quoniam sanata inmortalitate adque incorruptione natura vitia non habebit . . . non opus erit ut ratio vitiis, quae nulla erunt, imperet; sed imperabit Deus homini, animus corpori, tantaque ibi erit oboediendi suavitas et facilitas, quanta vivendi regnandique felicitas. Et hoc illic in omnibus adque in singulis aeternum erit aeternumque esse certum erit; et ideo pax beatitudinis huius vel beatitudo paci cuius summum bonum erit. (*De Civ. Dei*, xix, cap. xxvii, ed. cit., ii. 446–7.)

The concept of a further illumination by the Holy Ghost is, in essence, the most unambiguous pointer towards an apotheosis of history, but even here the status of history remained unclear. Montanus connected the Third Age with the imminent Second Advent and believed that the New Jerusalem was about to descend on Phrygia, where it would become the habitation of the saints.[1] Tertullian also spoke of the new illumination in terms of the New Jerusalem descending from heaven.[1] Thus the full illumination in the Age of the Spirit would only be realized after the Second Advent. Yet it was not conceived as being after the winding up of history: the Third Age is an age of history and the element of *this* earth was emphasized by Irenaeus when he wrote: '. . . in the very creation in which they endured servitude, they should also reign. . . . It is fitting, therefore, that the creation itself, being restored to its primeval condition, should without qualification be under the dominion of the righteous' (translated Cohn, op. cit., p. 11).

Thus medieval thought started with an ambiguity about the 'end' of history which (in different terms) is with us still. Optimistic and pessimistic elements are closely juxtaposed, materialistic and spiritual dreams intermingle, human and divine agencies compete. It is, on the whole, the second in each of these pairs which represented the stronger, more orthodox Christian tradition and shaped early medieval thought. The Millennium was often interpreted as covering the whole period between the First and Second Advents rather than a special age to come. The Sabbath Age was safely relegated by such influential leaders as Isidore of Seville and Bede to a position

---

[1] Cohn, op. cit., p. 9.

almost, if not quite, beyond history. The full hope of a final and special flowering of human institutions within history could not be developed until all the possibilities of a third illumination in a third age of history had been grasped. Only the Trinitarian structure of history as elaborated by Joachim could give the necessary framework; only within this could the two concepts of Millennium and Sabbath Age clearly symbolize a crowning age of history, set in the future and therefore not yet attained, whilst unmistakably within the time-process, preceding the winding-up of history in the Second Advent and Last Judgement.

Yet to some extent, in the period preceding Joachim, the question of giving an optimistic or a pessimistic twist to history remained an open one, or at least it was possible to combine an expectation of a material Age of Gold with a recognition that evil would increase until slain by divine intervention. This came about because hope was fed from the classical stream which flowed into western medieval thought through the channel of Sibylline oracles. The cyclical Age of Gold, of course, was diametrically opposed to Joachim's Trinitarian view of history: it offered, not a final fruition of human life, attained after long pilgrimage through history, but the periodic return of an age of ease which did nothing to refine mankind and ended in retribution for evil. None the less, as a hope to counter the gloom of the pessimistic downward trend of history, it was seized on eagerly. In the development of the Sibylline prophecies we see the desire for a human triumph in history struggling with the conviction that only divine intervention can overcome the inherent evil in Man. From this conflict of ideas emerges the figure of a human saviour, a Last Emperor who achieves a partial triumph before the final onset of evil and the final supernatural intervention.

The oldest of these oracles known to medieval Europe was the Tiburtine which appeared in the mid-fourth century.[1] It proclaimed the expectation of a mighty Greek Emperor, Constans, of fine physique and radiant countenance, who would reign for 112 (or 129) years. This would be an age of peace and plenty in which a great triumph of Christianity would be consummated. The heathen would be converted or destroyed, the Jews converted, and finally Gog and Magog, with all their multitudes, would be annihilated. When his tasks were accomplished, the Emperor would go to Jerusalem, lay down his crown and robe on Golgotha and surrender his rule and

[1] E. Sackur, *Sibyllinische Texte*, pp. 177–87.

care of Christendom to God. Only then would Antichrist appear in the final fury of evil to reign in the Temple at Jerusalem. Here human agencies would be of no avail: the Archangel Michael would appear to destroy him and, immediately after, history would be wound up at the Second Coming. Thus the glory of a Last World Emperor was combined with an orthodox pessimistic conclusion to history and this became a popular programme of Last Things. The emphasis could be placed either on the Emperor's triumph or on his final surrender, and so the degree of optimism or pessimism varied at will.

The figure of the Last World Emperor was greatly popularized by a tract known as the *Pseudo-Methodius*, composed in the Eastern Empire towards the end of the seventh century and disseminated in the eighth at the court of Charlemagne in a Latin translation.[1] This emphasized a rising crisis of evil culminating in the conquest of Christendom by Ishmaelites. When evil was at its height, there would arise from slumber a 'rex Gregorum sive Romanorum in furore magna'. He would subdue the Ishmaelites and inaugurate a reign of felicity:

> Et tunc pacificabitur terra, que ab eis fuerat destituta et rediet unusquis-
> que in terram suam . . . et multiplicabuntur homines super terra, que
> desolata fuerat, sicut locustae in multitudinem. . . . et sedebit terra in
> pace et erit pax et tranquillitas magna super terra qualis nondum esset
> facta, sed neque fiet similis illa eo quod novissima est et in fine saecu-
> lorum. . . . In hac igitur pace sedebunt homines super terra cum gaudio
> et laetitia comedentes et sese potantes, nubentes et dantes ad nuptias . . .
> et non erit in corde eorum timor vel solicitudo. (Sackur, *Sibyllinische
> Texte*, pp. 90–1.)

Finally, however, this period of blessedness would be rudely shattered, the gates of the north would burst open and all the peoples shut in by Alexander sweep forth to burn and to kill. A period of devastation and terror would follow. At last the Emperor would go to Jerusalem to await the onslaught of Antichrist and when the son of perdition appeared he would perform the traditional surrender and give up the ghost: 'Et cum apparuerit filius perditionis, ascendit rex Romanorum sursum in Golgotha. . . . In quo loco . . . tollit rex coronam de capite suo et ponet eam super crucem et expandit manus suas in caelum et tradit regnum Christianorum Deo . . .' (ibid.,

---

[1] Sackur, op. cit., pp. 53 seq.

p. 93). Then Antichrist would reign until the true Christ appeared
in clouds of glory to destroy His last enemy and sit in judgement. As
in the Tiburtine oracle, we see here once again the desire for an
Age of Gold merging into the pessimistic conviction that against the
cosmic power of evil no human institution will stand. The reign of
peace is not the Millennium or the reign of the Saints with Christ.
Indeed, the description of eating and drinking, marrying and giving
in marriage suggests the carefree materialism of the human race
before the Flood, rather than the triumph of righteousness and the
beatitude of saints. So when Gog and Magog swoop down, only God
can save. In face of Antichrist the Emperor can only go to Golgotha
and surrender his office: the final cosmic battle and the final rule of
blessedness are Christ's alone.

In the tenth century this pattern of Last Things, including a
detailed life and career of Antichrist, was finally worked out by the
Burgundian Abbot Adso, whose *Libellus de ortu et tempore Antichristi*
became the standard book of reference on this subject.[1] Thus the
most widely accepted medieval tradition incorporated the hope of
a Last World Emperor, but gave him a strictly limited role and
allowed little hope of an earthly Millennium, for the Sabbath of
history was placed firmly beyond the final events of history. None
the less, the promise of a last emperor gave scope for racial aspirations
and there quickly developed, first, a French tradition of a Second
Charlemagne, and then a German tradition of a Last Emperor.

Norman Cohn has shown that the period of the First Crusade saw
a heightening of interest in prophecies of a Last World Emperor,
while the crusade itself brought the expectation to a sharp focus.[2]
Thus under the year 1095 Ekkehard of Aura recorded the circulation of a *fabulosum confictum* concerning the resurrection of Charlemagne, who would once more lead the Christian to triumph against
the infidel and bring in the era of peace and plenty.[3] On the other
side, shortly before the First Crusade, Benzo of Alba was addressing
a poem to the Emperor Henry IV in which he saw him as the heir to
all the great emperors of the past—Theodosius, Justinian, Charlemagne—and prophesied for him the programme of the Last World
Emperor: the conquest of Byzantium and the infidel and the establishment of a universal empire at Jerusalem which would endure till

[1] Sackur, op. cit., pp. 99–113.   [2] Op. cit., pp. 40 seq.
[3] Ekkehard v. Aura, *Hierosolymita*, ed. H. Hagenmayer (Tübingen, 1877), p. 120;
Chronicon Universale, MGHS vi. 215.

the end of the world.[1] In this case we may notice an unusually positive attitude to the conquest of evil, since Benzo actually expected Henry himself to meet and overcome Antichrist at Jerusalem. There are many traces of a hope in a Saviour–Emperor in the annals of the First Crusade, not least among the poor and illiterate. Thus Emmerich, Count of Leiningen, was able to impose himself as the Last World Emperor on the masses who swarmed through the Rhineland on the People's Crusade.[2]

By the twelfth century new versions of the Sibylline oracles, under the names of both the Tiburtine and Cumaean Sibyls, were giving wide currency to the expectation of a Last World Emperor, whether as *Carolus Redivivus* or *Rex Romanorum*. Without attempting to survey all the twelfth-century material on this theme, we may take Otto of Freising and Godfrey of Viterbo as examples of those who regarded the promises of the Sibyls seriously. Otto of Freising begins his *Gesta Friderici Imperatoris* with a prophetic prologue. Here he comments on a French oracle which, found in Sibylline books, clearly looks forward to the last great Emperor, designated in the mysterious letter C (Constans).[3] Godfrey of Viterbo, writing *c.* 1186/7, expects a 'Rex Romanorum nomine et animo Constans' to realize the full programme of the Last Emperor.[4] Sibylline predictions promise that he will be the King of Kings, destined to lead the crusade, crush the infidel, and proclaim his universal dominion from Jerusalem. He must rule gloriously for 122 years, but, like most other versions of the Sibylline oracles, this programme ends with the depositing of the imperial crown at Golgotha: 'Et cum cessaverit imperium Romanum, tunc revelabitur manifeste Antichristus.'

Thus, in spite of the warnings of orthodoxy, the dream of a last human glory under a Last World Emperor was one which men could not abandon. It was cherished not only by the crazy and fanatical, but by sober historians and politicians. Yet the hope was usually tempered by a final capitulation to pessimism. Joachim's exposition of the Trinitarian structure of history revived a conception which, so far as we can see, had been virtually neglected. This put the expectation for the future on an entirely new basis. Joachim, we

---

[1] Benzo, *Ad Heinricum IV Imperatorem Libri VII, MGHS* xi. 605, 617, 623, 668–9.

[2] Ekkehard, *Hierosolymita*, p. 126.

[3] Otto v. Freising and Rahewin, *Gesta Friderici Imperatoris*, ed. G. Waitz (Hanover, 1884), p. 8.

[4] *MGHS* xxii. 146–7. See also the *Vaticinium Sibillae* printed at the end of Godfrey of Viterbo's work, p. 376.

must reiterate, did not lose sight of orthodox pessimism: he saw that
no age of human history could achieve the perfection beyond history
and so he postulated a final recrudescence of evil. He himself quotes
the text in St. Matthew which prophesies a deteriorating situation at
the end. But he did believe that the major victory against Antichrist
was to be won before the apotheosis of history and he believed this
because he believed in a third 'act of God', to be manifested in
a third stage of spiritual illumination. Thus Joachim's age of bliss
is placed after Antichrist and before the Second Coming and Last
Judgement, precisely because it stems from a belief about the structure of the whole of history. Within this Trinitarian framework he
could give a new force to both the concepts of the Millennium and
the Sabbath Age. Joachim's teaching, therefore, forms a turning-
point in medieval thought about Last Things. In the following centuries the full force of his doctrine of the Third Age was rarely
grasped, but it profoundly influenced the form which prophetic
expectation took in the later Middle Ages and indeed right down to
the early seventeenth century.

In Joachim's writings the agencies for ushering in the third *status*
are naturally clearer than its institutions. On the new orders of
spiritual men we have many passages; on authority in Church and
State in the third *status*, almost nothing. The reason for this lies in
Joachim's double pattern of twos and threes. What we may call
'historical institutions' are seen in twos: *Populus Judaicus/Popu-
lus Gentilis*; Hebrew Kings/Roman Emperors; *Synagoga/Ecclesia
Romana*. Although in this last case a sequence of threes can be made
with *Ecclesia Spiritualis*, nowhere in Joachim's writings is there any
clear support for the idea that this is a new institution, superseding
the Roman Church. The third *status* is within history, yet not a third
set of institutions: rather, a new quality of living which transforms
former institutions. This is perhaps why Joachim is so unclear about
its place in the final generations of history. In the sense in which it
proceeds from both the first two *status*, the third *status* takes one of
its beginnings from as far off as the days of Elijah in the Old Testament.[1] Under the figure of the Seven Days Joachim sometimes
speaks of the Sixth and Seventh as running concurrently.[2] In his
calculations of generations he is not clear as to whether there will
be any measurable generations beyond the forty-second after Christ.[3]
The third *status* cannot be tied down to generations.

[1] *Lib. Conc.*, ff. 16ᵛ–17ʳ.   [2] *Expos.*, f. 9ʳ.   [3] *Lib. Conc.*, ff. 12ᵛ, 134ʳ.

Because, as Joachim made quite plain, he expected the Roman
Church to endure till the end of time, the concept of an Angelic
Pope does begin to emerge in his writings. We shall be examining
this is the next part. With regard to the secular authority, it is
notable that Joachim was not in the least tempted to follow the
tradition of a Last World Emperor. It is true that he entertained the
concept of a beneficent ruler as symbolized in David, under whom
the Jewish people reached a momentary climax of peace and beatitude. This he paralleled with the state of the Gentile People under
Constantine,[1] but when he expressed this in two diagrams of the
Liber Figurarum,[2] three points strike one at once: first, that this is
a pattern of twos in which there is no suggestion of a third great
empire of peace; second, that the 'movement' of both figures is
circular, dictating a descent from greatness into captivity for the
second time; third, that in fact David is here paralleled, not with
the Emperor Constantine, but with Pope Silvester. Thus David is
given a priestly character and the apotheosis is seen in terms of
Church rather than State.

Joachim shared the common view that the Roman Empire had
been ordained to keep the peoples of the world within their prescribed
limits. When it lusted after illicit conquest itself, it ceased to fulfil
this function and therefore judgement would fall upon it. It had
become the New Babylon, to be destroyed as proclaimed in the
Apocalypse. This would happen in the sixth age of the Church.
Joachim saw the Roman Empire as the River Euphrates which dries
up when the Sixth Angel pours his phial upon it; it would be overrun
by kings from the east and the fall of New Babylon would be final.[3]

Thus there was no place in Joachim's expectation for a Last World
Emperor. The great rulers of Jewish history—Joseph, David, Solomon, Zorobabel—were interpreted in a priestly rather than an
imperial sense, and when Joachim prophesied a future great *dux*
symbolized by Zorobabel, he was conceived as a religious leader.[4] At

[1] *Lib. Conc.*, ff. 17ᵛ, 38ᵛ–39ᵛ, 66ᵛ, 92ᵛ, 134ᵛ; *Expos.*, ff. 62ʳ–63ʳ.
[2] *Lib. Fig.* II, Pls. V, VI; cf on these figures, Reeves, Hirsch-Reich, *Studies*, pp. 186–91.
[3] *Expos.*, ff. 190ʳ–192ʳ; see also f. 134ʳ⁻ᵛ, where Joachim sees the disaster which
overwhelmed Frederick Barbarossa and his army as the beginning of this judgement:
'Dictum est autem quod siccande essent aque Eufratis, ut preparetur via Regibus ab
ortu solis: quod sine gemitu dicendum non est: initiatio quedam terribilis iam precessit:
super eo sc. quod nuper accidit: super inclyto illo exercitu Frederici magni et potentis-
simi Imperatoris et aliis exercitibus populi Christiani, qui transeuntes mare in infinita
multitudine, vix in paucis reliquiis pene sine effectu remearunt ad propria' (f. 134ᵛ).
[4] *Lib. Conc.*, ff. 55ᵛ–56ʳ.

the same time Joachim was not violently against the Roman Empire. In spite of denouncing it as the oppressor of the Church, he did not usually find in it the most extreme symbols of evil. It is true that in one of his interpretations the Dragon's fifth head is the Emperor Henry IV, but this is an alternative to *Mesemothus*;[1] the sixth is Saladin, and Joachim gives no grounds for the later popular belief that the seventh would be a Roman Emperor. On the contrary, the Antichrist who is to be the worst tyrant comes from outside as an infidel: he is the beast from the sea, whereas the beast from the land is a false pontiff.[2] Again, the very final tyrant of all, figured in Antiochus, *radix peccati*, arrives from beyond the Caucasus with the tribes of Gog and Magog.[3] Joachim, it seems, did not cast a Roman ruler for the worst role, but neither did he envisage a secular emperor in the third *status*. The agencies for converting the Jews and infidels and for bringing back the Greek Church to its true obedience were the orders of new spiritual men. Beyond this he only saw life in the liberty of the Spirit, until the final deterioration set in.

Joachim was quite specific in his writings that mankind could not pass even from the seventh age to the eighth without the sharpness of tribulation. This is the significance of Gog and Magog's appearing right at the end of time, as the tyrant Antiochus Epiphanes appeared right at the end of the Old Dispensation. But in spite of this final concession to pessimism, Joachim's central message remained his affirmation of a real—though incomplete—achievement of peace and beatitude within history. This was quickly vulgarized into dreams of world-wide empire. What distinguished these later dreams from the pre-Joachimist ones was that the decisive battle of history against the greatest Antichrist was to be won *before* the apotheosis of history took place. In this sense Joachimism exercised a decisive influence on political prophecy. Moreover, the concept of the *renovatio mundi* transformed merely political dreams into hopes of a genuine spiritual empire. *Renovatio* had, of course, a note of return to a golden past, but, transformed by the forward thrust of the Joachimist conception, it clearly expressed the expectation of a process which was not a renewal so much as a final consummation within history.

[1] *Expos.*, f. 196ᵛ, cf. *Lib. Fig.* II, Pl. XIV. See also *Expos.*, f. 10ʳ.
[2] *Expos.*, ff. 162ʳ seq., 166ᵛ.
[3] *Lib. Conc.*, f. 56ᵛ; *Expos.*, ff. 9ʳ, 10ᵛ–11ʳ, 212ᵛ seq.; *Lib. Fig.* II, Pl. VIII.

II

THE WORST ANTICHRIST AND THE
LAST EMPEROR

POLITICAL hopes and rivalries soon entered eschatological history. The temptation to allot the roles of worst tyrant and most glorious emperor was irresistible. Thus when, about the middle of the thirteenth century, Joachites began to realize the implications of Joachim's third *status*, they immediately sought to apply these politically. In contrast to the Abbot's own works, the pseudo-Joachimist writings are full of political prophecy. Already in the *Super Hieremiam* the writer begins to give shape to the third age beyond the catastrophe of Antichrist on which attention had so far been focused. Tribulation, of course, still looms large. The *ecclesia contemplativa* of the third *status* lies between the two tribulations of Antichrist and Gog at the close of history, or, to use the common metaphor, between the seventh head of the Dragon and its tail. To reach it (changing the metaphor) the hazardous crossing of the first gulf must be made: the ark must be carried over Jordan and the 'passio vel tribulatio futura ecclesie generalis' must be suffered.[1] The tribulation of Antichrist will be brief but 'ferox et dura'.[2] It will be threefold in form, for the Church must be afflicted by the *Imperium*, the infidel, and the heretic. The Ark of the Church will be almost submerged in the tempestuous seas of the Roman *Imperium* but finally it will ride triumphantly on the waves.[3] The cosmic evil which dominates the work is the German *Imperium*, for 'ab aquilone pandetur omne malum' and 'Alemanorum imperium semper extitit nostris durum, dirum et mirum'.[4] The work purports to be addressed by Joachim to the Emperor Henry VI, and to the Hohenstaufen line are applied the prophecies 'de radice colubri egredietur regulus et semen eius absorbens volucrem' and 'in terra tribulationis et augustie . . . leena et leo et ex eis vipera et regulus volans'.[5] The

---

[1] *Super Hier.*, f. 18ᵛ. [2] Ibid., f. 24ʳ.
[3] Ibid., ff. 2ʳ, 3ʳ, 19ᵛ, 38ʳ, 46ᵛ, 47ᵛ, 58ᵛ.
[4] Ibid., ff. 3ᵛ, 4ʳ, 12ʳ, 46ʳ.
[5] Ibid., ff. 14ʳ, 45ᵛ (cf. Isa. 14: 29); f. 46ʳ (cf. Isa. 30: 6).

prophecies are always handled so as to point forward to a worse portent, a supposedly 'future' Frederick II who is described as the 'leo saevus de aquilone', the 'regulus colubri', the Leviathan, the terrible *aquila*, the sixth or seventh head of the Dragon.[1] There will be a monstrous coalition between Roman *Imperium* and the Saracen and also between the heretic (the Patarin) and the infidel, i.e. the beast from the land and the beast from the sea; a pseudo-pope and a *rex impudicus facie* will occupy the seats of power.[2] Thus in the *Super Hieremiam* the wicked characters begin to take their places.

This work, as we have seen,[3] undoubtedly emanated from an Italian group. As one would expect, therefore, the chief character of the third *status* is not an emperor but a *pastor bonus*:[4] the figure of the Angelic Pope just begins to emerge. The future in the third *status* belongs chiefly to a rejuvenated Roman Church. At the sound of the seventh trumpet the mystery of labour will be completed, the partial life of action will pass away and the perfect life of contemplation will appear, resuscitating the sevenfold spiritual intelligence.[5] The Greek Church will return to the true fold, the Jews will be converted, and the day of liberty for the Church will dawn.[6] When the third *status* dawns—'quem et in ianuis iam tenemus'[7]—the only authority remaining will be the *ecclesia contemplantium*:

Videsne lector quod sicut Romanum imperium fuit erectio ecclesie, sic et modo diebus istis novissimis sit iactura. Unde Ezechiel: Finis venit: venit finis. Finis utique senescentis ecclesie clericorum et finis superbientis similiter novorum imperii caldeorum. Neque proinde finis mundi: quia relinquetur adhuc sabbatismus populo Dei: ut ecclesia contemplantium habitet in fiducie tabernaculis et requie opulenta.

(Super Hier., f. 58ᵛ.)

It is largely from the similarity of their political outlook and use of Biblical imagery to express this that we can group the other pseudo-Joachimist works which follow within the next two decades with the *Super Hieremiam* as forming the Italian school of Joachimism. But the *Vaticinium Sibillae Erithreae*, the *De Oneribus*, and the *Super Esaiam* represent successive stages in the development of this viewpoint. The pseudo-Joachimist gloss on the oracle of the Erithrean Sibyl is now dated to the period before the death of Frederick II.

---

[1] *Super Hier.*, ff. 11ᵛ, 14ʳ, 15ᵛ, 18ᵛ, 45ᵛ–46ᵛ, 58ᵛ, 62ʳ
[2] Ibid., ff. 10ʳ, 18ᵛ, 20ᵛ, 45ᵛ. [3] *Supra*, pp. 151–6.
[4] *Super Hier.*, f. 53ʳ. [5] Ibid., f. 23ʳ.
[6] Ibid., ff. 57ᵛ–58ᵛ. [7] Ibid., f. 35ʳ.

That event shook the faith of the prophet-managers, and there is little doubt that it had really caught out the Italian Joachites. When Salimbene was at Hyères, it will be recalled, the focus of conversation was Joachim's prophecies concerning the Emperor Frederick.[1] When the Hohenstaufen died in his bed without more ado, Salimbene was sadly shaken: 'Sed postquam mortuus est Fridericus, qui imperator iam fuit, et annus MCCLX est elapsus, dimisi totaliter istam doctrinam et dispono non credere nisi que videro.'[2] But in fact neither Salimbene nor others could give up their Joachimism. They could not believe that the Hohenstaufen had done his worst: he must either be resurrected or be reborn in one of his brood. The *Vaticinium Sibillae Erithreae* had already anticipated the rumour: 'Oculos eius morte claudet abscondita, supervivetque; sonabit et in populos "Vivit, non vivit".'[3]

In the *De Oneribus* this suspicion of evil yet to come was already crystallized into the prophecy of a Third Frederick. Since this was probably written before 1260, it is curious that, while others of the Hohenstaufen brood yet survived, the name of Frederick should already have established itself. But there is no doubt that the Hohenstaufen house was still the cosmic centre of evil, the *malleus ecclesie*. Once again the symbols of the adder, the lion, the viper, and the flying serpent were applied to it.[4] The *Super Esaiam*, written about a decade later, represented another shift in time. The year 1260 was now passed and it was necessary, by calculating the generations from the Passion instead of the Nativity, to shift the crucial date on to 1290. The German Emperors were still portrayed as the source of all evil, of which a new manifestation was expected. But this was not named the Third Frederick. At one point Frederick II is openly designated the seventh head of the Dragon,[5] but there is constant reference to his evil progeny and even to a nameless eighth head.[6] It is probable that Manfred was the object of this and other enigmatic prophecies and that the work was written on the eve of his final struggle with Charles of Anjou. The Third Frederick as the worst tyrant only reappeared when the last of the direct Hohenstaufen brood had been crushed.

[1] *Supra*, p. 166.   [2] Salimbene, pp. 302–3.
[3] *NA* xv. 168.
[4] *De Oneribus*, ff. 38ᵛ, 39ʳ, 39ᵛ, 40ᵛ, 41ʳ, 42ʳ, 42ᵛ, 43ʳ, 43ᵛ, 44ʳ.
[5] *Super Esaiam*, f. 59ʳ. See also some versions of the dragon-figure in the *Praemissiones* preceding the *Super Esaiam*.
[6] Ibid., ff. 3ʳ, 15ʳ, 19ʳ, 20ʳ, 27ʳ, 29ᵛ, 35ʳ, 37ʳ, 38ʳ, 39ᵛ, 40ᵛ, 42ᵛ, 46ᵛ, 47ʳ, 47ᵛ, 49ᵛ, 59ʳ.

It is significant that, apart from the isolated example of Gebenon,[1] some of the first rumours of Joachimism to reach Germany were political. The prophecy which Albert of Stade recorded in 1250 was taken from the *Super Hieremiam* and obviously embodied the Italian viewpoint, but it was cleverly chosen from the theme of Imperial triumph before ultimate defeat: 'Superabitur Francus, capietur pontifex summus, praevalebit imperans Alemannus.'[2] The question of how the *Super Hieremiam* reached Germany is a puzzling one. Cardinal John of Porto, the carrier of certain prophetic verses, has been suggested.[3] More likely it was one of the Franciscan preachers, such as Berthold of Ratisbon, who met both John of Parma and Salimbene in 1249, or even perhaps Salimbene's Joachite acquaintance, Rudolf of Saxony.[4] Even more obscure are the beginnings of what we may call German political Joachimism. It was to be expected that a German counterblast to Italian propaganda would be forthcoming but the initial problem is the extent to which the Emperor Frederick II himself had encouraged a kind of Imperial Joachimism for purposes of propaganda.

There is no doubt about the heightened language used by Frederick and his servants to describe his role in history. For us the most significant point is the use of Biblical symbolism to express this. Frederick hailed his own birth-place, Jesi, as a second Bethlehem and dared to adapt the words of the prophet Micah: 'Unde tu, Bethleem, civitas Marchie non minima, es in generis nostri principibus. Ex te enim dux exiit, Romani princeps imperii qui populum tuum reget . . .'[5] In a letter to the city of Worms (1241) he claimed that God has raised up again in him the spirit of Elijah—and, since one of the key texts for Joachites was 'Helias cum veniet restituet omnia', the eschatological overtones here would not be lost.[6] Frederick's servants and admirers carried further the application of Messianic texts to the Emperor. Pier della Vigna identified him as

[1] *Supra*, p. 39.
[2] Cf. *Super Hier.*, f. 60ᵛ: 'Superatur Francus: capitur summus pontifex: dominabit alemanus Imperator.'
[3] See Bloomfield, Reeves, *Speculum* xxix. 790–1, for a discussion of this point.
[4] Ibid., p. 791; cf. Salimbene, pp. 559–63.
[5] J. Huillard-Bréholles, *Historia Diplomatica Friderici Secundi* (Paris, 1857), v (i). 378; cf. Mic. 5: 2.
[6] Ibid., v (ii) (1859), p. 1131; cf. Matt. 17: 11. Elijah appears prominently at the end of history in *Lib. Fig.* II, Pls. II, IV, VII, X. In Joachim's writings we find innumerable references; see especially *Lib. Conc.*, ff. 32ᵛ, 97 seq.; *Expos.*, f. 10ᵛ, 137ʳ⁻ᵛ,140ʳ, 146 seq., 166ᵛ; *Quat. Evang.*, pp. 6, 24 seq., 95 seq., 141 seq., 191 seq.

the *Aquila grandis* of Ezekiel 17: 3, again a Messianic text of significance to Joachim,[1] and applied to him the prophecy of Jeremiah:
'Replebo te hominibus quasi botro.'[2] The application of Biblical
prophecy was extended to Pier himself. Thus the notary Nicholas de
Rocca audaciously made him the corner-stone upon which the new
Church would be founded. The first Peter denied his master three
times, but the new Peter would not do it once.[3] 'O felix vinea',
Nicholas exclaims, '. . . Haec est vinea cujus radices grandis aquila in
terra negociationis de Libano . . . transplantavit.'[4] Other friends,
playing on the same theme, made the Emperor address to him the
words of Christ: 'Petre, amas me, rege oves meas', and pictured his
relationship to Frederick as that of Peter to Christ at the Last
Supper.[5] Huillard-Bréholles asked himself if all this could be taken
seriously and decided that it probably should be. That is to say,
whatever Frederick himself thought, there were those around him
who found this Messianic language really expressed their expectation. As we have already argued,[6] this bold adaptation of Biblical
prophecy and symbol betrays a Joachimist current of influence. It
implies a sequence of threes, making possible the claim that as
events and persons in the Old Testament foreshadowed those in the
New, so both would be paralleled by their counterparts in the new
age. No doubt the Joachimist basis of this mode of thinking was
generally unrealized, but the emotional overtones of these writings,
propagandist though they may be, were eschatological. To his supporters Frederick was the ultimate *renovator mundi* and in him the
Biblical promises were finally fulfilled.

Whether or not stimulated by Imperial propaganda, there is clear
evidence of a group in Swabia committed to the expectation of
a *renovatio mundi* which would be brought in by the Hohenstaufen.
In 1248 Albert of Stade recorded the appearance of an abominable
sect in Swabia teaching that the pope was heretical and all ecclesiastical authority void.[7] Between 1248 and 1250 one of its leaders, Frater

[1] J. Huillard-Bréholles, *Vie et Corréspondance de Pierre de la Vigne* (Paris, 1865),
pp. 222, 425. On Joachim's use of Ezekiel's eagles see Reeves, *Arbores*, pp. 128, 133.
[2] Huillard-Bréholles, *Vie*, p. 425; cf. Jer. 51: 14.
[3] Huillard-Bréholles, *Vie*, pp. 290–1. Nicholas also calls him *novus legifer Moyses* and
alter Joseph.
[4] Ibid., p. 291; cf. Ezek. 17: 3, 4. He uses the same text as Pier.
[5] Huillard-Bréholles, *Vie*, pp. 431, 433.
[6] *Supra*, pp. 177, 210. For a discussion of the influence of Joachimism on Frederick
II see E. Kantorowicz, *Frederick the Second, 1194–1250*, tr. E. Lorimer (New York,
1931), pp. 395–6, 506–7.   [7] *MGHS* xvi. 371.

Arnold the Dominican, published his manifesto, *De Correctione Ecclesiae*, addressed to Frederick II.[1] He believed that the sixth age now approaching had been given to the Church for correction and that afterwards would come the seventh of peace, justice, and renovation. The agencies to effect this spiritual revolution were the Dominican brethren the Emperor himself, and his son Conrad. Fr. Arnold ended with a direct appeal to Frederick: 'Unde Karissimi vestram in domino obsecro Karitatem, ut omnem timorem abicientes restauracioni uniformiter studeamus' (op. cit., p. 18). It is clear that the writer's entire hope was focused on the belief that after present tribulation and the death of Antichrist there would be peace in the Church. Here for the first time we meet what is really Joachim's third *status* recast in political terms. The need was felt to seek an alternative agent to the papacy in the work of renewal and it was naturally to the second great luminary of the world that the German turned. So the two streams—of Joachimism and of the ancient World Emperor tradition—finally met in this political programme to bring in the seventh age of renewal. It will be observed at once that Joachim's vision of a spiritual revolution had made a significant difference to the image of the great World Emperor, in that he was now seen as the just chastiser and renewer of a depraved Church. For the future the portrait of the Last Emperor will often include this feature of his position as the agent of spiritual renewal and he will be called the *Rex pudicus facie* as a counterblast to the *Rex impudicus facie* of the opposite camp.[2]

The next stage is seen in a prophecy which was recorded in the Minorite Chronicle of Erfurt in 1268 under the name of Joachim.[3] It was said to have been sent into Germany by the Cardinal Bishop of Porto, but all we can safely say is that it must have emanated from a Ghibelline source.[4] It begins by 'foretelling' the end of Manfred and Conradin, and then focuses the hope for the future on a new Third Frederick who was almost certainly Frederick, Landgrave of Thuringia, a grandson of Frederick II:

Regnabit Menfridus bastardus a flatu mezani usque ad finem regni. Contra quem veniet rex ultramontanus, leo Francie propter audaciam et severitatem, qui debellabit eum et auferet dyadema de capite suo. Tunc

[1] Ed. E. Winkelmann (Berlin, 1865).
[2] See Dan. 8: 23 for the source of the *Rex impudicus facie*. The positive version is a bold counter-stroke.   [3] *MGHS* xxiv. 207.
[4] For a discussion of this question see Bloomfield, Reeves, *Speculum* xxix. 790.

surget filius aquile, et in volatu suo debilitabitur leo, et XXI die post conflictum filius aquile incidet in os leonis et post hec leo modico tempore regnabit. Orietur enim ramus de radice regni Fridericus nomine orientalis, qui debellabit leonem et ad nichilum rediget, ita ut memoria sua non sit amplius super terram. Cuius potencie brachia extendentur usque ad finem mundi. Ipse enim imperans imperabit, et sub eo summus pontifex capietur. Post hec Theutonici et Hyspani confederabuntur et regnum Francie redigent in nichilum. (*MGHS* xxiv. 207.)

In the period which saw the downfall of the Hohenstaufen prophetic oracles circulated briskly. A second Ghibelline prophecy attributed to Joachim had a wide distribution.[1] Its opening lines reveal an anti-French bias: 'Gallorum levitas Germanos justificabit, Et tribus adiunctis consurget aquila grandis'; while the Imperial triumph is expressed thus: 'Papa cito moritur, Caesar regnabit ubique.' Two sides in the prophetic contest now emerge clearly, for the next verse, dated by Holder-Egger as after 1268, envisages an anti-Hohenstaufen champion who will destroy Frederick's brood and support the papacy in bringing all nations into one fold:[2]

> Rex novus adveniet totum ruiturus in orbem . . .
> Hic Siculos pravamque tribum sevi Frederici
> Conteret, ulterius nec sibi nomen erit.
> Cuncta reformabit que trux Fredericus et eius
> Subvertit soboles seva suusque sequax.
> Hic sub Apostolico Romanos ponet in artum
> Vim dantes Rome sic patientur onus.
> Post trahet ad Christum Machometi Marte sequaces:
> Sic et ovile unum, pastor et unus erit.
>
> (*NA* xxx. 383–4.)

Thus it would seem to have been the drama of the Hohenstaufen house and the political passions which it engendered that first produced a political Joachimism in two opposed versions and juxtaposed on the stage of history the Antichrist–tyrant and the Saviour–Emperor. Whichever side they support these prophecies all point

[1] Ed. Holder-Egger, *NA* xxxiii. 125–6, from MS. Vat., Lat. 3822, f. 6ᵛ. Other manuscript references are: Vat., Lat. 3816, f. 62ʳ; Ottobon. 1106, f. 24ʳ; Reg. Lat. 132, f. 201ᵛ. A slightly different prose version occurs in MS. Yale, Univ. Lib., T. E. Marston 225, f. 41ʳ. It is quoted in the following works: B. Cotton, *Historia Anglicana*, RS, p. 239; Walter of Coventry, *Memoriale*, RS, i. 26; Appendix to Peter of Langtoft, *Chronicle*, RS, ii. 450; *Annales Monastici*, RS, iv. 514; *Last Age of the Church*, ed. J. Todd Dublin, 1840), p. xxxiii. For sixteenth-century reference to this verse see *infra*, p. 371.
[2] Holder-Egger, *NA* xxx. 380–4. It is found in MSS. Vat., Lat. 3822, f. 100ᵛ; Florence, Bibl. Ricc., 688, f. cxiiʳ.

to a sharp crisis leading to a decisive and final political triumph and a period of peace beyond tribulation which embodies at least an echo of Joachim's third *status*.

We catch the mood of disillusionment which overcame the German Imperialists after the Hohenstaufen had disappeared in the writings of Alexander von Roes. In the *Notitia Seculi*, written in 1288, he took his structure of history from that curious work, *De Semine Scripturarum*, so often attributed to Joachim but in fact emanating from a different quarter.[1] From this Alexander adopted the calculation that the end of the world would come in 1500, i.e. 6,000 years from the foundation of the world when the six 'Days' of Creation had been completed. Thus the Sabbath Age for Alexander was beyond history and it is clear that he had not been influenced by Joachim's hope of the third *status*. None the less, from the *De Semine* he derived a more limited and transitory hope in a revival of the Roman *Imperium* and a period of peace and prosperity, when the Holy Land would be recovered and men would enjoy the riches of this world until the inevitable deterioration set in and the destruction of the Roman *Imperium* heralded the onset of Antichrist. He expected, therefore, an immediate change for the better in the fortunes of the Empire which had sunk so low in the contest with the *Sacerdotium*.

To support his hope Alexander turned, in the *De Translatione Imperii*, written *c.* 1281, to the prophecies.[2] As far as the Hohenstaufen tradition goes, he seems to know only the prophecy against them and gives us the legend of the Third Frederick as the worst tyrant in its definitive form. There has, he says, for a long time been circulating in Germany a prophecy which runs: 'De huius Frederici germine radix peccatrix erumpet Fredericus nomine, qui clerum in Germania et etiam ipsam Romanam ecclesiam valde humiliabit et tribulabit vehementer' (op. cit., p. 31). This forces him to turn in quite a different direction for the promise of a glorious ruler. It is the old Charlemagne legend which he revives: 'Dicunt praeterea aliud ibidem esse vulgare propheticum, quod de Karlingis, id est de stirpe regis Karoli et de domo regum Francie, imperator suscitabitur Karolus nomine, qui erit princeps et monarcha totius Europe et

---

[1] *Notitia Seculi*, MGH, *Staatsschriften des Späteren Mittelalters*, i (Stuttgart, 1958), pp. 149–71. On *De Semine Scripturarum* see *supra*, p. 58.

[2] Ed. H. Grundmann, *Alexander v. Roes, De translatione Imperii u. Jordanus v. Osnabrück, De Prerogativa Romani Imperii* (Leipzig, 1930).

reformabit ecclesiam et imperium sed post illum nunquam alius imperabit' (op. cit., p. 30). This, of course, must be coupled with his claim that Charles was a Teuton and that the Empire had been translated to the German monarchy. Thus in Alexander von Roes's works we encounter for the first time the Third Frederick as tyrant and the Second Charlemagne as saviour placed in a dramatic juxtaposition in which we shall meet them many times. The agents both of *tribulatio* and of *renovatio* are imperial and, indeed, as we shall see, the line between the evil oppressor and the just chastiser is not very clear-cut. We may observe also the use of the symbol of a new branch springing from an old root or stem for both the good and bad rulers. The one probably carries an echo of the 'rod out of the stem of Jesse' and the other of the evil tree of Antiochus Epiphanes.[1]

It is strange that twice within a century the University of Paris should have been disturbed by the speculations of Joachites. In 1297 the mysterious Arnold of Villanova wrote his *De Tempore Adventus Antichristi* and in 1300 roused an academic storm in Paris over his views.[2] Unlike Gerard of Borgo San Donnino he was not immediately concerned so much with the advent of the third *status* as with the imminence of the last and worst Antichrist which should precede it. Nevertheless, it was the Joachimist context of his message which aroused the opposition, for instead of the old convention of Antichrist, he proclaimed a Joachimist structure of history with the Age of the Spirit beyond the crisis of evil:

Quod autem post tempus Antichristi non sit seculum uno centenario duraturum, ex predictis patet acceptis . . . Et beatus qui expectat et pervenit ad MCCCXXXV annum . . . Ideo vero beatus dicitur, qui pertinget illud tempus . . . quia veniet ad tempus universalis tranquillitatis et pacis ecclesie, in quo per universum orbem cognoscetur veritas et adorabitur Christus et 'erit unus pastor et unum ovile'. Hoc est tempus apertionis septimi sigilli . . . 'Et cum aperuisset septimum factum est silentium in celo', id est, pax et tranquillitas in ecclesia, 'quasi dimidia hora'. Per quod expresse testatur, quod modicum in illa tranquillitate

---

[1] See Isa. 11: 1 and 1 Macc. 1: 10. The *radix peccatrix* was first applied to the Hohenstaufen in the *Super Esaiam*, ff. 19ʳ, 27ʳ.

[2] On Arnold of Villanova, see H. Finke, *Aus den Tagen*, ii. 210 seq., cxvii–ccxi; P. Diepgen, *Arnald v. Villanova als Politiker u. Laientheologe* (Berlin and Leipzig, 1909); Douie, *Fraticelli*, pp. 32–5; Lambert, *Franciscan Poverty*, pp. 179–80; Pou y Marti, *Visionarios*, pp. 36 seq.; F. Pelster, 'Die Quaestio Heinrichs v. Harclay ueber die Zweite Ankunft Christi u. die Erwartung des Baldigen Weltendes zu Anfang des XIV. Jahrhunderts', in *Archivio italiano per la storia della pietà*, i. 33–5; R. Manselli, *La Religiosità d'Arnaldo da Villanova* (Rome, 1951).

permanebit ecclesia, ut quasi dimidio anno aut medio centenario vel
circiter iuxta principia huius considerationis predicta. Et cum tunc nulla
tribulatio sit ventura quantum ad seculum presens, necesse est ut veniat
tribulatio repentina generalis iudicii. (Finke, *Aus den Tagen*, p. cxxxiii.)

Here the Joachimist order of events is unmistakable: first, the crisis
of wickedness under Antichrist, then the Sabbath of the world
under the opening of the Seventh Seal, and finally the 'tribulatio
repentina' of the Last Judgement. In a later passage he enlarges on
this time of peace which he calls the 'tempus plenitudinis gentium':

. . . quod illud tempus in quo plenitudo gentium ingredietur ecclesiam,
est tempus centenarii quarti decimi a Christi nativitate. Quod centenarium
inchoabit quando finietur computatio presentis anni, quo ecclesia numerat
annos domini mille trecentos, quod idcirco fuit appositum, quoniam
Erithea prenuntiat evidenter quod infra sequens centenarium dissipabitur
secta Machometi non solum in membris, set in suo capite. Prenuntiat
etiam quod in eo unus erit pastor et unum ovile in orbe toto. Cum
igitur iam nobis emergat tempus plenitudinis gentium in quo . . . tenebit
secure populus fidelis possessionem terrene Jerusalem, patet quod . . .
nunc tamen . . . confidenter accingi possunt non solum ad adquirendam
illius possessionem . . . set insuper ad secure amodo vel pacifice retinen-
dam. (Ibid., p. cli.)

The reaction of the academics at Paris and also at Oxford was
sharp. It was a conflict between mystics, for whom 'die Welt der
Konkordanzen, der Zahlensymbolik, der apokalyptischen Schrift-
deutung noch eine Welt der vollen Wirklichkeit ist', and scholastics
'die nicht nur metaphysische, sondern auch exegetische und histo-
rische Kritik mehr und mehr ansübt'.[1] According to Fr. Pelster,
the protagonist of the scholastics against Arnold was Henry of
Harclay, Chancellor of Oxford University, whilst in a middle position between the two sides stood the Dominican, John Quidort or
John of Paris. John Quidort's treatise on Antichrist shows a genuine
interest in the subject but very different from Arnold's passionate
concern; he cites Joachimist prophecies, however, with a sense of
urgency. On the scholastic side a Paris master, Peter du Croc of
Auvergne, wrote four *quaestiones* on the coming of Antichrist in
which he strenuously opposed all speculation and averred that
Antichrist had already appeared in mystical form.[2] Guido de
Terrena, a Carmelite of Calabria, also wrote against Arnold,[3] and
the issue was still a live one when in 1310 Nicholas of Lyra devoted

[1] Pelster, op. cit., p. 28.   [2] Ibid., pp. 41-3.   [3] Ibid., p. 45.

the first of three *Quodlibeta* to the question: 'Utrum possimus scire an Antichristus sit natus vel non natus adhuc.'[1] Significantly, it was Joachim rather than Arnold whom he attacked for his erring views on Antichrist.

Henry of Harclay spoke for Oxford. His *Quaestio*—'Utrum Astrologi vel Quicumque Calculatores possint probare Secundum Adventum Christi'—was a weighty and serious treatment of a subject which had suddenly become important.[2] He, too was as much concerned with Joachim as with Arnold of Villanova, and it is evident that his study of the Joachimist writings, both genuine and spurious, had been careful and interested. He condemned Arnold's calculations on the coming of Antichrist out of hand, accusing him of Jewish tendencies and laying down categorically: 'Ista opinio est heretica, sicut et omnis alia, que conatur asserere certum tempus adventus Christi.'[3] In passing he remarked sardonically: 'Ego credo quod si iste magister viveret in anno predicto 1356 ab incarnacione et videret quod istud non esset impletum, ipse adhuc fingeret novam calculacionem annorum.'[4] Turning then to Joachim he gave a careful analysis of the method of calculating the Last Things used supposedly by Joachim in the *De semine Scripturarum*, and then of the calculations according to the concords of generations in Joachim's genuine *Liber Concordie*.[5] He also quoted the *Expositio in Apocalypsim* on the opening of the Seven Seals and the *Psalterium decem chordarum*, as well as the pseudo-Joachimist *De Oneribus Prophetarum*.[6] His treatment of Joachim shows much more respect than for Arnold. This respect is based on two things: first, his belief that Joachim had truly foretold the coming of the two Mendicant Orders; second, the very sound observation that Joachim was much more cautious in his prognostications than his disciples:

Verum est autem quod idem Joachim verum prophetavit de multis sicud de duobus ordinibus post tempus suum venientibus, de Frederico imperatore et eius deposicione et de multis aliis. Tamen de fine mundi omnino erravit, si certum tempus determinare voluit. Nescio tamen si voluit vel non voluit. Nam alibi in libro *De Psalterio decacordo* versus finem libri secundi dicit expresse tempus esse incertum secundi adventus Domini ad iudicium . . . Item inferius in eodem libro, [dicit] loquendo de istis generacionibus in quibus finietur mundus, sic: 'Utrum autem generaciones iste future sint dierum an mensium an annorum, quot annos et

[1] Pelster, op. cit., p. 44   [2] Ibid., pp. 53–82.   [3] Ibid., p. 59.
[4] Ibid., p. 68.   [5] Ibid., pp. 73–4.   [6] Ibid., pp. 75–6.

menses per singulas scient illi qui ibi futuri sunt.' Ecce ergo quod non determinat aliquod tempus certum finis illarum generacionum. (Pelster, op. cit., pp. 75–6.)

Here, as with some other opponents of Joachim, we get the impression of someone who, in spite of his disapproval, has read the Joachimist literature eagerly and has not been altogether impervious to its influence.

The row in Paris was an academic one and not political. No mention appears to have been made of speculation about a Last World Emperor nor of the *renovatio mundi*. Yet Arnold himself was deeply concerned with the practical consequences of his speculations. He constantly pressed on Boniface VIII the imminence of crisis and in 1304 summoned Benedict XI to prepare the Church for the 'persecutio maxima Antichristi' and to support those ordained 'ad renovandum evangelice veritatis perfectionem', that is, the Spiritual Franciscans.[1] Although Antichrist seemed to dominate his thoughts, *renovatio* was a vital part of his eschatological programme. When the papacy failed to respond to his pleas, he turned to a secular agent, Frederick of Aragon, who became King of Trinacria or Sicily. There was already close friendship between them, and Arnold dreamed that Frederick might be the divine instrument of the *renovatio mundi*.[2] Church and State must be cleansed, the Saracens converted, and all men led into the true evangelical life. With passion Arnold poured out his dream to the King: God would raise up an Angelic Pope who, together with the King, would bring the whole world into one fold. Frederick was not unmoved. Perhaps of all the candidates for the role of Last World Emperor he took his religious vocation most seriously. Thus at the court of Sicily in the early fourteenth century we witness a unique attempt to realize on the plane of politics the eschatological dream of a *renovatio mundi*.

Others observed, too, that Frederick of Trinacria was the Third Frederick and descended from the Hohenstaufen. He caught the

---

[1] Finke, op. cit., pp. clxxvii–cxcv.

[2] See Manselli, op. cit., pp. 20–3, for Arnold's plan of reform. Manselli appears to regard Joachimist influence on Arnold's thought as slight, although Arnold certainly knew the three main works of Joachim as well as some pseudo-Joachimist ones. In my view Arnold's Joachimism consisted in the conjunction of the proclamation of Antichrist and the call to *renovatio*. His plan of reform has an eschatological setting. It is true that in some statements he appears to see reform as purification in preparation for Antichrist, but the passages quoted from the *De Tempore Adventus Antichristi* seem to me to postulate quite unequivocally a time of beatitude *after* Antichrist.

prophetic imagination of the Fraticelli, many of whom he sheltered. Similarly, Fra Dolcino expected him to fulfil the programme of the Apostolic Brethren.[1] A Catalan chronicle of this period hailed him as the Third Frederick and expected him to become 'senyor del imperi e de la major part del món'.[2]

It was chiefly the political dreamers, the men with a programme to further, an axe to grind, who turned to the emperor prophecies. A prince of such political prophets was Cola di Rienzo. The eloquent series of his letters published by Burdach[3] shows that for him the focus of expectation was not so much the tribulation of Antichrist as the new outpouring of the Holy Spirit. In this he was deeply a Joachite. Again and again he claimed to be inspired and led by the Spirit, 'per quem dirigimur et fovemur'.[4] Again and again in glowing words he expressed his expectation of the *renovatio* to come, not, as he disclaimed, that 'alius novus Spiritus Sanctus' would come: 'sed amplificacionem Spiritus Sancti, super omnem eciam carnem venire promissam, illuminaturam et renovaturam orbis faciem universam . . . Nam flante Spiritu Sancto suo, omnia ubilibet' simulachra corruent, fides christiana exaltabitur "et fiet ovile unum . . . eciam pastor unus" ' (op. cit., pp. 313–14). The source of his Joachimism can be traced to the Fraticelli group at Majella with whom he sojourned in hiding for some time.[5] Their leader, a hermit Angelus de Monte, revealed to him the secrets of the universal reformation which he must expect and seek to bring in. That Rienzo's mentors were by origin Spiritual Franciscans is clear from the prominence he gave to St. Francis. At Majella, no doubt, he found the pseudo-Joachimist *Oraculum Cyrilli*, the enigmatic words of which he studied and in his letter to the Archbishop of Prague applied to himself.[6] When accused of vain imaginings, he defended his belief in his prophets warmly: 'nam totum Testamentum vetus et novum, totumque Scripturarum corpus Ecclesie plenum iacet, quod per appariciones, visiones et sompnia multis multa Dominus revelavit' (op. cit., p. 211).

Rienzo's Age of the Spirit was, however, as political a form of Joachimism as we shall meet anywhere. Primarily it was the City of

[1] *Supra*, pp. 245–6.

[2] Ed. K. Lanz, *Chronik des edlen En Ramon Muntaner* (Stuttgart, 1844), p. 331.

[3] Burdach, *Vom Mittelalter* ii, Pt. iii.   [4] Ibid., p. 55.

[5] Burdach, *Vom Mittelalter* ii, Pt. v, pp. 292 seq.; Muratori, *Antiquitates Italicae Medii Aevi* . . ., iii (Milan, 1740), col. 509.

[6] Burdach, *Vom Mittelalter* ii, Pt. iii, p. 267.

Rome which, he believed, must arise to new life and, adorned as a bride, receive again its spouse, the Roman pontiff. Rienzo saw himself as called 'ad reformacionem et renovacionem iusticie, libertatis et securitatis statusque pacifici prefate Romane Urbis ac tocius provincie'. Rome would be restored to her pristine glory, 'ut pacis gustata dulcedini floreat per gratiam Spiritus Sancti melius quam unquam floruit inter ceteras mundi partes'.[1] The central agent of this great revival was always in Rienzo's mind the *pastor angelicus*, but after his retreat into the Appennines and apparently under the influence of his hermit prophet, he addressed himself to the Emperor Charles IV to carry out the great work of emancipating Rome and bringing in the *reformacio*. His two letters to Charles[2] reveal the type of political programme he designed for his emperor–saviour. Within a year and a half he expected events to begin to move and by 1357 'erit una fides, videlicet fides Christi apud sarracenos . . . Item dixit, dominum imperatorem electum una cum summo pontifice futuro feliciter prosperari, si modo observent fideliter viam Dei' (op. cit., p. 197). If Charles would only believe the prophets and start his campaign in Italy, he would receive prosperity and empire. Rienzo promised him the fulfilment of the oracle of Cyril, 'Grandis aquila, nigra pennis'.[3] Italy would be conquered in seven months and Rome, the new Jerusalem, would become the head of the world. This was an Italian dream for a German Emperor, since he was envisaged as the ally rather than the chastiser of the papacy. For this revised Ghibelline programme of prophecy, however, Charles IV of Bohemia was much less apt than Henry VII of Luxemburg had been for the role Dante designed for him. Charles would listen neither to Rienzo nor to the ambassadors from Majella who, according to the *Chronicon Estense*, waited on him to announce the advent of the Age of the Holy Ghost.[4]

---

[1] Burdach, *Vom Mittelalter* ii, Pt. iii, p. 22.   [2] Ibid., pp. 191–213.
[3] Ibid., p. 297.   [4] Ibid., Pt. v, p. 295.

III

THE SECOND CHARLEMAGNE

I N spite of Dante and Rienzo, however, the German star was in
eclipse in the fourteenth century. The rising star was the French
monarchy and the gathering of prophecies around it saluted the
new hope. So far, in the pseudo-Joachimist works emanating from
Italy, France had played a minor role, usually that symbolized by
Egypt, the broken reed of Isaiah 36: 6.[1] But it only needed an
enthusiastic Joachite of French political outlook to marry up the old
Second Charlemagne prophecies with the Joachimist *renovatio mundi*.
Already the thirteenth-century Carmelite, St. Angelo, was credited
with a vision in which the liberator of the Holy City was expected:
'. . . unus sanctus et potens Rex de domo Franciae et iste amabitur
ab omnibus Regibus Christianorum . . . et habebit Passagium cum
meo Vicario et cum multis Christianis . . .' (AS, 2 May, p. 821).
Another version of this prophecy ran: 'Surget tandem Rex antiqua
de gente et stirpe Francigena . . . et terra et mari crescit potentia
eius . . . et Pontifici Romano iunctus, purgatis Christianorum erroribus, et Ecclesia ad statum bonis optatum restituta, copias transmit-
tet . . . Ipse vero instructa classe fretus transfretabit et perditas
restituet ecclesias et liberabit Ierusalem . . .' (AS, loc. cit.). In the
early fourteenth century Pierre Dubois was claiming a cosmic role
for the French monarch in his *De recuperatione Terre Sancte* and
deliberately linking this claim with the descent from Charlemagne.[2]
From this source alone, he believed, could flow the universal peace
desired by all. So the Imperial title must be transferred to the French
royal house and, the Holy Land recovered, the French Emperor
must rule a federation of nations from Jerusalem. This was political
aspiration based, it seems, on the sober study of Roman Law rather
than flights of prophecy. But prophecies could be used to support it.
The first hint of a French Joachimism comes in the *Liber de Flore*,
where the first Angelic Pope is expected to be partnered by a *rex*

---

[1] See, for example, *Super Hier.*, ff. 7ᵛ–8ᵛ, 43ᵛ, 60ʳ; *Super Esaiam*, ff. 6ᵛ, 10ʳ, 16ᵛ,
44ʳ–45ᵛ; *De Oneribus, NA* xxxiii, pp. 140–1, 174–6.
[2] Ed. C. Langlois (Paris, 1891), pp. 98–9.

generosus from the line of Pipin,[1] but the full programme of political Joachimism was only worked out later for the French monarchy by Jean de Roquetaillade. The secret of the influence exercised by his works probably lies partly in their fusion of national aspirations and Joachimist dreams. His prophetic politics were convincingly simple in their range of black and white.

Roquetaillade's commentary on the *Oraculum Cyrilli*, written between 1345 and 1349, set out the pattern clearly.[2] The source of all political evil lay still in the accursed seed of the *serpens antiquus*, Frederick II, a poisoned race, heretic, Ghibelline, Luciferian. From Frederick had sprung Frederick of Trinacria and from him would spring Louis of Sicily, the future *Antichristus magnus*. Louis of Bavaria had prefigured him as the *Antichristus mysticus*, but the final Antichrist must arise from the Hohenstaufen in conjunction with the scorpion house of Aragon which was the instrument of Antichrist and always opposed to the realm of France. Linked with Frederick II as a begetter of evil was Brother Elias: the bad sons of St. Francis, together with the proud and wealthy prelates, are the adjutants of Antichrist. Between the years 1360 and 1365, Roquetaillade declared, the Curia would return from Avignon to Rome. When this happens, open your eyes: it is the prelude! About 1365 Antichrist will be elected Emperor in Rome and with him the Antipope, the Beast from the Land.

The forces of good stand in gratifyingly clear contrast. At the outset Roquetaillade interprets the Sun which triumphs over the Beast as Charles of Anjou who fought the enemies of the Holy See, the posterity of Frederick II. Therefore at the election of Antichrist the one non-participant will be the King of France, for there is always great antipathy between the race of Antichrist and the Catholic Kings of France, and, consequently, a close alliance between the Holy See and France. Thus it will be in France that the true Pope will find refuge. Roquetaillade expects a holy Pope, *corrector et reparator*, whom he describes under the figure of the *ursus admirabilis*. For a time the forces of good will be beaten down: the

---

[1] Grundmann, *HJ* xlix. 71. He will assist in ending the schism of the Greek Church, become the King of Sicily, conquer Jerusalem, and end his life as a Franciscan. Cf. *infra*, p. 326, for the use made of this prophecy by Telesphorus of Cosenza, and p. 406 for French manuscripts which pick up this prophecy.

[2] The following summary of Roquetaillade's main works is drawn mainly from Bignami-Odier, *Roquetaillade*, to which I am heavily indebted. For the *Commentary on Cyril*, see pp. 53–109.

true Pope will flee, the Franciscan remnant will hide in caves, many righteous will be martyred. In the final battle against Antichrist, the *ursus* will triumph, aided politically by the King of France and religiously by the true children of St. Francis. Then there will be a new outpouring of the Holy Spirit, Antichrist will be destroyed, and the whole world will submit in peace to the Vicar of Christ. Schismatics, Jews, Saracens, and other infidels will be converted and there will be one flock and one shepherd. This period of beatitude will be the Millennium from the death of Antichrist to the appearance of Gog, precursor of the Second Coming. The only three institutions which clearly survive the crisis of Antichrist are the papacy under its Angelic head, the true part of the Franciscan Order, and the French monarchy.

In his next book, the *Liber Secretorum eventuum*,[1] written in 1349, Roquetaillade proclaimed the same programme but certain points stand out more clearly. Antichrist he now saw as a series of evil tyrannies, first under Frederick II, then under Louis of Bavaria, then under a horrible union of tyrants to arise against the Emperor Charles IV, and finally under a conjunction of three: Louis of Sicily, his false prophet, and an eastern tyrant. The most important, however, was still Louis, born of the accursed Hohenstaufen seed. Among the terrors to herald Antichrist Roquetaillade announced famine and plague—a sinister note in the year 1349. The role of the blessed race of the French princes, new Maccabees, stands out: they would arise to defend the Church, but to aid Antichrist Satan would bring against them the English. So the world would be lined up in two camps: Antichrist and his allies, the Ghibellines of Italy, the kings of Spain, the tyrants of Germany, the king of England, against the true Pope, the King of France, and Charles IV of Bohemia. In these days the King of France would have to choose whether to bow to the yoke of Antichrist or to be despoiled of his realm by the allies of Antichrist, and he would submit patiently to the latter. Antichrist, according to Roquetaillade, would be smitten down by Christ Himself, *c.* 1370, but wars would continue until the Millennium, due to begin in 1415. Joachim, says Roquetaillade, had most accurately prophesied concerning 'this new state of being'. Such a plenitude of the Holy Spirit would fall that Paradise will seem to have descended upon men. All would turn towards the contemplative life.

The *Liber Ostensor*, written during his Avignonese imprisonment and finished in 1356, is a lengthy and complex work with many allusions to contemporary history.[1] In its loyalties it still revolves round the two poles of adherence to the true Franciscan party and belief in the French monarchy. The French disasters in the Hundred Years War are seen as the work of Antichrist, yet there is still hope of triumph. In previous works Roquetaillade had merely assigned the role of aiding the Angelic Pope to the French monarchy; now he goes further and declares that in the final period of beatitude the temporal power will be exercised by a king of the race of Pipin who will reign in Jerusalem. Here is an echo of the Second Charlemagne, deliberately invoked when French fortunes were at their nadir.

The best known of Roquetaillade's works was the *Vade mecum in tribulatione*, written at the end of 1356 and forming a final summary of the future he expected.[2] Two Antichrists now stood out clearly, an 'oriental' who would preach in Jerusalem and seduce the Jews; an 'occidental' who would be a heretical Emperor, a new Nero appearing between 1362 and 1370. The appearance of the Angelic Pope was now specifically stated to mark the beginning of the third *status* of the world. The King of France, contrary to custom, would be elected as Roman Emperor and the entire world would submit to him. The Emperor and Pope together would carry out the final programme of reform:

Ipse [i.e. the Pope Reparator] est post Christum pro principio tertii status generalis orbis, lapis abscissus de monte sine manibus, qui Babylonicam statuam percutiet . . . et implebit lapide Christo, et eius lege universam terram, ubi Gog remanebat, convertendo ad Christum. . . . Regem Francorum, qui veniet in principio suae creationis ad videndam angelicam claritatem eiusdem, assumet, contra morem Alamanicae electionis, in Imperatorem Romanum, cui Deus generaliter subjiciet totum orbem occidentem et orientem et meridiem; qui tantae sanctitatis existet, quod ei Imperator aut Rex similis in sanctitate non fuit ab origine mundi . . . Hic Imperator renuet coronari corona aurea, ad honorem spinarum Coronae Jesu Christi: hic Imperator sanctissimus erit executor omnium mandatorum reparatoris praedicti: per illos duos totus orbis reparabitur et ab eis destruetur tota lex et tyrannica potentia Mahometi: ambo, tam Papa, quam Imperator, Graeciam et Asiam personaliter visitabunt,

---

[1] Bignami-Odier, *Roquetaillade*, pp. 140–8.
[2] Published in *Fasciculus rerum expetendarum et fugiendarum, prout ab Orthuino Gratio . . . editus est Coloniae . . . 1535 . . . una cum appendice . . . scriptorum veterum . . . qui Ecclesiae romanae errores et abusus detegunt et damnant . . . opera et studio Edwardi Brown* (London, 1690), ii. 496–507. See Bignami-Odier, *Roquetaillade*, pp. 157–72.

destruent schisma, Graecos liberabunt a Turcis, Tartaros fidei subjuga-
bunt, regna Asiae reparabunt; . . . hic destruet Italiae schisma Guel-
phorum et Ghibellinorum; et terras Ecclesiae sic disponet, ut Papa eas
Ecclesias in aeternum non impugnet: avaritiam omnem et superbiam
extirpabit, a clero haereses annullabit; . . . (*Vade Mecum*, pp. 501–2.)

The rapid dissemination of these Francophile prophecies is illustrated from the *Diario d'Anonimo Fiorentino*[1] which records a prophecy said to have been made 'per uno Frate minore nel 1368', in
which the Angelic Pope, 'Riparatore del mondo' was to arise after
1378 and, together with 'lo Re di Francia, imperadore di Roma',
reform the world. This is, in fact, taken from the *Vade Mecum*.
Roquetaillade's works, however, are found, not only in France and
Italy as one would expect, but also in countries where the prophetic
programme would obviously be unpalatable—England, Germany,
and particularly in Catalonia.[2] Perhaps the reason lay partly in his
good luck in prognostication: it was obviously a good scoop to have
foretold in the mid-fourteenth century disaster to France, a great
plague, and a great schism. But beyond this, the vogue enjoyed by
his works exemplifies the continuing fascination exercised by the
themes of Antichrist and the Joachimist *renovatio*. To those with
pro-French sympathies the emergence of the French Last World
Emperor who, together with the Angelic Pope, would rule the
Joachimist third *status*, satisfied aspirations which had only found
partial expression in the old pseudo-Methodian legend and married
them to the haunting desire for a renewed papacy and an evangelical
Church. An interesting example of attention focused on the World
Emperor is to be found in a French manuscript of the fourteenth
century, now in the library of Yale University, entitled *Sibylla. De
Imperatore*. Among various Sibylline prophecies, this contains a text
(ff. 24ʳ–29ʳ) which I have not yet identified, but which, in its style
and its expectation of a holy Emperor and Pope, clearly has an
affinity with Roquetaillade's writings.[3]

Roquetaillade's works undoubtedly sparked off the mysterious

---

[1] *Diario d'Anonimo Fiorentino dall'anno 1358 al 1389*, ed. A. Gherardi in *Documenti di storia italiana*, vi (Florence, 1876), pp. 389–90. See passage quoted *infra*, p. 418.

[2] See the bibliography of manuscripts in Bignami-Odier, *Roquetaillade*, pp. 235–54. Translations of his works are found in English, German, and Catalan.

[3] MS. Yale, Univ. Lib., T. E. Marston 225 (see W. Bond, *Supplement to the Census of Mediaeval and Renaissance MSS. in the United States and Canada* (New York, 1962), p. 90). See J. Leclercq, 'Textes et manuscrits cisterciens dans les bibliothèques des États-Unis, *Traditio* xxii (1961), pp. 166–9.

Telesphorus of Cosenza.[1] Whether or not he was really a hermit of Calabria by origin, he was certainly a Francophile Joachite, inspired by the *Oraculum Cyrilli* and Roquetaillade's interpretation of it. In his prefatory letter Telesphorus tells us that he had a vision of angels on Easter Sunday, 1386, directing him to search the oracles of Cyril, Joachim, and others, concerning the Schism and its outcome and the 'futurum ecclesie regimen per Spiritum Sanctum' to come afterwards.[2] In obedience to a command to search for these books he set out for Calabria with a friend named Eusebius of Vercelli. There, in Cosenza and elsewhere, they found, not only the *Oraculum Cyrilli*, but:

libros omnes prefati magni prophete Joachimi et maxime ipsius singulares libros missos Henrico de Suevia Imperatore VI. Et alium singularem librum ipsius intitulatum Liber de Flore de summis pontificibus . . . Item invenimus unum singularem librum qui incipit Revelatio que de Orastopo intitulatur . . . Item invenimus quendam parvum librum intitulatum Hec revelatio Merlini . . . Item invenimus multas alias prophetias et visiones sanctorum . . . (*Libellus*, f. 8ᵛ.)

All these, with various chronicles, Telesphorus studied diligently, claiming 'per quos libros clare cognovi instans scisma eiusque causas predictis viris sanctis fuisse monstrata et revelata' (f. 9ʳ).

The dating of the vision and consequent search in Calabria present problems, since elsewhere he dates the inception of his book to 1356.[3] After a detailed examination Donckel reached the conclusion that the prophecies originated in the period 1356–65 and that the *libellus* took its final form between 1378 and 1390.[4] Thus Telesphorus may have been turning to prophecy just at the time when Roquetaillade was writing his final prognostications. It is with schism between an Angelic Pope and a pseudo-pope such as Roquetaillade foresaw that Telesphorus was in the first instance preoccupied and he may well have been already thinking in these terms when the Great Schism in 1378 confirmed his reading of the signs.

It is clear that Telesphorus had been able to gather together most of the pseudo-Joachimist works as well as the *Liber Concordie*, at least, of Joachim's genuine writings. He makes a complete synthesis of the south-Italian Joachimist tradition and the French nationalist

---

[1] The most complete study of the author and the various redactions and manuscripts of his work has been made by E. Donckel, *AFH* xxvi. 29–104.

[2] *Libellus*, f. 8ᵛ.

[3] MS. Paris, Bib. Nat., Lat. 3184, f. 124ʳ: 'inceptus est hic liber anno nativitatis Domini 1356.'   [4] Donckel, *AFH* xxvi. 74 seq.

prophecy. He begins with an exposition of the pseudo-Joachimist commentary on the *Oraculum Cyrilli* and, indeed, his whole work is in part a gloss upon this. From all his various sources he proves that this last and most monstrous schism had long been foretold by the Holy Spirit. Its cause is God's anger at the sins of the clergy. The sins of the Mendicants, as well as the wealth and pride of other clergy, have brought down on them affliction and destruction. The agents of destruction are a 'Rex alemanus qui ultimus alemanorum imperator erit' and a pseudo-pope of the same nation 'eligendus malitia dicti imperatoris'.[1] Telesphorus's original *exordium*—as distinct from that printed in the Venetian edition—specifically names the German tyrant as Frederick III:

Incipit libellus fratris Thelofori presbyteri ac heremite secundum auctoritates prescriptorum prophetarum et verarum cronicarum de causis, statu, cognitione ac fine instantis scismatis et tribulationum futurarum, maxime tempore futuri regis aquilonis vocantis se Fredericum imperatorem III usque ad tempora futuri pape vocati angelici pastoris et Karoli regis Francie, futuri imperatoris post Fredericum III supradictum. (Paris, Bibl. Nat., MS. Lat. 3184, ff. 106ʳ–107ᵛ.)

In naming the tyrant Frederick III Telesphorus is consciously calling up the old Hohenstaufen bogey from the pseudo-Joachimist works, and in his exposition of the forces of evil he uses in particular the oracle of the Sibyl Erithrea, written just before Frederick II's death. The German Antipope will crown the diabolical Frederick III and then the stage is set for the great conflict between the forces of Antichrist and those of the *nova religio sanctissima*[2] in Joachim's third *status*, which come to a focus in the Angelic Popes.[3]

It is in this final clash between good and evil that the French King appears—*nomine Karolum* and 'generosus rex de posteritate Pipini'.[4] Here Telesphorus is taking over a prophecy from the *Liber de Flore*.[5] The French King's role, of course, is to aid the true Pope against the German *Aquila* and the pseudo-pope. Both these latter are eventually destroyed and the Angelic Pope crowns the French King as Emperor, thus depriving the German electors of their right. Then

---

[1] *Libellus*, f. 14ᵛ.

[2] *Infra*, p. 423, for the passage in which these words occur.

[3] Ibid., ff. 11ʳ–14ʳ.

[4] MS. Venice, Bibl. Marc., Lat. Cl. III, 177, ff. 26ᵛ, 28ᵛ. The name *Karolus* is omitted in the printed editions.

[5] For the reference to the *Liber de Flore* see *supra*, p. 321.

in a holy partnership Emperor and Pope will reform the Church and undertake the seventh and last crusade to recover the Holy Land: 'Qui imperator cum pastore angelico qui ipsum coronabit reformabit ecclesiam in statu paupertatis . . . Et ipse imperator cum pastore ecclesie faciet septimum et ultimum passagium pro terra sancta quam recuperabunt' (*Libellus*, f. 20ᵛ). There follows the period of the Millennium, for the Angel of the Lord will bind Satan and thrust him into prison.

At this point there occurs a significant variation in the pattern. Telesphorus believes that the second *status* of Joachim ended in 1260, when the tribulations inflicted on the Church by Frederick II were ended. He regards himself as already living in the third *status*, but this is clearly not yet free from tribulation and evil. So he sees his own time as the sixth rather than the seventh age of history. Although the peace and joy of the Millennium will be great, at the end of it Satan must once more be unbound for a season; so it is at the end of the third *status* that the *ultimus antichristus* or Gog, the persecutor of the *ecclesia contemplantium* must come. Then the tribes once shut up by Alexander will burst forth and at the onslaught of this last Antichrist the French Emperor will deposit his crown on the Holy Sepulchre and carry out the old programme of the Tiburtine Sibyl.[1] Here it will be seen that, in spite of his Joachimist belief in the third *status*, Telesphorus reverts to the old pessimistic tradition in which finally human institutions seem to fail. Yet this is not the end, for he still has the seventh or Sabbath Age of history in reserve. He cites Joachim as his authority for believing that after the death of the last Antichrist the end of the world would not come at once. So there yet remains the 'tempus septimum pacis et letitie'.[2] Here the only surviving institutions seem to be the papacy whom all the world will obey and the *Ecclesia contemplativa* of Joachim's vision. But for those with political interests it was the first age of beatitude in which the French World Emperor took the place of the German *Aquila* that caught the attention. Telesphorus had finally incorporated the Second Charlemagne myth into the Joachimist programme.

Of the great vogue enjoyed by Telesphorus's *libellus* there can be no doubt. The numerous manuscripts of the fifteenth to seventeenth centuries are found scattered in libraries of Italy, France, Germany, and Austria, while among fragments found in other manuscripts is

---

[1] *Libellus*, f. 30ᵛ.   [2] Ibid., ff. 19ᵛ, 34ʳ.

one in the British Museum.[1] Many are embellished with pictures graphically depicting the programme of Last Things. Two manuscript translations in French and two in German have survived. In the early sixteenth century it was with Telesphorus's *libellus* that the Augustinian Silvestro Meuccio started his series of editions of what he believed to be the works of Joachim. Two editions appeared in 1516 and there were possibly other Italian editions. In France there was a Paris edition, one at Lyon in 1572, and a translation, entitled the *Livre Merveilleux*, made at Rouen in 1565.

In the Vatican library there is a collection of prophecies—MS. Reg. Lat. 580—which was finished in 1387 and includes what must, therefore, be one of the earliest manuscripts of Telesphorus's *libellus*. The illustrations pick out especially the four Angelic Popes and the Last Emperor, including one of the crowning of the 'Second Charlemagne'. This is followed immediately by a separate prophecy which was destined to become one of the most widely disseminated oracles of the next two centuries and which will be referred to throughout the rest of this book as 'the Second Charlemagne prophecy':

Karolus filius Karoli ex natione illustrissimi Lilii habens frontem longam, supercilia alta, oculos longos, nasum aquilinum, circa sue etatis annum XIII coronabitur et in anno XIIII magnum exercitum congregabit omnesque tirampnos sui regni destruet. Nam ut sponsa cum sponso sic erit justicia sociata cum eo; usque ad XXIIII annum suum deducet bella, subiugans Anglicos, Hyspanos, Aragones, Burgales, Lungobardos, Ytalicos; Romam cum Florentia destruet et igne comburet; duplicem coronam obtinebit, postmodum mare transiens cum exercitu magno intrabit Greciam. Et Rex Grecorum nominabitur. Caldeos, Thucenos, Yspanos, Barbaros, Palestinos, Giorgianos subiugabit, faciens edictum ut quicunque Crucifixum non adoraverit morte moriatur et non erit qui possit ei resistere, quia divinum brachium semper cum ipso erit et fere dominium universe terre possidebit. His factis sanctus sanctorum vocabitur, veniens ad sanctam Jerusalem et accedens ad montem Oliveti, orans ad Patrem deponensque coronam de capite, Deo gratias agens cum magno terremotu, signis et mirabilibus, emittet spiritum suum anno regni XXXI. Hic coronatus erit ab Angelico pastore et primus Imperator post Federicum tercium, post presens scisma et tribulationes et persecutiones pseudoprophetarum et dicti Federici. (Vat., MS. Reg. Lat. 580, f. 52r.)

The prophecy is not explicitly ascribed to Telesphorus in this manuscript, yet in a Venetian manuscript written in 1467[1] it also occurs in exactly the same position, following directly after Telesphorus's *libellus*. Moreover it clearly has close affinities with his prophecies, its last sentence expressing in summary form the whole Telesphorean future. This text, in fact, remains persistently associated with the name of Telesphorus.

Yet it seems doubtful if he actually wrote it. M. Chaume discovered and published another version, which he has shown to have been transcribed between 27 October 1381 and 29 June 1382 in the Côte d'Or, and to have been composed in honour of Charles VI between 16 September and 4 November 1380.[2] The text is a slightly fuller version of that given above, with few significant variations until the end, where it stops short before the last sentence. But this omission makes all the difference. Without this last sentence the prophecy is little more than a revival of the old Byzantine myth of the Last Emperor, as it had long since been applied to *Carolus redivivus*. The physical description, though peculiar to itself, is probably based on the Tiburtine Sibyl;[3] the programme of conquest follows the same tradition, although geographically brought up to date. The conclusion, it is true, has not the deep gloom of the old tradition, in which human history ends when the Last Emperor resigns his crown on Golgotha and goes down before the forces of Antichrist; here, the Second Charlemagne is favoured of God and lays down his *imperium* in a cloud of glory and sanctity—on Olivet, be it noted, not Golgotha—but there is no indication that he has wrestled with Antichrist in any form or that he has a real place in the eschatology of Last Things. The additional sentence in the Vatican and Venetian manuscripts is awkwardly tacked on, but it clearly gives a new slant to the prophecy: by placing the Second Charlemagne after the pseudo-prophets and the Third Frederick (manifestations of Antichrist), and by crowning him by the Angelic Pope (representing the third *status* of Joachim), the author of the addition

---

[1] MS. Venice, ref. *supra*, p. 326 n. 4, f. 35ᵛ. J. Valentinelli, *Bibliotheca Manuscripta ad S. Marci Venetiarum* (Venice, 1868), ii. 215, thought that this prophecy was the *incipit* of the *Tractatus de Antichristo* of John Quidort which follows it without a break. For this manuscript see *supra*, p. 173, and *infra*, pp. 343–6, 431.

[2] M. Chaume, 'Une prophétie relative à Charles VI', *Revue du Moyen Âge latin*, iii (1947), pp. 27–42.

[3] For an analysis of the sources of the Second Charlemagne prophecy see Chaume, loc. cit., pp. 37–42. A physical description occurs in the *Interpretatio sibyllinorum librorum*, *PL* cx. 1181–6, and in Godfrey of Viterbo's *Pantheon*, *MGHS* xxii. 146–7. See also R. Folz, *Le Souvenir et la légende de Charlemagne* (Paris, 1950), pp. 138–9.

contrives to place this triumph of human history within an eschatological framework and to make it the embodiment of an expectation
which is Joachimist in origin, if not in form. Assuming that the
French version of M. Chaume is the original one,[1] it seems most
likely that the text was seized upon by Telesphorus or one of his
followers and disseminated, with the additional last sentence, in the
company of his own prophecies.

From the number of quarters in which it turns up, it would seem
that this Second Charlemagne text enjoyed the greatest vogue of any
political prophecy in the fifteenth and sixteenth centuries. We shall
meet it with variations in its beginning, according to its application
in differing political situations, and in its ending, according to its
association or otherwise with the Telesphorean programme, but
always the Last Emperor bears the same physical features and
carries out roughly the same programme. The same Venetian manuscript, for instance, which contains the text given above also gives
(fol. 49ᵛ) a much extended version under the heading *Prophezia
Karoli Regis Francorum*.[2] Here there is no Joachimist last sentence,
but the *pius pastor* with whom the Emperor is associated may be
a vestige of the Angelic Pope. In a Paris manuscript (Bib. Nat., Lat.
3598, f. 45) the prophecy follows the *Visiones fratris Joannis de
Rupescissa* but, again, does not contain the last sentence. On the
other hand, Vat., MS. Chigiano A. VII 220, a Renaissance manuscript which contains the *libellus* of Telesphorus, gives the Telesphorean conclusion to this prophecy with a beautiful illustration of
a king in a mitre-crown surmounted by a cross, holding a sceptre in
his left hand and raising his right in blessing. Two examples stand
by themselves. About 1468 Johannes Peregrinus of Bologna, of the
monastery of St. Anthony in Venice, copied the Second Charlemagne prophecy with the Telesphorean end into a miscellany. His
account of his source is as follows: '. . . ex quodam antiquissimo

---

[1] This seems most likely, but in one detail the version in the Vatican and Venetian
manuscripts is more correct: it gives the age of Charles VI at his coronation correctly as
13, not 14. M. Chaume uses the erroneous age of 14 in his argument to show that the
prophecy was written before Charles's coronation on 4 November 1380. He may be
right, in which case the Italian version has been corrected; or, on the other hand, the
original may have been 13, wrongly transcribed as 14, in which case the prophecy need
not have been written as early as Chaume supposes.

[2] The text has been edited by A. Graf, *Roma nella memoria e nelle immaginazioni del
medio evo* (Turin, 1883), ii. 489 n. 37. It is the only version in which the physical
features have been altered. In its extension also it stands apart from other texts. For
a note at the end of this prophecy see *infra*, p. 345.

libro quem apud me habeo, qui liber antiquus scriptus fuit anno domini M.CCCC.XIII per quendam Blasium Mathei die XVII Maii et ista est prophetia IX illius Abbatis Joachim Libro tertio regum Capitulo XIII.' This is found in two manuscripts, one at Florence and one, according to Bezold, at Munich. In both cases the ascription is exactly the same: the unsolved puzzle is in what unknown pseudo-Joachimist work Peregrinus, or rather the writer he copied, discovered this text.[1] The prophecy is also found in a number of fifteenth- and sixteenth-century manuscripts listed in Appendix B. These are widely distributed and include an English translation. We further find an echo of the Second Charlemagne prophecy at the end of the chronicle of Gilles le Bel.[2] Winding up his history at the turn of the fourteenth/fifteenth century, he devotes two pages to prophecies in which he announces the prophetic programme of a King of France named Charles in terms which clearly point to our prophecy. It was an unfortunate moment, for Charles VI had recently become irrevocably insane.

[1] MS. Florence, Bibl. Naz. Cen., II. xi. 18, f. 8^r. Bezold, *Kaisersage*, p. 600. One would expect Peregrinus's source to have been the book at St. Georgio Maggiore from which MS. Venice, Bibl. Marc., Lat. Cl. III. 177, was made, but the precise reference he gives does not match this at all.

[2] K. de Lettenhove, 'Les chroniques inédites de Gilles le Bel', *Bulletins de l'Académie Royale des Sciences, des Lettres et des Beaux-Arts de Belgique*, 2nd series, ii (1857), pp. 442–3. There is possibly another echo in a prophecy written in Paris in 1395, now in the Newberry Library, Chicago, Case MS. 31. 2, f. 15^v. I owe this reference to Fr. Leclercq, O.S.B.

IV

THE THIRD FREDERICK

IT was inevitable that the period of the Schism and the Councils should produce once more a Teutonic counterblast to French claims. The prophecies of Gamaleon, reputed to be a relation of Pope Boniface IX, were circulating in the early fifteenth century.[1] His first vision of a boy adorned with the seven planets and holding four swords carries prognostications of wars and tribulations.[2] Then he sees an armed man clothed in red and crowned with a ruby whom the boy proclaims as 'magnus ille rex de campo Liliorum ex Meridie'.[2] He is the French tyrant who seizes the Imperial title from the German race, bringing desolation and destruction on the Church and the peoples. Of this tyrant it is written: 'Tu es horribilis et quis tibi resistet?'[3] But in the Rhineland there will arise a prince whom the Germans will elect as Caesar. He will call a Council at Aachen and there the Patriarch of Mainz will be crowned as Pope. Then the German Emperor will destroy the French Emperor and prevail over all peoples, exterminating the Jews and reducing the clergy to Apostolic poverty. Rome will be remembered no more as the seat of the Apostles, for the Patriarchate of Mainz will be the centre of the Church: 'Germania nunc pie et Christiane vivet et honoribus adaugebitur.'[4] The version given by W. Lazius ends thus: 'Et sub isto Caesare Germanicae regiones ac nationes exaltabuntur et honorabuntur et Iudaei in omnibus terris affligentur, postea Germani Christiane vivent cum novo futuro pastore et erit tunc magna et ultima in terram sanctam expeditio.'[5] Here national hopes are clearly allied to the expectation of a spiritual *renovatio*.

---

[1] The chief sources for this prophecy are the long extracts given by W. Lazius, *Fragmentum*, f. Hii[v] and J. Wolf, *Lect. mem.* i. 720–1. A version of it is also printed by F. v. Bezold, *Kaisersage*, pp. 604–6. On p. 728 Wolf gives a shorter version as from a sermon preached in Hamburg by Johann Wünsschelburg in 1409. In Bezold's version this date is given as 1439. A vernacular version is printed by A. Reifferscheid, *Neun Texte zur Geschichte der religiösen Aufklärung in Deutschland* (Greifswald, 1905), Document 9. See also F. Kampers, *Die deutsche Kaiseridee* (Munich, 1896), p. 127.

[2] Wolf, *Lect. mem.*, p. 720.   [3] Lazius, *Fragmentum*, f. Hii[v].

[4] Wolf, *Lect. mem.*, p. 721.

[5] Lazius, *Fragmentum*, f. Hii[v]. Lazius's version differs considerably from Wolf's in detail, yet they are clearly versions of the same thing.

The name of Frederick was still a potent word with which to conjure, for the legend of a resurrected Frederick or Third Frederick had been kept alive during the preceding two centuries by folk tradition and fanatical claimants.[1] Always he appears with the enhanced stature of one who in the programme of Last Things is either the chastiser or renovator of Christendom. In a fifteenth-century Munich manuscript[2] Gamaleon's vision is followed by a version of the Third Frederick prophecy, and when in the mid-fifteenth century the mysterious title of Frederick III was at last embodied in flesh and blood, this naturally gave a boost to the prophecy. Thomas Ebendorfer, winding up his *Cronica Regum Romanorum*[3] at this time, allowed his thoughts to move into the future. What kind of portent would this Frederick prove to be—the embodiment of good or evil? Ebendorfer, taking care to distinguish his history *sine fictione*[4] from this doubtful stuff, quoted a current prophecy which is clearly a version of the pro-Hohenstaufen Third Frederick oracle, brought up-to-date politically:[5]

Veniet aquila, cuius volatu debellabitur leo et veniet pullus aquile et nidificabit in domo leonis, cuius fructus alimento paterno carebit. Et illic eligetur unus, cui honor regis non exhibetur. Tandem conspirabunt principes Alemanie et magnates terre Bohemie opprimentur et leopardus

---

[1] See Cohn, pp. 107 seq.; G. Schultheiss, *Die deutsche Volkssage vom Fortleben u. der Wiederkehr Kaiser Friedrichs II* (*Histor. Studien* 94, Berlin, 1911), pp. 1–133. Among those who wrote of these beliefs in the fourteenth and fifteenth centuries see especially J. Rothe, *Düringische Chronik*, ed. R. v. Liliencron, *Thüringische Geschichtsquellen*, iii (Jena, 1859), pp. 426, 466; John of Winterthur, *Chronik*, *MGHS*, N.S., iii. 280; Theodoric Engelhus, *Chronicon*, ed. G. Leibniz, *Scriptores rerum Brunsviciensium* . . . (Hanover, 1707–11), ii. 1115; Oswald der Schreiber, ed. Zarncke, *Abh. Ges. Wissensch. Leipzig*, vii (1879), pp. 1004 seq.; Peter v. Zittau, *Chronicon*, ed. J. Loserth, *Fontes Rerum Austriacarum*, viii. 424 seq.; *Die Detmar Chronik v. Lübeck*, *Chroniken der deutschen Städte*, xix (1884), pp. 333, 367; Ottokar, *Oesterreichische Reimchronik*, *MGH*, *Deutsche Chroniken*, v, 1, pp. 423 seq. In Cologne people believed that at his coronation Sigismund received the new name of Frederick (Bezold, op. cit., p. 584).

[2] F. Lauchert, 'Materialen zur Geschichte der Kaiserprophetie im Mittelalter', *HJ* xix (1898), p. 846.

[3] Ed. A. Pibram, *Mittheilungen des Instituts für oesterreichische Geschichtsforschung*, Ergänzungsband III (Innsbruck, 1890), pp. 38–222.

[4] Ibid., p. 143. Ebendorfer introduces the prophecy thus: 'Unum tamen in calce huius hystorie, quam sine fictione didici et sine invidia communicare ac exarare disposui, addicere [*sic*] volui, quod quidam timoratus michi in partibus Reni ab antiquissimo libro se professus est excerpsisse [et] sua manu scriptum obtulit, eciam presentibus annectere pro memoriali in hac forma . . .'

[5] Ibid., cf. *supra*, pp. 311–12. Another version of this prophecy in its original form, beginning '*Regnabit Manfredus*', is quoted by the fifteenth-century German historian Theodoricus Paulus in his *Speculum historiale*, ed. W. Focke (Halle, 1892), p. 78. *Infra*, p. 361, for further references to this text.

devorabit eos. Et exurget radix de radice aquile, nomine Fredericus orientalis, hic regnans regnabit, imperans imperabit et extendet ramos usque ad ultimos fines terre, tempore illius summus capietur pontifex et clerus dilapidabitur.

But he also knew the legend of Frederick III as the embodiment of evil, disseminated through 'istius Theolophori heremite figmenta, ... qui de tercio Friderico evomuit sine fundamento'.[1] We find him quoting from Alexander von Roes, without acknowledgement, the passages cited above on Frederick as the *radix peccatrix* and the future Carolingian Emperor.[2] He was not prepared to let the French win hands down, but felt impelled to add—albeit with somewhat of a sneer—the Second Charlemagne prophecy which we have quoted above in full.[3] He gave it in the Telesphorean form, with the correct coronation age and the complete Joachimist last sentence. This meant, of course, that Frederick III appeared in the role of villain-precursor to the Last World Emperor. Thus there were three figures on the prophetic horizon at this time: a good Frederick, a bad Frederick, and a good Charles. Be it noted, however, that they all had one thing in common: their role as chastiser of Rome and the clergy. Ebendorfer found the future entirely problematic. He hoped great things from Frederick III, whom he addressed thus: 'Assurge ergo Deo amabilis imperator . . . ut revivescat spes imperii et tua serenior appareat gloria.'[3] But clearly he was uncertain how this Frederick would shape.

On the other side of the picture we get an amusing sidelight from Aeneas Sylvius Piccolomini on the Italian attitude to Frederick III.[4] As he approached Rome for his coronation in 1452, Aeneas tells us, some tried to persuade Nicholas V that he was that future intolerable scourge of the clergy who, according to the oracles, would punish Rome and do mighty deeds. Nicholas was in two minds 'hinc timet, inde cupit; hinc dominatum amittere formidat, inde coronandi

---

[1] Ebendorfer, op. cit., p. 144.

[2] *Supra*, p. 313. The same passage from Alexander v. Roes is quoted in MS. Vindob. 3402 in fifteenth-century notes added to the *Chronicon pontificum et imperatorum Ratisponense*, see *MGHS* xxiv. 285 n. 2. F. Lot, 'Origine et signification du mot "carolingien"', *Revue historique*, xlvi (1891), p. 69, cites another example of this quotation from a Bavarian chronicle.

[3] Ebendorfer, op. cit., p. 149, cf. *supra*, p. 328.

[4] Aeneas Sylvius Piccolomini, *Historia rerum Friderici III imperatoris*, ed. J. Schilter, *Scriptores rerum Germanicarum* (Strasbourg, 1687), p. 45. MS. Vat., Lat. 3816 contains a collection of prophecies made in 1448 by an Italian who saw the Third Frederick as the final manifestation of evil (ff. 59ᵛ–62ᵛ) and expected the Second Charlemagne (f. 63ʳ) and Angelic Pope (f. 64ᵛ).

Caesaris gloriam expetit.' To this may be added a conversation between Pope and Emperor reported by the Abbot Trithemius:[1]

Inter prandendum fertur Papa dixisse ad Caesarem: Multa de te, glorio-sissime fili, praenuntiata sunt mala, quae sis facturus Ecclesiae, si fidem adhibere praedictionibus huiusmodi debeamus. Cui Imperator respondit: Mea intentio pro Ecclesia Dei bona et recta est; si Deus aliud de me aut per me ordinare voluerit, in ipsius potestate est, qui solus omnia novit, potest et disponit secundum suam rectissimam voluntatem.

Even Frederick himself could not evade his ordained role: only time could tell if he were in truth the Third Frederick of prophecy.

As a candidate for a part in the drama of Last Things it is difficult to think of any historical character more disappointing than the Emperor Frederick III. Two contemporary poets appear to believe in his prophetic role,[2] but a tract, written from a German viewpoint well on in his reign, reflects the confusion into which he had thrown prophetic expectation. The *Tractatus de Turcis*,[3] composed in 1474, was a compilation of prophecies made by some Dominicans to strengthen men's hearts against the menace of the Turks. It is based on the famous pseudo-Methodian prophecy of the ultimate defeat of the infidel[4] and includes among its prophets Joachim, Cyril, Hilde-garde, Merlin, the Sibyl, and St. Bridget. The pseudo-Joachimist commentary on the *Oraculum Cyrilli* is cited on the affliction of the Church for her many sins by the Turk,[5] but none of the current

[1] J. Trithemius, *Chronicon Hirsaugiense* (St. Gall, 1690), ii. 423. The author continues: 'Et notandum quod multi spiritum sibi Prophetiae temeraria praesumptione usurpantes multa de Friderico Imperatore III mala praedixerunt esse futura, quod videlicet esset futurus Ecclesiae Romanae persecutor, Romanorum Pontificum, Praelatorum Ecclesiae Universalis inimicus et destructor, Cleri et pauperum oppressor, tyrannus impius, crudelis, maleficus, infidelis et fidei Christianae hostis, desertor et osor, quae omnia, frivola, ficta, falsa et mentita fuerunt. Constat enim omnibus qui noverunt eum, quod cunctis diebus regni sui simul et Imperii per annos 53 in fide Christi semper princeps fuit Catholicus et Christianissimus, nunquam Ecclesiae molestus, nunquam tyrannus, nunquam crudelis. . . . Manifestum est ergo praedictiones de illo malas omnes extitisse mendaces.'

[2] Rudolf Montigel, ed. R. v. Liliencron, *Die historischen Volkslieder der Deutschen vom 13. bis 16. Jahrh.* (Leipzig, 1866), ii. 26; Hermann v. Sachsenheim, *Die Moerin*, ed. E. Martin, *Bibliothek des Historischen Vereins in Stuttgart*, cxxxvii (Tübingen, 1878), pp. 209-10.

[3] The main title reads: 'Incipit Tractatus quidam de Turcis prout ad presens ecclesia sancta ab eis affligitur collectus diligenti discussione scripturarum a quibusdam fratribus praedicatorum ordinis . . .'   [4] See Sackur, *Sibyllinische Texte*, pp. 53 seq.

[5] *Tractatus*, f. 6ʳ. To prove that Rome must be destroyed, the authors cite 'quedam dicta Merlini et quedam alia dicta cuiusdam discipuli abbatis Joachim que eciam in quadam antiqua biblia regis Aragonum reperiuntur, que expressissime videntur loqui de quadam devastacione Ytalie fienda per Turcos et hec prophetie communiter habentur in Ytalia in plerisque civitatibus' (f. 4ᵛ).

oracles on the agents of the *renovatio* are utilized. This is not because
the Dominican authors were afraid to use prophecies associated with
a name of such doubtful repute as Joachim's.

Nam constat ipsum spiritum habuisse propheticum presertim in illa
postilla super Hieremiam in qua inter cetera de duobus ordinibus in fine
seculi futuris, fratrum scilicet predicatorum et minorum locutus est.
Unde secundum beatum Thomam, licet in quibusdam erraverit, quia
tamen correctioni ecclesie se submisit et excellentissimum ingenium
habebat, ideo eius dicta merito admittuntur. (f. 7r.)

Their difficulty lay, it would seem, in their reluctance to admit the
expectation of a French Second Charlemagne as victor over the
Turk and their inability to see Frederick III in this role. Some,
indeed, saw him as the symbol of evil; others, following popular
Sibylline oracles ('dicta etiam sibille solum habentur in libris vul-
garibus et non latinis vel autenticis'), believed he would be the
saviour of Christendom; but our authors were certain he was neither,
for actual embodiment in the flesh had reduced the huge symbol of
the *Fredericus tertius* to ordinary human stature.[1] The extermination
of the Turk would not be accomplished by the present Emperor,
nor would the future Christian King whom they expected be like
him. So, turning away from current tradition, they looked for a
saviour of Christendom 'de exiguis Christianorum regibus' and put
forward a tentative candidate in Mathias Corvinus of Hungary. It is
possible, indeed, that the purpose of the tract should be related to
Mathias's candidature as King of the Romans, but the authors were
doubtful if this were he for whom they looked.[2] The one certain
thing was that the apotheosis of history would be brought in by

[1] Tractatus, ff. 20v–21v: '...Secundo quod de imperio Romanorum erit idem rex non
quo ad sanguinis notabilitatem aut rei publice gubernacionem prout ipse presens Fridericus
tercius gubernacula imperii tenens existit. Tertio, quod de exiguis et non de maioribus
Christianorum regibus idem rex futurus regnabit ... Hec particula sic declaratur quia
futura victoria obtinenda in exterminium Turcorum non fiet per presentem imperatorem Fridericum tercium sed per aliquem de exiguis Christianorum regibus ...' The
case for Frederick is then examined, including his probity, but is dismissed: 'Ex quibus
concluditur quod licet in imperatore videatur probitas vite, hoc est tamen quo ad
privatam suam personam. Quantum vero existit communis persona quo ad regimen et
tuitionem ecclesie, ibi plurimum asseritur defectuosus utpote qui nec proprias oves ab
incursibus infidelium defendit, qui tamen totius ecclesie advocatus existit et hoc patuit
in depopulatione Karinthie et Carniole provinciis ...'

[2] Ibid., ff. 21v–22r: '... Licet de rege hunorum sive ungarorum alique scripture
faciant mentionem, in dubium tamen vertitur an de presenti vel alio aliquo futuro tales
scripture fuissent locute ... Unde per presentem regem ungarorum plures estimant
terminari presentem afflictionem. Sed hec omnia manent in divina dispositione.'

a great Christian king: 'Et per ipsum regem magnificabitur regnum Christianorum super omnia regna mundi.'¹ The whole tract reflects belief in the Joachimist future together with disillusionment concerning the Third Frederick. The death of the Emperor Frederick III seemed indeed to be the death of the Third Frederick, whose epitaph is best supplied by Stefano Infessura in his *Diario della Città di Roma*: 'A.D. 1493. Mortuus fuit imperator Federicus et cum eo perierunt omnes prophetiae . . .'²

Prophetic verses were again circulating in Italy at this time. One such,³ in the style of those attributed to Tomassuccio or Stoppa, looked forward to a great German Emperor who would do all the proper things:

> Costù sarà signor di tuto il mondo
> Fazendo iusticia a quadro e a tondo,
> Sposo de l'Italia, questo non ascondo,
> E Imperatore.
>
> .   .   .   .   .   .
>
> Costù mantegnerà pace in ogni lato
> Deschezando dal mondo ogni peccato,
> Non se trovarà che sia superchiato
> Dal so vicino.
>
> Convertirasse a la fede el Saracino
> E Tartaria con tuto el so camino,
> Poy intrarà in quello loco divino
> Sanctificato.
>
> E quando Roma tornarà in so stato
> E tuto quanto el mondo sarà ripossato
> Li santi preyti del mondo stato
> Tuti predicarano.
>
> Tuti li infideli se convertirano
> Vestiti tuti d'uno aspro panno
> E senza proprio sempre viverano
> In la povertade.
>
> .   .   .   .   .   .

---

¹ Tractatus, f. 22ᵛ. *Infra*, p. 340, for the continuation of this passage.
² S. Infessura, *Diario della Città di Roma*, ed. O. Tommasini (Rome, 1890), pp. 292–3.
³ A. Hilka, 'Über einige italienische Prophezeiungen des 14. u. 15. Jahrh. vornehmlich über einen deutschen Friedenskaiser', *Sonderabdruck aus dem 94. Jahresbericht der Schlesischen Gesellschaft für vaterl. Cultur* (Breslau, 1917), pp. 1–11.

Al mondo may non sarà più bataglia,
Sarà in obprobrio ogni ferro e maglia,
Ne may più cara sarà la vitualia
Certamente.

Remarrà sopra la terra poche gente,
E ogni spirituale sarà alora gaudente
Per ho pregamo Dio che conducha ogni gente
A bon stato.

El can con l'orso sarà pacificato
El lupo con l'agnello acompagnato
El serpente starà nel fossato
A manducare.

(Loc. cit., pp. 10–11)

Another set of Italian verses on the Emperor–Restorer was circulating in the second half of the fifteenth century under the name of Pelligrino Allegri,[1] and the theme continued to be popular in Italian prophetic verse down to the early sixteenth century.[2]

The figure of the King–Chastiser now begins to play an important prophetic role, popularized by prophecies associated with St. Bridget. During her lifetime her revelations had been collected in seven books, the *Liber coelestis revelationum*. Later the *Liber magnus* was extracted from these and *c.* 1433 J. Tortsch of Leipzig compiled the brief *Onus mundi* from all the revelations.[3] St. Bridget probably believed in a coming Age of the Spirit, Joachim's *third status*,[4] but this was to be preceded by a terrible chastisement of Christ's Judgement, the executor of which is variously described as *Dux venturus*,[5] *Arator*,[6] and *Venator*.[7] In the authentic revelations St. Bridget seems uncertain whether the Chastiser will be Christian, heretic, or pagan, but he is clearly an involuntary agent of God's judgement, an evil instrument of divine purpose. In the popular oracles which begin to circulate under Bridget's name during the fifteenth century the role of the Chastiser was developed further. One, beginning 'Sub aquila

---

[1] Messini, *Misc. Franc.* xxxix. 129–30. For similar prophetic verses see *infra*, pp. 419–20.   [2] Ibid., p. 130.

[3] On the various collections of St. Bridget's prophecies see J. Jørgensen, *St. Bridget of Sweden*, tr. I. Lund (London, 1954), i. 300 seq.

[4] This is the view taken by Jørgensen, op. cit. ii. 78, 223, though it is difficult to find precise proof of this in the *Revelations*.

[5] *Libellus qui intitulatur Onus mundi* (ed. undated, no pl. of pub., no pag.), cap. 8: 'De Duce venturo qui erit future tribulationis executor.'

[6] *Liber celestis Imperatoris ad Reges* (ed. undated, no pl. of pub., no pag.), Bk. IV, cap. xxii.   [7] Ibid., Bk. VIII, cap. xviii.

grandi',[1] gives a stark picture of the German race trampling down the Church, whilst another prophesies the destruction of Rome.[2] Another popular Brigittine oracle, however, reverses the role of chastiser: by a daring transformation of the *Rex impudicus facie* prophesied in the book of Daniel into the *Rex pudicus facie*,[3] the wicked tyrant becomes the godly chastiser. He will not only chastise but also reform the Church; he will rule everywhere and he will be a German. A third of these Brigittine oracles concerns the Lily (i.e. France), ending with the peaceful union of the Lily and the Eagle and the submission of the former to the latter.[4] These pseudo-Brigittine prophecies, which quickly established themselves in the general prophetic currency, on the whole favoured the German side

[1] See Lichtenberger, *Prognosticatio*, i, cap. 3: 'Unde Brigida in Libro Revelationum: Sub aquila grandi que ignem fovebit in pectore conculcabitur ecclesia et vastabitur. Nam potens est Deus alemanos altos provocare contra ecclesiam que magis de humana potentia quam Dei confidant [*sic*]. Iusto iuditio hostilibus incursibus conculcabitur navicula Petri et clerus turbabitur. Et necesse est ut Petrus succinctus effugiat ne squalorem publice servitutis incurrat. Et sic videat ipsa ecclesia occidentalis ne sit sibi baculus harundinis ponata [*sic*] gallicana in qua confidit cui siquis innitur perforat manus eius. Datur intelligi quod Alemani scorpioniste confederationem inibunt cum rege Francie sub quo ecclesia crucem lamentationis humeris propriis probabit.' See also *Mirabilis liber* (Paris, 1522), f. xii[r], and for another version Lazius, *Fragmentum*, f. Kii[r]. The author of this text, whether Bridget or another, is almost certainly quoting pseudo-Joachimist works in the following phrases: 'que ignem fovebit in pectore', *Vat. Sibillae Erithreae*, p. 168; 'necesse est ut Petrus succinctus effugiat', *Super Hier.*, f. 3[v]; 'ne sit sibi baculus harundinis ponata gallicana in qua confidit cui siquis innitur perforat manus eius', ibid., f. 7[v].

[2] Cited by W. Aytinger, *Tractatus de revelatione beati Methodi* (Basle, 1498, no pag.), cap. 2. A prophecy attributed to Bridget, beginning 'O desolata civitas', is associated with the *libellus* of Telesphorus in MSS. Vat., Lat. 3816, f. 62[r], and Venice, Bibl. Marc., Lat. Cl. III. 177, f. 16[r], and also in the Venetian printed edition of 1516, f. 5[v].

[3] See Dan. 8: 23. The essential core of this oracle is as follows: 'Exsurget tunc Rex pudicus facie qui regnabit ubique sub quo Ecclesiae collapsae status reformabitur et clerici plurimum molestabuntur . . . ultimo Franciae Rex succumbet et Rex pudicus facie regnabit ubique et ingredietur nidos veterum Aquilarum et imperium solus obtinebit ab Oriente ad Occidentem.' This is quoted or referred to in the following: *Tractatus de Turcis*, written in 1474, printed at Nuremberg in 1481, ff. 18[r-v], 22[v]; Lichtenberger, *Prognosticatio* ii, caps. 3, 17; Aytinger, op. cit., cap. 2; Maister Alofresant, *Alle alten Prophecien v. Keyserlichen Maiestat* (Strasbourg, no date), f. 9[r] (in German); P. Gengenbach, *Der Nollhart* (Basel, 1517, no pag.); *Mirabilis liber*, f. xii[r]; Lazius, *Fragmentum*, f. Kii[r]; *Prophetia de santa Brigida* (Venice, 1525, no pag.) (in Italian verse). Lichtenberger and Alofresant also associate St. Francis with this prophecy.

[4] The central core of this runs: 'Nam de bono gallo antiquum propheticum invenietur ita: aquilae grandi sociabitur lilium et movebitur ab occidente in orientem contra leonem, leo carebit auxilio et decipietur a lilio. Fragrabit lilium in Alemania, unde laus sua ultima volabit sub aquila.' See Lichtenberger, *Prognosticatio*, ii, cap. 17; *Mirabilis liber*, f. xxviii; A. Torquatus, *Prognosticon* (Antwerp, 1544), f. 9[v] (quoting the last phrase only).

of the contest; they also supported the Joachimist expectation. Thus a late fifteenth-century tract used the Brigittine oracles in this context:[1]

Et per ipsum regem magnificabitur regnum Christianorum super omnia regna mundi. . . . Quintum, commendabile est conversio infidelium per novam praedicationem evangelii. . . . Sextum, commendabile quod per eundem regem cum conversione infidelium erit ecclesie innovatio. Hec materia ad longum tractatur in revelationibus Sancte Birgitte in quibus tractatur de novis praedicatoribus evangelii et conversione infidelium et nove sponse electione, ad que omnia prefatus rex diligentissime cooperabitur. . . . Septimum commendabile est pax et concordia super terram qualis antea non fuit.

Here, to the traditional programme of the Last World Emperor, the Brigittine prophecies add the Joachimist *renovatio*.

With Gamaleon and Bridget there often appears an unknown Frater Reinhard, whose prophecy, probably dating from the early fifteenth century, is preserved in several later collections.[2] In one such extract there is a strong echo of Joachim's method in concords worked out between the last age of the Old Testament and the coming crisis of the New Dispensation:[3]

Ista futura tribulatio assimilatur praeteritae tribulationi, quae fuit tempore Machabaeorum, quia omnia in figuris contingebant illis ad nostram correptionem. Sicut ergo per regem Antiochum templum in Hierusalem fuit profanatum et sacerdotium turbatum, deinde iterum templum restitutum, ac populus Dei liberatus, sic a simili per dictum tyrannum Ecclesia et clerus ob sua et populi peccata turbabitur. Qui quidem tyrannus nequam Papam intrudet in Ecclesiam, cuius tandem status una cum Christiana republica per quendam bonum principem reformabitur, sectaque Mahumetica destruetur.

Here again the wicked tyrant and the reformer–prince are juxtaposed.

As a focal point for Teutonic expectation Frederick III's predecessor Sigismund had seemed promising. There are hints of an enhanced stature accorded to him by prophecy in the titles *lux*

---

[1] *Tractatus de Turcis*, f. 22ᵛ. See Aytinger, op. cit., cap. 5, quoted *infra*, pp. 353–4.
[2] See the extracts quoted 'de revelationibus fratris Reynhardi lolhardi' by Lichtenberger, *Prognosticatio*, ii, caps. 3, 5, 13, 26; Aytinger, op. cit., cap. 7; Alofresant, op. cit., f. 9; Lazius, *Fragmentum*, f. Kiiiʳ (cf. Lichtenberger, ii, 3); Wolf, *Lect. mem.* i. 748. Alofresant calls him 'bruder Rainhards des Nolhards' and he can probably be connected with Gengenbach's *Der Nolhart* (*infra*, p. 360). Regiselmo, *Vaticinia* XXVI, quotes a four-line verse from him on the Eagle. Wolf dates his prophecy 1413.
[3] Wolf, *Lect. mem.* i. 748; cf. *Lib. Conc.*, ff. 56ʳ, 127ʳ.

mundi, secundus David, and *Charlemagne*, given to him by contemporaries.[1] A prophecy of Hildegarde was also applied to him.[2] But the connection of Sigismund with prophetic expectation is most clearly brought out in the *Reformation Kaiser Sigmunds*, a vernacular tract produced *c.* 1439.[3] This was based on a Latin programme of reform prepared for the Council of Basle, but the German tract became the vehicle of social and political aspirations which were focused on a prophetic future. There is a strong overtone of Joachimist prophecy in a Latin oracle spoken by the Biblical Esther concerning a *sacer pusillus* who will arise *tempore terno et novo*: 'dominabitur a mare usque ad mare, pes suus calcabit turbines,... plebs exultet, gaudet iusticia.'[4] At the end the vision of the future is summed up in a prophecy put into the mouth of the Emperor Sigismund, recently dead.[5] He foretells the coming of a priest–king and describes the rule of spiritual blessedness and social righteousness that he will inaugurate. The fact that the priest–king is named as Frederick of Lantnaw (either the author of the tract or the prophet for whom it was written)[6] did not prevent this programme for a German *renovatio* from achieving wide circulation during the following century.[7]

Prophecies seem to be indestructible. As we shall see, the Third Frederick legend recovered from the career of the actual Frederick; equally, that of the Second Charlemagne survived the madness of Charles VI. There was a strange French group in the mid-fifteenth century inspired by Jean Carrier who had been the Vicar-General of Benedict XIII and, after his death, gathered round a certain

[1] A. Altmann, *Eberhart Windeches Denkwürdigkeiten zur Geschichte des Kaisers Sigmund* (Berlin, 1893), p. 1; Theodoricus de Monasterio, *Panegyricus in Concilio Constantiensi dictus*, ed. C. Walch, *Monumenta Medii Aevi* (Gottingen, 1757), i. 2, 96; D. Schilling, *Schweizerchronik* (Lucerne, 1862), p. 42.

[2] *Altmann*, op. cit., p. 350.

[3] Ed. W. Boehm, *Friedrich Reiser's Reformation des Kaisers Sigmund* (Leipzig, 1876); K. Beer, *Die Reformation Kaiser Sigmunds* (Stuttgart, 1933); H. Koller, *MGH, Staatsschriften des Späteren Mittelalters*, vi.

[4] Boehm, op. cit., pp. 238–9. Cf. *Lib. Conc.*, f. 69ᵛ: 'Futurus est enim ut ordo unus convalescat in terra similis ioseph et salomonis ... et dominabitur a mari usque ad mare et a flumine usque ad terminos orbis terrarum ...' The common quotation from Ps. 72: 8 could be coincidence but the words 'tempore terno et novo' suggest that the author is thinking in Joachimist terms, while the figure of Esther symbolized to Joachim the Third Age, cf. *Lib. Conc.*, f. 119 seq., especially 122ᵛ, where the sublimation of the papacy is foretold in the exaltation of Mordecai.

[5] Boehm, op. cit., pp. 242 seq.; Beer, op. cit., pp. 138–43; Koller, op. cit., pp. 332 seq.

[6] Boehm, op. cit., pp. 242, 246; Beer, op. cit., p. 72; Koller, op. cit., pp. 332, 343.

[7] Bezold, *Kaisersage*, pp. 591–2.

blacksmith, Jean Trahinier.[1] They believed that Jean Carrier was
still alive and was the true Pope, Benedict XIV, and they expected
a King of France, 'Charles, son of another Charles', to discover the
legitimate Pope in hiding and place him at the head of Christendom.
This is a pathetic echo from Telesphorus. More serious are the
'conseils et prédictions' presented by an obscure Jean du Bois to
Charles VII in 1445, when he was at the height of his successes.[2]
Jean had steeped himself in all the prophetic literature he could find
of the Sibyls, Hildegarde, Joachim, John of Bassigny, John of
Bridlington, Telesphorus, and so on. The results of this research
he now submitted to the King and his court. If France would repent
of her sins and seek reconciliation with God, a great future would
open up before her. He cited the Second Charlemagne prophecy
itself and proved its applicability by the fact that Charles had
really won his crown at Arras in the thirteenth year of his reign.[3]
The programme he announced was largely drawn from Telesphorus:
it included the persecuting Third Frederick, the Angelic Pope, and
the most holy Emperor 'de nobilissimo sanguine et semine Francorum regum'.[4] After the tribulations seven great years of peace and
felicity would descend on France. The year 1451 would see 'an
abundance of peace' and on Easter Day that year, guided by the
Holy Spirit, the King would gather thirteen other Christian kings in
Paris. There, in the sight of the kings and all the people, an angel
would descend to present to the King of France a shining sword and
a ruby ring.[5] After that the triumph of the Second Charlemagne
would go forward according to the accustomed programme:[6] Charles
would march into Italy, destroy Rome and another culpable but
unnamed city, and be crowned by the Angelic Pope as emperor, not
only of France, but also of Germany, Rome, Greece, and Jerusalem.
He would reunite under his rule East and West, reconquer the Holy
Places, and become universal monarch. After 37 years of ruling he
would deposit his crown at the Holy Sepulchre and many pagans
would be converted at the sight. In laying this glittering future
before Charles VII, Jean du Bois did not express complete faith in
it, but none the less he asked to be rewarded by exemption from all

[1] N. Valois, *La France et le Grand Schisme d'Occident* (Paris, 1902), iv. 475–7.
[2] N. Valois, 'Conseils et prédictions adressés à Charles VII en 1445 par un certain
Jean du Bois', *Annuaire Bulletin de la Société de l'Histoire de France*, xlvi (1909), pp. 201–
38. I owe this reference to Mr. Peter Lewis.
[3] Ibid., p. 226.   [4] Ibid., pp. 225, 231.
[5] Ibid., p. 232.   [6] *Supra*, p. 328.

taxes. There is no record of Charles's reaction either to the prophecies or to the request.

All the figures of political prophecy—wicked tyrant and pseudo-
pope, Second Charlemagne and Angelic Pope—appear in a remarkable Venetian compilation which shows by its successive layers
a continuing interest in the Joachimist political future.[1] First, in the
mid-fifteenth century, *c.* 1454, there was a Venetian, Domenico
Mauroceno, who compiled a book of prophetic excerpts. To him, as
we have seen,[2] the Dominican, Fr. Rusticianus, addressed a Dedicatory Letter when, at Mauroceno's request, he set to work on the
large volume of prophecies, 'a te mihi nuper adlatas', to select,
abbreviate, and set in order the confusion of material which had
been culled from Telesphorus and others. The core of his work was
the *libellus* of Telesphorus. This was preceded by his own Dedicatory Letter and by prophecies from St. Bridget and a Fr. Antonius de
Yspania, written in 1383.[3] In the text of Telesphorus's work his chief
additions were picture-sections in which each illustration was introduced by a caption or brief text. A number are Biblical (e.g. Apocalyptic angels blowing trumpets and pouring phials) but some illustrate
the Joachimist future and are of real interest.[4] His own political
programme, as set out in his Dedicatory Letter, was the Telesphorean one: the *Antichristus mixtus* was at hand, 'quidam pseudo-
papa germanus origine quem imperator vi ac fraude creabit'; he
would crown the false German Emperor, the expected Frederick III,
and together they would overturn France, devastate Italy, perse-
cute the clergy, and profane St. Peter's; there would be the three
other false Popes, but all the evil agencies would be overthrown by
the divine partnership of the *papa angelicus* and the 'generosus rex
de posteritate Pepini', who would bring in the Age of Tranquillity.
The French Emperor, the embodiment of piety and power, would
journey to view the brightness of the Angelic Pope and recover
Jerusalem.

Some of Rusticianus's picture-additions to Telesphorus's *Libellus*
point up this programme vividly: three pseudo-popes are crowned
by devils; Frederick III's armed forces arrive by sea—two boat-
loads—and by land, with eagle banners flying and the king at their

[1] *Supra*, p. 263 n. 5.
[2] *Supra*, p. 173.
[3] MS. Venice, Bibl. Marc., Lat. III, 177, ff. 15ᵛ–17ᵛ. This manuscript is linked in
content with MS. Vat., Lat. 3816, compiled in 1448.
[4] Ibid., ff. 27ᵛ, 28ʳ, 29ʳ, 29ᵛ, 30ʳ, 31ʳ, 33ᵛ, 34ᵛ, 35ʳ.

head; the holy monk sits outside his prison as the deputation which has come to proclaim him Angelic Pope kneels in awe; the crowned Angelical in turn crowns the King of France with thorns.[1] The following Angelic Popes are displayed in a series of enigmatic pictures and the culminating illustrations show God blessing His *populus sanctus* and the reprobate roasting in a curious receptacle.[2] This mid-fifteenth-century Venetian plainly accepted the prophetic roles of German Emperor and French King, but how far, one wonders, did he really expect these deeds from the contemporary Frederick III and Charles VII? The conjunction of names, of course, made Telesphorus once more particularly apt. Although the original Great Schism had long since ended, Rusticianus retains Telesphorus's language, as, for instance, 'in presente scismate', and only partially adapts the dates.[3]

The Venetian manuscript which we have is not Rusticianus's original work but a copy made in 1469 by Andreas, a monk of St. Cyprian's, from an exemplar belonging to St. Georgio Maggiore at Venice. It is not quite clear how much was added by the compiler of the St. Georgio book. As Rusticianus's Dedicatory Epistle does not occur till f. 15ʳ, the preliminaries appear to belong to this other compiler. They include some crude and startling pictures by a priest named Lazarus of Pavia. One shows the Pope and Emperor Frederick III locked in a wrestling match in which Frederick is being worsted. In his left hand the Pope manages to hold the symbols of the French monarchy and scales which represent Rome. Pope and Emperor stand balanced on a lion (*dux burgundie*), a wheel (*patriarcho*), and the mast of a boat (*civitates imperatoris*) which, beneath them, represents various other political powers of Europe. On the left the stump of a tree-trunk (*hierusalem*) has a shield hanging on it.[4] A second picture has a huge bull-figure with a tail and various appendages to represent Antichrist.[5] The rest of the preliminary pages are taken up with pictures and text from the *Vaticinia de summis pontificibus*.[6]

[1] Ibid., ff. 27ᵛ–28ʳ.

[2] Ibid., f. 29ʳ. See *infra*, p. 431, for the 'angelic' pictures.

[3] In one passage he makes the tribulation run from 1364 to 1490, but elsewhere he allows the *ultimus Antichristus* to appear in 1433; see ibid., ff. 30ʳ, 31ʳ, 35ʳ.

[4] Ibid., f. 10ᵛ, Cf. *infra*, p. 462 n. 1, for another example of this illustration.

[5] Ibid., f. 11ʳ.

[6] Ibid., ff. 13ʳ–15ʳ. These are garbled versions of *Vaticinia* XXVII–XXX. Interpolated on f. 13ʳ is a note on Joachim's supposed visit to Pope Urban bringing with him the *Papalista*. On ff. 13ᵛ, 14ʳ, 14ᵛ, there are interesting extensions of the prophecies.

Pius II and Paul II are identified and two more—Angelic Popes—
are to come. We shall return to these in the next part.

Immediately following the *libellus* of Telesphorus and almost continuous with it is the Second Charlemagne prophecy which we have
already discussed.[1] Since this is so closely associated with the
Telesphorean work, it seems extremely likely that it was part of
Rusticianus's original compilation, as also was the *Tractatus de
Antichristo* of John of Paris, which again follows straight on in the
same handwriting.[2] At this point the work of Andreas stops; this
is also probably the end of the compilation made by Rusticianus,
though not necessarily of the St. Georgio book. Here in 1495 a note
on Andreas was added by order of the Abbot of St. Cyprian,[3] which
stresses his prudence and good reputation, suggesting that some
defence was thought necessary in view of the contents of his book.
This was not, however, the end of the manuscript nor of an interest
in prophecy at St. Cyprian's. On f. 43ʳ a different hand takes up the
pen in 1476 to continue with a prophetic anthology of shortish
pieces which includes a prophecy of Fr. Bardellino de Bardellini,
citizen of Mestri, and one of the old Eagle oracles.[4] Then follow
sequences of papal prophecies in different hands and in some confusion: one set of the so-called Prophecies of St. Malachy must have
been inserted in the seventeenth century, but some of the last pages
were filled towards the end of the fifteenth.[5] Here there occurs the
unusual, extended version of the Second Charlemagne prophecy
already mentioned.[6] A note at the end gives us the source and supposed date of the prophecy: 'Haec prophetia superius transcripta
fuit ex exemplari antiquissimo quod havitum fuit a domino Iohanne
Marcello de Sancto Vitali de verbo ad verbum, sicut ibidem erat,
non obstante inconcina latinitate que in ea est. A.D. MCCCCXV
quinto martii' (MS. Lat. Cl. III, 177, f. 50ʳ). Thus in Venice a continuous current of interest in these prophetic figures flows right
through the fifteenth century to the time, probably just before the
advent of Charles VIII in Italy, when this last text was copied into
the St. Cyprian's manuscript. In 1495 Petrus Delphino, the Venetian
General of the Camaldolesi, wrote from Florence, in connection
with the Angelic Pope prophecy, to ask a certain monk if he would
borrow the *Papalista* from Domenico Mauroceno, whom Delphino

[1] Ibid., f. 35ᵛ. [2] Ibid., ff. 35ᵛ–42ᵛ.
[3] Ibid., f. 42ᵛ. [4] Ibid., f. 43ʳ⁻ᵛ.
[5] Ibid., ff. 44ʳ–46ʳ. [6] Ibid., ff. 49ᵛ–50ᵛ; cf. *supra*, p. 330.

obviously knew as a student of these prophecies.[1] In the next
generation we find Silvestro Meuccio making his 1516 edition of
the Telesphorean prophecies from what must have been a closely
connected manuscript. Later still another Venetian, Pasqualino
Regiselmo, came across Domenico Mauroceno's original manuscript—written, he says, a hundred and thirty years earlier—when
he was pursuing his researches into the authorship and interpretation of the *Vaticinia de summis pontificibus*.[2]

---

[1] Martène et Durand, *Ampl. Coll.* iii, cols. 1152–3. It is, perhaps, no accident that
in the first quarter of the sixteenth century Lichtenberger's *Prognosticatio* appeared
in a whole group of Venetian editions.

[2] Regiselmo, *Vaticinia*, Preface.

V

THE EAGLE AND THE LILY

BEFORE the death of Frederick III a new star was already rising in the German firmament. This was first saluted in the famous *Prognosticatio* of Johann Lichtenberger, published in 1488.[1] Lichtenberger was Astrologer to Frederick III—'astrorum iudex sacri imperii'—and in earlier works he had, like others, placed his hopes in this Emperor to fulfil the prophecies. But by 1488 he had become disillusioned with the Third Frederick and his chief work, which rapidly became a best-seller, looked elsewhere for the fulfilment of prophecy. The *Prognosticatio* is not a coherent work, putting forth neither a philosophy of history nor even one clear prophetic programme. It consists, in the first place, of two disparate elements—astrological and prophetic. The former is largely a piece of plagiarization from Paul of Middelburg[2] and it consorts ill with the latter, as Paul was not slow to point out in his *Invectiva . . . in supersticiosum quendam astrologum*, written in 1492 against Lichtenberger.[3] The latter is a gathering together of prophecies and oracles from many quarters, often in seeming contradiction with each other But so many of them derive at either first or second hand from pseudo-Joachimist sources that Lichtenberger can fairly be called a political Joachite in the sense that he looked for the Joachimist

---

[1] See full reference in Select Bibliography. For the most up-to-date study see D. Kurze, *Johannes Lichtenberger* (Lubeck and Hamburg, 1960). Lichtenberger's work was printed in many editions, translated into German, French, Dutch, Italian, and English, and reproduced unacknowledged in two French publications, the *Mirabilis liber* and *La Prophétie merveilleuse de madame saincte Brigide* (for these cf. *infra*, p. 379). D. Fava, 'La fortuna del pronostico di Giovanni Lichtenberger', in 'Italia nel Quattrocento e nel Cinquecento', *Gutenberg Jahrbuch*, v (1930), pp. 126–48, shows that it was brought to Italy, probably by German students, and published as early as 1490–2 at Modena. He has located thirteen editions in Latin and Italian at Modena, Venice, and Milan between 1490 and 1532. Kurze thinks that the popularity of Lichtenberger in Italy was due to his blend of fashionable astrology and Joachimist prophecy.

[2] Paulus Almanus de Middelburgo Zelandie, . . . *Prognosticatio* . . . (no pl. of pub., date, or pag.). See Kurze, op. cit., pp. 16 seq., 34–5; A. Chastel, 'L'Antéchrist à la Renaissance', *Cristianesimo e ragion di Stato, Atti del II congresso internazionale di studi umanistici*, ed. E. Castelli (Rome, 1952), pp. 180–1.

[3] Chastel, loc. cit., p. 181.

third *status* in the political terms into which it had by now been translated. Although so eclectic in his use of materials, his *Prognosticatio* none the less seems to point in one particular direction.

Lichtenberger addressed his prophetic words in three parts, to the Pope, the Emperor, and the laity. Part Two contains the clearest indication of his pattern for the future. He had gathered his material, as we have said, from every kind of source, but notably from the genuine Joachim (the *Liber Concordie*), the pseudo-Joachim (chiefly the *Super Hieremiam*, the *Oraculum Cyrilli*, and the *Vaticinium Sibillae Erithreae*), Telesphorus, Reinhard, and St. Bridget.[1] Clearly he was much influenced by the contemporary vogue of the pseudo-Methodius and believed that the final tribulation of Church and Christian people was imminent.[2] In accordance with this tradition he expected the Imperial Saviour to vanquish the Turk,[3] but after this point, like the authors of the *Tractatus de Turcis*, his expectation

---

[1] Lichtenberger's quotations from Joachimist sources are as follows: (1) Pt. I, cap. 2. *Joachim Super Hier.*: 'Est et alia ficus . . .': abbreviated from *Super Hier.*, f. 3ʳ⁻ᵛ; (2) cap. 3. 'Unde Brigida in libro Revelationum: Sub Aquila grandi . . .': a quotation from the Brigittine oracles which itself incorporates phrases from *Super Hier.*, ff. 3ᵛ, 7ᵛ; (3) Pt. II, cap. 3. 'Unde in libro multarum tribulationum dicitur Moab et Amon duo filii Loth...': quotation from a short work of Joachim, see MS. Reggio, ff. 1ᵛ–2ᵛ; (4) cap. 5. 'Unde in libro multarum tribulationum Joachim dicit ad ruinam ihericho ...': ditto; (5) cap. 6. 'Joachim abbas super Jheremiam dicit in ulciscendo principes doctores sacri imperii sunt isti septem angeli...': one phrase from *Super Hier.*, f. 3ᵛ, the rest of the quotation is unidentifiable (but similar to a passage in *Lib. Conc.*, f. 98ʳ); (6) cap. 7. 'Nam ab anno M.CCCCLXXXVIII (ad) M.CCCCXCIX mihi suspecta sunt tempora et momenta in quo novo ordine Samuelis exorto . . .': adapted with revised dates from the Preface, *Super Hier.*; (7) cap. 13. 'ut habetur 5⁰ et 6⁰ c. libri Cyrilli: In quo tempore tribulatio magna erit et resurget novus ordo et nova restauratio . . .': a general reference probably to the *libellus* of Telesphorus; (8) cap. 13. 'Unde Sibilla Erithrea . . .': 'Post hec veniet altera Aquila . . .': *NA* xv. 168-9, Telesphorus, ff. 15ᵛ, 20ᵛ; (9) cap. 14. 'Erit in insidiis sponse agni, depauperans cultum eius et erunt sponsi tres adulteri, unusque legitimus . . .': *NA* xv. 169, Telesphorus, f. 20ᵛ; (10) cap. 15. 'Unde in libro lamentationum Jheremie ... dicit Joachim Certe vita contemplativa olim in veteri lege viguit sub helia et heliseo...': this quotation cannot be found in the *Super Hier.* and must be presumed to belong to a lost work under this title; (11) cap. 35. 'Unde quidam servus nomine theophilus pro presbitero in libro prophetiarum . . .': general reference to Telesphorus, ff. 10ᵛ–15ʳ; (12) cap. 35. 'Continetur insuper in eodem libro Cirilli quod antequam ecclesia renovetur deus permittet vacante papatu oriri maxima scismata . . .': general reference to Telesphorus, f. 11ʳ; (13) cap. 36. 'Sicut Joachim in libri concordie dicit Vir magna sanctitate in Romana sede sublimatus ...': not a direct quotation from *Lib. Conc.*, but probably based on ff. 89ʳ, 122ᵛ. Lichtenberger's 'quotations' seem often to be adaptations containing a few identifiable phrases.

[2] Lichtenberger, *Prognosticatio*, i, caps. 2, 3; ii, caps. 2, 7, 9, 13, 15, 19, 35; iii, caps. 1–8.

[3] Ibid. ii, caps. 21, 22, 25, 26. He also holds the traditional view that 'cessante enim sacro Imperio, necesse est saeculum consumari' (ii. 7).

took on a shape which was Joachimist rather than Methodian, for attention was focused, not on the coming of Antichrist to end the Emperor's reign, but on the *nova reformatio* which would be inaugurated by the overthrow of the Turk.[1]

When he turned to the agents of the *renovatio*, he had two difficulties to overcome. In the first place, his catholic taste in prophecies involved him in the use of two conflicting traditions—the anti- and the pro-German. In the anti-German tradition, as we have seen, the wicked German tyrant persecutes the Church and makes schism, while the *renovatio* is in the hands of the Angelic Popes, with the later addition of the Second Charlemagne. In the pro-German tradition the great *Aquila* both chastises the Church and renews it, ushering in the Age of Beatitude. Lichtenberger combined the two roles in one Emperor-Chastiser, but since he quoted a number of the anti-German oracles without mitigating their force,[2] it is not always clear if this role is good or bad. The contradiction was resolved for him, however, in the Brigittine oracle of the *rex pudicus facie* who would lead the German nation in its terrible mission and

---

[1] See, for instance, the following passages: ii, cap. 13 (quoting the *Oraculum Cyrilli*): 'In quo tempore tribulatio magna erit et resurget novus ordo et nova restauratio in ecclesia et multi pseudo-pontifices erunt ante reformationem . . .': ii, cap. 35: 'Unde quidam servus nomine theophilus [i.e. Telesphorus] pro presbitero in libro prophetiarum . . . in quo libro spiritualiter continentur omnia que futura sunt de regimine ecclesie et qualiter debeat renovari, sicut Deus longo tempore revelavit servo suo Joachim abbati et sancto Cyrillo . . .'; iii, cap. 14: 'Depost stabit renus [*sic*] et ecclesiastica persona in bona pace et sceptrum discordie auferetur ab eis eritque nova reformatio, nova lex, novum regnum.'

[2] Ibid. ii, cap. 4 (entitled *cap. Decimum*): 'Unde Sibilla Chumaea prophetico spiritu loquitur in vaticinio suo: Post hec, i.e. post modicum temporis, egredietur aquila de Germaniae rupibus multis associata griffonibus . . .' (source unknown, see *infra*, p. 353 n. 1); ii, cap. 9: 'O plebs misera . . . quia regulus novus surrexit in te, non gubernator sed desolator fidelium, non consolator sed depredator spiritualium, non protector sed depressor orphanorum et viduarum in tota alta Alemania. Novus destructor . . . radix peccati a scorpionistis esurget peior Anthiocho . . .' (*supra*, pp. 306, 313, for the thirteenth-century sources from which the *regulus* and the *radix peccati* derive); ii, cap. 13: 'Unde Sibilla Erithrea: . . . Post hec veniet altera Aquila que ignem fovebit in gremio sponse Christi et erunt tres adulteri, unusque legittimus qui alios vorabit . . .' (*supra*, p. 308, for the thirteenth-century source); ii, cap. 35: 'Continetur insuper in eodem libro Cirilli quod antequam ecclesia renovetur Deus permittet vacante papatu oriri maxima scismata inter imperatorem alemanum, qui de sua confisus potentia intendet ordinare ac constituere papam et romanos ac ytalos qui resistere conabuntur aquile grandi, que aquila furore incensa non solum alemanos sed et de omni genere gentes pessimas quas poterit associabit ad suum exercitum et armata manu intrabit Romam . . .' (based on the *libellus* of Telesphorus). This passage is followed by a picture with the caption: 'Hic Imperator ingreditur Romam cum sevitia et eius timore fugiunt Romani clerici et laici ad petras et silvas et multi detruncabuntur.'

yet was the good agent of God.[1] His second problem was where to find a suitable candidate for this part, one in whom the prophecies of the Lily and the Eagle might be reconciled. Lichtenberger ruled out Frederick III,[2] and the care he took to dismiss the candidature of Mathias of Hungary suggests that he may have been deliberately writing a counterblast to the suggestion in the *Tractatus de Turcis*.[3] Although often obscured by the contradictory prophecies quoted, the real point of the *Prognosticatio* seems to lie in its salutation of Maximilian I as the *rex pudicus facie* and his family as that in which all the prophecies would be fulfilled.[4] For, prophetically speaking, Maximilian was in a strong position, since his marriage with Mary of Burgundy made it possible for the first time to resolve the prophetic dilemma and unite in one the oracles of both the Lily and Eagle. It was a Burgundian World Emperor that Lichtenberger expected to arise as a Second Charlemagne in the region where the first once had his capital. His hint as to who this will be is quite plain: 'Et dicitur in libro regum Francorum quod de Karlingis, i.e. de stirpe regis Karoli Franci suscitabitur Imperator in novissimis nomine P. qui erit princeps et monarcha tocius Europe, reformabit ecclesias et clerum et post illum nullus amplius imperabit'

[1] Ibid. i, cap. 3: 'Unde Brigida in libro Revelationum: Sub aquila grandi que ignem fovebit in pectore conculcabitur ecclesia et vastabitur. Nam potens est Deus alemanos altos provocare contra ecclesiam qui magis de humana potentia quam Dei confidunt . . .' (*supra*, p. 339 n. 1, for the continuation of this passage); ii, cap. 3: 'Unde Franciscus et Brigida canunt: Surget rex pudicus facie. Multi dicunt hunc regem esse Fridericum tercium. Ego volo quod sit Maximilianus quia sub eo conculcabitur ecclesia clerusque turbabitur ubique . . . demum gallus succumbet et pudicus facie regnabit ubique.'

[2] *Supra*, p. 348 n. 3.

[3] Lichtenberger, *Prognosticatio*, ii, cap. 21: 'Tu solus clipeum crucis Christi adversus Thurcum erexisti . . . Sed post te exurget maior te, flagellum longiturniter percutiens canes infidelissimos. . . . Ipseque reformabit ecclesiam Pragensem et sancte Zophie templum Constantino [*sic*]. Scandetque ad ardua inter catholicos sed non de sanguine Mathie sed de rupibus alemanie orietur et exiet rex sincerissimus.' See also ii, cap. 20.

[4] *Supra*, n. 1. See also ii, cap. 4 (entitled *cap. Decimum*): 'O Maximiliane, isti duo eunuchi sunt infideles subditi tui, qui fraudis et malicie venenum gestantes contra pudicam faciem tuam, ut fideles tuos et te interficiant'; cap. 5: 'unde in libro multarum tribulationum Joachim dicit ad ruinam Ihericho . . . reges multi contra Israhelitas Alemanos advenient sed expugnabuntur propter Maximilianum quia sublime clipeum elevabit expectando auxilium non solum ab hominibus sed a Domino et resurget volando ad ardua.' Lichtenberger seems to associate Reinhard in particular with the prophecies of Maximilian (which would suggest a later date for Reinhard than that assigned by J. Wolf, *supra*, p. 340 n. 2), but it is difficult to tell when Lichtenberger is quoting and when adapting Reinhard's oracles. See especially ii, cap. 26: '. . . Sub monarcha Maximiliano vel primogenito Acharlingis [*sic*] purum ac nitidum felicitatis tempus accidet.'

(*Prognosticatio*, ii, cap. 16). Thus for the first time Philip, the son of Mary of Burgundy and Maximilian, comes into the prophecies.

At the moment of writing, Lichtenberger felt himself to be on the verge of the great crisis of history. Adapting the words of the pseudo-Joachimist *Super Hieremiam*, he wrote:[1] 'Nam ab anno MCCCCLXXXVIII (ad) MCCCCXCIX mihi suspecta sunt tempora et momenta.' His confidence in the future lay in his belief that the consummation of history would be achieved through the union of German and French aspirations. Quoting a Brigittine prophecy he summed up the political shape of the future thus:[2] 'nam de bono gallo antiquum propheticum invenitur ita: aquile grandi sociabitur lilium et movebitur ab occidente in orientem contra leonem, leo carebit auxilio et decipietur a lilio. Fragrabit lilium in Alemania unde laus sua ultima volabit sub aquila' (*Prognosticatio*, ii, cap. 17). In the midst of these political expectations the figures of the Angelic Popes are somewhat perfunctorily introduced. It is interesting that the one passage which Lichtenberger cited from the genuine *Liber Concordie* is one of the few in which Joachim himself foreshadows a last great Pope.[3] He also drew on the later pseudo-Joachimist tradition of a series of Angelic Popes,[4] but left unclarified their relation to the Emperor–Reformer.[5] It seems plain that his main interest was in the political future of the German *Imperium*.

In the expectation which now became focused on Maximilian and his son Philip two strands were joined. There was, in the first place, the pseudo-Methodian prophecy. Here, as already pointed out, there was no Joachimist Third Age: the Roman Empire must finally succumb before Antichrist, but before this, the last King of the Romans would triumph completely over the infidel.[6]

---

[1] Ibid. ii, cap. 7, adapting *Super Hier.*, Preface.   [2] Cf. *supra*, p. 339 n. 4.

[3] Lichtenberger, *Prognosticatio*, ii, cap. 36: 'Depost esurget quidam vir solitarius magna sanctitate perspicuus sicut Joachim in libro concordie dicit: Vir magna sanctitate in Romana sede sublimatus ut apostolicus per illum faciet Deus tanta miracula quod omnis homo reverebitur illum nec quisquam audebit contraire suis constitutionibus.' *Supra*, p. 348 n. 1, for the source of this 'quotation'.

[4] Lichtenberger, *Prognosticatio*, ii, cap. 37: 'Subsequenter confestim Deus suscitabit alios tres viros sanctissimos unum post alium, in virtutibus et miraculis consimiles, qui facta et dicta antecessoris confirmant. Sub quorum regimine status ecclesie recrescet. Et hi appellabuntur pastores angelici.'

[5] The only specific statement is ii, cap. 35: 'Tandem extirpatis et eradicatis vepribus et spinis malorum hominum [by the German eagle], veniet vir sanctus, pacabit ipsam aquilam cum ecclesia.'

[6] The relevance of the Methodian prophecy is demonstrated by the number of

352   *Antichrist and Last World Emperor*

Maximilian, around whom prophetic expectation had gathered since his youth,[1] was the natural focal point for Methodian hopes. In 1495 Sebastian Brandt prefaced his *De origine et conversatione bonorum Regum et laude civitatis Hierosolymae cum exhortatione eiusdem recuperande*[2] with a frontispiece of Maximilian, King of the Romans, outside Jerusalem and ended his epilogue thus:

> Perge igitur rex sancte cito: te fulmen acerbum
> Thurcorum: voluit maximus esse deus.
> Qui stabile efficiat regnum tibi: sceptra beando
> Sub pede dum teneas secula cuncta. Vale.

In 1498 he published an edition of the *Revelations of Methodius*, edited and expounded by W. Aytinger,[3] with a preface of his own expressing the same appeal to Maximilian. Here the second, the Joachimist, strand also appears, for, besides the victory over the infidel, both Brandt's preface and Aytinger's following tract on the Apocalypse stress the renovation of the Church. Brandt strikes an unmistakably optimistic note: although it is not permitted to calculate the time of the End,

Dubitare tamen utique non debemus: antea non esse venturum finem nisi prius fructificante ecclesia, universus a mari usque ad mare impleatur orbis et gentium prius ut apostolus ait intret plenitudo. Nemo igitur doctus negare ausit gloriosum hunc ecclesie catholice triumphum . . . Maturet Deus optimus maximus hanc sanctissimi sui nominis credentium plenitudinem, presertim invictissimi Christianissimique regis nostri Maximiliani ductu et auspitio felicissimo, cuius regnum et imperium vitamque et fortunam divina adaugeat tueaturque clementia. (Op. cit., Preface.)

editions at the end of the fifteenth century. Besides those mentioned here, it was published at Cologne in 1475 and at Memmingen in 1497. Note, too, that the *Reformation Kaiser Sigmunds* was first printed in 1476 and reprinted in 1480, 1484, 1490, 1494.

[1] The name Constantine, with its pseudo-Methodian implications of Last Emperor, was given to him; see H. Ulmann, *Kaiser Maximilian I* (Stuttgart, 1884), i. 205. On popular expectations centring around Maximilian see also E. Gothein, *Politische u. religiöse Volksbewegungen vor der Reformation* (Breslau, 1878), p. 97. On the expectations of a humanist see J. Knepper, *Jakob Wimpfeling* (Freiburg im Breisgau, 1902), pp. 156-7.

[2] Published at Basle, 1495, no pag.

[3] *Supra*, p. 339 n. 2, for full reference. Aytinger's work had already been published at Augsburg in 1496. Brandt published a second edition in 1515. He also wrote a German poem summoning Maximilian to a high destiny; see R. v. Liliencron, op. cit. (ref. p. 335 n. 2), ii. 307-8. The exhortation to Maximilian is repeated in another poem as late as 1518, ibid. iii. 215. For another collection of prophecies belonging to the same period see H. Haupt, 'Ein oberrheinischer Revolutionär aus dem Zeitalter Kaiser Maximilians I', *Westdeutsche Zeitschrift für Geschichte u. Kunst*, Ergänzungsheft viii (Trier, 1893), pp. 196-7.

The Church must first be punished by the German Emperor and, in delineating his role as chastiser and destroyer of Rome, Aytinger draws on the pseudo-Joachimist works, the Brigittine oracles, the Sibyls, Reinhard, and the latest prophet, Lichtenberger.[1] Finally, the King of the Romans assumes the dual role of Methodian saviour of Jerusalem and Joachimist reformer of the Church. The contrast between the pessimistic and optimistic traditions is strikingly illustrated in the endings of the pseudo-Methodian tract, which is placed first, and Aytinger's, which follows it: in the first, after the overthrow of the Turk and the recovery of Jerusalem, Christendom will be overwhelmed by Gog and Magog and Antichrist, while the King of the Romans expires on Olivet; in the second, Aytinger focuses attention on the *renovatio* and the great peace which passes into the eternal peace. Here he repeats Lichtenberger's prophecy placing the double task on Maximilian's son.[2]

Quia legitur in legenda Karoli magni regis Francie quod de stirpe eius suscitabitur quidam in novissimis temporibus nomine P. qui erit princeps et monarcha totius Europe, qui terram promissionis recuperabit et ecclesiam atque clerum reformabit. Post illum nullus amplius imperabit ... Qui rex Romanorum, de quo dicit Methodius, reformabit ecclesiam et clerum dispersum liberabit de suis necessitatibus, renegatos Christianos castiget, terram infidelium sibi subiiciet, novos predicatores evangelii

[1] References are to his *Tractatus super Methodium* which follows the Methodian prophecy. He knows Joachim chiefly from a reputed prophecy of the failure of Frederick I's crusade (capp. 1, 4). Two quotations in cap. 2 from Joachimist works are taken from Lichtenberger's *Prognosticatio*, ii, caps. 15, 35, cf. *supra*, p. 348 n. 1; one passage (cap. 5) appears to be quoted directly from *Super Hier.*, but in fact is only loosely based on cap. 49, ff. 60–61ʳ. Other passages from the Sibyls, Bridget, and Reinhard appear to be taken mainly from Lichtenberger. In cap. 2 Aytinger quotes a prophecy beginning 'Egredietur aquila de Alemanie rupibus multis associata griffonibus', which Lichtenberger (ii, cap. 4, quoted *supra*, p. 349 n. 2) cites under the authorship of the Cumaean Sibyl but which I have been unable to trace further back than Lichtenberger himself. Aytinger prefaces it by another Sibylline prophecy beginning 'Postquam I. octavus et F. Tertius delati fuerint et A. Sextus nascetur . . .'. This was obviously written after the election of Alexander VI and is therefore not the work of Lichtenberger, but possibly of Aytinger himself. It becomes amalgamated with the prophecy following it and the two are cited as one prophecy from the Sibyl Erithrea in a vernacular prophecy of 1522 (*infra*, p. 360 n. 1); by Purstinger, *Onus Ecclesiae*, cap. 41; by Lazius, *Fragmentum*, f. Kʳ; by T. Graminaeus, *Mysticus Aquilo* (Cologne, 1576), p. 154 (as from the Cumaean Sibyl).

[2] In the 1515 edition Brandt substituted for the *nomine P.* of this prophecy *nomine Petrus*. In 1496 Joseph Grünpeck, historiographer and secretary to Maximilian, published his *Prognosticon*, which was in part copied directly from Lichtenberger's work. In his *Buch v. der Reformation der Christenheyt u. der Kirchen*, he takes up the prophecy of the *Rex pudicus facie* (see D. Kurze, 'Prophecy and History', *Journal of the Warburg and Courtauld Institutes*, xxi (1958), p. 65).

eliget et novam reformationem ecclesie faciet. Et de illis reperitur in revelationibus Sancte Brigite et Hildegardis. Item per eundem magnifica-bitur cum auxilio Christi regnum Romanorum super omnia regna mundi. Ultimo universalem pacem in mundo et maximam faciet ut per presentem pacem mereamur pervenire ad eternam. (Cap. 5.)

The hope that a great king would appear to fulfil these two func-tions also at this time inspired the pen of an Italian who served no special candidate. In the pontificate of Sixtus IV a Dominican, Giovanni Annio of Viterbo, wrote a *Tractatus de futuris Christia-norum triumphis in Saracenis* or *Glosa super Apocalypsim de statu ecclesiae ab anno MCCCCLXXXI usque ad finem mundi*.[1] He ad-dressed his work to the Pope, the Kings of France and Spain, and the Senate of Genoa. His paramount belief was that at the last the Pope and a future prince, working in perfect harmony, would bring in the final state of beatitude in the Church.[2] This triumph would involve the destruction of all Saracens and the union of the Churches. The writer insisted that this age of felicity was the temporal rule of Christ preceding the Last Judgement, that is, the Millennium of history in which Satan was bound, not the eternal felicity beyond history.[3] Its agents would be men; Satan would be bound by a great prince symbolized in the Angel of the Apocalypse descending from the sky, which, in his interpretation, signified the Church.[4] When the peace had been established there would be a patriarch, a king, and a guardian angel ruling in each of twelve divisions of the world.[5] Even the language of the last chapter of the Apocalypse was claimed for this state of temporal beatitude: 'Vidi novum celum, i.e. novum statum ecclesie et terram novam sive novum statum laicorum', and he also used a typically Joachimist phrase: 'sequitur ergo tercius status in reformatione ecclesie.'[5]

In 1485 the magic name of Charles returned to the French monarchy. It is not surprising that the mantle of the Second Charlemagne fell on Charles VIII and, indeed, his fantastic

[1] Published at Louvain, undated, unpag. The current expectation that this saviour would be a French king was utilized by Pius II when seeking to persuade Louis XI to lead a crusade: 'nam pugnare cum Turcis et vincere et Terram Sanctam recuperare Francorum regum proprium est' (cited by Chaume, op. cit. [ref. p. 329 n. 2], p. 36).

[2] *Commentary on Apoc.*, capp. xviii, xix.

[3] Cf. *infra*, pp. 463-4.

[4] *Commentary on Apoc.*, capp. xviii, xix, xx. The verse Apoc. 20: 1, 'Vidi alium angelum descendentem de celo, etc.', was interpreted by Joachim in terms of the ushering in of the third *status* (*Expos.*, ff. 210ʳ-211ᵛ).

[5] *Commentary on Apoc.*, cap. xxi.

ambitions may well have been nourished on prophecy.[1] Much was
expected of him. The poet André de la Vigne dreamed that Christianity, in the form of a woman, implored Charles to rescue her from
the infidel.[2] Michael Tarchianota Marullus, of Constantinople, in
his *Epigrammata et hymni*,[3] exhorted Charles to take up his appointed
role. Jean Michel, his doctor, had a prophetic vision which he presented to Charles as a treatise, *De la nouvelle réformation du siècle et
de la récupération de Jérusalem à lui destinée.*[4] Finally Guilloche, a poet
of Bordeaux, unearthed the very Second Charlemagne prophecy
once written for Charles VI, and expanded it in vernacular verse.[5]

It was extraordinarily apt, for Charles VIII was actually crowned
in his fourteenth year, and the early part of his career could already
be made to conform fairly well to the prophetic programme:

> Charles huitiesme de ce nom,
> Filz de très noble nacion
> Et très illustres fleur de lis,
> En soy aura haultes sourcis,
> Semblablement aura long front,
> Les yeulx longuetz comme seront
> Le nez agu . . .   (Chaume, 32)

Thus the young king assumes the prophetic features, the 'frons
longa, supercilia alta, oculi longi, nasus aquilinus' of the Second
Charlemagne.

[1] For the prophetic background to Charles VIII's expedition see C. de Cherrier,
Histoire de Charles VIII (Paris, 1868), i. 394; H. Delaborde, *L'Expédition de Charles
VIII en Italie* (Paris, 1888), p. 314; H. Hauser, *Les Sources de l'histoire de France: XVIᵉ
siècle*, i (Paris, 1906), pp. 107–8, 243–5, 264.
[2] Prologue to the *Vergier d'Honneur*, summarized in *Archives curieuses de l'Histoire de
France* (Paris, 1834), i. 316. See also Marquis de la Grange, *La Prophécie du Roy Charles
VIII de Maître Guilloche Bourdelois* (Paris, 1869), p. xxvi; de Cherrier, op. cit. i. 394.
[3] Published at Strasbourg in 1509, no pag. The poem is addressed *Ad Carolum Regem
Franciae.*
[4] Ed. J. de la Pilorgerie, *Campagne et Bulletins de la Grande Armée d'Italie commandée
par Charles VIII* (Nantes/Paris, 1866), pp. 431–3. The title continues: *'et qu'il sera de
tous les roys de terre le souverain et dominateur sur tous les dominions et unique monarche du
monde.'* The climax of his triumph is described in these eschatological terms: 'Et tu
seras très plein de felicité, roy des roys et seigneur des seigneurs et prince des princes
de la terre, et non pas tout seulement seras nommé Charles roy de France; mais le
fervent et integerrime reformateur . . . juste et misericors du monde . . . l'expectation
des gens, le désir de tous . . . et benoist de choses spirituelles et temporelles . . .' (p. 432).
[5] Printed in full by de Cherrier, op. cit. i. 487–90; de la Grange, op. cit., pp. 1–9,
with a commentary pp. 10–50; Chaume, op. cit., pp. 32–4. Guilloche appears to have
used the original French version, for the coronation age is given as 14 and the Telesphorean ending is lacking, cf. *supra*, pp. 329–30.

> . . . sera couronné
> L'an quatorze, quant il sera né
>
> .   .   .   .
>
> L'an dixe septiesme, autre foys
> Aucuns des grans princes françoys
> Hors du royaume s'en yront,
> Et contre luy se leveront;
> Mais tout ce rien ne leur vauldra
> Car victoire contr' eulx aura.   (Chaume, 32)

Here the poet expands the promise made in the original text: *Omnesque tyrannos sui regni destruet*, and with some grounds for regarding this as fulfilled, he turns to the future with confidence:

> L'an trente troys, celles parties,
> Il fera de si grant batailles
> Qu'il subiuguera les Ytailles,
> Espaigneulz et Aragonnoys,
> Lombards, aussi bien Yrlandoys,
> Et d'autres gens subiuguera,
> Et puis après conquestera
> Vaillamment la cité de Romme
> Et obtiendra double couronne,
> Nommé sera roy des Rommains
> Oultre le vouloir des Germains,
> C'est assavoir des Alemans;
> Et puis après incessammens
> Par feu et par sang destruyra
> Un'autre cité qui sera
> Nommée la cité de pechié.   (Ibid. 33)

Here a note identifies this city as Florence. From this point the poem proceeds with the whole programme of the Second Charlemagne text. He will conquer Greece and be acclaimed King of the Greeks; he will conquer the Turk and all barbarians; all Christian kings will submit to him. He will issue the edict of death against all who refuse to honour the Cross and no man will be able to resist him.

> Il possédera, en sa vie,
> La très-haultaine seigneurie
> De ceste terre universelle.   (Ibid. 34)

His career ends at the climax of the original text without the additional Telesphorean ending:

> En Jhérusalem entrera
> Et mont Olivet montera,

Priant Dieu le père et le filz
Et le benoist sainct Esperis;
Déposant ces troys couronnes,

. . . . .

A Dieu rendra son esperit,
Lors seront signes merveilleux,
La terre mouvant en tous lieulx,
Du règne dudit Roy Françoys,
L'an qui sera cinquante troys.　　　　(Chaume, 34)

　　How far Charles VIII was influenced by this prophetic programme it is impossible to say with any certainty. Lauréault de Foucemagne, writing on his Italian expedition in the eighteenth century, concluded that a vital element throughout was the crusading motive and recalled the prayers and processions Charles offered for victory against the infidel.[1] Charles's programme suggests the dual prophetic role most clearly: as Joachimist chastiser and reformer of the Church he must conquer Florence and Rome; as Methodian saviour he must lead the Crusade. The inclusion of Florence in his programme immediately recalls the Second Charlemagne prophecy,[2] and it is perhaps permissible to seek here a clue to Charles's unusual and unexpected route south through Italy.[3] We may get an echo of his belief in the prophecies from the *Diaria de Bello Carolino* of Alessandro Benedicto: 'et quaedam vaticinia de se ipso augurari confidentius professus est', after which follows what is obviously a summary of the Second Charlemagne prophecy.[4] We may also note Guicciardini's report that, to flatter Charles, reference was made to 'quello gloriosissimo Carlo, il cui nome voi ottenete'.[5]

---

[1] Cited by Marquis de la Grange, op. cit., p. xxiv. It is reported that when Charles saw the mystery play of David and Goliath he interpreted it as his fight with the Turks.

[2] So far as I am aware, Florence was not coupled with Rome as the chief objects of the destruction carried out by the King–Chastiser until the Second Charlemagne prophecy.

[3] i.e. his crossing of the Apennines and advance down the west side instead of either going by sea from Genoa, as many French invaders of Naples had done, or following the Via Emilia into the Romagna, as the Papal–Neapolitan army expected him to do.

[4] Published, probably at Venice, 1496, no pagination. See Bk. I (beginning). The quotation continues: 'Ita ut eius auspiciis Hispania, Germania et Italia perdomita facile Graecia, Asia, Syria, ac Egyptus illum tanquam Deum veneraretur. Et adepta Hierosolyma deposita humi corona sepulchrum Christi veneraretur, victor triumphans suprema die in coelum raperetur.' Notice the triumphant apotheosis in place of the Methodian collapse.

[5] F. Guicciardini, *La storia d'Italia*, ed. A. Gherardi (Florence, 1919), i. 22–3. Guicciardini's report shows that all the arguments of prophecy and the portents of the heavens were being used to forecast unprecedented calamities in Italy and an unparalleled role of glory for Charles (ibid., pp. 22–3, 52–3).

Whilst the question of Charles's own state of mind remains uncertain, there is no doubt that contemporaries were expecting a crisis of history which would see the fulfilment of prophecies. In a number of sources we meet references to the prophecy circulating at this moment under the name of St. Cataldus and the awe-inspiring circumstances in which it was discovered at Tarento and sent to King Ferdinand to warn him of approaching calamities.[1] Tizio's *Historia Senensium* told of presages, phantoms, and astrological conjunctions of dreadful import.[2] There was a prophet crying woe in Rome in 1490,[3] while a Benedictine monk of Vallombrosa, Angelo Fondi, hailed Charles as the final Emperor and exhorted Florence and the Papacy to believe the prophecies and support him.[4] Above all, as evidence of the prevailing mood, we have the phenomenon of Savonarola.[5] By a curious coincidence a Hebrew writer of the time also placed Charles VIII in a Messianic context, believing that, with the arrival of the King of France in Naples, the Messianic era had begun.[6]

At first the pattern of Charles's career in Italy seemed to fit the prophecies wonderfully. The rapid conquest of Florence and Rome, the presence of Maximilian and Ferdinand of Spain to play the role of wicked kings, the appearance of Savonarola as the herald of the *Papa angelicus*—all fitted miraculously into place. But the wicked rulers played their parts too effectively for the prophets and Charles was back home again before the Joachimist future had well advanced.

---

[1] *Prophetia S. Cataldi . . . reperta A.D. 1492 in ecclesia tarentina vivente adhuc et regnante Ferdinando Alphonsi primi filio, nuper autem . . . in lucem edita per fratres S. Marie Montis Oliveti, a quibus inventa fuit in Sicilia in biblioteca regis Alphonsi secundi . . .* On the finding of the oracle see Infessura, op. cit., p. 1240; Alexander ab Alexandro, *Genialium diariorum libri sex* (Paris, 1539), ff. 67ᵛ–68ʳ; B. Moroni, . . . *Cataldiados . . . libri sex* (Naples, 1614), pp. 173 seq.; *Cronica di Napoli di Notaro Giacomo*, ed. P. Garzilli (Naples, 1845), p. 173; Petrus Galatinus, *De ecclesia destituta*, MS. Vat., Lat. 5569, f. cxliiiᵛ. The text, or part of it, appears in S. Tizio, *Historia Senensium* (cited Delaborde, op. cit., p. 317); *Mirabilis liber* (Paris, 1522), f. xlʳ; Galatinus, MS. cit., f. cxliiiᵛ seq. There is a mention of this prophecy in a late manuscript collection of prophecies in the Bodleian Library, Laud Misc. 588, f. 2ᵛ.

[2] Cited Delaborde, op. cit., p. 317.

[3] Infessura, op. cit. [ref. p. 337 n. 2], pp. 264–5; cf. *infra*, p. 430.

[4] Cited Hauser, op. cit., p. 264.

[5] On Savonarola and Joachimism see *infra*, pp. 435–6.

[6] S. Krauss, 'Le Roi de France, Charles VIII, et les espérances messianiques', *Revue des études juives*, li (1906), pp. 87–95.

VI

CONSTELLATION OF PROPHECIES
CHARLES V

AFTER the death of Charles VIII of France the advantage in this duel of prophecies swung back heavily in favour of the German house.[1] The Hapsburg Charles carried the magic name, while his Burgundian lineage enabled him to pose as the heir to both traditions. In a late fifteenth-century hand at the back of a manuscript now in Cambridge[2] the Second Charlemagne prophecy is written out under the heading *Prophetia abbatis Joachimi A.D. 1180.* It begins: 'Carolus philippi filius ex natione illustra lilii.' Thus it marks the second stage in the appropriation of this Prophecy by the Burgundian–Hapsburg house: from the *nomine P.* we have moved to *Carolus philippi filius.*

Spanish expectation, too, contributed to Charles's prophetic position. Crusading hopes had not disappeared with the Conquest of Granada but had found a new focus in the destiny opening up before the Spanish monarchy at the end of the fifteenth century. New lands were to be won for Christ, the Turk was to be finally vanquished, all people were to be brought into the *unum ovile* and this work was the prophetic destiny of the Catholic sovereigns. Cardinal Ximenez de Cisneros himself had been caught in the emotional current of these hopes.[3] In 1509 Charles de Bovelles (Bobillus) wrote an exultant letter to the Cardinal proclaiming the imminence of this prophetic future and in 1512 there was a Fray Melchior who announced a similar message. Again in 1523 a Franciscan, Francesco de Ocaña, prophesied the final reforming mission of Charles V. But

---

[1] Giovanni Baptista Spagnuoli or Mantuanus continued, however, to celebrate in verse the expected French saviour, see *Fastorum libri duodecim* (Lyons, 1516), p. 5, 'De sancto angelo Carmelita' and 'Exhortatio ad insubres', which is a eulogy of Louis XII.

[2] MS. Cambridge, Univ. Libr., Kk. VI. 16, f. 185ᵛ.

[3] The material in this paragraph is derived from M. Bataillon, *Érasme et l'Espagne* (Paris, 1937), pp. 55–70, 199–200; *Raccolta di documenti e studi pubblicati dalla R. Commissione Colombiana pel quarto centenario dalla scoperta dell'America* (Rome, 1894), Pt. I, vol. ii, *Scritti di Cristoforo Colombo*, ed. C. de Lollis, *Libro de las profecías*, pp. 76–160; see also pp. 202, 434–5. See *infra*, pp. 446–7, on Melchior and Ocaña.

perhaps the most striking example of these Spanish-centred prophets
is Christopher Columbus himself. In 1501–2 he wrote the *Libro de
las profecías* in which he tried to search into the prophetic future.
One of his authorities was: 'El abad Johachín, calabrés, diso, que
había de salir de España quien havía de redificar la Casa del monte
Sion' (op. cit., p. 83). His collection of prophecies gives a somewhat
confused programme of Last Things, but through it runs the thread
of the expected Age of Gold and the role of the Spanish monarchs
in it. Amongst other things he quoted an unidentifiable letter of
Genoese ambassadors in 1492 to the Spanish monarchs, which again
made Joachim the authority for expecting a Spanish king 'qui arcem
Syon sit reparaturus'.

Round the period of the Imperial election of 1519 the prophecies
gathered thickly. In 1517 a curious little German pamphlet was
produced by Pamphilius Gengenbach, a Swiss poet, in which
prophetic pronouncements were gathered together from a hermit
named Nollhart, from Bridget and the Sibyls, Methodius, Joachim,
and Reinhard.[1] The chief point of its rhymed German verses seems
to lie in the fact that the prophets are interviewed by the Kaiser and
the King of France and that the latter is rejected as a candidate for
world empire. The marriage of French and German traditions
appears in the pamphlet of Master Alofresant of Rhodes, *Alle alten
Prophecien von Keyserliche Maiestat*, published at Munich and
Strasbourg in 1519. Here the galaxy of prophetic witnesses is impressive: the Sibyls and Cyril, Hildegarde and Bridget, Joannes de
Rupescissa, Gamaleon, Reinhard, and Lichtenberger, all pronounce
their oracles in favour of Charles. On the one side, Charles's Burgundian inheritance is stressed, for the historical background sketched
is that of the descendants of John the Fearless, Duke of Burgundy,
and the prophecies of the Lily are made to focus on his fourth direct
male descendant. On the other hand, the Hohenstaufen prophecies
are revived, notably the one which first pointed to a glorious Third
Frederick. We have already found this used, in a revised form, by

---

[1] Gengenbach, *Ditz sind die prophetien sancti Methodii u. Nollhardi* (Basel, 1517).
Kurze, loc. cit. (ref. p. 353 n. 2), p. 67, calls this a carnival play, part of which reads
like a rhymed extract from Lichtenberger, with variations. In another version of this,
Von ainem Waldbrüder wie er underricht gibt Babst Kaiser König u. allen ständen (no
pl. of pub., 1522), the Pope, the King of France, the Kaiser, and others question the
Waldbrüder, Bridget, and the Sibyl on the future, with the same outcome: that the
future *Imperium* belongs to the German Kaiser. There are echoes of Lichtenberger
here, and the prophecy 'Postquam I. octavus . . .' discussed *supra*, p. 353 n. 1, is given
by the Sibyl in a vernacular version.

Thomas Ebendorfer in the fifteenth century; now, in a newly revised form with the tell-tale name omitted, it is applied to Charles V:[1]

Volabit Aquila, cuius volatu debellatur Leo, qui regnabit Ierosolymis septem annis. Tandem conspirabunt principes Almaniae, et magnates Bohemiae opprimentur. Et Leopardus devorabit eum. Tunc surget Rex de radice Aquilae Orientalis, et veniet pullus Aquilae, et nidificabit in domo Leonis et fructu alimentoque paterno carebit. Et eligetur Rex, cui honor regis non exhibetur. Hic regnabit, ac imperans imperabit, extendetque ramos suos usque ad ultimos fines terrae. Tempore illius summus capietur pontifex. Et clerus dilapidabitur, nam depravat fidem. Heu pessima vita cleri.

It is clear that the Second Charlemagne text was circulating in favour of Charles V at this time. In 1505 it was found in an 'old book' in Italy;[2] later it appeared at Louvain.[3] A German vernacular version, beginning 'Karolus ein sun Philippi', was now current.[4] In 1519 Sanuto, the Venetian ambassador, sent back to Venice from England an entirely independent English version of the Second Charlemagne prophecy.[5] It is interesting to observe here how the original French–Joachimist context has been lost in the opening and closing sentences: 'Charles the son of Philip, of the illustrious Caesarean race'—thus an Imperial origin has been substituted for the descent from the Lily. The last sentence, in the Telesphorean version, had set the Emperor in relation to the two other Joachimist symbols of the Third Frederick and the Angelic Pope. Since then, however, the Third Frederick had appeared without displaying any hint of superhuman stature. In Sanuto's version, as also in the German vernacular one then current, the last Telesphorean sentence survives, but both symbols have lost their pregnant meaning: 'He will, with signs and miracles, breathe his last in the thirty-fifth year

---

[1] Alofresant, *Alle alten Prophecien* (ref. p. 339 n. 3), f. 9ᵛ. He says that this was taken in 1498 from an ancient book by Maternus Hatten of Spire. For earlier versions of this prophecy see *supra*, pp. 311–12, 333–4. Wolf, *Lect. mem.* i. 722, quoted it from Alofresant, and in 1630 Cornelius Crull, probably quoting from Wolf, applied it to the Elector Frederick of the Palatinate; see J. Praetorius, *Alectryomantia seu divinatio magica* (Frankfurt/Leipzig, 1680), pp. 70–1. Alofresant also uses the other thirteenth-century pro-Imperial verse, *Gallorum levitas*; cf. *supra*, p. 312.

[2] A pamphlet published in 1532, *Erzelung der Künigreich in Hispanien . . . Mer ein alte Prophecy Kay. Carl betreffend*, introduces the prophecy at the end thus: 'Dise Prophecey ist gefunden worden in Italien, in der stadt Verona in einem fast alten buch.' See also Lazius, *Fragmentum*, Kivʳ, giving the date 1505, and B. Purstinger, *Onus Ecclesiae*, cap. 48.

[3] Lazius, *Fragmentum* f. Nivᵛ.   [4] *Supra*, n. 2.

[5] *Calendar of State Papers*: Venice II, 1509–1527 (London, 1867), No. 1301, p. 566.

of his reign, and be crowned by the angel, being the first crowned Emperor since Frederick III.'[1]

The Second Charlemagne prophecy was known to Berthold Purstinger, the reforming bishop of Chiemsee, who wrote his *Onus Ecclesiae* in 1519.[2] This work affords an interesting example of a thoroughgoing Joachimist scheme of history into which the old tradition of the World Emperor is fitted. The framework is that of the three *status* and seven ages as constructed by Joachim and his Franciscan disciple, Ubertino da Casale.[3] The sixth age of the Church, 'in quo nunc sumus',[4] is given for reform, beginning with St. Francis and St. Dominic and lasting until the great Antichrist. It is typified in the Church of Philadelphia in the Apocalypse and will see schism and persecution by tyrant and pseudo-pope. Here Purstinger does not hesitate to use the anti-German Joachimist oracles,[5] although he does not believe in the sinister role cast for the German people by Telesphorus: the tyrant from the north need not necessarily be a German. In any case, he believes that the good Emperor to be raised up by God is Charles V, and here he quotes the Second Charlemagne prophecy which, he says, has been circulating since 1505.[6] But to this reforming bishop the chief instruments of the *renovatio* which will end the sixth age will be Angelic Popes, not Emperors. They will bring in the seventh age or third *status* of the world, when Satan will be bound. In this Sabbath of Tranquillity, to endure until the Last Judgement, the world will be ruled jointly by a new pontiff and a new king.[7] Thus, while accepting the prophecy of Charles V, Purstinger did not put it in the context of the final Age of Blessedness, which lies further ahead.

It seems that prophecy even penetrated the Imperial electoral chamber in 1519. Some of the speakers in the debate attached great significance to the issue of this election, declaring that the salvation of Europe hung on it, that he who could sustain this office must be of heroic mould and vast strength, and that he must be comparable to

---

[1] Cf. the German vernacular version in the pamphlet cited *supra*, p. 361 n. 2: 'und mut wunderparlichen zaychen seinen geyst auffgeben im fünff und dreyssigsten jar seines Reichs, und wirt dasselbst gekrönt werden von dem Engel, und wirt werden der erst gekrönt Keiser nach Keyser Friderich dem dritten.'

[2] Published anonymously, 1524, and under his name, 1531, no pl. of pub., no pag.

[3] *Infra*, pp. 467–8 on Purstinger's Joachimism.

[4] Purstinger, *Onus Ecclesiae*, cap. 2.

[5] Ibid., capp. 16, 38, 39, 41.

[6] Ibid., cap. 48.

[7] Ibid., capp. 60, 61, 66, 69.

an Alexander.[1] The magic name of Charlemagne was invoked, but, it was insisted, the *imperium* belonged to the Germans.[2] The Bishop of Trier remembered a prophet of Maximilian's election who swore he would be the last German Emperor, but the Elector of Brandenburg had a better prophecy for these times. 'Fata etiam his temporibus promittunt Imperatorem, qui majores, magnitudine potentiae, superaturus sit. Et addunt alteram laudem, multo gratiorem: futurum ut bonitate et clementia praeter caeteros reges excellat, nec alium nisi Carolum vaticinor. Quare opto Deus Imperium ipsi committat, eumque gubernet, ad salutem orbis terrarum' (Sabinus, op. cit., p. 26). This may well be an echo of the Second Charlemagne prophecy, while the same heightened expectation seems to inspire the tones in which the new Emperor was hailed in the *Libertas Germaniae* of H. Gebviler.[3] Thus on Charles V's career the prophetic expectation of both traditions—the Lily and the Eagle—became focused.[4]

The *Prognosticon* of Torquatus, an Italian astrologer, ostensibly

---

[1] G. Sabinus, *Erudita et Elegans Descriptio Electionis et Coronationis Caroli V Imperatoris* . . . (Helmstadt, 1612), pp. 25–6, 37.

[2] R. Folz, op. cit. (ref. p. 329 n. 3), p. 561.

[3] H. Gebviler, *Libertas Germaniae* . . . (Strasbourg, 1519, no pag.), cap. x: 'Quem [i.e. Charles V] toto Christiano orbe pacato, et Romane ecclesie monstroso statu in melius reformato, ferocissimam immanium Turcarum gentem oppressurum, ac Christiane religionis suavissimo iugo facile subditurum, dubitamus minime . . . Cui proculdubio Caroli magni vestigiis innixuro, totus orbis olim acclamabit: Carolo Augusto, a Deo coronato, magno et pacifico Imperatori vita, victoria.' See also the following contemporary pamphlets: Franz von Sickingen, *Eyn Sendbrieff* . . . (Württemberg, 1521), hailing Charles as, without doubt, the great champion against Antichrist; G. Sauromanus, *Hispaniae consolatio* (? Louvain, 1520, no pag.), *Hypotheses sive argumenta spectaculorum* . . . (Antwerp, 1520, no pag.):

Iam nova lux terris oritur, Pax alma redibit
Et positis armis aurea soecla fluent.
Carolus Europae Rector Lybiamque Asiamque
Asseret imperio victor ubique suo.
Nunc implebuntur prudentum oracula vatum,
Grex unus terris, Pastor et unus erit.

Commenting on this literature, Folz, op. cit., p. 561, says: 'Sur ce plan . . . l'élection du petit-fils de Maximilien ne fut pas que le triomphe de la technique financière des Fugger, mais, dans une large mesure, celui du Charles allemand.'

[4] The *Reformation Sigmunds*, with references to Charles V, was published anew in 1520, 1521, and 1522. In 1519, in two editions at Augsburg and Landshut, the German legends were disseminated in the *Volksbuch vom Kaiser Friedrich* (ed. M. Haupt, *Zeitschrift für Deutsches Altertum*, v (1845), pp. 250–68). In 1521 Hermannus a Nuenare addressed his edition of Einhard's *Vita et gesta Karoli Magni* to Charles V, ending his preface: 'Tu vero huius viri sanctimoniam imitatus, iure optimo Karolus Maximus appellaberis.'

addressed to Mathias of Hungary in 1480 but probably composed in 1527,[1] underlined the prophetic significance of events in Charles V's reign. The rise of the pseudo-prophets, the final schism, and the arch-heresiarch[2] are 'prophesied' in terms which pointed to Luther's Germany. The conflict with the Turk, the Battle of Pavia, and the Sack of Rome are there too. A copy of the 1544 edition in the British Museum is studded with marginal notes applying his 'forecasts' to sixteenth-century events. These 'fulfilments' would lead men forward in expectation of those hopes against which '*nondum impletum*' was still written. Torquatus expected the renewal of the Church and the triumph of the Empire. The Turk would be conquered and converted and then would be accomplished that union of interests which had been expressed in the Brigittine prophecy: 'Gallorum laus sub aquila volabit.'[3] The manuscript note 'nondum impletum renovatio in Ecclesia' sums up the hope with which such prophecies were read.

In the second quarter of the sixteenth century Charles V was clearly the prophetic favourite. Ariosto saluted him in words which echo the old Imperial dream:[4]

> E vuol che sotto a questo imperatore
> Solo un ovile sia, solo un pastore.
> (*Orlando Furioso*, xv. 26)

Giangiorgio Tressono made the same salute to the Eternal Empire.[5] Much more significant than these casual gestures was the deep passion with which Egidio of Viterbo appealed to Charles V. His dreamed-of golden age was, as we have seen, at once humanist and mystical, political and religious. The grand sweep of history, the 'storia assoluta della umanità sub specie aeternitatis',[6] had come to a second great focus in his age. All events proved this—for there was no distinction between secular and sacred history—and the whole of

---

[1] Published in Latin editions of 1534, 1535, and 1544, and in a German edition of 1535. The edition used here is that of Antwerp, 1544. Cantimori, *Eretici*, pp. 18–20, clearly takes the view that this work was written after the Sack of Rome, but D. Kurze, loc. cit., p. 68, indicates that Cantimori gave his support orally to the opinion that it was written as early as 1492. Although no precise *post-eventum* prophecy can be located, the whole sequence of happenings down to 1527 seems far too close to history to be genuine prophecy.

[2] Note the description of Luther: quoted *infra*, p. 447.

[3] Torquatus, op. cit., f. 9ᵛ.

[4] Cited F. Yates, *Charles Quint et l'Idée d'Empire* (Paris, no date), p. 81.

[5] In *L'Italia liberata dai Goti*, cited Yates, op. cit., p. 94.

[6] E. Massa, 'Egidio da Viterbo e la metodologia del sapere', *Pensée humaniste et tradition chrétienne aux XVᵉ et XVIᵉ siècles* (Paris, 1950), p. 208.

the past showed the present direction of history. In his *Historia Viginti Saeculorum*[1] Egidio worked out in great detail the parallels between the two sets of ten centuries before and after Christ and the whole pattern led inevitably to the great climax of the twentieth century. In the *Scechina*,[2] written at the instigation of Clement VII and addressed to Charles V, Egidio moved from the theology of history to an outpouring of hope inspired at once by Jewish mystical studies and the great contemporary signs of the times. This was the right century and Charles had the right number, therefore he was called to do the work of the Holy Spirit: 'Audi quem appellet Rex meus a gradu quinto: si simile haeret simili: non alium apellare potuit nisi Carolum quintum ut ego decima: decimo saeculo: primum vocavi decimum vocavi. Sic nunc Rex caeli: terrarum regem: princeps principem: regem rex: quintus quintum: . . . Audi quintas vires, Carole quinte . . .' (*Scechina*, p. 99). Charles was the new Moses to lead the human race into liberty, the new Caesar to overcome all barbarian tyrannies, the Pastor, like David, to gather all sheep into one fold. He could even be compared with advantage to the Apostles: '. . . per illos orbem notum: per te incognitum: acquisivere: per illos partem: per te totum circuiere . . .' (*Scechina*, p. 161). His fame must be announced to all the islands (Britain and Hibernia included) and he must open up the new lands which now begin to appear in a marvellous vista before amazed eyes: '. . . partem orbis maioribus ignotam adinvenire a Gadibus occidentem et ad antipodas fere fugientem solem sequi: sancti Johannis insulam: Hispaniolam Cubam ad Cancri tropicum: novi orbis terras ad antarticum mortalibus patefacere: novos homines: novas gentes: admirantium oculis ostentare' (*Scechina*, p. 145). Charles is apostrophized in the most extravagant terms:

Tu Caesar: quem post apostolos ad tam divinum opus accersimus: cui tantum honoris, dignitatis, gloriae reservavimus contemni nos: abiici nos: oblivioni nos dari patieris? Qui ostendisti partes orbis terrarum occultas: ne sis caelo quam terris avarior, ostende occultas partes Scripturarum. Latuere ante te libri archanorum non Numae: non Pythagorae: non mortalium: sed eorum divinorum munerum quae ego in Sinai Mosi aperui . . . (*Scechina*, p. 161.)

---

[1] This work is still unpublished. The archetype is MS. Lat. IX B14 in the Bibl. Naz., Naples. See bibl. no. 8.815. I have drawn on L. Pélissier, *De 'Historia Viginti Saeculorum'* (Montpellier, 1896).

[2] Ed. F. Secret (Rome, 1959).

His cosmic task is finally summed up thus: 'Quaere magnanime Caesar tu ad quem qua imperator: orbem invenire, emendare, componere: qua advocatus Ecclesiae illam fovere, erigere, propagare pertinet' (*Scechina*, p. 219). If he fulfils this role the promise of the future is unbounded: 'Vides hic terram novam: ac caelum novum: novam Asiam: novam Africam: novam Europam: maria item nova: novas insulas: quae tibi uni cognoscenda ut exemplaria sunt: . . .' (*Scechina*, p. 224).

Egidio did not belong with the mere disseminators of prophecy and oracle. His expectation was based on profound search for the meaning of history, both within history and in the mystical Jewish studies of letter- and number-symbolism. But his mood and hope he shared with many. This heightened sense of the vast significance of contemporary events lent excitement to their interpretation and when history presented one with a figure-head of the stature of Charles V, it is hardly surprising that he was magnified into the final colossus of history.

Also in Rome at the same time as Egidio and probably well known to him was Petrus Galatinus, the Franciscan.[1] In 1524 he dedicated his Commentary on the Apocalypse[2] to Charles V, whom he hailed as the athlete elected by God to assist the Angelic Pope in the final reformation of history. He did not name his pope but expected him in time to form a splendid partnership against the infidel: 'ita sub angelico Pastore et Carolo quinto Romanorum Imperatore (ut speramus) humiliata defectura sit ut quasi et mortua appareat . . .' (i.e. the Saracen sect) (f. ccvi^v). Elsewhere he spoke of the *magnus rex* who would overthrow the infidel first in Africa and then in Europe[3] and quoted Amadeus: *erit ter maximus: maximus videlicet Pontifex, maximus Rex et maximus Dominus.*[4] His sense of the positive imperial role led him to make Zorobabel the type of a great prince—rather than the great pontiff of Joachim—who would reform the principalities of the imperium.[5] Galatinus's vision of world unity was a political dream as well as a religious one: 'Tunc enim non unus tantum pastor erit et unum ovile, verum unus quoque Deus coletur in orbe . . . una lex a cunctis gentibus observabitur: unus princeps potentissimus, ac Deum timens orbi imperabit' (MS. 5578,

---

[1] On Petrus Galatinus see *supra*, pp. 234–8, and *infra*, pp. 442–5.
[2] MS. Vat., Lat. 5567, f. 1^v.
[3] MS. Vat., Lat. 5578, ff. 18^v–19^r.
[4] Ibid., f. 24^r.
[5] Ibid., f. 29^r; for Joachim's interpretation see *supra*, p. 304.

f. 30ʳ). He even composed a *carmen* on the expected partnership of
Pope and Emperor:

> Pauper et hinc subito surget, qui legibus orbem
> Formabit sanctis: nam regnans unus ubique
> Pastor erit: rexque unus mundi vasta tenebit
> Climata, iam Christo populis terrisque subiactis.
>
> (MS. 5579, f. 10ʳ)

With this ideal picture of co-operation before his eyes, what, one
asks, were the reactions of Galatinus to the events of the year 1527?
We do not know.

The Sack of Rome in 1527 by the armies of Charles V was a major
prophetic event. It fulfilled so dramatically the prophecies of the
King–Chastiser who should destroy Rome that it was difficult not
to see it in this context. The double tradition of the good and bad
chastisers, of course, allowed interpretation in two opposite senses.
The various Italian prophets who cried Woe! Woe! in the streets
during the months prior to the Sack, announcing the imminent
punishment of the Church for her sins, had prepared the minds of
Pope and ecclesiastics to see in these terrible events a manifestation
of Antichrist.[1] The rise of the great heresiarch Luther with his
'locusts' from the bottomless pit, the schism in the Church, the Sack
of Rome—all were part of the long-expected crisis of Antichrist, and
the German Emperor and nation were traditionally agents in this.
Yet the destruction of Rome and the just chastisement of the Church
also belonged to the roles of the Second Charlemagne and the
Brigittine *rex pudicus facie*. Thus the Catholic German interpretation of these events separated the forces of Antichrist, represented
by the Protestants and Turks, from the work of chastisement and
renewal which belonged to the Last Emperor: the Sack of Rome
confirmed Charles in this role.[2] It is significant that both Italian and
German interpreters of this crisis believed that *renovatio* would
shortly follow tribulation.[3]

A few years later there was a revival of prophetic propaganda in

---

[1] Wolf, *Lect. mem.* ii. 295; L. Guicciardini, *Il Sacco di Roma* (Paris, 1664), p. 174;
G. Pecci, *Memorie storico-critiche della Città di Siena* (Siena, 1755), iii. 248; Pecci,
Notizie storico-critiche sulla vita di Bartolomeo da Petrojo chiamato Brandano (Lucca,
1763), p. 20; D. Bernino, *Historia di tutte l'heresie*, iv (Rome, 1709), pp. 368, 375; O.
Raynaldus, *Annales ecclesiastici*, xiii (Lucca, 1755), pp. 1, 10; Pastor, *History of the
Popes* ix. 379–81.

[2] Lazius, *Fragmentum*, ff. Hiiiʳ, Kiiᵛ, Kiiiᵛ, Kiiiiᵛ.

[3] Ibid., f. Hiiiᵛ; Guicciardini, op. cit., p. 174.

favour of Charles V. In 1532 Berthold Purstinger again published
his *Onus Ecclesiae*. At the same time the Second Charlemagne
prophecy appeared once more at the end of a German pamphlet on
Spain.[1] In this year Charles conducted an expedition against the
infidel in North Africa and to some this seemed an occasion of
prophetic import. When the *De Bello contra Barbaros* of Benedetto
Accolti the Elder was printed in 1532, the publisher thought the
times to be crucial and appended various oracles, one of which
brings together in a strange medley the Book of Daniel and the
classical Age of Gold, the Joachimist Angelic Pope and the divine
Caesar.[2] It catches the mood of those who believed themselves to
be standing on the threshold of the greatest evil and the highest
beatitude in history: 1535 is to be the key year. In 1532 Johann Eck
published a pamphlet *Sperandam esse in brevi victoriam adversus
Turcam*,[3] in which he firmly pinned his hope on Charles V and his
brother Ferdinand for a speedy triumph over the Turks. Though he
used them cautiously, the testimony of the usual prophetic band
is invoked: Methodius, Hildegarde, Merlin, Cyril, Joachim, and
Bridget, these all supported his expectation. Again, Johannes Carion,
winding up his chronicle of empires in 1532, also passed over from
Charles' expedition into prophetic speculation. He remembered
a Greek promise of restoration to Constantinople eighty years after
its fall: Lichtenberger's prophecies came to mind and those of the
Abbot Joachim, St. Bridget, and others. The heavens declared their
portents and the prophets were all of one mind in expecting the
great Emperor.[4] So Carion, too, believed himself to be ending his
history on the eve of the *renovatio*.

[1] *Supra*, p. 361 n. 2.

[2] *De bello contra Barbaros* (Venice, 1532), appendix: 'Apolinei Vatis Oraculum: . . .
Foelix igitur ac nimium foelix cui septima fulserit aetas, annus scilicet 1530. Sed mage
beatus qui superaverit Annum 1535. Siquidem tunc sacrosancta ecclesia reformabitur
et aetas aurea passim per multos vigebit annos sub quodam pontifice beatissimo et Divo
Caesare clementissimo, et antequam talis reformatio fiet, interim maior pars hominum
morietur fame, gladio, peste, ac timendum erit quod vix media aut tertia pars hominum
totius orbis supervivet tunc temporis.' It is curious that in 1564 a younger Benedetto
Accolti was involved in a plot to remove Pope Pius IV in order to bring in 'quel pontifice che ordinariamente dal populo Romano è chiamato pontifice angelico' (cf. *infra*,
pp. 450–1).

[3] Published Augsburg, unpag. See the dedication and *Sermo Secundus*. There was
a Turkish oracle in circulation which prophesied the end of Turkish domination and
this was used to support the belief that Christians would easily and in a brief space of
time overcome them and bring them into the 'unum ovile sub uno pastore' (*Aulae
Turcicae Othomannicicae Imperii Descriptio* (Basle, 1577), pp. 305–14).

[4] J. Carion, *Chronica* (Lat. ed. Paris, 1551), pp. 577–9. The first edition was published

Martin du Bellay supplies evidence as to the actual effect of prophecy on politics at this time. In 1536 he noticed 'un grand et merveilleux cours de prophetes et prognostications qui toutes promettoient à l'Empereur heureux et grand succes et accroissement de fortune'.[1] He observed the effects of these rumours: how Charles was convinced, 'et quand plus il y adiustoit de foy, de tant plus en faisoit l'on semer et publier de nouvelles'; how the Marquis of Saluzzo changed sides hastily, showing pity for his French friends 'qui perdroient leurs biens, parce qu'on ne pouvoit aller contre les oracles de Dieu, dont les prophetes estoient denontiateurs'; how Frenchmen were terrified, but Francis I stoutly opposed these superstitions and pursued his designs undismayed.

As late as 1547 a learned man could still believe in Charles's prophetic destiny. Wolfgang Lazius was a Doctor of Vienna and historian to Ferdinand I. He had written four books on Viennese history, twelve on the Roman Empire, two on the genealogy of the House of Austria;[2] finally, he made an excursion into the future, gathering together in his *Fragmentum vaticinii cuiusdam Methodii*[3] a compilation of oracles and prophecies from every possible source in honour of the Emperor. He saw at this time a consonance between event and prophecy which was most convincing. He knew that the Joachimist programme expected the final crisis of wickedness to be twofold: the infidel and the heretic, the beast from the sea and the beast from the land.[4] The menace of the infidel was obvious and now the prophecies of schism and pseudo-prophets seemed to be clearly fulfilled in Lutheranism. To establish the coming of the great heresiarch, Lazius produced a formidable crowd of witnesses, quoting

in 1532. He cites from the *Super Hieremiam* a text beginning 'Veniet Aquila grandis quae vincet omnes'. This is not traceable as a direct quotation in the printed edition, but must be derived from ff. 58ᵛ seq., a passage which is anti-German in sense. He quotes from a Neapolitan astrologer, Lorenzo Miniati, and a hundred-year-old prophecy from Magdeburg: 'Ex sanguine Caroli Caesaris et regum Galliae imperator orietur Carolus dictus, dominabitur is in tota Europa, per quem et ecclesiae collapsus status reformabitur et vetus imperii gloria restituetur.' On Carion see F. v. Wegele, *Gesch. des Deutschen Historiographie seit dem Auftreten des Humanismus* (Munchen/ Leipzig, 1885), pp. 190–1.

[1] Martin du Bellay, *Mémoires* (Paris, 1569), v, f. 142ᵛ; vi, f. 167ʳ. For the case of the Marquis of Saluzzo see also M. de Montaigne, *Essais* (Paris, 1598), Livre I, chap. 11: '*Des Prognostications*', p. 34, and P. Massé, *De l'Imposture et Tromperie des Diables, Devins* . . . (Paris, 1579), ff. 165ʳ–170ʳ.

[2] A. Mire, *Bibliotheca ecclesiastica* (Antwerp, 1639–49), *sub nom.*

[3] For full details see select bibliography.

[4] *Expos.*, ff. 8ᵛ, 162ʳ–168ʳ, 190ᵛ; *Super Hier.*, ff. 20ᵛ, 45ᵛ; Telesphorus, ff. 15ʳ⁻ᵛ, 29ᵛ.

in full Torquatus's supposedly prophetic description of Luther: 'Veniet a septentrione heresiarcha magnus subvertendo populos contra vota Romanae sedis . . .'[1] Obviously Luther was to be identified with the *pseudo-Papa Germanicus* of Telesphorus's programme, but the difficulty of using this pro-French source was that it made the German *Aquila* the chief instrument of evil. Lazius adapted Telesphorus skilfully, laying emphasis on the pseudo-popes, identifying the wicked king vaguely as a certain Frederick, and suppressing references to the Eagle, as here: 'et exurgent ab eo tempore multi Antichristi, praecipue sub Friderico Rege, sub quo multi Papae, qui universum orbem turbabunt, et Germaniae terram in errores collocabunt' (f. Hiii[r]). His intention is presently made clear from a marginal note suggesting that this Frederick is Duke Frederick of Saxony, the patron of Luther.[2]

Leaving the agents of wickedness, Lazius turns to his real purpose, that of proving that by his double lineage Charles V is heir to all the good prophecies. On the one hand he was descended from the Lily,[3] and in appropriating the Second Charlemagne prophecy, Lazius was able to claim: '. . . et Caesaris nostri Caroli praeter nomen et stirpem (quam a Carolo magno et Pipino, nobili ac vetusta Francorum sive Franciae Regum Lilifera primum omnium prosapia, tam quo ad paternum gens Habspurgen, quam maternum Burgundiae trahit) affabre omnia corporis etiam liniamenta depingunt' (f. Hiiii[r]).

He had met the text of our Second Charlemagne prophecy in various sources,[4] and related it to the whole Telesphorean programme, in which *Carolus rex de lilia Franciae* was elected and crowned by the *Papa angelicus* and called to conquer and reform the world.[5] On the other hand, the one-time Hohenstaufen prophecy,

[1] Lazius, *Fragmentum*, ff. Liii[v]–iv[r], cf. *supra*, p. 364.

[2] Ibid., f. Hiiii[v]: 'Itemque Papae Germanici haeresiarchae, ac cuiusdam Regis Friderici factionum haeresiumque [Telesphorus] mentionem addit. [marginal note:] Forte Saxoniae ducem sic insinuavit propheta.' He also interprets a prophecy of Reinhard as referring to the Schmalkaldic League (f. Kiii[r]).

[3] Ibid., f. Hiiii[r]. See also f. H[v]: 'Porro Caesares nostros processisse de Burgundiae et Habspurgensi stirpibus, quarum utraque a Carolo Magno et veteribus Franciae Regibus defluxit, inconfesso est et a nobis in commentariis rerum Austriacarum ostensum.' Lazius quotes a passage beginning: 'In veteri Caroli magni historia' which must derive from the same source as Lichtenberger's prophecy 'Et dicitur in libro regum Francorum' (cf. *supra*, p. 350). See also ff. Hiii[r], L[r].

[4] Ibid., f. Hiiii[r] (ascribed to Telesphorus); f. Kiiii[r] (found at Verona and also quoted by the Bishop of Chiemsee); f. Liii[r] (found at Verona and Louvain).

[5] Ibid., ff. Hiii[r]–iiii[r]. Lazius quotes long extracts which appear in the printed edition

'Veniet aquila grandis quae vincet omnes',[1] and many other oracles of the Eagle were pressed into service: 'Hoc nomine Carolus noster ab omnibus vatibus nuncupatur, videlicet Aquila grandis.'[2] He took his oracles from many sources: from Pilsen in Bohemia came one of the thirteenth-century verses, 'Gallorum levitas';[3] from Magdeburg a prophecy, 'Dominabitur is in tota Europa', and from Saxony another;[4] from the monastery of Plass in Bohemia, a prophecy of Rupescissa.[5] The galaxy of prophets is overwhelming: Rabanus, Methodius and the Sibyls, Cataldus, Cyril and Merlin, Joachim, Rupescissa and Telesphorus, Gamaleon, Bridget and St. Vincent Ferrer, Reinhard, Lichtenberger, Torquatus, Carion, and Paracelsus —all were made to speak with one voice in honour of this last great ruler.[6] Once again, the role of the chastiser of the Church formed an important point in interpretation. Lazius separated it into two: in its wickedness it devolved on Frederick of Saxony, but for the Emperor he built up a typically Germanic role of chastiser–reformer. He proved that the *Rex aquilonis* of Jeremiah 50 was a liberator, not an oppressor,[7] he showed that the Emperor was the *Rex pudicus facie,*

of Telesphorus's *libellus*, ff. 20ʳ–25ᵛ. From this he passes straight to the beginning of the Second Charlemagne text: 'Carolus autem coronatus ab isto angelico Papa, spinosa et lignea corona, filius Caroli magni erit, serenissimi lilii Francorum, habebit longam frontem...' This differs from the usual opening (*supra*, p. 328), which is that given by Lazius on f. Kiiiiʳ, and, as we have seen, the Second Charlemagne prophecy is not to be found in the regular text of Telesphorus's work; cf. *supra*, p. 329. Did Lazius find the unusual version in a manuscript of the *libellus*? He insists with great emphasis that this prophecy exactly fits Charles V (f. Kiiiiʳ).

[1] Ibid., f. Kiiᵛ. Like Carion, Lazius ascribes this prophecy to Joachim at the end of the *Super Hier.*, but the only passage from which it could be derived cites the anti-German Erithrean Sibyl text. Cf. *supra*, p. 368 n. 4.

[2] Ibid., f. Kiiᵛ. Among other eagle prophecies Lazius cites an oracle from Pilsen, Bohemia (f. Hviᵛ); a prophecy which he ascribes to the Erithrean Sibyl but which must have been composed at the end of the fifteenth century: 'Egredietur Aquila postquam I. octavus...' (f. Kʳ, cf. *supra*, p. 353 n. 1.); prophecies from Reinhard of the *grandis aquila* and of two eagles, interpreted as Maximilian and Charles V (f. Kiiiʳ⁻ᵛ, cf. *supra*, p. 340); a prophecy from Cyril: 'Imperio grandis Aquila, rige pennis, ocyus expergiscere...' (f. Kiiiᵛ), for the original of which (beginning *Imperio grandis aquila, nigra pennas*) see *Oraculum Cyrilli*, p. 308, and Telesphorus's *libellus*, f. 16ʳ. This last prophecy is correctly quoted by Purstinger, *Onus Ecclesiae*, cap. 38.

[3] Lazius, *Fragmentum*, f. Mᵛ; cf. *supra*, p. 312. This is also included by Wolf, *Lect. mem.* i. 722.

[4] Lazius, *Fragmentum*, ff. Kivᵛ–Lʳ.   [5] Ibid., f. Mᵛ.

[6] Among the more obscure prophets cited are: St. Sigebold (ff. Hʳ seq.), St. Carsianus (f. Hiiiiᵛ), Turkish prophecies (ff. Liiʳ–iiiᵛ), Lorenzo Miniati (f. Liiiᵛ), P. Cataneus (f. Liiiᵛ) in a prophecy ending: 'Tunc fiet unum ovile et unus pastor, et unus dominus, qui mundum omnem suo imperio obtinebit, et aurea etas declarabitur.'

[7] Ibid., f. Miiiʳ.

not the *Rex impudicus facie*,[1] he quoted prophecies indicating the Emperor's specific duty to reduce the Church to apostolic poverty.[2] The truth of these prophecies had already been demonstrated in the Sack of Rome, and Lazius looked to the Emperor to carry through the chastisement that was part of reform.

Thus to Wolfgang Lazius in 1547 the hope of the world stood in Charles V. The events of his life proved it: he had overcome and imprisoned the Lily, he had brought down Rome and Florence, he had gone over the seas to Africa against the infidel and contended with the heresiarch. True, the Lily had escaped, the Sack of Rome had unfortunate repercussions, the infidel remained unbeaten, and the heretic increased, but the programme was only half-completed. That the future was in the hands of the Emperor this German collector of prophecies did not doubt. In his conception of the *renovatio* the Angelic Pope remained a shadowy figure and, though he quoted the usual descriptions from Rupescissa and Telesphorus, at least once he added: 'Quae etsi ad Pontificem etiam quendam possint accomodari, tamen de Carolo nostro etiam Caesare esse intelligenda, docent caetera vaticinia.'[3] For the reformation of the Church his faith was in the Emperor and the Council of Trent, not the Papacy. The prophecies supported him: 'Quae satis ostendunt omnem nostram spem, post Deum immortalem, in Carolum sanctissimum Imperatorem nostrum, et sacrosanctum Tridentinum Concilium ponendam esse.'[4] In 1547 he believed the consummation of history and the end of prophecy to be very near: 'infra tempus 1548 annorum totum saeculum congregabitur in unum ovile . . . et fiet unum ovile et unus pastor.'[5]

A Protestant answer to such an interpretation as Lazius's can be seen in the claim that Frederick of Saxony fulfilled the role of the good Third Frederick. Thus Luther himself wrote in 1521:[6]

---

[1] Lazius, Fragmentum, f. Kii[v]. Citing the Brigittine text: 'Exsurget tunc Rex pudicus facie', he caps it thus: 'per Regem pudicum facie Carolum Caesarem nostrum citra omne dubium figuravit.' A curious little anecdote in the *Zimmerische Chronik*, ed. K. Barack (Freiburg/Tübingen, 1881), iii. 241, illustrates both the popularity of Lichtenberger and the dissemination of the image of the *rex pudicus facie*: as a compliment, a young girl was abducted and brought to Charles at night, but he, discovering the circumstances, sent her home under honourable escort, whereat the chronicler applied to him Lichtenberger's (i.e. the Brigittine) prophecy: 'rex pudicus facie regnabit ubique.'

[2] Lazius, *Fragmentum*, Hii[v], Hiiii[r], Hv[r–v].

[3] Ibid., f. Kiii[v].   [4] Ibid., f. Hiii[v].

[5] Ibid., f. Hv[r]. See also p. 371 n. 6.

[6] M. Luther, *De abroganda missa privata . . . sententia*, in *Werke: Kritische Gesammt-*

Celebris est in terris istis me puero saepe cantata prophetia, Esse redimendum sepulchrum dominicum per Fridricum imperatorem. Et, ut mos est prophetiarum, quae pro obscuritate ante implentur, quam intelliguntur, tum longe in aliud spectant, quam vulgo sonant, videtur mihi et ista in hoc Fridrico nostro impleta. Quod enim sepulchrum domini rectius intelligas quam divinam scripturam, in qua veritas Christi per Papistas occisa sepulta iacuit, custodientibus militibus, id est, mendicantium ordinibus et pravitatis haereticae inquisitoribus, ne discipulorum quisquam eam raperet? Nam sepulchrum illud corporale, quod Saraceni tenent, non magis est curae Deo, quam boves illi esse curae Paulus dicit. Negari autem non potest, apud vos sub Fridrico isto scripturae vivam veritatem refloruisse.

This idea that Frederick of Saxony had fulfilled the ancient prophecy of the Third Frederick by freeing the 'Holy Sepulchre' of the Scriptures was later picked up by J. Wolf in his great Protestant anthology.[1] He also asserted that prophecy could have been fulfilled by the election of Frederick of Saxony as Emperor, but for his refusal in favour of Charles V. The *Reformation Sigmunds*, which was circulating again at this time, also provided Protestant ammunition in the claim that the priest–king Frederick, whose coming was foretold in it, was really Frederick of Saxony.[2] In the *Practica deutsch* of Tarquinius Schnellenberg[3] we find this friend of Luther and Melanchthon still drawn towards the prophecies of a great Kaiser, gathering them all together from the pseudo-Joachim, Bridget, Lichtenberger, and others. But he no longer named the Emperor as Charles V and emphasized the revolutionary aspect of the Eagle role.

A curious line of Catholic defence against these Protestant prophetic claims appeared later in the century in Theodorus Graminaeus's two works: *Oratio in Esaiam et Prophetiam sex Dierum Geneseos* and *Mysticus Aquilo, sive Declaratio vaticinii Ieremie Prophetae: Ab Aquilone pandetur malum super omnes habitatores terrae*.[4]

---

ausgabe, viii (Weimar, 1889), pp. 475–6; (in German) *Vom Miszbrauch der Messe*, pp. 561–2.

[1] Wolf, *Lect. mem.* ii. 114. Luther's words are again cited (through Wolf) in an oration by Cornelius Crull in 1630, quoted by Praetorius, op. cit. [ref. 361 n. 1], p. 70.

[2] Wolf, *Lect. mem.* i. 809.

[3] This work was printed by F. Tetzer, 'Tarquinius Schnellenberg u. sein Werk Practica deutsch', *Zeitschrift f. Bücherfreunde*, N.F. iii (1911), pp. 173–6. Schnellenberg quotes a prophetic verse of Lorenzo Miniati, the Neapolitan astronomer, Joachim (a bogus quotation from the end of the *Super Hier.* beginning 'Veniet Aquila grandis', also used by Carion), Lichtenberger, an Egidius Abbas (1460), and Bridget.

[4] Published Cologne 1571 and 1576.

The author, as a German, addressed his second work to the Emperor Maximilian II, yet the whole burden of his argument was that the role of the northern peoples was to bring tribulation on the Church. To this end he used the pseudo-Joachimist works extensively, especially the *Super Hieremiam* and the *libellus* of Telesphorus. In the earlier work he concentrated the prophetic burden squarely on Saxony itself: 'Si vero inquiratur quid per aquilonem intelligatur, respondet Abbas Joachim et Vincentius Dominicanus . . . esse gentem Alemanorum, cuius mater sit Saxonia. Hoc loco egregie deducto, alterum Apocalypsios cap. 16 scriptum de Luthero . . . luculenter interpretatur Lutherum Draconem et bestiam affirmans, de cuius ore pseudoprophete et spiritus tres immundi in modum ranarum exierint' (*Oratio*, 17). Naturally he brought home the charges of schism and heresy against the Lutherans, but to establish their guilt he was prepared to jettison the pro-German oracles altogether, with their promise of a German Last World Emperor.

VII

FRENCH COUNTER-CLAIM

A FRENCH counter-attack, though hampered by the unprophetic names of the French kings, was not lacking. It was in 1516 that Silvestro Meuccio published the *libellus* of Telesphorus with its strong pro-French programme. His source for this edition was a manuscript very close in contents to the Venetian compilation of Andreas of St. Cyprian which we have already examined.[1] But a number of small textual variations make it certain that he did not actually use this one. A note on f. 54ᵛ—'extracta in bibliotheca sancti Georgii maioris Venetis'—suggests that the whole preceding part of his edition was taken from the original book which had been copied by Andreas and others.[2] Silvestro omitted, adapted, and added to suit the contemporary situation. His chief omissions were the preliminary pictures and sequences of popes and both the original and the longer versions of the Second Charlemagne prophecy, suppressed perhaps because the name of Charles was embarrassing at that moment to a Francophile. His adaptations consisted mainly in substituting phrases such as *futurus rex aquilonis* and *imperator alemanie* for the specific mentions of Frederick III,[3] in suppressing too specific dates or substituting vague phrases for them,[4] and in omitting to name the French king as *Karolus*.[5] The additions consist of more extensive picture-series, of the same type as those introduced by Rusticianus, but adding many new subjects. In no case are these pictures copied from the St. Cyprian manuscript.

[1] MS. Venice, Bibl. Marc., Lat. III, 177, cf. *supra*, pp. 343–5.

[2] On f. 42ᵛ occurs the note on Andreas's death (cf. *supra*, p. 345). There follows a medley of prophecies in different hands, some of which were copied in before the end of the fifteenth century. A group of these (ff. 43ʳ⁻ᵛ, 49ᵛ) corresponds to prophecies on ff. 51ᵛ–54ᵛ of Silvester's edition, but with considerable variations. Thus it appears that St. Cyprian monks went on copying from the same book at San Giorgio as that which was afterwards used by Silvester, both, perhaps, doing their own editing.

[3] See, for example, ff. 8ᵛ (MS. f. 18ʳ), 14ᵛ (23ᵛ), 15ʳ (24ʳ), 20ʳ (26ʳ), 20ᵛ (27ᵛ), 21ʳ (27ʳ), 25ʳ⁻ᵛ (28ʳ⁻ᵛ), 28ʳ (31ᵛ).

[4] See, for example, ff. 9ʳ (MS. f. 19ʳ), 20ʳ⁻ᵛ (26ʳ⁻ᵛ, 27ʳ).

[5] See, for example, ff. 20ᵛ (MS. f. 26ᵛ), 25ᵛ (28ᵛ), 29ʳ (32ᵛ); also a passage (MS. f. 29ʳ) beginning 'Angelicus pastor . . . qui coronat Karolum regem francie', which is omitted from the printed edition.

These illustrations, with their short paragraphs of text, break up the original Telesphorean text in a most confusing way and without any indication that they are additional material. They give us, however, at some points a fascinating, even amusing, light on prophetic politics in early sixteenth-century Venice. The first set (ff. 9^v–10^v) is mainly on subjects from the Apocalypse and does not call for special comment. The second set (ff. 15^v–16^v) shows the coronation of the true Pope, the series of three anti-popes, the German anti-pope with his Emperor and the latter's fleet. Although differently placed, this corresponds roughly to pictures in the St. Cyprian manuscript on ff. 27^v–28^r, but adds an interesting note on the fleet:

Hac classis seu armata in mari infidelium cum insignis etiam imperatoris alemani: aggreditur classem unionis ecclesie, sc. Venetorum, regis Francie, et Anglie, qui omnibus ab infidelibus superantur. Unde sciendum quod quia primo coronati fuerint antipapa germanus et suus imperator: statim quasi ex insperato superveniet eorum flagellum contra verum papam et sequaces, terrestre videlicet et navale: ita ut paucis detur spacium fugiendi et precipue in italia . . . (f. 16^v.)

The next really interesting interpolations occur in a picture-section from f. 18^r to 19^r. This begins: 'Notandum ut dicit iste noster auctor quod rex Francie in uno magno conflictu qui forte secundum aliquos erit in agro Brixiano inter suum exercitum et imperatoris alemani et antipape . . . capietur et incarcerabitur et tandem miraculose liberabitur, et eligetur imperator ab· universali ecclesia, et coronabitur a papa angelico . . .' (f. 18^r). The accompanying picture shows the French king released and crowned by the Angelic Pope. Then the anti-pope is killed by an angel. After a short amount of original text there follows another picture-section (ff. 21^r–25^r) in which are repeated a number of themes which had really been misplaced in the earlier sections. First we return to the discovery of the Angelic Pope: the Angel indicates to the ambassadors where he is to be found and it is at this point that Silvestro inserts his claim that the Angelic Pope will be an Augustinian Hermit;[1] the ambassadors lead him forth from the prison in which the devil had incarcerated him and he is crowned by the Angel. Then the theme of the King of France's capture, imprisonment, and miraculous release is repeated. Next Silvestro introduces a holy patriarch of the Venetians who will lead his people into virtue at the time of the Angelic Pope and he

[1] Cf. *supra*, p. 266.

supports this expectation with the words of his own special local prophet: 'De hoc autem sancto patriarcha mihi interroganti multas egregias virtutes retulit quidam venerabilis eremita Parentinus, spiritum prophetie habens, qui adhuc vivit, meque charitatis vinculo non parum diligit' (f. 22ʳ). Finally the English and the Venetians appear together on the side of the angels. Silvestro derives his expectation of a good English king from the prophecies of Merlin, but it is apparently his own idea to unite the two seafaring races—'boni marinarii'—in a great and holy naval enterprise 'pro republica Christiana'.[1] The King of England is a holy prince who will reform the life of his people, but he is also 'vir strenuissimus', strong and robust in body, a new Samson.[2] He will lead his people 'in partibus transmarinis' and, by order of the Church, capture the wicked German Emperor and deliver him into servitude. The Venetians will be led by a great Captain who will first accomplish a successful embassy to England to establish the coalition and then, on his return, be elected 'generalis Capitaneus totius classis marittime Venetorum et unionis sancte ecclesie'.[3] The English King and Venetian Captain together will win a great naval victory over the infidel and then the scene is all set in which the Angelic Pope, new French Emperor, King of England, and Venetian Captain will reform the political world:

Facta cede pseudopontificis . . . mortuoque imperatore alemano et mediantibus angelico pastore ac novo imperatore: omnibus malis ac bellis in Italia et occidentali ecclesia sedatis: a predictis convocabitur generale concilium pro passagio contra infideles et ad recuperandam sanctam Hierusalem. Et fiet classis seu armata atque exercitus terrestris et maritimus magnus valde totius sancte unionis ecclesie . . . sc. Regis Francie novi imperatoris, Regis Anglie, et Venetorum. . . . Capitaneus . . . erit Venetus. (f. 22ᵛ.)

All this programme is set out in a series of vivid little pictures which convey the hopefulness of these political dreamers and culminate in scenes of great rejoicing: 'Hic est magnum gaudium.'[4] The

---

[1] f. 22ᵛ.

[2] Ibid.: 'Hic est rex Anglie qui erit vir strenuissimus qui in Italia et in partibus transmarinis pro republica christiana magnalia facturus est et maximam contra infideles simul cum Venetis inde victoriam reportaturus.'

[3] Ibid.: 'Hic est generalis Capitaneus totius classis marittime Venetorum et unionis sancte ecclesie, qui post legationem suam in Anglia, in qua ita prudenter omnia sibi commissa perficiet, post annum suc reversionis ex Anglia eligetur generalis Capitaneus magne armate.' [4] f. 24ᵛ.

unanswerable question with which one is left is what relation all this bears to Venetian politics *c.* 1516: was the new Samson intended as a portrait of Henry VIII, was there an actual candidate for the role of Venetian Captain, did a French alliance seem most desirable?

In the final political apotheosis of Silvestro's book the French King emerges clearly as the Last Great Emperor who will reconquer Jerusalem and reunite the Eastern and Western Empires for ever. All arms will be forbidden, the sea will offer no more hazards to travellers, and there will be 'pax summa et tranquillitas . . . in toto orbe'.[1] This first tranquillity will last until at the onslaught of the *Antichristus ultimus* the French Emperor will render up his soul to God. The last pages of Silvestro's book,[2] in which the text of Telesphorus is liberally interspersed with pictures, deal with the sequence of Angelic Popes, scenes from the Apocalypse, the final tribulation, and the final tranquillity in which all political forces have given way entirely to religious forces. It will be observed here how skilfully the editor combines the old pessimistic tradition with the Joachimist, making the Emperor go down before Antichrist, yet carrying the triumph of the Church forward into the Sabbath Age beyond Antichrist, but still within history.

It is significant that a French translation of the Telesphorean prophecies was published under the title of the *Livre Merveilleux* at Lyons in 1565 during the reign of Charles IX, the only French king of this name in the sixteenth century.[3] Furthermore, in 1570, J. Baptista Nazarus of Brescia was once more putting forward the Telesphorean programme and quoting again the Second Charlemagne prophecy.[4] We also know of the existence of a Latin manuscript of Telesphorus's *libellus* and a sixteenth-century translation

[1] f. 21ᵛ.   [2] f. 25ʳ.

[3] The full title runs: *Livre Merveilleux Contenant en Bref La Fleur et Substance de Plusieurs traittez, tant des Propheties et revelations, qu'anciennes Croniques, faisant mention de tous les faictz de l'Église universelle, comme des schismes, discords et tribulations advenir en l'Église de Rome, et d'un temps auquel on ostera et tollira aux gens d'Église et Clergé leurs biens temporelz, tellement qu'on ne leur laissera que leur vivre et habit necessaire. Item aussi est faicte mention des souverains Evesques et Papes, qui apres regneront et gouverneront l'Église. Et speciallement d'un Pape qui sera appellé Pasteur Angelique. Et d'un Roy de France, nommé Charles sainct homme.* This title is derived from, but not a translation of, the original *incipit.* Whereas the Venetian editor in 1516 deleted the name *Karolus* from the title, this edition restores it.

[4] I have not seen this work. It is cited at length by Wolf, *Lect. mem.* ii. 884-97. For the Second Charlemagne text, beginning 'Exurget Rex Lilii qui frontem habebit longam...', see p. 893. Bezold, *Kaisersage*, p. 600, says that this prophecy was actually applied to Charles IX.

made from it, belonging to Messire Francois de Chevriers, 'gentil-homme Lyonnois'.[1] Possibly Benoist Rigaud, the publisher of the *Livre Merveilleux*, used this manuscript. He had already published in 1545 *La Prophétie Merveilleuse de madame sainct Brigide et iusques à presente trouvée veritable depuis lan Mil. CCCC. LXXXIIII iusques à cette presente année Mil. CCCCCXLV.* This was actually a complete, unacknowledged translation of the *Prognosticatio* of Lichtenberger, and closely related to the Latin version in the *Mirabilis liber.*[2] In 1603 Rigaud published *Les Pléiades* of Chavigny, to which we shall be turning shortly. Thus there are some indications of a group of people in Lyons interested in the French applications of the prophecies.

The most considerable French anthology of prophecies in the sixteenth century was the *Mirabilis liber*, supposedly published in Venice in 1514; now known in Paris editions of 1522 and later. Its purpose, according to the preface, was to prove that all prophecies pointed towards the Angelic Pope and the last great emperor of the French monarchy.[3] The oracles, collected from all periods, represent various stages in the evolution of the Joachimist programme.[4] The *Vaticinia de summis pontificibus*, ascribed to Joachim, is reproduced entire,[5] though without the illustrations; Joachim, Rupescissa, Telesphorus, Catherine of Siena, St. Vincent Ferrer, and Bridget are among those cited; the *Prognosticatio* of Lichtenberger, again reproduced without acknowledgement, and the *Revelationes* of Savonarola represent the latest prophets.[6] Many of the oracles have been collected from manuscripts in the libraries of French religious houses and the whole forms a curious hotchpotch

[1] A. de Landine, *Manuscrits de la Bibliothèque de Lyon* (Paris/Lyon, 1812), i. 181; *L'Amateur d'autographes*, ed. E. Charavay, x (1872), pp. 63–5.

[2] *Supra*, p. 347 n. 1; *infra*, p. 433.

[3] See the author's preface on the title-page: 'Ex his prophetiis et revelationibus intimis ocullis perlustratis facile cognosci poterit: pontificem maximum vite sanctitate prefulgentem: brevi ex religiosissimo Francorum regno futurum: qui Deo optimo maximo duce pacem inter Christicolas omnes componere: statusque hominum . . . iniuria fortasse temporum deformatos: diligentissime reformare curabit: terras Palestinorum . . . Grecorum, Turcorum et alias quam plurimas expediet: omnesque a Christiana fide abhorrentes: veritatis lumine illustrabit.' Fol. 1ᵛ contains a dedication to the French king and seven proofs from prophecy of the great future foretold for him.

[4] The earlier prophecies represent the pre-Joachimist or pseudo-Methodian tradition: f. iiʳ *Liber Bemecholi Episcopi*; f. iiiiʳ *Prophetia Siibllc*; f. viiᵛ *Prophetia Sancti Severi.*

[5] *Mirabilis liber*, ff. xxxᵛ–xxxiiiᵛ.

[6] Cf. *infra*, p. 435.

of traditions. The pre-Joachimist Methodian view of the Last World
Emperor, who goes down before Antichrist, is represented, whilst,
on the other hand, the early fourteenth–century Joachimist prophecies of the Angelic Popes are used, allied to material from
Telesphorus on the 'Rex de posteritate Pipini' who will be co-agent
with the Angelic Popes in the *renovatio*.[1] Rupescissa and Telesphorus
are, of course, most apt, but it is interesting to observe that Lichtenberger's *Prognosticatio* can easily be pressed into service for the rival
house, since it contains, on the one hand, much from the anti-
German Joachimist tradition and, on the other, prophecies of the
Lily ascribed to Bridget. The Second Charlemagne prophecy is
given without name or initial letter from a source not yet traced:
'ex libro catalogi finis seu cataldi finii (*sic*) undecimi capitis de
Italia'.[2] The book names no names, lays down no dates, and ven-
tures on no applications of prophecy. It is, however, plainly an
anthology in support of the French claim to the Last World
Emperor.

Another author who in the reign of Francis I was busy trying to
fit the prophecies to the French monarchy was Symphorien Cham-
pier (or Symphoriano Campeggio). In his *De Monarchia Gallorum*,
published in 1537,[3] he revived the old prophecy that Antichrist
would not appear as long as the Roman empire endured and then
transferred the hope of the world from the Germanic monarchy
to the French. Everyone could see, he argued, that the Germanic
Empire was almost ruined and near collapse in face of the Turkish
menace. He could produce an alarming passage from Nicholas of
Cusa pointing to the deadly sickness of the *imperium Germanicum*
and prophesying that men would seek the *imperium* in Germany and
would not find it. So Symphorien exhorted Charles V and the
German princes to read the signs of the times: either Antichrist was
near or one must look elsewhere for salvation. This, of course, was
to be found in the French monarchy. History showed that, whereas

[1] Cf. *infra*, pp. 404, 423–4.
[2] *Mirabilis liber*, f. xlʳ. This passage is not to be found in the *Prophetia Sancti Cataldi*
(*supra*, p. 358 n. 1), nor does it agree with the passage quoted by Lazius, f. 38ʳ⁻ᵛ,
although there are affinities. It consists of one long paragraph containing a reference to
the Lily Prince ('tunc nascetur inter lilia princeps pulcherrimus cui nomen novum
inter reges erit') and the Second Charlemagne prophecy in a separate paragraph
beginning: 'Surget rex ex natione illustrissimi lilii habens frontem longam ...'
[3] *De Monarchia Gallorum Campi Aurei: Ac Triplici Imperio, vid. Romano Gallico,
Germanico: una cum gestis heroum ac omnium Imperatorum* (Lyon, 1537, unpag.).

the German rulers had always fought the Papacy, the French monarchy had always been faithful to the Church. The Gallic kings had been hallowed by a divine unction; the Gallic kingdom was the 'vine elect' planted by God according to the prophecy of Isaiah;[1] it was the white cloud seen by St. John in Apocalypse 13; it was even the holy city descending from heaven of Apocalypse 21.[2] Finally, Symphorien turned to the old prophecy which asserted 'quod unus de regibus Gallorum Romanum imperium ex integro tenebit: qui in novissimo tempore erit et ipse maximus et omnium regum ultimus qui postquam regnum suum feliciter gubernaverit, ad ultimum Ierosolymam veniet et in monte Oliveti sceptrum et coronam deponet. Et is erit finis et consummatio Romani imperii' (lib. iv, cap. iiii). It seemed clear to this mid-sixteenth-century reader of the signs that, whereas the decline of the Germanic empire had gone on continuously, with fatal heresies that had been its undoing, the French monarchy had remained pure in faith, while all the prophecies pointed to this monarchy as destined by God to hold the final *imperium*.

The *Livre Merveilleux* should almost certainly be connected with the strange Guillaume Postel, perhaps actually being his work, or that of a disciple. With it F. Secret links the *Liber Mirabilis* to which Postel himself refers.[3] These were the sort of works on which Postel's imagination fed, but we must remember that he was also an expert of his day in linguistic studies and interested in the textual criticism of the Bible. In his combination of humanist and medieval mystical approaches, as also in his passionate vision of a possible *concordia mundi*, he invites comparison with Egidio of Viterbo, although manifestly much more unstable in character. As we have seen,[4] at an early stage he fixed on the Jesuit Order as God's chosen instrument in carrying out the cosmic programme of Postel's vision. But even before this, his eyes had turned towards the French monarchy as God's political agency. He himself described an interview which he had with Francis I before he left for Rome to join the Jesuits in which, in Hebrew fashion, he proclaimed the choice before the King: if he reformed Church and State, he would be monarch of the universe, if not, evils worse than any previous would come

---

[1] Ibid., Bk. iii, cap. vi, cf. Isa. 5: 2.
[2] Ibid., cf. Apocalypse 14: 14 and 21: 2.
[3] Secret, *Studi francesi* I, p. 389.
[4] *Supra*, p. 287.

upon him. It was, however, not until 1548 that his conviction about the divine mission of the French king and people was clearly expressed in the work entitled *Candelabri typici in Mosis tabernaculo ...interpretatio*.[1] In an autobiographical passage he tells us that this knowledge was given by divine illumination:

> ... Que combien que j'eusse receu du Ciel par Divine et a moi tres certaine lumière que la Monarchie qui, necessairement, sera en ce bas monde, partira de la Gaule et y prendra origine, et que le Roy de la Gaule par vertu et non par sang esleu et tres chretien de faict sera le Monarche reformateur de l'Eglise et du monde universel, et ledict Roy debvoir estre le premier quiconque vouldra entendre a tele vocation ... (Quoted Bernard-Maître, *RSR* xxxviii. 214.)

Nor was it to be shaken by the death of one French monarch, as a letter of Ignatius Loyola points out:

> ... il a attendu qu'arrivât le moment qu'il avait défini pour l'accomplissement de ses prophéties. Et le roi de France est mort, lui qu'il voulait être monarque universel pour le temporel, et malgré cela il s'est appliqué à justifier de mensonge, ses prophéties, en disant que, par son incrédulité, le Roi François avait empêché ce que Dieu avait décidé et que son fils l'accomplirait, comme Josué au lieu de Moïse ... (Quoted Bernard-Maître, *Le Passage*, p. 237.)

During the period following his expulsion by the Jesuits he bombarded the French Kings and people with appeals to realize their great destiny and, when Henry II and Francis II in turn were deaf, he began to threaten them with the fate of Moses and Saul.[1] In the same period he was plunging into a frenzy of linguistic and cabbalistic studies, seeking to work out his world religion through contacts with Ethiopians, Arabs, Jews, and others. In the 1550s he was publishing tracts, writing letters to influential people and travelling ceaselessly, proclaiming urgently that all the auguries pointed to 1556 as the fateful date. In despair at French heedlessness, he turned at one time to the Emperor Ferdinand who, interested in his philological and missionary plans, appointed him to a chair in the University of Vienna.[2] So Postel sketched an Imperial version of the future: Rome was to be the temporal capital of the world, Jerusalem the spiritual; then there would be a general reformation, the earthly paradise would be restored and the purpose of

---

[1] Bouwsma, *Concordia Mundi*, pp. 216 seq.   [2] Ibid., pp. 20, 227.

the world would have been fulfilled. But *au fond* his was a Gallican passion and he returned to it, proclaiming as late as 1579 the imminence of the Millennium and exhorting the French king to initiate the necessary reformation.[1]

The source of Postel's belief in the cosmic role of the French monarchy was almost certainly the Joachimist writings. From Joachim himself he possibly drew the significance of the Lily as the symbol of the third *status*[2] and, of course, the inspiration for the series of mystical threes which he uses. But the role of the French monarchy he obviously drew from Roquetaillade and Telesphorus. In the great *renovatio* the French king must take the lead because of the corruption of the Roman Curia. Aided by a General Church Council, he must establish a universal monarchy and a universal church. Postel's case for the French king and people is built up on every possible symbol and argument.[3] The claim goes back to Japhet, to whom Noah gave the temporal monarchy of the world, and, of course, to Charlemagne. The symbol of the Lily, as it appears in the Old Testament and in Joachim's writings, points to the French monarchy. The attributes of the French people, such as intellectual leadership, reveal their destiny. The German Caesar is advised that to become true Emperor he must first become King of France—only it is simpler for the King of France to become Emperor. Postel's programme of action is both peaceful and military, for he longs to convert the infidel to a rationalized Christian faith as well as to conquer him. At the last, he believes, every man, in all the peoples of the earth, will understand the truth of God for himself and achieve that illumination which should be the aim of all human experience in the temporal order. The final world-order envisaged by Postel follows a Joachimist number-symbolism: there will be three heads—a sovereign king, a sovereign pope, and a sovereign judge—who, of course, represent the Trinity and beneath this triple authority the world will be ruled in twelve sees, corresponding to the twelve tribes and apostles. With the papal part in this programme we shall be dealing later.

---

[1] Bouwsma, *Concordia Mundi*, p. 27.

[2] In Joachim's famous passage (*Lib. Conc.*, f. 112[r]) on the sequences of threes, lilies represent the third *status*, while in the *Lib. Fig.*, Pl. VI, the Eagle which carries the implication of the third *status* is decorated with lilies.

[3] Bouwsma, *Concordia Mundi*, pp. 219–26. He comments: 'As a whole his argument probably constitutes the most comprehensive justification for French world leadership in the sixteenth century.'

In spite of his craziness Postel was attended to, read, and admired by many contemporaries. He struck exactly the twin notes of apprehension and exultation which chimed in with the sixteenth-century mood. His warnings were full of foreboding but the tremendous horizons of his vision lifted the heart. Moreover, paradoxical though it may seem in an age of intensifying national feeling, his ecumenism caught on. In a curious manner typical of his time, he combined national aspiration with a universalism that really desired the brotherhood of all mankind. And, again typically, he saw the master-plan of Providence in the achievements and discoveries of Man:

Today we see clearly that, quite suddenly, Greek, Latin and Hebrew letters, along with all learning, divine and human, have made more progress in fifty years than in the previous thousand, while at the same time the Ismaelites today no longer possess either letters or learning. Thus it is evident that the advantage of truth has returned to us, so that we can oppose their power and doctrine with authority and reason. And we see another great change and marvel when we consider how, during the last ten years, through the efforts of sailors and merchants, the new world, which is greater than our own, has not only been discovered and conquered, but also converted to the Christian religion, this being done under the Spanish power, the navigation of the Portuguese having made a start ... I do not mention the arts of artillery and printing, discovered among the Latin Christians, the one to consummate the wisdom of the world, the other the power, which has been given to the Christians by Providence, in order that they may see it is God alone who kills and revives. (Tr. Bouwsma, op. cit., p. 271.)

Postel did not lack disciples. In 1587 one of them, Vincent Cossard, published a book with the title *Totius Galliae onus prodeat ex Ioachimi abatis opere selectum, donec totius universi onus prodeat ex Bibliotheca V. Cossardi*.[1] The *Livre Merveilleux* was published again in 1577 and 1588. In 1580 Giordano Bruno visited France at a time when Henry III was seeking a politico-religious alliance with England. This seems to have awakened in him the old concept of a peaceful and universal French monarch. In 1585, in his *Spaccio della Bestia Trionfante*, Bruno put forward once more the plan of universal reform and pointed to Henry III as a suitable initiator:[2]

---

[1] Secret, *Studi francesi* I, p. 388. I have not been able to see this work.

[2] Ed. G. Gentile, *Opere Italiane*, ii (Bari, 1927). I owe this reference to F. Yates, 'Considérations de Bruno et de Campanella sur la monarchie française', *L'Art et la pensée de Léonard de Vinci*, *Actes du Congrès Léonard de Vinci* (Paris, 1954), pp. 6-7.

Questo Re cristianissimo, santo, religioso e puro può securamente dire:
Tertia coelo manet, perchè sa molto bene che è scritto: Beati li pacifici . . .
Ama la pace, conserva quanto si può in tranquillitade e devozione il suo
popolo diletto; non gli piaceno gli rumori, strepiti e fragori d'instrumenti
marziali che administrano al cieco acquisto d'instabili tirannie e prenci-
pati de la terra; ma tutte le giustizie e santitadi che mostrano il diritto
camino al regno eterno. (Ed. cit., pp. 225–6.)

But the French monarchy supplied no effective candidate for the role
of great pacific ruler until the advent of Henry of Navarre. It was
at the moment of Henry's conversion to catholicism that Bruno,
returning to Italy, eagerly began to canvass a universal solution for
the problems of politics and religion in a holy alliance of Pope and
French king which would bring in a new Age of Gold. His dream
and its repercussions in Italy were satirized thus by Agrippa
d'Aubigné:[1]

. . . J'avois appris qu'à Rome les disputes publiques avoient pour thèses
ordinaires la comparaison du Roi d'Espagne et de lui [Henry IV]. Les
devineurs de là trouvoyent par figure de Geomance, par oracles, par le
nom fatal de Bourbon, que ce prince doit convertir les hiérarchies à
l'Empire, la chaire en throsne, et les clefs en espées, qu'il doit mourir
Empereur des Chrestiens. Les Venitiens adoroient ce Soleil levant avec
telle dévotion, que quand il passoit par leur ville un Gentilhomme
François, ils couroient à lui . . . A la cour de l'Empereur et en Pologne, on
oyoit vœux publics, pour mettre l'Empire en ses heureuses mains, avec
disputes pour la réunion des religions, ou la tolérance de toutes, force
discours d'amener l'Italie à cette raison, et de rendre les tiltres d'Empereur
de Rome efficatieux, et non point tiltres vains . . . (Yates, loc. cit., p. 8.)

But the prophets are never deterred. In 1592 Henry was hailed in
a pamphlet with the title *Carolus Magnus redivivus*.[2] It was inevitable
that all the old oracles would be gathered once more round the figure
of Henry IV of France. In Paris the famous Nostradamus was the
centre of a group which sought the future from oracle and star.
One of the group, the Sire de Chavigny, tells us that Nostradamus
was the first to apply the Joachimist prophecies to Henry IV. In *Les*

[1] Agrippa d'Aubigné, *Œuvres complètes*, ed. E. Réaume and F. de Caussade, ii (Paris,
1877), p. 327. See Yates, loc. cit., pp. 7–8.
[2] J. Stuckius, *Carolus Magnus Redivivus* . . . (Tigurinus, 1592). A preliminary verse
runs:

> Carolus ecce tibi redivivus: pellege: dices
> Henricus nunc est, Carolus ante fuit.

Pléiades, which he dedicated to Henry in 1603,[1] Chavigny embodied these expectations. There are seven *Pléiades* and the first of these is none other than a French translation of our Second Charlemagne text, written for Charles VI, applied in turn to Charles VIII and the Emperor Charles V, and now applied to Henry IV. Chavigny, who cites it from the same source as the *Mirabilis liber*,[2] knows that it was once applied to Charles VIII, but by omitting name or initial he is able to prove satisfactorily that it really designates Henry IV. Neither the villainous Third Frederick nor the Angelic Pope have survived in this version, but the Last World Emperor, with the same physical features and the same career, remains. The following *Pléiades* set forth the well-known prophetic future: great wars and tribulations, the overthrow of thrones and the multiplication of heresies, 'mais après cela viendra un regne meilleur et une saison plus douce'.[3] Thus the Joachimist hope of renewal emerges once more, but this is a Protestant's Age of Gold, for 'il n'y a rien plus doux à l'homme . . . que de vivre avec liberté . . .; telle que preschent par tout les nouveaux Evangelistes du iourd'hui'.[4]

The two great figures of medieval political prophecy, the *Rex Romanorum* and the *Rex Christianissimus*, the Eagle and the Lily, still confront each other at the end of the sixteenth century. The search for a universal monarch is not yet dead. The dream of a world united in peace and justice is still fused with a Joachimist theology of history which sees the whole of it as building up to this final age. A political hope can still at this late date have an eschatological background and that hope can still be focused on an international

---

[1] Sire de Chavigny, *Les Pléiades, Ou en l'explication des antiques Propheties conférées avec les Oracles du célèbre et célébré Nostradamus est traicté du renouvellement des siècles, changement des Empires et avancement du nom Chrestien. Avec les prouesses, victoires et couronnes promises à nostre magnanime Prince, Henri IV Roy de France et de Navarre* (Lyons, 1603).

[2] Ibid., p. 1. He describes it as 'une vaticination de S. Cathalde, iadis Evesque de Trente, retirée d'une livre intitulé, Des calamitez de l'Italie'. His version begins: 'Un Roy sortira de l'extraction et tige du lis tres-illustre, ayant le front eslevé, les sourcils hauts, les yeux longuets, le nez aquilin . . .'

[3] Ibid., p. 56. The *renovatio mundi* appears also in the title: *renouvellement des siècles*, cf. *supra*, n. 1.

[4] Ibid., p. 96. Commenting on an oracle of Lorenzo Miniati, which is translated as follows: 'L'age meilleur qui bien tost suivra cestuy-cy, retranchera beaucoup de choses de nostre religion, dures par trop et aspres à supporter: et corrigera toutes sortes d'abus et les pompes sacrées. Et donnera un Roy clement et benin, qui avec toute equité et droiture gouvernera le monde. Cestuy regira vertueusement les peuples et soubsmettra à son empire la gent rebelle et fière. Et dominera sur tout l'univers' (p. 95). Lazius, op. cit., f. Liii, also quotes a prophecy of Lorenzo Miniati, cf. *supra*, p. 371 n. 6.

rather than a national goal. In the last examples of this which we shall look at, the Middle Ages are seen extending into the seventeenth century.

Tommaso Campanella was not a Calabrian for nothing.[1] Joachim was only one among a number of authorities to whom he appealed in his writings, but, once more, his ardent expectation of a new world order was founded on a Joachimist structure of history. Unlike so many of the political prophets we have studied, he tried to push on the inevitable apotheosis of history by taking part in a curious revolt in south Italy in 1599.[2] This put him into the hands of the Inquisition for many years but he never ceased to seek for his ideal order. As it is expressed in the *Città del Sole*,[3] this seems far removed from politics: the head of the ideal city is the Sun, an abstract figure, at once prince and priest. In the *Monarchia Messiae*[4] the one world state, with one religion, is gathered under Christ the Messiah and His Vicar, the Pope. But none the less, Campanella perceived that a political agency was needed to build his City of the Sun, so he sought for the true inheritor of the role of universal monarch. In his *De Monarchia Hispanica*[5] he argued that this role had been handed down through various world empires to Spain. Like Joachim he saw the history of the Church prefigured in Hebrew history and found the symbol he required in Cyrus, King of Persia:

Ille igitur qui Ecclesiam hisce malis liberabit, evadet universalis Monarcha, quia fungetur officio Cyri Christiani, quem suscitabit Deus, sicut Esaias dicit, ad subiugandum totum mundum, restaurandam Hierosolymam, solvendam captivitatem et aedificandum templum Dei . . . Igitur officium Cyri spectat ad regem Hispaniarum qui postquam jam a Papa Rex Catholicus appellatus est, facile ad principatum mundi poterit eniti. (*De Monarchia Hispanica*, pp. 28–31.)

[1] On Campanella see L. Blanchet, *Campanella* (Paris, 1920), R. de Mattei, *La politica di Campanella* (Rome, 1927).

[2] Yates, loc. cit., p. 8.

[3] Ed. E. Solmi (Modena, 1904).

[4] *Monarchia Messiae* (Jesi, 1633), pp. 11–21.

[5] Pub. Amsterdam, 1640; see especially pp. 25–33. As with Egidio of Viterbo and Galatinus, his expectation is heightened by contemplation of the world empire of Spain: 'Hispania namque circuit per Brasiliam, fretum Magalanicum, Philippinas, Iapponem, Chinam, Archipelagus Lazari, Calecuttam, Goam, Bengalam, Ormum, Caput bonae spei, Civitatem Africae, insulas fortunatas: in eadem Hispania mundus cum sole circumagitur . . . Res stupenda sane et signum evidentissimum, regnum in immensum diffusum est, in quo continuo preces pro Ecclesia et Rege funduntur . . .' (pp. 32–3). He supports his view by reference to a number of prophets, including the Abbot Joachim (p. 23).

In 1634, however, when Campanella removed to France, he shifted his prophetic allegiance from the Spanish to the French monarchy. In his *Aphorismes*[1] he argued that all the signs of history and the stars pointed to the decline of the Spanish monarchy and the rise of the French. Spain now represented the end of the Fourth Monarchy of Daniel which must go down before Antichrist. But now a Fifth Monarchy was arising, that of the Most Christian King whose destiny was to aid the Pope in bringing in the old promise of one fold and one shepherd. Campanella built up from every kind of proof the case for the final world-empire of the French, arguing in the seventeenth century, as Miss Yates points out, a case almost exactly that argued by Pierre Dubois in the thirteenth.[2] This in itself is perhaps not so surprising: we have met other examples of late dreamers who still lived in this earlier world. What is of more significance is the good reception which Campanella received both from king and court and from learned men. Like Postel he was read and attended to by many in high places. His last works show Campanella writing a panegyric of Louis XIII, propaganda for the French monarchy in Italy, and an appeal to Richelieu to build the City of the Sun.[3] His final gesture was a poem to salute the birth of Louis XIV who would bring in the Age of Gold:[4]

> Cantabit Gallus, sua Petrus corriget ultro:
> Cantabit Petrus, Gallus super evolat orbem,
> Subiicit et Petro, et Petri aurigatur habenis.
>
> .   .   .   .   .   .
>
> Nam labor est iocus, in multos partitus amice,
> Quippe unum agnoscent omnes patrumque Deumque.
> Conciliabit amor fraternus cognitus omnes;
>
> .   .   .   .   .   .
>
> Conveniunt reges, populorumque agmina in urbem
> ('Heliacam' dicent) quam construet inclytus heros.
> Et templum in medio statuet coelestis ad instar:
> Praesulis aulam summi, regificumque senatum,
> Sceptraque regnorum Christi deponet ad aras,
>
> .   .   .   .   .   .

---

[1] This was published in 1635. It is printed by L. Amabile, *Fra Tommaso Campanella ne'castelli di Napoli, in Roma, ed in Parigi* (Naples, 1887), ii. 291 seq.

[2] Yates, loc. cit., p. 11.   [3] Ibid., p. 12.

[4] T. Campanella, *Poésie*, ed. G. Gentile (Bari, 1915), pp. 201–2. I owe this reference to Miss Yates.

Unanimes populi cantantes 'Gloria Patri'
Perpetuum alleluia sonent pacemque beatam.

Here the French *Coq* has quite displaced the German *Aquila*.

The Imperial rival for the role of Last World Emperor now stood in a poor position, partly owing to the division of the great claim of Charles V between the Spanish and Austrian Hapsburgs. A German writing in the seventeenth century was wiser to leave his great ruler nameless. Bartholomew Holzhauser (1613–58),[1] in *Interpretatio in Apocalypsin*, worked out a pattern of history within the framework of the seven ages of the Church. He believed that the fifth state of the Church—*status afflictionis*—had begun with Leo X and Charles V and would run 'usque ad Pontificem Sanctum et Monarcham illum fortem qui venturus est nostro saeculo et vocabitur auxilium Dei, hic est restituens universa'.[2] These would inaugurate the sixth state—*status consolationis*—which was especially typified in the Angel to the Church of Philadelphia.[3] In this age all nations would return to the unity of the orthodox Catholic faith, all heretics would be crushed, 'et florebit maxime status clericalis et sacerdotium'. This state is prefigured in the Sixth Day of Creation when Man was created and all things subjected to him, and also in the Sixth Age of the Old Testament when the Jews returned from captivity to restore Jerusalem and the Temple. In the sixth state of the Church the sixth spiritual gift—*spiritus sapientiae*—will be poured out on all men: there will be an 'open door' to the 'sensum clarum et apertum Sanctae Scripturae' which no heretic may close, and a multiplicity of sciences will flourish.[4] 'In sexto enim statu erit Ecclesia Catholica sublimis et gloriosa et magnificabitur a mari usque ad mare et non erit controversia aut quaestio amplius quae sit vera Ecclesia.'[5]

Holzhauser paints this vision against a black background of present woes, of wars and calamities, of violence done to monarchs, of the Catholic Church beaten down by pestilential heretics.[6] Yet even now the triumphs of the Society of Jesus and the spreading of the Catholic faith to Asia and the Americas inaugurate the new reign.[7] The agents to bring it in are the old pair—the Angelic Pope and the World Emperor—but it is clear that for Holzhauser the chief figure

[1] See the article *sub nom.* in Wetzer u. Welter, *Kirchenlexicon*, vi (1889), pp. 183–96.
[2] *Interpretatio in Apocalypsin* (Vienna, 1850), p. 53.
[3] Ibid., pp. 69–70.
[4] Ibid., pp. 70–2.
[5] Ibid., p. 75.
[6] Ibid., pp. 53–65.
[7] Ibid., pp. 185–6.

is the *Monarcha fortis*. He will destroy all republics, break the
Turkish Empire, reign over east and west alike, and give peace and
justice to the entire world.[1] This will be the Millennium of Satan
bound. So powerful in his mind is the spiritual role of this Monarch
that, whereas Joachim had seen in the various Angels of the Apocalypse new religious orders to inaugurate the Age of the Holy Ghost,[2]
Holzhauser instantly sees the Emperor typified both in the '[vidi]
angelum fortem descendentem de coelo amictum nube, et iris in
capite eius',[3] and in the one 'super nubem sedentem similem filio
hominis, habentem in capite suo coronam auream'.[4] He finds the
great Pope symbolized in others of the angels, and the *status sacerdotalis* in the Angel with the Eternal Evangel,[5] but it is the symbolism
of those representing the great Monarch that he works out in most
detail: *angelum fortem*, strong in battle; *descendentem de coelo*, born
in the bosom of the Church; *amictum nube*, humble in all things; *iris
in capite eius*, bringing the peace of God to the whole world; *facies
eius sicut sol*, the splendour, sanctity, and glory of Empire and highest
wisdom which adorn him; *pedes tanquam columnae ignis*, the breadth
and power of his Empire sustaining the Catholic Church; *in manu
sua libellum apertum*, the future General Council over which he will
preside and which will declare the clear sense of the Scriptures.[6]

The close relationship of this spiritual *status* to the Joachimist
Third State will be apparent. Holzhauser, however, demonstrates
strikingly the tendency which we have traced throughout Part III
of this book to seek a reconciliation between the older, pessimistic
tradition and the idea of the *renovatio*. He accepts therefore the
orthodox view that history must go downhill to Antichrist by placing
after his great sixth age a seventh—*status desolationis*—beginning
with the birth of Antichrist and enduring until the Second Advent.[7]
Here he departs sharply from Joachim's great conception of the
Sabbath Age of history, and, indeed, we have no indication that he
knew the works of the Abbot directly. His idea of the *renovatio*
probably came to him through such writers as Berthold Purstinger.
Yet his vision of a spiritual consummation of history to which the

[1] *Interpretatio in Apocalypsin*, pp. 69–70, 186.
[2] Cf. *Expos.*, ff. 88ᵛ, 89ᵛ, 175ᵛ–176ᵛ.
[3] Holzhauser, op. cit., pp. 185–6; cf. Apocalypse 10: 1.
[4] Holzhauser, op. cit., pp. 264–5; cf. Apocalypse 14: 14.
[5] Holzhauser, op. cit., pp. 256, 261, 265.
[6] Ibid., pp. 185–8.
[7] Ibid., pp. 78, 200.

last coming of Antichrist seems quite external and irrelevant places him with the Joachites.

The early seventeenth century also provides an example of an English Protestant who could not abandon the chimera of a Last World Emperor. James Maxwell's *Admirable and notable Prophesies*[1] was mainly concerned with the defection, tribulation, and reformation of the Church, but within this framework he collected a large number of political prophecies, including most of the Eagle and Lily ones. He seems to have had no particular candidate in mind and turned from the Eagle to the Second Charlemagne in some confusion. He knew that the Second Charlemagne prophecy had been applied to both Charles VIII of France and the Emperor Charles V. He had also seen the *Pléiades* with the application of the prophecies to Henry IV of France.[2] But he was convinced that the 'Lilly-King' was still to come. When he came he would 'recover the Virgin-Land of Palestine and water and bedewe the infected countries and corners of the world with the living water of the Christian Religion . . .'.[3] He would be like a cedar of Lebanon surmounting all the rest, a dispenser of justice and right. When he held in his hands the reins of the Empire, 'the King, the Nation and the Religion or law . . . shall taste of an admirable change'.[4] Towards the end of the book Maxwell begins tentatively to suggest that the agents of the *renovatio* might come out of England[5] and in support of this he leaves the Eagle and Lily prophecies to quote the pseudo-Joachimist oracle: 'Flores rubei aquam odoriferam distillabunt.'[6] With this he couples a prophecy of Paracelsus to suggest that from the Roses (i.e. England) might spring a 'rosie Prince' who would purify the Church with sweet water.[7] He did not, however, hint at a possible candidate.

A last echo of the Second Charlemagne prophecy is found in the Apocalypse-Commentary of David Pareus, a Protestant theologian of Heidelberg. Wishing to emphasize the future destruction of Rome, he seized on the Second Charlemagne text from an old manuscript 'found in the house of Salezianus and lately sent to me'.[8] Thus the Second Charlemagne ends his career by becoming merely the

[1] For full title and a further description of this work see *infra*, p. 499.
[2] *Admirable and notable Prophesies*, pp. 32–5, 47.
[3] Ibid., p. 45. [4] Ibid., p. 47. [5] Ibid., p. 84.
[6] Ibid., p. 86. This is the caption to No. XIV of the *Vaticinia* in the usual arrangement.
[7] Ibid., p. 86.
[8] D. Pareus, *Commentary upon the Divine Revelation*, tr. E. Arnold (Amsterdam, 1644), p. 440.

divine instrument for the destruction of Rome. If the final form of
the prophecy, as it appears in an English translation of Pareus's
work published in 1644, is compared with the original, it will be
seen how faithfully the circumstantial details—especially the physical features—have been preserved and how completely the pregnant
phrases of the Joachimist hope have been lost:

There shall arise a King out of the Nation of the most illustrious Lilie,
having a long forehead, high brows, great eyes, an Eagle's Nose: He shall
gather a greate Army, and destroy all the Tyrants of his kingdome: and
slay all that flye and hide themselves in Mountaines and Caves from his
face. For righteousness shall be joyned unto him, as the Bridegroome to
the Bride: with them he shall wage warre even unto the fourtieth yeere,
bringing into subjection the Ilanders, Spaniards and Italians: Rome and
Florence he shall destroy and burne with fire, so as Salt may bee sowed on
that Land. The greatest Clergymen who have invaded Peters Seat he
shall put to death: and in that same yeere obtaine a double Crowne. At
last going over Sea with a greate army, he shall enter Greece, and be
named King of the Greeks. The Turks and Barbarians hee shall subdue,
making an Edict: that everyone shall die the death that worshippeth not
the Crucified one. And no one shall be found able to resist him: because
an holy arme from the Lord shall allwayes be with him. And he shall
possesse the Dominion of the Earth. These things being done, he shall be
called the rest of holy Christians. Thus far the Prophecie.

PART FOUR

ANGELIC POPE AND *RENOVATIO MUNDI*

———

I

ECCLESIA ROMANA AND
ECCLESIA CONTEMPLATIVA

ALTHOUGH there is certainly ambiguity in Joachim's statements
about the Church of the third *status*, it must be asserted
firmly that institutionally this was never anything but the
Roman Church in his mind. He might contrast the *ecclesia laborantium* with the *ecclesia contemplantium*; he might speak in terms of the
Church of Peter and the Church of John which came dangerously
near implying that the latter would supersede the former in the
third *status*. But, as we have already pointed out, these contrasts are
qualitative, not institutional: Peter symbolizing the church that
preaches and labours, or the order that must first be consummated,
stands in a context quite other than that of Peter the rock on which
Christ has built the *Una Ecclesia Catholica* to endure to the end of
time. Joachim most accurately expresses his thought when he speaks
of the *vita activa* and *vita contemplativa* of Peter and John. For the
great immovable institution, the *Mater Ecclesia*, Joachim has certain
designations which recur constantly: it is the *Ecclesia Romana, quasi
altera Hierusalem*,[1] or the *spiritualis Hierusalem*, or the *nova Hierusalem*;[2] once it is described as . . . *novam Hierusalem que est Petri
navicula*.[3] As David won the kingdom from Saul, so the Church of
Peter, that is Rome, won the authority from the Church of Ephesus.[4]
In the *Liber Figurarum* Pope Silvester is matched with David[5] and
there is no question but that the 'kingdom' rightfully belongs to the
Roman Church to whose obedience the Greek Church must return.
Reflecting on the great vision of the Church as Mount Sion in the
Apocalypse, Joachim exclaims: 'Magnus Petrus apostolorum prin-
ceps et totius prelatus ecclesie: sed o quam felix Joannes est . . .

---

[1] *Expos.*, f. 17ᵛ.
[2] *Lib. Conc.*, ff. 125ʳ, 134ᵛ; *Expos.*, ff. 7ᵛ, 24ʳ, 142ᵛ, 145ᵛ; *Psalt.*, f. 276ᵛ; *Quat. Evang.*,
p. 105; *Enchir.* (ed. Huck), p. 298.
[3] *Vita S. Benedicti*, pp. 83–4.
[4] *Lib. Conc.*, f. 92ʳ. See also *Expos.*, f. 61ᵛ.
[5] *Lib. Fig.* II, Pls. XV, XVI. See also *Lib. Conc.*, ff. 17ᵛ, 38ᵛ, 92ᵛ; *Expos.*, ff. 62ʳ–63ʳ.

Ille maior in gloria: iste felicior in amore.'[1] This seems to sum up both Joachim's loyalty and the focus of his affection.

If the Church of Rome is unshakeable in authority, none the less there is to be a transition from one quality of living to a higher. That the Papacy itself makes the transition follows from Joachim's analogy with David who first rules in Hebron and then in Jerusalem; even so the papacy: 'Prius ergo regnavit David in Hebron et postea in Hierusalem. Quia occurrit pontificibus romanis preesse ecclesie laborantium: postea ecclesie quiescentium: prius desudantium in vita activa: postea exultantium in vita contemplativa' (*Lib. Conc.*, f. 92ᵛ). When we ask the further question what type of leadership belongs to the Papacy in the third *status*, we only get the answer in symbols. In the forty-second generation after Jacob Zorobabel the priest, returned from Babylon, ascended to Jerusalem and rebuilt the Temple. In the corresponding generation of the New Dispensation it will be the same: 'In qua vero generatione peracta prius tribulatione generali et purgato diligenter tritico ab universis zizaniis, ascendet quasi novus dux de Babylone universalis scilicet pontifex nove Hierusalem, hoc est sancte matris ecclesie' (*Lib. Con.*, f. 56ʳ). Again, the final domination of Joseph over his brethren and over the Egyptians represents the final position of the Papacy: '. . . ut fiat unus populus cum gentili: et erit dominatio populi sanctorum designati in Joseph. In ipso enim erit tunc successio romani pontificis a mari usque ad mare et a flumine usque ad terminos orbis terrarum . . .' (*Lib. Conc.*, f. 89ʳ). Finally, in the last histories of the Old Testament we find the Roman pontiff typified in those heroes who emerged triumphant through great tribulation, Mordecai and Judas Maccabaeus, and last of all in *Michael princeps magnus*, who intervenes on behalf of God's people.[2] In the story of Esther she herself represents both the *ecclesia contemplativa* and the Church of Rome which is preferred above all others: 'Placuit itaque Assuero sublimare Hester: placuit et Christo preferre omnibus Romanam ecclesiam.'[3] Mordecai is the successor of Peter who will triumph over all enemies:

Porro Mardocheus exaltatus est nimis et data est ei a rege potestas et gloria Aman: quia successor Petri qui erit in tempore illo, quasi fidelissi-

---

[1] *Expos.*, f. 170ᵛ.

[2] *Lib. Conc.*, f. 132ᵛ. See also f. 95ᵛ where Joachim looks forward to the 'nova religio . . . que omnino erit libera et spiritualis, in qua romani pontifices potiti pace ecclesie continebunt [*sic*]'.   [3] *Ibid.*, f. 121ʳ.

mus vicarius Christi Iesu elevabitur in sublime. Ut compleatur illud quod scriptum est in Isaia propheta: Erit in novissimis diebus preparatus mons domus domini in vertice montium et elevabitur super colles et fluent ad eum omnes gentes et ibunt populi multi et dicent: Venite ascendamus ad montem domini . . . (*Lib. Conc.*, f. 122ᵛ.)

Thus the Roman pontiff in the last days will be both the great champion in the tribulation and the focus to which all the tribes will flow. It is important to stress that Joachim's third *status* is characterized not only by spiritual understanding and holy liberty but also by ecumenism. Again and again he stresses the return of the Greek Church to its true obedience and the conversion of the Jews in the last age of history. This emphasis is particularly striking in his last work, the *Super Quatuor Evangelia*. Such a vision presupposes the institutional authority which Joachim places unquestioningly in the Roman Church and its head. Transition and immutability are together summed up thus: 'Non igitur . . . deficiet ecclesia Petri que est thronus Christi . . . sed commutata in maiorem gloriam manebit stabilis in eternum' (*Lib. Conc.*, f. 95ᵛ).

From whatever quarter they emanated, the first group of pseudo-Joachimist works display a different attitude to the Roman pontiff. The author of the *Super Hieremiam* could not forget the 'unjust' condemnation of 1215 and the responsibility of the papacy for this.[1] Traces of the same feeling appear in the *De Oneribus* and the *Super Esaiam*.[2] So in some respects the Roman hierarchy is already under attack. The *Super Hieremiam* starts by expecting disaster on the Church, prefigured in the fall of Eli and his sons.[3] The attack on the wealth, worldliness, and pride of the Roman Church is developed and from this springs a more revolutionary attitude towards the transition from the second to the third *status*. A violent gesture, either by the papacy itself or by others towards it, begins to appear in the expected programme. Peter must cast off his coat and plunge naked into the waves,[4] or the Church must 'fall among thieves' on the road from Jerusalem to Jericho.[5] The Ark must almost be submerged, yet ride the waves: 'In aquis enim gentium et tribulationis immense natabit Petrus ecclesie, sed nudus: quia revera non liberabitur in aquis diluvii archa sive onera mundi reiiciet sive reformetur de lignis in tribulationis ascia levigans' (*Super Hier.*, f. 38ʳ). There are

[1] *Supra*, pp. 149–50.   [2] *Supra*, p. 151.   [3] *Super Hier.*, preface.
[4] Ibid., f. 3ᵛ.   [5] Ibid., f. 10ʳ.

enigmatic hints of a pseudo-pope, another Herod, yet still it is the
Roman Church which is the one true Church, producing from her
womb the two new orders of spiritual men,[1] or sending forth the
new fishers of men,[2] and to Rome, as Sion, the Greek Church must
return *novissimis diebus.*[3] Once at least the Roman pontiff is represented as Christ suffering again: 'Et iccirco crucifigetur Petrus,
summus pontifex occidetur sc. doctores, dispergentur oves con-
ventuales . . . Nescio tamen si post tres dies vel annos resurgat
pastor bonus et dux domus Israel.'[4] This is the nearest that the
Super Hieremiam gets to the concept of the Angelic Pope.

The other two works linked with the *Super Hieremiam,* the *De
Oneribus* and the *Super Esaiam,* have much the same viewpoint on
the Roman Church and, indeed, use exactly the same figures, but
neither gives a hint of a transformed role for the papacy in the new
age. They are obsessed by the waves of tribulation about to break
over the ship of the Church and the commonest image which pre-
sents itself to them is that of the naked Peter battling in those seas.[5]
But the Roman Church is still the *mater ecclesiae,* the *altera Jerusalem,* Mount Sion, Judah, the *ecclesia perfecta.* For this reason it
must always be persecuted by the Roman Emperors and cannot
make concord with them any more than Mordecai could with
Haman.[6] To these Italian Joachites tribulation and persecution
loomed largest. They constantly asserted that they were on the verge
of the third *status* but could hardly see into it.[7] Pseudo-popes and
false prelates, as well as persecuting Emperors, must come first, but
somehow—through revolutionary violence—the Roman Church
would survive into the new age.

Thus in the first group of pseudo-Joachimist works there is little
suggestion of the Angelic Pope, and positive hope, when it emerges,
is almost wholly focused on the two new orders of spiritual men. The
same blank is encountered in the scanty records we have of John of
Parma and Hugh de Digne and other early Spirituals. The conversations at Hyères, as reported by Salimbene, do not touch the
future position of the papacy but are concentrated on the *Aquila* and

---

[1] *Super Hier.,* f. 35ʳ.   [2] Ibid., f. 37ᵛ.
[3] Ibid., f. 10ᵛ.   [4] Ibid., f. 53ʳ.
[5] *Super Esaiam,* ff. 15ʳ, 20ᵛ, 28ᵛ, 58ᵛ; *De Oneribus,* ff. 38ʳ, 39ʳ, 39ᵛ.
[6] *Super Esaiam,* ff. 2ᵛ, 15ʳ; *De Oneribus,* ff. 38ᵛ, 42ᵛ.
[7] The affirmation of the transition across Jordan and the beginning of the third
status is made a number of times; see *Super Esaiam,* ff. 27ʳ, 29ᵛ, 30ʳ, 33ᵛ, 34ᵛ, 58ᵛ; *De
Oneribus,* f. 42ᵛ; *Super Hier.,* ff. 1ᵛ, 12ʳ.

Antichrist. Gerard of Borgo San Donnino's gloss on Joachim's works apparently only referred to an expected pseudo-pope and schism.[1] The revolutionary aspect of the transition to the third *status* had to be developed first. When the idea that the seat of Peter must be seized by demonic forces had taken hold, then recovery by an angel-pontiff would appear as the divine eschatological answer. There is, however, one clear reference to the Angelic Pope in the mid-thirteenth century, not, curiously enough, from a confirmed Joachite but from Roger Bacon, whose statements on this subject we have already quoted in full.[2] There can be little doubt that, though his is an almost isolated reference, its background is a prophetic tradition which goes back close to Joachim's time and that he is referring not simply to a good pope, but to the divinely appointed agent to carry out the final programme of history. This programme includes the return of the Greek Church, the conversion of the Tartars, and the destruction of the Saracens—a variation on Joachim's ecumenical theme—and its climax is in the famous words from John 10: 16, which form the motif of so many of the World Emperor and Angelic Pope prophecies: 'et fiet unum ovile et unus pastor.' We must conclude that Bacon was not just voicing an idea of his own but a Joachimist prophecy already in circulation by 1267, even though there is so little trace of it elsewhere at this date. There is, however, a small echo of it in the chronicle of Salimbene who recorded, on the death of Gregory X in 1276, some verses circulated first among the Friars Preacher which clearly looked forward to a *papa sacer* of *angelice vite* who would carry out a programme of reform:

> Hunc Deus ornabit et mire clarificabit,
> Sanctificabit, magnificabit, glorificabit.
> Mundum pacabit et Ierusalem renovabit,
> Fructus terra dabit, Deus orbem letificabit . . .
> (Salimbene, pp. 492–3)

This Golden Age was to be preceded by a horrible apparition. Salimbene actually cited Joachim in the discussion on this prophecy and the juxtaposition of great evil and great good clearly points to a Joachimist origin for these verses.

[1] *ALKG* i.122–3.
[2] R. Bacon, *Opus Tertium*, ed. J. Brewer, *Opera Inedita*, RS, p. 86. Cf. *supra*, p. 47, where these passages are quoted.

Probably the development of the concept of Angelic Pope was stimulated by the shaping of its institutional counterpart, the World Emperor. As long as the *imperium* meant the dreaded German Eagle, no concord was possible for the Italian Joachites, but when the Pope was seeking other candidates for political rule, prophecy could join the two powers in a final alliance. Thus, as we have seen, the anti-Hohenstaufen verse beginning 'Rex novus adveniet' ends with reform and an ecumenical programme in which we begin to see the holy alliance of last ruler and Angelic Pope. In the *Oraculum Cyrilli*, the latest of the thirteenth-century pseudo-Joachimist works, the prophetic future of the papacy begins to take more shape. There is clear emphasis on a final schism, symbolized now in Rehoboam, the true king, and Jeroboam, the false.[1] It was this point upon which Telesphorus seized a hundred years later. Secondly, when the *verus pontifex* has been vindicated, the future papacy is represented under symbols which suggest the spiritual revolution. In one passage the expected pope is the *ursus mirabilis*[2] and in another, a new flower: 'Ex hoc intelligo futurum pontificem odorifere vite aut fame futurum ac novitates magnas facturum. Flos quidem habet odorem in tactu et novitatem in ortu. Hec autem novitas, quam committet, poterit contingere multipliciter et maxime in officiis et dignitatibus Romane Ecclesie conmutandis et renovandis' (*Oraculum Cyrilli*, p. 295).

---

[1] *Oraculum Cyrilli*, pp. 288–90. For the verse 'Rex novus adveniet', *supra*, p. 312.

[2] *Oraculum Cyrilli*, p. 292.

II

THE EMERGENCE OF THE IDEA OF THE
ANGELIC POPE

ONE of the extraordinary aspects of the history of the Angelic Pope is the sudden embodiment of the dream in action before, so it seems, the dream itself had been fully articulated in written form. It is almost impossible now to assess the various currents of emotion, aspiration, and political scheming which flowed together in the election of the hermit pope, Celestine V, in 1294. Once chosen, he was certainly hailed in Messianic terms—by a crowd at Aquila, for instance—as he journeyed from the wilderness meekly riding upon an ass to take up office.[1] But the lack of evidence for a wide-spread expectation of an Angelic Pope before this date makes one doubtful as to how far a Joachimist view actually influenced the election. What is quite clear is that once this astonishing event had taken place it 'precipitated' the image of the Angelic Pope in clear and powerful form. Celestine V became the prototype of the angel–pontiff to be. Moreover, the tragedy of his fate underlined the stark juxtaposition of good and evil which characterized the Joachimist programme. Since the forces of Antichrist were expected to capture the high places and thrust in a pseudo-pope, it was tempting to see the drama of Celestine V and Boniface VIII in these terms. We have an almost immediate reaction to these events in the visions of Robert d'Uzès, written before 1296. He stops well short of equating Boniface VIII with Antichrist, but expresses strongly both the exultation at the advent of the Holy Pope and the horror at his deposition.[2] The important thing, however, is that this single drama had become for him a symbol of more portentous happenings. He expected persecution of and judgement on the Church, but *renovatio* through an Angelic Pope, who now assumed the image of the hermit pope preaching evangelical poverty. Strangely enough for a Dominican, in one vision this future saviour was seen as a Minorite.[3]

[1] Messini, *Misc. Franc.* xxxvii. 51.   [2] *AFP* xxv. 281–2, 285–7.
[3] Ibid., pp. 279, 281–2.

The form in which the image of the Angelic Pope now finally crystallized was moulded both by the drama of Celestine V and Boniface VIII and by the continuing experience of persecution suffered by the Spiritual Franciscans. As we have seen,[1] it was in one of the circles of Spiritual Franciscans that the first set of fifteen *Vaticinia de summis pontificibus*, the *Liber de Flore*, and its accompanying tracts probably originated. These were men whose fortunes had risen and fallen with the succession of popes, who had been raised to a pitch of high expectation by Celestine V and cast into the depths by his successor. For them the immediate juxtaposition of good and evil was a close reality. It was easy to believe that the final drama of history would be played out in such terms—by an abomination of desolation followed instantly by an angelic *renovatio*. So the transition to the third *status* became a sharp revolution, a sudden salvation. This revolution would take place within the Papacy itself. No disloyalty to the Roman See was yet hinted at, but the personalities of the popes suddenly became important, as expectation of the great moment crystallized into the substitution of a holy for an unholy series of pastors. All the experiences and hopes of Spiritual Franciscans seem to be embodied in these *Vaticinia* of the popes and it was no accident that they took this form of a series of portraits, partly historical and partly prophetical.

The dating of this group of writings can be accurately determined by establishing where this crucial point of all time, the change-over from history to prophecy, is placed. The *Vaticinia de summis pontificibus* clearly start with Nicholas III, the Orsini Pope, pictured with little bears besieging him and accompanied by a text beginning 'Genus nequam ursa catulos pascens'.[2] The captions, pictures, and texts plainly indicate the following series of historical characters, including Celestine V and Boniface VIII, down to Benedict XI. There history seems to stop and here the prophetic series seems to begin. Thus this work should probably be dated to the months prior to the election of Clement V. By the same reasoning the *Liber de Flore* and the *Horoscopus*, which is an astrological appendix to it, belong to the same period, but the gloss on the *Liber de Flore* which is attributed to 'Rabanus' must be dated after the election of Clement, since it speaks of two popes between Boniface VIII and

---

[1] Grundmann, (i) *AK* xix; (ii) *HJ* xlix.
[2] No. XVI in the early printed editions.

the expected prophetic series.[1] So in 1303–5 the great moment seemed very near. The emotions of these expectant Joachites are vividly portrayed in the pictures of the *Vaticinia*. Thus the 'unholy' series of mitred and politically occupied pontiffs is dramatically interrupted by a monk holding a sickle and a rose to represent Celestine V, with the caption: *Elatio, Obedientia, Paupertas, Castitas, Temperantia, Ypocrisorum Destructor*. This is immediately followed by the mitred and seemingly prayerful Boniface VIII, with the caption 'Incisio hypocrisis in abominatione erit'.[2] Then, after another Orsini, the prophetic series begins with a judgement on Rome ('Heu, heu miser civitas!') and an exaltation of the monastic life in the caption *Potestas cenobia*. The next again judges Rome ('Veh tibi civitas septem collis'), but with the caption 'Potestas unitas erit'. After this the true series of Angelic Popes begins, all portrayed in attitudes of devotion and humility with the symbols of simony and political power conspicuously absent. The first is mitred, with the caption 'Bona gratia Simonia cessabit'. The next is an almost naked hermit meditating on a rock, watched by a devout monk, with the caption 'Bona oratio'. Then a haloed monk in pontificals places his mitre over the flock to guard it, with the caption 'Bona intentio caritas abondabit'. In the next two the Pope is first crowned by an angel, and then, mitred and enthroned, is supported by two angels; the captions are 'Pro honorate concordia erit' and 'Bona occasio'. Finally, a holy monk tames and places his mitre over a crowned and horned animal which probably in the original intention represents the *imperium*.[3] Thus, at the last, the Angelic Pope is expected to dominate over both secular and spiritual spheres. Although, as Grundmann shows, the originals of these enigmatic pictures and texts go back to the Byzantine Leo oracle,[4] it is evident that the Joachites have adapted them strikingly to convey their own feelings and one can draw from the latter ones some idea of the sequence of the divinely controlled history which they expected.

The *Liber de Flore* is a series without pictures and related to the earlier group of the pseudo-Joachimist works rather than to a Byzantine source. It begins earlier than the *Vaticinia* with Gregory IX,

---

[1] Grundmann (ii), pp. 40–1.

[2] The numbers vary in the printed editions, since the original order is not always observed.

[3] The angelic series is usually numbered XXV–XXX in the printed editions. Note that later the animal in the last picture is variously interpreted as Antichrist and as the seven-horned Lamb.   [4] Grundmann (i), pp. 83–90.

the reason being, according to Grundmann, that this Pope first
began the modification of the Franciscan Rule.[1] Its chief differences
are a greater attention to political forces, its more specific angelic
portraits, and—most significant   its expectation of political aid to
the Pope from the French house. This, indeed, is the first sign of the
type of French Joachimism we traced in Part III of this book. The
four Angelic Popes who form the climax of the series have lost their
mysterious quality and are delineated in historical terms.[2] The first,
though of unnamed nationality, is probably intended to be an
Italian. He will be a poor hermit, 'pauper et nudus', sought out and
crowned by an angel. Then he will form an alliance with a 'generosus
rex de posteritate Pipini' who will come to salute the 'claritatem
gloriosi pastoris'. The Pope will bestow on him the dual empire of
east and west, with the title *Bicephalus*. After this the typical programme of Second Charlemagne and Angelic Pope will be carried
out together; the Greek Church will return to its true obedience and
the French king will conquer Jerusalem, afterwards resigning his
kingdom to a successor in order to become a Franciscan. Under this
Pope the Roman See will renounce all temporal wealth and a
General Council will ordain that all clergy shall live on bare neces-
sities alone. The next Angelic Pope will be of French nationality and
will visit Germany to reform its abuses and then France to bless
its people. After this will come an Italian Franciscan, while the
last Angelic Pope will be a Gascon who will be a great and wise
preacher and make long pilgrimages throughout the world. Finally,
in Palestine, the two barbarous folk Gog and Magog will meet him
with palms and songs and he will rule the world as Christendom
until the appearance of Antichrist. In this programme there is a clear
modification of the old pessimistic tradition towards a Joachimist
optimism, in that the Second Charlemagne does not disappear with
a gesture of despair but becomes a Franciscan, and that Gog and
Magog—those final scourges—are tamed and won over. Right at the
end, however, tradition reasserts itself in the conventional introduction of the Antichrist.

The first fifteen *Vaticinia* are sometimes found alone in manuscripts of the fourteenth and fifteenth centuries, but usually in the

[1] Grundmann (ii), p. 47.

[2] Ibid., pp. 70–4, where the text of all four is summarized. Neither the *Liber de Flore*
and its gloss nor the *Horoscopus* has yet been published in full. For manuscripts see
Appendix A, p. 523.

later ones preceded by the second fifteen *Vaticinia* and associated with the mythical name of Anselm, Bishop of Marsico, as well as Joachim. Already before 1314 the Dominican Francesco Pipini was describing these prophecies which, he said, were attributed to the Abbot Joachim,[1] while the Franciscan Bernard Delicieux also had the *Papalarius* of Joachim in his hands very soon after its production.[2] In 1319 Hugh of Novocastro gives us what is also a very early reference to the 'libellus in quo romanorum pontificum figure describuntur'.[3] When Benvenuto da Imola wished to characterize 'il Calvarese abbate' whom Dante placed in the *Paradiso*, he pointed to this book 'quem dicitur fecisse de pontificibus, in quo effigiavit mirabiliter unumquemque in diversa forma et figura, ut saepe notavi'. The manuscripts are innumerable and widely disseminated.[4]

The striking features of the manuscripts are the great variety of style and workmanship in the execution of the figures and the eagerness with which the prophecies are identified by marginal notes, in later readers' hands. Thus, to take only a few examples, MS. Reg. Lat. 580 in the Vatican has the whole thirty done in beautiful and careful paintings and a second finely illuminated set in the Vatican is found in the Renaissance MS. Chigiano A. VII. 220. Vat., Lat. 3816 has pen-and-ink drawings and Vat., Lat. 3819 has some unusual and vivid illustrations. In England, MS. Cambridge, Corpus Christi College, 404, ff. 88^r–95^r, gives the first set in fine, clear pen-and-ink drawings, identified in a later hand down to Urban VI, and at an earlier point (f. 41^r), the last five of the second set. In the British Museum we have MS. Arundel 117 with rough-painted pictures and scrawled identifications, MS. Additional 15691[5] with

---

[1] Muratori o.s. ix, cols. 724, 726, 727, 728, 736, 741, 747, 751, giving all the series down to the eighth and identifying them from Nicholas III to Clement V.

[2] *AFH* xvii (1924), pp. 332–3 n. 3.

[3] *Tractatus de victoria Christi contra antichristum* (Nuremberg, 1471, unpag.), cap. xxviii.

[4] Benvenuto de Rambaldis de Imola, *Comentum super Divinam Comediam*, ed. J. Lacaita (Florence, 1887), v. 90. For manuscripts see Russo, *Bibliografia*, pp. 44–8, where fifty are cited in a still incomplete list. In Yale University Library there is a set of the earliest fifteen *Vaticinia* alone. The illuminations (ff. 16^r–23^r) are delicately drawn, with the special feature that the various bears become neat little dogs. The manuscript, entitled *Sibylla De Imperatore*, was written in France in the fourteenth century; cf. *supra*, p. 324.

[5] The popes are identified up to Eugenius IV, but a later hand has added the next two: 'D. Amadeus dux sabaudie Felix V papa' and 'D. tomas de sazzana cardinalis bononiensis deinde Nicolaus quintus papa'.

delicate illuminations in pen-and-colour wash, and MS. Harley 1340 with superb Renaissance miniatures, which have been claimed to be from the hand of the Master of the San Miniato altar-piece.[1] We shall be examining the most important printed editions later.[2] In all there were about twenty-five, including translations into Italian, German, and French. The whole set found a place in the *Mirabilis liber*[3] and engaged the attention of a variety of commentators. In the seventeenth century there was an Italian manuscript version made from an edition of 1625 (now MS. Florence, Bibl. Laur., Ashburnham 933) and there were reprints with a new Preface as late as 1646 and 1670.

The *Liber de Flore* never obtained anything like the same vogue as the *Vaticinia*, nor was it published as such in the sixteenth century. The enigmatic oracles of the *Vaticinia* were endlessly adaptable as history unrolled, especially when the second fifteen had been added. The *Liber de Flore* was too historically precise in its past and too clear-cut in its future to be easily bent to the game of finding new solutions. On the other hand, its much clearer political loyalties—above all its pro-French attitude—made it potent material for those who wanted their political loyalties embodied in the future. Thus it was seized on by Telesphorus of Cosenza. Thus, too, we find it in a French manuscript at Arras.[4] An early fifteenth-century manuscript at Paris contains excerpts on the Angelic Popes and the promised French king.[5] The latter extract is headed: 'Prophecia Karoli regis Francie coronati in imperatorem per angelicum pastorem corona spinea nolentis coronari corona aurea.' The Venetian manuscript which contains Fr. Rusticianus's compilation begins with some curious original pictures of which four are prophecies of Popes.[6] The short texts accompanying the four pictures are drawn from numbers, 27, 28, 29, 30 of the *Vaticinia*, that is, portraits of the Angelic Popes. Although the first two of these are here applied to Pius II and Paul II, the last are clearly intended as angelicals and the whole sequence is interspersed with longer extracts from the *Liber*

---

[1] See B. Berenson, 'Miniatures probably by the Master of the San Miniato altar-piece', *Essays in honor of George Swarzenski* (Chicago, 1951), pp. 96–102. The popes are identified as far as Eugenius IV.

[2] *Infra*, pp. 453–62.   [3] *Supra*, p. 379.

[4] See Appendix A, p. 523.

[5] MS. Paris, Bib. Nat., Lat. 14726, ff. 98ʳ–103ᵛ.

[6] MS. Venice, Bib. Marc., Lat. III, 177, ff. 13ʳ–14ᵛ. Here the horned animal in the last picture is identified as Antichrist. Cf. *infra*, pp. 455, 457–8.

de Flore. An additional note records that in 1185 Abbot Joachim 'de partibus Calabrie' presented the *Papalista* to Pope Urban, in which he showed the state of the supreme pontiffs, as revealed to him by God, until the end of the Age.[1]

The revolutionary concept of the Angelic Pope evolved only as the Spiritual Franciscans were pressed into an impossible dilemma by the inexorable logic of two incompatible principles. These are well represented in the apologetic tracts of Petrus Joannis Olivi. In one he affirmed categorically his belief that the true Pope could not err: '. . . quod sedes romana existens sedes vera non potest errare; aut quod papa existens verus papa et verum caput ecclesie non potest errare . . . de hac clarum est quod nec papa nec sedes romana potest in fide pertinaciter errare . . . impossibile est quod papa sic errans sit verus papa et verum caput ecclesie' (*ALKG* iii. 524). But in the same moment he was affirming with equal strength and passion that to amend the Rule was the deed of Antichrist, betraying the life of the future:

. . . quod status evangelicus est et esse debuit omnino immobilis et indissolubilis . . . Ex hiis autem patet quod papa in predictis non potest dispensare nec absolvere . . . ut de statu simpliciter perfectiori descendat ad statum imperfectiorem. . . . Si quis autem profundius inspiceret, quomodo per vitam Christi et renovationem eius circa finem ecclesie consistat illustratio et exaltatio universalis ecclesie et ineffabilis appertio scripturarum et destructio antichristi . . . et introductio Judeorum et consummatio omnium . . . videret clarius quomodo istius status et regule laxatio et obfuscatio in tantum est pestilens quod ex ea sequatur denigratio totius fidei, introductio antichristi et omnium temptationum finalium et dissipatio omnis perfecti boni, et tunc indubitabiliter certissimum esset, quod a nullo vivente dispensationem recipere potest. (*ALKG* iii. 528–30.)

He repudiated unorthodox views of the renunciation of Celestine V and would not question the justice of the condemnation of Joachim in 1215, denouncing such deviations among Spiritual Franciscans severely.[2] Yet the logic of the passages quoted above pushed the argument the other way: the true Pope could not err, the Rule could not be modified, therefore a pontiff who did so and manifestly erred must be the pseudo-Pope of prophecy, presiding over the carnal

[1] f. 13ʳ.
[2] *AFH* xi (1918), pp. 340 seq., 370; ibid., xxvii (1934), p. 431; ibid., xxviii (1935–6), pp. 146–7.

church of Babylon. To Olivi the cosmic conflict between St. Francis and the carnal Christians was inevitable and the figures he used in the *Postilla* to represent the carnal church and its head—the Babylonish Whore, Caiaphas the pseudo-pope, the *Antichristus misticus*, the Beast from the land[1]—gave a concrete meaning which was all too easily identified with the Roman Church. Manselli, while defending Olivi's obedience to Rome right to the end of his life, shows how for Olivi the forces of good and evil were expected to range themselves more and more sharply against each other: on the one side, the true Church under the true Pope, backed by faithful Franciscans; on the other, the carnal church and pseudo-pope.[2] Nearly all the clergy and people would leave the true Pope and the conflict would not be resolved without a violent reversal. Here Olivi used a 'concord' with dangerous implications: as the Jewish synagogue was rejected when the 'new man' Christ established His new Law, so in the sixth age the carnal church would be rejected when the 'new man' Francis has established his Rule.[3] The fall of the new Babylon would be celebrated by a jubilee of the true Church comparable to the triumph of the Jews at the fall of the old Babylon.[4] Olivi, apparently, had no vision of an Angelic Pope, but all the other elements pointing to a revolution in the Church are present in his *Postilla*, although probably unrealized in their implications.

The position of the other two Spiritual leaders, Angelo Clareno and Ubertino da Casale, was perhaps somewhat nearer to revolution. Angelo and his companions were closely involved with Celestine V and took the extreme step—condemned by Olivi—of breaking from the Franciscan Order and forming a new group authorized by Celestine himself. Celestine's renunciation became for Angelo an eschatological event, the date from which the 28 years of the sixth tribulation were to be counted.[5] Yet the position of both Angelo and Ubertino remained ambiguous. When cross-examined by the Pope, Ubertino defended his secession in terms of the overriding claims of the Rule, yet declared his obedience to the Pope,[6] while Angelo reiterated that he had not broken from the Rule of St. Francis and

[1] See references given *supra*, p. 199.
[2] Manselli, *Lectura*, pp. 174–5, 183–5, 219–28.
[3] See passage quoted *supra*, p. 198.
[4] Baluze, *Miscellanea* ii. 269.
[5] *ALKG* ii. 126.
[6] For Ubertino's defence to Pope Clement V in 1310 and other apologetic statements see *ALKG* iii. 51–89, 162–95.

placed himself in the hands of the Pope.[1] That the authorities saw revolution in the words and deeds of Angelo is clear from the charges he refuted in his *Epistola Excusatoria*:

Quod autem auctoritas papalis non esset, et dominus papa Bonifatius non esset papa, et quod iamdiu ab ecclesia auctoritas defecisset et in nobis resideret, quamdiu reformaretur ecclesia, et quod nos soli et similem nobis spiritum habentes erant veri sacerdotes et sacerdotes facti auctoritate et ordinatione papali et aliorum episcoporum non vere (essent) ordinati . . . et quod ecclesia Orientalis esset melior quam Occidentalis, nec angelis nec apostolis ista mihi cum miraculis asserentibus credidissem; et nunquam fui tam levis vel stultus . . . quod ista ab aliquo audire supportassem . . . Unde certus sum et semper certus fui de fide romane ecclesie et nunquam dubitavi de ea . . . (*ALKG* i. 522–3.)

But he continued to walk his knife-edge, as this passage from a letter shows:

. . . Responsio recta, vera, fidelis, sancta: quia et obedire ecclesie et summo pontifici, et fideliter et plena promissa, si volumus, servare valemus . . . Nam et ecclesia et summus pontifex non prohibent bene facere nec Deo sancte promissa persolvere; . . . non enim est potestas contra (Christum) dominum et contra evangelium sed novam religionem facere et novum habitum assumere; . . . de ecclesia et sacramentis et auctoritate et fide male sentire, spernere et iudicare . . . prelatorum auctoritatem; frangere et rescindere fidei et ecclesie unitatem . . .; curam animarum arroganter . . . assumere; animaliter et damnose contra Christi spiritum et fidelium subversionem et scandalum segregari et superiorum regimen contemnere . . .: hec Deus et ecclesia odit . . . Quod si quando a quocunque sive rege sive pontifice aliquid sibi mandaretur, quod esset contra fidem eius et fidei confessionem et caritatem et fructus eius, tunc obediet Deo magis quam hominibus . . . (*ALKG* i. 560–1.)

Always in the background was the image of the pseudo-pope and the persecution in high places which the Spirituals expected. Angelo claimed that St. Francis specifically prophesied a 'pontifex non catholice electus qui male sentiet de Christi vita et regula'.[2] The Pope might become a heretic but, said Angelo, we cannot condemn him. In his final *Apologia pro vita sua*[3] he went through the whole argument again, reiterating his faith both in the Rule and the *Una*

---

[1] *ALKG* i. 521–33 for the *Epistola Excusatoria*; pp. 558–69 for further letters expounding and defending his position.

[2] Ibid., p. 566.

[3] V. Doucet, 'Angelus Clarinus ad Alvarum Pelagium. Apologia pro Vita Sua', *AFH* xxxix (1946), pp. 63–200.

Ecclesia, justifying the secession authorized by Celestine and declaring his belief that the Spirit was able to raise up supreme pontiffs to lead the Church 'ad perfectionis prime et novissime celestia fundamenta. Sub quo habitu vel quo nomine non est ponderandum . . .'[1] Thus Angelo drew back from the radical prophecy which carried so many later Fraticelli into trouble.

Possibly Ubertino went further than Olivi or Angelo. He took a more extreme view of Celestine's renunciation—'illa horrenda novitas reiectionis Celestini pape et usurpationis successoris super ecclesiam'.[2] Yet he defended Olivi against the charge that he had called the Roman Church the *meretrix magna*.[3] But his long sojourn and struggle at Avignon perhaps brought him to the point of believing that the Avignonese Papacy had become the carnal church of Babylon. It is curious that none of these three leaders developed the idea of the Angelic Pope in juxtaposition to the pseudo-pope of the carnal church. What they did supply was a revolutionary logic which others would take further: the Rule was the immovable evangel; the true Pope could not gainsay it; if a pontiff in any way denied it, he was no true Pope but the minister of Antichrist. A cosmic conflict between the carnal church and the true Church had been foretold by prophets, including St. Francis himself, and events suggested that it had begun. From this point it was a short step to dating the defection of the Roman Church from the deposition of Celestine (or, later, the pontificate of John XXII) and declaring that henceforth the Roman Church was no longer the true Church but the Church of Babylon.

The followers of Olivi in the south of France at once drew this logical deduction. Repeatedly in the Inquisitorial proceedings we read such a confession as that of Raymund de Buxo who, having read concerning the *magna meretrix* in Olivi's *Postilla*,

---

[1] *AFH* xxxix (1946), p. 109.

[2] *Arbor*, f. ccxxv^v. See also f. ccxxvi^v: '...quod canonice non intravit vivente Celestino: cuius resignatio cum tanta malitia et fraude procurata per hunc seductorem et alios complices suos non valuit: qui nullo modo potuit resignare...'; f. ccxxvii^v: '... sic etiam impossibile est quod Jesus caput ecclesie renunciet regimen ecclesie peregrine. Sic impossibile multi reputant quod eius vicarius et universalis sponsus summus pontifex possit separari ab officio regiminis ecclesie et maxime modo fraudulento et fallaci: sicut fuit utique celestinus. Et quia antichristus apertus illam unionem divinam Christi Iesu separare nitetur: ad quid disponit assertio possibilitatis separationis summi pontificis ab ecclesia? Idcirco dixerim quod hic est error antichristianus et quod inventor huius erroris est misticus antichristus illius magni precursor.'

[3] Baluze, *Miscellanea* ii. 275.

... exponit quod per dictum meretricem magnam intelligitur Romana ecclesia non quantum ad fideles et electos sed quantum ad reprobos ... et subdit in dicta postilla quod sicut in fine primi status ecclesie fuit factum judicium de synagoga que Christum crucifixerat propter quod fuit destructa et dejecta, sic in fine secundi status ecclesie qui durat usque ad Antichristum fiet judicium de ecclesia carnali que persequitur vitam Christi in viris spiritualibus qui volunt tenere paupertatem Christi secundum regulam sancti Francisci, et destructa ecclesia carnali post mortem Antichristi erigetur ecclesia tercii status in viris spiritualibus. (Limborch, *Hist. Inquis.*, p. 298.)

Many openly asserted that John XXII was the pseudo-pope or *Antichristus misticus*.[1] As for the 'third church', they saw this mainly in terms of the *viri spirituales*, the true sons of Francis who would constitute it in poverty, humility, and gentleness on the ruin of all other churches. Again, there is little hint here of the *Papa Angelicus*.

Accusations against Fraticelli in Italy show the same development of ideas. A deposition of 1334 accused Angelo Clareno's group in these terms:

... audivit de fraticellis de paupere vita in pluribus locis conversando cum eis, quod dictus papa Johannes non est papa, sed nominant eum Jacobum de Caturcho et dicunt ... quod dictus dominus papa Johannes amputavit capud vite Christi, quia cassavit fraticellos, et quia fecit decretalem, quod Christus habuit in proprio et communi ... Et dixit quod habetur una profecia quod ecclesia Romana facta est meretrix et ad hoc, ut possit melius fornicari, transivit ultra montes ... (*ALKG* iv. 9.)

A deposition of 1362 declared: 'Omnes tamen concordabant quod papa Johannes fuit hereticus et quod nullus post eum fuit verus papa.'[2] Now there began to appear the theme that the beginning of evil in the Roman Church went back to the wealth acquired by the Donation of Constantine.[3] If the true church, the *ecclesia spiritualis*, was now separate from the Church of Rome, from which spiritual authority had departed, the next step was to look for the true pastor, wherever he might be concealed. One group of Fraticelli, at least, thought he might be Philip of Majorca,[4] but the image of the *Papa Angelicus* really required a poor religious. Thus, according to one

[1] See, for example, Limborch, *Hist. Inquis.*, pp. 304, 315, 316.
[2] *ALKG* iv. 100. See also similar depositions, pp. 11, 12, 113–14, 120, 122.
[3] L. Fumi, *Eretici e ribelli nell'Umbria* (Todi, undated), pp. 158–9.
[4] Ibid., p. 164.

deposition, 'summus pontifex debet esse pauper et incedere excalceatus visitando oves suas per mundum et . . . propter oppositum modum vivendi multa incommoda facit Ecclesia Dei.'[1] We recall that at Majoreti there was an inscription dating from 1419 which spoke of a Fr. Gabriel who was called the Pope of the Philadelphian Church, the last and universal Church.[2] Here clearly a Fraticelli group had set up its own Angelic Pope. Where he could not be identified, the Angelic Pope could still be the hope to sustain through persecution, as in the pathetic declaration of the martyred Michele Calci that he would submit himself to 'il papa santo da venire'.[3]

Two works throw some light on the attitudes of the later Fraticelli, though from different geographical quarters. The first is the later series of fifteen *Vaticinia de summis pontificibus* associated with the name of an apocryphal Bishop Anselm of Marsico and later placed before the earlier fifteen to form the thirty in circulation in the fifteenth and sixteenth centuries. This series was probably the work of Tuscan Fraticelli just before 1356.[4] Like the earlier ones it began with Nicholas III and took the same form of picture, caption, and text. But obviously the moment of hope in 1304 had gone and the series gives a longer line of straight political portraits. The Fraticelli viewpoint is expressed in the harsh indictments of wealth, political intrigue, and nepotism, and the roles allotted to Celestine and Boniface stand out dramatically. Celestine is represented by a holy mitred pope being blessed, with a text that begins 'Benedictus qui venit in nomine Domini', but there is a fox tugging at his robe from behind. The next, with the caption 'Fraudulenter intrasti . . .', shows Boniface at his worst, piercing the dove of peace and embroiled with the Cock and the Eagle, while behind him the rejected holy monk sits disconsolate.[5] Indignation against the Avignonese is fierce in the next portraits. If our dating is correct, the last three, that is, after Innocent VI, are real prophecies. It is difficult to see what was

[1] N. Papini, *Notizie sicure della morte, sepoltura, canonizzazione e traslazione di San Francesco d'Assisi* (Foligno, 1824), p. 275.

[2] *Supra*, p. 225.

[3] Ed. Zambrini, F., *Storia di Fra Michele Minorita, Scelta di curiosità letterarie . . .*, (Bologna, 1864), p. 22.

[4] Grundmann, *AK* xix. 120–4. But Grundmann's date (1377/8) is too late, since there is a reference to this second set of *Vaticinia* in Roquetaillade's *Vade mecum*, p. 501: '. . . ac in commentario meo libri prophetici de summis pontificibus qui incipit Ascende calve' (written in 1356).

[5] These should be numbers V and VI in the original order.

intended by two of these, but the last is clearly Antichrist, the only one in which the Pope is represented by a beast, with the caption: 'Terribilis es, quis resistet tibi?' (No. XV). This is an uncompromising assertion that Antichrist will appear in the supreme pontiff's seat and that the papacy as such is doomed. Here attention is so strongly focused on absolute indictment, that there is no looking beyond to an angelic series of pastors.

The second production, also partly pictorial, is the *Summula seu Breviloquium super concordia Novi et Veteris Testamenti*, a Catalonian work of *c.* 1351–54 to which we have already referred.[1] Here again we get a number of references to the carnal church and to the expected pseudo-pope.[2] The violent end of the present regime is represented dramatically by an extension of Joachim's Tables of Concords. In these original tables Joachim had paralleled the generations of the Old Testament kings with the sequences of popes in the New Dispensation. This is now modified and extended to bring the end crisis down to a point after 1350 (the forty-fifth generation A.D.).[3] Here, foreshadowed by the original Babylonish Captivity, the Roman Pontiff suffers a violent fate:

Futurum quidem est per concordiam modernis temporibus ut novus Rex Babilonis insurgat et cum magno exercitu Caldeorum veniet Jerusalem et capto Ieconia Rege Iuda seu summo pontifice cum magna parte populi sc. ecclesiastici exceptis pauperibus et cum omnibus thesauris domus Domini ducatur in Babilonem captivus ut transmigracio Babilonica misterialiter impleatur. (f. 88ʳ.)

This is accompanied by the symbol of the mitre and keys violently overthrown. Then comes the Abomination of Desolation. But after this, following Joachim himself, the new Zorobabel returns to Jerusalem, figured as a new pope.[4] At an earlier point in the *Breviloquium* there is also a reference to the 'sanctum pastorem' who, after the Fall of Babylon, 'cum ceteris regibus ad sanctum sepulchrum transibit et alias infidelium partes ad conterendum eorum superbiam et divino cultui subjugandum.'[5] At the end the writer is uncertain how many pontiffs there will be in the third *status* after the new Zorobabel, but he is certain that the Church will not be left without a pastor.[6]

---

[1] *Supra*, pp. 223–4. [2] See MS. Egerton 1150, ff. 29ᵛ–30ʳ, 34ᵛ–35ʳ, 88ᵛ.
[3] Ibid., f. 88ʳ⁻ᵛ. [4] Ibid., f. 89ʳ⁻ᵛ. [5] Ibid., f. 26ʳ.
[6] Ibid., f. 90ʳ⁻ᵛ.

It is interesting to compare these two later pictorial or diagrammatic series with the earlier *Vaticinia* of 1304. Then, the angelic regime was confidently expected in the last eight portraits; now, for the Tuscan Fraticelli an Antichrist in Rome is much more certain than anything else, while for the Spaniard, although he accepts Joachim's new Zorobabel, collapse and overthrow are far more evident in his representations of the last stages of history than *renovatio*, until the extreme end. There his table of the New Dispensation ends most enigmatically.[1] He carries it on beyond Zorobabel, using names from the Old Testament genealogy until the fifty-seventh generation in Joseph, after which he goes backwards from Jareth to the beginning. At Enoch there is a final cataclysm, with the second violent overthrow of the pontiff, the appearance of *Antichristus apertus et ultimus*, and the Second Coming to Judgement. This all happens at the sixty-second generation where there is a blank in the table. But after this the last generations are still designated in Seth and Adam, and represented in each case by a monk with keys and cross. Does this signify a final *Ecclesia contemplativa* to be reborn in the Second Adam after the final cataclysm?

The most extreme revolutionaries were the groups such as that of Fra Dolcino, who had no doubt at all that the existing Church, *illa meretrix*, would be overthrown with violence and that Pope and prelates would be killed. After this, according to Dolcino, would come 'unus papa sanctus a Deo missus mirabiliter et electus, et non a cardinalibus'.[2] It will be remembered that in Dolcino's sequence of churches this Angelic Pope was symbolized by the final Church of Philadelphia. In his second letter, written in 1303 after Anagni, Dolcino gave his own pattern of popes: good, bad, bad, good.[3] These were Celestine V, Boniface VIII, the third his unnamed successor, the fourth the *papa sanctus*. The accusations against Dolcino went further and attributed to him both the belief that all spiritual power had now been transferred to the *Apostoli* and the claim that he himself would assume the seat of Peter as the *papa sanctus*.[4] Whatever his real belief about himself, Dolcino's repudiation of the existing hierarchy was complete. His followers, although forced

---

[1] See MS. Egerton 1150, ff. 90ʳ–92ʳ.
[2] Muratori N.S. ix, Pt. v, p. 21.
[3] *Supra*, pp. 245–6.
[4] Muratori, vol. cit., p. 26. See also statements of followers, ibid., pp. 57, 69.

to abandon his immediate programme, continued to hold that the deterioration of the Roman Church had gone on since the days of Constantine and Pope Silvester, that the Church must be forcibly reduced to poverty again, and that this would happen in the time of a certain holy pope 'qui debet esse de fide et credencia dicti Dolcino'.

[1] Muratori, vol. cit., p. 61.

III

PROPHECY IN THE PERIOD OF BABYLONISH CAPTIVITY AND GREAT SCHISM

BABYLONISH Church, schism, pseudo-pope or *Antichristus misticus*, Angelic Pope—these were already established elements in prophecy by the mid-fourteenth century. Against a background of the Avignonese papacy Jean de Roquetaillade worked these into a prophetic programme which firmly linked the Angelic Pope with an idealized political force in a partnership to bring in the Age of Gold. For obvious reasons this prophetic partnership was conceived in French terms. Here Roquetaillade was picking up a suggestion in the *Liber de Flore*,[1] but the programme as a whole was first popularized in his tracts.

His Spiritual Franciscan principles dictated his revolutionary viewpoint: a worldly hierarchy in the Church was the antithesis of the true evangelical Church and therefore a manifestation of Antichrist. Thus one or more pseudo-popes were inevitable and from this would follow schism between the false church of Antichrist and the true one. The true Pope would be stripped, persecuted, and forced to flee into the desert, perhaps to hide himself in the realm of France. In the *Liber Secretorum Eventuum* the schism between the falsely elected pope and the true *papa angelicus* is so violent that the false cardinals lay sacrilegious hands on the true Pope.[2] But throughout Roquetaillade's works, though the false church of Antichrist nearly overwhelms the true Church, the victory of the forces of righteousness, represented by the true Pope and his ever-faithful servant, the King of France, is never in doubt.

The *Papa Angelicus* appears under a number of figures: he is the *Corrector*, the *Reparator*, the *Reformator*;[3] he is Rehoboam against Jeroboam;[4] more especially he is the *ursus admirabilis*, a figure derived from the *Oraculum Cyrilli* and most fully expounded in

---

[1] *Supra*, pp. 320–1.
[2] Bignami-Odier, *Roquetaillade*, p. 119.
[3] Ibid., p. 70.
[4] Ibid., p. 80.

Roquetaillade's Commentary on this.[1] He will resemble both St. Francis and Celestine V, and like the latter be elected at Perugia.[2] He will be a hermit called forth from the rock.[3] He is also called the Dove of the Holy Spirit and will be endowed with the Seven Gifts.[4] In one passage Roquetaillade expects him to be chosen from the Minorites and he will himself choose evangelical men of poverty for his cardinals.[5] Together with the French king he will carry out the great programme, visiting Greece and Asia and bringing all, even Turks and Tartars, under their rule. Peace will be made in Italy, all schism ended, and the clergy drastically reformed.[6] He will then leave the political role to the French king 'of the race of Pipin', who will execute the mandates of the *Reformator* throughout the world.[7] He himself will be wholly occupied with the spiritual power. After the conversion of the Jews he will transfer the Holy See from Rome to Jerusalem.[8] He will hold seven general church councils concerned with the conversion of the world. The New Jerusalem will be constructed but no secular ruler allowed therein for fear of contaminating the clergy.[8] Then there will be such an outpouring of the Holy Spirit that Paradise will seem to have descended again. All will desire the contemplative life and will live according to the Rule of St. Francis. Forty-five years after the death of Antichrist there will be one Empire embracing the whole earth, unbelief will exist no more, and there will be one flock and one shepherd.[9]

Roquetaillade's vision of unity, as we have already seen, caught on. Mme Bignami-Odier's studies have demonstrated the wide distribution of some of his works. Troubled thoughts over the Avignonese exile, general unease and gloom caused by plague and war, made men pay attention to such speculations. We have already referred to the diary of an anonymous Florentine which reported part of Roquetaillade's *Vade Mecum* as circulating in the year 1368.[10] The extract begins by prophesying disaster on the Avignonese papacy and the cardinals, announcing the near approach of Antichrist from the east. There will be terrible tribulations, tempests,

---

[1] Bignami-Odier, *Roquetaillade*, p. 82; cf. *supra*, p. 400. He is also the *ursus terribilis* against Antichrist, ibid., p. 82.

[2] Ibid., pp. 82, 88.   [3] Ibid., p. 82.

[4] Ibid., p. 82. He is also called there the *papa mirabilis*.

[5] Ibid., p. 96.

[6] Ibid., pp. 171–2. See also passage quoted *supra*, pp. 323–4.

[7] Ibid., p. 171.   [8] Ibid., p. 125.   [9] Ibid., pp. 103, 125.

[10] *Supra*, p. 324.

floods, and the Church will be despoiled of all temporal goods. But in 1378 will arise 'el detto sommo Pontifice riperatore del mondo'[1] to meet the forces of evil:

... il quale sarà da Dio mirabilemente liberato ... discaccierà della Santa Chiesa tutti sacierdoti lussoriosi e avari . . ., gastigando la superbia de' chierici, e dividerà e' lupo dal popolo santo; ed eleggierà lo Re di Francia imperadore di Roma, il quale signioreggierà tutto el mondo e annullerà in Italia la setta ch'è tra guelfi e ghibellini, e acquisterà i Reame di Gierusalem . . . E se non fosse che Iddio provvedrà . . . col predetto Riparatore, el qualle nuovamente ne riformerà l'Ordine de' Frati Minori, rimarrebbono distrutti come gli altri. . . . E pone che innanzi al 1378 anni, quasi tutti gl'Infedeli si convertiranno alla fede di Cristo, e . . . el Papa e Cardinali e Vescovi con tal ordine chericato saranno ridotti a stato perfettissimo di vita di Cristo, però ch' altrimenti o l'Infedeli non si convertirebbono. (Op. cit., p. 390.)

It was, perhaps, speculation about the state of the papacy which drove Fr. Gentile to look back among prophecies collected thirty years earlier, when he wrote his Commentary on *Ve mundo in centum annis* (*c.* 1345). Among the oracles he resurrected was the following:

Audivi tamen Parisius tempore pape Bonifatii a quodam illustri viro, qui erat antiquus religiosus et magister in theologia, quod ecclesia Romana debebat transferri in Galliam et ibi morari XL annis. Et in ista prophecia dicitur quod ibi debet ipsam persecucionem recipere. Legi in alia prophecia, iam sunt anni forte XXX, quod tempore istius persecucionis ecclesie pauci cardinales, qui remanserint, venient Romam latenter . . . Et cum aliquo tempore erunt simul congregati ad eligendum papam volentes unum eligere de se ipsis, tunc, exibit vox sanctuario dicens: Ite ad occidentem septicollis et querite in syndone beati Johannis pauperum nudum meum. Et illum eligent papam. Et ille erit primus reformator ecclesie ad statum primum paupertatis et sanctitatis. Set quia erit multum antiquus, modico tempore vivit. Verumptamen illud, quod ipse inceperit, alius papa subsequens persequitur. Et tercius papa similiter. Qui tercius papa simul cum imperatore, qui erit sibi filius et subditus, cum pace et crucibus intrabit in Jherusalem et recipientur gratanter a Sarracenis . . . (Finke, *Aus den Tagen*, p. 220.)

This is an interesting and original version of the Angelic Pope prophecies, drawn in all likelihood from the *Liber de Flore*. It links this Gentile more closely to the Spiritual Franciscan circle of Angelo

---

[1] *Diario d'Anonimo Fiorentino dall'anno 1358 al 1389*, ed. A. Gherardi, *Documenti di storia italiana*, vi (Florence, 1876), p. 390.

Clareno, making it even more likely that he was Gentile of Foligno, Angelo's Augustinian friend.

Prophetic verses circulating in Italy during the Great Schism, or just after, expect a future saviour[1] who often appears to be an amalgam of pope and emperor, as in the following:

> Verrà nel sereno
> Delle benigne stelle
> Un'huom che rinnovelle
> Il mondo in altra forma . . .
> Per l'universo, pace
> Sarà dal cielo in terra,
> E follia e guerra
> Sarà in fondo messa.
>
> (*Misc. Franc.* xxxvii. 48 n. 1)

A later poem, attributed to Tomassuccio da Foligno, but actually written *c.* 1420, describes a *Restauratore universale* who is a mixture of Angelic Pope and Emperor:

> Et a ben fare verrà un cristiano
> E sarà un Papa vero e naturale
> Santissimo, giusto e governarà piano . . .
> Da poi avranno un giusto per Signore
> Che fia al mondo degno Imperadore
>
> .   .   .   .   .   .
>
> Sarà di questo stuolo capitano
> Un che terrà l'imperial corona,
> E fia seguito da ogni cristiano
> E ogni sua fattura sarà buona,
> E torrà la signoria al gran soldano . . .
> E della terra santa fia Signore
> Il franco santo vero imperatore.
> Costui sarà di povera natura,
> Avrà da Dio grande signoria . . .
> E fia tranquillità, pace e unione,
> Come al tempo del buon Ottaviano;

---

[1] The well-known *Apri le labbra mie* ends:

> Poi fie la Chiesa ornata di pastori
> Umili e santi come fur gli autori.

See G. Carducci, *Rime di M. Cino da Pistoia e d'altri del secolo XIV* (Florence, 1862), p. 267. A vision of Fr. Johannes de Firenze, dated 1361, ends with a vision of the ecumenical Church 'che face uno ovile e una patria'; see E. Narducci, *Catalogo di manoscritti ora posseduti da B. Boncompagni* (Rome, 1862), pp. 191–200.

E per un solo si terrà ragione
Che sarà uom prudentissimo e sano,
De' cristiani universal Signore,
E manterrà l'imperio Romano,
Ai cristiani darà pace ordinata,
E nulla guerra sarà ricordata.

(*Misc. Franc.* xxxix. 127–8)

A partnership of Pope and Emperor appears in another fifteenth-century poem where, after describing the 'imperatore di casa David', it continues:

Vedrai el pastor romano
Della Chiesa capitano
Sancto sarà et soprano
Del mondo unitore.

(*Misc. Franc.* xxxix. 129)

Although it seems likely that much of this prophetic verse emanates from Fraticelli groups, its circulation was much wider, and the number of Italian manuscripts in particular containing prophecies which centre on the tribulation of the Church, schism, *renovatio*, and angelic partnership of Pope and Emperor throws light on the general state of feeling during the end of the Avignonese papacy and the Great Schism.[1]

Among the voices calling the Pope back to Rome in eschatological terms was that of Cola di Rienzo.[2] His great dream was that by the time of the 1350 jubilee-year the Pope would have returned to a renewed and purified Rome and Italy, upon which the Holy

---

[1] Thus in the Vatican MS. Reg. Lat. 580, written in 1387, is a beautifully illuminated collection of prophecies including the whole series of thirty *Vaticinia de summis pontificibus*, the *libellus fratris Thelofori*, with illustrations, amongst others, of the four Angelic Popes, and the Second Charlemagne prophecy. The fifteenth-century MS. Ottoboniani 1106 contains Telesphorus's work, with a selection of prophetic verses and other oracles attributed to Joachim. MS. Chigiano A. VII. 220 is a beautiful Renaissance volume following the earlier Reg. Lat. 580. MS. Vat., Lat. 3816 is a fifteenth-century paper book, with neat pen-and-ink pictures illustrating the *Vaticinia* and Telesphorus's work, with various prophetic verses, and MS. Vat., Lat. 3817 is similar. A manuscript in Florence, Bib. Ricc. 688, contains prophetic verses sent to Pope Clement in 1382. The Bibl. Naz. in Florence contains, besides a manuscript with the usual *Vaticinia* and Telesphorus's *libellus* (Magl. XXII, 22), a set of verses headed *Profetia del Beato Gioachino* in MS. Magl. A. XXV, 612, and in MS. II, xi, 18 a prophecy purporting to come from the Abbot Joachim compiled by a Frater Ioannes Peregrinus of Bologna. Besides these more specifically Joachimist examples, Hilka and Messini cite a number of manuscripts containing prophetic verses of the type quoted above.

[2] The material for this paragraph is drawn from Burdach, *Vom Mittelalter*, ii, Pts. 1, 2, 3, 5.

Spirit would be poured out. From Avignon in 1343 he wrote to the Senate and People of Rome to expect the coming of her Spouse and the new era which was to dawn:

Ecce quidem clementissimus agnus Dei peccata confundens, sanctissimus videlicet Romanus pontifex, pater Urbis, sponsus et dominus sue sponse, clamoribus, querelis et luctibus excitatus compaciensque suis cladibus, calamitatibus et ruinis, ad renovacionem ipsius Urbis, gloriam plebis sue ac tocius mundi leticiam et salutem, inspiracione Sancti Spiritus sinum clemencie sue graciosus aperiens, misericordiam vobis propinavit et graciam, ac universo mundo redempcionem promittit et remissionem gentibus peccatorum. (Burdach, *Vom Mittelalter*, Pt. 3, p. 6.)

For this Rome must prepare herself: '. . . ut civitas vestra, sponsa Romani pontificis, expurgata viciorum vepribus, suavibus renovata virtutibus, in odorem unguentorum suorum vernarum suscipiat sponsum suum . . .' (Burdach, *Vom Mittelalter*, Pt. 3, p. 7).

By 1347 Rienzo's letters were going in the other direction, to Avignon. To Clement VI he wrote of the great *renovatio* taking place in Rome under the influence of the Holy Spirit, and again later to declare his faith in the return of Rome's true Mistress: 'Et cum auxilio Spiritus Sancti spes certa me confovet, quod in anno Domini iubileo vestra Sanctitas erit Rome ac imperator vobiscum, quod unum erit ovile et unus pastor, per gracie eiusdem Spiritus Sancti unionem' (Burdach, *Vom Mittelalter*, Pt. 3, p. 113). When, disillusioned over the year 1350, he turned to the Emperor Charles IV, Rienzo still expected the prophetic partnership of Emperor and Pope to bring in the Golden Age by 1357. He declared:

. . . quod in brevi erunt magne novitates, presertim pro reformacione Ecclesie ad statum pristine sanctitatis, cum magna pace non solum inter Christicolas sed inter Christianos et eciam Sarracenos, quos sub uno proxime futuro pastore Spiritus Sancti gracia perlustrabit . . .; item quod ad huiusmodi spiritualis negocii prosecucionem electus sit a Deo vir sanctus, revelacione divina ab omnibus cognoscendus . . . et quod deinde idem pastor angelicus Ecclesie Dei quasi ruenti succurret, non minus eciam quam Franciscus, et totum statum Ecclesie reformabit . . . (Burdach, *Vom Mittelalter*, Pt. 3, pp. 194–5.)

A little later, St. Bridget of Sweden was also calling on the Pope to fulfil the destiny of history in returning to Rome. Amongst the prophets on the great approaching tribulation of the Church whom

she cited was the Abbot Joachim from the *Super Hieremiam.*[1] Once
more the greatest evil and the greatest good are juxtaposed in her
Revelations. She hears Christ proclaim the coming age: 'Now will
my friends bring to me a new bride, fair to look upon, joyful to
embrace, honourable in her conduct.'[2] Doing her part to bring
about fulfilment, St. Bridget calls on successive popes to return to
Rome, entreating Pope Gregory XI in particular: '. . . ut venies
Romam ad sedem tuam quam citius poteris . . . Veni igitur et noli
tardare . . . Incipe renovare ecclesiam meam . . . et renovetur et
spiritualiter reducatur ad pristinum statum suum sanctum' (*Liber
coelestis revelationum* (ref. *supra*, p. 338 n. 3), Lib. IV, cap. cxlii).
Again, the messages of St. Catherine of Siena are pitched in the
same key. To such visionaries the return to Rome is seen not as
a desirable political or moral move, but as an essential part of the
programme of Last Things. The Jordan of tribulation must first be
crossed before the Last Age can dawn and this implies a significant
element of discontinuity. The return to Rome itself is expected as
a revolutionary act: in St. Bridget's vision it is a *new* bride that Christ
will receive. The physical discontinuity between Avignon and Rome
is seen as symbolic of the deeper discontinuity between the sixth and
seventh ages of history.

The Great Schism brought into the sharpest possible focus all
the various elements of the prophetic tradition that we have been
tracing: the forces of Antichrist creating schism and persecution in
the Church, the expectation of terrible tribulation and judgement,
the prophetic summons of the Pope back to Rome to fulfil the full
destiny of the *renovatio ecclesie.* Above all, it was the fact of the
Great Schism itself which set the seal of truth on the prophets from
Joachim and St. Francis to Jean de Roquetaillade. Even Pierre
d'Ailly wondered whether this was 'illud magnum scisma quod esse
debet preambulum adventus Antichristi: de quo multa scripserunt
sancta Hildegardis et venerabilis abbas Joachim'.[3] He was writing in

[1] *Libellus qui intitulatur Onus Mundi . . .* (ref. *supra*, p. 338 n. 5), cap. xxvi. On St.
Bridget's message see J. Jørgensen, *St. Bridget of Sweden*, trans. I. Lund (London,
1954), ii. 78 seq.
[2] Ibid., p. 79.
[3] Petrus de Aliaco, *Concordantia astronomie cum theologia . . .* (Venice, 1490, unpag.),
cap. lix. See also his *Tractatus de materia*, ed. F. Oakley, *The Political Thought of Pierre
d'Ailly* (New Haven, 1964), pp. 315–16: 'Propterea ex tunc quidam spirituales mala haec
subtilioris intelligentiae oculo praevidentes, praesertim Ecclesiae persecutionem et huius
schismatis horrendam monstruosamque divisionem, subtractionem quoque oboedientiae
ab Ecclesia Romana, et alia plura scandalosa inde secutura praedixerunt, sicut patet in

1414, on the eve of the Council of Constance. Even while operating on a practical level to end the Schism, d'Ailly was alive to the possibility that the Church might be in the grip of cosmic forces to which the only certain guides were the prophets.

The interpretation of these portentous happenings was undertaken by Telesphorus of Cosenza. Here was the terrible schism so often prognosticated by Joachim, here was the pseudo-pope, the *Antichristus misticus*. Now was the ruin of the carnal church, the punishment of false clergy and mendicants. If Joachim's *nova religio sanctissima* was to come in, there must be violent revolution, with the ruin of the Roman Church as it stood. Under the pseudo-pope, *natione alemanus*, the *ultima persecutio* would be heavier and more inhuman than any before.[1] But the advent of the New Dispensation was undoubted. Telesphorus characterized it in words which he ascribed to the *Liber Concordie*, although only the first sentence is a direct quotation:[2] 'Item in libro concordie pluries et expresse tenet et clare quod insurget una nova religio sanctissima que erit libera et spiritualis in qua Romani pontifices potiti pace ecclesie se continebunt. Quam religionem et ordinem Deus super omnes alias diliget, quia perfectio illius vincet omnes alias aliorum ordinum' (Telesphorus, *Libellus*, f. 14ʳ). We can, perhaps find an indication that Telesphorus was not himself a Mendicant in the fact that he did not here use any of the pseudo-Joachimist prophecies but left the identification of the 'new order' entirely open. For the series of Angelic Popes he drew on the four portraits in the *Liber de Fiore*. Working in holy partnership, angelic pontiffs and new spiritual men will purify the Church and bring it *in statum paupertatis*. A general council will ordain poverty for all clergy and twelve will be elected from the *nova religio* to preach the gospel throughout the world.[3] In the final sabbath of Telesphorus's intricate programme, the spiritual power alone will rule the world in a regime which he again describes in an unidentifiable quotation from Joachim:[4]

libris Abbatis Joachim et Hildegardis, quos non esse contemnendos, quorundam magnorum doctorum probat auctoritas.' (In a footnote to this passage the editor refers to Telesphorus's *libellus*, which he erroneously states to be no longer extant.) For an opposite contemporary view, denouncing these phantasies and delusions, see J. Gerson, *Omnia Opera* (Antwerp, 1706), *De Distinctione verarum visionum a falsis*, col. 44.

[1] Telesphorus, *Libellus*, ff. 9ʳ–14ᵛ.
[2] *Lib. Conc.*, f. 95ᵛ. See also ff. 56ʳ, 89ʳ, 92ᵛ–93ʳ, 122ᵛ.
[3] Telesphorus, *Libellus*, ff. 20ᵛ, 25ʳ–27ʳ.
[4] Telesphorus gives a reference for this passage: *Joachim in Concordie*. But it is not a direct quotation, although it contains an echo of f. 89ʳ, where Joachim exalts the

Et Romanus pontifex in spiritualibus dominabitur a mari usque ad terminos orbis terrarum et erit reformatio status ecclesie . . . Et dictus status ecclesie et similitudo apostolorum erit non solum in summo pontifice et in ecclesia romana sed in omnibus aliis prelatis et collegiis, ac omnes reges et principes populi Romanum pontificem ut verum vicarium Christi honorabunt . . . secundum Joachim in libro concordie. (Telesphorus, *Libellus*, f. 39ʳ.)

In the fifteenth and sixteenth centuries the works of Roquetaillade and Telesphorus and the circulating Second Charlemagne prophecy in its Joachimist form kept alive the ideal partnership of French King and Angelic Pope. But on the German side it was more difficult to expect an *entente* between temporal and spiritual powers, since the tradition of enmity between Pope and German Eagle was so strong. As we have seen, the difficulty could be resolved by making the Emperor sole *reparator* and liquidating Rome altogether. The role of chastiser was much emphasized in the German tradition and received support from the Brigittine prophecies circulating in the fifteenth century. Sometimes these made the German nation the involuntary agent of God's wrath, trampling down the Church and destroying Rome. But the most interesting idea was that of the *Rex pudicus facie*,[1] the strong but godly king who must chastise the Church, but would also reform and restore it, like the Maccabees at the end of the Old Dispensation. Thus, alongside the picture of the golden alliance in a French future, there developed a starker image of a chastiser–reformer who must do the work of the Angelic Pope, for Rome could not produce him. It was a short step to assimilate the spiritual and secular roles in a ruler who would be priest–king. This expectation was actually put forward in the *Reformation Kaiser Sigmunds* and it is not without significance that this tract had a considerable vogue and was revived in the sixteenth century in Germany.[2] As we have seen, the idealism of political prophecy was by no means dead and various forms of partnership between spiritual ruler and secular were eagerly scanned in the search for the final combination that would initiate world peace.

It was always as an affirmation of optimistic expectation within history that the *Papa Angelicus* appeared. He might be revealed and elected by divine intervention but he was to be essentially a human

papacy under the figure of Joseph. For an explanation of Telesphorus's intricate programme, see *supra*, p. 327.

[1] Cf. *supra*, p. 339.　　　　　　　　　　　[2] Cf. *supra*, pp. 341, 363 n. 4.

being, occupying the historic Chair of Peter and initiating the great positive achievement of the Church before the end of time. The prophecies were most subject to attack from those who held that no such religious Age of Gold within history was to be expected, and the debate between the optimistic and pessimistic views of history turned most fiercely around these prophetic hopes. Thus in the fifteenth century we meet the deep pessimism of Jacobus de Paradiso reacting against the facile hope of *renovatio*.[1] Virtue is declining, the Roman See cannot reform itself nor do general councils achieve this:

Quid ergo? Putamusne Ecclesiam posse recipere reformationem generalem? . . . Ego iudico impossibile humano modo: . . . Persuaderi mihi
videor, quod nec aetas nostra, nec futura haec patietur: . . . Aestimo
igitur mundum dietim decrescere in pravis moribus, salva divina dispositione cuius consilium nemo novit, usque ad profundum delictorum,
quousque veniat filius perditionis. (Op. cit., pp. 110–11.)

An interesting study of fascination which turns to disillusionment has been made by Dr. Hirsch-Reich in her researches on Henry of Langenstein (de Hassia),[2] the most celebrated German scholar of the late fourteenth century, first as professor of theology at Paris and later as Vice-Chancellor of the University of Vienna. In 1383 in a letter to his friend Eckard of Ders, Bishop of Worms,[3] he revealed his eagerness in gathering together information about Antichrist from the 'nova Sibilla' and Hildegarde. In pursuing this he evidently came across Joachim, 'endowed with the spirit of prophecy', particularly his supposed work *De Semine Scripturarum*, which he quoted in a letter to the same friend shortly afterwards.[4] It was the tribulation of the Great Schism which no doubt set his mind both on the signs of approaching Antichrist and the hope of *reformatio*. The 'mystery of the letters' evidently took hold of him, for in 1388 he produced a tract *De Idiomate hebraico* in the second part of which he dealt with these mysteries.[5] Then in 1390, in a sermon on Ascension Day before the whole university, the Vice-Chancellor tackled the

[1] Jacobus de Paradiso, *De Septem Statibus Ecclesie in Apocalipsi mystice descriptis . . .*, pub. in *Antilogia Papae* (Basle, 1555). I have used the edition in E. Brown, *Appendix ad fasciculum Rerum Expetendarum et Fugiendarum* (London, 1690), ii. 102–12.
[2] I am greatly indebted to her for generously supplying much of the information in this paragraph.
[3] Ed. G. Sommerfeldt, *Epistola de ecclesie periculis*, *HJ* xxx (1909), pp. 43–61.
[4] Ibid., pp. 297–307.
[5] Cf. B. Walde, *Christliche Hebraisten Deutschlands am Ausgang des Mittelalters* (Münster, 1916), pp. 28 seq.

question which was haunting so many: Is it possible to predict the Last Things?[1] He examined various valid methods of investigation and accorded high praise to Joachim as one of the great men who had laboured to determine the Last Things from the Scriptures.[2] With astrology he would have no dealings, but the methods of Joachim, divine revelations, the mysteries of the letters—in all these he placed confidence. There is a certain note of defence in his stress that these methods should not be treated with contempt which suggests that he had already met with scepticism. Two years later he had, it would seem, made a complete volte-face. In his *Tractatus . . . contra quendam Eremitam de ultimis temporibus vaticinantem nomine Theolophorum*,[3] he launched a violent attack, not only on Telesphorus of Cosenza, but also on Joachim, Cyril, and all recent prophets. Who is this Joachim, he contemptuously asks, who is of no reputation in the Paris schools? 'Ibi enim nullius auctoritatis, sed habetur pro quodam suspecto conjecturatore de futuris ex industria humana.'[4] If he had the true Spirit, why did he err on the Trinity? 'Quomodo tantum deliravit, ut putaret, post legem Christi, adhuc legem Spiritus Sancti venturam esse, in quam transferenda esset lex Christi, sicut in illam transivit lex Moysi tanquam figura in figuratum, et umbra in lucem?' (op. cit., col. 522). If all these prophets—Joachim, Cyril, Merlin, Dandalus, and the rest—were holy men and true prophets of God, 'quomodo latuit hoc tam diu Ecclesiam et sanctos doctores?'[5] The bitterness of the attack suggests the extreme disillusionment of one who had placed his hope and faith in a quarter where they had been shattered. Dr. Hirsch-Reich suggests opposition and contempt from fellow academics as one reason for the change and the unacceptable politics of Telesphorus in boosting French claims as another. But deeper than either may have been the onset of a bitter gloom concerning the future. Could

---

[1] On the contents and manuscripts of this sermon see O. Hartwig, *Henricus de Langenstein dictus de Hassia* (Marburg, 1859), pp. 21 seq.; Sommerfeldt, loc. cit., pp. 45 seq. Dr. Hirsch-Reich used four fifteenth-century manuscripts in the Vienna State Library.

[2] 'Nam primo ex scripturis variis multi laboraverunt in determinatione ultimorum temporum, de quibus unus et magnus fuit abbas Joachim qui secundum aliquem modum spiritum prophetie habuisse dicitur. Hic in re illa multa laboravit super apocalypsim et in aliis opusculis suis' (Dr. Hirsch-Reich's transcription).

[3] Ed. B. Pez, *Thesaurus Anecdotorum Novissimus* (Augsburg, 1721), i, Pt. II, cols. 507–64.

[4] Ibid., col. 521.

[5] Ibid., col. 524. The main attack on the Joachites occupies cols. 521–9.

the Schism ever issue in the *renovatio* which Telesphorus and Joachim proclaimed? In refuting Telesphorus, Henry of Langenstein declared his now convinced pessimism:

. . . verisimile videtur, quod sub illis Ecclesia Christi continuo sit decensura in deterius, quemadmodum iam diu est. Declinare incepit a meridie suae perfectionis, sicut heu! manifestum est nimis comparando quo ad spiritualia, status singulos fidelium huius temporis ad status similes praecedentium laicorum et clericorum. Unde sicut mundus vadit senescendo, vergens continuo ad interitum praesentis dispositionis: ita et populus Christianus in fine seculorum constitutus tendit ad defectionem charitatis et fidei. . . . Non videtur ergo quod futura sit aliqua notabilis Ecclesiae reformatio usque post interfectionem manifestam Antichristi per Jesus Christum Dominum nostrum. Tunc enim Judaei et ceteri infideles . . . convertentur ad Deum . . . Hoc ergo modo videtur Ecclesia post tribulationem per Antichristum valde in omni populo et gente dilatanda ac in fide, charitate, spe, in omni virtute et sanctitate perficienda. (Op. cit., col. 532.)

It will be seen from this passage that the debate between the optimists and pessimists was never quite clear-cut. Henry of Langenstein did expect a space right at the end, after the intervention of Christ to destroy Antichrist, in which the Jews and others will be converted, while, on the other hand, those who stressed the *renovatio* usually expected a final declension and manifestation of Antichrist. In the various programmes of Last Things proposed there are many variations. Thus Nicholas of Lyra believed that the silence at the opening of the Seventh Seal did signify a period of tranquillity for the Church after Antichrist, but he gave it no emphasis as an Age of Gold and stressed its brevity.[1] Nicholas of Clémanges believed that the *magnum iudicium Domini* was at hand, but that between this and the *extremum iudicium* there would be an interval truly called the Sabbath 'propter tranquillitatem a fremitu bellorum strepituque turbinum'.[2] Nicholas of Cusa, writing in the mid-fifteenth century, expected a very positive resurrection of the Church after Antichrist:[3]

. . . resument sancti vires et redibunt ad cor, quia videbunt ecclesiam post sanctorum interemptionem gloriosiori fulgore resurgere post paucos dies. Et videntes infideles Antichristi praevaluisse ecclesiam et se victos, victori Christo cedent et ad ipsum revertentur omnes nationes, ut sit

---

[1] *Liber apocalipsis . . . cum glosis . . .* (no pl. of pub., no date, unpag.), cap. vii.
[2] *Opera omnia* (Lyon, 1613), pp. 357–8.
[3] *Coniectura de Novissimis Diebus* (Padua, 1514), f. 1ᵛ.

Christi haereditas in universo orbe, unum ovile unius pastoris. . . . Et reddet se ecclesia gloriosa resurrectione a pressura Antichristi . . . Et incipiet ecclesia in tranquillitate de aeterna pace meditari . . . Sed nondum statim finis . . .

These views show how often thoughts turned to the possibility of a final age of peace, but they do not go as far as the positive affirmation of the Joachimist *Papa Angelicus.*

IV

RENOVATIO MUNDI AND RENAISSANCE

IN the age of Savonarola and the Florentine Platonists the elements of despair and exaltation were strangely mixed.[1] Savonarola preached imminent woe and judgement, yet expected afterwards the *pastore angelico*; the Platonists were swept to a high excitement by the sense that the *plenitudo temporum* had arrived, yet at the same time were assailed by anxious expectations of Antichrist. It was to the astrologer Paul of Middelburg that Marsilio Ficino in 1492 wrote his famous letter[2] proclaiming the Age of Gold to have arrived and listing all its manifestations in the arts, in humane letters, in the art of printing, and so on:

Si quod igitur seculum appellandum nobis est aureum, illud est proculdubio tale, quod aurea passim ingenia profert. Id autem esse nostrum hoc seculum minime dubitabit, qui praeclara seculi huius inventa considerare voluerit. Hoc enim seculum tanquam aureum, liberales disciplinas ferme iam extinctas reduxit in lucem, grammaticam, poesim, oratoriam, picturam, sculpturam, architecturam, musicam, antiquum ad Orphicam Lyram carminum cantum. Idque Florentiae . . . Idque potissimum in Federico Urbinate duci . . . In te quoque mi Paule perfecisse videtur astronomiam, Florentiae quin etiam Platonicam disciplinam in lucem e tenebris revocavit. In Germania temporibus nostris imprimendorum librorum inventa sunt instrumenta.

Egidio of Viterbo, writing to Ficino, echoed this salutation of the Age of Gold.[3] Among this circle of humanist friends art and letters were in no sense divorced from religion in their expectation. Plethon was reported to have prophesied 'veram eamdemque religionem uno animo, una mente, una praedicatione, universum orbem paucis post annis esse suscepturum'.[4] Commenting on this, A. Chastel describes

---

[1] See A. Chastel, (i) 'L'Antéchrist à la Renaissance', *Cristianesimo e ragion di Stato, Atti del II Congresso Internazionale di Studi umanistici*, ed. E. Castelli (Rome, 1952), pp. 177–86; (ii) 'Art et religion dans la Renaissance', *Bibliothèque d'Humanisme et Renaissance*, vii (1945), pp. 20–37.

[2] M. Ficino, *Opera* (Basle, 1576), i. 944. On Paul of Middelburg see *supra*, p. 347.

[3] P. Kristeller, *Supplementum Ficinianum* (Florence, 1937), pp. 315–16.

[4] Cited Chastel, loc. cit. (i), p. 177 n. 2.

his mission thus: 'le platonisme était l'instrument d'une rénovation totale de la pensée théologique et des mœurs qui ouvrait une étape magnifique de l'histoire humaine.'[1]

In the same Italy, however, general anxiety was building up to a peak in the 1480s and 1490s. Luca Landucci reported a miracle in his Florentine Diary because everyone was awaiting great signs from God.[2] There were wandering prophets crying 'Woe!' in Siena in 1472, and in 1492 Fra Giuliano was inveighing against *l'avara Babilonia* in Milan.[3] Various prophets appeared with strange foreboding messages in the streets of Rome. In 1484 one who posed as a humanist, an astrologer, and a cabbalist rode through proclaiming imminent change to the whole world.[4] In 1490 Stefano Infessura described the advent of one 'natione incognitus, indutus veste vili more mendicantium' who threatened the Romans 'in hoc praesenti anno' with great calamity which would spread to the rest of Italy.[5] In this case there are traces of a positive Joachimism, both in his method— 'reducebat ad concordiam Testamentum Vetus usque ad Novum' —and in his final expectation: 'tertio anno MCCCCLXXXXIII clericus absque temporali dominatione reperietur; eritque tunc Angelicus Pastor, qui solum vitam animarum et spiritualia curabit ...' At this time the Sienese chronicler Tizio wrote a book on the end of the world, whilst, on the other hand, the Florentine canon Prospero Pitti prophesied the renewal of the Church and the advent of the Angelic Pope.[6] In these same years the strange and solemn prophecy attributed to St. Cataldus was striking like a knell on men's ears, and Paul of Middelburg's astrological prognostications were sweeping through Italy.[7] Again the emphasis here was on catastrophe and Antichrist, yet the conjunction of the stars in 1484 also pointed to the advent of a holy Reformer. A few years later Lichtenberger's *Prognosticatio*, with its popular mixture of astrology and prophecy, was attaining great popularity among Italians, especially in northern Italy.[8] The significant point to grasp is that we are not dealing here with two opposed viewpoints or groups—optimistic

---

[1] Cited Chastel, loc. cit. (i), pp. 177–8.

[2] Ibid., p. 178.

[3] A. Allegretti, *Diarium*, Muratori o.s. xxiii. 775, 780; F. Chabod, 'Per la storia religiosa dello Stato di Milano durante il dominio di Carlo V', *Annuario del R. Istituto storico italiano per l'età moderna e contemporeana*, ii (1936), p. 83.

[4] E. Garin, *Filosofi italiani del Quattrocento* (Florence, 1942), p. 501.

[5] S. Infessura, op. cit. (ref. p. 337 n. 2), pp. 264–5.

[6] J. Schnitzer, *Savonarola* (Munich, 1924), ii. 634–5.

[7] *Supra*, p. 347.   [8] *Supra*, p. 347 n. 1.

humanists hailing the Age of Gold on the one hand, and medieval-style prophets and astrologers proclaiming 'Woe!' on the other. Marsilio studied Paul of Middelburg's calculations; Pico della Mirandola and, later, Egidio of Viterbo studied the Cabbala; the Florentine Platonists at first welcomed Savonarola. Foreboding and great hope lived side by side in the same people. Now the juxtaposition of greatest tribulation and greatest earthly beatitude was already present in the Joachimist pattern of history which we have traced down to this moment. Thus the Joachimist marriage of woe and exaltation exactly fitted the mood of late fifteenth-century Italy, where the concept of a humanist Age of Gold had to be brought into relation with the ingrained expectation of Antichrist.

The evidence for a Venetian interest in Antichrist and *Renovatio* goes back to the mid-fifteenth century when Domenico Mauroceno, Rusticianus, Andreas, and the later writers of the St. Cyprian manuscript were collecting the prophecies of popes from the *Vaticinia*, from the *Liber de Flore*, and, above all, from Telesphorus of Cosenza's *libellus*. By illustration they attempted to delineate the Angelic Popes more closely. Thus the St. Cyprian manuscript begins with crude pictures of the final sequence of four popes from the *Vaticinia* and in the text of Telesphorus inserts pictures of all four Angelic Popes.[1] One of these from a leafy tree directs the gathering in of the harvest (f. 30ʳ); another preaches to a crowd of lay people (f. 31ʳ). An enigmatic 'figura nove religionis in qua summi pontifices erunt' shows a tonsured monk with a hatchet in a strange setting which appears to be some kind of garden (f. 29ᵛ). The *nova religio* is also shown as groups of pious monks prayerfully receiving God's Word from an angel (f. 29ᵛ). In the final part of Telesphorus's programme the picture-section emphasizes the fact that political saviours will be left behind in the period after the *Antichristus ultimus* and only the *populus sanctus et electus* under its angelic pastor will remain. God the Father appears in clouds to bless the kneeling people, while the note below explains: 'Hic est populus sanctus habens habitum monachorum et nove religionis. In quibus se continebunt omnes summi pontifices post ultimum antichristum.' This is followed by a picture of a mitred and haloed pope (f. 35ʳ). Among the later additions to the St. Cyprian manuscript are

[1] MS. Venice (ref. *supra*, p. 173 n. 1), ff. 13ʳ, 13ᵛ, 14ʳ, 14ᵛ (see *Vaticinia*, numbers XXVII to XXX); ff. 29ʳ, 30ʳ, 31ʳ. *Supra*, pp. 173, 343–5, for other pictures in this manuscript.

more sequences of popes, including those attributed to St. Malachy, written into the manuscript as late as 1666.[1]

The continuing interest in this type of prophecy is seen in Silvestro Meuccio's Joachimist editions. Particularly relevant to the theme of the Angelic Pope was the edition of Telesphorus's *libellus* which appeared in 1516. Silvestro's dedicatory letter emphasizes the approaching crisis of tribulation, and this is underlined in the other preliminaries, but the dedicatory letter of Fr. Rusticianus which Silvestro prints moves on from the desolation of Rome to the renewal under the Angelic Pope and the programme of *renovatio* is clearly brought out by the pictures which the editor adds to the text. When the Augustinian hermit, the Angelic Pope elect, has been sought out and crowned by the Angel and all the forces of evil have been quelled, the triumph of the *nova religio*[2] is expressed in pictures and captions of high exaltation.[3] The Angelic Pope will journey round the world bringing peace to all nations: the final unity of one flock under one shepherd is the only form of organization needed for the Last Tranquillity.

Silvestro Meuccio's handling of the fourteenth-century work reveals his strong sense of its contemporaneity and the interest expressed by Paolo Angelo reinforces this. This elusive person, only known to us through his relations with Meuccio and the two tracts he wrote, claimed descent from Byzantine Emperors.[4] The paramount influences upon his outlook appear to have been exercised by the Blessed Amadeus and by 'il confessor mio maestro Sylvestro eremita, che quasi tutte le opere dell'abbate Ioachino fece venir a luce'.[5] In 1524 he published an *Epistola . . . ad sanctissimum . . . patrem . . . Clementem . . . Papam septimum . . . In Sathan ruinam tyrannidis . . .* in which he translated long passages from the prophecies of Amadeus.[6] In 1530, in his second tract addressed to Andrea Gritti, the Venetian Doge, he summarized the work of Telesphorus in Italian.[7] Like Silvestro, his preoccupation was with two expectations: first, that of the *Anticristo misto* in the schism,

[1] MS. Venice, ff. 43ᵛ–46ʳ, 53ʳ–54ᵛ.

[2] For the passage describing the *nova religio* see *supra*, p. 423.

[3] Ed. 1516, ff. 24ᵛ–27ʳ, 32ʳ–34ʳ.

[4] The only study of Paolo Angelo known to me is that of Secret (ref. Select Bibliography).

[5] *Profetie certissime* (ref. *supra*, p. 264 n. 3), f. 2ᵛ.

[6] I have not seen this and rely here on Secret, *Rinascimento* XIII, pp. 211 seq. for its contents.   [7] Ref. *supra* (p. 264 n. 3), pp. 24–32.

with all the ills to follow; second, that of the *renovatio* to be carried
out by the 'angelico tanto espettato pastore con li successori vera-
mente santissimi'.[1] Paolo Angelo followed Silvestro's edition of
Telesphorus closely, naturally giving prominence to the Venetian
elements which had now been inserted in the *libellus*. His eastern
origin is perhaps betrayed in his emphasis on the union of the Greek
and Latin Churches for ever and in the idealized international relations to be established by the *Papa Angelico*, when men will be able
to go dry-foot from Europe to Asia because of three bridges to be
built.[2] In the conclusion he bases his faith in the 'tempo della
renovatione' on Joachim's writings and affirms that the death of
Antichrist will be followed, not, as many think, by the end of the
world, but by the end of the time of labour and the blessed epoch
when Satan will be bound.[3]

A further indication of prophetic interests is the *Mirabilis Liber*,
supposedly published in Venice (1514), but only known in a Paris
edition (1522) and later French editions. This, as we have seen,[4] was a
prophetic anthology which contrived to bring all the prophecies into
line in support of the French Last World Emperor. It included the
captions of the whole thirty *Vaticinia de summis pontificibus* (without
pictures)[5] and these were followed by a section 'De angelico pastore
et eius bonitate et virtute et operibus sanctis qui apparebit finitis
tribulationibus pie prophetatis in sua proprietate et operibus vir-
tuosis'. This section was drawn directly from the *Liber de Flore* and
the source cited for it was the library of St. Victor's in Paris 'in
libro abbatis Joachim'.[6] The purpose of this and other following
prophecies is always to work up to the splendid holy alliance of
Gallican king and Angelic Pope in the last age. The libraries of
France and Italy appear to have been combed in search of material.[7]

One of Domenico Mauroceno's correspondents was Pietro Delphino, the Venetian General of the Camaldolesi.[8] In a letter addressed to a monk, Hieronymus,[9] he reports the visit of Zenobius
Accaiuoli ('utraque lingua eruditissimus et eloquii nitore insignis')
who brought him prophecies to read. Amongst them was a 'vaticinium quoddam de Angelico futuro pontifice; quo elicitur et

---

[1] *Profetie certissime*, f. 4ʳ.
[2] Ibid., f. 29ʳ.
[3] Ibid., ff. 29–30.
[4] *Supra*, pp. 379–80.
[5] Ed. Paris, 1522, ff. xxxᵛ–xxxiiiᵛ.
[6] Ibid., f. xxxvʳ.
[7] See, for instance, notes of sources on ff. xxxvʳ, xxxviiᵛ, xxxixʳ.
[8] Martène et Durand, *Ampl. Coll.* iii, cols. 1107, 1152.
[9] Ibid., cols. 1152–3.

moriturum illum prius, et postea revicturum. Et quantum ex illo apparet, ipsius nomen per M futurum describitur.' This reminded Delphino that his magnificent and learned friend Mauroceno possessed a *papalista* about the Angelic Pope which he had urged Delphino to study. So now the General of the Camaldolesi asks Hieronymus to seek out the book and request permission to copy it for him.

This letter was written from Florence in 1495, where Delphino found himself in the thick of the Savonarola controversy and amid the hectic study of prophecy. Accaiuoli was a well-known humanist, later librarian to Leo X, and this little episode with Delphino seems typical of the way in which prophecies were circulating among the Florentine intelligentsia at this time.

The mysterious anxiety abroad in Italy provided the perfect sounding-board for Savonarola's message. Alessandro Benedicto of Verona gives the setting of astrological presage at the beginning of his history of Charles VIII's expedition:[1]

Eo tempore calamitatem ingentem in Italiam venturam astrorum periti praedixerunt . . . Saturno oeconomo, Marte adverso, Sole horoscopo incipientis anni, siderumque defectibus praeteritis augurantes. Elementa quoque non sine praesagio fuere, auctis supra modum in tota Italia fluminibus anno MVIID Octobri mense. . . . Religiosus praeterea quidam pari modo jejuniorum tempore sequenti anno cum Novariae pro more praedicaret, civibus ingentem cladem imminere: Hispanos, Gallos, Elvetios, Svevos, Teutones, Dalmatas, Macedones, Graecos, Turcas innumerasque alias nationes prope moenia audituros praedixit verissima quidem praedivinatione. (Op. cit., p. 1579.)

A hermit of Vallombrosa beseeches the Florentines and the Pope to receive Charles as ordained of God.[2] We meet again the strange phenomenon of a parallel Jewish foreboding and expectation which, with the advent of Charles VIII, began to take a messianic shape.[3] It was in 1494 that a layman, Luke of St. Gemignano collected together prophecies of Joachim, Merlin, the Sibyls, and others, adding to his collection this comment: 'Ego vero Lucas geminianensis ab ea copiavi in anno Domini 1494 die 10 maji, cum Carolus Francorum rex versaretur circa Romam cum multis militibus armatorum eundi causa expugnatum regnum neapolitanum, ut agebant' (ref. *supra*, p. 252 n. 5).

[1] Ref. *supra*, p. 357 n. 4.   [2] Ref. *supra*, p. 358.
[3] *Supra*, p. 358.

In such an atmosphere Savonarola's double message of chastisement and *renovatio* spoke at once to many. How far was he really
drawing on Joachimist expectation for this message? The question
of the relation between Savonarola's thought and Joachimism still
awaits thorough investigation. Opposite views have been taken by
writers of some of the recent lives, but no one has really tried
to study the problem in the light of the full development of the
Joachimist tradition right down to the end of the fifteenth century,
although D. Weinstein's *Savonarola and Florence: Prophecy and
Patriotism in the Renaissance* points the way.[1] When Savonarola first
announced his full message in the Florentine sermons of 1490, he
cited the Abbot Joachim and St. Vincent Ferrer as authorities.[2] His
statement at this time that after six days, when men had escaped from
the toils of material things, the sun would illuminate the world and
men would be brought to the mountain of contemplation where they
would receive true understanding of the Old and New Testaments,
sounds remarkably like an inspiration from Joachim himself. On the
other hand, it is well known that Savonarola later repudiated any
debt to Bridget and Joachim.[3] But the form in which he apparently
did this—a conversation with the Tempter, in which the latter accuses him of possessing these and other prophecies and Savonarola
replies that he had read none of Bridget and little of Joachim—
suggests that he was in fact attracted by these methods of foretelling
the future. The test lies in the content of his message rather than in
his declared attitude to former prophets. His violent denunciations
of Florence and Rome, of Italy as a whole and of the Church in particular, the announcement of imminent disaster, and the threat of
annihilation put Savonarola in the tradition of the Old Testament
prophets and many medieval ones as well. But when he goes on to
the message of *renovatio* it is difficult to see where his hope has been
fed except at some Joachimist spring. He announces the resurrection
of Jerusalem in place of Rome, the conversion of the Turks, and the
propagation of the faith throughout the world. The first city to be

---

[1] *Church History*, xxvii (1958), pp. 3–17.
[2] Ibid., pp. 5–6; P. Villari, *La storia di Girolamo Savonarola e de' suoi tempi*
(Florence, 1882), ii, XI (extract from Savonarola's unpublished *Lezioni sull'Apocalisse*).
[3] *Trattato delle revelatione della reformatione della Chiesa* . . . (Venice, 1536), f. 17ʳ:
(The Tempter says) 'Io ho inteso che tu hai le revelationi di santa Brigida e de lo abbate
Joachino e di molti altri con lequali tu vai prenunciando queste cose future. Rispuosi:
Io vi prometto padre che di queste tali lettioni io non mi diletto: ne ho letto mai le
revelationi di santa Brigida: e poco de lo abbate Joachino.'

renewed will be Florence, which is to be God's specially chosen instrument, and gradually, it seems, it is Florence which is to become God's New Jerusalem. In connection with this mission of Florence Savonarola uses the Old Testament figure of the Shunamite Woman in a way strongly reminiscent of Joachim's *Liber Concordie*.[1] Furthermore, in Bartholomew Redditi's account of Savonarola's message there is another striking echo of the *Liber Concordie*: as God elected the people of Israel to be led by Moses through tribulation to felicity in the Old Dispensation, so now the people of Florence have been called to a similar role, led by 'un huomo profeta', their new Moses.[2] In the fifth age of the world Antichrist must be endured and beaten, but the *renovatio* which is to follow will build up to the seventh Sabbath Age in which men will rejoice in the *Chiesa Nuovata* and there will be one flock and one shepherd. The extraordinary political circumstances in which Savonarola's message was delivered probably made him emphasize the political agency of the Second Charlemagne which fitted in so naturally with the traditional French connections of Florence, but the culminating point of his expectation is that of the *Papa santo* to be sent by God.[3] All this is of a piece with the Joachimist programme for the Angelic Pope and Last Emperor. By this time, of course, these ideas were so widely disseminated that their source was often forgotten. It is not a question of calling Savonarola a Joachite so much as recognizing that the particular form of millenarianism which inspired him was the Joachimist prophetic programme.

It is well known that Savonarola was in personal contact with some of the humanists and artists of Florence and if we refuse to make a sharp dividing line between the humanist Age of Gold and the religious *renovatio mundi*, we shall look for continuing echoes of Savonarola's message in many quarters. One is to be found in Sandro Botticelli's famous eschatological picture of the Nativity in which the Incarnation is seen as the symbol of a new divine event to take place in the future, when angels will embrace men and the

<hr>

[1] *Prediche italiane ai Fiorentini*, ed. F. Cognasso (R. Palmarocchi) (Perugia, Venice, 1930), i. 170–1. Cf. *Lib. Conc.*, f. 34^{r-v}.

[2] J. Schnitzer, *Quellen u. Forschungen z. Geschichte Savonarolas* (Munich, 1902), i. 37–40, cf. *Lib. Conc.*, *passim*, on the symbolism of the Exodus and wanderings in the Wilderness.

[3] *Profezie politiche e religiose di Fra Hieronymo Savonarola ricavate dalle sue prediche da Messer Francesco de' Guicciardini l'historico* (Florence, 1863), f. vii^r, a prophecy made in 1495: 'Manderà Dio uno Papa santo . . .'

Devil will be beaten down. This picture has long since been connected with Savonarola's inspiration, but it is worth pointing out
that the inscription, with its reference to the three and a half years
of the Book of Daniel and the Apocalypse, makes the eschatological
context certain. Joachim—and many others, of course—had used
this mysterious span of time to denote the length of time during
which the tribulation of Antichrist must be endured. For Joachim
there was always the implication of the third *status* which lay beyond
it and the ecstasy of Botticelli's picture, taken together with the
inscription, must surely carry the message of beatitude after tribulation, a new birth to be expected almost immediately.[1] In 1496
Giovanni Nesi, a pupil of Ficino's and well known in humanist
circles, published the *Oraculum de novo seculo*, in which the announcement of catastrophe and renewal are once more juxtaposed.
The poem culminates in what has been described as 'l'exaltation
typique du millénarisme piagnone, où revit en somme le vieux
joachimisme confiant dans le règne prochain de l'Esprit'.[2]

One of the most interesting cases of Savonarola's influence is that
of Francesco da Meleto, who in 1473 was in Constantinople seeking
contact with the Jews and learning from a great rabbi 'in gran
segreto . . . che io chiaramente vedrei tutti i giudei convertirsi alla
fede christiana, se il messia da loro aspettato non veniva per tucto
l'anno . . . mille quattrocento ottantaquattro'.[3] Later he was in
Florence where he was carried away by Savonarola's prophesied
renovatio ecclesie and gave himself up to studying when this would
begin. By the aid of the Holy Spirit, he declared, the year 1517 would
see the beginning of the renewal. The first of his two books, *Con-
vivio de' segreti della Scriptura Santa*, was possibly written in 1508,
the year in which Landucci records that once again there were
preachers in Florence crying 'grande tribolazione e la novazione della
chiesa'.[4] The second, *Quadrivium temporum prophetarum*, was written in Latin to present to Leo X. In this he set out to prove that 'A.D.
MDXXX reformationem universalem fore in Ecclesia Dei ita nempe
ut destructis heresibus et erroribus universis in toto terrarum orbe

[1] On the interpretation of this picture see H. Ulmann, *Sandro Botticelli* (Munich, 1893), pp. 148-9. F. Saxl, *Journal of the Warburg and Courtauld Institutes*, v (1942), p. 84, calls it one of the greatest documents of Joachimist thought.
[2] Chastel, loc. cit. (i), p. 183.
[3] S. Bongi, 'Francesco da Meleto', *ASI* iii (1889), p. 63 n. 2. The substance of this paragraph is drawn chiefly from this article. See also Chastel, loc. cit. (i), pp. 179, 184.
[4] Bongi, art. cit., p. 65.

fieret unum ovile et unus pastor'. Meleto had friends among humanists who secured him an audience with the Pope and helped him to publish the book. It envisaged a typical programme of tribulation and triumph, in which the conversion of Jews and Mohammedans would take place. Apparently the Papal Curia was not unfavourable and the book was published, but later both his works were condemned as dangerous by a Florentine Provincial Synod. This was probably the result of a campaign against Meleto by P. Orlandini, a poet and theologian who wrote 'contra prophetas vanos' as a direct attack on Meleto's writings and left behind him an *Expugnatio Miletana*.[1]

We also see the repercussions of Savonarola's message in a series of minor prophetic detonations which followed in Florence. In 1500 twenty of Savonarola's disciples from the lower classes formed a society with their own *Papa Angelicus*, Pietro Bernardino, and preached a new outpouring of the Holy Spirit.[2] It is interesting to note that, driven out of Florence, they eventually found refuge with the Count of Mirandola, an ardent admirer of Savonarola. In 1508 another hermit was preaching 'Woe to Italy' in Florence.[3] In 1516 Francesco de Montepulciano was there preaching tribulation and renewal.[4] In the same year a Fra Bonaventura announced himself the Angelic Pope in Rome and wrote a letter to the Doge of Venice beginning 'Bonaventura, chosen by God to be the Pastor of the Church in Zion, crowned by the hands of angels and commissioned to be the Saviour of the World, sends greetings and apostolic blessings to all believers in Christ'.[5] His programme must surely be linked with the edition of Telesphorus's *libellus* published in Venice in that same year,[6] for he calls on Venice to support the French monarchy which is destined by God to reform the Church and convert the Turks. At about the same time proceedings were being taken in Florence against a certain Theodore 'qui audens sedem ad Aquilonem ponere sibi Angelici Pastoris nomen usurpabat'[7] and whose heresy is specifically traced to Savonarola. Delphino, the General of the Camaldolesi, whom we have already seen interesting himself in the prophecies of Angelic Popes,[8] described him as

[1] Bongi, art. cit., pp. 69–70; 'Paolo Orlandini, poeta e teologo' (note signed E. G.), *Rinascimento* i (1950), pp. 175–8.   [2] Pastor, *History of the Popes* v. 214–16.
[3] Ibid., p. 217.   [4] Ibid., p. 219; Schnitzer, op. cit. (ref. p. 430 n. 6), pp. 863–4.
[5] Pastor, *History of the Popes* v. 224–5.   [6] *Supra*, p. 262.
[7] B. Moreni, *Memorie istoriche dell'Ambrosiana R. Basilica di S. Lorenzo* (Florence, 1704), ii. 208 n. 1.   [8] *Supra*, pp. 433–4.

a Greek and renegade monk, making the same allegation against him: 'Denique credi se fecit esse se illum papam Angelicum, quem idem fr. Hieronymus praedixit paulopost esse venturum . . .'[1] He suffered perpetual imprisonment at S. Miniato.

In spite of the proscription of Meleto's writings and a ban on similar preachings and prophesyings pronounced by the Council of Florence in 1517,[2] concern with Savonarola's message could not be killed. In 1530 Girolamo Benivieni wrote a letter to Pope Clement VII[3] pressing on his attention the essential and unchanged core of Savonarola's prophecies in four points: (1) 'il flagello d'Italia, massime di Roma', (2) 'la rinnovazione della Chiesa', (3) 'la conversione de' Turchi e de' Mori', (4) 'la felicità di Firenze'. He showed how many of Savonarola's predictions had proved true and were still being fulfilled. The role of Florence was the real focus of his expectation and he appealed passionately to the Pope to further the fulfilment of these prophecies by assisting the liberation of Florence. A few years later a Florentine Dominican, Luca Bettini, published an *Oracolo della renovatione della Chiesa*,[4] in which he claimed to have reduced into a compendium all Savonarola's doctrine. The essence of his message was the same as that of Benivieni and again the emphasis was on *renovatio* and the final role of Florence.[5] God will send *un Papa santo*; evil priests will be removed and holy men sent into the Church; the whole world will be converted to Christ; Jerusalem will become again the centre of the world, 'e sarà tanto spirito che parrà un paradiso'.[6] This does not detract from the holy position which Florence will occupy, after she has suffered, as the elect of God and the illumination of Italy. Thus the part of Savonarola's message which made the greatest impact was the vision of the *renovatio mundi* and in 1536 Bettini could still describe it in lyrical terms:

Et così era tutto il mondo in una charità et Giubilatione . . . Sarà allhora

---

[1] J. Schnitzer, *Peter Delphin. General des Camaldulenserorden, 1444–1525* (Munich, 1926), p. 364.

[2] Mansi, xxxv (Paris, 1902), cols. 273, 274.

[3] Printed by B. Varchi, *Storia fiorentina* (Florence, 1858), pp. 307–28.

[4] *Oracolo della renovatione della Chiesa secondo la dottrina del Riverendo Padre Frate Hieronimo Savonarola da Ferrara* (Venice, 1536).

[5] Bettini cites the Abbot Joachim by name (f. 81ᵛ) and then proceeds to give an unusual analysis of successive stages of world history which is reminiscent of the *Lib. Fig.* in its use of tree metaphors, although the pattern of history is different (ff. 81ᵛ–85ᵛ). It is difficult to know how much of this derives from Savonarola.

[6] Ibid., ff. 154ʳ–158ʳ.

tanta quiete et tanta pace che l'uno amico chiamerà l'altro alla chiesa . . .
Et ogn'uno guiderà l'un l'altro alle cose spirituali et empierasse il mondo
di dolcezza. Dolci saranno le scritture, gioconde le contemplationi, le
predicationi tutte soavi . . . Sarà la chiesa in grande amore, pace et
tranquillità. Et gli angeli stilleranno tutta dolcezza nella chiesa militante
. . . Veranno gli angeli a conversare, a parlare et habitare, con gli huomini
. . . (Op. cit., ff. 160ʳ–161ᵛ.)

Savonarola's proclamation of Angelic Pope and *renovatio ecclesie*
had necessarily become tainted with suspicion of heresy because of
his own fate and that of his more fanatical followers. His humanist
well-wishers withdrew their support and even swung over to denouncing him as Antichrist.[1] Much less dramatic in impact, but
pervasive in certain circles of theologians and humanists, was the
influence of the Blessed Amadeus or Joannes Menesius de Sylva. As
we have seen,[2] he was invited to Rome by Sixtus IV and allowed to
form his own congregation. He left behind him an *Apocalipsis Nova*
which, according to legend, had been dictated to him by the Angel
Gabriel. He also left a great reputation especially in Rome, where,
Postel tells us, his book was to be found in many households, including those of cardinals.[3] There is little doubt that the focus of this
interest was his proclamation of the Angelic Pope, whom he prophesied both in words and in a painting. Possibly he believed that
he was himself the Angelic Pope but this is not certain. One of his
writings is described thus:[4] 'De revelationibus et prophetiis pulcherrimum libellum composuit: Romanae Ecclesiae statum, angelicum quendam Pontificem, regnorum, dominiorum, atque religionis
mutationem concernentibus.' An Italian translation of some of his
utterances was made by the Byzantine Paolo Angelo who obviously belonged to the circle of his admirers.[5] The Latin title which
he gives runs thus: 'Prophetia fratris Amadei ordinis Minorum de
observantia reformatorisque, qui vidit iam illum hominem ab omni-
potente Deo electum, quo mediante opifex summus renovabit ecclesiam suam' (Secret, loc. cit., p. 216). In the Italian version
Amadeus enquires of Gabriel 'del novo Pastore et del tempo et del
advento expressamente del signore . . .' He is told that God has
already elected a future pastor: 'lui è adesso in Roma giovenetto,

[1] Chastel, loc. cit. (i), pp. 182–3.
[2] *Supra*, p. 233.
[3] See passage quoted *supra*, p. 234.
[4] N. Antonio Hispalensis, *Bibliotheca Hispania Vetus* (Madrid, 1788), ii. 317.
[5] F. Secret, *Rinascimento* XIII, pp. 211–20.

poverino, incognito . . . et a poco a poco lo acresce . . . et quando gia
serà vechio monstrarà in esso la virtù della potentia sua esso Dio,
el quale fa levare da terra el povero.' The angel then prophesies
a further chastisement of Italy which involves various political
happenings, some of them obviously prophesied *post eventum*: 'Et
Re deli gigli passarà como un fulgure, vincerà, ritornerà senza victoria et apena fugerà . . .' Undeterred by these gloomy prognostications, Amadeus, in the vision, rejoices solely in the prospect of the
Angelic Pope and aspires to see him: 'O si fusse digno de vedere
questo poverino et incognito.' To which the angel replies: 'Gia lo hai
visto ma non in quella maiestate . . .'[1]

The *post-eventum* prophecies make it obvious that these were not
literally the words of Amadeus but a popular form in which his
message was afterwards circulated. A study of these prophecies
shows us that in the first quarter of the sixteenth century there was
a considerable circle of people, centred perhaps mainly in Rome,
who were deeply concerned with the final programme of history and
looked for World Emperor and Angelic Pope as well as Antichrist.
They were scholars, humanists, and theologians, in some cases the
disciples of the Florentine Platonists of the previous generation.
They exchanged oracles and prophecies and sometimes wrote down
their ideas in the form of future history.

We have already noticed Egidio of Viterbo, one of the most
influential of these, inquiring from Silvester Meuccio concerning
the writings of Joachim when he was in Venice.[2] The *Scechina*
showed us Egidio fervently adjuring Charles V to take up his cosmic
role as Emperor, but this was always seen by the General of the
Augustinians in relation to the greater role of the papacy. In his
famous sermon at the opening of the Lateran Council in 1512 it was
Julius II to whom he looked for fulfilment of the final destiny of the
papacy;[3] his great *Historia Viginti Saeculorum* ended with a panegyric of Leo X who 'ab initio orbis electus est ut Christi mandata
atque opera perficeret, Christianorum fidem in aeternum confirmaret, pacemque Ecclesiae reduceret';[4] the *Scechina* was written at the

---

[1] Ibid., pp. 217–20.

[2] *Supra*, p. 268.

[3] J. Hardouin, *Acta conciliorum* (Paris, 1714), ix, cols. 1576–81. Note also the speech
of Cardinal Baldassare del Rio (ibid., cols. 1702–5), in a later session of the Council,
citing prophecies on the Turkish as well as the Christian side, which prove the impending world-wide triumph of the Church under Leo X.

[4] Quoted L. Pélissier, *De 'Historia Viginti Saeculorum'* (Montpelier, 1896), p. 37.

instance of Clement VII[1] and contains passages on the prophetic role of Pope as well as Emperor.[2] Egidio collected Joachimist prophecies as well as cabbalistic mysteries and gathered within his household a group of humanist scholars in Greek, Hebrew, and eastern languages who studied prophecies as well as linguistics.

Perhaps even more committed to this way of thought was Petrus Galatinus, probably a member of Egidio's circle. He, too, looked for the famous partnership between Emperor and Pope and he dedicated works to Maximilian I and Charles V, but the centre of his interest was the future restoration of the Church under the Angelic Pope and it was to popes and cardinals that several of his works were addressed.[3] Galatinus was a great collector of prophecies and it was probably through his writings that many of these were circulating in the mid-sixteenth century. He used a number of the genuine and spurious works of Joachim and amongst others the writings of Pierre Jean d'Olivi, Robert d'Uzès, Roquetaillade, St. Vincent, St. Hildegarde, and St. Bridget. He had seen for himself the famous prophecy of St. Cataldus 'in libro plumbeo scripta' which caused such a stir in Rome.[4] He collected a *Vaticinium Montis Gargani*, a *Vaticinium Romanum*,[5] another attributed to St. Severus, and a prophecy of St. Francis from Bartholomew of Pisa.[6] Above all he was impressed by the visions of Amadeus, particularly in relation to the Angelic Pope expected so shortly.[7] All this material was utilized in his numerous works. These were chiefly focused on the history and destiny of the Church and his main pattern can be simply demonstrated by the titles of three of them: *De Ecclesia instituta*, *De Ecclesia destituta*, *De Ecclesia restituta*. He found the corruption and deformity of the Church in such contemporary conditions as the

---

[1] Ed. F. Secret (Rome, 1959), p. 10.

[2] Ibid., pp. 98, 219–20, 233.

[3] See especially MS. Vat., Lat. 5578, ff. 86ʳ–106ᵛ, a *libellus* dedicated to Leo X, and MS. Vat., Lat. 5575, *Opus de Ecclesia instituta*, dedicated to Paul III.

[4] MS. Vat., Lat. 5569, f. cxliiiᵛ.

[5] Ibid., ff. xiiʳ, xxiiiʳ, xxxiiiiʳ, cxxxiʳ; MS. Vat., Lat. 5578, ff. 24ʳ, 27ʳ, 39ʳ, 54ᵛ, 58ʳ, 63ʳ, 70ʳ; MS. Vat., Lat. 5579, f. 27ᵛ, for references to these two prophecies. In MS. Vat., Lat. 5581, a manuscript addressed to Alessandro Spagnuoli of Mantua, these two prophecies are set forth and expounded. They both concern the Angelic Pope and the Monte S. Gargano prophecy gives a series of popes, ending with Clement VII, after which the Angelic Pope is described (f. 73ʳ⁻ᵛ). There is no trace of these two prophecies before the time of Galatinus and they would therefore seem to be the product of prophetic expectations in Galatinus's own circle.

[6] MS. Vat., Lat. 5569, ff. ccixᵛ, ccxixᵛ, cclvᵛ.

[7] References are innumerable throughout his works.

pestilence of Luther and believed that his own age was the sixth Age of Tribulation. But the time of 'restitution' was, he believed, at hand. One of his earlier works was a *libellus* to Leo X, *De Republica Christiana pro vera eiusdem reipublicae reformatione, progressu et felici ad recuperanda Christianorum loca expeditione*.[1] Later he expected Paul III to carry through the reformation,[2] but above all he wrote of the Angelic Pastor, urging continual prayer 'ut hunc sanctissimum Pastorem per quem haec omnia facturus est, nos cito videre faciat'.[3]

Joachim had seen various of the angels of the Apocalypse as symbols of the new spiritual men: Galatinus found the Angelic Pope and his disciples represented in the Angel of the Church of Philadelphia to whom God will give in the sixth *tempus* an open door; in the Angel descending 'amictus nube' with an open book in hand; in the Angel ascending from the east, having the sign of the living God.[4] He was, of course, familiar with the identification of this last angel as St. Francis, but firmly dissented from this interpretation, since St. Francis lived in the fifth, not the sixth *tempus*.[5] Finally, Galatinus did not hesitate to claim the Angel with the Eternal Evangel as the Angelic Pope to come.[6] He avoided any dangerous mention of Joachim here, but interpreted the Eternal Evangel as the *spiritualis intellectus* of the Scriptures and in numerous passages proclaimed the chief characteristic of the *Pastor Angelicus* as the mystical power to penetrate to the core and to lay bare all the mysteries of the sacred word. In words which almost echo Joachim's he wrote: 'oportebit sub angelico Pastore sacrarum scripturarum veritatem quasi ex noctis caligine splendescere et ad lucis meridiane claritatem venire.'[7] In another work Galatinus describes the Angelic Pope as descending from the contemplative state to assume the government of the Church with five specific tasks to perform: to reduce ecclesiastics to a pristine perfect poverty; to liberate the faithful from the persecution of evil forces; to reform the laity and make concords between

---

[1] MS. Vat., Lat. 5578, ff. 86ʳ–106ᵛ. In the Dedication the words *Leonem X* have been crossed out and *Hadrianum VI* substituted in a more hurried hand.

[2] See the Dedication in MS. Vat., Lat. 5575: 'Quia igitur hanc pro Dei voluntate reformationem Tuae Sanctitatis opera, maxime factum iri speramus.'

[3] MS. Vat., Lat. 5581, f. 68ᵛ (from the *explicit* of Galatinus's *explicatio* of the Rome prophecy).

[4] MS. Vat., Lat. 5567, ff. xxiᵛ, xxviʳ, xcvʳ–xcviiʳ, clviiiᵛ–clxiᵛ.

[5] Ibid., ff. clxʳ–clxiʳ.

[6] Ibid., f. ccxxxiiʳ⁻ᵛ.

[7] Ibid., f. xcviᵛ, cf. *Lib. Conc.*, f. 96ᵛ.

princes; to convert all infidels to Christ; to promote good clergy to positions of government in the Church.[1] In imitation of Christ he would cleanse the Temple and expel all traffickers. Reverting constantly in all his writings to this theme, Galatinus decided finally to put his thoughts together in one little tract, *De Angelico Pastore opusculum ex sacra veteris et novi testamenti scriptura excerptum*.[2] In this he rehearsed many of the points made in his Commentary on the Apocalypse, buttressing his hopes with passages from Joachim, Cyril, and Rabanus, as well as his favourite Amadeus. Here he used a number of the Old Testament figures dear to Joachim as symbols of the great hope: Moses leading forth the Israelites from Egypt;[3] Hannah, at first sterile but afterwards giving birth to Samuel;[4] the triumph of Esther and Mordecai over Vashti and Haman;[5] the great return of Zorobabel and the priest Zacharias to Jerusalem from captivity;[6] the work of Cyrus, King of Persia.[7] Amadeus had imprinted on his mind the spiritual physiognomy of the Angelic Pastor, and, indeed, almost the physical features, for apparently under the direction of the Angel Amadeus had painted a picture which Galatinus had seen:

Quum eius imaginem prout ei angelus revelaverat in pano lineo depingi fecisset: sub eius pedibus ita scripsit: Tu es secundus Petrus et super hac

---

[1] MS. Vat., Lat. 5569. *Secunda pars operis de ecclesia destituta*, f. xxiii[r-v].

[2] MS. Vat., Lat. 5578. Although this would seem to be a final summarizing of his hopes (see f. 1[r]), cross-references in his Commentary on the Apocalypse show that he was still working on this at the same time. Thus the dating of his works given by Kleinhans, *Antonianum* i. 327-8, needs modification.

[3] MS. Vat., Lat. 5578, f. 54[r-v]. He also, in a strikingly Joachimist style, links the Apocalypse angel with feet on sea and land (Apocalypse 10: 2) with the blessing of Manasseh and Ephraim (Gen. 48: 14) as figures of the Angelic Pope: 'Pastor ille angelicus per angelum hunc designatus ex utriusque testamenti littera, sensus spiritalis proferet veritatem. *Et bene dextrum super mare et sinistrum super terram posuit pedem.* Ex hoc enim innuitur *quod sicut Epphraim qui iunior erat tactus dextera Jacob quamvis Manasse seniori sinistra tacto praelatus est, ita novum testamentum tamquam si tempore posterius esset, dignitate tamen primum factum est'* (f. 10[v]). The italicized words are practically a quotation from Joachim's *Expos.*, f. 138[r], but Galatinus links them with the Angelic Pope.

[4] MS. Vat., Lat. 5578, ff. 32[r]-38[r]. Hannah symbolizes the *spiritualis ecclesia* persecuted until the Angelic Pope comes like a second Samuel: 'Tunc Deus ista faciet, quum spiritualis ecclesia quae sterilis prius erat pariet plurimos hoc est innumerabiles' (f. 38[r]). The symbol of the sterile woman who afterwards becomes fruitful is one of Joachim's favourite figures for the *ecclesia spiritualis*; see *Lib. Conc.*, ff. 18[r-v], 32[r-v], 42[r], 116[r-v]; *Expos.*, ff. 11[v]-12[v]; *Lib. Fig.* II, Pls. XX, XXI.

[5] MS. Vat., Lat. 5578, f. 56[r-v], cf. *Lib. Conc.*, ff. 119[r]-122[v].

[6] MS. Vat., Lat. 5578, ff. 26[r], 29[r]-30[v], cf. *Lib. Conc.*, f. 56[r-v].

[7] MS. Vat., Lat. 5578, f. 53[r], cf. *Lib. Conc.*, f. 104[v].

petra reaedificabo ecclesiam meam. Quae imago apud sanctum Petrum montis aurei de urbe servatur: quam ego oculis vidi . . . Et sicut Petrus tanquam ecclesiae fundamentum in secundi status mundi exordio fuit primae conversionis gentilium minister . . . Ita ipse Pastor angelicus erit primae notabilis infidelium conversionis minister quae fiet in tertio mundi statu . . . (MS. 5578, f. 75ᵛ.)

The second Peter was expected immediately. The manuscript of the Monte Gargano prophecy has a series of popes written in the margin from Paul II to Clement VII: after him comes the *Angelicus pastor*.[1] Galatinus lived long enough to revise this timetable and dedicate a work to Paul III, but the note of immediacy remains strong: 'quoniam cito cito apparitutus est, qui non solum (ut in Romano vaticinio praedicitur) orbem universum novis sanctisque legibus moribus et institutis reformabit; verum etiam (ut beato Amadeo angelus revelavit) et mundum ipsum a cunctis purgabit erroribus.'

We catch some traces of the group of early sixteenth-century scholars who shared these common interests in prophecy. In 1525 Galatinus sent a prophecy concerning Rome with his own *explicatio* to Alessandro Spagnuoli of Mantua, and Alessandro, in another letter to Francesco Calvo, *Chalcographo*, speaks of three other prophecies elucidated by Galatinus, those of Methodius, Cataldus, and Cyril, which he will send him to be printed.[1] Everybody knew about the famous prophecy of St. Cataldus, discovered at Tarentum in dramatic circumstances in 1492. Galatinus, as we have seen, copied and interpreted it, and we also find it in the *Libri Sex Genialium Dierum* of a Neapolitan lawyer, Alexander ab Alexandro, first published in Rome in 1522.[2] Galatinus probably knew him and exchanged this prophecy with him.[3] Guillaume Postel comes later into this circle and may not have known Galatinus personally, but he certainly read his works at the convent of Ara Coeli and he knew other members of this group. It is possible also that Paolo Angelo from Venice knew some of these people: he used the prophecy of Amadeus and addressed his writings to Popes Leo X

---

[1] *Supra*, p. 442 n. 5.

[2] Ed. Paris, 1539, unpag., iii, cap. xv. The prophecy is also mentioned by another Neapolitan, the notary Giacomo, *Cronica di Napoli*, ed. P. Garzilli (Naples, 1845), p. 173.

[3] Suggested by Secret, *Studi francesi* I, p. 379. B. Moroni, *Cataldiados . . . libri sex . . .* (no pl. of pub., 1614), pp. 173 seq. in giving an account of this prophecy, says that a certain brother in Rome found it in Galatinus's *De ecclesia destituta*, lib. viii, cap. 1, in the library of the Ara Coeli.

and Clement VII as well as Cardinal Bernardino da Carvajal.[1] Possibly he was in contact with Egidio of Viterbo through his friend Silvestro Meuccio. Finally, we may note that Galatinus was involved in an episode at Palermo in which the mysterious seven names of the archangels were 'discovered' in mosaics and in some way connected with a revelation of Amadeus. Galatinus evidently interested himself in this and in a document entitled *Sacramentum Septem Stellae* his evidence on the *Epistola de Secretis* of Paul de Heredia is given.[2]

We must also recall that the Iberian Peninsula, the refuge of earlier Joachites and the home of the Blessed Amadeus, was not immune from these influences. Cardinal Ximenez de Cisneros himself dreamed of a *renovatio mundi* in which, after the final crusade led by Spain, there would 'unum ovile et unus pastor' and he himself would celebrate Mass before the Holy Sepulchre.[3] It was to Ximenez that Charles de Bovelles wrote exultantly in 1509 concerning the imminent appearance of a great reforming Pope, and although his prophetic expectations were treated cautiously they received a hearing.[4] Fray Melchior, born of a *conversos* family in Burgos, was prophesying in 1512 tremendous happenings in the near future:[5] in a period of twelve years the Church would be transformed; seven had already passed and in the remaining five the Roman Empire, the kingdoms, the papacy, would all be overturned. All the clergy would be killed except the elect, preserved to accomplish the work of *renovatio*. Finally, the Church would be transferred to Jerusalem and humanity would live in virtue and happiness. This description comes from a letter of Cazalla to Cardinal Ximenez the tone of which shows secret admiration for this prophet and for the tradition of Saints Bridget, Catherine, and Vincent in which, Cazalla remarks, Fray Melchior stands.[6] There was, about 1523 a resurgence of what Bataillon calls this 'esprit messianique'[7] among Franciscans

[1] Secret, *Rinascimento* XIII, p. 213. On Paolo Angelo see *supra*, pp. 432–3.

[2] MS. Vat., Ottobon. 2366, ff. 300ʳ–302ʳ; see Secret, *Rinascimento* XIII, pp. 221–4.

[3] M. Bataillon, *Érasme et l'Espagne* (Paris, 1937), pp. 55 seq.

[4] Ibid., pp. 58–60. It is interesting to note that Bovelles had been to visit John of Trittenheim who, in spite of his caution about Joachim (*supra*, p. 104), collected prophecies on the Angelic Pope himself.

[5] M. Bataillon, *Érasme et l'Espagne*, pp. 66–70.

[6] Ibid., p. 70: '. . . de quibus loquebatur Brigida, Catherina de Senis, Vincentius et plerique alii scriptores prophetico spiritu.'

[7] Ibid., pp. 199–200. See further J. Phelan, *The Millennial Kingdom of the Franciscans in the New World* (Berkeley and Los Angeles, 1956).

of Escalona, articulated especially by Fr. Francisco de Ocaña, who prophesied victory to Charles V and a great reforming mission which would set a Spaniard on the seat of St. Peter.

How far did the actual course of history in the first half of the sixteenth century lend support to expectations of schism and revolution preceding *renovatio*? The advent of Luther and other heretics certainly gave weight to the prognostications of divisions in the Church, of noisome heresies arising like the locusts from the pit of hell. The astrologer Torquatus was able to delineate the great heresiarch to come in words which purported to have been written before 1500:

Veniet a septentrione heresiarcha magnus subvertendo populos contra vota Romanae sedis, cum magnorum principum septentrionalium auxilio, qui faciet ingentia et magna loquetur. Et apparebunt tunc temporis hypocriti multi quaerentes sibi exaltationes et honores atque dignitates ecclesiasticas ambient. Et erit confusio magna et persecutio in Dei ecclesia maxima. (*Prognosticon* [ref. p. 339 n. 4], f. 7ᵛ.)

The menace of the Turk, too, took its expected shape. Above all, the prophetic role of the great King–Chastiser—in all its ambiguity, good or bad, *pudicus facie* or *impudicus facie*—appeared to be fulfilled in the Emperor Charles V. Egidio of Viterbo, Petrus Galatinus, Postel, and others might dream of an ideal co-operation between Pope and Emperor, but what was commonly expected was drastic punishment of the papacy by God's appointed agent. The Second Charlemagne prophecy specifically stated that Rome must be destroyed, and prophecies circulating under the name of St. Bridget, St. Vincent, and others proclaimed the same message. In spite of the prohibitions of Church Councils, the menacing preacher continued to cry in Italian cities in the second and third decades of the sixteenth century. Milan reverberated with the anticlerical denunciations of Girolamo of Siena in 1516, in 1522–3 with the prophesyings of a Frate di San Marco, and in 1529 with the preaching of Fra Tommaso Nieti.[1] We have already mentioned the Florentine disturbances. In 1517 there was a Sienese hermit preaching in Bologna who may have been Girolamo of Siena. In Rome there are various ref. records of prophets crying 'Woe!' to the papacy.[2] Thus in 1516 Fra

[1] Pastor, *History of the Popes*, v. 223; Chabod, loc. cit. (ref. p. 430 n. 3), p. 83. Nieti preached *renovazione* as well as tribulation.

[2] Pastor, *History of the Popes*, v. 224; O. Raynaldus, *Annales Ecclesiastici* (Lucca, 1755), xiii. 1, 10; Bernino, *Historia di tutte l'heresie*, iv (Rome, 1709), pp. 368, 375.

Bonaventura announced himself as Angelic Pope there, excommunicating Leo X and the Curia and warning the faithful to separate themselves from the Roman Church. Giovanni Baptista Eremita, with the appearance of a veritable John the Baptist, was proclaiming his message of doom in 1525. The so-called Brandano arose with a similar message at the time of the Sack of Rome itself and later was found prophesying at Siena.[1] All these voices united in announcing a final judgement on Rome and thus it was that the Sack of Rome in 1527 came as an anticipated event of cosmic import to many Italian contemporaries. The idea that the terrible events formed the expected chastisement was more than half believed in the Roman Curia itself and the Pope addressed cardinals and prelates on the need for reform.[2] This mood is reflected in Luigi Guicciardini's account of the Sack: it was the vanity, pomp, and luxury of the Roman Curia which had brought this judgement, and Charles V had been the just agent of God.[3]

Looked at from a later perspective, the Sack of Rome was still an event of vast proportions, a true portent. To Protestants it was the proof that the Roman Church was the Babylonish whore, and J. Wolf, for instance, could find many ancient prophecies which foretold this retribution.[4] To Catholics it was part of the culminating crisis of catastrophe and punishment in which the bark of St. Peter, beset by waves of infidels, heretics, and chastisers, would all but founder. Thus, again, Wolfgang Lazius could dig up many old oracles to confirm this view from Telesphorus, Gamaleon, Lichtenberger, Torquatus, Bridget, Rabanus, Reinhard, and so on.[5] He was able to collect from Bohemia an oracle which placed the whole reign of Charles V in the context of the tribulation and renovation of the Church:

Ab anno 1520 usque ad 1547, cum multis castigationibus hominum, fiet unum ovile et unus pastor fidei Christianae in toto mundo . . .. Ab A.D. 1523 navicula Petri et fides Catholica multis undis quassabitur, ita ut pene submergitur. Inauditae novitates et controversiae erunt ab A.D. 1520 usque ad 1540 proditiones, Ecclesiae destruentur, diluvium maximum particulare, pestis, fames, clades coelo. Exurget pseudopropheta, qui ardentia et flammantia verba scriptaque evomet et multos

[1] See references *supra*, p. 367.
[2] Pastor, *History of the Popes* x. 16.
[3] L. Guicciardini, *Il sacco di Roma* (Paris, 1664), pp. 4 seq.
[4] Wolf, *Lect. mem.* ii. 295 seq.
[5] Lazius, *Fragmentum*, ff. Hii^v, Hv^v, Hvi^v, K^r-Kiiii^v, Miv^v.

cum suis discipulis seducet et hoc maxime in Alemania. Rex Franciae penitus eiicietur, infideles vastabunt Italiam et Rex Hispaniarum contra eos triumphabit, Turciae Hungariam et Poloniam et partem Germaniae occupabunt, totus mundus insurget contra Clerum et pugnabit, maximus persecutor Ecclesiae exurget et faciet tantam persecutionem in Ecclesia qualis non fuit. Vacante sede Apostolica, eligetur in Papam Canonice frater minor, sacco indutus, qui adsumet socium suum etiam sacco indutum arctissimae vitae in Cardinalem, et isti reformabunt et idem Papa contra morem electionis suae, Alemaniae adsumet Imperatorem qui recuperabit Constantinopolim . . . (Lazius, *Fragmentum*, f. M^v.)

This programme was apparently still relevant to Lazius as late as 1547.

Writing later in the century, Theodore Graminaeus sees contemporary history chiefly from the viewpoint of the old pseudo-Joachimist prophecy that 'ab Aquilone pandetur omne malum'.[1] The Roman Church, the true Jerusalem, was locked in conflict with Babylon. The forces of destruction included the Lutheran heretics and the 'populum Aquilonarem Europicum qui Romanam Ecclesiam infestet', as well as Ottomans and other infidels.[2] He quotes substantial passages from the pseudo-Joachimist *Super Hieremiam* and *Super Esaiam* to show both the oppression of the Church by the Teutons and the stripping off of worldly wealth which are necessary elements of God's judgement on her.[3] Ezekiel's wind from the north was the spirit of pride as seen in Luther and his doctrine,[4] and Graminaeus had no doubt that Joachim in his insistence on the evil from the north had foreseen the Lutheran sect.[5] Moreover, this plague from the north had been foretold by more recent prophets such as Torquatus, Lichtenberger, and Grunpeck.[6] The accumulated tribulations would pile up: devastations of Turks, infections of heresies, attacks of Germans, schisms, and false popes. But Graminaeus was a true

---

[1] *Mysticus Aquilo* (ref. p. 290 n. 1), *passim*.

[2] Ibid., pp. 7, 16–17, 64–6, 99–102, 128–36.

[3] Ibid., pp. 37, 61–5, 81, 139–40, 148. He also cites the *Vaticinia*, Cyril, Telesphorus, and the prophecy *Ve mundo in centum annis*.

[4] Ibid., p. 64; see also p. 66.

[5] Ibid., pp. 37–8. After quoting from the *Super Esaiam* Graminaeus writes: 'Haec Prophetia cum circa annum Domini millesimum ducentesimum ab ipso Abbate scripta sit, impudenter et temerarie mihi a Thaddaeo imputatur.' (Margin: 'Nota patriam Lutheri ante 350 et amplius annos praedictam'). Thaddaeus was the antagonist against whom the work was directed.

[6] Ibid., pp. 99–102, 156.

Joachite in his belief that after the ruin of Babylon the Roman Church would be restored, and he used Joachim's symbols to express this: the toil of Leah would give place to the rest of Rachel, and the tribe of Judah (Rome) would be elected instead of Ephraim (the Greek Church).[1] Micah's prophecy of the consolation of Jerusalem which will be born in Bethlehem designated the 'spiritualem intellectum processurum de parvulis in Latina Ecclesia, qui regnaturus sit in populo videnti Deum, ut iam non vivant homines secundum carnem sed secundum spiritum'.[2] Although he did not hazard an identification, Graminaeus actually turned to Joachim's original prophecy of the new hermit order for his agency of *renovatio*, quoting the key passage—'Surget enim ordo, etc.'—from the *Expositio*.[3] Here we have a world view in which the political forces of the age are seen as almost entirely evil and the renovation of the Church after calamity is thought of in spiritual terms exclusively. It is strange that Graminaeus did not draw on the prophecies of the Angelic Popes but returned instead to the initial Joachimist concept of the new order of spiritual men as the agency of his final reformation.

Elsewhere, however, the expectation of a miraculous *renovatio* could still be focused on revolutionary change in the papacy. In 1564 Benedetto Accolti, the illegitimate son of a cardinal, conspired with others to kill Pope Pius IV.[4] The plot crumbled because the unstable leader was seized with fear. Accolti's confessions reveal the basis of his dream. He believed that it would have been an act pleasing to God to remove Pope Pius IV because room must be made for the one to come: 'credo che sia aparechiato un home che in ogni evento che bisogni sia per essere il pontefice de Dio, e quel pontefice che ordinariamente dal popolo Romano è chiamato pontefice angelico' (op. cit., appendix, p. 486). Accolti expected him to be 'homo de santissima vita, di età senile che havesse spirito de Dio da poter mostrare la authorita sua come l'abbia havuto uno de quelli santi pontefici antiqui' (ibid.). He confessed that in this dream he had been influenced by the plot of Porcaro in the previous century and

---

[1] *Mysticus Aquilo*, pp. 14, 82–3.

[2] Ibid., p. 23.

[3] Ibid., p. 25: '. . . post ruinam novae Babylonis reformari oportet [i.e. Ecclesiam Romanam] in gradum pristinum... per ordinem videlicet Eremitarum, in extrema mundi aetate, divina gratia, in zelo ac Dei amore, veluti igne exardescenti, iam repurgata Ecclesia. *Surget enim ordo*, ut Abbas Ioachim ante quadringentos fere annos prophetico spiritu clarus praedixit . . .' (quotes *Expos.*, f. 176ʳ).

[4] Pastor, *History of the Popes* xvi. 383–9; appendix, pp. 485–97.

by reading books by Luther. It was, however, far more the general tradition of the Angelic Pope that drove him to look for 'un papa novo, onto, santo et angelico',[1] who would be monarch of the world and renovator of the Church.

Another would-be revolutionary, perhaps equally unstable, was Tomasso Campanella. His earliest concepts of an ideal world order were religious rather than political. When, against the atheism of the Machiavellians, he pressed his dream of the Golden Age celebrated by poets and philosophers, it was a world republic under the Church that he expected after the ruin of Antichrist.[2] In the *Monarchia Messiae* he developed the concept of one ruler and one religion throughout the world, and adduced many arguments for the priest-king, the supreme pontiff who should hold both material and spiritual swords. His dream is summed up in a chapter-heading: 'Foelicitatem Soeculi aurei existere, si totius mundi unus sit modo Princepes [*sic*] Sacerdotalis, absque Superiori: et unica Religio vera erga unum Deum . . .'[3] In the following pages he develops that blend of Renaissance Golden Age and medieval ecclesiastical ecumenism which is so characteristic of this time. In the *saeculum aureum* wars, pestilences, famines, schisms, and heresies will not arise. Men will live longer through the new arts of medicine. 'Item afflueret sapientia hominum ex abundantia pacis . . . Item si totus mundus regeretur ab uno, multiplicaretur scientia, ob tutas navigationes, et itinera, et mercaturas, et communicationes rerum, quae sciuntur . . .'[4] In this world unity there will be no barbarians, for the *Pontifex*, the *solum mundi caput*, will provide rulers for all nations: '. . . quando mundus totus unitus fuerit sub hac monarchia et evacuati fuerint Principatus et potestates eidem non subditae in omnibus . . . et diversitas Religionum sectarumque sublata fuerit, tunc apparebit soeculum aureum.'[5] Although Campanella does not allude directly to the prophecies of the *Liber de Flore* and of Telesphorus, he could hardly fail to have been influenced by his fellow Calabrians and, indeed, cites Joachim occasionally.[6] His philosophy was, of course, more sophisticated than the simple programme of the Angelic

---

[1] Pastor, *History of the Popes*, appendix, p. 489.
[2] *Atheismus Triumphatus* . . . (Rome, 1631), pp. 72 seq.
[3] *Monarchia Messiae* (Jesi, 1633), p. 14.
[4] Ibid., p. 15.
[5] Ibid., p. 21.
[6] See *Atheismus Triumphatus*, p. 83; *De Monarchia Hispanica* (Amsterdam, 1640), p. 23.

Popes, but the basic concept was the same. Later, as we have seen,[1] Campanella retreated from this extreme ultramontanist position and sought to recast his dream of the prophetic future in secular political terms.

[1] *Supra*, pp. 387–8.

V

THE *VATICINIA DE SUMMIS PONTIFICIBUS*

I F Telesphorus's *libellus* kept the Angelic Popes before men's eyes, the other pseudo-Joachimist work which continued to rouse speculation on the prophetic future of the papacy was the *Vaticinia de Summis Pontificibus* with all its numerous editions and commentaries.[1] As we have seen, the second, later set of fifteen did not embody the hope of the *renovatio* at all, but ended rather with a forecast of Antichrist. By the sixteenth century, however, the two sets had been put together with the later set first, so that the most menacing prognostication—'Terribilis es et quis resistet tibi?'— was placed innocuously in the middle and the sequence of thirty ended once more with the angelic portraits which originally closed the first fifteen. The first printed edition, by the Gesu brothers, appeared between 1501 and 1515 (?1505), followed by the Latin/Italian editions of Leandro Alberti (1515) and a second Gesu one (1527). These show no recognition of the doctrine of *renovatio* or expectation of Angelic Popes. In his Preface Alberti speaks of the consuming curiosity of mortals and, to judge by the scribbled notes in so many copies, the main attraction of the *Vaticinia* lay in identifying the past sequence of popes and determining the point at which history became prophecy.

Protestants were the first to seize on the *Vaticinia* as supplying a general prognostication concerning the papacy rather than particular oracles. Andreas Osiander, the Lutheran minister of St. Lawrence Church, Nuremberg, found copies of the work in the Ratsbibliothek and the library of the Carthusian monastery and in 1527 published an edition with a German Commentary and a verse for each picture by Hans Sachs.[2] It was easy to see in most of

---

[1] Montaigne writes: 'Je voudrois bien avoir reconnu de mes yeux ces deux merveilles: du livre de Joachim, Abbé Calabrois, qui predisoit tous les Papes futurs, leurs noms et formes; et celuy de Leon l'empereur, qui predisoit les Empereurs et Patriarches de Grece . . .' He then reflects on the extent to which his fellow men are deceived by the ambiguities of such prophecies and enticed into the game of interpreting them just as they wish. *Essais* (Paris, 1598), Livre i, ch. 11, 'Des Prognostications', p. 36.

[2] *Eyn wunderliche Weyssagung von dem Babstumb, wie es ihm biz an das endt der welt*

these pictures denunciations of papal worldliness, simony, political intrigue, and so on. Osiander made full use of this material in a Protestant polemic against the papacy. He did, indeed, recognize the saintliness of the original portrait of Celestine V, the Monk with the Rose (now number XX), and immediately applied it to Martin Luther, but of the angelic series from XXIII onwards he showed no awareness at all. Wolff's *Lectionum Memorabilium...Centenarii XVI* (1600) has Osiander's commentary on the *Vaticinia*, translated into Latin, under the name of Ioannes Adrasder, an anagram of Andreas Osiander.

A reply to this Protestant use of the *Vaticinia* came from Paracelsus at Nuremberg, *c.* 1530, in his *Expositio Vera Harum Imaginum olim Nurenbergae repertarum* . . .[2] This interpretation, again, does not attempt to apply the prophecies to individual popes but treats them as concerned with the general state of the papacy. Paracelsus's point of view is severely critical of the Holy See and pro-Imperial in sympathy: thus No. XXIII (f. 38ʳ), showing a walled city full of spears, is interpreted as the 'expugnatio urbis Romae sub Carolo quinto per Germanos facta'. Some of the pictures are sharpened in an anti-papal direction, yet this is not Protestant polemic, but rather a restatement of the Catholic revolutionary position, that is, a denunciation of the sins of the papacy linked to the expectation of revolution necessary to bring in the Angelic Popes. When he reaches the series of angelic portraits, it is clear that, in contrast to the Protestants, Paracelsus has grasped the meaning of at least the last four. Of number XXVII (f. 43ʳ) he writes: 'Transactis omnibus que dicta sunt, Papa veniet alius, sc. purus, mundus, et in linea Petri et Pauli constitutus . . .' Under XXVIII (f. 44ʳ) Paracelsus stresses that the Pope in the new regime will be chosen and crowned by God, through His angel, not by men. Again he uses the angels in the

gehen sol, in figuren oder, gemal begriffen, gefunden zu Nürmberg im Cartheuser Closter, und ist seher alt (Nuremberg, 1527). See, on this publication, R. Bainton, 'The Joachimite Prophecy: Osiander and Sachs', *Studies on the Reformation* (London, 1964), pp. 62–6. But Bainton goes astray on the dating of the *Vaticinia* (p. 64), as does also K. Sudhoff, *Bibliographia Paracelsica* (Berlin, 1894), pp. 38–9.

[1] See also a Frankfurt ed. of 1608: *Prophetia Anglicana et Romana...Addita sunt Vaticinia et praedictiones Joachimi Abbatis Calabri...una cum annotationibus et explicatione Johannis Adrasder.*

[2] On this edition see Sudhoff, op. cit., pp. 38–9. A German translation appeared in 1532. The edition I have used is that of 1570 (no. pl. of pub.) and the folio references are to this.

XXIXth picture to underline the new, revolutionary position of the papacy: '. . . significatur hic Papam istum a Deo, non ab hominibus, sedem et suam potestatem habiturum, et ista non humano sed angelico modo fieri' (f. 45ᵛ). The enigmatic XXXth picture he interprets not, like so many, as a seven-horned Antichrist, but as the culmination of the angelic regime in the papacy:

Postrema pictura vaticiniorum finem horum concludit in agno septicorni, qui Christum denotat. Papa coronam superponens ei, fatetur hoc ipso Christum Papam, et non miserum hominem talem fore, potestatemque hanc esse Christi, non hominum, item Papam humanum, ut Apostolum et perfectum ex Deo hominem fore debere, qui suis ovibus ad Christum viam ostendat: et sub tali potestate reducentur oves omnes in unum ovile, pastorem habebunt unum supra septem generationes hominum. Pastor iste vocatur redemptor, sub cuius potestate sic manebimus . . . laete beateque vivemus in aeternum . . . (f. 46ʳ⁻ᵛ.)

Then will supervene the blessed regime expected—but how hard, exclaims Paracelsus, it is to reach this, how impossible, unless God Himself destroys the Babylonish Whore and all heretics!

Paracelsus represents that strange mixture of interests which we have already met in some Italian humanists: vaticination, astrological prognostication, and the cabbala were as much grist to his mill as the classical and semi-scientific studies for which he is remembered. His pseudo-scientific works had a considerable vogue, especially his interpretation of the *Vaticinia*, which went into several editions.[1] He studied the *Prognosticatio* of Lichtenberger[2] and wrote a work *De Presagiis Vaticiniis Atque Divinationibus*, in which he surveyed different types of supernatural knowledge.[3] In 1549 he appeared with a collection of prophets in a tract which went into several editions: *Propheceien und Weissagungen . . . Doctoris Paracelsi, Johan Liechtenbergers, Joseph Grunpeck, Joannis Carionis, Die Sibyllen und anderer*.[4] His attitude towards the Church and towards the future can be deduced by putting together some remarks in his conclusion to the *Vaticinia* and some passages in a curious

---

[1] The following are known to me: *c.* 1530, 1532 (German), 1569 (German), 1570, 1577, 1600, 1620. Wolf, *Lect. mem.* i. 374–90, published *In imagines Joachimi Abbatis annotationes Theophrasti Paracelsi*.

[2] Sudhoff, op. cit., p. 12.

[3] Published Frankfurt, 1584. Here he mentions Lichtenberger's 'figuras magicas' and the 'figurae penes Charthusianos inventae' (pp. 34–61).

[4] Sudhoff, op. cit., p. 42.

Prognosticatio of his own which he published in 1536.[1] In the former
he shows his belief that the root of all evil lay in the Papal assumption
of temporal power and that there must be a sharp break between
the bad old regime and the new:

... prophetiam hanc numerare debeatis ab eo tempore quo Papa dominari
coepit in temporalibus, ad eaque primum assumptus fuit, in finem usque
depositionis eius: quo quidem tempore, cessabunt omnes sectae, nequi-
tiae, fraudes etc. nedum Ecclesiasticorum, verum etiam falsarum ovium,
et scabiosarum, quae simul omnes cum Papa cadent in interitum. Haec
omnia prior pars huius prophetiae continet, quae finem arboris malitiae,
dolique praefiguravit: altera vero mundas complectitur oves sub uno ovili,
pastore pariter unico feliciter Deoque viventes . . . (*Vaticinia*, f. 47ʳ.)

The *Prognosticatio* appears to be Paracelsus's own essay in producing
prophecies modelled on the *Vaticinia*. There are thirty-two figures,
each with an enigmatic text. They are dedicated to Ferdinand, King
of the Romans, and the XXVIth applies Sibylline prophecies to him.
The last two represent Paracelsus's vision of the coming Age of Gold,
not now in ecclesiastical terms so much as humanistic. Number
XXXI shows naked children dancing, with the following textual
comment: 'Tanta et talis futura est omnium rerum renovatio et
mutatio: ut plane aurea saecula redisse videantur, ubi plane puerilis
candor, simplicitas ac integritas regnabit, explosis omnibus versutiis,
astutiis et insidiis hominum . . .' Number XXXII pictures a man
reclining at ease under a tree with the sun shining on him. This is
the future Age of Rest: 'Multo sudore, et labore conatus es reformare
mundum, magnus ut ab integro nascatur saeculorum ordo, merito
itaque exacto labore quiesces, foelix is futurus, qui sub hac quiete et
somno proditurus est, malum enim non videbit: omnia tunc erant
pacata, restituta, ac in integrum redacta. Nemo potuit tuos sanctissimos conatus impedire . . .'

But Paracelsus's interpretation of the *Vaticinia*, albeit Catholic,
was too dangerous to be left unchallenged, so Paracelsus himself was
countered by another Catholic viewpoint in the edition of Paulus,
Princeps de la Scala or Scaliger or Schalich,[2] which was published
by Theodore Graminaeus at Cologne in 1570 with a Foreword to

---

[1] *Prognosticatio eximii doctoris Theophrasti Paracelsi* . . . (no pl. of pub. or date,
written 1536, unpag.). See also W. Peuckert, *Die Rosenkreutzer. Zur Geschichte einer
Reformation* (Jena, 1928), p. 25.

[2] On P. Scaliger see G. Krabbel, *Paul Skalich: ein Lebensbild aus dem 16. Jahrhunderts* (Münster, 1915): Secret, *Studi francesi* I, p. 384, calls him the *Picus Redivivus du
Nord*.

Maximilian II. The long title concludes: '. . . vaticiniorum et imaginum Joachimi Abbatis Florensis Calabriae . . . contra falsam, iniquam, vanam, confictam et seditiosam cuiusdam Pseudomagi, quae super nomine Theophrasti Paracelsi in lucem prodiit, pseudomagicam expositionem, vera, certa et indubita explanatio.' In order to withdraw these prophecies from this dangerous revolutionary interpretation, Scaliger goes back to the original of each oracle as applying to individual popes, not to the state of the papacy in general, as Paracelsus has so falsely assumed.[1] Taking each of the series in turn, down to Innocent VIII, the last one, Scaliger shows much ingenuity in rendering them innocuous by his limited interpretations. Thus his eulogy of Sixtus IV, who now qualifies for an angelic portrait, is most amusing.[2] By using this method, of course, he drains the figures of any but a strictly historical meaning. Joachim to Scaliger is a true prophet because he forecast actual popes and their acts, not because he foreknew the shape of history to come. The expectation of *renovatio* by the angelic series of popes has again utterly disappeared.

Scaliger has a sharp word for Paracelsus on the final figure which the latter had brought within the Angelic series by interpreting the animal as the seven-horned Lamb of God.[3] It is nonsense, says

[1] Scaliger's attack on Paracelsus is well illustrated by his notes on the first figure: 'Paracelsus, sive quisquis ille sit Pseudomagus, qui imagines ex Joachimi Abbatis et Anselmi Episcopi vaticiniis confectas, et ut ille ait, olim Nurenbergae repertas, se ex fundatissimo verae Magiae vaticinio deduxisse et exposuisse profitetur, splendidissime mentitur. Nam primam hanc imaginem dicit esse Rhomani Pontificis cum duobus ursis, alteri per os monetam ingerentis. Caeterum Joachimus ipsemet interpretatur non monetam sed grana esse. Ita istum pseudomagum aut solas imagines sine autoris adumbratione habuisse, consentaneum est, atque pro sua libidine et interpretatum esse et depravasse: aut si adumbrationes illas vidit, exquisita quadam malitia et impostura magica: non tam magice quam affectate, libidinose, nefarie et mera vesania, atque crudelitate Pseudomagice tractasse et consultasse . . . Neglectis igitur insani hominis opinionibus, ad rem veniamus, et quidnam voluerint Joachimus et Anselmus iuxta propriam illorum interpretationem, et historicam atque symbolicam veritatem dignoscamus' (pp. 3-4).
[2] Ibid., pp. 134-5: 'Hic vir certe non minus arte, quam ingenio clarus fuit, . . . labore incredibili ad divinarum humanarumque artium apicem conscendit . . . [gives a list of his theological works]. Et ut ante pontificatum adeptum, clemens, pius et in omnes mansuetus extitit, ita magistratu pontificio insignitus, omni virtute coepit caeteros praecellere . . . [gives a list of his good works, e.g. he protected refugees from Byzantium, rebuilt Rome, celebrated the Jubilee]. Et licet hic multos habuerit detractores (id quod viris sanctis proprium est) optimus tamen Pontifex fuit. Summa enim alacritate et animarum custos extitit et cupiditatem a se resecavit, et iras compressit et malitias extirpavit.' (Then he proceeds to apply the words of the angelic prophecy in detail, including an emphasis on Sixtus's role as peace-maker in Italy!)
[3] *Supra*, p. 455.

Scaliger, to turn this formidable beast into a lamb 'cui tamen nec vaticinium respondet, nec vetustissimum exemplar'.[1] The beast is in essence the German people, and here Scaliger displays the same viewpoint as his publisher Graminaeus.[2] However antiseptic his interpretations of the *Vaticinia*, we find at the end that he was not really immune from the prevalent disease of applying prophecies currently. He quotes from Joachim's *Super Esaiam*[3] on the evils to befall the Church from the north and then shows how this clearly prophesies the scourge of Luther:

. . . Huius Aquilonis mater est Saxonia: . . . Quid obsecro clarius dici poterat de Luthero? . . . Haec prophetia nova non est, sed A.D. 1178 Ioachimo tradita et postremo, quod sciam, typis Lazari Soardi Venetiis A.D. 1516 excusa, cuius exemplar penes nos est: cum tamen Lutherus coeperit insanire A.D. 1517. De hoc Luthero Ioannes Liechtenbergius A.D. 1488 Calend. Aprilis haec praedixit: Monachus . . . in cuculla et diabolus in scapulis eius retro . . . [He then quotes from Lichtenberger and describes his picture of a monk with a devil on his back and illustrates this] . . . Recte hic Lutherus depingitur. Fuit enim Monachus sub instituto Eremitarum beati Augustini. (Op. cit., pp. 147–9.)

The judgements of God must descend on an erring Church, but in the final analysis the Roman Church is the Tribe of Judah and Joachim affirms this: 'Unde abunde satis constat quid de potestate et principatu Rhomanae Ecclesiae, atque perpetuitate, et puritate fidei illius Joachim sentiat: quamvis a iustitiae operibus deflectat aliquando: quia militans est, non triumphans, quae et cadit et resurgit . . .' (op. cit., p. 151).

Yet another Catholic viewpoint on the *Vaticinia* is expressed by Pasqualino Regiselmo in his Venetian edition of 1589.[4] In his dedication to the Bishop of Treviso, Regiselmo speaks of the human propensity to be drawn into the investigation of curious matters rather than to pursue solid and useful knowledge. But some visions and mystical arts are worthy of study and among such are the *Vaticinia* of the Abbot Joachim. Yet these have been corrupted and twisted by a certain heretic to seduce many, and so the author has been roused to counter these false images. The heretic or *pseudo-*

---

[1] Scaliger, p. 151.   [2] *Supra*, pp. 373–4.
[3] Scaliger, p. 146, cf. *Super Esaiam*, ff. 10ᵛ, 19ʳ. He also quotes (p. 138) from Telesphorus's *libellus* in the 1516 ed., ff. 21ʳ, 26ʳ.
[4] *Vaticinia sive Prophetiae Abbatis Ioachimi et Anselmi Episcopi Marsicani* (Venice, 1589, unpag.), in Latin and Italian, preceded by the life of Joachim by Gabriele Barrio, who is here erroneously described as a Franciscan; cf. *supra*, p. 118.

magus, as he calls him elsewhere, is certainly Paracelsus. With that mixture of credulity and science characteristic of the sixteenth century, Regiselmo bases his claim to give the true interpretation on his scholarly researches, informing the reader in his Preface that he has examined eight manuscripts and seven printed editions in order to eliminate corruptions of the text and false interpretations. Among the manuscripts used was one which he judged to be more than three hundred years old, belonging to Antonio Magino of Padua, 'vir syderum cognitione praestans', and also the original compilation of Domenico Mauroceno, written one hundred and thirty years before. Regiselmo mentions the three modes of interpretation of those who affirm that all the prophecies have already been fulfilled, those who say that not all have yet been completed, and those who believe the meaning of the series to be cyclical. He also notices three theories of authorship—by Joachim and Anselm, Bishop of Marsico, by Joachim alone, and by a certain Rabanus, named by Mauroceno. To these he adds the view of some recent Greeks that the originals of all these pictures could be found under the name of Leo in Constantinople. The scholarship which has in fact shown the truth contained in this theory[1] was unfortunately too far ahead of Regiselmo and he dismissed this foolish tale, preferring the evidence of others: '. . . percontatus sum peritissimos viros et clarissimos qui Constantinopoli diu fuere, ipsi haec non modo risere sed etiam asseruere nihil extare . . .' (Annotations to the Preface.)

Regiselmo's notes on the text are partly devoted to manuscript variations and efforts to establish the correct order of the prophecies, partly to the refutation of false interpretations. He joins Scaliger in his attack on the *pseudomagus*, Paracelsus, but he also criticizes Scaliger's interpretations. Here he relies heavily on his very old manuscript. Thus he writes: 'Nescio quodnam vetustissimum exemplar Paulus Scaliger viderit et quid ille Pseudomagus confinxerit . . .: hoc unum scio meum illud manuscriptum ab hinc trecentis annis (ut in eo adnotatum scriptoris manu videre licet) exscriptum . . .'[2] By the time of Regiselmo interpreters of the *Vaticinia* were faced with the problem that to give the prophecies a general interpretation came dangerously near the Protestant position, but to give them individual interpretations, starting according to tradition with Nicholas III, meant that the series of thirty was now closed, no longer prophecy, but history. This latter was the line taken by Scaliger, but Regiselmo

---

[1] *Supra*, p. 193.   [2] Note to Fig. XIX.

cannot relinquish the idea of prophecy. He gets out of his dilemma
ingeniously. The prophecies, he argues, do represent individual
popes, but not in continuous sequence. They occur at intervals and
therefore extend into the future by some secret mathematical principle. Here he introduces an interesting point, namely that Joachim
learnt these principles from the orient, since he was born in *magna
Graecia*, where Greek is still spoken today, and went east on pilgrimage.[1] So Regiselmo is able to criticize both Scaliger's pictures
and texts, and his applications of the prophecies. Among the later
ones Regiselmo applies XXI to Julius III and XXIV to Pius V. He
refuses to name number XXV, and by XXVI he is clearly in the
future. Thus, although he does not emphasize them greatly, the
angelical series is expected and Regiselmo's recognition of a prophetic future is seen in his reference under number XXVI to other
prophets who have also foretold mighty events.[2] Under XXVIII he
considers whether Luther or Calvin represents Antichrist but concludes that this applies to future, not past, times, and focuses attention rather on those future and holy pontiffs who will restore the
Church and gather together the scattered flock of Christ, for in the
time of this twenty-eighth Pontiff, or a little after, Israel will begin
to return to the true fold and seek salvation in the true Messiah. At
this point Regiselmo's ancient manuscript fails him, for the end has
been torn out (perhaps by a child, he says),[3] but he is able to give
the final two *vaticinia* from other sources, including pictures in S.
Macro to which he has already referred a number of times.[4] No. XXX
represents the final Pontiff in whose time Antichrist will be revealed.
He calculates that this will be soon after 1700. He supports his
calculations from Pico della Mirandola, remarking that 'per l'Arith-
metica non materiale ma formale, s'ha buonissima strada alla Profetia naturale' and that Joachim 'non caminò per altra strada nelle
sue Profetie che per i numeri formali'.

The extraordinary fascination exercised by these enigmatic series
of papal prophecies is seen in the proliferation of imitative series
in the sixteenth century. Regiselmo adds three of these at the end

[1] Note to Fig. XV.
[2] Under Figs. XXVI and XXVII he cites Iodochus Palmerius, Johannes Heremita,
Johannes Capistranus, and Magister Reinhard Ord. Praed., giving a verse composed by
the latter. He also quotes the Cyril prophecy 'Grandis Aquila infra surget' (cf. *supra*,
p. 319).
[3] Note on Fig. XXVIII.
[4] Notes on Figs. IV, VI, XXVII, XXIX.

of his book. One, entitled *Prognostica de Successoribus Petri a Martino usque ad Antichristum, ex libro Ioachimi Abbatis*, names the popes from Martin V to Gregory XIV. The second set of twenty purports to derive 'ex libro antiquissimo Fratris Egidii Poloni' and to prophesy the popes from Pius II to Gregory XIV. The *Rota* of the Blessed Iodochus Palmerius gives a sequence from Paul IV to Gregory XIV. The most famous of these imitative series was that which went under the name of St. Malachy. It achieved great fame. The vogue for this type of prophecy is strikingly represented in a Bodley manuscript, Laud 588, a late sixteenth-century prophetic anthology. Here all possible series of papal prophecies seem to be gathered together, many of them illustrated by naïve pen-and-ink drawings. The series given by Regiselmo appears here, as well as that of St. Malachy and a number more. Most of them name the series as far as Sixtus V or an adjacent pope and then end with enigmatic, unfulfilled prophecies. Thus the object of these exercises appears to be twofold: to describe under cover of prophecy actual popes, often in uncomplimentary terms, but also to embody in oracular form the continuing hopes and fears for the future. These are often extremely confused and enigmatic, but one characteristic stands out strikingly in the Laud collection: almost every series ends in one way or another with the figure of the Angelic Pope. Thus a series under the name of Nicholas of Toledo places immediately after Sixtus V the following: 'Succedet Angelicus pastor, hinc ecclesia Dei exaltabitur, lux orbi constituetur' (f. 12ᵛ). Again, the series ascribed to Egidius Polonus culminates in a portrait of the Angelic Pope: 'Hic pastor est ordinis monachorum. Praedicabit evangelium in toto mundo. Iste pastor est Angelicus, vir bonus, et dabit suavem odorem in ecclesia Dei, et multi venient ad baptismum . . .' (f. 34ʳ). The most interesting of the texts in the Laud manuscript is a long visionary dialogue between the angel Gabriel and an unnamed author which is mainly focused on the expected Angelic Pope (ff. 4ᵛ–7ᵛ). This seems to be a version of the prophecy of Amadeus, since phrases in it correspond to quotations made from Amadeus's revelation by Paolo Angelo and Petrus Galatinus.[1] Probably this text of Amadaeus's vision exists elsewhere but I do not know of another example. This gives the Laud text a particular interest. It expresses eloquently the great longing and expectation, the idealized angelic portrait, the ecumenical vision which inspired

---

[1] *Supra*, pp. 366, 432.

Amadeus in the fifteenth century, as it had the authors of the
original *Vaticinia* in the fourteenth, and as it could still do at the end
of the sixteenth century when the Laud manuscript was written.[1]

[1] This Laud manuscript would repay a detailed study. It belongs to a genre of
which there may be many other examples. It is certainly related to a much more beautifully executed manuscript from the Philips collection, No. 17267, now MS. Ital. C. 73
in the Bodleian Library. One intriguing feature is a picture cut out of a printed book
stuck in on f. 19ᵛ, showing emperor and pontiff locked in conflict, balanced on a boat,
with various emblems around them. I do not know the printed source from which this
comes, but it reproduces almost exactly an illustration in MS. Venice, Bibl. Marc.,
Lat. III. 177, f. 10ᵛ. Another Joachimist collection, made by a Renaissance antiquary
and entitled 'Les propheties qui sont vulgairement attribuées a l'abbé Joachim', is found
in the Bibl. Inguimbertine, Carpentras, MS. 340. I owe this information to Mr. John
Fleming.

VI

RENOVATIO MUNDI AND CATHOLIC EXEGESIS

IT can be argued that most of those who expected revolution and renovation in the Church were on the periphery of the main lines of thought in their period, just as those who looked for a political saviour were hardly in touch with the political realities of their time. The men who played with interpretations of the *Vaticinia*—though hardly frivolous—may not have been very profound in their belief. The evidence of a continuing tradition of 'optimistic' thinking about history among theologians and Biblical scholars of repute gives a more solid basis to the argument that prophetic expectation was a factor of real importance in the thought of this period.

Giovanni Annio of Viterbo was very conscious of making just such a positive affirmation of *renovatio mundi* when he wrote his *Glosa super Apocalypsim de statu ecclesie ab anno ... MCCCCLXXXI usque ad finem mundi ...*[1] He knew that there were objectors to the concept of a terrestrial age of bliss and he met them squarely. To those who quoted 'My kingdom is not of this world', he said:

Ad hoc firmissime tenentes respondemus quod nedum in futuro seculo sed etiam in presenti Christus solus habet monarchiam iuridicam. Ergo monarchia Christi universalis est, nedum celestis, sed temporalis . . . Et ita regnum temporale Christi dissipabit omnia alia regna . . . Ergo Christo et vicario eius data est monarchia nedum celestis sed etiam terrestris. (Op. cit., cap. xvii.)

To the objection that the victory of Christ which figures in the Apocalypse is to be thought of in celestial, not terrestrial, terms, he replied firmly that this victory must apply to the temporal monarchy of the Church, first, 'quia totus iste liber ad litteram est de statibus ecclesie militantis in terra, non triumphantis in celo': second, because after this victory the Devil will be bound for the stated time but then released for a space, 'ergo intelligitur de monarchia que erit

---

[1] Pub. at Louvain, undated, unpag.

ante iudicium'.[1] With these and other arguments he satisfied himself that an era of terrestrial triumph was to be expected and so he
developed the concept of a double resurrection of the Church:
'prima resurrectio est totius ecclesie ad universalem unionem sub
uno pastore . . . secunda autem resurrectio erit corporum.'[2] One
agent in achieving this universal victory would be a great prince
instituted by the Church, but the real universal monarch in this age
of beatitude and felicity would be the Roman pontiff. Annio did
not try to portray his Angelic Pope but sketched a world government
with twelve regions, each ruled by a patriarch and a king and 'unus
custos angelus'. This twelvefold division was, of course, derived from
the twelve gates of the New Jerusalem, and it was indeed the New
Jerusalem descending from heaven, 'quia tanta reformatio terrestris
a celo veniet'.[3] He emphasized this point: 'Vidi novum celum, i.e.
novum statum ecclesie et terram novam, sive novum statum laicorum.'[3] Although he only quoted Joachim once—or rather, the
pseudo-Joachimist *Super Hieremiam*[4]—he actually used the Joachimist phrase: 'sequitur ergo tercius status in reformatione ecclesie.[3] Annio's final stage of history was undoubtedly the Joachimist
Third Age.

Of the same school of thought, although not a Catholic, Francis
Lambert of Avignon, also wrote on the Apocalypse.[5] He, too,
argued strongly for a genuine historical seventh age, after the fall
of Babylon and the defeat of Antichrist, at the end of the
sixth age and before the Last Judgement. Like Joachim he found
the quintessence of this symbolized in the half-hour's silence at the
opening of the Seventh Seal. In this space peace would reign, truth
would prevail, and the saints would be free; in a word, the world
would be renewed and, as it were, raised from the dead.[6] The angel
with the open book signified the preaching of the Gospel throughout
the world, and this would be the work of 'unum summum Evan-
gelistam, multos habentem cooperarios', whom Lambert found
typified in the various angels of the Apocalypse.[7] He did not cite
Joachim, but his exegesis was very close to the Abbot's and he used

[1] Giovanni Annio, op. cit., cap. xix.   [2] Ibid., cap. xx.
[3] Ibid., cap. xxi.
[4] Ibid., cap. xvii, prophesying the final defeat of the Saracens.
[5] F. Lambert, *Exegeseos in sanctam divi Joannis Apocalypsim Libri VII* (Basle,
1539). His dates were 1487–1530.
[6] Ibid., pp. 306–7: '. . . mundus renovatus et quasi a mortuis suscitatus videbitur.'
[7] Ibid., pp. 353–8.

a similar number-symbolism.[1] All these events were now at hand: 'puto omnino in ianuis esse magni Antichristi adventum.'[2] How long the seventh age would last he would not venture to say. It would probably be brief 'quia tam gloriosa et admirabile pax non potest diu esse in hac valle miseriarum, sanctis adhuc in fragili carne viventibus.'[3] Thus Lambert clearly saw this as a Golden Age within history, stating more sharply than most its essential limitations of the flesh. None the less he concluded: 'Summa autem causa est, ut magnificetur, foelicissimum illud spiritus regnum in quo vel brevissimum tempus pro longissimo erit . . .'[4]

In the next generation Damián Hortolá is an interesting example of this school of thought. Born at Perpignan in 1493, he became Abbot of the monastery of Ville-Bertrand and was sent by Philip II to the Council of Trent. The work in which he expresses his view of the future is a Commentary on the Song of Solomon.[5] He still uses the medieval pattern of concords between the history of the Synagogue and that of the Church, plotting both in parallel mounting graphs of tribulation up to the sixth age. The climax of iniquity in Antichrist is now at hand: as the waves of enemies once rose against Judah, so now the mounting tide rolls in on the Church:

Incredibile est, quam stupendis incrementis a trecentis quadraginta annis Mahumetis, et Antichristi Regnum in Affrica, et Asia superato Sultano, confirmavit: et inde in Graeciam atque Europam se effundens, omnem orientalem ecclesiam, et quicquid in Oriente reliquum fuerat Romani Imperii, expugnata Bizantio, inundarit . . . et nuper aggressa Occidentale Imperium, florentissimum Ungarie Regnum totius Imperii propugnaculum, expugnarit . . . Reliquum tandem quod eius Regni superest, atque adeo Germaniam . . . occupatura, Deo sic permittente et propter schismaticos et . . . rebelles Germanorum animos, in saevissimi Tyranni potestatem tradente . . . (*In Canticum*, p. 319.)

In interpreting contemporary events as the onslaught of Antichrist Hortolá did not directly cite Joachim, but he did use the pseudo-Joachimist *Oraculum Cyrilli* as well as prophecies attributed to Methodius, St. Bridget, and St. Vincent.[6] The signs of impending

[1] See, for instance, pp. 403–5, 478–9 (on the seven *etates* and the numbers six and seven).
[2] Ibid., p. 480.   [3] Ibid., p. 581.   [4] Ibid., p. 582.
[5] *In Canticum Canticorum Salomonis . . . Explanatio* (Venice, 1585). On Hortolá see Glaire, *Dictionnaire Universel des Sciences Ecclésiastiques* (Paris, 1868), *sub nom.*
[6] *In Canticum*, pp. 320–1.

disaster and revolution in the sixth age are very clear, yet the constant theme of his interpretation of the Song of Solomon is the beauty and the glory of the Church in the seventh age. Here at once we meet the familiar agencies of blessedness: the *Papa Angelicus*, a pious emperor, an angelic order of world-wide preachers, two orders of 'perfect men', twelve apostolic men—all detected in the various symbols of the Song and the Apocalypse, and applied in a style akin to that of Joachim.[1] The Angelic Pope is described in terms which suggest the revolution in the lives of the clergy which must form part of the *renovatio*:

. . . ac tunc demum creandum sanctissimum quendam pontificem, qui propter admirandam morum, et vitae integritatem ac puritatem Angelicus dicendus sit. Atque hunc revocaturum fore ecclesiasticam disciplinam, et universam vivendi rationem ab Apostolis olim . . . institutam: nec quicquam clericis praeter alimenta et quibus tegantur permissurum: atque omni cura et administratione rerum temporalium clero interdicturum, Evangelium Christi per orbem Ierosolymam usque peregrando sancte, et sine sordibus ullis praedicaturum in hoc ipsum delectis duodecim sociis, quorum opera longe lateque disseminando verbum Dei universum orbem Christo subjicere aggredientur: cui tres continenter alius post alium succedentes Pontifices pari sanctitate et integritate, pari etiam felicitate Apostolico munere defungentes . . . perficient . . . (Ibid., p. 336.)

Under the text 'Veni in hortum meum soror mea sponsa, etc.'[2] Hortolá writes eloquently and at length on the return of the Jews to the true garden of Christ and on the flowing together of all the nations into that garden which will follow the universal preaching. This, he claims, has been foretold by prophets ancient and modern. The only past time to which this could be compared is that in which Pope Silvester and Constantine co-operated for the peace of the world,[3] but the approaching seventh age is not really seen as a returning cycle but as the culmination of history. Hortolá boldly uses the symbols of the new heaven and earth and the New Jerusalem descending to earth to describe this last age of history:

Ac tunc demum Ioannes novum celum videt et terram novam, (h.e.) genus hominum utraque sui parte tam inferiore, quam superiore renova-

---

[1] *In Canticum*, pp. 336, 337 ('Angelicus ille ordo praedicatorum'), 338, 349, 351, 353 ('Sub pio . . . Imperatore et sub Angelico Pontifice summo, ut olim Romae sub Constantino et Sylvestro . . .'), 364 ('duos illos ordines perfectorum'), 375 ('duodecim Apostolicis viris'), 386–7.

[2] Ibid., pp. 353 seq.

[3] Ibid., p. 358, cf. *Lib. Conc.*, ff. 52ʳ, 92ᵛ; *Expos.*, f. 62ʳ⁻ᵛ; *Lib. Fig.* II, Pl. XVII.

tum. Nec mare usquam est, quia omnis turbulentia et fluctuatio de ecclesia tunc erit sublata. Videt civitatem sanctam Hierusalem novam descendentem de caelo . . . Ac talis quidem est species, et admiranda civitatis Christianae, quae Ioanni per Spiritum Sanctum ostensa est, magnificentia. Talis sub finem temporum quae sexto sigillo et magna parte septimi revelantur, nobis a Ioanne depingitur futurus ecclesiae status. . . . Id vero regnum septimo ecclesiae statu in hoc mundo constabiliendum, et confirmandum fore, ille locus Apocalypsis indicare videtur. (Ibid., pp. 377–80.)

Pushing the point home, he firmly challenges the pessimists who hold that this blessed *renovatio*, foretold by the prophets, belongs to eternity, not history:

Quae omnia, et multa alia a prophetis et Apostolis dicta de ecclesia ad statum beatorum, qui post universale iudicium futurus est, referre, ut per multos referre video, hominum mihi videtur esse refugium, qui dum nimis iniqui iudices in seipsos sunt tam foelicem Reipublicae Christianae statum in terris unquam fore ut credant, in animum suum inducere nequeunt . . . (Ibid., p. 381.)

A contemporary of Hortolá's, but in quite a different setting, was Bertold Purstinger, born in Salzburg and becoming Bishop of Chiemsee in 1508. He was associated with reforming movements in the province of Salzburg, and his *Onus Ecclesiae*, written in 1519, first appeared anonymously in 1524.[1] Purstinger was much more avowedly a Joachite than Hortolá. His work is devoted quite specifically to the seven ages of the Church, the pattern of which he takes directly from Ubertino da Casale. He draws a good deal from Joachim himself and cites many of the pseudo-Joachimist writings under the names of Merlin, Cyril, Raynier, Dandalus, Rabanus, Telesphorus, as well as prophecies attributed to SS. Francis, Vincent, Hildegarde, Bridget, and Catherine of Siena. His closeness to Joachim is seen in many passages, such as this on the *spiritualis intellectus*:

Quod olim sancti doctores, a Deo missi, tanquam lucernae fuerunt illuminati lumine mystice intelligendi sacram scripturam, quae antea obscura fuit et literaliter exposita . . . Nam lumen intellectus, quo sacra scriptura intelligitur, procedit a lumine supernaturali a Deo pendente, quo lumine superbi et flagitiosi carent ob amoris propriis [*sic*] nubem: quae excaecat spirituales oculos. Ideo isti intelligunt sacram paginam literaliter iuxta corticem exteriorem, non gustantes interiorem medullam scripturae. Sic

---

[1] For full title, see Select Bibliography.

hodie Luterani et alii quidam temeraria et ambitiosa disputatione alter-
cantes pro sua audacia sacras literas torquent . . . (*Onus Ecclesiae*, cap. xii.)

Purstinger, as so often, places himself at the end of the fifth or
the beginning of the sixth *status* of the Church, the fifth having
ended with the fall of Constantinople in the time of Frederick III.[1]
For the final drama he adopts the programme of Telesphorus:
schism and anti-pope, the tyrant from the north and the *Antichristus
mixtus*, then the triumph of the Church and the time of peace until
the great Antichrist, and finally the Sabbath of Tranquillity ending
with Gog and Magog and the Judgement.[2] In the first *renovatio* we
get the Second Charlemagne[3] and the Angelic Pope and his successors, as delineated by the *Liber de Flore* and by Telesphorus, with
the renunciation by the Church of all worldly goods, union of the
Greek and Latin churches, and preaching throughout the world.[4]
The final tranquillity is the seventh age of the Church, the Sabbath of
history.[5] Purstinger's sense of immediate contemporary relevance
is very strong. The locusts conjured up by the sixth trumpeting
angel are already present in the Lutherans;[6] the Fall of Constantinople, as once of Jerusalem, has taken place;[7] the prophecies of
Cyril began to be fulfilled in the intolerable wars of Italy from 1510.[8]
In the end it is the true Joachimist framework of the three *status* of
the world's history in which he places himself. He expounds these
in a chapter 'De triplici status totius mundi',[9] quoting Joachim when
he compares his own position between the second and third *status*
to that of Zacharias between the first and second. The climax of the
third *status* is expressed in Joachimist terms: 'Talis forsitan intelle-
ctualis visio apprehendetur in tertio mundo statu: quia tunc clarius
quam nunc aperietur veritas. . . . Tunc enim incipiet regnum Dei et
clare splendescet intelligentia sacrarum scripturarum . . .' (*Onus
Ecclesiae*, cap. lxvii.)

Two commentators on the Apocalypse in the later part of the
sixteenth century both expect the Golden Age in the seventh *status*

---

[1] *Onus Ecclesiae*, capp. ii, vi, vii.
[2] Ibid., cap. xxxix seq.
[3] *Supra*, pp. 326–7.
[4] *Onus Ecclesiae*, cap. lx.
[5] Ibid., cap. lxvi.
[6] Ibid., capp. xli, xlii.
[7] Ibid., cap. lxv.

[8] Ibid., cap. xxxix. In cap. xlix the prophecy of Bridget is cited concerning the
destruction of Rome by the intestine warfare of Christians.

[9] Ibid., cap. lxvii. He also adopts the pseudo-Joachimist concept of the three advents of Christ, the second being 'in spiritu reformationis, quo salvator ecclesiam
. . . generaliter reformabit' (cap. lxii).

of the Church between the death of Antichrist and the *consummatio saeculi*. Coelius Pannonius (alias Francesco Gregorio) does not directly base himself on Joachim but interprets many of the Apocalypse figures in a Joachimist sense.[1] The various angels are types of preachers of the Gospel and in particular the three angels of Apocalypse 14 typify the three final orders of universal preachers who will convert the whole world and bring in the time of great joy after the death of Antichrist.[2] To the theme of the final Age of Gold and the universal exultation to be experienced then, Pannonius returns several times[3] in passages of lyrical passion. In his Preface he already states clearly that the seventh Sabbath Age, the *aurea etas*, will fall between the death of Antichrist and the brief appearance of Gog and Magog. Whether it will be long or short does not matter compared with the intensity of joy:

Durabit tamen pax illa aliquanto utique tempore eo quod in donis suis bonus Deus cupiat se suamque bonitatem suis effundere . . . In qua re hoc solum pro certo habemus, quia foelicissimum illud futurum est ecclesiae regnum, cuius vel brevissimum tempus pro longissimo merito sui computabitur, quando pii exultabunt et inenarrabili laetitia iucundabuntur, et de Antichristi interitu et de eorum pace, praesertim vero de Christi gloria, quasi quodammodo foelicitatem ultimam forent assequuti. . . . Quod dum fiet, pulchra admodum tranquillitate conticescent universa. Tunc laetiores in suo cursu dies erunt, sol blandior spiculis ludentibus irradiabit, non mugiet horrendo tonitruo caelum, nec fulmina irati Dei iacientur. Tum ros et hymber complutu tellurem amplius foecundabunt, ridebunt exortu astra . . . Quid plura? Tunc redibunt aurea saecula . . . (Op. cit., p. 888.)

After this comes Judgement, and then the Eighth Day, the perpetual Sabbath.[4]

The second commentator, Serafino da Fermo, who was a Regular Canon, wrote on the Apocalypse in both Italian and Latin.[5] Like Purstinger, he drew directly on Joachim and Ubertino da Casale, adopting the latter's seven *status* of the Church. For him the great rejoicing was farther off, for he placed his own age in the fifth, not sixth, *status*[6] and he was deeply oppressed by the manifestations of

[1] *Collectanea in sacram Apocalypsin* (Paris, 1571).
[2] Ibid., pp. 375, 394–8, 402, 408, 412, 432, 488, 658–60, 667–71.
[3] Ibid., pp. 372–3, 520, 843–5, 854, 887–8, 899.
[4] Ibid., p. 918.
[5] *Sopra l'Apocalisse* (Piacenza, 1569); *Opuscula: In Apocalipsim* (Piacenza, 1570).
[6] *In Apocalipsim*, pp. 624, 647.

Antichrist already appearing, especially in the sinister phenomenon
of Luther and his followers. The great star falling from heaven was
Luther, while other falling stars were Zwingli, Melanchthon, and
the Anabaptists. Again, Luther was the Beast from the land.[1] The
various angels of the Apocalypse were divinely appointed human
agencies—'hic enim per Angelos semper viri intelliguntur angelici et
illustres'[2]—and he envisaged three final orders of preachers.[3] He did
not specifically name the Angelic Pope, but the Angel of Apocalypse 10 descending from the heaven will be 'magnus quidam Dei
servus qui tenebroso eo in tempore mundo apparebit', and will convert the heathen and renew the Church.[4] Like Egidio of Viterbo
and others, he found confirmation that through all the expected
tribulation God's great purpose was working towards the Golden
Age in the discovery of new worlds and especially of America.[5] God's
Word must go forth into the four corners of the earth and now the
fourth has been discovered.[6] It will not be until the final age that all
people will flow into the City of God, but perhaps already the signs
of this appear in the evangelization of new lands: 'Et iam fortasse
caepit in nova predicatione ad novam regionem et insulas, tum ad
Occidentalem plagam, tum et ad Meridionalem . . .' (op. cit., p. 698).
The end is certain, when the Church will enter her state of bliss on
earth, when all the poisons of heresies will vanish and great joy will
be universal.

Finally, we must turn again to Bartholomew Holzhauser, the German commentator on the Apocalypse[7] in the early seventeenth
century. He took his own line in interpreting the seven *status* of the
Church, but none the less belonged to the optimistic school. Holzhauser, like Serafino, placed himself in the fifth *status*—the *status
afflictionis*[8]—and expected the sixth—the *status consolationis*—to be
the Age of Felicity,[9] but the seventh, contrary to the usual pattern,
would be the *status desolationis*, beginning with the birth of Antichrist and running until the *consummatio seculi*.[10] The fifth had begun
with Leo X and Charles V, and its experience had already been one

---

[1] *In Apocalipsim*, pp. 639, 647, 655, 675–6.   [2] Ibid., p. 641.
[3] Ibid., pp. 679–80.   [4] Ibid., p. 661.
[5] Ibid., pp. 664, 698.   [6] Ibid., p. 665.
[7] *Interpretatio in Apocalypsin* (Vienna, 1850).
[8] Ibid., p. 53: '. . . Status afflictionis incipiens a Leone X et Carolo V usque ad
Pontificem Sanctum et Monarcham fortem . . . qui venturus est nostro saeculo et
vocabitur auxilium Dei, h.e. restituens universa.'
[9] Ibid., pp. 69–75, 185–8.   [10] Ibid., pp. 78 seq., 200.

of wars, heresies, and calamities, but it would culminate in the appearance of the 'pontificem sanctum et monarcham fortem' sent by God to restore all things and bring in the Age of Felicity.[1] Holzhauser's view of the *renovatio* was in some respects a very German one. As we have seen,[2] he gave a major place to the last great monarch, whom he actually identifies with the Angel of Apocalypse 10, 'angelum fortem descendentem de coelo amictum nube, et iris in capite eius . . .', applying all the symbols of the description to aspects of his imperial rule. The longing for a strong, universal, and just secular arm must have been very great in Germany on the eve of the Thirty Years War, and Holzhauser's reiteration of all the great monarch would do has a pathetic ring. None the less it was basically an ecclesiastical and orthodox Catholic Age of Gold that he expected, one in which all dissentient heretic voices will be for ever silenced: 'Reducentur enim omnes gentes ad fidei catholicae et orthodoxae unitatem et florebit maxime status clericalis et sacerdotium et homines omni sollicitudine requirent Regnum Dei et justitiam eius' (op. cit., p. 69). This sixth *status* was typified in the creation of Man on the Sixth Day, for the Monarch would have dominion over all the beasts, that is 'super efferas gentes, populos rebelles, respublicas haereticas, et dominabuntur homines passionibus suis malis'.[3] It would be characterized by the sixth spiritual gift—the *Spiritus sapientiae* which would be abundantly poured forth at that time: 'erunt quoque scientiae multiplices et perfectae super terram, et sacra scriptura intelligetur unanimiter sine controversia et errore haeresum, et erunt homines illuminati tam in naturalibus quam in coelestibus scientiis.'[3] Again, the sixth *status* is symbolized by the Church of Philadelphia and the open door promised to her can be interpreted in two senses:

. . . describitur futura huius sexti status felicitas, quae consistit (i) in vero, claro et unanimi sensu Sanctae Scripturae quo sextus Ecclesiae status fugatis et dissipatis tenebris . . . haereticorum . . . clarificabitur . . . *Quod nemo potest claudere*, h.e., quem sensum nemo haereticorum potest pervertere, quia in sexto statu celebrabitur maximum totius mundi concilium generale . . . (ii) Consistit haec felicitas in copiosissimo grege fidelium; confluent enim in tempore illo omnes gentes et populi et nationes ad ovile unum et intrabunt per januam unam quae est sola et vera fides catholica et orthodoxa. . . . *Et erit unus Pastor et unum ovile . . .* (Ibid., pp. 71–2.)

[1] *Supra*, p. 389.　　[2] *Supra*, p. 390.　　[3] *Interpretatio in Apoc.*, p. 70.

For the present the calamities, the depredations of the heretics (*bestia horrenda*), and the pestilences of war must be borne. God in His goodness had always sent consolations and in this age there were four: the Society of Jesus, the work of the Council of Trent, the spread of the Catholic faith through new worlds, and the provision of Catholic emperors such as Ferdinand II.[1] But the real *renovatio* must await the descent of the angel *amictus nube*, the great monarch, and the holy pontiff to come.[2] Then would be accomplished the unity of a Catholic Christendom which was the dream of so many: 'In sexto enim statu erit Ecclesia Catholica sublimis et gloriosa et magnificabitur a mari usque ad mare et non erit controversia aut quaestio amplius quae sit vera Ecclesia' (ibid., p. 75).

[1] *Interpretatio in Apoc.*, p. 185. Note especially the third consolation of the Latin Church: '. . . per novam et copiosam sobolem, qua iam floret et foecunda est America, quantum enim in Europa a fide Catholica discessum, tantum in Indiis, Japonia, China et aliis plurimis insulis et terris, imo plus incrementi vera Catholica fide sumpsit.'

[2] Ibid., pp. 185–8, in which he expounds this figure of the Apocalypse phrase by phrase to prove the exaltation of the Church in the sixth *status*; cf. *supra*, p. 390.

VII

RADICAL VIEWS OF THE
RENOVATIO MUNDI

S IDE by side with Catholic revolutionaries of varying shades
there continued to exist throughout the later Middle Ages more
extreme revolutionaries whom we chiefly know from the condemnations of the Church. In the sixteenth century this type of
protest is swept into one or other of the radical Protestant groups.
With the earlier ones our problem is to distinguish those who spring
from Joachimism from a number of others with certain common
characteristics. Thus we meet records of groups belonging to the
category of Brethren of the Free Spirit who, with their emphasis on
new spiritual illumination by the Holy Spirit, seem to approach
closely to Joachimism. In so far as they may stem from the teaching
of the Amalricians there is still an unsolved problem here, for
Amaury of Bènes apparently taught a doctrine of the three *status* in
history which is remarkably like Joachim's, and we have as yet found
no clear means of determining whether or no there was any relationship between them. But in so far as these later sects display the
general characteristics of pantheism, they can be distinguished from
those of Joachimist origin. The test is whether or not their doctrine
of the Spirit is related to a philosophy of history. For the Joachites
the only ground for claiming or expecting a new state of spiritual
illumination was belief in a Trinitarian pattern of history which was
established by the concords of past history. There was to be a clear
new stage of history, a new regime which applied to all men, not just
to an inner group of *illuminati*. As a consequence they tended to see
the manifestation of the Spirit not so much in terms of individual
enlightenment as of the establishment of a new illumined order in
society. I have applied this test in examining the Radical groups for
signs of Joachimism.

We meet in the Process of a so-called Beghard group in 1381 one
article which suggests that these people looked for a new stage of
history in which a new society would be established: the leader,

474   *Angelic Pope and* Renovatio Mundi

when interrogated, admitted that he believed himself to be a second
Adam, sent with power from God to evangelize the whole world,
and that he would be the beginning of the 'third generation of men'.[1]
In 1411 members of the sect of 'homines intelligentiae' were
examined by Peter d'Ailly.[2] These made a clear affirmation of the
three stages of history and of the new law of the Spirit to be expected:

> 18. Item dicunt tempus veteris legis fuisse tempus Patris et tempus
> novae legis tempus Filii, et pro nunc esse tempus Spiritus Sancti, quod
> dicunt esse tempus Heliae, quo reconciliabuntur scripturae; ut quae prius
> tamquam vera habebantur, jam refutentur, etiam et catholica doctrina . . .
> . . . quod praedicationes et doctrinae antiquorum sanctorum et docto-
> rum cessabunt et supervenient novae et quod scriptura clarius revela-
> bitur quam hucusque notificata sit, et quod Spiritus Sanctus clarius
> illuminabit intellectum humanum quam hucusque fecerit, etiam in
> apostolis, quia non habuerunt nisi corticem, et quod instabit tempus quo
> revelanda erit illa lex Spiritus Sancti et libertatis spiritualis et tunc
> praesens lex cessabit . . . (Fredericq, op. cit., i. 272–4.)

They expected Jews and pagans, even the Devil, to be saved and all
to be ultimately gathered into one fold under one shepherd in one
general salvation. Both these examples belong to the Rhineland and
Netherlands, but in Thomas of Apulia, whose book was condemned
at Paris in 1388, we meet an evangelist of the Age of the Holy
Spirit who may well have been nourished more directly on the
surviving Joachimist doctrine of south Italy.[3] Yet another isolated
piece of evidence shows a connection between Lollardy and Joachimist tenets. Appended to *A Brefe Chronycle concernynge the Examyna-
cyon and death of the blessed martyr of Christ, Syr Johan Oldecastell*
. . . are extracts from *Prophecyes of Joachim Abbas*, translated into

---

[1] H. Haupt, 'Ein Beghardprozess in Eichstädt vom Jahre 1381', *ZKG* v. 487–98,
especially 497.

[2] P. Fredericq, *Corpus Documentorum Inquisitionis Haereticae Pravitatis Neerlandicae*,
i (1889), pp. 269–79; D'Argentré, *Collectio Judiciorum de Novis Erroribus*, i (Paris,
1728), ii. 201–14; Baluze, *Miscellanea*, pp. 288–91.

[3] D'Argentré, op. cit., p. 151: 'Liber vero ab eo scriptus de Ecclesiastici Ordinis
statu, in quo multa continebantur adversus B. Virginem, Ecclesiam et Ecclesiasticos
proceres, multa vero pro haereticis, ut quod mundus non amplius a Patre vel Filio, sed
a Spiritu Sancto regeretur . . .' See also *Chronique du Religieux de S. Denys*, ed. M.
Bellaguet *Collection des documents inédits sur l'histoire de France* (Paris, 1839), i. 574:
'. . . qui se a Spiritu Sancto missum ad confundendum errores et virtutes exaltandum
firmiter asserebat . . . Quemdam nempe librum quem docente Spiritu Sancto ut docebat,
didiscerat et scripserat, ostendebat . . . Mundum eciam non amplius a Deo patre vel
Filio sed a Spiritu Sancto regi debere astruebat usque ad finem ipsius; et cum eius lex
sit simpliciter amoris mortales ecclesiasticis sacramentis dicebat non indigere . . .'

English.[1] Here we find an adaptation of the doctrine of the three
status to the needs of revolutionary heretics:

In the latter dayes shall apere a lawe of lyberte. The Gospell of the
kyngedome of Christ shall be taught, and the church shall be pourged as
wheate is from chaff and tares. More clerelye shall menne than be lerned.
The kyngedome of the fleshe shall be done awaye, and these thynges
shall be fulfylled towarde the ende of the worlde. The holye ghost shall
more perfyghtlye exercyse his domynyon in convertynge peoples by the
preachers of the latter tyme, than by the Apostles. . . . The churche of
Rome shall be destroyed in the thyrde state, as the synagoge of the
Jewes was destroyed in the second state. And a spirituall churche shall
from thens forth succede to the ende of the worlde . . .

These all remain sporadic, isolated outbursts; they do, however,
reveal the power which this Trinitarian doctrine of history continued to exercise.

    Dr. Kestenberg-Gladstein has pointed to Joachimist influences in
Bohemia[2] and an examination of tenets ascribed to the so-called
Picards of Bohemia (i.e. the Taborites) in 1422 reveals again this
association of an outpouring of the Spirit with a programme for the
last age of history.[3] They held that now, in this present year, would
be the *consummatio seculi*, in the sense of the end of this time and the
extermination of all its evil forces: 'post quod erit aliud seculum,
i.e. tempus et evangelium hominum viantium et fulgentium ut sol
ab omni prorsus macula in regno patris supradicto usque ad finem
mundi duraturo . . .'[4] In embryo this 'regnum reparatum hominum
viantium', as it is elsewhere called,[5] already existed in the five cities
of refuge under Taborite control, but there must be a Second
Advent or Resurrection of Christ to inaugurate it fully. This would
occur a long while before the third and final Advent.[6] In this *regnum*
nothing evil would be able to mix with the good and therefore all

---

  [1] *A brefe Chronycle* was collected and published by John Bale in 1544. A note says
that the prophecies are drawn from Guido of Perpignan's *Summa de haeresibus*, written
c. 1342 and this is, in fact, so. It is not quite clear if the linking of Joachim's prophecy to
the Lollard martyr was made by a Lollard or by Bale himself. I am inclined to think the
former. It is striking that the account of Joachim's views written by an enemy should
have been seized on and adapted so successfully to express the Lollard hope in terms of
a new Age of the Spirit.

  [2] Kestenberg-Gladstein, loc. cit. (ref. p. 258 n. 4), pp. 254–6.

  [3] These are printed from a Viennese manuscript by I. v. Döllinger, *Beiträge 2.
Sektengeschichte des Mittelalters*, ii (Munich, 1890), pp. 691–700. See also Kestenberg-
Gladstein, loc. cit., p. 255.

  [4] Döllinger, op. cit., p. 697; see also p. 694.

  [5] Ibid., p. 695.   [6] Ibid., pp. 694–5.

evil towns, castles, dwellings, etc., would be destroyed.[1] The glory of
the *regnum reparatum* would be greater than that of the primitive
Church[2] and the illumination of the Spirit will be poured out upon
this redeemed society:

> . . . quod in regno reparato ecclesiae militantis sol humanae intelligentiae
> non lucebit hominibus, hoc est, quod non docebit unusquisque proximum
> suum, sed omnes erunt docibiles Dei. quod lex Dei scripta in regno
> reparato ecclesiae militantis cessabit et bibliae scriptae destruentur, quia
> lex omnibus superscribetur in cordibus et non opus erit doctore. (Döl-
> linger, op. cit., p. 698.)

Despite this emphasis upon individual illumination, the doctrine of
the Taborites clearly centres upon a new regime within history,
a final stage of the Church Militant herself, neither an extra-historical
paradise nor a private stage of beatitude. In this sense it bears the
marks of Joachimism.

A connection between this Bohemian heresy and certain outbursts
in Germany is likely but not clear. In 1446 Nicholas of Buldersdorf
was condemned at the Council of Basle for views which again reveal
a Joachimist philosophy of history.[3] His expectation, it appears, was
structured both on the seven ages of history and the three Dispensations. He possessed a book the doctrine of which he expounded thus:
the sixth age of the world is passing and the seventh dawning in
which an Angelic Shepherd, the leader of a new order, would bring
men into the Third Dispensation. In this case there was no hesitation on the question of Testaments, for Nicholas declared that there
would certainly be three Testaments—the Old and the New, belonging to Father and Son, and the third, the Eternal Evangel of the
Holy Spirit.

Dr. Kestenberg-Gladstein[4] connects both Nicholas of Buldersdorf and the Wirsberger brothers,[5] who appeared twenty years later in

---

[1] Döllinger, op. cit., p. 695.   [2] Ibid., p. 698.
[3] The chief source for Nicholas of Buldersdorf is the account given of his doctrine by
the *Bassler Chronick*, ed. C. Wurstisen (Basle, 1580), p. 405.
[4] Kestenberg-Gladstein, loc. cit., pp. 256–7.
[5] On Janko and Levin Wirsberger, the chief sources are: N. Glassberger, *Cronica*,
AF ii (Ad Claras Aquas, 1887), pp. 422–6; *Annales Mellicenses, Continuatio, MGHS* ix.
521; L. Hochwart, *Catalogus Episcoporum Ratisponensium*, ed. A. Oefele, *Rerum
Boicarum Scriptores*, i (Augsburg, 1763), p. 223; a letter of Jobst v. Einsiedel, ed.
F. Kurschner, *Archiv f. österreichische Geschichte*, xxxix, Pt. I (1868), pp. 280–2;
the articles of 1467, ed. G. Ritter, 'Zur Geschichte des häretischen Pantheismus in
Deutschland im 15. Jahrhunderts', *ZKG* xliii (1924), pp. 158–9. See also Döllinger,
op. cit., pp. 625–6; O. Schiff, 'Die Wirsberger . . .', *Hist. Vierteljahrsschrift*, xxvi

the diocese of Ratisbon, with the Bohemian group, but in the case
of the Wirsbergers there is a possible alternative source of Joachimist
influence in the Observantine Franciscan convent of Eger, from
a member of which the two leaders claimed to have learnt their
doctrine.¹ On the other hand, they appear also to have had Bohemian
connections, for Livin appealed at one point to George Podiebrad,
and is termed an 'infidel Bohemian'.² Our knowledge of the views
of Janko and Livin Wirsberger is derived chiefly from a letter to the
Bishop of Ratisbon and the articles of deposition before the ecclesiastical convocation of Ratisbon in 1467. They were said to have
many books on their doctrine and to use the Scriptures for their
own purposes. The central point they proclaimed was the immediate advent of one whom they called the 'Unctus Salvatoris', who
was mysteriously born of the 'Mulier amicta sole' of Apocalypse
12: 1.³

His advent would mark the obliteration of the whole present state
of the Church and the immediate passage to the third *status*, for he
would introduce the 'tertium et finale testamentum' and would be
'ille pastor de quo Christus dicit quod erit unus pastor et unum
ovile, per quem omnes in eum credentes debent illuminari speciali
et interiori luce etiam ad cognoscendam sanctam Trinitatem'.⁴ Here
we meet a clear conjunction of the mystical, inner-light theme and
the idea of a last great age in history, for the Wirsbergers declared
that the 'Unctus Salvatoris' would be followed by all peoples and rule
over the whole world *'sicut Caesar imperator et Deus'*.⁵ They pushed
their interpretation of the Scriptures so far as to claim that its great
promises applied far more to the 'Unctus Salvatoris' *spiritualiter* than
they did to Christ *corporaliter*.⁶ Like Christ the new saviour had his
precursor, called *Iohannes de Oriente*, whom the authorities assumed
to be Janko himself.⁷

The two brothers and their sect disappeared quickly enough, in
spite of their claim that an irresistible multitude in Germany would
rise in their support. But the outburst of argument over Joachim's
third *status* at Erfurt in 1466 must surely be connected with the

(1931), pp. 776–86; H. Haupt, 'Zur Geschichte des Ioachimismus', *ZKG* vii (1885),
pp. 423–5.
¹ Glassberger, p. 425; *Annales Mellicenses*, p. 521.   ² Schiff, p. 781.
³ Glassberger, p. 423; *ZKG* xliii. 158; Döllinger, p. 625.
⁴ Glassberger, p. 423; Döllinger, p. 625.
⁵ Glassberger, p. 423.
⁶ Ibid., p. 424; *ZKG* xliii. 158.   ⁷ Glassberger, p. 425; Döllinger, p. 625.

Wirsberger infection. The pernicious doctrine was traced to its Joachimist source and, as we have seen,[1] the Augustinian John Dorsten was moved to expound in public his *quaestio*: 'Utrum tertius mundi status quem Joachim abbas ymaginatur et hereticorum conventiculum minatur Catholice venturus astruatur postquam annus dom. millesimus CCCCLXXI compleatur.' Although Dorsten does not here mention the Wirsbergers by name, the introduction to the text makes it clear that this was no academic discussion, but an urgent problem raised by a sudden wave of religious excitement[2] which called for the firmest possible intellectual guidance to prevent people from going off the rails. The anxiety with which the proposition of the third *status* was debated shows how tempting it could be and therefore how menacing. As already suggested, it would seem from the way he handled the issue that Dorsten himself was sufficiently attracted to this doctrine to be extremely sensitive to its danger. Having expounded Joachim's own views carefully and refuted the doctrine of the third *status*, he dealt with the tenets of 'quidam scandalosi heretici' who had resurrected this dangerous matter.[3] Here it was the social and political consequences that concerned him more than the religious heresy: he understood well that Joachim's third *status*, adopted by the poor and outcast, spelt revolution. The concept of a final era as expected by these heretics meant the fall of the Church with the fall of the second *status*, and this Dorsten branded as the work of the Devil. Here the Angelic Pope of Catholic hopes was suddenly seen in a ruder form when, as the 'Unctus Salvatoris', he was expected to overthrow the existing order absolutely and bring in the third *status de novo*. That people in Erfurt did not cease to play with fire after Dorsten's magisterial attempt to stamp it out is shown by another *quaestio*, twenty years later, held at the request of many monks and laymen, concerning the problems of the last age, which were in this case specifically linked with the teaching of the Wirsbergers.[4] The clue to these sporadic

---

[1] *Supra*, pp. 258-9.

[2] Kestenberg-Gladstein, loc. cit., p. 267: 'Quia diebus istis videlicet circa annum domini MCCCCLXV quidam periculosi ac venenosi de latebris suis exeuntes heretici erroris sui multipliciter virus in ecclesiam Dei nequiter evomentes, inter cetera sue delirationis commenta tertium quendam statum, novum testamentum removentes, et destructionem confixerant quem ante annum domini MCCCCLXXI asserunt venturum . . .'   [3] Ibid., pp. 274 seq.

[4] Ibid., p. 264. Dr. Kestenberg-Gladstein suggests that marginal notes to MS. Giessen 696 which she used show a continuing interest in the Joachimist ideas themselves.

outbursts of revolutionary Joachimism in Bohemia and Germany
lies surely in social conditions. As Norman Cohn[1] has demonstrated
fully, the coming Age of the Spirit meant for these groups the life
from which they were excluded in the present.

Out of quite a different background and development another
type of revolutionary Joachimism comes to life in the final phase of
Postel's extraordinary career. As we have seen,[2] he tried to make
existing institutions do the work of revolution and pinned his faith
both on the Jesuit Order and on the French monarchy. When these
failed him, he gradually drifted into a mystical state in which the
key to the future age came to rest in his own hands. This phase is
bound up with his experiences in Venice, where he met a mysterious
woman, the 'Mater Mundi' or 'new Eve', and where he also appears
to have been fascinated by the so-called mosaics of the Abbot
Joachim and by the representation of a woman's head which he
called the 'Vièrge vénitienne' and attributed to Joachim.[3] These
influences, together with the prophecies of Amadeus and Galatinus,[4] led him to focus attention increasingly on the mystical *Papa
Angelicus* as the instrument of the revolution he expected. Finally,
about 1551 he had a vision, through the medium of the Venetian
Virgin, that he was himself the great instrument of the future, that
he had been reborn as the *Shekinah*, the Holy Spirit. As the first-
born of the new age, it would be his mission to bring in the *renovatio
mundi* and he saw himself even as a 'lower Messiah'. Postel's conception of two Messiahs corresponds to his theory of the double structure
of the world on masculine and feminine principles. Christ Himself
was the higher Messiah to save the realm of the intelligence, but
Postel would be concerned with the lower realm, the feminine sphere.[5]

The period following his great vision was full of frenzied activity,
publishing books and broadsides, appealing to influential people all
over Europe, preaching and travelling incessantly. His plans fluc-
tuated as he turned in different directions for allies—back to the
King of France at times, to the Emperor Ferdinand, and even to the
extreme left-wing Protestants.[6] He never appealed to the papacy to

[1] Cohn, op. cit. (ref. p. 295 n. 1), pp. 217 seq.
[2] *Supra*, pp. 287–8, 381–2.
[3] Bouwsma, *Concordia Mundi*, pp. 15–17; Secret, *Studi francesi* I, pp. 381–3, 393
(quotation from Postel's *Thrésor ou Receuil des Prophécies*).
[4] Bouwsma, *Concordia Mundi*, pp. 17, 153, 161–3.   [5] Ibid., p. 163.
[6] R. Bainton, 'Wylliam Postell and the Netherlands', *Nederlandisch Archief voor
Kirkgeschiedenis*, N.S. xxiv (1931), pp. 161–7. The Joris papers at Basle show frequent

carry out his programme and at times almost identified it with Antichrist. Yet Postel was essentially a Catholic revolutionary. He was horrified to find himself linked with Joris.[1] His constant dream was the ecumenical one of a universal Christian order and authority which would embrace all religions. There must, however, be a revolution of which the instruments—besides himself—would be the great monarch and people and a General Church Council, and he believed it to be Christ's will that the Pope of the reformation should transfer his seat to Jerusalem.[2] His two most passionate concerns are expressed in his two key phrases: *Concordia Mundi* and *Restitutio omnium*: to bring all peoples of all faiths into one fold and to restore the whole creation to its pristine glory. The two points are brought together in his manifesto to the Emperor Ferdinand in 1560:

Led by the *mater mundi* who is right reason, I have proposed a method by which the Christian Republic may be preserved uninjured and undisturbed. This is to be accomplished by a universal empire which will enable the teachings of the Christian religion, confirmed by right reason, to be set forth. In this way Christ will be seen to restore as much as Satan has destroyed and it will be as though Adam had never sinned. (Translated by Bouwsma, *Concordia Mundi*, pp. 115–16.)

To accomplish this there must be a tremendous world-wide missionary effort, involving attempts to rationalize the Christian faith as well as the study of many languages. Alongside this, however, there must be a great campaign of arms to bring the whole world under one sway.[3] His concept of world unity goes far deeper than the common dream. Its final structure is envisaged by Postel as a division into twelve sees, the rulers of which will be responsible to a trinity of sovereign pope, sovereign king, and sovereign judge. It embraces religious unity in one synthesized world religion, social unity through the abolition of private property, and cultural unity as expressed in the abolition of separate languages.[4]

Postel's eschatological dream of the *concordia mundi* embodies in the most extreme form the view of history in which the greatest

---

references to Postel, including extracts copied from his works. Postel's works circulated in Anabaptist circles under the name of Elias Pandochius. See also Bouwsma, *Concordia Mundi*, pp. 19–20, 276.

[1] Bainton, loc. cit., p. 161.
[2] Bouwsma, *Concordia Mundi*, pp. 177–81, 277 seq.
[3] Ibid., pp. 231–40, 273–4.   [4] Ibid., pp. 277–80.

pessimism and the greatest optimism are juxtaposed. He believed
that the whole pattern of history had been gradually building up to
this final climax in his own age. In some respects he saw his own
world as in greater darkness than ever before since Christ came.
Yet, as with all the Joachites, his age also displayed the most
miraculous signs of the new dawn. In the passage quoted in Part III
of this book[1] he expatiated on four of these: the new progress in
learning, the new geographical discoveries, the invention of artillery,
and the invention of printing. At last the instruments and conditions
were to hand which would enable every man on earth to understand
the truth of God for himself. So the conversion of the whole human
race would carry the drama of history to its climax and restore the
original order of all creation: 'in ea fiat ex toto orbe terrarum unum
ovile et unus pastor.'[2] In one sense, of course, the climax is to be
a great *restitutio*, for everything that Satan has destroyed will be
renewed and resurrected, yet Postel's pattern of history is not really
cyclical, for the whole of history is leading forward to its great
climax in the Sabbath Age. In seeking to place this fantastic dreamer
within his contemporary setting, the facts which must not be forgotten are that Guillaume Postel had been a professor in the University of Paris, that he was listened to at times both by the King of
France and the Emperor Ferdinand, and that his books were
bought and read by many anxious men who thought that the signs
of the times demanded such an interpretation.

The compound of humanist expectation, evangelical regeneration,
and Joachimist philosophy of history produced some unusual revolutionaries among Italians of the mid-sixteenth century. As Cantimori
has shown in his study of them,[3] they form a group with many inter-
connections and many contacts with Protestants, especially in Basle
and Geneva. The rediscovery of the truth of regeneration in Christ
could lead simply to an individualistic evangelical fervour that in
itself had few revolutionary implications for society. It was when the
belief in the 'new man' was married to the expectation of a new era in
history that far-reaching consequences followed. Among those who
visited Basle was the humanist Curione, who combined in his view
of history great pessimism about the present position of man with
great optimism concerning the future Christian perfection to be

---

[1] *Supra*, p. 384.
[2] Bouwsma, *Concordia Mundi*, p. 79.
[3] D. Cantimori, *Eretici* (see Select Bibliography).

attained.[1] We are, he contended, still held captive in Babylon but liberation is at hand. In a discussion with Mainardi he put forward the view that there would be an intermediate Coming of Christ on earth between the first and the final Advent.[2] This is developed in his *De Amplitudine Beati Regni Dei*. The 'middle Advent' would be the reform and renovation of the Church prophesied by Cyril and Joachim.[3] Curione believed he could see it already dawning in his present time. It would bring all people into one religion, including those of the newly-discovered Americas, and would be marked especially by the conversion of the Jews. Above all it was to be recognized in the beginning of the diffusion of light upon earth after the darkness, and thus he called it the 'adventus . . . divinae claritatis et lucis'.[4] For Curione 'light' meant a mixture of humanist understanding and evangelical truth. As it took God six days to make the world, it had taken six thousand years to perfect true religion, but the dawn of the seventh age was inevitable. Man was the crown of the Creation on the Sixth Day and it was the *verus homo*, i.e. the *sanctus populus*, whose emergence would crown the sixth age and make the seventh.[5] It was the humanist's dream of the perfect man which Curione placed within the old medieval framework of history. In the end optimism wholly triumphs over pessimism; Christ had asked 'When the Son of Man shall come, shall he find virtue upon earth?', but this doubt cannot possibly apply to the Last Age in which 'praedicato per totum terrarum orbem Evangelio, infinita erit credentium multitudo'.[6] It is certain that Christ will come in judgement, but with equal certainty Curione asserts: 'sed ventura prius aurea secula, in quibus omnes gentes et nationes, in unam sint coagmentandae religionem, atque altissima in terris pace, quieteque fruiturae.'[7]

At Basle Curione met and talked with both David Joris and the Savoyard humanist and Biblical scholar, Sebastian Castellione. Cantimori regards it as typical of the atmosphere in which these men thought that Castellione translated the *oracula sibyllina* into Latin and commented on a number of prophecies. In his preface to his translation of the Bible he avers that the Age of Gold announced in the Scriptures has not yet come and must be awaited with expecta-

[1] Cantimori, *Eretici*, pp. 88 seq.　　　[2] Ibid., pp. 187-9.
[3] Coelius Secundus Curio, *De Amplitudine Beati Regni Dei Dialogi sive Libri Duo* (no pl. of pub., 1554), pp. 42-61 (reference to Joachim, p. 52).
[4] Ibid., p. 42.　　　[5] Ibid., pp. 63-70.
[6] Ibid., p. 46.　　　[7] Ibid., p. 60.

tion.[1] Another member of the Basle group was the Sienese Bernardino Ochino, once General of the Observantine Franciscans, later of the Capuchins, but finally a preacher in exile in Augsburg, England, Basle, and Zurich.[2] He too was profoundly interested in a doctrine of history and Cantimori finds an echo of Joachimism in his division of history into three periods: natural law to Moses; written law to Christ; law of the Spirit or Grace under Christ.[3] He did not—it will be noticed—follow a Trinitarian pattern, but, in fact, like Curione, put the emphasis not so much on the Incarnation for the inauguration of the third stage as on the spiritual manifestation of Christ about to dawn now, when the evangelical faith would be diffused throughout the whole world and all men would live in Christian liberty under the law of love. It has been noticed that the catalogue of his original Sienese convent lists two copies of Joachim's *Liber Concordie*, three works of Petrus Joannis Olivi, and one of Ubertino da Casale. Thus Spiritual Franciscan influences may have been his starting-point.[4]

A generation later humanist and Joachimist hopes were renewed in the Florentine Francesco Pucci, born *c.* 1540 and influenced by the works of Meleto and Curione.[5] Astrological speculations gathered round the comet of 1577 and Pucci saw in this a portent of approaching crisis, as also in sinister circumstances attending the election of Sixtus V. His vision of the future started at a humanist level with an emphasis on education and on the expected intellectual and moral regeneration of Christendom, which was to be achieved through education, since he believed in the perfectibility of man. His ideas, however, became more apocalyptic. From Curione he took the idea of an intermediate coming of Christ to renew Christendom, convert all pagan peoples, and establish the reign of peace and felicity. He plunged into the interpretation of Scriptural prophecy, especially the Apocalypse, of natural revelation, and of pagan prophecies. Although he never repudiated the authority of the papacy, Pucci found that judgement upon the sins of the Roman Curia had long since been pronounced in the prophecies of Joachim and Bridget. He expected a General Church Council, illumined by revelation and

[1] Cantimori, *Eretici*, pp. 115–19.

[2] On Ochino see Cantimori, *Eretici*, pp. 120–6, 255–6; K. Benrath, *Bernardino Ochino of Siena*, trans. H. Zimmern (London, 1876); R. Bainton, *Bernardino Ochino* (Florence, 1940).

[3] Cantimori, *Eretici*, p. 121.   [4] Bainton, op. cit., p. 14 n. 2.

[5] Cantimori, *Eretici*, pp. 380–6.

reason, to bring in the Age of Reform and establish a perfect society which would cure all political ills in Christian love and unity. In this the Roman Curia would be abolished. His two final institutions remain very much in the Joachimist tradition: 'uno nuovo ordine' and 'uno supremo pastore'.[1]

In these circles there was much thought on the doctrine of the Trinity. It was perhaps through their reaction against scholastic treatments of the subject that some of these thinkers first met Joachim as the antagonist of Peter Lombard. In their break-away from an over-intellectualized dogma and search for a more imaginative vision of the work of the Holy Spirit in history, some recognized Joachim as a prophet of this new thought. Thus, when Biandrata traced the history of the dogma of the Trinity[2] he hailed Joachim as the first to react against the obscurantism of the theologians, especially Peter Lombard:

Post decreta illa tyrannica Longobardi, sancti et eruditi homines magis ac magis reclamare, et sese huic quoque Sophisticae doctrinae opponere coeperant. Inter ceteros primus fuit qui in Longobardum surrexit Ioachymus Abbas sui temporis Propheta insignis, et qui de futura Romanae Ecclesiae (quam nunc videmus) vastatione ad unguem vaticinatus est. Is in concilio sub Gregorio Nono coacto, palam Quaternitatis Longobardum convicit, et libellum de eadem egregium nobis reliquit, quem Papa tum primum prohibuit, cum Ioachymum Senis relegasset damnatum. Vide de summa Trinitate, et fide Catholica, capite Damnamus. Hic in Apocalypsim scribens, de tempore (quo isthaec Quaternitas palam mundo fieri deberet) prophetavit dicens: *cum missantium turba cessabit, quaternitas detegetur.* (Op. cit., p. 107.)

The vision which traced the Spirit at work bringing history to its fruition was just what these reformers sought and found in Joachim. The outstanding example here is that of Servetus. He twice referred to Joachim in his polemic against metaphysical views of the Trinity,[3] but it was in his whole philosophy of history, in his conception of

---

[1] Cantimori, *Eretici*, pp. 381–2. See also F. Pucci, *Omnibus veritatis studiosis divinam lucem charitatemque precatur*, ed. D. Cantimori and E. Feist, *Per la storia degli eretici italiani del secolo XVI in Europa* (*R. Accad. d'Italia. Studi e documenti* 7, Rome, 1937), p. 155: 'In qua sententia me confirmant multa oracula, per Prophetas et Apostolos edita, quae nil magis spectant, quam renovationem rerum adventante Domino futuram, et felicissimum illum Ecclesiae Dei statum . . .'

[2] Biandrata, *De Falsa et Vera Unius Dei Patris Filii et Spiritus Sancti Cognitione Libri Duo*, ed. Cantimori and Feist, op. cit., pp. 104 seq.

[3] R. Bainton, *Michel Servet* (Geneva, 1953), pp. 18 seq., referring to (i) De Trinitatis Erroribus, pp. 33*a*, 39*a*; (ii) *Christianismi Restitutio*, pp. 39, 40.

divinity as a continuing activity working in the process of history, that he came closest to Joachimist thought: 'L'eco della concezione gioachimita della storia della cristianità si unisce alla passione riformatrice per affrontare il pensiero scolastico . . .'¹ The reign of Christ, begun in the new liberty of evangelical truth, was indeed the Third Dispensation of history, the Age of the Spirit, the humanist Age of Gold, and to this vision the Joachimist conception gave a more substantial and universal framework than the inner conviction of new life could supply.

The framework of history is very evident in parts of Servetus's *Christianismi Restitutio*.² He works out close concords between the Old and New Dispensations in a pattern of twos,³ he interprets the Dragon's seven heads as seven persecuting monarchies,⁴ he sees the number-symbolism of the six Seals and the seventh as the six ages of labour and tribulation and the seventh Sabbath of rest.⁵ But it is in his understanding of the significance of threes in history that Servetus finds his real vision of history.⁶ There is a threefold presence of Christ in history—'ante incarnationem in umbra', 'per incarnationem in corporis infirmitate', 'post resurrectionem in gloria et potentia'⁷—and this is an analogue of all the world's mysteries. He then develops a series of sequences of three: three manifestations of the lamenting Rachel, three appearances of Elijah, three rulers of this world who oppose Christ (Absalom, Caiaphas, the papacy), three deaths and burials of the Lord, three callings of the Son of God from Egypt. Each time the sequence is *sub umbra, corporaliter,* and *spiritualiter*. Threefold is the voice of one crying in the wilderness: first in the time of Cyrus; second in John the Baptist; 'tertia erit nunc vox liberatorum ab horribili et vasta hac Babylonis et Antichristi captivitate, ut nulla deserti vastitas impedire possit, quo minus viae nostrae dirigantur, et Papistici illi montes, ac Babylonici colles humilientur.'⁸ Finally, Servetus reaches his climax in the threefold *missio* of the Holy Spirit, symbolized in the threefold sending of the dove by Noah from the Ark. First the Spirit was sent forth at the Creation and secondly at Pentecost, but even at the second time it found no permanent resting-place, returning to heaven, the ark.

¹ Cantimori, *Eretici*, p. 45.
² *Christianismi Restitutio* (no pl. of pub., actually Vienne-en-Dauphiné, 1553).
³ Ibid., pp. 399–401.   ⁴ Ibid., p. 404.
⁵ Ibid., p. 408.   ⁶ Ibid., pp. 457–62.
⁷ Ibid., p. 457.   ⁸ Ibid., p. 460.

Tertio nunc repetito post Christum novae hebdomadae mysterio, denuo mittitur columba, et spiritus paracletus, qui nobiscum perpetuo manebit, et nos docebit omnia. Prima fuit missio spiritus in umbra. Secunda fuit corporalis missio, quando corporaliter visi sunt aperiri caeli et corporali specie descendere spiritus sanctus. Tertia erit nunc spiritualis et interna missio admodum necessaria. Necessarium est Christum denuo regnum assumere . . . Necessaria est per Paracletum nova consolatio, post novam desolationem. Post Antichristi glorificationem necessaria est nova Christi glorificatio. (Op. cit., pp. 460–1.)

Thus Servetus combined a Christocentric evangelicalism with a doctrine of the Spirit working in history. It was the intensity of the new life in Christ and the promise of release from the forces of Antichrist (usually identified by him with Rome) which made him affirm that Christ must come anew in a third Dispensation. Joachim's principle that the greatest Antichrist must be fought and overcome before the Age of the Spirit began exactly fitted the hopes of these sixteenth-century reformers, who saw Antichrist embodied in the Roman Curia, or in the whole Roman Church, and expected that it would shortly be beaten down. In some calculations, based like Joachim's on the 1260 days, Servetus brought the crucial period to 1565 or 1585.[1] He would not specify too closely, but believed that the days were near when the reign of Antichrist would end and the new reign of Christ in the Spirit be inaugurated.

The line of demarcation between Catholic and Protestant revolutionaries at this time was not as clear-cut as might be supposed. At one point Postel turned to the Protestant leaders Melanchthon and Bullinger as possible supporters and his works were disseminated among Anabaptists.[2] He corresponded with one of their leaders, probably Caspar Schwenckfeld, about the approaching *restitutio*.[3] When accused of a connection with David Joris, Postel repudiated this, but the Joris papers at Basle contain extracts from Postel's writings and letters which suggest that they were in touch with one another at one time.[4] Again, the Italian Curione frequented Joris's preachings when he was in Basle. The common ground was the expectation of the new age, and thus it is among some of the more radical Protestant groups that we shall find our last traces of Joachim's philosophy of history. But among more conservative Reformation leaders the Abbot Joachim had another use which must first claim our attention

[1] Bainton, op. cit., p. 86.
[2] See *supra*, p. 479 n. 6.
[3] Bouwsma, *Concordia Mundi*, p. 20.
[4] Reference, p. 479 n. 6.

briefly. They were interested in any ammunition from history which could be used against the Roman Church and therefore turned to Joachim and his disciples as prophetic voices denouncing the sins of Babylon. In particular they fastened eagerly on Joachim's famous but misleading statement that Antichrist was already born in Rome.[1] On the other hand, they also found the infamous scandal of the Eternal Evangel very much to their liking as a shocking episode.[2] In the great collections of historical material made to support the Reformation position by Mathias Flacius Illyricus and by Johann Wolf, Joachites find a prominent place. Flacius picks out various supposed prophecies of Joachim which are damaging to the papacy, emphasizing, in his account of Joachim,[3] both his harsh judgements on the papacy and also his expectation of reformation which has now been fulfilled: 'In alio quodam libello predicit etiam fore, ut Christus Ecclesiam suam repurget: et ratio reformationis praesentium temporum rebus pulchre consonat.' Besides the *Vaticinia de summis pontificibus*, he also knows and quotes from the *Super Hieremiam*, choosing not only a passage against the worldliness of the Latin Church, but also one on the new liberty of the last age:[4] '. . . tempus aestimat esse periculosum futurum ab A.D. 1200 usque ad ultimos dies, in quibus apparebit (inquit) lex libertatis: evangelium regni Christi tunc predicabitur, et Ecclesia purgabitur, ut a palea et zizaniis triticum' (op. cit., p. 681). From Foxe he gathers Howden's story of the meeting at Messina, quoting Joachim's exposition of the seven heads as well as the statement on Antichrist 'quod is iam in urbe Roma prognatus esset'. Among Joachites Flacius includes Jean de Roquetaillade,[5] Arnold of Villanova,[6] the heresiarchs Segarelli and Dolcino,[7] and Petrus Joannis Olivi.[8] He also mentions some verses associated with Joachim's name and Osiander's edition of the *Vaticinia*.[9] Flacius had certainly seen the application of Joachim's third *status* to the Reformation, but he was only mildly interested in it; his use of Joachimism is, in the main, negative.

Johannes Wolf's mighty collection includes a large amount of

[1] *Supra*, p. 7.   [2] *Supra*, pp. 108–9.

[3] *Catalogus Testium Veritatis qui ante nostram aetatem Pontifici Romano atque Papismi erroribus reclamarunt* (Lyon, 1597), ii. 680–1. (The account of Joachim is slightly fuller in this enlarged edition than in that of Basle, 1566.)

[4] The passage against the Latin Church is the oft-quoted 'Est et alia ficus . . .'; cf. *Super Hier.*, f. 3^{r-v}.

[5] *Catalogus*, ii. 788–91.   [6] Ibid., pp. 667–8.

[7] Ibid., p. 770.   [8] Ibid., p. 775.

[9] Ibid., pp. 135, 136, 675.

material from Joachimist sources of one kind or another.[1] From
Joachim himself he takes an interesting set of extracts from the
Liber Concordie[2] emphasizing the pre-eminence of the Holy Spirit,
the sins of prelates, the meaning of the Babylonish Woman, and the
defections of the fourth order in the Church, the hermits and virgins.
Of pseudo-Joachimist works he quotes the *Super Hieremiam*,[3] *Super
Esaiam*,[4] and *Liber de Flore*.[5] He also reproduces the whole thirty of
the *Vaticinia*, with a survey of the various editions and annotations
on them.[6] The life of Joachim by G. Barrio is included, the usual
reference to Antichrist from Howden, and a long list of references to
those who have praised Joachim.[7] Besides all this, scattered throughout his volumes, there are numerous references to Joachites such as
Arnold of Villanova, Ubertino da Casale, Olivi, and Roquetaillade,
as well as various Joachimist verses and oracles.[8] There are long
extracts from Telesphorus's *libellus* which he must have known
in Meuccio's edition, for he fastens eagerly on the picture of the
Papa Angelicus in the habit of an Augustinian hermit, applying it to
Luther himself: 'Quidam arcanorum periti viri hoc de Luthero
intelligendum esse putant.'[9] A great deal of his material is negative:
he can cite thirty authorities to prove that the Roman Church equals
Babylon, of whom Joachim is the nineteenth.[10] But towards the end
of his long work he begins to put together a potpourri of prophecies
from Bridget, Telesphorus, Rusticianus, and others, which go
beyond the programme of schism and tyrant to the *renovatio mundi*
under the Angelic Pope.[11]

We have an interesting example of an English theologian who
actually read Joachim's *Expositio* for himself in William Perkins,
whose *Idolatrie of the last times* appeared in a 1605 edition of his

[1] For full reference, see Select Bibliography.
[2] Wolf, *Lect. mem.* i. 489–91; ii. 891. I have identified passages corresponding to *Lib. Conc.*, ff. 27ʳ, 27ᵛ, 41ʳ, 41ᵛ, 66ᵛ, but these are not taken from the printed edition.
[3] *Lect. mem.* i. 491; ii. 839, 843.   [4] Ibid. i. 488.   [5] Ibid. i. 490.
[6] Ibid. i. 443–87, especially the annotations of Regiselmo, Paracelsus, and Adrasder.
[7] Ibid. i. 497–502.
[8] Ibid. i. 443, 602, 623 seq., 662–9, 721–2, 728, 748; ii. 104–11, 886–95.
[9] Ibid. i. 668–9. See pp. 662–9, where the whole section is drawn from Telesphorus's *libellus* with pictures. The use of the 1516 edition is also indicated by his quotation from John of Paris's *De Antichristo*, followed by the prophecy found at Mestri exactly as in the printed edition (i. 602).
[10] Ibid. ii. 839 seq., Joachim, p. 842.
[11] Ibid. ii. 889 seq., ending with contemporary prophets such as Nostradamus. Wolf's collection of prophecies is so extensive that it forms a major source for the study of this type of material. It is worth listing the chief prophets whom he cites (not to

writings.[1] Perkins used Joachim in the entirely negative sense of fastening on his interpretations of Babylon and its members. He was not at all interested in a doctrine of the third *status* or the revolutionary nature of the new era. It is, however, worth setting his quotations from the *Expositio* beside the original text to show how easily a sixteenth-century Protestant could pick out what he wanted from Joachim's writings:

Abbat Ioachim in his commentarie upon the Revelation hath these words: Some that carry a shew of the seat of God, that is, the Catholike Church, are made the seat of the beast, which is the kingdome of Antichrist, raigning everywhere in his members, from the beginning of the Church. Againe, We have, by Tradition from our fathers, that Rome is spiritually Babylon. Againe, the Marchants of the earth are Priests themselves who sell prayers and Masses for pence [*note*: pro denariis], making the house of prayer a place of marchandise. Againe, We know that not onely Bishops and Priests are intangled in the affaires of Babylon that they may grow rich: but also some Abbats, Monkes and religious persons or rather which seeme to be so and are not. (Op. cit., p. 841.)

. . . et tamen nonnulli sub specie eiusdem sedis Dei facti sunt sedes bestie que est regnum antichristi regnantis ubique a principio ecclesie in membris suis . . . (*Expos.*, f. 189ᵛ.)

. . . et ex presenti loco traditum est nobis a patribus quod Roma sit in spiritu Babylon . . . (Ibid., f. 198ʳ.)

Negotiatores terre qui sicut superius dictum est. Ipsi sunt sacerdotes bruti qui nesciunt que Dei sunt: sacerdotes animales qui dati sunt in atrium exterius . . . qui vendunt orationes et missas pro denariis facientes domum orationis apothecam negotiationis. (Ibid., f. 200ᵛ.)

Scimus autem quod non solum nonulli episcopi et sacerdotes implicantur negotiis babylonis ut divites fiant: verumetiam nonnulli abbates et monachi et alii atque alii religiosi: immo non qui sint, sed qui esse videntur. (Ibid., f. 202ʳ.)

mention a large number of anonymous oracles and verses): Hildegarde, Joachim, John of Paris, Arnold of Villanova, Ubertino da Casale, Petrus Joannis Olivi, Rabanus, Dante, Occam, Nicholas of Lyra, Jean de Roquetaillade, Telesphorus of Cosenza, Petrarch, Bridget, Catherine of Siena, Mathias of Cracow, Gamaleon, Mechthilde, Rusticianus, Reinhard, Vincent Ferrer, Jacobus de Paradiso, Nicholas de Clémanges, Nicholas of Cusa, John Capistranus, Alofresant, Adrasder, Paracelsus, Regiselmo, P. Scaliger, Maternus Hatten of Spires, Kaiser Sigmund, Lichtenberger, Ioannes Carion, Lorenzo Miniati, Torquatus, Purstinger, Johannes Baptista of Siena, Grunpeck, Theodorus Graminaeus, S. Severus, S. Cataldus, Nostradamus, Iacobus Procardus, Ioannes Rasch, Ioannes Rosinus. The list might almost form an index to this book.

[1] William Perkins, *Works* (Cambridge, 1605). I owe this reference to Dr. Conrad Russell.

Thus among conservative Protestants Joachim was more often used as a prophet denouncing Babylon than as the proclaimer of a *renovatio mundi*. It is true that Luther was identified as the *Papa Angelicus* portrayed in Meuccio's edition of Telesphorus and also as the monk with the rose in the *Vaticinia*, originally the portrait of Celestine V. We have seen[1] that Luther himself interpreted one of the old prophecies of the 'good' Third Frederick as foretelling the work of Frederick of Saxony in rescuing Scriptural truth from the sepulchre where the false papalists had buried it. This application of Luther's was later picked up by J. Wolf[2] and by Cornelius Crull in an oration of 1630, *de heroica constantia Elect. Sax. in religione Evangelica*.[3] Wolf himself was interested enough to collect prophecies of *renovatio*. But these stray applications are all that one finds in the main Reformed traditions. Both Luther and Melanchthon in their correspondence commented on the identification with the portrait in the *Vaticinia*,[4] but neither appears to have taken the idea of Luther as the *Papa Angelicus* of prophecy at all seriously. The forms and symbols of the Joachimist *renovatio mundi* did not express the objectives of the conservative reformers.

The real Joachites among the Protestants were those who felt that they must interpret their new religious experience in terms of a new era of history, for the Joachimist philosophy of history still had power to influence religious revolutionaries. Thomas Müntzer openly acknowledged his debt to Joachim through the *Super Hieremiam* which he had studied: 'Bei mir ist das Zeugnis Abbatis Joachim gross. Ich hab ihn allein über Jeremiam gelesen.'[5] Müntzer believed that in the third stage of enlightenment the elect would come into possession of the key of David to unlock the Book with Seven Seals, and that he himself had been chosen to bring in this new age of

---

[1] *Supra*, pp. 372–3.   [2] Wolf, *Lect. mem.* ii. 114.

[3] Quoted by J. Praetorius, *Alectryomantia seu Divinatio Magica* (Frankfurt and Leipzig, 1680), p. 70.

[4] E. Enders, *Dr. Martin Luthers Briefwechsel*, vi. 43, 52; *Corpus Reformatorum*, ed. C. Bretschneider, i (Letters of Melanchthon), p. 565. On the other hand, we must notice that Luther was interested enough in prophecy and astrology to publish an edition of Lichtenberger's *Prognosticatio* with his own preface and Melanchthon believed that 1484 (the year of the great constellation supposed to herald a great reformer) must have been the year of Luther's birth, though it was in fact 1483 (see Kurze, op. cit. [ref. p. 347 n. 1], pp. 71–2). Luther also developed an eschatological view of the Turkish struggle, but does not seem to have linked it with a concept of a golden age within history; see H. Buchanan, 'Luther and the Turks', *Archiv f. Reformationsgeschichte*, xlvii (1956), pp. 157–8.

[5] Quoted G. Williams, *The Radical Reformation* (Philadelphia, 1962), p. 51.

spiritual understanding. In his Prague manifesto he put forth a programme for the new Church of the Spirit in which the elect would be
directly instructed by a sevenfold outpouring of the Spirit, superseding all previous religious authority.[1]

With variations of emphasis and patterns of history this expectation is common to a whole group of radical reformers who—as
distinct from those with quietist tendencies—affirmed the new era
to be a definite and wholly new era of history. They believed themselves to be witnessing its inauguration and to be called as the active
agents of its inevitable triumph. The consequence of this view
of history was a shift of focus from the historical Christ. In G.
Williams's words: 'With the overriding conviction that they were
living at the opening of a new age, the Radical Reformers began to
alter their conception of the redemptive role of Christ.' Thus, he
says, 'the Trinitarian scheme of Joachim of Flora was especially
pervasive' among Reformation eschatologies.[2]

Melchior Hofmann[3] was one who developed the threefold pattern
in terms of Church History: (i) apostolic times to the reign of the
popes, (ii) the period of the unlimited power of the popes, (iii) the
period of the Spirit, already prepared by Hus and now beginning, in
which the papacy would be deprived of all power and the Letter
transformed into the Spirit. Hofmann used concordances between
the Old and New Testaments in a Joachimist way. He saw himself
and his followers as the Israelites sent into the wilderness in the Old
Testament and as the Woman clothed with the Sun in the Apocalypse fleeing, as the bride of Christ, into the wilderness.[4] Hofmann
fastened particularly on the role of the two witnesses in the Apocalypse and more and more came to think of himself as either Elijah
or Enoch in the final age. As Rome was the spiritual Babylon, so
he expected Strasbourg to be the spiritual Jerusalem from which
144,000 heralds of world regeneration would go forth.[5] His approach
is well represented in the following extract in which there is probably
a confused echo of Joachimism:

And now again such a time has come that the proclamation of God's

---

[1] On Müntzer see Williams, op. cit., pp. 45–55; *Mennonite Encyclopedia* (Pennsylvania
and Kansas, 1956) [= *ME*], ii. 785–9.   [2] Williams, op. cit., pp. 858, 861.
[3] On Hofmann see Williams, op. cit., pp. 259–308; G. Williams and A. Mergal,
Spiritual and Anabaptist Writers (Library of Christian Classics, xxv, London, 1957),
pp. 186–9; *ME* ii. 778–85.
[4] Williams and Mergal, op. cit., pp. 187–8; Williams, op. cit., pp. 307–8.
[5] Williams, op. cit., p. 263.

Word shall go out to all peoples as a witness and absolutely none shall be excepted. But rather to all tribes, pagans, tongues and nations the gospel shall be revealed to their enlightenment, yea the whole world shall be brought into a clarity of enlightenment . . . And now in this final age the true apostolic emissaries of the Lord Jesus Christ will gather the elect flock . . . and lead the Bride of the Lord into the spiritual wilderness. . . . For in the New Covenant the Third Day, that third lunar festival, i.e. the spiritual Feast of Tabernacles, will be in the spiritual wilderness; and the last appearance of all that is lunar. (Translated Williams and Mergal, op. cit., pp. 186–9.)

Another echo of Joachimism is found among the High-German Anabaptists who called Old Testament time yesterday, New Testament time today, and the future time tomorrow.[1] As we know,[2] Postel's works were circulating among Anabaptists, and Professor Bainton's examination of the Joris papers has shown clearly that David Joris made extracts and translations from Postel's works and discussed his views both orally and in letters. It was very possibly through this channel that Joris received his Joachimist inspiration.[3] Characteristic of his thinking was the pattern of threes in history. He called himself the third David, in succession to the first, the historic David, and the second, that is, Christ. Though he did admit Christ to be greater, he believed that he himself was the chosen instrument of the Spirit in the third age to break the tyranny of the 'dead-letter' faith in the Bible and reveal the spiritual secrets, or—in the Old Testament figure—to smite off the head of Goliath and liberate Israel. The three Davids were the focal points for Joris's three ages of history, which he expounded in his most important work, *'t Wonderboek*, in 1542. Here he characterized the ages in terms which culminated in a third age surprisingly close to Joachim's original thought: the first, the age of the Old Testament, had been polygamous; the second, the age of the New Testament, was monogamous; now, the dawning age of the Spirit would be celibate.[4]

A final, far-distant echo of Joachim's three ages appeared without any known context in England in 1646, where in London a Mrs.

---

[1] *ME* iii, *sub nom.* Joachim of Fiore.

[2] *Supra*, p. 479 n. 6.

[3] On David Joris see R. Bainton, 'David Joris, Wiedertäufer u. Kämpfer f. Toleranz im 16. Jahrhundert', *Archiv f. Reformationsgeschichte*, vi (Leipzig, 1937), pp. 11–82; Cantimori, *Eretici*, pp. 108 seq.; Williams, op. cit., pp. 382 seq.

[4] Bainton, loc. cit., pp. 30–6; Williams, op. cit., pp. 382–3.

Atomy or Attaway was reported as preaching heresy. Among the errors listed in Edwards's *Gangraena* is the following:[1]

Error 166. That God the Father did reign under the Law, God the Son under the Gospel, and now God the Father and God the Son are making over the kingdom to God the Holy Ghost, and he shall reign and be poured out upon all flesh.

That there shall be a generall restauration wherein all men shall be reconciled to God and saved . . . (*Gangraena*, p. 35.)

In her preaching she again used the wilderness symbol, telling her hearers that 'for her part she was in the Wildernes, waiting for the powring out of the Spirit'.[2]

In more general terms we find the idea of the *renovatio* or *restitutio mundi* held by several radical reformers. Bernard Rothmann's *Restitutio mundi* is an outstanding exposition of this view.[3] Man had fallen under the Old Covenant and been restored in Christ, but there had been a second fall under the New Covenant from the second century onwards. Now the second restitution, begun under Luther and Hofmann, must be extended to all. This would be a restitution not by and for the learned, but for the common man. Dietrich Philips expounded the history of the Church in terms of Origins, Primordial Fall, and Restoration, believing that the last era had now begun in the New Jerusalem which had already descended from heaven to earth.[4] The restored Church of God had been born from above and would be exalted above all the kingdoms of the earth. In it the saints would have spiritual authority and would be conquerors of the whole world. It is, however, not clear whether this spiritual reign is conceived as being in time or eternity, and we reach here the point at which belief in a final manifestation of divine illumination within history and before the Last Judgement passes over into a more general chiliasm which expects the saints to reign with Christ after His final Advent when history has been wound up. Thus Sebastian Franck dreamed of the invisible Church of God as finally gathered together out of all nations by Christ in triumph, to reign with him for the thousand years of the old chiliastic belief.[5] Again, Hans Hut

[1] T. Edwards, *Gangraena* (London, 1646), pp. 35, 87. See also R. Jones, *Studies in Mystical Religion* (London, 1909), pp. 419–20, quoting a contemporary description of her as 'the mistress of all the she-preachers in Coleman Street'.

[2] Edwards, op. cit., p. 87.

[3] On Bernard Rothmann see Bainton, op. cit., pp. 21–4; *ME* iv. 367–70.

[4] Dietrich Philips, *The Church of God*, ed. Williams and Mergal, op. cit., pp. 255–60.

[5] Sebastian Franck, *Letter to John Campanus* (Strasbourg, 1531), ed. Williams and Mergal, op. cit., pp. 149–60. See also *ME* ii. 363–7.

also preached the imminent advent of Christ to rule with his saints. The Turkish tribulation was a sign of the Last Things: three and a half years were allowed for repentance; then would come the Last Judgement and after that the saved would rule the earth.[1]

In a loose way Joachimism has often been cited as one of the influences behind these chiliastic dreams of the left-wing reformers. But if we use a more rigorous set of categories, these cannot really be claimed as Joachimist: they belong rather to the general millenarian tradition in which the emphasis is on the Second Coming as the final event of history, with the Millennium as an extra-historical state beyond. The true mark of a Protestant Joachimism is the third historical Dispensation with its assignation of historical roles matching those in the Old and New Testaments which represent the first and second Dispensations. This third Dispensation may be ushered in by an intermediate or second 'coming' of Christ, but this will manifest itself in a new outpouring of the Spirit and is clearly to be distinguished from the Final Advent at the end of this last era of history.

One Protestant theologian who had certainly grasped the full significance of Joachimism for his age was Giacopo Brocardo, who wrote an exposition of the Apocalypse at the end of the sixteenth century.[2] Here we start at once with the three *status* of man, of which the third, belonging to the Holy Spirit, will be the Sabbath of 'opened prophecy'.[3] We also get the seven ages of the world in which the sixth is reckoned as that of the new prophets and the seventh as that

---

[1] *ME* ii. 846–50. It is of significance to note that the Hutterites drew on Petrus Joannis Olivi's thought: facts about him are mentioned in the early part of the Hutterite chronicle and they possessed his *Postilla* on the Apocalypse, which probably reached them about 1530 and has been preserved in a Hutterite manuscript of 1593; see *ME* iv. 1113.

[2] Brocardo is presumably the *Iacobus Procardus* who in 1581, according to Wolf, *Lect. mem.* ii. 937, 'edidit librum de prophetia in quo inter alia multa monstrat, in omnibus sacris libris inesse prophetiam usque ad postrema tempora...'. Wolf mentions him again (ibid., p. 752) as Iacobus Brocardus. Among his works *De Prophetia Libri Duo* (Lyon, 1581); *The Revelation of St. John reveled . . . Englished by J. Sanford* (London, 1582); *Mystica et Prophetica Libri Levitici Interpretatio* (Lyon, 1580); *Mystica et prophetica libri Geneseos interpretatio . . .* (Bremen, 1585) all contain relevant material. From the preface to the latter we learn that it was written at Bremen in the midst of the preaching of the New Evangel and that Brocardo was in touch with Protestants in Heidelberg and also in France, England, and Holland. Some autobiographical details occur in *The Revelation*, from which we learn that as a young man he fled from the Inquisition in Venice to Strasbourg and then to Basle (f. 45ᵛ). See also f. 98ʳ. J. Moltmann's article in *ZKG* lxxi (1960), pp. 110–29, which I found too late to use here, gives further information.

[3] *The Revelation*, f. 5ʳ.

of the Second Coming. And again, he reckons seven divisions to the *status* of the Son – in which the seventh 'began to shyne as the mornynge doth' when Luther renewed the preaching of the Gospel— and seven seasons to the *status* of the Holy Ghost. Of these latter, the first was from the preaching of Luther to the preaching in Switzerland, the second and third covered the preaching elsewhere, such as in England and Denmark, and the fourth 'commeth to the French troubles'. These four seasons were marked by four new prophets corresponding to the four Angelic Popes. The fifth ran 'even unto the universall slaughter of the Gospellers', and the sixth would last until 'the conflicte of hostes, when in thicke cloudes of the sky Chryst shalbe present to turne his Judgement agaynst ye Papistes'.[1] Thus Brocardo saw himself as already living in the third *status* and the seventh age, in which the Second Coming of Christ (which he distinguished clearly from the Third) would mark the vanquishing of Antichrist.

Brocardo acknowledges the source of this view of history quite openly.[2] In the sixth age, he says, a preparation began to be made: 'Chryst sendeth the Abbot Ioachim and many others whom Theleasphorus recordeth, who sayth that the Lordes comming is to bee looked for, and that there must needes be an innovation or renewing, to weete of the Gospell' (*The Revelation*, f. 7ʳ). The new prophets, of course, did not know everything; they told some things truly, some not, and they could not open all the mysteries of God's Book. Yet 'stronge was the Voyce of the Abbot Ioachimus wrytinge and foretellinge many thinges, of Frear Robert, of Saynte Vincente, of John Hus . . .'.[3]

Joachim is the key prophet of the sixth age and the chief medieval influence upon Brocardo's thought. This is made clear not only by the number of references[4] but also by his use of characteristic symbols from Joachim which he adapts in his own way. The 'wheel within a wheel' from Ezekiel is one of these. Brocardo uses it to explain

---

[1] *The Revelation*, f. 5ᵛ.

[2] Ibid., f. 17ᵛ: 'And that there are three states as we sayd . . . it is spoken of in ye beginning of Genesis and elsewhere oftentimes: and the Abbot Joachimus and others have allowed them by the worke of the Father, by the worke of the Son, and by the worke of the Holy Ghoste.'

[3] Ibid., f. 71ᵛ.

[4] In the works I have read the following occur: *The Revelation*: ff. 7ʳ, 17ᵛ, 55ᵛ, 71ᵛ, 85ᵛ, 131ʳ, 131ᵛ, 132ᵛ, 167ʳ; *Mystica . . . Levitici Interpretatio*, pp. 77, 99, 100, 159, 165, 203; *Libri Duo*, pp. 76, 81, 84, 102. Brocardo uses all three main works of Joachim, as well as those of Ubertino and Telesphorus.

how the seventh age will contain seven seasons: 'that a season may be brought within a time, as a wheele in the middle of a wheele'.[1] Again, he insists in a number of passages, as does Joachim, on the co-existence of all three Persons of the Trinity in all three *status*, and uses the wheel symbol to show the centrality of the Second Person in this mystery:

In this order, then, the Sonne of God draweth into Himselfe the firste seconde and thirde state, as a wheele amiddest a wheele: which turneth aboute it the first state of the Father into the thirde of the Holy Ghoste, both meeting together upon one very large wheele, whereof it is spoken in ye first Chapter of Ezechiell: and . . . then there ariseth a deeper cogitation, that Christe may drawe together all times or seasons into Himselfe and all the bodily worlde. (*The Revelation*, f. 10ʳ.)

A second symbol is that of the trumpet, that is, the preaching of the Gospel in all ages, which Brocardo adapts from Joachim[2] while still linking it with the Trinity:

This Trumpet is stretched very far in length: therefore farre behinde us we are to heare the voices of God's word even untill the first beginning unto the first chapter of Genesis and that even from thence the worde of God in Moyses Trumpet stretched out to the Prophetes and Apostles doth sownde the thinges which belong to the Father, and to the Sonne, and to the Holy Ghost in all ages and Churches even until . . . the ende of this worlde . . . (*The Revelation*, f. 29ᵛ.)

From the *Liber Concordie* he draws another symbol dear to Joachim —the sacrifice of Elijah on Mt. Carmel.[3] But it is in the fascination of letters that Brocardo most shows the influence of Joachim's ways of thought. Joachim, says Brocardo, had used the forms of letters (i.e. the Alpha and Omega) in the *Psalterium* to demonstrate the mystery of the Trinity,[4] but he, Brocardo, is now determined to discover these same mysteries in a comparison of three whole alphabets, for the Hebrew represents the work of the Father, the Greek the work of the Son, and the Latin that of the Holy Ghost. Here he finds a figure at once embodying both the unity and diversity of the Trinity in which

---

[1] *The Revelation*, f. 5ᵛ; cf. Ezek. 1: 16. In Joachim's writings references to this symbol are innumerable. He uses it particularly to represent the relationship of the Old and New Testaments (cf. *Lib. Fig.* II, Pl. xv), an interpretation which Brocardo does not use, although his second reference to the wheels (quoted below) approaches it.

[2] Cf. *Expos.*, f. 40ᵛ, and *Lib. Fig.* II, Pl. xviii *a, b*.

[3] Cf. *Lib. Conc.*, ff. 101ʳ seq.

[4] Cf. *Psalt.*, ff. 256ᵛ–257ʳ. See also *Expos.*, ff. 34ʳ seq.; *Lib. Fig.* II, Pl. xi *a, b*.

Joachim himself might have revelled: 'The Alphabets are doubt-lesse dystinct, as there is a distinction of the three persons in Divinity: but because there is one meaning in these three tongues, we understand God the Father, ye Son and ye holy Ghoste in one essence . . .' (*The Revelation*, f. 167^r). There ensues a long passage in which by a study of the orders in the several alphabets he shows the relationship of the Persons:

And here it seemeth to be done for a great cause, that the Hebrew and Greeke letters are writen in a contrary order, that the Sonne is knowne to be one with the Father and the Father with the Son, that the Son of God which commeth in ye middle of tymes through the conjunction of A with A . . . may bee knowne, I say, as the Father in ye Sonne . . . And as the Greeke Alphabet stretcheth out from ye middle unto the ende, in running from ye left hand to ye right, we have knowne the continued worke of ye Sonne from the time of his first comming unto ye ende of times: so contrariwise in the Hebrewe Alphabet, while A which was the beginning, is made the ende, there is made a recourse in the worke of the Father from the time of the Sonnes coming to the beginning of times. But because A and A are joyned together, all the Hebrew Alphabet runneth into all the Greeke Alphabet, and contrarywise all the Greeke Alphabet runneth agayne into all the Hebrew Alphabet. . . . The Latin Alphabet . . . comprehendeth at once and bryngeth together in one measure the things which belong to the Hebrew and Greeke Alphabets: the Holy Ghoste contayneth in his worke the worke of the Father and the Sonne, whilest the Latine Alphabet is measured with the Hebrew and Greeke . . . But whilest the three measures are matched in one and are brought to one measure, the three Alphabets come to one, that by these thou mayest have a patterne or example of the distinction of the Persons and of the unity of God's essence, of the severall worke and mutuall worke of the Father, the Sonne and the Holy Ghoste . . . (*The Revelation*, ff. 167^v–168^r.)

These selections from a long argument have been given to show how closely Brocardo shares Joachim's thought on the Trinity and how easily he uses the same type of figurative exposition. There is, however, one notable difference in his treatment. Both here and in the passage quoted above on the Wheels we are struck by an empha-sis on the work of the Son as central to the mystery of the Persons. Here was a Protestant reorienting Joachim's thought on the Trinity to accord with an evangelical Christology.[1]

---

[1] Brocardo erroneously ascribes to Joachim himself the concept of the three Advents

The detailed exposition of the Apocalypse by this Protestant Joachite makes fascinating reading. Under the figures of the Seven Churches of Asia he gives an interesting account of the state of Protestantism in various parts of Europe.[1] The Pope is, of course, Antichrist and the Church of Rome the Babylonish Woman. The bottomless pit is the Inquisition and the locusts which rise from it, the Jesuits.[2] The Seven Angels with trumpets stand for things spoken by the new prophets, such as Joachim, Savonarola, and Luther,[3] while the Angel with the Eternal Evangel is the preaching touching the Lord's Second Coming foretold by Joachim, 'as the wrytings of that Abbot and others doe testifie, which foretellyng was reported through all the Chrystian people, wherein was contayned the everlasting Gosple to be opened unto all Nations'.[4] The two following Angels are others who told the same thing 'and drewe all men to a newnesse of life as every man may perceave by the Booke of Theolosphorus'.[5] It does not really please this Protestant to find the blessedness of the Sabbath Age symbolized in the silence of the Seventh Seal-Opening, so he interprets the silence as the time from Savonarola to Luther—and then writes with exultation of the voices of the preachers now ringing everywhere.[6] Brocardo finds his ideal state not in the silence of contemplation, but in the 'voice of many waters': 'as wee now see in Germany, Fraunce, Italy and in many other Countryes that an innumerable number of People doth speake the selfe-same worde of God'.[7] For the final bringing in of the third *status* there must be a council of 'true catholicks and gospellers' who will guide men into open prophecy and erect a Church of all Christian people.[8] This council, so Brocardo believes, will be situated in Venice.[9] The first heaven and earth, i.e. the popish ecclesiastical state, will pass away and the new heaven and earth will represent the new *status* wherein Satan shall be cast away and the City will need neither sun nor moon in the shape of an ecclesiastical hierarchy, for the Holy Ghost will instruct in full open revelation. The diffusion of

---

of Christ which was one of the means by which the central work of Christ could be harmonized with belief in a further revelation of the Spirit (see *The Revelation*, f. 131ʳ; *Libri Duo*, p. 81).

[1] *The Revelation*, ff. 40ʳ seq.   [2] Ibid., ff. 97ʳ seq.
[3] Ibid., ff. 92ᵛ seq.   [4] Ibid., f. 132ᵛ.   [5] Ibid., f. 133ʳ.
[6] Ibid., f. 92ᵛ.
[7] Ibid., f. 36ʳ; and again, the voice of a great thunder, i.e. gospellers preaching throughout the world (f. 131ᵛ).
[8] Ibid., f. 60ᵛ (where the council is the 'door opened in heaven'), 153ʳ.
[9] Ibid., ff. 152ʳ–153ʳ.

the Gospel throughout the world is seen in Christ's bright garment which is compared to Aaron's with bells and pomegranates:

(These) signifie the last age of the worlde, wherein Christes Garment is more inlarged and comprehendeth the whole world, when everywhere there shal be little Belles and Pomegarnates, that is, Churches, and the preaching of the Gosple shalbe in the whole worlde. No other religion, no other lawe, and rule to heare then that of the Gosple shall be heard. (*The Revelation*, f. 32ᵛ.)

Then shall be the kyngdom of God in the state of the Holy Ghost untyll that when the Saboth is fynished in this worlde, hee bryngeth us in his thyrde comming to Heaven. (*The Revelation*, f. 153ʳ.)

One last example, taken from early seventeenth-century England, provides us with a distinctive blend of Protestantism and Joachimism. James Maxwell, who published his *Admirable and notable Prophesies* in 1615,[1] had collected the prophetic expectations of nearly everyone mentioned in this book. His range of reading and research in this type of literature is notable. Among the prophets Joachim stands out as having been, in Maxwell's view, 'extraordinarily inspired';[2] indeed, he devotes a special section to the prophecies and writings of the Abbot.[3] Maxwell's objective is to demonstrate the defection, tribulation, and reformation of the Church of Rome. He uses the denunciatory prophecies in no uncertain terms to chastise the Roman Church, yet his categories of reformation are strikingly medieval—much more so than Brocardo's. He looks for the old partnership of World Emperor and Angelic Pope, using all the familiar Joachimist and Telesphorean prophecies in support. We have already looked at his description of the last great ruler.[4] His portrait of the Angelic Pope is a blend of various sources with his own additions:

Baptista Nazarus writing of the future and expected victory against the Turk, telleth how that ancient Predictions do promise that there shall be a holie league between the Lyon and the mitred Lamb and the crowned Cock against the dragon or serpent. *Unio conspirat sancta incursura colubrum.* Where by the mytred Lambe is to be understood the Angelicall Pastour, or the reformed and reforming Bishop of Rome, or first Patriarch promised by S. Cyrillus and S. Telesphorus . . . as also by Joachimus Abbas, Merlinus, Ioannis de Rupescissa etc. As for Abbot Joachim in his

---

[1] J. Maxwell, *Admirable and notable Prophesies, uttered in former times by 24 famous Romain Catholickes, concerning the Church of Romes defection, tribulation and reformation* (London, 1615).

[2] Ibid., p. 17.   [3] Ibid., pp. 132–44.   [4] *Supra*, p. 391.

Booke *Of the agreement of the two Testaments* he doth foretell how that
God shall raise up certaine Popes or Romaine Bishops which shall reform
the Church and restore the primitive puritie of God's worship. There shall
arise (saith he) a man renowned for his great holinesse, preferred to sit in
the Apostolicall See, who within a short while shall mervailously reforme
the whole Church and ordaine the Clergie to live of the oblations and
tithes. He shall likewise forbid the pompe and excesse of apparell and all
dishonest things, as also all lascivious daunces and songs. He shall
ordaine women to walke honestly and modestlie without gold and pretious
stones, and make the Gospell to bee preached everywhere. This holie man
shall continue in the Popedome but a short while, even foure yeares, the
which being passed, hee shall depart blessedly to the Lord. After him
God shall raise up successively other three most holie men which shall con-
firme the sayings and doings of their Antecessour, and reforme the whole
Church, so that under their government the state of the Church shall
bee renued and these are called Angelicall Pastors. (Op. cit., pp. 67–8.)

To Maxwell the *renovatio* is still to come—it has not already arrived
through the reforming churches—but perhaps, he thinks, the agencies for transforming the old institutions will come from a new
quarter. *Renovatio* could mean the healing of the breach between old
and new if *angelicus* were translated into *anglicus*. So Maxwell
brings the prophecies to a head in the expectation of an angelic
agent from England:

The Good Bishop or Pope that should thus reforme the Church is commonly called Pastor Angelicus, Angelicall Pope, and who knoweth but
he may even be a Pastor Anglicus, a Pastor or Bishop sent from the
Countrie of England. England hath been more fertile of converters of
Nations and Countries to the Christian faith then any other Land else;
so is it not unlikely but that God will have the same Countrie to be more
fertile of reformers of other corrupt Churches, especially that of Rome,
then any other Land whatsoever. And that as there is in no other Countrie
or Nation of the world to be found so many learned and eloquent
Preachers, nor so many complet Devines, for Iudiciousnes, Ingenuousnes
and Moderation, and for fitnesse to deserve well of the peace of the
Church, as there is in England; so it may well bee that God will honour
this same Island with the reforming of the Church of Rome and her
daughters by sending foorth from thence such godly, iudicious, zealous and
moderate men as shall reclame them from their abuses . . . (Op. cit., p. 84.)

Some of these last Protestant Joachites suggest a comparison with
the Spiritual Franciscans. In each case a vivid religious experience
of such inner veracity had so taken hold as to implant the conviction

that this was a New Coming of Christ. In each case they were driven to erect this new experience into a new Dispensation in history. This third Dispensation became quickly identified with the Age of the Spirit in the Trinitarian pattern of Joachim. Yet the concept remained strongly Christocentric in each case: the Spiritual Franciscans believed the new era had begun in St. Francis, because he represented afresh in a mystical way the life of Christ; many of the Protestants we have considered believed that Christ would be, or was already, manifest in a Second Coming in their time, as distinct from the Third and Last Coming. The concept of three Advents is common to both thirteenth-century Franciscans and sixteenth-century Protestants. The Trinitarian framework of Joachim could thus be used in different ways and in different periods to express a hope about history which was primarily based on an inner religious experience.[1]

It can perhaps be further claimed that Joachimist thought played its part, more generally, in developing among Protestants a positive approach to history. E. L. Tuveson has argued that the classical attitude of the Protestant reformers towards history was one of pessimism: all things must decline; decay is the essential fact of history.[2] But he finds also an optimism which seems to break through irresistibly. God has done so many great works in these last days that it is impossible not to look forward with expectancy. He quotes from Sheltoo a Geveren, a passage in which this exultant feeling bursts forth:

For God in this last age hath shewed his singular and marveylous good wyll towards mankynd: especially . . . by raysing up some, Valla, Agricola, Erasmus, Melancthon and others, which, with great study and payne, have brought all sciences and knowledge of the tongues to their puritie and delivered unto us a more easie way to the attaynyng the perfect knowledge of them all by which almost all Europe is set free from barbarousnes. (*Millennium and Utopia*, p. 46.)

Here, remarks Tuveson, is the germ of a new attitude but 'ideas of progress could not develop until the Protestant interpretation of history itself had undergone a reorientation'.[3] He finds the source of

---

[1] A further example, found too late to be studied here, is that of the Rosicrucians. W. Peuckert relates their expectations to Joachimism in *Die Rosenkreutzer* (Jena, 1928), pp. 38 seq., 77 seq.

[2] E. L. Tuveson, *Millennium and Utopia* (Berkeley and Los Angeles, 1949), pp. 45 seq.

[3] Ibid., p. 59.

this new viewpoint in a new interpretation of the Apocalypse and of the eschatological pattern which looked forward to some great transforming event rather than to inevitable decay. Thus he arrives at the interesting conclusion that the forebears of modern concepts of progress must be sought in the seventeenth-century apocalyptic theorists.[1] But this interpretation of the Apocalypse was not new. The evidence assembled in this chapter shows a continuous stream of interpretation, stemming from the headwaters of Joachimism, which proclaimed the culmination of history in a final glorious achievement. One cannot study sixteenth- and seventeenth-century apocalyptists without putting them in the perspective of their medieval ancestry. If Tuveson is right in detecting a swing among Protestants from a pessimistic towards an optimistic view of history, this must surely be traced, in part at least, to Joachimist sources. This legacy, of course, provided a doctrine very far from the modern one of inevitable progress: it expected an apocalyptic event, that is, a divine event, but nevertheless one which brought human history to its final fruition. This affirmation, in combating both the cyclical view and the expectation of inevitable decay, became perhaps an element of considerable importance in forming modern expectations of progress.

There is little need to press home further the point that expectation of the *renovatio mundi* remained a continuing hope right through to the seventeenth century. It was fostered wherever fervent groups gathered round their special prophet or leader; it was fed by oracles and prophecies from many periods of history; it was reinvigorated through the printing press. There were in it, certainly, elements which looked back to a past Golden Age, to the pristine glory of the Apostolic Church. But what is abundantly clear is that this last age was not really conceived as a renewal, so much as the ultimate goal of all history. It sprang, not from a cyclical view of history, but a linear one which directed men's aspirations towards a positive end within history. Its source can be traced back to Joachim's philosophy, or rather, theology of history. However various the forms in which the hope of *renovatio* was expressed, the basis was a belief that there would be a manifestation of God's spirit in a new age, and this derived from Joachim's Trinitarian conception of history, concealed though the source often was. The idea of novelty rather than return is seen in the excited references to all the new manifestations of the

[1] Tuveson, *Millennium and Utopia*, pp. 75 seq.

age—the new lands, the new learning, the new books, the new missionaries. If the signs of greatest good are juxtaposed with warnings of greatest evil, both pile up a last act of the drama which is ultimate and unrepeatable: the victory over Antichrist and the apotheosis of history to follow.

It is both surprising and illuminating that the medieval symbol of the Angelic Pope retained for so long its central place in the expectation of *renovatio*. It could, of course, be interpreted in many different ways. Fundamentally, the word 'angelic' implied a revolution. This could, however, be interpreted by the orthodox as an expectation that God's angel would set all things right when he indicated the hidden *Papa Angelicus*. It could lead more revolutionary Catholics to expect violent judgement on the papacy as a prelude to a complete reversal of existing worldly standards and the establishment of an entirely new regime. It could betray the fanatical and unstable into claiming the role for themselves or for their chosen candidate. It could be used by the real revolutionaries among the Protestants to prove their claim that the *renovatio mundi* had begun with the violent transfer of authority from the Babylonish Church to the true one. Except in special cases, the concept of the Angelic Pope was not such an important one to Protestants. It appears, however, to be a vital lifeline to a number of Catholics, enabling them to express in extreme terms their horror of existing evils and their expectation of violent change, while loading on to the impeccably Catholic figure of the Angelic Pope all their dreams for a future millennium. It was, after all, the Latin Church that they expected to triumph over all other sects and religions, and this confirmed their orthodoxy. Thus, in a period of much ferment and perturbation of spirit, the concept of the Angelic Pope was important as a symbol upon which unquiet minds could focus without being carried to extremes. The hope of an Angelic Pope neutralized revolutionary tendencies in many, though not all. Thus men like Amadeus, Egidio of Viterbo, Petrus Galatinus, could believe in their revelations and hold their views unmolested because their dream was projected into the future, was Catholic in conception, and was to be brought about by angelic agency.

A second striking feature of this hope in *renovatio* is the reiterated motif of 'unum ovile sub uno pastore' which runs like a continuum through so many of the prophetic aspirations. The unity, not just of Christendom, but of the whole world is the passionate desideratum of the later Joachites, and this at a time when the limits of the known world had been so astonishingly expanded. But while geography was widening the vision, politics was narrowing it. This ecumenical dream in Church and State, of unity in one faith and peace under one rule, is found widely disseminated precisely in the period when all the political realities were working in the opposite direction. It is pathetic but true that in the very age when religious and national divisions were hardening irrevocably, men so often turned back to the apparently irrelevant ideal of the *unum ovile*. This must be recorded, since men's dreams are as much a part of history as their deeds.

CONCLUSION

EXPLORING over a number of years these peculiar ways of thought has raised in the mind a number of reflections and questions about the relationship of human beings to their own past and future. There seems strong evidence for concluding that, from the beginning of the Christian era, over a number of centuries at least, the meaning of history was a major preoccupation of men in Western Europe. They lived their lives in a vivid, if often naïve, relation to the great past of Jewish and Christian history, and precisely because the past was so immediate in their lives, the future pressed upon them as a reality in which they, too, must participate. It is often claimed that history has only been discovered in the post-Renaissance world and that a distinguishing feature of modern civilization is its historical-mindedness. This may be so at the level of conscious philosophizing about the nature of history—the attraction of the type of study embodied in this book illustrates our fascination with problems of this nature—but, at the level of a deep involvement in a continuing drama, medieval thinkers seem to me to have participated much more fully in both the past and the future, even though their conceptions of both were, to our way of thinking, mythological. They rarely thought of themselves as spectators of history.

The word 'pattern' has occurred frequently in this book. The obsession with the discovery of shape in events is surely an outstanding characteristic of man's relation to history. Medieval interpretations of history are very largely mythologies of pattern and shape, and perhaps the basic reason for the popularity of Joachim's doctrine was his skill with the symbolism of patterns and the visual imagination which could translate history into *figurae*. Most mythologies of history have been based on one or other of two contrasted shapes: the cyclical and the linear. In medieval patterns there are often elements of both and it has been fascinating to study their interplay. The cyclical is, of course, fundamentally the pessimistic view: all things are returning whence they came, all must decay and die. In Christian thought this finds an echo in the oft-quoted text from Matthew (24: 12): 'And because iniquity shall abound, the love of many shall wax cold.' Yet, on the other hand, the very hope of *renovatio* contains within it a notion of return to pristine glory which made it possible in the Renaissance period for a Christian idea of *renovatio* to be married to the concept of the returning Age of Gold. The linear pattern, however, is the one most natural to Christian thought about history. In so far as this presupposes an 'end' to history—and in Christian thought this 'end' must ultimately be the triumph of God's purposes—the linear view is optimistic.

As we have seen, however, there has been a deep ambiguity in Christian thought about how the 'end' will be achieved. Would there be a mounting battle between good and evil, reaching its climax in the reign of Antichrist, the collapse of history, and the triumph of supernatural forces of righteousness? This was a widely accepted view which combined pessimism concerning the fate of history with faith in the achievement of the goal beyond itself. The study of Joachimism, however, shows how strong was the urge to find a basis for a more positive affirmation about the meaning of history itself. The linear pattern of successive stages must lead to a final stage of achievement within history itself. Joachim's Trinitarian pattern supplied the theological basis for this, and although his doctrine of the Trinity in history was frequently lost to sight, his optimistic expectation caught on to a most astounding extent. The reality of Antichrist remained as a constant experience and fear, but the juxtaposition of the greatest tribulation with the highest triumph, both within history itself, provided the balance men sought for between pessimism and optimism. Old traditions of Antichrist and -of Gog and Magog were married to the expectation of an apotheosis of history in the Last Age.

A further ambiguity is found in considering the nature of the transition to the Last Age. How violent and revolutionary would this transition be? Would there be continuity or discontinuity in institutions and authorities? This problem goes back to Joachim himself and we have traced a series of varying answers, in which the violence of the break goes all the way from the reforming hope of a Catholic theologian to the extremism of a heretical sect. All felt that drastic chastisement of existing sin must form the first stage of the transition, all believed that the qualitative difference of life in the Last Age necessitated a real break. In the figure used by Joachim, the life designated in Peter must give way to that designated in John. Yet if this was to be achievement within history and not beyond it, it must be the triumph of historical institutions, the working out to their final fulfilment of things already known in the past. The Age of the Holy Ghost was not a millennium descending from the heavens, but the illumination of existing history. Thus, as we have emphasized, in Joachim's third *status* the Church (as distinct from the 'life') of St. Peter stands, the two Testaments are unmoved, the *Novus Ordo* takes within itself existing orders. The Joachimist view demands a certain type of continuity in history, although the nature and degree of the equally necessary break between the sixth and seventh ages (or second and third *status*) varies greatly from thinker to thinker. Some of the most interesting examples of ways in which this problem was dealt with occur in connection with the concept of the Angelic Pope. The very idea implies continuity, yet the word 'angelic' often means more than 'the most saintly possible'. As the angelic portraits in the *Vaticinia* show, in some mysterious way through His angels, God is expected to intervene directly to point out or elect the chosen agent who is yet to be a man. The implication that the traditional method of choosing a pope was not sufficiently under divine guidance to be adequate for this particular moment of history is surely a most significant, not to say surprising, conclusion, when we remember how widely these expectations were accepted in unquestionably orthodox circles.

The outstanding impression which remains from these studies is the significance of the motif of optimism about history. This unites the medieval and Renaissance periods in an unexpected way. Renaissance people changed neither their patterns nor their expectations of history. Humanist hopes fastened eagerly on medieval symbols of the Golden Age and in a quite extraordinary way the new discoveries, new learning, new printing, new religious orders, fell into the pattern as fulfilments of old expectations and portents of the new age dawning. Nowhere, perhaps, are medieval and humanist thought so closely linked as in this view of history. The most universal of these shared hopes—and to us, perhaps, the most poignant—was that of the 'unum ovile sub uno pastore'. It cannot have escaped notice that this text becomes the theme-song in the latter part of this book. One comes to expect that every utterance of prophetic expectation will culminate thus. It is the most hard-worked text of prophecy. This ecumenical hope for both political and religious unity expresses the point at which the history of the future presses most sharply on the present. It will also have been observed, however,

that between the thirteenth and sixteenth centuries the concept
of ecumenism has changed. In the earlier period, although the
Greeks and sometimes the Jews are expected to be brought within
the fold, unity is to be achieved mainly through the extermination
of the chief enemies, that is, all infidels. By the sixteenth century
this has given place to a dream of one world religion, in which unity
will be achieved by the willing conversion of all races to Christianity.
There is even sometimes a hint that the world religion will be a process of synthesis rather than one of simple conversion.

Prophecy was thus one of the bonds between medieval and Renaissance thought. This was so because there was still a shared experience of history. But prophecy has now ceased to be of importance,
except on the fringes of modern civilization. When did this change
take place? Certainly not at the time when scholars began to apply
modern, so-called scientific, methods in their scholarship, for, as
we have seen, sixteenth-century thinkers could hold together new
concepts of knowledge and belief in the efficacy of ancient oracles.
When did these two begin to reveal themselves as impossible
bedfellows? In seeking to answer this question we may be able to
illumine an important aspect of the whole problem of transition
from the medieval to the modern world. At the end of the seventeenth century the Bollandist, Daniel Papebroch, in some ways so
forward-looking in his scholarship, could still take Joachim's
prophecies seriously. The reason was undoubtedly his sense of
involvement in the divine purposes of history inherited from the
medieval tradition. Perhaps we might say that only when intelligent
and educated men ceased to take prophecy seriously were the Middle
Ages truly at an end. The contention here is that this change hinges
on a change in our whole attitude to history and to our own parti-
cipation in it.

APPENDICES

APPENDIX A

THE GENUINE AND SPURIOUS WORKS OF JOACHIM

As Professor Bloomfield has said,[1] the task of establishing a canon of the genuine works of Joachim is an urgent one. F. Russo in his *Bibliografia Gioachimita* attempts to divide the works into *Opere Autentiche*, *Opere Dubbie*, and *Opere Apocrife*, but this work is riddled with errors, omissions, and confusions.[2] E. Donckel, *AFH* xxvi. 51–2, gives two lists under the headings *Echte Werke* and *Unechte Werke*, but his category of genuine works is still incomplete and also contains some confusions. The attempt made here to divide the writings clearly into genuine and spurious does not claim any finality. There is general agreement on the main books which Joachim wrote, but still disagreement on some of the minor tracts, some of which have only recently been identified. Doubts are chiefly expressed concerning items 11 to 16 in list I below. On 11 see Reeves, Hirsch-Reich, *RTAM* xxi. 226–31. The case for the genuine character of the items under 13 and 14 rests (*a*) on their presence in MS. Padua 322, regarded as the most reliable early collection of Joachim's works; (*b*) the absence of obvious anachronisms or particular interests which would be served by forged prophecy; (*c*) internal characteristics which, though in no case particularly strong, link them with the established works of Joachim. On 14 (*d*) see *supra*, p. 4, but note that Tondelli, *Lib. Fig.* I, pp. 119–20, rejects it. The case for the genuine character of the *Liber Figurarum* (15) has been hotly disputed. It rests mainly on internal evidence, particularly on the close relations of its figures to the textual figures in the three main works of Joachim. The case is fully argued in Reeves, Hirsch-Reich, *Studies*. On the general problem, see the following: Denifle, *ALKG* i. 91–6; Huck, *Joachim v. Floris*, pp. 127–227; Buonaiuti, *Quat. Evang.*, introd., pp. lxiv–lxxi; *De Articulis Fidei*, introd., pp. lviii–lix; Donckel, *AFH* xxvi. 50–1; Tondelli, *Lib. Fig.* I, pp. 116–22; Grundmann, *NF*, pp. 15–31; Bloomfield, *Traditio* XIII, pp. 251–60; Tondelli, 'Gli Inediti dell'Abate Gioacchino da Fiore', *ASCL* xii. 1–12.

---

[1] *Traditio* XIII, p. 251 n. 3: 'A definitive bibliographical and canonical work on Joachita and pseudo–Joachita cries out to be done. It is an absolute preliminary to the long-hoped-for definitive edition of all his works.' See now, bibl. 3.323, 3.324.

[2] See the review article by B. Hirsch-Reich, *RTAM* xxiv. 27–44.

The lists of manuscripts are not intended to be exhaustive: I have included only the earliest and/or most interesting.

I. GENUINE

1. LIBER CONCORDIE NOVI ET VETERIS TESTAMENTI
(Usually preceded by Joachim's Testamentary Letter)

Inc. Quia labentis et perituri saeculi perurgere ruinam

MSS.	Rome, Vatican, Lat. 4861, ff. 1–199	13th century
	Rome, Bibl. Corsin., 41. F. 2, ff. 2–115 (known to come from S. Giovanni in Fiore)	early 13th century
	Paris, Bibl. Nat., Lat. 16280, ff. 1–262	13th century
	Paris, Bibl. Nat., Lat. 10453, ff. 1–91	13th century
	Paris, Bibl. Nat., Lat. 15254, ff. 233–334	13th century
	Rome, Vatican, Borgh. 190, ff. 5–181	13th century
	¹Troyes, Bibl. Munic., 249 ff. 1–36 (Bks. I–IV only)	13th century
	Dresden, Sächs. Landesbibl., A. 121, ff. 2–56 (incomplete)	late 13th century
	Bamberg, Staats-Bibl., Msc. Bibl. 152, ff. 1–101	2nd half 13th century
	Padua, Bibl. Anton., 328, ff. 1–139	1st half 14th century
	Florence, Bibl. Laur., Conv. Soppr. 358, ff. 1–116	early 14th century
	Florence, Bibl. Laur., Plut. VIII, dextr. x, ff. 1–168	early 14th century
	Paris, Bibl. Nat., Lat. 3320, ff. 1–101 (incomplete)	14th century
	Chalons-s-Marne, Bibl. Munic., 68, ff. 64–162	14th century
	Rome, Bibl. Casanaten., 1412, ff. 1–103	14/15th century
	Rome, Vatican, Urb. Lat. 8, ff. 1, 10–164	15th century
	Leipzig, Universitäts. Bibl., 194, ff. 141–232 (Bks. I-IV only)	15th century

Editions: Venice 1519, prefaced by the Testamentary Letter, the letter of Clement III to Joachim and a short extract from Joachim's *Expositio.*

Reprinted Frankfurt-a-M., 1964, 1983.

E. R. Daniel, ed., Abbot Joachim of Fiore. *Liber de Concordia Novi ac Veteris Testamenti. Trans. of the American Philosophical Society*, 73, Pt. 8 (1983). (Bks. I-IV only).

---

¹ Both these break off in the middle of a sentence, the *Lib. Conc.* at f. 67ʳ and the *Expos.* at f. 151ʳ in the Venetian editions. The foliation given here is my own, starting from the beginning of the Joachimist material.

2. Expositio in Apocalypsim

Inc. Quam propensioribus studiis a viris catholicis

MSS. [1]Troyes, Bibl. Munic., 249, ff. 38–107	13th century
Milan, Bibl. Ambros., H. 15,	
inf. misc., ff. 65–160	13th/14th century
Rome, Vatican, Chig. A. VIII, 231, ff. 1–104	14th century
Rome, Bibl. Casanaten., 1411, ff. 1–191	14th century
Nuremberg, Städtbibl., Cent. II, 51, ff. 127–373	
London, Brit. Mus., Harley 3049,	
ff. 137 (135)–220 (218)	15th century
Rouen, Bibl. Munic., A. 450, ff. 1–131	16th century

Edition: Venice, 1527, prefaced by the Testamentary Letter and the letter of Clement III to Joachim, printed Frankfurt-a-M., 1964.

3. Apocalypsis nova (an independent, short commentary on the Apocalypse)

Inc. Apocalypsis ihesu christi quam dedit illi deus

MSS. Dresden, Sächs. Landesbibl., A. 121, ff. 100–31	13/14th century
Rome, Vatican, Lat. 4860, ff. 55–8, 85–141	13th century

Unedited.

4. Enchiridion super Apocalypsim

Inc. Quam propensioribus studiis a viris catholicis

This is a longer version of the *Liber Introductorius* which opens the *Expositio*. It is often found separately and at Pavia in one of the earliest manuscripts of Joachim's work.

MSS. Pavia, Bibl. Univ., Aldini 370, ff. 1–78	early 13th century
Paris, Bibl. Nat., Lat. 2142, ff. 103–33	13th century
Paris, Bibl. Nat., Lat. 427, ff. 46–94	13th century
Rome, Vatican, Reg. Lat. 132, ff. 58–95	14th century
London, Brit. Mus., Harley 3049 (fragment),	
ff. 137(135)–140(138)	15th century

In its longer form this tract is unedited.

---

[1] Both these break off in the middle of a sentence, the *Lib. Conc.* at f. 67^r and the *Expos.* at f. 151^r in the Venetian editions. The foliation given here is my own, starting from the beginning of the Joachimist material.

5. ENCHIRIDION SUPER APOCALYPSIM
Inc. Apocalypsis liber ultimus est
MSS. Rome, Vatican, Lat. 3822, ff. 104–8   late 13th century
   (fragment)
   Wroclaw, Bibl. univ., Rediger 280,
   ff. 47–53   14th century
Edition: E. K. Burger, Studies and Texts, 78 (Toronto, 1986) pp. 1–6.

6. PRAEPHATIO SUPER APOCALYPSIM
Inc. Apocalypsis liber ultimus est librorum omnium
MSS. Rome, Vatican, Lat. 3822, ff. 100–8   end of 13th century
   (fragments)
   Rome, Vatican, Reg. Lat. 132, ff. 49–53   14th century
   Paris, Bibl. Nat., Lat., 2142, ff. 96–103   13th century
   Paris, Bibl. Nat., Lat. 682, ff. 41–5   13th century
   London, Brit. Mus., Harley 3969, ff. 216–24   13th century
   (fragment)
   Dresden, Sächs. Landesbibl., A.
   121, ff. 97–100   13/14th century
Editions: Huck, *Joachim v. Floris*, pp. 287–305.
   Selge, K-V., *DA* (1990), pp. 85–101.

7. PSALTERIUM DECEM CHORDARUM
Inc. Antiqua Patrum traditione perlatum est
MSS. Pauda, Bibl. Anton., 322, ff. 1–42   first half of 13th century
   Paris, Bibl. Nat., Lat. 427, ff. 1–45   13th century
   Rome, Vatican, Lat. 4860, ff. 145–9, 160–92   13th century
   Rome, Vatican, Lat. 5732, ff. 1–36   14/15th century
   Dresden, Sächs. Landesbibl., A. 121, ff. 56–83   13/14th century
   Nuremberg, Städtbibl., Cent. II 51, ff. 2–92   16th century
Editions: Venice 1527, bound with the *Expositio*, ff. 225–79.[1]
   Reprinted Frankfurt-a-M., 1965, 1983.

8. TRACTATUS SUPER QUATUOR EVANGELIA
Inc. Liber generationis Jesu Christi. In exordio sacrae huius lectionis
MSS. Padua, Bibl. Anton., 322, ff. 81–136   first half of 13th century

---

[1] But see La Piana, 'Joachim of Flora', *Speculum*, vii (1932), p. 267 n. 2, who says that there was a separate edition of the *Psalterium* printed at the same time by the same printers and that there is a copy in the Harvard library.

¹Reggio Emilia, Bibl. Semin., R², ff. 21–6   13/14th century
(fragment)
Dresden, Sächs. Landesbibl., A. 121, ff.
179–221   13/14th century
Edition: Buonaiuti, Rome, 1930.

9. DE ARTICULIS FIDEI
Inc. Rogasti me, attentius, fili Johannes
MSS. Padua, Bibl. Anton., 322, ff. 156–62   first half of 13th century
Florence, Bibl. Laur., Plut. IX, dextr. xi,
ff. 58–66   14th century
Reggio Emilia, Bibl. Semin., R², ff. 20–5   13/14th century
Nuremberg, Städtbibl., Cent. II 51, ff. 92–8   16th century
Edition: Buonaiuti, *De Articulis Fidei di Gioacchino da Fiore, Fonti per la Storia d'Italia*, 78 (Rome, 1936).

10. DIALOGI DE PRAESCIENTIA DEI ET PRAEDESTINATIONE ELECTORUM
Inc. Volo, si possum, frater carissime Benedicte, vetustissimae illi quaestioni
MSS. Padua, Bibl. Anton., 322, ff. 43–56   first half of 13th century
Rome, Vatican, Urb. Lat. 8, ff. 165–99   15th century
Reggio Emilia, Bibl. Semin., R², ff. 12–20   13/14th century
Editions: Huck, *Joachim v. Floris*, pp. 278–87.
Leo, P. De, *Gioacchino da Fiore* (ref. n. 3.314), pp. 65–123.

11. TRACTATUS DE VITA S. BENEDICTI ET DE OFFICIO DIVINO SECUNDUM EIUS DOCTRINAM
Inc. Legimus in libro Genesis, qui primus est
MSS. Padua, Bibl. Anton., 322, ff. 141–9   first half of 13th century
Rome, Vatican, Lat. 4860, ff. 35–44   13th century
Nuremberg, Städtbibl., Cent. II, 51, ff. 104–23   16th century
Edition: Baraut, *Analecta Sacra Tarraconensia*, xxiv (1951), pp. 42–118.

12. ADVERSUS (*or Contra*) JUDAEOS
Inc. Contra vetustam duritiam Judaeorum
MSS. Padua, Bibl. Anton., 322, ff. 57–71   first half of 13th century

¹ In the absence of any catalogue numbers for the two Reggio manuscripts I have designated them R¹ and R². See Tondelli, *Lib. Fig.* I, pp. 3 seq. for a descritpion of these.

Reggio Emilia, Bibl. Semin., R², ff. 2–11   13/14th century
Dresden, Sächs. Landesbibl., A. 121, ff. 223–35 13/14th century
¹London, Brit. Mus., Add. 11439, ff. 78–98   1377
Prague, Bibl. Cap. Metrop. ad S. Vitum, C.XCV,
    ff. 1–13   13th century

Edition: Frugoni, A., *Fonti per la Storia d'Italia*, 95 (Rome, 1957).

13. DE SEPTEM SIGILLIS

Inc. Sub hoc tempore continetur de Abraham, Ysaac et Jacob

MSS. Paris, Bibl. Nat., Lat. 11864, f. 152   early 13th century
      Paris, Bibl. Nat., Lat. 3595, ff. 25–28   14th century
      Oxford, Corpus Christi College, 255 A, f. 4 early 13th century
      Padua, Bibl. Anton., 322, f. 166   first half of 13th century
      Dresden, Sächs. Landesbibl., A. 121, ff. 221–2   13/14th century
      Rome, Vatican, Lat. 3822, ff. 1–2   13/14th century
      New York, Pierpont Morgan Lib., 631, ff. 47–8   14th century
      Milan, Bibl. Ambros., H. 15. inf. misc., f. 64   13/14th century
      Wroclaw, Bibl. universytecka, Rediger
         280, ff. 11–13   14th century

Editions: Reeves, Hirsch-Reich, *RTAM* xxi. 239–47.
           Bloomfield, M., Lee, H., *RTAM* xxxviii (1971), pp. 137–142.

14. DE ULTIMIS TRIBULATIONIBUS

Inc. De ultimis tribulationibus disputantes in opusculis nostris

MSS. Padua, Bibl. Anton., 322, ff. 151–3.   first half of 13th century
      Rome, Vatican, Lat. 4860, ff. 47–50   13th century
      Rome, Vatican, Lat. 3822, ff. 15–17   13/14th century
      Florence, Bibl. Laur., Plut. IX, dextr. xi, ff. 54–57 14th century
      Reggio Emilia, Bibl. Semin., R², ff. 1–2   13/14th century
      Dresden, Sächs. Landesbibl., A. 121, ff. 235–7   14th century
      Wroclaw, Bibl. universytecka, Rediger
         280, ff. 39–42   14th century

Edition: Daniel, E. R., *Prophecy and Millenarianism* (ref. 1.1), pp.
         173–89.

_____

¹ Frugoni was unaware of the existence of this copy.

15. EPISTOLA UNIVERSIS CHRISTI FIDELIBUS

Inc. Universis Christi fidelibus ad quos littere iste prevenerint ... Loquens Dominus Iezechieli

MSS. Padua, Bibl. Anton., 322, f. 166

(fragment)	first half of 13th century
Rome, Vatican, Lat. 3822, f. 1^{r-v}	13/14th century
Rome, Vatican, Lat. 2034, ff. 195–7	15th century
Rome, Vatican, Borgh. 190, ff. 2–4	13th century
Florence, Bibl. Laur., Plut. LXXXIX, inf. xli, ff. 109–12	14th century
Paris, Bibl. Nat., Lat. 11864, f. 152^v	early 13th century
Paris, Bibl. Nat., Lat. 3595, f. 19^v–21^v	14th century
Paris, Bibl. Nat., 16397, ff. 119–23	14th century
London, Brit. Mus., Royal and Kings 8. F. xvi, ff. 35–7	14th century
London, Brit. Mus., Add. 11439, ff. 76–7	1377
Milan, Bibl. Ambros., H. 15, inf. misc., ff. 47–8	13/14th century
Wroclaw, Bibl. universytecka, Rediger 280, ff. 10–11	14th century

Edition: Bignami-Odier, *MAH* liv. 220–3.

16. VARIOUS LETTERS AND SERMONS

(a) Epistola Domino Valdonensi

Inc. Domino Valdonensi Dei gratia monasterii abbati

MSS. Rome, Vatican, Lat. 3822, f. 4   13/14th century
Paris, Bibl. Nat., Lat. 3595, f. 34   14th century
Wroclaw, Bibl. universytecka, Rediger
280, f. 13   14th century

Edition: Bignami-Odier, *MAH* liv. 226–7.

(b) Super flumina Babilonis

Inc. Sollempne est et notorium, fratres charissimi
MS. Padua, Bibl. Anton., 322, ff. 71–4   first half of 13th century
Editions: Tondelli, *Lib. Fig.* I. pp. 100–7 (part).
            Antoni, G. De, *Il sermo in septuagesima "Super flumina Babilonis"*. Thesis, Univ. of Padua, 1989/90.

(c) Intelligentia super calathis ad Abbatem Gaufridum

Inc. De spiritualibus autem visum est
MS. Padua, Bibl. Anton., 322, ff. 136–9   first half of 13th century
Edition: Leo, P. De, *Gioacchino da Fiore* (ref. no. 3.314), pp. 135–48

(d) *Expositio de prophetia ignota*
Inc. Beatus Augustinus quasdam peregrinas prophetias
MS. Padua, Bibl. Anton., 322, ff. 149–51   first half of 13th century
Edition: McGinn, B., 'Joachim and the Sibyl' (ref. no. 3.322), pp.
     129–38.

(e) Sermon
Inc. Sumam ego de medulla cedri
MS. Padua, Bibl. Anton., 322, ff. 162^{r-v} first half of 13th century
Edition: Buonaiuti, *De Articulis Fidei* (ref. no. 9 supra), Appendix, pp.
     81–93.

(f) Group of short sermons
MS. Padua, Bibl. Anton., 322, ff. 164^r–165^v first half of 13th century
Edition: Buonaiuti, op. cit., pp. 94–108.

(g) Sermon
Inc. Usitatem inter plurimos questionem
MS. Padua, Bibl. Anton., 322, ff. 139–40   first half of 13th century
Edition: Leo, P. De, *Gioacchino da Fiore* (ref. no. 3.314), pp. 157–63.

17. LIBER FIGURARUM
MSS. Oxford, Corpus Christi College, 255 A,
ff. 4–14	13th century
Reggio Emilia, Bibl. Semin., R¹, ff. 1–20	13/14th century
Dresden, Sächs. Landesbibl., A. 121,	
ff. 87–96	13/14th century
Rome, Vatican, Lat. 4860, ff. 198–204	
(6 figs. with texts)	13th century
Rome, Vatican, Lat. 3822, ff. 2–3, 4^v, 7^r–8^r	
(3 figs., text only)	13/14th century
Paris, Bibl. Nat., Lat. 11864, f. 151	
(1 fig. with text)	early 13th century
Paris, Bibl. Nat., Lat. 3595, ff. 22–5, 29–34	
(3 figs., text only)	14th century
Milan, Bibl. Ambros., H. 15, inf. misc.,	
f. 63 (1 fig., text only)	13/14th century
Florence, Bibl. Laur., Conv. Soppr. 358,	
ff. 92–3 (1 fig., without text)	14th century
Rome, Vatican, Urb. Lat. 8, ff. 132–3	
(text of one figure only)	15th century

Edition: Tondelli, Reeves, Hirsch-Reich, *Il Libro delle Figure di Gioac-
     chino da Fiore*, ii (Turin, 1953).

18. Two Poems: *(a) Hymnus de Patria Coelesti et de Gloria Sanctorum*
(b) Visio Admiranda de Gloria Paradisi

Inc. (a) O felix regnum Patriae supernae
(b) Visionem admirandae ordiar historiae

MSS. Padua, Bibl. Anton., 322, ff. 165–6   first half of 13th century
      Florence, Bibl. Laur., Plut. IX, dextr. xi, f. 66   14th century

Editions: Psalterium Decem Chordarum (Venice, 1527), ff. 279–80.
      G. Falcone, *Poeti e Rimatori Calabri* (Naples, 1899), i. 48–53.
      Huck, *Joachim v. Floris*, pp. 186–9, *(b)* only.
      Reeves, M., Fleming, J., *Two Poems attributed to Joachim of*
      Fiore (Princeton, 1978).

II. SPURIOUS

1. Epistola Subsequentium Figurarum

Inc. Genealogia sanctorum antiquorum

Date: probably in the first generation after Joachim's death (cf. *supra*,
   p. 42.

MSS. Rome, Vatican, Lat. 3822, ff. 3–4   13/14th century
      Paris, Bibl. Nat., Lat. 11864, ff. 151–2   early 13th century
      Paris, Bibl. Nat., Lat. 3595, ff. 28–9   14th century

Editions: Bignami-Odier, *MAH* liv. 224–6.
      Tondelli, *Lib. Fig.* I, pp. 41–3.

2. Liber contra Lombardum

Inc. Cum a pluribus dubitetur de confessione fidei

Date: soon after 1234.

MS. Oxford, Balliol College, CCXCVI, ff. 219–49   14th century

Edition: Ottaviano, *Joachimi Abbatis Liber contra Lombardum* (Rome,
   1934).

3. Super Hieremiam Prophetam

Inc. Verba Hieremiae filii Elchiae

Generally preceded by a supposed letter to the Emperor Henry VI.

Inc. Henrico sexto inclito Romanorum augusto

Date: before 1248, probably before 1243.

MSS. Rome, Vatican, Lat. 4860, ff. 206–74 (excerpts)   13th century
      Rome, Vatican, Lat. 3822, ff. 21–4, 39–100
        (excerpts)   13/14th century
      Florence, Bibl. Laur., Plut. IX, dextr. xi, ff. 1–55   14th century
      Florence, Bibl. Laur., Plut. XX, xix, ff. 1–85   14th century
      Perugia, Bibl. S. Pietro, 15, ff. 70–115   13/14th century
      Paris, Bib. Nat., Lat. 13428, ff. 1–43   15th century

Paris, Bib. Nat., Lat. 15637, ff. 203–42	13th century
Dresden, Sächs. Landesbibl., A. 121, ff. 132–75	14th century
Brussels, Bibl. Roy., Lat. 11956–66, ff. 1–71	13th century
London, Brit. Mus., Add. 11439, ff. 2–73	1377
Wolfenbüttel, Herzog August. Bibl., Lat.	
Helmst. 1064, ff. 1–140	13th century

[Note: see also Moynihan, bibl. no. 3.412].

Editions: Venice, 1516.
Venice, 1525.
Cologne, 1577.

4. VATICINIUM SIBILLAE ERITHREAE

Inc. Exquiritis me o illustrissima turba Danaum

Date: 1249 (?), perhaps earlier.

This exists in two forms: A, the original, longer version; B, a shorter version.

MSS. A. Brussels, Bibl. Roy., 11956–66, ff. 89–92	13th century
Rome, Vatican, Reg. Lat. 132, ff. 97–101	14th century
Florence, Bibl. Ricc., 881, ff. 1–4	14th century
Paris, Bibl. Nat., Lat. 3595, ff. 15–17	
(fragment), 37–53	14th century
Paris, Bibl. Nat., Lat. 6362, ff. 64–8	15th century
Paris, Bibl. Nat., Lat. 14726, ff. 82–95	15th century
Paris, Bibl. Nat., Lat. 3455, ff. 37–45	16th century
B. Rome, Vatican, Lat. 3822, ff. 19–20, 24–5	13/14th century
Rome, Vatican, Lat. 3820, ff. 37–8	15th century
Rome, Vatican, Lat. 2034, ff. 201–2	15th century
Rome, Bibl. Vitt. Eman., 14. S. Pant. 31,	
ff. 49–51	13/14th century
Florence, Bibl. Laur., Plut. LXXXIX, inf. xli,	
ff. 105–8	14th century
Paris, Bibl. Nat., Lat. 3319, ff. 1–5	14/15th century
London, Brit. Mus., Add. 11439, ff. 73, 75	1377
(fragments)	
Cambridge, Univ. Lib., Mm. 1. 16, ff. 24–46	14th century
Cambridge, Corpus Christi Coll., 138,	
pp. 179–82	14th century
Hague, Bibl. Reg., 71. E. 44, ff. 104–12	1500
Nuremberg, Städtbibl., Cent. IV, 32, ff. 29–34	13th century
Wroclaw, Bibl. universytecka, Rediger	
280, ff. 9–10	14th century

Edition: Holder-Egger, *NA* xv. 155–73 (A); xxx. 328–35 (B).[1]

---

[1] C. Alexandre, *Oracula Sibyllina*, ii, excursus (Paris, 1856), p. 291, mentions an edition published by Lodovicus de Tovat (? Toval) in Spain in 1508 but says he has not been able to find it.

5. De Oneribus Prophetarum

Inc. Henrico sexto inclito . . . Pie petis

Date: probably 1255–56.

MSS. Rome, Vatican, Borgh. 190, ff. 183–91	13th century
Rome, Vatican, Lat. 3822, ff. 28–33	13/14th century
Rome, Vatican, Lat. 5732, ff. 57–71	14/15th century
Rome, Vatican, Lat. 3820, ff. 14–26	15th century
Rome, Bibl. Vitt. Eman., 14. S. Pant. 31, ff. 39–47	14th century
Perugia, Bibl. S. Pietro, 15, ff. 115–26	13/14th cenutry
Milan, Bibl. Ambros., H. 15, inf. misc., ff. 52–62	13/14th century
Paris, Bibl. Nat., Lat. 3595, ff. 1–15	14th century
Paris, Bibl. Nat., Lat. 13428, ff. 44–56	15th century
Paris, Bibl. Nat., Lat. 14726, ff. 77–81	15th century
Paris, Bibl. Nat., Lat. 16397, ff. 125–36	14th century
London, Brit. Mus., Royal and Kings 8. F. xvi, ff. 38–44	14th century
Brussels, Bibl. Roy., 11956–66, ff. 82–7	13th century
Hague, Bibl. Reg., 71. E. 44, ff. 101–3, 143–5 (extracts)	1500
Wroclaw, Bibl. universytecka, Rediger 280, ff. 21–9	14th century

Edition: Holder-Egger, *NA* xxxiii. 139–87 (but note that the version in the British Museum manuscript differs in order, omits some parts, and contains further material).

6. Expositio Abbatis Joachimi super Sibillis et Merlino

Inc. Interpretari tua serenitas imperat Merlinum

Date: probably before 1250.

MSS. Brussels, Bibl. Roy., 11956–66, ff. 72–82	13th century
Rome, Vatican, Lat. 5732, ff. 51–7	14/15th century
Rome, Vatican, Lat. 3820, ff. 1–14, 27–36	15th century
Rome, Bibl. Vitt. Eman., 14. S. Pant. 31, ff. 29–39, 51–8	14th century
Paris, Bibl. Nat., Lat. 3319, ff. 9–25, 28–38	14th century
Paris, Bibl. Nat., Lat. 14726, ff. 50–1	15th century
Nuremberg, Städtbibl. Cent. IV, 32, ff. 23–9, 39–45	13th century
Hague, Bibl. Reg. 71. E. 44, ff. 99–100	1500

Unedited

7. Prophetia Abbatis Joachim Ordinis Cisterciensis transmissa Henrico Imperatori Alemannie de Tribus Statibus Sancte Ecclesie

Inc. Tres sunt status in ecclesia

Date: probably 1250–60.

MS. Paris, Bibl. Nat., Lat. 2599, ff. ccxliv–ccxlix   14th century

Note: This has close affinities with No. 3 above, from which several short passages are taken. But it is not simply a selection from the longer work. The quotations are worked into a slightly different scheme of ideas and vary verbally. Some parts are original, while, on the other hand, important sections of the *Super Hier.* are not used. See Bignami-Odier, *Roquetaillade*, pp. 235–6. Passages from the *Super Hier.* are used as follows: f. ccxliv^v: *S.H. Prefatio*, f. 23^r; f. ccxlv^r: *S.H.* ff. 23^r, 14^r; f. ccxlv^v: *S.H.* ff. 1^v, 18^v, 13^r, 51^v; f. ccxlvi^r: *S.H.* ff. 53^r, 46^v; f. ccxlvii : *S.H.* 46^r; f. ccxlvii^v: *S.H.* f. 49^v.

Unedited

8. SUPER ESAIAM PROPHETAM

Inc. Joachim ad fratrem Raynerium de Pontio super prophetas

Usually preceded by a small figure-collection with text to which the name *Praemissiones* is here given (see No. 9).

Date: probably 1260–66.

MSS. Rome, Vatican, Lat. 4959, ff. 5–61   13th century
Rome, Vatican, Lat. Ross. 552, ff. 6–65   end of 13th century
Perugia, Bibl. S. Pietro, 15, ff. 6–69   13/14th century
Venice, Bibl. Marc., Lat. I, 74, ff. 5–65   14th century
Vienna, Staatsbibl., 1400 (Theol. 71), ff. 91–156   14th century
London, Brit. Mus., Add. 11439, ff. 103–23 (part only)   1377
London, Brit. Mus., Cotton, Tib. B. V, Part II,
ff. 92–143   14th century
Prague, Mus. Nat., XIV B. 17, ff. 7–
72 (*olim* Roudnice, Bibl. Lobkowicz,
VI. Fc. 25)   first half of 14th century

Edition: Venice, 1517.

9. THE PRAEMISSIONES

A small figure-collection usually associated with No. 8.

Date: probably 1260–66.

MSS. Rome, Vatican, Lat. Ross. 4959, ff. 1–4 (9 figs.)   13th century
MSS. Rome, Vatican, Lat. Ross. 552, ff. 1–5
(11 figs.)   end of 13th century
Perugia, Bibl. S. Pietro, 15, ff. 1–5 (11 figs.)   13/14th century
London, Brit. Mus., Add. 11439, ff. 99–103 (11 figs.)   1377
Vienna, Staatsbibl., 1400 (Theol. 71), ff. 21–5
(11 figs.)   14th century

Prague, Mus. Nat., XIV B, 17, ff. 2–6 (II figs.)

  (*olim* Roudnice, Bibl. Lobkowicz, VI. Fc. 25)   14th century

Venice, Bibl. Marc., Lat. I, 74, ff. 2–4 (8 figs.)   14th century

London, Brit. Mus., Cotton Tib. B. V., Pars II,

  ff. 89–91 (8 figs.)   14th century

Editions: prefacing *Super Esaiam*, Venice, 1517.

  prefacing *Super Hier.*, 2nd edn., Venice, 1525.

  prefacing *Expos.* and *Psalt.*, Venice, 1527.

10. ORACULUM CYRILLI CUM EXPOSITIONE ABBATIS JOACHIM

This has various elements: (*a*) Prologue (often with a later Commentary) by a Frater Gilbertus Anglicus; (*b*) supposed Letter of Cyril to Joachim; (*c*) supposed Letter of Joachim to Cyril; (*d*) Oraculum Cyrilli; (*e*) supposed Gloss by Joachim.

Inc. (*a*) *Frater Gilbertus anglicus ille magnus theologus, qui et ipse hunc librum*

  (*b*) *Domui totius divine sapientie, septiformi columpna*

  (*c*) *Stelle manenti in ordine sanctitatis*

  (*d*) *Tempore annorum Christi millesimo ducentesimo quinquagesimo quarto*

  (*e*) *Millesimo ducentesimo quinquagesimo quarto: puto hoc tempus hic prescriptum*

Date: probably 1280–90 (with the addition of (*a*) in the 14th century).

MSS. Rome, Vatican, Lat. 3819, ff. 131–4   14th century

Rome, Vatican, Lat. 3816, ff. i–xi   15th century

Rome, Vatican, Lat., 3820, ff. 46–62   15th century

Rome, Bibl. Vitt. Eman., 30, ff. 1–51   14th century

Rome, Bibl. Vallicel., J. 32, ff. 1–54   17th century

Paris, Bibl. Nat., Lat. 4126, ff. 282–94   14th century

Paris, Bibl. Nat., Lat. 2599, ff. 1–244 (with the Commentary of Jean de Roquetaillade)   14th century

Paris, Bibl. Nat., Lat. 14726, ff. 51–76   15th century

Paris, Bibl. Nat., Lat. 2598, ff. 1–19   14/15th century

Paris, Bibl. Nat., Lat. 3184, ff. 90–108   15th century

[1]Berlin, Staatsbibl., Lat. qu. 54, ff. 50–9   14/15th century

Cambridge, Corpus Christi Coll., 404, ff. 67–88   14th century

Cambridge, Gonville and Caius Coll., 388/608, ff. 103–25   14/15th century

Hague, Bibl. Reg., 71. E. 44, ff. 70–99   1500

[1] The present location of this MS. is uncertain. After 1945 it was in the Universitäts Bibliothek, Tübingen.

Nuremberg, Städtbibl., Cent. IV, 32, ff. 1–16	13th century
Wroclaw, Bibl. universytecka, Rediger	
280, ff. 54–60	14th century

Editions: *Divinum Oraculum S. Cyrilli Carmelitae... Cui adiungitur Commentarius B. P. F. Philippi a Sanctissima Trinitate Carmelitae discalceati* (Lyon, 1663).

P. Puir in Burdach, *Vom Mittelalter*, II, iv, Appendix, pp. 241–327.

11. VATICINIA DE SUMMIS PONTIFICIBUS *(first fifteen)*

Inc. Principium malorum ... Genus nequam

Date: ? 1300–1305.

MSS. Rome, Vatican, Lat. 3822, f. 6^{r-v}	
(incomplete)	early 14th century
Cambridge, Corpus Christi College,	
404, ff. 88^r–95^r	early 14th century
Oxford, Bodl. Libr., Douce 88,	
ff. 240^r–47^r	early 14th century
Florence, Bibl. Ricc., 1222B, ff. 1^r–8^v	14th century
Lunel, Bibl. de Louis Médard à Bibl. Munic.,	
7, ff. 4^r–22^v	14th century
Yale, Univ. Libr., T. E. Marston	
225, ff. 15–22	14th century
Paris, Archiv. Nat., JJ. 28, ff. 285^r–91^v	14th century
Monreale. Bibl. Comun., XXV, F.17, ff. 1^r–17^r	14th century
Rome, Vatican, Lat. 3819, ff. 147^r–50^r	14th century

Joined to the later set of *Vaticinia*, attributed to Anselm, Bishop of Marsico, and placed as numbers 16 to 30 in the series of 30, this work appears in many manuscripts of the late 14th century onwards. Only early manuscripts in which it appears alone have been listed here.

Editions: (with the later 15) numerous; see Russo, *Bibliografia*, pp. 44–8.

12. LIBER DE FLORE

Inc. Tempore colubri leaenae filit

Date: 1303–1305.

MSS. Arras, Bibl. Munic., 138, ff. 85–106	14th century
Rome, Bibl. Vallicel., J. 32, ff. 2–18	17th century
Rome, Bibl. Vallicel., J. 33, ff 106–48	17th century

Edition: Grundmann, *HJ* xlix, 80–4 (parts only).

Grouped with the above are two small tracts also composed 1303–5:

(a) a commentary on the *Liber de Flore* usually attributed to Rabanus;
(b) the *Horoscopus* written by Dandalus.

13. SUMMULA SEU BREVILOQUIUM SUPER CONCORDIA NOVI ET
VETERIS TESTAMENTI

*Inc. Prologus. Exposita sunt tempora per dicta prophetarum
Breviloquium. Cum non sit nostrum nisi divina revelatione*

Date: probably 1351–54.

MSS. Madrid, Bibl. Nat., 6972 (formerly S. 247), ff. 1–50 *c.* 1368–70
Tarragona, Bibl. Civil., R. 79. S. XV. R. 232,

ff. 1–65	15th century
London, Brit. Mus., Egerton 1150, ff. 1–92	1455
Rome, Vatican, Lat. 11581, ff. 1–65	1488

Five other MSS. contain excerpts.

Edition: Lee, H., Reeves, M., Silano, G., *Western Mediterranean Prophecy* (ref. no. 7.72), pp. 164–322.

14. PROPHETIAE ET EPISTOLAE JOACHIMI ABBATIS FLORENSIS PERTINENTES
AD RES KALABRAS

Inc. Quibus accesserunt expositiones tum literales tum allegoricae

Date: 17th century.

MS. Rome, Vatican, Rossiano 480, ff. 1–5   17th century

Edition: Tondelli, *Sophia* xix, 374–7 (part only).

Note: MS. Vatican Ferraioli 728, ff. 371^r–372^v, contains a *Vaticinium B.
Joachim Abbas, inc. Audite Reges Iudicium Domini.* This is extracted,
with other prophecies attributed to Joannes de Aquitania and Joannes
Kalà, from the *Opusculum D. Ioannis de Bonatio De Prophetis Sui
Temporis,* published Naples 1660. It is connected with the above
prophecies, since all appear to emanate from the same forging source
(cf. *supra,* pp. 119–21 on Stocchi, the forger). The presence of these
prophecies in the late sixteenth-century Ferraioli manuscript seems
to throw back the origin of these forgeries to a somewhat earlier date.

Two other works must be mentioned here:

1. *De Semine Scripturarum*

This is not a pseudo-Joachimist work at all, having been written *c.* 1204.
But it was persistently attributed to Joachim during the later Middle
Ages. On this work see B. Hirsch, 'Zur "Noticia saeculi" u. zum "Pavo" ',
Mitteilungen des Instituts f. österreichische Geschichtsforschung, xxxviii.

571–610; B. Hirsch-Reich, 'Alexander v. Roes Stellung zu den Prophetien', ibid. lxvii (1959), pp. 306–16.

2. *Expositio magni prophete Joachim in librum beati Cyrilli* or *Liber de
magnis tribulationibus . . . compilatus a Theolosphoro de Cusentia*
(Telesphorus)

This is not strictly a pseudo-Joachimist work because never attributed to
Joachim himself, but it is closely related to several of the above works,
notably nos. 10 and 12. A full account of the manuscripts and editions of
this work has been given by Donckel, *AFH* xxvi. 33–49.

APPENDIX B

SOME SHORT PROPHECIES ATTRIBUTED TO JOACHIM, OR ASSOCIATED WITH JOACHIMIST PROPHECIES

1. VERSE ON ANTICHRIST

Inc. Cum fuerint expleti anni mille ducenti

Date: before 1250.

Text: *supra*, p. 49.

References: *supra*, pp. 49–51, 56.

2. PROPHECIE IOACHIM IN MAIORI LIBRO DE CONCORDANCIIS

Inc. Anno Incarnacionis MCCL (or later date) *corruent nobiles*

Date: before 1250.

Text: *supra*, p. 50.

References: *supra*, pp. 51, 84, 92, 94.

3. PROPHETIC VERSES SUPPOSEDLY EXCHANGED BETWEEN FREDERICK II AND INNOCENT IV

Inc. (1) *Roma diu titubans*; (2) *Fata monent, stelleque docent*

Date: before 1254.

Text: Holder-Egger, *NA* xxx. 336–7.

References: see the long list of manuscripts, chronicles, etc., given by Holder-Egger, pp. 335–69.

4. *Inc. Oculus eius morte claudet abscondita*

(Part of the pseudo-Joachimist Sibyl Erithreae but circulating separately. Sometimes only the sentence 'Sonabit in populis: *Vivit* et *non vivit*' is quoted).

Date: 1249 or earlier.

Text: Holder-Egger, *NA* xv. 168; xxx. 334.

References: *De Oneribus*, f. 40ᵛ.
        Salimbene, p. 243.
        A. Milioli, *Liber de Temporibus, MGHS* xxxi. 568–9.

5. *Inc. In die illa elevabitur draco repletus furore*

Date: 1260–4, according to Tondelli, *Studi e documenti*, iv. 7–9.

Text: Tondelli, loc. cit., pp. 5–6.

References: MSS. Padua, Bibl. Anton., 90. Misc. 2a, f. 44ʳ.
Reggio Emilia, Bibl. Munic., Tutti D. 2, f. 131ᵛ.
Paris, Bibl. Nat., Lat. 14726, ff. 76–7.
Nuremberg, Städtbibl., Cent. IV, 32, ff. 45–6.
Florence, Bibl. Laur., Plut. XVIII, sin. v, inside end cover, fragment, *inc. Post celestinum.*

6. *Inc. Regnabit Manfridus bastardus*; (later) *Inc. Veniet aquila cuius volatu debellabitur*

Date: c. 1268.

Text: *supra*, pp. 311–12, 333–4, 361.

References: *supra*, pp. 74, 311–12, 333 n. 5, 361 n. 1.

7. *Inc. Gallorum levitas*

Date: c. 1268.

Text: Holder-Egger, *NA* xxxiii. 125–6.

References: *supra*, pp. 312 n. 1, 371.
(See also Holder-Egger, *NA* xxxiii. 119–24.)

8. *Inc. Rex novus adveniet*

Date: after 1268.

Text: *supra*, p. 312; Holder-Egger, *NA* xxx. 383 (line 41)–384.

References: *supra*, p. 312 n. 2.
(See also Holder-Egger, *NA* xxx. 380–4.)

9. *Inc. Hic Siculos pravamque tribum sevi Frederici* (part of No. 8)

Date: after 1268.

Text: Holder-Egger, *NA* xxx. 384 (line 47).

Reference: MS. Florence, Bibl. Ricc., 688, f. cxii.

10. *Inc. De huius Frederici germine radix peccatrix erumpet*

Date: after 1268.

Text: *supra*, p. 313.

References: Alexander v. Roes, *De Translatione Imperii* . . . (Leipzig, 1930), p. 31.
T. Ebendorfer, *Cronica Regum Romanorum* (ref. p. 333 n. 3), p. 143.
MGHS xxiv. 285 n. 2, for a 15th-century reference in MS. Vindob. 3402.
F. Lot, *Revue historique*, xlvi (1891), p. 69, for a reference in a Bavarian chronicle.

11. *Inc. Erunt duo viri, unus hinc, alius inde*

Date: between 1251 and 1274.

Text: Bartholomew of Pisa, *De Conformitate*, pp. 53–4, cited as from the *Lib. Conc.* This must be an interpolation, possibly at *Lib. Conc.* v, cap 118, f. 133ᵛ. Now edited by J. M. Arcelus Ulibarrena, see bibl. 6.283.

References: *supra*, pp. 100, 182 n. 2, 239 n. 4.

12. PROPHECIA JOACHIM DE ORDINE FRATRUM MINORUM ET PRAEDICATORUM

Inc. Dixit idem ioachim quod primus status seculi terminavit in dispersione

Date: possibly mid-thirteenth century.

Text: unedited.

References: MS. Dublin, Trinity College, 347, f. 35ʳ⁻ᵛ.

Note: After a statement of the three *status*, the text concentrates on the prophecy of the two orders. It contains passages from the *Super Hier.*, ff. 20ᵛ, 25ᵛ, 26ʳ, in a shortened form, with verbal variations. In the opinion of the Librarian at Trinity College the manuscript is probably a thirteenth-century one.

13. ANOTHER PROPHECY OF THE TWO FUTURE ORDERS

Inc. Sed et circa finem seculi

Date: probably mid-thirteenth century.

Text: unedited.

Reference: MS. Padua, Bibl. Univ., 2063, ff. 81ʳ–82ᵛ.

Note: This uses most of the Biblical figures denoting the two orders which are found in the genuine and pseudo-Joachimist works. It purports to have been written in the fortieth generation after Christ, i.e. A.D. 1200, and in style resembles the non-political parts of the *Super Hieremiam* and *Super Esaiam*.

14. FRATER RAYNERIUS JOACHIMO

Inc. Decem plagas quibus affligetur Egyptus

Date: This seems to belong to the same group as Nos. 4–7 in Appendix A. II. Probable date *c.* 1250–60.

Text: unedited.

References: MSS. Rome, Vatican, Lat. 3820, ff. 26ʳ–27ᵛ.
Rome, Bibl. Vitt. Eman., 14. S. Pant. 31. 8, f. 48ʳ.
Paris, Bibl. Nat., Lat. 3319, ff. 26ᵛ–28ʳ.

Note: This short text draws concords between the ten plagues of Egypt, belonging to the Old Dispensation, and the seven phials poured forth by the seven angels in the Apocalypse which signify the seven plagues of the New Dispensation. Characteristic Joachimist notes are the double tribulation in the sixth age, the assignation of the four orders and the *sedes Dei* to the first five ages, the placing of the present in the sixth age and the expectation of the Sabbath Age. A reference to the Erithrean prophecy helps to date this.

15. TRACTATUS ABBATIS JOACHIM SUPER ILLO PASSU APOCALIPSIS DE NUMERO BESTIE

Inc. Quia semper in stipendariis propriis

Date: c. 1252–60.

Text: unedited.

References: MSS. Rome, Vatican, Lat. 3822, f. 14ʳ⁻ᵛ.
Rome, Vatican, Lat. 5732, f. 62ᵛ (with *inc. Tenebre erant*).
Rome, Bibl. Vitt. Eman., 14. S. Pant. 31. 8, f. 47ʳ (with *inc. Tenebre erant*).
Paris, Bibl. Nat., Lat. 3319, ff. 25ᵛ–26ᵛ.
Paris, Bibl. Nat., Lat. 3595, ff. 15ʳ–17ʳ.
Brussels, Bibl. Roy., 11956–66, ff. 87–9 (with *inc. Tenebre erant*).

Note: This short piece is an exposition of the number of the Beast: 666. It is interpreted in terms of the six *etates mundi*, the six *tempora ecclesiae*, and the *tercius numerus ceteris brevior sex in quibus persecutio gravis erit*. References to the Sibyl Erithrea prophecy and to Frederick II show that it belongs to the same group of writings as No. 14. It is found also in a shorter version, *inc. Tenebre erant super faciem abyssi*.

16. JOACHIM DE REGNO SICULO

Inc. Cum ad me ruine miseriam predixerit frater Raynerius

Date: *c*. 1252–60.

Text: unedited.

References: MSS. Rome, Vatican, Lat. 3820, f. 45^v.
Paris, Bibl. Nat., Lat. 3319, f. 40^{r-v}.

Note: A political prophecy on Sicily which, because of its reference to Frater Raynerius, should probably be assigned to the same group of writings as Nos. 14 and 15.

17. PROPHECIA ABBATIS JOACHIM DE REGNO BOEMIE

Inc. In etate sexta huius seculi

Date: 1271–3.

Text: R. Kestenberg-Gladstein, 'A Joachimite Prophecy concerning Bohemia', *The Slavonic and East European Review*, xxxiv (1955), pp. 35–9.

References: MSS. Prague, Bibl. Univ., XII E. 13, f. 122^v.
Prague, Bibl. Metrop. Capit., G. XXIV, f. 528^v.
Vienna, Staatsbibl., 1291, f. 1^v.
Vienna, Staatsarchiv, 22, f. 20^r.
Munich, Staatsbibl., Clm. 14, 3134, f. 26^v.
Wolfenbüttel, Herzog August. Bibl., 42. 3. Aug., f. 304^v.

Note: This list of references is taken from Dr. Kestenberg-Gladstein's article, p. 34 n. 2.

18. SIBILLA SAMIA

Inc. Excitabitur Romanus contra Romanum

Date: If the argument for the genuine character of No. 14 (*d*) in Appendix A. I is correct, this prophecy, which is quoted there, must go back to the 12th century.

Text: Holder-Egger, *NA* xv. 178.

References: MSS. Padua, Bibl. Anton. 322, ff. 149–51 (with Joachim's Commentary).
Rome, Vatican, Lat. 3822, ff. 17^r, 100^r (called Sibylla Delphica).
Rome, Bibl. Vitt. Eman., 14. S. Pant. 31. 8, f. 49^v.
Paris, Bibl. Nat., Lat. 3319, f. 3^v.

19. *Inc. Imperio grandis aquila nigra pennas ocius expergiscere*

A passage from No. 10 in Appendix A. II which circulated separately in a corrupted form.

Date: 1280–90.

Text: see References.

References: quoted Purstinger, *Onus Ecclesiae*, cap. xxxviii.
Lazius, *Fragmentum*, f. Kiiiᵛ.
P. Regiselmo, *Vaticinia* (Venice, 1589), No. XXVIII.
MS. Oxford, Bod. Lib., Laud 588, f. 22ᵛ.

20. *Inc. In illo tempore aquila veniens a septentrione*

Date: uncertain.

Text: unedited.

References: MSS. Rome, Vatican, Lat. 3816, f. 62ᵛ.
Rome, Vatican, Ottobon. 1106, f. 24ᵛ.
Venice, Bibl. Marc., Lat. Cl. III. 177, f. 43ʳ.
Paris, Bibl. Nat., Lat. 3455, f. 34ᵛ.

21. *Inc. Veh mundo in centum annis*

Date: incorporated by Arnold of Villanova into his work *De cymbalis ecclesie*, written in 1301.

Text: Pou y Marti, *Visionarios*, pp. 54–5.
Finke, *Aus den Tagen*, pp. 218–22 (extracts in footnotes).

References: MSS. Rome, Vatican, Lat. 3824, ff. 95–6.
Paris, Bibl. Nat., Lat. 15033, ff. 236–7.
Paris, Bibl. Nat., Lat. 14669, f. 133.
Tours, Bibl. Munic., 520, ff. 18–32 (with commentary by Roquetaillade).
Rouen, Bibl. Munic., 1355, f. 97ᵛ.
Vienna, Staatsbibl., 545, ff. 107ʳ–111ᵛ.
Printed work: Purstinger, *Onus Ecclesiae*, cap. XLI.

22. Dᴇ Aɴɢᴇʟɪᴄᴏ Pᴀsᴛᴏʀᴇ ᴇᴛ ᴇɪᴜs Bᴏɴɪᴛᴀᴛᴇ ᴇᴛ Vɪʀᴛᴜᴛᴇ ᴇᴛ Oᴘᴇʀɪʙᴜs Sᴀɴᴄᴛɪs ϙᴜɪ ᴀᴘᴘᴀʀᴇʙɪᴛ Fɪɴɪᴛɪs Tʀɪʙᴜʟᴀᴛɪᴏɴɪʙᴜs

Inc. Viso et prenotato per quos et qualiter

Date: end of 14th century.

Text: this consists of selected parts of the *libellus* of Telesphorus of Cosenza, which was printed at Venice in 1516 (see Appendix A, p. 524).

References: MSS. Paris, Bibl. Nat., Lat. 14726, ff. 98ʳ–115ʳ.
Hague, Bibl. Reg., 71. E. 44, ff. 118ʳ–122ʳ.

Note: The selections begin on f. 25ʳ of the Venetian printed edition, but diverge considerably from it. They follow closely MS. Venice, Bibl. Marc., Lat. III, 177, ff. 28ʳ–35ʳ with earlier extracts, corresponding to ff. 26ʳ seq., inserted later. In the Paris manuscript captions and sometimes blank spaces indicate that the selections were made from a copy with the original pictures. It must be remembered that in the printed edition more extensive picture-sections were added which make collation with this text more difficult. The parts selected in this text deal mainly with the Angelic Pope and his three successors.

23. SECOND CHARLEMAGNE PROPHECY

Inc. Karolus filius Karoli ex natione illustrissimi Lilii habens frontem longam

Date: 1380.

Text: *supra*, p. 328.

M. Chaume, 'Une prophétie relative à Charles VI' *Revue du Moyen Âge latin*, iii (1947), p. 29.

References: MSS. Rome, Vatican, Reg. Lat. 580, f. 52ʳ.

Rome, Vatican, Lat. 4872, ff. 167ᵛ–168ᵛ.

Rome, Vatican, Chig. A. VII. 220, f. 50ᵛ.

Venice, Bibl. Marc., Lat. Cl. III, 177, f. 35ᵛ; (another version, f. 49ᵛ).

Modena, Bibl. Estense, M. 5. 27, f. 42ᵛ.

Paris, Bibl. Nat., Lat. 3598, f. 45ʳ.

Rouen, Bibl. Munic., 1355, ff. 87ᵛ, 97ᵛ.

Munich, Staatsbibl., Clm. 313, f. 40ʳ.

London, British Mus., Add. 24663, f. 10ᵛ (English trans.).

Cambridge, Univ. Lib., Kk. VI. 16, f. 185ᵛ.

Florence, Bibl. Nat., Cent. Cod. II. xi. 18, f. 8ʳ, contains this prophecy with the following introduction: 'Hec prophetia compillata est per me fratrum Ioannem peregrinum de Bononia monasterii sancti Antonii de Venetiis ... et ista est prophetia IX illius Abbatis Joachim Libro tertio regum Capitulo XIII.' Bezold, *Kaisersage*, p. 600, cites a similar example in Munich, for which he gives the reference Cod. lat. Monac. 14. 668, ff. 43–4.

Printed Works:

K. de Lettenhove, 'Les chroniques inédites de Gilles le Bel', *Bulletins de l'Académie Royale des Sciences, des Lettres et des Beaux-Arts de Belgique*, 2nd series, ii (1857), pp. 442–3.

N. Valois, 'Conseils et prédictions adressés à Charles VII en 1445 par un certain Jean du Bois', *Annuaire-Bulletin de la Société de l'Histoire de France*, xlvi (1909), p. 226.

T. Ebendorfer, *Cronica Regum Romanorum*, ed. A. Pibram, *Mittheilungen des Instituts für oesterreichische Geschichtsforschung*, iii (Innsbruck, 1890), p. 149.

Guilloche of Bordeaux, *La Prophécie du roy Charles VIII* (the original prophecy translated into French and expanded). Text printed in full in the following: C. de Cherrier, *Histoire de Charles VIII* (Paris, 1868), i. 487–90; Marquis de la Grange, *La Prophécie du Roy Charles VIII de Maître Guilloche Bourdelois* (Paris, 1869), pp. 1–9; Chaume, op. cit., pp. 32–4.

A. Benedictus, *Diaria de Bello Carolino* (probably Venice, 1496), unpag. Bk. I (beginning).

Calendar of State Papers, Venice II, 1509–27 (London, 1867), No. 1301, p. 566 (an English version sent back to Venice by Sanuto in 1519).

Purstinger, *Onus Ecclesiae*, cap. XLVIII.

Erzelung der Kunigreich in Hispanien . . . Mer ein alte Prophecy Kay. Carl betreffend (no pl. of pub., 1532), unpag., at the end (German trans.).

Lazius, *Fragmentum*, Hiiii^r, Kiv^r.

Mirabilis Liber (Paris, 1522), f. xl^r.

J. Baptista Nazarus, a work cited by Wolf, *Lect. mem.* ii. 893.

Sire de Chavigny, *Les Pléiades* (Lyon, 1603), p. 1.

J. Maxwell, *Admirable and notable Prophesies, uttered in former times by 24 famous Romain Catholickes* . . . (London, 1615), p. 44.

D. Pareus, *Commentary upon the Divine Revelation*, trans. E. Arnold (Heidelberg, 1644), p. 440.

24. *Inc. Veniet Aquila grandis quae vincet omnes*

Date: cited as from the *Super Hieremiam*, but the first example I have found is in 1532. Not a direct quotation, but may be derived from *Super Hier.*, ff. 58^v seq.

Text: see References.

References:

J. Carion, *Chronica* (2nd edn. Halle, 1537), f. 301^v.

Lazius, *Fragmentum*, f. Kii^v.

T. Schnellenberg, *Practica deutsch*, ed. T. Tetzer, 'Tarquinius Schnellenberg u. sein Werk Practica deutsch', *Zeitschrift f. Bücherfreunde*, N.F. iii (1911), p. 174.

25. *Inc. Post haec . . . egredietur Aquila de Germaniae rupibus multis associata griffonibus*

Date: first cited by Lichtenberger from the Sibyl Cumaea in 1488.

Text: see References.

References:

Lichtenberger, *Prognosticatio*, ii, cap. 4.

W. Aytinger, *De revelatione beati Methodii* (Basle, 1498), cap. 2, with a new sentence tacked on the front, 'inc. Egredietur Aquila postquam I. octavum'.

Lazius, *Fragmentum*, f. K^r, in the Aytinger version.

Echoes are also found in P. Gengenbach's vernacular prophecy, *Der Nollhart* (Basle, 1517) and in the republished version, *Von ainen Waldbrüder* (1522).

APPENDIX C

EXAMPLES OF PROPHETIC ANTHOLOGIES

Note: 'Anthology' is here used to describe a collection of short pieces. With the exception of No. 5, I have usually excluded longer works and extracts from them. In some cases the 'anthology' itself forms a unit within a larger collection of works and excerpts (e.g. Nos. 2 and 3).

1. MS. PARIS, BIBL. NAT., LAT. 11864, ff. 151ᵛ–152ᵛ

Date: first decade of the thirteenth century; northern scriptorium.

Contents:

1. f. 151ᵛ Tables of Concords (from the *Lib. Fig.*)
2. f. 152ʳ *De septem sigillis*
3. ff. 151ᵛ–152ʳ *Epistola subsequentium figurarum* See Nos.
    (written across the bottom of two pages in four short 2 and 4
    columns)
4. f. 152ᵛ *Universis Christi fidelibus*

Description: Tondelli, Reeves, Hirsch-Reich, *Lib. Fig.* II, p. 34.

2. MS. ROME, VATICAN, LAT. 3822

Date: end of thirteenth century; probably south Italian.

Contents:

1. f. 1ʳ   *Universis Christi fidelibus*
2. f. 1ᵛ   *De septem temporibus (sigillis)*   cf.
3. ff. 2ᵛ, 3ʳ Tables of Concords   No. 1
4. f. 3ᵛ   *Epistola subsequentium figurarum*   See No. 4,
5. f. 4ʳ   *Epistola Domino Valdonensi*   items 5–11
6. ff. 7ʳ, 4ᵛ Tree-figure
7. ff. 7ᵛ, 8ʳ Dragon-figure (text only from *Lib. Fig.*)
8. f. 5ʳ   Different dragon-figure with different text

Description: Holder-Egger, *NA* xxxiii. 97–105.
             Bignami-Odier, *MAH* liv. 219–34.
             Reeves, Hirsch-Reich, *MARS* iii. 177–9.

3. MS. ROME, VATICAN, LAT. 4860

Date: late thirteenth century; probably south Italian.

Contents:

1. ff. 198ᵛ–200ʳ Tables of Concords
2. f. 201ʳ Dragon-figure
3. ff. 201ᵛ–203ʳ *Mysterium Ecclesie* (figure)
4. ff. 203ᵛ–204ʳ *Dispositio novi ordinis* (figure)
5. f. 204ᵛ Three *status* (figure)

Description: Bignami-Odier, *MAH* liv, pp. 235–41.

4. MS. PARIS, BIBL. NAT., LAT. 3595

Date: fourteenth century; probably Italian.

Contents:

1. f. 1ʳ *De Oneribus*
2. f. 15ʳ *Quia semper in stipendariis*
3. f. 15ʳ *Commentatio in prophetiam Sybille Erythreae*
   (fragment)
4. f. 17ʳ *De ultimo antichristo*
5. f. 19ᵛ *Universis Christi fidelibus*
6. f. 22ʳ Tables of Concords
7. f. 25ᵛ *De septem sigillis*
8. f. 28ʳ *Epistola subsequentium figurarum*
9. f. 29ᵛ Tree-figure (text)
10. f. 31ʳ Dragon-figure (text)
11. f. 34ʳ *Epistola Domino Valdonensi*

} See Nos. 1 and 2, items 1–7, but drawn from an older pre-1260 version

12. f. 35ᵛ *Prophetia . . . quedam virgo . . . de teutonicis imperatoribus*
13. f. 37ʳ *Exquiritis me o illustrissima turba danaum*

Description: Reeves, Hirsch-Reich, *MARS* iii. 180–2.

5. MS. PARIS, BIBL. NAT., LAT. 16397

Date: fourteenth century; French. Copied except for item 4 in fourteenth-century English MS. Brit. Mus., Royal 8, F. xvi, and Milan, Bibl. Ambros., MS. H. 15, inf. misc.

Contents:

1. f. 61ʳ *Liber Concordie*
2. f. 98ᵛ *Liber Introductorius in Apocalypsim*
3. f. 108ʳ *Psalterium decem chordarum* (excerpts)
4. f. 109ʳ *Super Hieremiam* (excerpts)
5. f. 119ʳ *Universis Christi fidelibus*
6. f. 125ᵛ *De Oneribus*

6. MS. PARIS, BIBL. NAT., LAT. 3319

Date: late fourteenth century.

Contents:

1. f. 1ʳ   *Vaticinium Sibille Erithre. Inc. Exquiritis me*
2. f. 3ᵛ   *Sibilla Samia. Inc. Excitabitur Romanus*
3. f. 4ʳ   *Inc. Nascetur aquila sine plumis*
4. f. 5ʳ   *Vaticinium Merlini Britannici*
5. f. 9ᵛ   *Expos. Ab. Joachimi super Sibillis et Merlino*
         Inc. Interpretari tua serenitas imperat
6. f. 25ᵛ   *Inc. Quia semper in stipendariis*
7. f. 26ᵛ   *Inc. Frater Raynerius Joachimi . . . decem plagas*
         quibus affligetur egyptus
8. f. 28ʳ   *Interpretari tua serenitas imperat*
9. f. 38ᵛ   *Versus Joachim Ab. Inc. Cum fuerint anni*
         completi
10. f. 40ʳ   *Inc. Cum ad me ruine miseriam predixerit*
         Fr. Raynerius

Except for items 2, 3, 4, 6, see No. 8; except for items 3 4, 10, see No. 7

11. f. 41ʳ   Gebenon, Prologue, followed by Hildegarde, *Speculum futurorum temporum*

7. MS. ROME, BIBL. VITT. EMAN., 14. S. PANT. 31
Date: late fourteenth century.
Contents:

1. f. 29ʳ   *Inc. Interpretari tua serenitas imperat*
2. f. 39ʳ   *De Oneribus*
3. f. 47ʳ   *Inc. Tenebre erunt super faciem abyssi* (= 6 in
         6 *supra*)
4. f. 48ʳ   *Inc. Fr. Raynerius Joachimi . . . decem plagas quibus*
         egyptus affligetur
5. f. 49ᵛ   *Inc. Excitabit Romanus contra Romanum*
6. f. 49ᵛ   *Inc. Exquiritis me o illustrissima turba danaum*
7. f. 50ʳ   *Verba Sibille*
8. f. 51ᵛ   *Inc. Interpretari tua serenitas imperat*
9. f. 57ᵛ   *Inc. Cum fuerint anni completi*

Except for item 2, see No. 6; except for items 3, 5, 7, see No. 8

Description: Holder-Egger, *NA*, xx. 174–5.

8. ROME, VATICAN, LAT. 3820
Date: fifteenth century.
Contents:

1. f. 1ʳ   *Inc. Interpretari tua serenitas imperat*
2. f. 14ᵛ   *De Oneribus*
3. f. 26ʳ   *Inc. Frater Raynerius Joachim decem plagas*
4. f. 27ᵛ   *Inc. Interpretari tua serenitas imperat*
5. f. 37ʳ   *Versus Joachimi Ab. Inc. Cum fuerint com-*
         pleti
6. f. 37ʳ   *Inc. Exquiritis a me illustrissima turba*
         danaum

Except for items 2, 8, see No. 6; except for items 7, 8, see No. 7; except for items 3, 7, see No. 9

7. f. 45ᵛ *Inc. Cum ad me ruine miseriam predixerit Fr. Raynerius*
8. f. 46ʳ *Oraculum Cyrilli*
9. f. 62ʳ *De Oneribus Provinciarum* (from the *Super Esaiam*)

9. PARIS, BIBL. NAT., LAT. 14726
Date: early fifteenth century; French (St. Victor).
Contents:
1. f. 50ʳ *Inc. Interpretari tua serenitas imperat* ⎫ Except for
2. f. 51ʳ *Oraculum Cyrilli*   ⎪ item 3, see
3. f. 76ᵛ *Inc. In die illa elevabitur dracho repletus furore* ⎪ No. 8. See
4. f. 77ʳ *Versus. Inc. Cum fuerint completi anni* ⎬ also No. 17
5. f. 77ᵛ *De Oneribus*   ⎪ for all items,
6. f. 82ʳ *Inc. Requiritis me o illustrissima turba danaum* ⎪ except 3
7. f. 95ᵛ Roquetaillade's gloss on the prophecies of Merlin ⎭
8. f. 98ʳ *De angelico pastore*
9. f. 125ʳ Prophecies of Hildegarde

10. MS. ROME, VATICAN, LAT. REG. 132
Date: fourteenth century.
Contents:
1. f. 49ʳ *Prephacio Joachimi Ab. super Apoc.*
          Inc. Apocalipsis liber ultimus est
2. f. 58ᵛ *Enchiridion super liber Apocalipsis* (i.e. *Lib. Introd.* to the
          Expositio)
3. f. 95ᵛ *Inc. visio et prophecia Norsei viri Dei*
4. f. 97ʳ *Inc. Exquiritis me o illustrissima turba danaum*
5. f. 101ᵛ *Inc. Gallorum levitas*
6. f. 202ʳ Various other prophecies

11. ROME, VATICAN, LAT. 3819
Date: fourteenth century.
Contents:
1. f. 1ʳ *De semine scripturarum*
2. f. 19ʳ *Joachim super Apocalipsim* (but Alexander of Bremen's work)
3. f. 131ʳ *Oraculum Cyrilli*
4. f. 147ʳ *Vaticinia de summis pontificibus* (first set); *Inc. Genus nequam*
   f. 151ʳ Expl.
5. f. 223ʳ *De provincialibus presagiis* (from the *Super Esaiam*)

12. MS. ROME, VATICAN, REG. LAT. 580
Date: 1387. Copied in MS. Vatican, Chig. A. VII. 220.
Contents:
1. f. 1ʳ *Vaticinia de summis pontificibus* (second set); *Inc. Ascende calve*
2. f. 17ʳ *Inc. Epistola fratris Thelofori*
3. f. 18ᵛ *Inc. Libellus fratris Thelofori*

4. f. 52ʳ Second Charlemagne Prophecy
5. f. 53ʳ *Inc. Visio quam vidit monachus . . . monasterii sancti Ambrosii*

13. MS. ROME, VATICAN, LAT. 3816

Date: 1448.

Contents:
1. f. 1ʳ   *Oraculum Cyrilli*
2. f. 15ʳ   *Vaticinia de summis pontificibus* (second set first); *Inc. Ascende calve*
3. f. 33ʳ   *Libellus Thelesfori*
4. f. 56ʳ   Notes on Antichrist from St. Augustine *et al.*
5. f. 59ᵛ   Fifteen Signs of the Last Judgement
6. f. 60ᵛ   Prophecies of the Third Frederick, etc.
7. f. 62ʳ   Various prophecies, including
             O desolata civitas (attributed to Bridget)
             Gallorum levitas (attributed to Merlin)
8. f. 62ᵛ   *Inc. Aquila . . . descendet in Liguriam*
9. f. 63   Further summaries of Joachimist prophecies
10. f. 63ᵛ Miscellaneous prophecies, including *Egredietur Aquila*
11. f. 64ʳ Telesphorus's dedicatory epistle
12. f. 64ᵛ Prophecies of Angelic Popes adapted from Joachimist sources.

14. MS. ROME, VATICAN, OTTOBON. 1106

Date: fifteenth century.

Contents:
1. f. 2ᵛ   *Libellus fratris Thelofori*
   f. 18ᵛ   *Expl.*
2. f. 24ʳ   *Veniet dracho contra . . . imperium*
3. f. 24ʳ   *Gallorum levitas*
4. f. 24ᵛ   *Prophecia Joachim . . . Inc. In illa die Aquila veniens a septentrione descendet in Ligurias*

15. MS. VENICE, BIBL. MARC., LAT. CL. III, 177

Date: fifteenth century; Venice.

Contents:
1. f. 10ᵛ   Illustration of Pope and Emperor locked in combat
   f. 11ʳ   Illustration of a bull-figure
2. f. 13ʳ   Inaccurate versions of *Vaticinia de summis pontificibus*, Nos. XXVII–XXX
3. f. 15ʳ   *Inc. Frater rusticianus suo karissimo dominico*
4. f. 16ʳ   *Prophetia beate Brigide. Inc. O desolata civitas*
5. f. 16ᵛ   Prophecy on Italian states, etc.
6. f. 18ʳ   *Inc. Libellus fratris theoloffori de cusencia*
   f. 35ᵛ   *Expl. Liber fratris theolophori*

7. f. 35ᵛ Second Charlemagne prophecy. *Inc. Karolus filius Karoli ex natione illustrissimi lilii*
Picture of Emperor
8. f. 35ᵛ John of Paris. *Tractatus de Antichristo*
f. 42ᵛ *Expl. tractatus*
9. f. 43ʳ *Inc. In illo tempore aquila veniens a septentrione*

Note: on the compiler of the book up to this point. The end of the book contains miscellaneous prophecies, including Nos. 20 (f. 43ʳ), 23 (f. 49ᵛ, in a longer version), and 7 (f. 50ᵛ) in Appendix B, and also the prophecies attributed to S. Malachy on the Popes (ff. 44ʳ seq.).

16. MS. CAMBRIDGE, CORPUS CHRISTI COLLEGE, 404[1]

Date: fourteenth century; from Bury St. Edmunds.

Contents:

1. f. 1ʳ   Prophecies attributed to the Sibyls, Methodius, Eusebius, etc.
2. f. 9ʳ   Hildegarde, *Speculum temporum futurum*
3. f. 38ᵛ   Various prophecies attributed to the Sibyl, Joachim, etc.
4. f. 41ʳ   *Vaticinia de summis pontificibus*, last 5 of the later 15, i.e. Nos. XI–XV in the printed editions
5. f. 42ᵛ   Note on Joachim in a later hand, from C. Gesner, the sixteenth-century bibliographer
6. f. 44ʳ   Pseudo-Joachim, *De seminibus literarum*
7. f. 65ʳ   *De Antichristo et fine mundi*
8. f. 66ʳ   A summary of Joachim's exposition of seven seals and persecutions, taken from *libro visionum apud Sibecone et apud Coggeshale* (f. 66ᵛ)
9. f. 67ᵛ   *Oraculum Cyrilli*: (*a*) Preface of Frater Gilbertus Anglicus
   f. 68ʳ   (*b*) Letter of Cyril to Joachim
   f. 68ᵛ   (*c*) Letter of Joachim to Cyril
   f. 70ʳ   (*d*) *Inc. oraculum*
10. f. 88ʳ Joachim. Prophecies of the popes, the earlier 15 of the *Vaticinia de summis pontificibus*, *Inc. Genus nequam*
11. f. 96ʳ *Inc. prophetiis de regibus anglorum* (political prophecies)
12. f. 100ʳ *Prophetie ioachim in maiori libro de concordanciis* (see Appendix B, No. 2)
13. f. 100ᵛ *Visio mirabilis in civitate tripolis. Inc. Cedrus alta libani succidetur*
14. f. 102ʳ Various prophecies
15. f. 103ᵛ Letter of Jean de Roquetaillade (see Bignami-Odier, *Roquetaillade*, pp. 174–5)

[1] ff. 39ᵛ to 42ʳ are blank. This has thrown out the foliation. For later items I give the numbers as written, not the actual folio number.

542   *Appendix C*

17. MS. THE HAGUE, BIBL. REG., 71. E. 44

Date: 1500.

Contents:

1. f. 2ᵛ   Judgements of the learned on the authors included (post-1662)
2. f. 6ʳ   Gebenon, Prologue, followed by Hildegarde, *Speculum tem-
           porum futurorum* (*Pentachronon*)
3. f. 70ʳ   *Oraculum Cyrilli* (all five parts)
4. f. 99ʳ   *Inc. Interpretari tua serenitas imperat*
5. f. 101ʳ *Versus. Inc. Cum fuerint anni completi*
6. f. 101ʳ Summary and short extract from *De Oneribus*
7. f. 104ʳ *Inc. sibila erithrea babilonis*
           Inc. Excerpta libro qui dicitur Basilographus
           Inc. Requiritis me o illustrissima turba danaum
8. f. 112ʳ *Sibilla tiburtina. Inc. Sibille generaliter omnes dicuntur femine*
9. f. 116ʳ Extracts from prophecies of Merlin with gloss by Jean de
           Roquetaillade
10. ff. 118ʳ-22ʳ *De angelico pastore et eius bonitate*
    ff. 123ʳ-31ᵛ (Extracts from the *libellus* of Telesphorus)
11. f. 122ʳ *Ex prophecia sidrac de papis*
           (Oracles on the Popes, the first two of which are Nos. XIV,
           XV in *Vaticinia de summis pontificibus*.)
12. f. 131ᵛ *Determinationes profunde de fine seculi*
13. f. 142ᵛ Extract from prophecies of Hildegarde
14. f. 143ᵛ Extracts from *De Oneribus*
15. f. 145ʳ *Invectiva ezechielis contra pseudo pastores*

Items 2, 3, 4, 5, 6, 7, 9, 10, 13, 14 form almost the whole of No. 9.

SELECT BIBLIOGRAPHY I

WITH ABBREVIATIONS USED IN REFERENCES

WORKS OF JOACHIM (for full list, see Appendix A)

1. *Liber Concordie Novi ac Veteris Testamenti* (Venice, 1519). [*Lib. Conc.*]

2. *Expositio in Apocalypsim* (Venice, 1527). [*Expos.*]

3. *Psalterium Decem Chordarum* (Venice, 1527, with *Expos.*). [*Psalt.*]

4. *Tractatus super Quatuor Evangelia*, ed. E. Buonaiuti (Rome, 1930). [*Quat. Evang.*]

5. *De Vita Sancti Benedicti et de Officio Divino secundum eius doctrinam*, ed. C. Baraut, *Analecta Sacra Tarraconensia*, xxiv (1951), pp. 42–118. [*Vita S. Benedicti*]

6. *Enchiridion in Apocalypsim* (i) unpublished, see Appendix A; (ii) ed. J. Huck, *Joachim von Floris und die joachitische Literatur* (Freiburg im Breisgau, 1938), pp. 287–305. [*Enchir.*]

7. *De Septem Sigillis*, ed. M. Reeves, B. Hirsch-Reich, *Recherches de Théologie ancienne et médiévale*, xxi (1954), pp. 239–47. [*Septem Sigillis*]

8. *Liber Figurarum*, ed. L. Tondelli, M. Reeves, B. Hirsch-Reich, *Il Libro delle Figure dell'Abate Gioacchino da Fiore*, vol. II (2nd edn., Turin, 1954). [*Lib. Fig. II*]

PSEUDO-JOACHIMIST WORKS

9. *Joachimi Abbatis Liber contra Lombardum*, ed. C. Ottaviano (Rome, 1934). [*Lib. contra Lombardum*]

10. *Super Hieremiam Prophetam* (Venice, 1516). [*Super Hier.*] (Where the 1526 edition is used, this is indicated.)

11. *Super Esaiam Prophetam* (Venice, 1517). [*Super Esaiam*]

12. *De Oneribus Prophetarum*, ed. in one version O. Holder-Egger, *Neues Archiv der Gesellschaft für ältere deutsche Geschichtskunde*, xxxiii (1907), pp. 139–87; unless *NA* version is specifically indicated, citations here are from MS. Brit. Mus., Royal and Kings, 8. F. XVI, ff. 38ʳ–44ᵛ [*De Oneribus*]

13. *Vaticinium Sibillae Erithreae*, ed. Holder-Egger, *NA* xv (1889), pp. 155–73. [*Sibyl Erithrea*]

14. *Oraculum Cyrilli*, ed. P. Puir, in Burdach, *Vom Mittelalter* (see below), ii, Pt. iv, Appendix, pp. 220–327. [*Oraculum Cyrilli*]

15. *Vaticinia de Summis Pontificibus*, many editions, cited here by editor. [*Vaticinia*]

16. *Expositio magni prophete Joachim in librum beati Cyrilli* . . . (otherwise) *Liber de magnis tribulationibus* . . . *compilatus a* . . . *Theolosphoro* [Telesphorus of Cosenza] . . . *Incipit libellus fratris Theolosphori de Cusentia* . . . (Venice, 1516). [*Libellus*]

PRIMARY SOURCES

1. COLLECTIONS OF SOURCE MATERIAL

17. *Acta Sanctorum*, see especially May, vol. vii, Day 29, *Joachimus Abbas*, cited [*AS*]. Other references are cited *AS*, followed by month and day.

18. *Archiv für Literatur und Kirchengeschichte des Mittelalters.* [*ALKG*] I (1885), H. Denifle, *Das Evangelium aeternum und die Commission zu Anagni*, pp. 49–142; F. Ehrle, *Die Spiritualen, ihr Verhältnis zum Franziscanerorden und zu den Fraticellen*, pp. 509–69.

II (1886), F. Ehrle, *Die Spiritualen, ihr Verhältnis zum Franziscanerorden und zu den Fraticellen* (cont.), *Angelo Clareno, Historia septem tribulationum ordinis minorum*, pp. 106–164, 249–336.

III (1887), F. Ehrle, *Zur Vorgeschichte des Concils v. Vienne*, pp. 1–195; *Petrus Johannis Olivi, sein Leben u. seine Schriften*, pp. 409–552; *Die Spiritualen, ihr Verhältnis zum Franziscanerorden und zu den Fraticellen* (cont.), pp. 553–623.

IV (1888), F. Ehrle, *Die Spiritualen, ihr Verhältnis zum Franziscanerorden und zu den Fraticellen* (concluded), pp. 1–190.

19. S. Baluze, *Miscellanea*, ed. Mansi (Lucca, 1761). [*Miscellanea*]

20. M. Bouquet, *Recueil des historiens des Gaules et de la France.* [Bouquet]

21. N. Eymerich, *Directorium Inquisitorum* (Venice, 1607). [*Direct. Inquis.*]

22. P. a Limborch, *Historia Inquisitionis, cui subjungitur Liber Sententiarum Inquisitionis Tholosanae 1307–1323* (Amsterdam, 1692). [*Hist. Inquis.*]

23. G. Mansi, *Sacrorum Conciliorum nova et amplissima Collectio.* [Mansi]

24. E. Martène et V. Durand, *Veterum Scriptorum et Monumentorum* . . . *Amplissima Collectio* . . . (Paris, 1724–33). [*Ampl. Coll.*]

25. *Monumenta Germaniae Historica. Scriptores.* [*MGHS*]

26. *Monumenta Ordinis Fratrum Praedicatorum Historica.* [*MOPH*]

27. L. Muratori, *Rerum Italicarum Scriptores*, (i) old series, (ii) new series. [Muratori O.S./N.S.]

28. *Patrologia Latina.* [*PL*]

29. *Quellen und Forschungen aus italienischen Archiven und Bibliotheken.* [*QFIAB*]

30. *Chronicles and memorials of Great Britain and Ireland during the Middle Ages.* [RS]

2. OTHER WORKS

31. Bartholomew of Pisa, *De Conformitate Vitae Beatae Francisci ad Vitam Dom. Jesu. Analecta Franciscana*, iv (1906). [*AF* iv]

32. Gregorio de Laude (or Lauro), *Magni Divinique Prophetae B. Jo. Joachim Abb. Sacri Cist. Ord. Monasterii Floris, et Florensis Ord. Institutoris Hergasiarum Alethia Apologetica, sive Mirabilium Veritas Defensa* (Naples, 1660). [*Apologetica*]

33. B. Gui, *Manuel de l'Inquisiteur*, ed. G. Mollat (Paris, 1926). [*Manuel*]

34. W. Lazius, *Fragmentum vaticinii cuiusdam . . . Methodii . . .* (Vienna, 1527), unpag., no numbered chapters; references are to the gatherings; H*. and H. indicate two consecutive gatherings with the same letter. [*Fragmentum*]

35. J. Lichtenberger, *Prognosticatio* (Strasbourg, 1488), unpag. [*Prognosticatio*]

36. B. Purstinger, *Onus Ecclesiae temporibus hisce deplorandis Apocalypseos suis aeque conveniens Turcarumque incursui iam grassanti accomodatum, non tam lectu quam contemplatu dignissimum . . .* (no. pl. of pub., 1532), unpag. [*Onus Ecclesiae*]

37. Joannes de Rupescissa (Jean de Roquetaillade), *Vade Mecum*, ed. E. Brown, *Appendix ad Fasciculum Rerum Expetendarum et Fugiendarum ab Orthuino Gratio editum Coloniae MDXXXV*, II (London, 1690), pp. 496–507. [*Vade Mecum*]

38. Fra Salimbene, *Cronica*, *MGHS* xxxii. [Salimbene]

39. Ubertino da Casale, *Arbor Vitae Crucifixae* (Venice, 1485). [*Arbor*]

40. L. Wadding, *Annales Minorum* (Rome, 1731). [*Annales*]

41. L. Wadding, *Scriptores Ord. Minorum Supplementum*, H. Sbaralea (Rome, 1806). [*Scriptores*]

42. A. Wachtel (ed.), *Alexander Minorita Expositio in Apocalypsim*, *MGH* (Weimar, 1955). [*Expositio*]

43. J. Wolf, *Lectionum memorabilium et reconditarum centenarii XVI* (Laving, 1600). [*Lect. mem.*]

SECONDARY SOURCES

1. WORKS

44. E. Benz, *Ecclesia Spiritualis* (Stuttgart, 1934). [*Ecclesia Spiritualis*]

45. J. Bignami-Odier, *Études sur Jean de Roquetaillade* [Joannes de Rupescissa] (Paris, 1952). [*Roquetaillade*]

46. M. Bloomfield, *Piers Plowman as a fourteenth-century apocalypse* (New Brunswick, 1961). [*Piers Plowman*]

47. G. Bondatti, *Gioachinismo e Francescanesimo nel Dugento* (S. Maria degli Angeli, Porziuncola, 1924). [*Gioachinismo e Francescanesimo*]

48. W. Bouwsma, *Concordia Mundi. The career and thought of Guillaume Postel (1510–1581)* (Cambridge, 1957). [*Concordia Mundi*]

49. E. Buonaiuti, *Gioacchino da Fiore, i tempi, la vita, il messaggio* (Rome, 1931). [*Gioacchino da Fiore*]

50. K. Burdach, *Vom Mittelalter Zur Reformation*:
I (Berlin, 1913); II, Pt. i (Berlin, 1913); Pt. ii (Berlin, 1928); Pt. iii (Berlin, 1912); Pt. iv (Berlin, 1912); Pt. v (Berlin, 1929). [*Vom Mittelalter*]

51. D. Cantimori, *Eretici italiani del Cinquecento* (Florence, 1939). [*Eretici*]

52. A. Crocco, *Gioacchino da Fiore* (Naples, 1960). [*Gioacchino*]

53. D. Douie, *The Nature and Effect of the Heresy of the Fraticelli* (Manchester, 1932). [*Fraticelli*]

54. H. Finke, *Aus den Tagen Bonifaz VIII* (Munster, 1902). [*Aus den Tagen*]

55. F. Foberti, *Gioacchino da Fiore, Nuovi studi critici sulla mistica e la religione in Calabria* (Florence, 1934). [*Gioacchino I*]

56. F. Foberti, *Gioacchino da Fiore e il Gioacchinismo antico e moderno* (Padua, 1942). [*Gioacchino II*]

57. H. Grundmann, *Studien über Joachim von Floris* (Leipzig, 1927). [*Studien*]

58. H. Grundmann, *Neue Forschungen über Joachim von Floris* (Marburg, 1950). [*NF*]

59. J. Huck, *Joachim von Floris und die joachitische Literatur* (Freiburg im Breisgau, 1938). [*Joachim v. Floris*]

60. M. Lambert, *Franciscan poverty* (London, 1961). [*Franciscan Poverty*]

61. R. Manselli, *La 'Lectura Super Apocalipsim' di Pietro di Giovanni Olivi* (Rome, 1955). [*Lectura*]

62. M. Menéndez y Pelayo, *Historia de los Heterodoxes españoles* (Madrid, 1880). [*Heterodoxes*]

63. L. Pastor, *History of the Popes*, trans. and ed. E. Antrobus (London, 1891–8), vols. i–vi; trans. and ed. R. Kerr (London, 1908–33), vols. vii–xxiv. [*History of the Popes*]

64. Pou y Marti, *Visionarios, Beguinos y Fraticelos Catalanes (Siglos XIII–XV)* (Vich, 1930). [*Visionarios*]

64A. M. Reeves, B. Hirsch-Reich, *Studies in the Figurae of Joachim of Fiore* (now published, see bibl. II, 3.312). [*Studies*]

65. F. Russo, *Bibliografia gioachimita* (Florence, 1954). [*Bibliografia*]

66. F. Russo, *Gioacchino da Fiore e le fondazioni florensi in Calabria* (Naples, 1958). [*Gioacchino*]

67. F. Tocco, *Studii Francescani*. Nuova biblioteca di letteratura, storia ed arte, vol. iii (Naples, 1909). [*SF*]

68. L. Tondelli, *Il Libro delle Figure dell'Abate Gioacchino*, vol. i (2nd edn., Turin, 1953). [*Lib. Fig. I*]

69. B. Töpfer, *Das kommende Reich des Friedens* (Berlin, 1964). [*Das kommende Reich*]

70. E. Sackur, *Sibyllinische Texte u. Forschungen. Pseudo-Methodius, Adso u. die tiburtinische Sibylle* (Halle, 1898). [*Sibyllinische Texte*]

2. ARTICLES

71. C. Baraut, 'Las Antiguas Biografias de Joaquin de Fiore y sus Fuentes', *Analecta Sacra Tarraconensia*, xxvi (1953), pp. 195–232. [*AST* xxvi]

72. E. Benz, 'Joachim-Studien I. Die Kategorien der religiösen Geschichtsdeutung Joachims', *Zeitschrift für Kirchengeschichte*, l (1931), pp. 24–111; 'Joachim-Studien II. Die Exzerptsätze der Pariser Professoren aus dem Evangelium Aeternum', ibid. li (1932), pp. 415–55; 'Joachim-Studien III. Thomas von Aquin und Joachim de Fiore', ibid. liii (1934), pp. 52–116. [*ZKG* l/li/liii]

73. H. Bernard-Maître, 'Le Passage de Guillaume Postel chez les Jésuites', *Mélanges offerts à Henri Chamard* (Paris, 1951), pp. 227–43. [*Le Passage*]

74. H. Bernard-Maître, 'Aux origines françaises de la Compagnie de Jésus. L'Apologie de Guillaume Postel', *Recherches de Science Religieuse*, xxxviii (1952), pp. 209–33. [*RSR* xxxviii]

75. F. von Bezold, 'Zur deutschen Kaisersage', *Sitzungsberichte der philosoph.-philologisch. u. historisch. Classe der K. bayer. Akademie der Wissenschaften zu München*, xiv (1884), pp. 560–606. [*Kaisersage*]

76. J. Bignami-Odier, 'Notes sur deux manuscrits de la Bibliothèque du Vatican contenant des traités inédits de Joachim de Fiore', *Mélanges d'Archéologie et d'Histoire*, liv (1937), pp. 211–41. [*MAH* liv]

77. J. Bignami-Odier, 'Les Visions de Robert d'Uzès, O.P.', *Archivum Fratrum Praedicatorum*, xxv (1955), pp. 258–310. [*AFP* xxv]

78. M. Bloomfield, 'Joachim of Flora', *Traditio*, XIII (1957), pp. 249–311. [*Traditio* XIII]

79. M. Bloomfield, M. Reeves, 'The Penetration of Joachism into Northern Europe', *Speculum*, xxix (1954), pp. 772–93. [*Speculum* xxix]

80. A. Crocco, 'La formazione dottrinale di Gioacchino da Fiore e le fonti della sua teologia trinitaria', *Sophia*, xxiii (1955), pp. 192–6. [*Sophia* xxiii]

81. E. Donckel, 'Die Prophezeiung des Telesforus', *Archivum Franciscanum Historicum*, xxvi (1933), pp. 29–104. [*AFH* xxvi]

82. H. Grundmann, 'Kleine Beiträge über Joachim von Fiore', *Zeitschrift für Kirchengeschichte*, xlviii (1929), pp. 137–65. [*ZKG* xlviii]

83. H. Grundmann, 'Die Papstprophetien des Mittelalters', *Archiv für Kulturgeschichte*, xix (1929), pp. 77–159. [*AK* xix]

84. H. Grundmann, 'Die *Liber de Flore*', *Historisches Jahrbuch*, xlix (1929), pp. 33–91. [*HJ* xlix]

85. H. Grundmann, 'Dante u. Joachim v. Fiore, zu Paradiso X–XII, *Deutsches Dante-Jahrbuch*, xiv (1932), pp. 210–56. [*DDJ* xiv]

86. H. Grundmann, 'Joachim von Floris und Rainer von Ponza', *Deutsches Archiv für Erforschung des Mittelalters*, xvi (1960), pp. 437–546. [*DA* xvi]

87. H. Haupt, 'Ein Beghardenprozess in Eichstadt vom Jahre 1381', *Zeitschrift für Kirchengeschichte*, v (1882), pp. 487–98. [*ZKG* v]

548 Select Bibliography I

88. H. Haupt, 'Zur Geschichte des Joachimismus', *Zeitschrift für Kirchengeschichte*, vii (1885), pp. 372–425. [*ZKG* vii]

89. B. Hirsch-Reich, 'Eine Bibliographie über Joachim v. Fiore u. dessen Nachwirkung', *Recherches de Théologie ancienne et médiévale*, xxiv (1957), pp. 27–44. [*RTAM* xxiv]

90. O. Holder-Egger, 'Italienische Prophetien des 13. Jahrhunderts', *Neues Archiv der Gesellschaft für altere deutsche Geschichtskunde*, xv (1889), pp. 143–78; xxx (1904–5), pp. 323–86; xxxiii (1907–8), pp. 97–187. [*NA* xv/xxx/xxxiii]

91. P. Kleinhaus, 'De vita et operibus Petri Galatini O.F.M., scientiarum biblicarum cultoris (*c.* 1460–1540)', *Antonianum*, i (1926), pp. 145–79, 327–56. [*Antonianum* i]

92. A. Messini, 'Profetismo e profezie ritmiche italiana d'ispirazione Gioachimito-Francescana nei secoli XII, XIV e XV', *Miscellanea Francescana*, xxxvii (1937), pp. 39–54; xxxix (1939), pp. 109–30. [*Misc. Franc.* xxxvii/xxxix]

93. C. Ottaviano, 'Un nuovo documento intorno alla condanna di Gioacchino da Fiore nel 1215', *Sophia*, iii (1935), pp. 476–82. [*Sophia* iii]

94. M. Reeves, B. Hirsch-Reich, 'The Seven Seals in the Writings of Joachim Fiore', *Recherches de Théologie ancienne et médiévale*, xxi (1954), pp. 211–47. [*RTAM* xxi]

95. M. Reeves, B. Hirsch-Reich, 'The *Figurae* of Joachim of Fiore: Genuine and Spurious Collections', *Mediaeval and Renaissance Studies*, iii (1954), pp. 170–99. [*MARS* iii]

96. M. Reeves, 'The *Liber Figurarum* of Joachim of Fiore', *Mediaeval and Renaissance Studies*, ii (1950), pp. 57–81. [*MARS* ii]

97. M. Reeves, 'The Abbot Joachim's Disciples and the Cistercian Order', *Sophia*, xix (1951), pp. 355–71. [*Sophia* xix]

98. M. Reeves, 'The *Arbores* of Joachim of Fiore', *Studies in Italian Medieval History presented to Miss E. M. Jamison, being Papers of the British School at Rome*, xxiv (1956), pp. 124–36. [*Arbores*]

99. F. Russo, 'Il libro delle Figure attribuito a Gioacchino da Fiore', *Miscellanea Francescana*, xl (1941), pp. 326–44. [*Misc. Franc.* xl]

100. F. Russo, 'S. Francesco ed i Francescani nella letteratura profetica gioachimita', *Miscellanea Francescana*, xlvi (1946), pp. 232–42. [*Misc. Franc.* xlvi]

101. F. Russo, 'Un documento sulla condanna di Gioachino da Fiore nel 1215', *Archivio Storico per la Calabria e la Lucania*, xx (1951), pp. 69–73. [*ASCL* xx]

102. F. Secret, 'Guillaume Postel et les courants prophétiques de la Renaissance', *Studi francesi*, Anno I (1957), pp. 375–95. [*Studi francesi* I]

103. F. Secret, 'Paulus Angelus, Descendant des Empereurs de Byzance et la Prophétie du Pape Angélique', *Rinascimento*, Anno XIII (1962), pp. 211–24. [*Rinascimento* XIII]

104. L. Tondelli, 'Gli Inediti dell'Abate Gioacchino da Fiore', *Archivio Storico per la Calabria e la Lucania*, xii (1942), pp. 1–12. [*ASCL* xii]

SELECT BIBLIOGRAPHY II

RELEVANT PUBLICATIONS ON
JOACHIMIST STUDIES SINCE 1968

1. BIBLIOGRAPHICAL SURVEYS

1.1. Bloomfield, M., 'Recent Scholarship on Joachim of Fiore and his Influence', *Prophecy and Millenarianism*, ed. A. Williams (London, 1980), pp. 23–52.

1.2. McGinn, B., 'Awaiting an End. Research in Medieval Apocalypticism 1974–1981', *Medievalia et Humanistica*. n.s., II (1982), pp. 267–78.

1.3. Fraja, V. de, 'Gioacchino da Fiore: bibliografia 1969–1988', *Florensia*, II, 1–2 (1988), pp. 7–59. [These bibliographies correct and complement Appendix A.]

2. CONFERENCE PAPERS AND COLLECTIONS OF ESSAYS

2.1. *Ricerche sull' influenza della profezia nel basso Medioevo*, ed. R. Manselli (Rome, 1973) [collection of essays involving critical examination of my book].

2.2. *Joachim of Fiore in Christian Thought*, ed. D. West, 2 vols. (New York, 1975) [collection of reprinted articles from G. La Piana (1932) onwards].

2.3. *Storia e Messagio in Gioacchino da Fiore*, Atti del I Congresso Internazionale di Studi Gioachimiti, ed. F. Russo (S. Giovanni in Fiore, 1980).

2.4. *Atti del Simposio Internazionale Cateriniano-Bernardiniano*, ed. D. Maffei, P. Napoli (Siena, 1982).

2.5. *L'Età dello Spirito e la fine dei Tempi in Gioacchino da Fiore e nel Gioachimismo Medievale*, Atti del II Congresso Internazionale di Studi Gioachimiti, ed. A. Crocco (S. Giovanni in Fiore, 1986).

2.6. *The Use and Abuse of Eschatology in the Middle Ages*, ed. D. Verhelst et al. (Leiden, 1988).

2.7. *L'Attesa della fine dei tempi nel Medioevo*, ed. O. Capitani, J. Miethke (Bologna, 1990).

2.8.   *Il profetismo gioachimita tra Quattrocento e Cinquecento, Atti del III Congresso Internazionale di Studi Gioachimiti*, ed. G. Potestà (Geneva, 1991).

3.   LIFE, THEOLOGY AND WRITINGS OF JOACHIM OF FIORE

3.11.   Daniel, E. R., Introduction to the edition of *Liber de Concordia Novi et Veteris Testamenti*. I–IV (Philadelphia, 1983) [dates main phases of life and spiritual experiences, cf. pp. 4–15, 21–25].

3.12.   Lerner, R., 'Joachim of Fiore's Breakthrough to Chiliasm', *Cristianesimo nella storia*, 6 (1985), pp. 489–512 [dating of mystical experiences, cf. pp. 21–25].

3.13.   Selge, K-V., 'L'origine delle opere di Gioacchino da Fiore', *L'attesa della fine dei tempi* (ref. 2.7), pp. 87–130 [dating of life and works, cf. Appendix A].

3.14.   Gonnet, G., 'Gioacchino da Fiore e gli eretici del suo tempo', *Storia e Messagio* (ref. 2.3), pp. 57–69.

3.15.   Dickson, G., 'Joachim and the Amalricians', *Florensia*, 1 (1987), pp. 35–45 [cf. p. 473].

3.2.   THEOLOGY

3.211.   Lerner, R., 'Refreshment of the Saints: the Time after Antichrist as a station for Earthly Progress in Medieval Thought', *Traditio*, 32 (1976), pp. 97–144 [traces antecedents of Joachim's theology of history].

3.212.   Reeves, M., 'The Originality and Influence of the Abbot Joachim of Fiore', *Traditio*, 36 (1980), pp. 269–316 [seeks to define more clearly Joachim's specific contribution to the later medieval view of history].

3.221.   McGinn, B., *The Calabrian Abbot. Joachim of Fiore in the History of Western Thought* (New York, London, 1985) [a masterly survey of the whole field].

3.222.   West, D., Zimdars-Swartz, S., *Joachim of Fiore. A study on Spiritual Perception and History* (Bloomington, IN, 1983).

3.223.   Wessley, S., *Joachim of Fiore and Monastic Reform* (New York, 1990) [cf. G. Potestà, 'Gioacchino reformatore monastico nel *Tractatus de vita S. Benedicti* e nel la coscienza dei primi florensi', *Florensia*, VI (1992), pp. 73–93].

3.231.   Reeves, M., 'The Abbot Joachim's Sense of History', *1274. Année charnière. Mutations et continuités* (Paris, 1977), pp. 781–96 [on

Trinitarian theology in relation to history and the senses of scripture].

3.232. Daniel, E. R., 'The Double Procession of the Holy Spirit in Joachim of Fiore's Understanding of History', *Speculum*, 55 (1980), pp. 469–83 [cf. pp. 16–27].

3.233. McGinn, B., 'Symbolism in the Thought of Joachim of Fiore', *Prophecy and Millenarianism* (ref. 1.1), pp. 145–64.

3.234. Lee, H., 'The Anti-Lombard Figures of Joachim of Fiore: A Reinterpretation', *Prophecy and Millenarianism* (ref. 1.1), pp. 129–42.

3.235. McGinn, B., ' "After Moyses": il ruolo di Bernardo di Clairvaux nel pensiero di Gioacchino da Fiore', *Florensia*, VI (1991), pp. 17–25.

3.241. Crocco, A., 'Genesi e significato dell' "età dello Spirito" nell' escatologia di Gioacchino da Fiore', *Storia e Messagio* (ref. 2.3), pp. 197–224.

3.242. Id., 'Il superamento del dualism agostiniano nella concezione della storia di Gioacchino da Fiore', *L'Età dello Spirito* (ref. 2.5), pp. 141–61.

3.243. Manselli, R., 'Il problema del doppio Anticristo in Gioacchino da Fiore', *Geschichtsschreibung und geistiges Leben im Mittelalter*, ed. K. Hauck, H. Mordek (Köln, Wien, 1978), pp. 427–49.

3.244. Id., 'Gioacchino da Fiore e la fine dei tempi', *Storia e Messagio* (ref. 2.3), pp. 429–45.

3.245. Pasztor, E., 'Ideale del momachesimo ed "età dello Spirito" come realtá spirituale e forma d'utopia', *L'Età dello Spirito* (ref. 2.5), pp. 57–124.

3.3 GENUINE WRITINGS

3.311. Daniel, E. R., Introduction (ref. 3.11) [cf. pp. 16–20].

3.312. Reeves, M., Hirsch-Reich, B., *The* Figurae *of Joachim of Fiore* (Oxford, 1972) [a study of Joachim's use of *figurae* leading to the *Liber Figurarum* appears in footnote references as *Studies*].

3.313. Mottu, H., *La Manifestation de L'Esprit selon Joachim de Fiore* (Neuchatel, Paris, 1977) [studies the unfinished *Tractatus super Quatuor Evangelia* and its radical implications, cf. pp. 395–97].

3.314. Leo, P. De, *Gioacchino da Fiore. Aspetti inediti della vita e delle opere* (Cosenza, 1988) [includes eds. of several smaller writings, pp. 67–125].

3.321. Bloomfield, M., Lee, H., 'The Pierpont Morgan Manuscript of *De Septem Sigillis, RTAM*, 38 (1971), pp. 137–42 [gives an ed. of this particular text].

3.322. McGinn, B., 'Joachim and the Sibyl. An Early Work of Joachim of Fiore from MS. 322 of the Biblioteca Antoniana in Padua', *Citeaux. Commentarii Cistercienses*, 24 (1973), pp. 97–138 [discusses dating questions and edits the short tract *Propheta ignota*].

3.323. Selge, K-V., 'Elenco delle opere di Gioacchino da Fiore', *Florensia*, III–IV (1989–90), pp. 25–35 [reviews MSS. and editions of genuine works, cf. Appendix A].

3.324. Id., Eine Einführung Joachims von Fiore in di Johannes-apokalypse', *Deutsches Archiv für Erforschung des Mittelalters*, 46 (1990), pp. 85–131 [discusses short tracts on the Apocalypse and edits one, cf. Appendix A].

3.325. Leo, P. De, 'Una nuova opera di Gioacchino da Fiore? Il *Super Cantica Canticorum Anonymi Commentarium* (cap. IV)', *L'Età dello Spirito* (ref. 2.5), pp. 437–88 [gives an ed. of the text].

3.326. Potestà, G., 'Ger. 24 nell' interpretazione di Gioacchio da Fiore', *La Cattura della Fine. Variazioni dell' escatologia in regime di cristianità*, ed. G. Ruggieri (Geneva, 1992), pp. 65–88 [studies a minor work, 'Intelligentia super calathis'].

3.331. Leo, P. De, ' "Reliquiae" florensi. Note e documenti per la ricostruzione della biblioteca e dell' archivio protocenobio di S. Giovanni in Fiore', *Storia e Messagio* (ref. 2.3), pp. 369–427.

3.332. Troncarelli, F., Gioia, E. di, 'Scrittura, testo, immagine in un manoscritto gioachimito', *Scrittura e civiltà*, 5 (1981), pp. 149–86 [studies MS. Cors. 797 (41.F.2)].

3.333. Troncarelli, F., 'Nuove reliquie dello "Scriptorium" di Fiore', *L'Età dello Spirito* (ref. 2.5), pp. 319–29.

3.334. Gioia, E. di, 'Un codice con Note Autografe di Gioacchino da Fiore (Vat. Barb. Lat. 627)', *Scriptorium*, XLIII (1989), pp. 3–34.

3.335. Gioia, E. di, 'Note su un manoscritto di Gioacchino da Fiore', *Storia e Messagio* (ref. 2.3), pp. 505–20 [on MS. Cors. 797 (41.F.2)].

3.336. Adorisio, A., *Codici latini calabresi produzione libraria in Val di Catri e in Sila tra XII e XIII secolo* (Rome, 1986).

3.337. Gelinas, Y., 'Joachim of Fiore, "Expositio in Apocalypsim": Approach to the study of the Textual Transmission', *Manuscripta*, 23 (1979), p. 9.

4. PSEUDO-JOACHIMIST WORKS

4.11. Simoni, F., 'Il "Super Hieremiam" cd il gioachimismo francescano', *Bollettino dell' Istituto Storico Italiano per il Medioevo*, 82 (1970), pp. 13–46.

4.12. Moynihan, R., 'The Development of the 'Pseudo-Joachim' Commentary "Super Hieremiam": New MS. Evidence', *Mélanges de l'Ecole française de Rome. Serie Moyen Âge et Temps Modernes*, 90 (1986), pp. 109–42 [argues for a text developed from a genuine core. cf. pp. 149–53].

4.21. Gioa, E. Di, 'Un manoscritto Pseudo-Gioachimita: Bibl. Naz. Centrale di Roma Vittorio Emanuele 1502', *Federico II e l'arte del duecento italiano*, 2 (Galatino, 1980), pp. 85–111 [deals with the *Praemissiones*, cf. pp. 154–60].

4.31. Reeves, M., 'Some Popular Prophecies from the Fourteenth to the Seventeenth Centuries', *Popular Belief and Practice*, ed. G. Cuming, D. Baker (Cambridge, 1972), pp. 107–34 [studies the *Vaticinia de Summis Pontificibus*, but on origins questioned by Lerner, see 4.35 below, cf. pp. 193–94, 402–7. An edition of the *Vaticinia* is in preparation].

4.32. Wilckens, L. von, 'Die Prophetien über die Papste in deutschen Handschriften zu Illustrationen aus der Pariser Handschrift Lat. 10834 und aus anderer Manuskripten der ersten Halfte des 15 Jahrhunderts', *Wiener Jahrbuch für Kunstgeschichte*, XXVIII (1975), pp. 171–80.

4.33. Fleming, M., 'Metaphors of Apocalypse and Revolution in Some Fourteenth-century Pope Prophecies', *The High Middle Ages*, ed. P. Mayo (Binghamton, N.Y., 1983), pp. 131–46.

4.34. Lerner, R., Moynihan, R., *Weissagungen über die Papste: Vat. Ross. 374 (Einführungsband zur Faksimile ausgabe des Cod. Vat. Ross. 374)*. (Zurich, 1985).

4.35. Lerner, R., 'On the origins of the earliest Latin pope prophecies: A Reconsideration', *Falschungen im Mittelalters*, MGHS, 33 V (Hanover, 1988), pp. 611–35. [cf. pp. 193–94, 402–7].

4.36. Guerrini, P., 'Per l'interpretatione iconografica dei "Vaticinia" nell' Angelicano 1146 e nel Chigiano A.V.152', *Scrittura biblioteche e stampe a Roma nel '400*, ed. M. Miglio (Città del Vaticano, 1983), 733–47.

4.37. Id., 'Federico da Montefeltro e Sisto IV nei "Vaticinia" nell' Angelicano 1146 e nel Chigiano A.V.152', *Federico da Montefeltro. Lo stato, le arti, la cultura*. I. La cultura, ed. G. Cerboni-Baiardi et al. (Rome, 1985), pp. 131–35.

4.38. Rehberg, A., 'Kardinalsorakel-Kommentar in der "Colonna" Handschrift Vat. Lat. 3819 und die Entstehungesstände der Papstvaticinien', *Florensia*, V (1991), pp. 45–112.

5. JOACHIM OF FIORE'S REPUTATION

5.11. McGinn, B., 'The Abbot and the Doctors: Scholastic Reactions to the Radical Eschatology of Joachim of Fiore', *Church History*, 40 (1971), pp. 30–47 [stresses Joachim's radicalism, cf. pp. 66–69, 179–81].

5.12. Gélinas, Y-D., 'La critique de Thomas d'Aquin sur l'exégèse de Joachim de Fiore', *Tommaso d'Aquino nel suo settimo centenario*, I (Naples, 1975), pp. 368–76.

5.13. Meinhold, D., 'Thomas von Aquin und Joachim von Fiore und ihre Deutung der Geschichte', *Speculum*, 27 (1976), pp. 60–76.

5.14. Saranyana, J., *Joaquin de Fiore y Thomas de Aquino* (Pamplona, 1979) [discusses the 1215 condemnation as well as Aquinas' view, cf. pp. 28–33, 127–29].

5.15. Robb, F., 'Did Innocent III personally condemn Joachim?', *Florensia* (forthcoming) [shows that Innocent borrowed from Joachim's Trinitarian imagery, cf, pp. 28–33, 127–29].

6. JOACHIM AND THE RELIGIOUS ORDERS

6.1. Bischoff, G., 'Early Premonstratensian Eschatology: the Apocalyptic Myth', *The Spirituality of Western Christendom*, ed. E. R. Elder (Kalamazoo, MI, 1976), pp. 41–71 [a pre-Joachimist model for the 'viri spirituales'?].

6.2. FRANCISCANS

6.211. Flood, D., OFM, 'A Study of Joachimism', *Collectanea Francescana*, 41 (1971), pp. 131–40 [raises critical questions on the 'Spiritual Franciscans', cf. pp. 175–212].

6.212. Daniel, E. R., 'Apocalyptic Conversion. The Joachite Alternative to the Crusade', *Traditio*, 25 (1969), pp. 127–54.

6.213. Id., *The Franciscan Mission in the High Middle Ages* (Kentucky, 1975) [argues that the Order developed an eschatological sense of mission independently which was only reinforced by Joachimism, cf. pp. 175–90].

6.221. Ratzinger, J., *The Theology of History in St. Bonaventure*, trans. Z. Hayes, OFM (Chicago, 1971) [studies the influence of Joachim on St. Bonaventure, cf. pp. 179–81].

6.222. McGinn, B., 'The Significance of Bonaventure's Theology of History, *The Journal of Religion Supplement*, 58 Supplement (1978), pp. S64–81 [cf. pp. 179–81].

6.223. Daniel, E. R., 'St. Bonaventure's Debt to Joachim', *Medievalia et Humanistica*, n.s., II (1982), pp. 61–75 [cf. pp. 179–81].

6.224. Weber, E., OP, 'Au principe de l'interprétation par San Bonaventure de l'eschatologisme de Joachim de Flore', *Florensia*, V (1991), pp. 27–43.

6.231. West, D., 'The Education of Fra Salimbene of Parma: The Joachite Influence', *Prophecy and Millenarianism* (ref. 1.1). pp. 193–215 [cf. pp. 184–85].

6.241. Manselli, R., 'La terza Età, Babylone e l'Anticristo mistico (a proposito di Pietro di Giovanni Olivi)', *Bullettino dell' Istituto Storico Italiano per il Medioevo*', 82 (1970), pp. 47–79.

6.242. Burr, D., *The Persecution of Peter Olivi. Transactions of the American Philosophical Society*, n.s., 66, Pt. 5 (Philadelphia, 1976) [considers Joachim's influence on Olivi, cf. pp. 194–201].

6.243. Id., 'Olivi's apocalyptic timetable', *The Journal of Medieval and Renaissance Studies*, II, 2 (1981), pp. 237–60.

6.244. Id., 'Olivi, Apocalyptic Expectation and Visionary Experience', *Traditio*, XLI (1985), pp. 273–88.

6.245. Pasztor, E., 'L'escatologia gioachimitica nel francescanesimo: Pietro di Giovanni Olivi', *L'Attesa della fine* (ref. 2.7), pp. 169–93.

6.251. Potestà, G., 'Un Secolo di Studi Sull' "Arbor Vitae". Chiesa ed Escatologia in Ubertino da Casale', *Collectanea Francescana*, 47 (1977), 3–4, pp. 217–67 [cf. pp. 207–9, 408–10].

6.252. Id., *Storia ed escatologia in Ubertino da Casale* (Milan, 1980).

6.253. Davis, C. T., 'Ubertino da Casale and His Conception of "Altissima Paupertas" ', *Studi Medievali*, 3rd ser., XXII, 1, (1981), pp. 1–56.

6.261. March, G., 'The enemies in Angelo Clareno's History of the Franciscan Order', *Use and Abuse* (ref. 2.6), pp. 385–92 [confirms Clareno's Joachimism, cf. pp. 191–94, 209–12].

6.262. Potestà, G., 'Gli Studii su Angelo Clareno, Dal Ritrovamento delle Raccolta Epistolare alle Recenti Edizione', *Rivista di Storia e Letteratura Religiosa*, XXV (1989), pp. III–43 [questions the extent of Clareno's Joachimism, cf. pp. 191–94, 209–12].

6.271. Bignami-Odier, J., *Etudes sur Joannes de Rupescissa*, rev. ed., *Histoire Littéraire de la France*, 41 (Paris, 1981), pp. 75–284 [cf. pp. 225–28, 321–24].

6.281. Lee, H., Reeves, M., Silano, G., *Western Mediterranean Prophecy. The School of Joachim of Fiore and the Fourteenth-Century Breviloquium* (Toronto, 1989) [introduction and edition of the Catalonian *Breviloquium super Concordia Novi et Veteris Testamenti*, cf. pp. 223–24, 413–14].

6.282. Pou y Marti, J., OFM, *Visionarios, Beguinos y Fratecelos Catalanes (Siglos XIII–XV)*, rev. ed., with substantial introduction by J-M. Arcelus Ulibarrena, surveying research since original ed. (Madrid, 1991).

6.283. Arcelus Ulibarrena, J-M., 'El Cod. 9.29 de la Biblioteca del Cabildo de la Catedral de Toledo: "Abbas Joachim, in Concordia maiori de novem ordinibus, sic scribit de Sancto Francesco"', *Florensia*, VI (1992), pp. 45–54 [edits this short text, cf. p. 182].

6.291. Rusconi, R., 'San Francesco nell' prediche volgari e nei sermoni latini de Bernardino da Siena', *Atti del Simposio Internazionale Cateriniano-Bernardiniano*, ed. D. Maffei, P. Nardi (Siena, 1982), [cf. pp. 230–33].

6.292. Zimdars-Swartz, S., 'Joachite themes in the Sermons of St. Bardardino of Siena', *Il profetismo* (ref., 2.8), pp. 47–59 [cf. pp. 230–33].

6.3. DOMINICANS

6.31. Gelinas, Y-D., 'L'influence du prophétisme joachimite dans l'ordre dominicain au XVIème siecle', *Il profetismo* (ref. 2.8), pp. 183–93 [examines my argument and carries it further, cf, pp. 161–74].

6.4. AUGUSTINIANS

6.411. McGinn, B., 'Circoli gioachimiti veneziani (1450–1530)' *Cristianesimo nella storia*, 7 (1986), pp. 19–39 [cf. pp. 262–67, 329–31, 343–46].

6.412. Moynihan, R., 'The MS. Tradition of the "Super Hieremiam" and the Venetian Editions of the Early Sixteenth Century', *Il profetismo* (ref. 2.8), pp. 129–37.

6.413. Reeves, M., 'Cardinal Egidio of Viterbo: A Prophetic Interpretation of History', *Prophetic Rome in the High Renaissance Period*, ed. M. Reeves (Oxford, 1992), pp. 91–109 [cf. pp. 267–68].

7. THE DISSEMINATION OF PROPHECIES IN THE LATER MIDDLE AGES

7.11. *Il profetismo gioachimita tra Quattrocento e Cinquecento* (ref. 2.8) (for précis of papers, see E. Pasztor, *Florensia*, V [1990], pp. 115–26).

7.12. Rusconi, R., *L'Attesa della Fine. Crisi della società, profezia ed Apocalisse in Italia al tempo del grande scisma d'Occidente (1378–1417)* (Rome, 1979) [critical of my treatment, cf. pp. 169, 171, 254, 325, 416–28].

7.13. Lerner, R., *The Powers of Prophecy. The Cedar of Lebanon Vision from the Mongol Onslaught to the Dawn of the Enlightenment* (Berkeley, Los Angeles, London, 1983).

7.14. Lubac, H. de, *La postérité spirituelle de Joachim de Flore*, I (Paris, 1979).

7.15. Manselli, R., 'Ricerche sulle influenza della profezia nel basso medioevo,' *Bullettino dell' Istituto Storico Italiano per il Medioevo*, 82 (1970), pp. 1–12.

7.16. Selge, K.-V., 'Die Überlieferung der Werks Joachims von Fiore im 14/15 Jahrhunderts', *Das Publikum politischer Theorie im 14 Jahrhundert*, ed. J. Miethke (Oldenbourg, 1992), pp. 49–59.

7.17. Rusconi, R., 'Il presente e il futuro della Chiesa: unità, scisma e reforme nel profetismo tardomedievale', *L'Attesa della fine* (ref. 2.7), pp. 195–200.

7.18. Vasoli, C., 'L'influenza di Gioacchino da Fiore sul profetismo italiano della fine del Quattrocento e del primo Cinquecento', *Il profetismo* (ref. 2.8), pp. 61–79.

7.19. Reeves, M., 'The Medieval Heritage', *Prophetic Rome* (ref. 6.413).

7.21. Emmerson, R., *Antichrist in the Middle Ages* (Manchester, 1981).

7.22. Vázanez Janeiro, I., OFM, 'Anticristo mixto, Anticristo mistico, varia fortuna de dos expressiones escatologicas medievale', *Antonianum*, 63 (1988), pp. 522–50 [cf. pp. 199, 343, 408–11, 423].

7.23. Guerrini, P., 'L'Anticristo "Bestia terribilis" nelle profezia figurali del Quattrocento e del Cinquecento', *Il profetismo* (ref. 2.8), pp. 87–96.

7.31. McGinn, B., 'Angel Pope and Papal Antichrist', *Church History*, 47 (1978), pp. 153–73 [cf. pp. 401–24].

7.32. Id., ' "Pastor Angelicus": Apocalyptic Myth and Political Hope in the Fourteenth Century', *Santi e santità nel secolo XIV* (Assisi, 1989), pp. 221–51 [cf. pp. 416–24].

7.33. Alexander, P., 'The Diffusion of Byzantine Apocalypses in the Medieval West and the Beginnings of Joachimism', *Prophecy and Millenarianism* (ref. 1.1), pp. 55–106.

7.34. Id., *The Byzantine Apocalypse Tradition*, ed. D. Abramse (Berkeley, Los Angeles, London, 1985) [provides essential background to the medieval concept of a Last World Emperor, cf. pp. 299–305].

7.35. Lerner, R., 'Frederick II, Alive, Aloft and Allayed in Franciscan-Joachite Eschatology', *Use and Abuse* (ref. 2.6), pp. 359–84 [gives new evidence of MSS. and dating, cf. pp. 309–12, 332–46, 518–22].

7.36. Berg, D., 'L'impero degli Suevi e il gioachimismo francescano', *L'Attesa della fine* (ref. 2.7), pp. 133–67.

7.41. Spence, R., 'MS. Syracuse University Von Ranke, 90 and the "Libellus" of Telesphorus von Cosenza', *Scriptorium*, XXXIII (1979), pp. 271–74.

7.42. McGinn, B., 'Circoli gioachimiti veneziani (1450–1530)', *Cristianesimo* (ref. 6.41), pp. 19–39 [cf. pp. 343–46].

7.43. Rusconi, R., 'Les collections prophétiques en Italie à la fin du moyen âge et au début des temps modernes', *Mélanges de l'Ecole Française à Rome*, 102 (1990), pp. 481–511 [see *Florensia*, II (1988), pp. 61–90, for an earlier Italian version].

7.51. Beaune, C., 'De Telesphore à Guillaume Postel. La diffusion du *Libellus* en France aux XIV-ème et XV-ème siècles', *Il profetismo* (ref. 2.8), pp. 195–208 [cf. pp. 327–31, 342, 378–85].

7.52. Rusconi, R., 'Alla ricerca delle autentiche tracce di Gioacchino da Fiore nella Francia meridionale', *Florensia*, VI (1992), pp. 57–71.

7.61. Patschowsky, A., 'Eresie escatologiche tardomedievale nel regno teutonico', *L'Attesa della fine* (ref. 2.7), pp. 221–44 [cf. pp. 258–59, 475–79].

7.62. Id., 'Die Wirsberger: Zeugen des Geisteswelt Joachims von Fiore in Deutschland während des 15 Jahrhunderts?', *Il profetismo* (ref. 2.8), pp. 225–57.

7.63. Zimdars-Swartz, P., 'John of Dorsten's Response to Apocalyptic Prophecy in the 1466 Erfurt *Quaestio*: A Prelude to an Apocalyptic Theology of Papal Grace', *Il profetismo* (ref. 2.8), pp. 259–71 [re-examines the possibility of Joachim's influence on Dorsten, cf. pp. 258–59, 478–79].

7.64. Cegna, R., 'Appunti per una tipologia della *status Spiritus libertatis* nella riforma boema e del Centro Europa del Quattrocento e degli inizi del Cinquecento', *Il profetismo* (ref. 2.8), pp. 351–78.

7.71. Lee, H., ' "Scrutamini Scripturas": Joachimist Themes and *Figurae* in the Early Writings of Arnold of Villanova', *Journal of the Warburg and Courtauld Institutes*, 37 (1974), pp. 31–56.

7.72. Lee, H., Reeves, M., Silano, G., *Western Mediterranean Prophecy* (ref. 6.281) [cf. pp. 223–24, 413–14].

7.73. Perarnau, J., 'Profetismo gioachimita catalano da Arnau de Vilanova à Vicent Ferrer', *Il profetismo* (ref. 2.8), pp. 401–14.

7.74. Hauf, A., 'El "De triplici statu mundi" di fr. Francese Eiximensis', *Estudio Universitaris Catalans*, 23 (1979), pp. 265–83 [cf. pp. 222-23].

7.81. Kerby-Fulton, K., Daniel, E. R., 'English Joachimism 1300–1500: The Columbinus Prophecy', *Il profetismo* (ref. 2.8), pp. 313–50.

7.82. Kerby-Fulton, K., *Reformist Apocalypticism and 'Piers Plowman'* (Cambridge, 1990) [cf. pp. 82–88].

8. PROPHECY IN THE RENAISSANCE PERIOD

8.11. Vasoli, C., *Profezia e ragione* (Naples, 1974) [cf. pp. 429–46].

8.12. Id. 'Umanesimo ed escatologia', *L'Attesa della fine* (ref. 2.7), pp. 245–75.

8.13. Tognetti, G., 'Note sul profetismo nel Rinascimento e la letteratura relativa', *Bullettino dell' Istituto per il Medioevo*, 82 (1970), pp. 129–57.

8.14. Rusconi, R., ' "Ex quodam antiquissimo libello". La tradizione manoscritta delle profezie nell' Italia tardomedioevale: dalle collezioni profetiche alle prime edizioni a stampa', *Use and Abuse* (ref. 2.6), pp. 441–72.

8.15. Rotondò, A., 'Anticristo e Chiesa romana. Diffusione e metamorfosi d'un libello anteromana del Cinquecento', *Forme e Destinazione del Messagio Religioso. Aspetti della Propaganda Religiosa nel Cinquecento*, ed. A. Rotondò, Florence, 1991, pp. 19–164.

8.16. Zambelli, P., 'Profeti-astrologi nel medio periodo. Motivi pseudogioachimiti dibattuto italiano e tedesco sulla fine del mondo per la grande congiunzione del 1524', *Il profetismo* (ref. 2.8), pp. 273–85.

8.211. Morisi, A. *Apocalypsis Nova. Ricerche sull' origine e la formazione del testo dello pseudo-Amadeo (Istituto Storico Italiano per il Medio Evo. Studi Storici* 77, Rome, 1970) [fundamental study of a key text, cf. pp. 233–34, 461–62].

8.212. Vasoli, C., *I miti e gli astri* (Naples, 1977) [see, *inter alia*, on Annio of Viterbo, pp. 17–49; Giovanni Nesi, pp. 51–128, cf. pp. 354, 463–64, 437].

8.213. Niccoli, O., *Profeti e Popolo nell' Italia del Rinascimento* (Rome, Bari, 1987), trans. L. Cochrane, *Prophecy and People in Renaissance Italy* (Princeton, 1990), [breaks new ground on popular prophecy, cf. pp. 430, 447–48].

8.214. Vasoli, C., 'L'influenza di Gioacchino da Fiore sul profetismo italiano della fine del Quattrocento e del primo Cinquecento', *Il profetismo* (ref. 2.8), pp. 61–85.

8.215. Morisi-Guerra, A., 'The "Apocalypse Nova". A Plan for Reform', *Prophetic Rome* (ref. 6.413), pp. 27–50 [see above, 8.211].

8.221. Chastel, A., *The Sack of Rome*, trans. B. Archer (Princeton, 1983) [cf. pp. 367, 448].

8.222. O'Malley, J., *Praise and Blame in Renaissance Rome: Rhetoric, Doctrine and Reform in the Sacred Orators of the Papal Court c. 1450–1521* (Durham, N.C., 1979).

8.223. Id., *Rome and the Renaissance: Studies in Culture and Religion* (London, 1981).

8.224. Troncarelli, F., ed., *La Città dei Segreti, Magia, astrologia e cultura esoterica a Roma* (XV–XVIII) (Milan, 1985), [includes an essay on prophecy in Rome].

8.225. Reeves, M., ed., *Prophetic Rome* (ref. 6.413).

8.226. Tognetti, G., 'Sul "romito" e profeta Brandano da Petroio', *Rivista storica italiana*, 72 (1970), pp. 20–44 [cf. pp. 448–49].

8.227. Minnich, N. M., 'Prophecy and the Fifth Lateran Council (1512–1517)', *Prophetic Rome* (ref. 6.413), pp. 63–87 [studies the attention paid to prophecy by participants at the Council].

8.228. Rusconi, R., 'An Angelic Pope Before the Sack of Rome', *Prophetic Rome* (ref. 6.413), pp. 157–87 [on Petrus Galatinus, cf. pp. 234–38, 366–67, 442–47].

8.229. McGinn, B., 'Notes on a Forgotten Prophet: Paulus Angelus and Rome', *Prophetic Rome* (ref. 6.413), pp. 189–99 [cf. pp. 264, 432–33].

8.231. Weinstein, D., *Savonarola and Florence: Prophecy and Patriotism in the Renaissance* (Princeton, 1970) [cf. pp. 434–40].

8.232. Vasoli, C., 'Profezie e profeti nelle vita religiosa e politica fiorentina', *Magia, Astrologia e Religione nel Rinascimento* (Wroclaw, Warsaw, Krakow, Gdansk, 1974), pp. 16–29.

8.233. Id., 'Un notaio fiorentino del Cinquecento: Ser Lorenzo Violi', *Il notariato nella civilità toscana* (Rome, 1985), pp. 391–418.

8.241. McGinn, B., 'Circoli gioachimiti veneziano', *Cristianesimo* (ref. 6.41), pp. 19–39 [cf. pp. 262–67, 344–46].

8.242. Niccoli, O., ' "Profetie di Musaicho". Figure e Scritture Gioachimiti nella Venezia del Cinquecento', *Forme e Destinazione* (ref. 8.15), pp. 197–227 [cf. pp. 73, 96–100, 164–65, 479].

8.243. Britnell, J., 'Jean Lemaire de Belge and Prophecy', *Journal of the Warburg and Courtauld Institutes*, XLI (1979), pp. 144–66 [cf. pp. 97–98].

8.244. Moynihan, R., 'The MS. Tradition of the "Super Hieremiam" and the Venetian editions of the early Sixteenth Century', *Il profetismo* (ref. 2.8), pp. 129–37 [cf. p. 262].

8.31. Britnell, J., Stubbs, D., 'The "Mirabilis Liber": Its Compilation and Influence', *Journal of the Warburg and Courtauld Institutes*, XLIX (1986), pp. 126–49 [argues that the so-called Venetian ed. of 1514 is unknown, cf. pp. 379–80].

8.321. Postel, G., *Le Trésor des Prophéties de l'Univers*, with introduction by F. Secret (La Haye, 1969).

8.322. Secret, F., Recueil d'articles (1955–1973) (Paris, 1973) [collection of articles on Postel, cf. pp. 287–89, 381–84, 479–81].

8.323. Id., 'D'Athenas à Jerusalem ou la politique de Guillaume Postel', *Théories et pratiques politique à la Renaissance* (Paris, 1977).

8.324. Kuntz, M., *Guillaume Postel Prophet of the Restitution of all Things* (London, 1981).

8.325. Vasoli, C., 'Postel, Galatino e l'Apocalypsis Nova', *Guillaume Postel 1581–1981 Actes du Colloque International d'Avranches 5–9 sept., 1981* (Paris, 1985), pp. 97–108.

8.41. Kurze, D., 'Popular Astrology and Prophecy in the fifteenth and sixteenth centuries: Johann Lichtenberger', *"Astrology Hallucinati". Stars and the End of the World in Luther's Time*, ed. P. Zambelli (Berlin, New York, 1986), pp. 177–93 [cf. pp. 347–51].

8.42. Russell, P., 'Joseph Grünpeck', *Forme e Destinazione* (ref. 8.15), pp. 165–95 [deals with Lichtenberger as well as Grünpeck, cf. p. 449].

8.51. Prosperi, A., 'Attese millenaristiche e scoperta del Nuovo Mondo', *Il profetismo* (ref. 2.8), pp. 433–60 [this group of writings expands on the eschatological significance of the New World discoveries, cf. pp. 174, 284, 287, 359–60, 365–66, 384, 470, 480–83].

8.52. Id., 'New Heaven and New Earth: Prophecy and Propaganda at the time of the Discovery and Conquest of the Americas', *Prophetic Rome* (ref. 6.413), pp. 279–303.

8.53. Arcelus Ulibarrena, J. M., 'Cristóbal Colón y los primeros evangelizadores del Nuevo Mundo; Lección de profetismo joaquinista', *Il profetismo* (ref. 2.8), pp. 475–504 [cf. p. 360].

8.54. Freitas Carvalho, J. A. de, 'Joachim de Flore au Portugal: XIII-ème-XVI-ème siècles. Un itinerare possible', *Il profetismo* (ref. 2.8), pp. 415–32.

8.61. Morisi, A., *Apocalypsis Nova. Ricerche sull' Origine e la formazione del testo dello pseudo-Amadeo* (ref. 8.21) [cf. pp. 233–34, 461–62].

8.62. Morisi-Guerra, A., 'The "Apocalypsis Nova". A Plan for Reform', *Prophetic Rome* (ref. 6.413), pp. 27–50.

8.63. Rusconi, R., 'An Angelic Pope Before the Sack of Rome', *Prophetic Rome* (ref. 6.413), pp. 157–87 [cf. refs. under 8.228].

8.64. Jungic, J., 'Joachimist Prophecies in Sebastiano del Piombo's Borgherini Chapel and Raphael's Transfiguration', *Prophetic Rome* (ref. 6.413), pp. 321–43.

8.65. Id., 'Prophecies of the Angelic Pastor in Sebastiano del Piombo's Portrait of Cardinal Bandinello Sauli and Three Companions', *Prophetic Rome* (ref. 6.413), pp. 345–70 [these two articles develop the theme of Joachimist prophecy in Renaissance art, cf. pp. 436–37].

8.66. Hudon, W., 'Marcellus II, Girolamo Seripando and the Image of the Angelic Pope', *Prophetic Rome* (ref. 6.413), pp. 373–87 [argues that Marcellus's election embodies a late echo of the Angelic Pope prophecy].

8.67. Giommi, E., *La monaca Arcangela Panigarola madre spirituale de Denis Briçonnet. L'attesa del 'pastore engelico' annunciato dall' Apocalypsis Nova del Beato Amadeo fra il 1514 e il 1520* (Università negli Studi di Firenze: Facoltà di Lettere e Filosofia, Ph.D. thesis).

8.71. Headley, J., 'Germany, the Empire and *Monarchia* in the Thought and Policy of Gattinara', *Das römischdeutsche Reich im politischen System Karls V*, ed. H. Lutz (Munich, Vienna, 1982), pp. 15–34.

8.72. Id., 'Rhetoric and Reality: Messianic, Humanist and Civilian Themes in the Imperial Ethos of Gattinara', *Prophetic Rome* (ref. 6.413), pp. 241–69 [these two essays develop the theme of Gattinara's prophetic vision of empire].

8.811. O'Malley, J., *Giles of Viterbo on Church and Reform* (Leiden, 1968) [for this group of essays, cf. pp. 268–71, 364–66].

8.812. O'Reilly, C., ' "Maximus Caesar et Pontifex Maximus": Giles of Viterbo Proclaims the Alliance between Emperor Maximilian I and Pope Julius II', *Augustiniana*, 22 (1972), pp. 80–117.

8.813. Id., '"Without Councils we cannot be saved...": Giles of Viterbo addresses the Fifth Lateran Council', *Augustiniana*, 27 (1977), pp. 166–204.

8.814. Martin, F. X., OSA, 'Giles of Viterbo as Scripture scholar', *Egidio da Viterbo, OBA, ed il suo tempo; Atti del V congresso dell' Istituto Storico Agostiniano* (Rome, 1983), pp. 191–222.

8.815. Id., 'The Writings of Giles of Viterbo', *Augustiana*, 29, 1–2 (1979), pp. 141–8.

8.816. Reeves, M., 'Cardinal Egidio of Viterbo: A Prophetic Interpretation of History', *Prophetic Rome* (ref. 6.413), pp. 91–109.

8.821. Minnich, N. H., 'The Role of Prophecy in the Career of the Enigmatic Bernardino Lopez de Carvajal', *Prophetic Rome* (ref. 6.413), pp. 111–20.

8.831. Vasoli, C., 'Giorgio Benigno Salviati e la tensione profetica di fine '400', *Rinascimento*, 2nd ser., 29 (1989), pp. 53–78.

8.832. Id., 'Giorgio Benigno Salviati (Dragišić)', *Prophetic Rome* (ref. 6.413), pp. 121–56 [Vasoli's two essays fill a gap in the book].

8.841. Id., 'Profezie e astrologia in uno scritto di Annio da Viterbo', *I miti e gli astri* (Naples, 1977), pp. 17–49 [cf. pp. 354, 463–64].

8.851. Lerner, R., 'The Prophetic MS. of the "Renaissance Magus" Pierleone of Spoleto', *Il profetismo* (ref. 2.8), pp. 97–116 [fills a gap in the book].

9. REFORMATION THEMES

9.11. Seibt, F., 'Gioacchino da Fiore e l'utopia nella Riforma', *Il profetismo* (ref. 2.8), pp. 287–94.

9.12. Heffner, D., *"Eyn Wunderliche Weyssagung von dem Babstumb": Medieval Prophecy into Reformation Polemic*, doctoral thesis (Univ. of Pennsylvania, 1991, UMI Dissertation Services, Ann Arbor, Michigan 48106) [Reformation use of the pope prophecies, cf. pp. 453–54, 487–88].

9.13. Id., 'The Use of Medieval Prophecy in Reformation Polemic', *Il profetismo* (ref. 2.8). pp. 295–304.

9.14. Burigana, R., 'Gioacchino da Fiore in Lutero', *Florensia*, VI (1992), pp. 95–102 [gives new evidence on Luther's knowledge of Joachim, cf. p. 490].

9.21. Hill, C., *Antichrist in Seventeenth-Century England* (Oxford, 1971).

9.22. Reeves, M., 'History and Eschatology: Medieval and Early Protestant Thought in some English and Scotish Writings', *Medievalia et Humanistica*, 4 (1973), pp. 99–123 [gives evidence for Joachimist echoes in the 16th and 17th centuries, cf. pp. 107–9, 475 n.1, 488–89, 499–500. Note 26 in this article modifies the view given in 475 n.1].

9.23. Bauckham, R., *Tudor Apocalypse* (Sutton Courtenay, 1978).

9.24. Jones, N. L., 'Matthew Parker, John Bale and the Magdeburg Centuriators', *The Sixteenth Century Journal*, 12 (1981), pp. 35–49.

INDEX OF MANUSCRIPTS

GENERAL INDEX

Aaron, 147–8, 499.
Abbott, R., author of *Antichristi Demonstratio . . .*, 107 n. 4.
Abraham, 183 n. 1, 223.
Absalom, 485.
Accaiuoli, Z., 433–4.
Accamandolus of Foligno, Augustinian Friar, 251.
Accolti, B., the elder, 368; B., the younger, 368 n. 2, 450–1.
Acta Sanctorum, Joachim included in, 3: Papebroch's defence of Joachim in, 119–25; life of Loyola in, 275–6; Joachim prophet of the Jesuits in, 285–7.
Adam, 183 n. 1; first *status* initiated in, 18–20; second Adam, 414, 474.
Adam, Cistercian, Abbot of Persigny, interview with Joachim, 3 n. 1, 12–14.
Adhémar de Mosset, 220–1.
Adrasder, J., 454, 488 nn. 6, 11.
Adrian VI, Pope, 443 n. 1.
Adso, Abbot, author of *Libellus de ortu et tempore Antichristi*, 301.
Advents of Christ, First, 282; First and Second, 6, 19, 298; Second, 55, 275, 284, 289, 303, 322, 390, 414, 493–5; Third, 198, 208, 291–2, 468 n. 9, 475, 482–3, 494–5, 497 n. 1, 501. *See also* Last Judgement.
Aemilius, P., 101 n. 1.
Agostino Trionfo, Augustinian Friar, 88–9, 256.
Agricola, R., 501.
Agrippa, H. C., of Nettesheim, author of *De incertitudine et vanitate scientiarum et artium*, 102.
Agrippa d'Aubigné, 385.
d'Ailly, P., Cardinal, 422, 474.
Alberic Trium Fontium, 65 n. 1.
Albert of Stade, 50; quotes *Super Hier.*, 56; reports Joachimist prophecies, 74, 309; refers to sect of Fr. Arnold, 170, 310.
Alberti, L., editor of *Vaticinia circa Apostolicos Viros . . .*, 101 n. 1, 453.
Albertus Magnus, Dominican, 235.
Albi, 201.

Albornoz, Cardinal, 219.
Alcázar, Jesuit, author of *Vestigatio arcani sensus in Apocalypsi*, 282–3.
Alemani, Joachimist prophecies concerning, 74; Joachim's attitude towards, 156 n. 2; Emperor of, scourge of Church, 263 n. 5, 267, 326, 367, 380–1; Pseudo-Joachimist works on, 306–8; prophetic role of, 321–2, 332, 339, 349–54, 362–3, 374, 375–7, 449, 458; pseudo-pope from, 326, 423. *See also* Roman *Imperium*.
Alexander, King of Macedonia, 300, 327, 363.
Alexander III, Pope, 30–1, 45.
Alexander IV, Pope, 61, 64 n. 2.
Alexander VI, Pope, 353 n. 1.
Alexander ab Alexandro of Naples, 358 n. 1, 445.
Alexander of Bremen (Bexhövede), Franciscan, 50, 147; quotes *Super Hier.*, 56; author of *Expos. in Apocalypsim*, 177–8.
Alexander v. Roes, author of *Notitia Seculi* and *De Translatione Imperii*, 313–14, 334.
Allegretti, A., 430 n. 3.
Allegri, Pelligrino, 338.
Allo, E., author of *St. Jean. L'Apocalypse*, 281 nn. 1–3.
Alofresant of Rhodes, 339 n. 3, 340 n. 2, 360, 361 n. 1, 488 n. 11.
Alpha and Omega, symbolism of, in Joachim's writings, 19–20, 23; Joachim's interpretation cited, 85, 86, 114, 197 n. 1, 496; Galatinus on, 235.
Alphonso de Castro, Franciscan, author of *Adversus omnes haereses Libri XIII*, Joachim classed as a heretic by, 103, 105, 279.
Alvaro y Pelayo, 252 n. 4.
d'Alverny, T., 80 n. 3, 90 n. 5, 93 nn. 1, 2.
Amadeus of Portugal (Joannes Menesius de Silva), 233–4, 442; influence of, 235, 238, 432, 440–1, 444, 446, 461–2, 479, 503.
Amaury of Bènes, 65 n. 1, 473; Amalricians, 44 n. 4, 473.

Zacharias, Pope, 5 n. 1.
Zacharias, Old Testament priest, 444, 468.
Zangari, D., 120 n. 1.
Zara, A., Bp of Petina, 278.
Zechariah, prophet, 143, 146-7.
Zedekiah, King of Judah, 149-50, 151 n. 1.

Zimmerische Chronik, 372 n. 1.
Zimmerman, B., dates *Oraculum Cyrilli c.* 1287, 57 n. 7.
Zorobabel, type of future leader, 304, 366, 396, 413-14, 444.
Zwingli, 470.